Handbook of Prosocial Education

Volume 2

EDITED BY
PHILIP M. BROWN
MICHAEL W. CORRIGAN
ANN HIGGINS-D'ALESSANDRO

D1606926

ROWMAN & LITTLEFIELD PUBLISHERS, INC.
Lanham • Boulder • New York • Toronto • Plymouth, UK

Published by Rowman & Littlefield Publishers, Inc.
A wholly owned subsidary of The Rowman & Littlefield Publishing Group, Inc.
4501 Forbes Boulevard, Suite 200, Lanham, Maryland 20706
www.rowman.com

10 Thornbury Road, Plymouth PL6 7PP, United Kingdom

British Library Cataloguing in Publication Information Available

Library of Congress Cataloging-in-Publication Data
Handbook of prosocial education / edited by Philip M. Brown, Michael W. Corrigan, and Ann Higgins-D'Alessandro.
   p. cm.
   Includes bibliographical references and index.
   ISBN 978-1-4422-1119-3 (hardback) — ISBN 978-1-4422-1121-6 (electronic)
   1. Affective education—Handbooks, manuals, etc. 2. Moral education—Handbooks, manuals, etc. 3. Social learning—Handbooks, manuals, etc. 4. School improvement programs—Handbooks, manuals, etc. I. Brown, Philip M., 1942– II. Corrigan, Michael W. III. Higgins-D'Alessandro, Ann.
   LB1072.H36 2012
   370.15'3—dc23
                                                                       2012008990

∞™ The paper used in this publication meets the minimum requirements of American National Standard for Information Sciences—Permanence of Paper for Printed Library Materials, ANSI/NISO Z39.48-1992.

Printed in the United States of America

Contents

CHAPTER 13

Positive Youth Development

FRANK J. SNYDER AND BRIAN R. FLAY

A fourth-grade student at Discovery Bay Elementary School in Byron, California, could teach us all a lesson about what it means to be positive. Tyler Page participates in lessons every day at school where he learns that you feel good about yourself when you think and do positive actions, and there is always a positive way to do everything. His teachers, other school staff, fellow students, and parents provide positive reinforcement and support for him and his fellow students in the classroom, on the school grounds, and elsewhere.

One day while watching TV, Tyler found a way to take positive action. Inspired and moved by an Oprah show that exposed parents selling their children into slavery in Ghana, Africa, he devised a plan to raise money to assist those children. Tyler knew that $240 could support one rescued child for an entire year. Along with twenty-five other kids and the help of parents and local businesses, he organized a car wash fund-raiser and raised $1,705—enough to support seven children. The kids worked all day, only stopping to eat. Some who had scheduled sports or other activities did not want to leave, and everyone asked Tyler when the next fund-raiser would be. Within seventeen months, Tyler had led the charge in raising $50,000—enough to support two hundred children. Tyler's positive assets and actions united an entire community behind a common cause. Two hundred children's lives were positively changed because one group of children across the world applied the concepts and skills they were learning to civic action in real life.

What would you prefer? To be praised for your positive assets, or to be told that you are merely problem free? Should you support a safe-school initiative or fight in the war on drugs? Would you rather attend a peace rally or an antiwar protest? A positive perspective is often semantically best, and a positive perspective toward youth development helps movement away from the negative paradigm that has been predominant in scientific thinking for decades (J. V. Lerner, Phelps, Forman, & Bowers, 2009). A positive youth development (PYD) perspective views youth as people to be nurtured, not problems to be managed (Benson, Scales, Hamilton, & Sesma, 2006; Roth & Brooks-Gunn, 2003a). While this perspective acknowledges the risk and difficulties youth face (Damon, 2004), its key components include (1) a focus on youth strengths or assets and potential for positive individual development; (2) the value of supportive (asset-rich) contexts; and (3) the bidirectional interactions between person and context (Benson, 1997; R. M. Lerner, Almerigi, Theokas, & Lerner, 2005).

PYD is grounded in the premise that every child has the potential to succeed and the capacity for positive development (R. M. Lerner, Dowling, & Anderson, 2003). Of course, this development is influenced by a myriad of intrapersonal, interpersonal, and cultural-environmental factors (Flay, Snyder, & Petraitis, 2009). Youth tend to manifest positive development when their environment is rich with assets that mesh with their strengths (Benson, 2003; R. M. Lerner, 2005). In addition to social-emotional skills, optimal youth development requires clear parental boundaries, supportive teachers, and caring communities that provide a venue for youth to contribute to society. However, only in recent decades have more researchers, practitioners, and policy makers taken a PYD approach that acknowledges these concepts. For most of the twentieth century, adolescence and young adulthood were seen as times of turbulence and stress (Hall, 1904, as cited in R. M. Lerner, 2005). Many researchers and the public cast a suspicious eye on youth, seeing them as susceptible to hazards and prone to risk behaviors that endanger themselves and disrupt society.

More recently, studies and advancements in knowledge have begun to shift the established views of youth. Now there is greater recognition of positive youth–adult interactions and motivated youth (Larson, 2006) thriving in their development (R. M. Lerner, Brentano, Dowling, & Anderson, 2002; R. M. Lerner et al., 2003; Settersten & Ray, 2010). In fact, while youth do face challenges, most youth do not have a turbulent second decade of life (adolescence; R. M. Lerner, 2005) or third decade (young adulthood; Settersten & Ray, 2010). Actually, they often value good relationships with their parents, frequently develop altruistic values, and select friends with similar core values.

A variety of work has bolstered support for the PYD perspective. Toward the end of the twentieth century, researchers began to accrue empirical evidence of neural plasticity, or experience-induced changes in the brain. This breakthrough was instrumental in understanding human development (Nelson, 1999). Further, theoretical understanding, along with a discussion among practitioners and policy makers, helped form a foundation upon which the PYD approach was built. Research and practice expanded the comprehensive and evolving set of constructs that PYD subsumes. Additionally, integrative theories have been developed that unify multiple influences into a more cogent view of human development and behavior (Flay & Petraitis, 1994; Ford & Lerner, 1992). Integrative theory has informed the PYD perspective and can help bring order to the confusion that may accompany a complex system of behavioral influences.

Current researchers have learned that behaviors, both positive and negative, are correlated and have the same distal influences and ultimate or fundamental roots and causes (Flay, 2002). Similarly, program developers and evaluators have found that many school-based programs have had limited results because most have been problem specific and have not addressed the distal and ultimate influences that have far-reaching influences on numerous behaviors (Flay, 2002; Flay et al., 2009; Romer, 2003). These distal factors, such as prosocial norms, are key in creating nurturing environments (Komro, Flay, Biglan, & Promise Neighborhoods Research Consortium,

2011). Several programs have evolved from problem-specific approaches to more comprehensive (i.e., including youth, school personnel, families, and communities) and integrative (i.e., addressing multiple risk and protective factors for co-occurring behaviors) approaches (e.g., Bierman et al., 2004; Flay & Allred, 2010; Flay, Graumlich, Segawa, Burns, & Holliday, 2004; Pentz et al., 1989). This new understanding that behaviors are linked and recent recognition that programs can address multiple influences have the potential to unite many disciplines.

Indeed, PYD is a multidisciplinary field, with many individuals involved who have found common ground after inquiry and experience. In this chapter, we provide a thematic review of the field rather than an exhaustive one; we are unable to be inclusive of all the researchers and practitioners who use the term *PYD* and conduct related work. To date, this relatively new and multidisciplinary field involves considerable overlap with multiple approaches to prosocial education, such as character education (Berkowitz & Bier, 2004, 2007); social and emotional learning (SEL; Durlak, Weissberg, Dymnicki, Taylor, & Schellinger, 2011; Payton et al., 2000; Weissberg & O'Brien, 2004); social and character development (SACD; Flay, Berkowitz, & Bier, 2009; Haegerich & Metz, 2009); and social-emotional and character development (SECD; Elias, 2009). We use the term *PYD related* to denote this overlap among various areas of prosocial education and to express that some approaches, such as public policy, are related to PYD. Prosocial education, in its principles and goals given in chapter 1, is an umbrella concept that is informed by PYD and the other approaches provided in this book.

Disparate inclusion criteria determine which programs were included in reviews on different areas of prosocial education, thus generating program overlap across the reviews. Readers who compare recent reviews of character education programs (Berkowitz & Bier, 2007); PYD programs (Catalano, Berglund, Ryan, Lonczak, & Hawkins, 2004); and SEL programs (Durlak et al., 2011) will find multiple programs that are included in two or all three of these reviews. Further, there are substantial overlaps in terminologies and strategies across disciplines; however, the best programs incorporate most, if not all, of the strategies described in the reviews. Listed in this chapter's first paragraph, three key components of PYD (a focus on youth strengths or assets, the value of supportive environments, and acknowledgment of bidirectional person–context interactions) help clarify what comprehensive PYD programs include and how they differ from other programs. A PYD program that includes these components can, as we will discuss herein, promote positive youth development and, simultaneously, prevent unhealthy behaviors without ever addressing an unhealthy behavior specifically.

Overall, PYD is a rather new perspective with a complex history. Although PYD may be a common "buzzword" in present-day scientific and colloquial dialogue, there is mounting empirical evidence that supports its concepts, characteristics, and strategies. Accordingly, this chapter provides a discussion of PYD in historical context; a detailed overview of what PYD is and its constructs; theories that informed the conception of PYD and unifying, integrative theories that facilitate understanding of PYD; empirical research on characteristics, strategies, and outcomes of effective programs; examples of effective research and programming; PYD-related policy; implications for prosocial education; and paths for future research.

HISTORICAL CONTEXT

The PYD perspective originated in biological and psychological research related to ontogenesis (i.e., the study of an organism's life span) and the plasticity of development, and it grew out of work related to child and human development (J. V. Lerner et al., 2009; R. M. Lerner, 2005; R. M. Lerner, Abo-Zena, et al., 2009) and juvenile delinquency (Benson et al., 2006). Further, it propagated from a discussion among practitioners and policy makers as well as funding initiatives that aimed to enhance the development of youth (Benson, 2003; Benson et al., 2006). Overall, PYD has many historical roots, and several scholars have blazed a path of research that emerged in the 1990s.

Integral in advancing the PYD movement during the last two decades are the contributions of groups led by Peter Benson (Benson, 1997; Benson & Pittman, 2001; Benson et al., 2006) and Richard Lerner (R. M. Lerner, 2005; R. M. Lerner et al., 2003; R. M. Lerner, Lerner, et al., 2005; R. M. Lerner, von Eye, Lerner, & Lewin-Bizan, 2009). Their efforts have provided vocabulary and insight about the strengths of youth, the importance of context, and approaches to enhance youth development. This chapter highlights many of their contributions toward and vision of PYD. These include Benson's forty developmental assets (Benson, 1997) and Lerner's theoretical and empirical work (Ford & Lerner, 1992; R. M. Lerner, 2006), including the 4-H Study of Positive Youth Development (R. M. Lerner, Lerner, et al., 2005).

Other key scholars interested in youth development and enhancement, including health promotion, have contributed toward a PYD approach (Catalano, Hawkins, Berglund, Pollard, & Arthur, 2002; Catalano, Oesterle, Fleming, & Hawkins, 2004; Damon, 2004; Flay, 2002; Larson, 2000). Moreover, although the PYD perspective did not originate from work related to positive psychology (R. M. Lerner, 2005; R. M. Lerner, Abo-Zena, et al., 2009), research conducted by such scholars as Seligman (2000) had similarities to and application toward PYD. Lastly, PYD is an aspect of another field, applied developmental psychology, which emphasizes the study of bidirectional and changing relationships of human development and contexts throughout the life span in ways that simultaneously add to both foundational knowledge and the development of new or adapted practices.

Also related to PYD, as mentioned briefly earlier, is the understanding that most, if not all, behaviors have common developmental determinants (Flay, 2002). Behaviors do not develop or exist in isolation from one another (Biglan, Brennan, Foster, & Holder, 2004; Botvin, Schinke, & Orlandi, 1995; Flay, 2002; O'Connell, Boat, & Warner, 2009). Research offers clear support that both positive and negative youth outcomes are influenced by similar protective and risk factors (Catalano, Hawkins, et al., 2002; Donovan, Jessor, & Costa, 1993; Flay, 2002). For instance, a clear relationship was established between academic achievement and violence, substance use, and other unhealthy behaviors (Fleming et al., 2005; Malecki & Elliott, 2002; Wentzel, 1993).

With this research showing that behaviors are linked and in an effort to tackle the narrow reach of many programs, there has been a movement in recent years toward more comprehensive, integrative PYD-related programs that address co-occurring behaviors and that involve families and communities. These programs generally appear to be more effective (Battistich, Schaps, Watson, Solomon, & Lewis, 2000; Bierman et al., 2004;

Flay, 2000; Flay et al., 2004; Hawkins, Catalano, Kosterman, Abbott, & Hill, 1999; R. M. Lerner, 1995). That is, a comprehensive, integrated, promotive-preventive approach that addresses multiple determinants of behavior, not a narrow problem-specific approach, is likely to improve such diverse behavioral outcomes as academic skills and achievement, prosocial behaviors, truancy, substance use, risky sexual activity, and violence (Battistich et al., 2000; Botvin et al., 1995; Catalano, Hawkins, et al., 2002; Flay, 2002).

Scholars have suggested a need to focus on risk reduction (i.e., a prevention science perspective) *and* asset development (i.e., the PYD perspective) because they acknowledge that positively developing youth are involved in some number of risk behaviors (Catalano, Hawkins, et al., 2002; J. V. Lerner et al., 2009). Empirical evidence suggests that it is possible to promote PYD and *simultaneously* reduce multiple risk behaviors with a PYD approach (Beets et al., 2009; Lewis et al., 2011; Li et al., 2011; Riggs, Greenberg, Kusché, & Pentz, 2006; Snyder, Vuchinich, Acock, Washburn, & Flay, in press; Snyder et al., 2010, 2011; Washburn et al., in press). Therefore, prosocial education can enhance youth development and, at the same time, prevent unhealthy behaviors. In fact, equipped with an understanding of PYD and more detailed knowledge of health behaviors and the components of effective programs, researchers have evaluated more comprehensive, integrative programs, such as the Positive Action program described herein. These types of programs have a greater likelihood of affecting multiple co-occurring behaviors, partly through positively influencing context; they promote positive behaviors while reducing risk concomitantly.

Before we discuss effective strategies and exemplar programs, it is useful to explore PYD constructs and related theory. Taken together, the aforementioned research has led to a better understanding of what PYD is and what constructs it includes.

POSITIVE YOUTH DEVELOPMENT: DEFINITIONS, CONCEPTS, AND CONSTRUCTS

PYD is broad and encompasses many descriptions and constructs. To date, no universally accepted definition of PYD exists (Benson et al., 2006; J. V. Lerner et al., 2009), perhaps because of its relative newness and cross-disciplinary nature or its complexity. As table 13.1 demonstrates, PYD can be thought of as (1) a perspective; (2) a construct (at minimum a second-order latent construct; Phelps et al., 2009); and (3) a program or policy approach. That is, PYD is a point of view (focusing on youth assets and their context), it is multidimensional and thus requires multiple measures to capture, and it is a comprehensive approach to intervention, aligned with program or policy activities, atmosphere, and goals. With such an inclusive term, definitions and constructs comprising PYD are many and varied. Paralleling the three concepts above, we describe PYD with three definitions:

1. *As a perspective*, PYD emphasizes youths' strengths and supportive contexts, along with acknowledging bidirectional youth–context interactions (e.g., when youth engage in civic activities, they are reinforced, and the community learns to place greater value on such activities and to encourage more of them).
2. *As a construct*, PYD is multidimensional and is assessed by multiple measures related to the strengths of youth and the assets in their social environments.

3. PYD *programs* support youth by focusing on developing their strengths, providing supportive and reinforcing contexts, and presenting opportunities for bidirectional youth–context interactions (e.g., school efforts affect youth and youth, in turn, affect their contexts).

The thoroughness of PYD can be grasped by examining a representative sample of several key literatures. Benson and colleagues, for example, have hypothesized that forty developmental assets are essential for all youth (Benson, 1997, 2007; Benson et al., 2006; Scales, 1999). The list includes both external, environmental, contextual asset types (e.g., support, empowerment, boundaries and expectations, constructive use of time) as well as internal, intrapersonal, individual asset types (e.g., commitment to learning, positive values, social competencies, positive identity). Further, these categories encompass several distinct assets. For instance, among the external asset types, "support" includes family support, positive family communication, other adult relationships, a caring neighborhood, a caring school climate, and parent involvement in schooling. Among the internal asset types, "commitment to learning" incorporates achievement

Table 13.1. Descriptions of Positive Youth Development

Description	Reference
Four defining features of this field: comprehensive (a host of inputs in a variety of contexts); promotion (increase access to strength-building inputs and building personal strengths); developmental (recognizes the growth process and stages, and the role youth play navigating through those stages); and symbiotic (drawing ideas, strategies, and practices from many disciplines).	Benson & Pittman, 2001, ix
Core ideas: community (i.e., family, school, neighborhoods, programs, congregations, peers, workplace); view of the child; developmental strengths; reduction in high-risk behaviors; promotion of health; well-being; and thriving.	Benson et al., 2006, 896–897
Approaches that seek to achieve one or more of the following objectives: promotes bonding, fosters resilience, promotes social competence, promotes emotional competence, promotes cognitive competence, promotes behavioral competence, promotes moral competence, fosters self-determination, fosters spirituality, fosters self-efficacy, fosters clear and positive identity, fosters belief in the future, provides recognition for positive behavior, provides opportunities for prosocial involvement, fosters prosocial norms.	Catalano, Berglund, et al., 2004, 101
The positive youth development approach aims at understanding, educating, and engaging children in productive activities rather than at correcting, curing, or treating them for maladaptive tendencies or so-called disabilities.	Damon, 2004, 15
This approach is not viewed as replacing the focus on preventing problems, but rather as creating a larger framework that promotes positive outcomes for all young people.	Eccles & Gootman, 2002, 3
Initiative (i.e., related to the capacity for agency or for autonomous action) is a core quality of positive youth development.	Larson, 2000, 170
The five Cs: competence, confidence, connection, character, and caring. A possible sixth C, contribution.	Lerner, Phelps, et al., 2009, 545
All concepts are predicated on the ideas that every young person has the potential for successful, healthy development and that all youth possess the capacity for positive development.	Lerner et al., 2003, 172
Three distinguishing features of youth development approaches: program goals, atmosphere, and activities.	Roth & Brooks-Gunn, 2003a, 97–98

motivation, school engagement, completing homework, bonding to school, and reading for pleasure. These forty assets have been found to affect seven thriving-related outcomes: school success, leadership, valuing diversity, physical health, helping others, delay of gratification, and overcoming adversity (Scales, Benson, Leffert, & Blyth, 2000). More recently, Benson has taken these concepts and written about ways for parents to help youth succeed by igniting their potential, called "sparks" (Benson, 2008).

Benson and colleagues' efforts coincide with work by the Committee on Community-Level Programs for Youth. Their work has considered personal assets (knowledge of essential life skills, good self-regulation skills) and social assets (connectedness, sense of social place and integration, ability to navigate in different cultural contexts) that facilitate positive youth development (Eccles & Gootman, 2002). Community partnerships, such as Children First, have used these concepts, and R. M. Lerner and others (J. V. Lerner et al., 2009; R. M. Lerner, 2005) have discussed the forty assets in their own work.

Richard Lerner and colleagues have sought to examine constructs related to indicators of PYD. They have hypothesized that indicators of PYD are comprised of the five Cs (competence, confidence, connection, character, and caring), and possibly a sixth C, contribution (R. M. Lerner, Almerigi, et al., 2005). The five Cs are derived from work by Roth and Brooks-Gunn (2003b) and are defined as follows (Phelps et al., 2009, p. 573):

1. Competence: Positive view of one's actions in domain-specific areas including social, academic, cognitive, and vocational. Social competence pertains to interpersonal skills (e.g., conflict resolution). Cognitive competence pertains to cognitive abilities (e.g., decision making). School grades, attendance, and test scores are part of academic competence. Vocational competence involves work habits and career choice explorations.
2. Confidence: An internal sense of overall positive self-worth and self-efficacy; one's global self-regard, as opposed to domain-specific beliefs.
3. Connection: Positive bonds with people and institutions that are reflected in bidirectional exchanges between the individual and peers, family, school, and community in which both parties contribute to the relationship.
4. Character: Respect for social and cultural rules, possession of standards for correct behaviors, a sense of right and wrong (morality), and integrity.
5. Caring and compassion: A sense of sympathy and empathy for others.

The sixth C, contribution, recognizes that PYD occurs over time (Larson, 2000) and that adult life should ideally include contributions to one's own health and well-being and to various realms of society (e.g., family, school, neighborhood; R. M. Lerner, 2004).

Other scholars, such as Damon, have echoed related components of PYD and have highlighted constructs such as noble purpose and morality (Damon, 2004, 2010). Noble purpose involves youth moving beyond self-interest (assuming that their basic needs are met) to pursue a purposeful life and engage in actions that strengthen the world around them. Morality involves children's natural moral sense and the guidance required of caregivers in a supportive context to promote youth to act in a caring and ethical manner as they mature into honorable adults.

These descriptions and constructs, along with work from other like-minded researchers and practitioners (Keyes, 2005; Larson, 2000; Seligman, 2000), have created a vocabulary that shares a common focus on enhancing youth development. The varying terminology reflects the heterogeneity of theory that has contributed to PYD. As research and theory progress, integrative theories may help generate greater consistency across this field.

UNDERLYING AND UNIFYING THEORIES OF POSITIVE YOUTH DEVELOPMENT

By the term *underlying*, we refer to theories that helped inform the process leading to the conception of PYD. This process includes a myriad of child and human development theories that, along with the study of plasticity and the nature-nurture synthesis, led to the development of systems theories of development (R. M. Lerner, 2006). "Unifying" theories make reference to these systems theories and other metatheories (such as the theory of triadic influence described herein) that are integrative and acknowledge the importance of nature- and nurture-based factors and their interaction. Unifying metatheories, such as developmental systems theory (Ford & Lerner, 1992; J. V. Lerner et al., 2009; R. M. Lerner, 2005), helped inform PYD and were at least part of the impetus for PYD by serving as the basis for the articulation of developmental assets. As Benson stated, "the concept of developmental assets, first posited in 1990 (Benson, 1990), is grounded in the large metatheory known as developmental systems theory (Ford & Lerner, 1992; Gottlieb, 1997)" (Benson, 2007, p. 36). Developmental systems theories include features noting the importance of both biological and environmental factors and the interactions or relationships between them (R. M. Lerner, 2006).

Certain developmental theories, such as attachment theory and social learning theories, have long been influential in developmental research (Cairns & Cairns, 2006). Developmental theory components are included as core concepts in dynamic systems theories that describe the behavior of complex biological and physical systems (Thelen & Smith, 1998). Dynamic systems theories overlap with developmental systems models that acknowledge concepts such as individual and contextual relations and the temporality and relative plasticity of human development (J. V. Lerner et al. 2009; R. M. Lerner, 2005; R. M. Lerner et al., 2009). These theories are similar to bioecological models in that they are evolving theoretical frameworks for the study of human development over time (Bronfenbrenner & Morris, 2006). They generally propose that by promoting intra- and interpersonal processes and environments, human developmental potential is enhanced (Bronfenbrenner & Ceci, 1994). Simply put, these theories highlight that personal, human relationship, and environmental factors all interact in myriad ways to influence development and outcomes.

As much as we admire well-thought-out theory and recognize its importance, we agree with Baltes and colleagues who explained, "It is important to recognize that present theoretical preferences are in part the direct result of historical contexts of science and cultural scenarios rather than of carefully elaborated theoretical arguments" (Baltes, Lindenberger, & Studinger, 2006, p. 571). Understanding of PYD is also informed by research and program advancement, such as the movement from problem-specific interventions to those that address more distal factors that influence multiple behaviors (Flay, 2000, 2002; Flay et al., 2009; Romer, 2003). Further, practitioners provide additional knowledge through experience on the "front lines" of PYD work. Benson noted that "the articulation of a developmental theory of positive youth development is itself an ongoing and dynamic process emerging several decades after the birthing of positive youth development as a field of practice" (Benson et al., 2006, p. 902). He described in detail a broad and comprehensive theory of PYD that includes theories of human development, context and community influence, and context and community change (Benson et al., 2006).

The Theory of Triadic Influence

Recently, researchers have recommended the theory of triadic influence (TTI; Flay & Petraitis, 1994; Flay et al., 2009) as an integrative, comprehensive theoretical framework with applicability to PYD (Catalano, Gavin, & Markham, 2010). Consistent with the holistic nature of PYD (i.e., considering environments in relation to the whole child; Damon & Gregory, 2003) and the reciprocity between person and context (Benson, 2007), the TTI has the potential to unify and clarify the many concepts of PYD.

Due to the "newness" of the PYD field and related theory, and the multidisciplinary and often comprehensive nature of PYD, there is sometimes inconsistency in what it encompasses across related disciplines. Moreover, an unclear picture arises from the complex puzzle of influences that affect PYD and result in behavior. Therefore, we believe that some new ideas regarding PYD can be derived from the TTI and have implications for prosocial education in general and PYD in particular. The comprehensive, integrative metatheory was developed to organize the scores of factors that influence behavior and to clearly focus one's view of (1) what causes behaviors and (2) how to effectively promote positive behavior, a key goal of prosocial education and PYD.

The theory was introduced during the time that PYD efforts began to expand in the 1990s. Faced with a complex mass of theories and variables, particularly in the field of substance use, Petraitis, Flay, and Miller (1995) examined the literature and concluded that variables can be organized along two dimensions: the *social-ecological streams of influence* (i.e., intrapersonal, interpersonal, and cultural-environmental influences) and *levels of causation* (i.e., ultimate causes, distal influences, and proximal predictors). From these findings, Flay and Petraitis (1994) proposed the TTI (see figure 13.1 for more detail) to acknowledge that a complex "web of causation" (Krieger, 1994) affects behaviors and that these causes can be organized into a cogent framework to provide a structured and testable integrated theory.

The TTI provides a detailed ecological approach and suggests that distal and ultimate influences on behavior produce larger and sustained effects on PYD. Further, the theory can provide PYD researchers with a detailed theoretical framework to guide research, program design, and evaluation. In fact, the Positive Action program that we discuss herein maps well onto the TTI.

The TTI arranges variables that affect behavior into three levels of causation: *ultimate*, *distal*, and *proximal*. Ultimate-level causes are factors that individuals possess little control over such as cultural practices, mass media, politics, socioeconomic status, school availability, parental values, and their own personality and neurocognitive skills. However, these factors affect multiple behaviors, are the most mediated, and if changed are likely to have the greatest and longest-lasting impact on PYD. Distal-level influences are factors reflecting the relation between individuals and context (social-personal nexus; e.g., general self-concept and self-control, bonding to parents and/or

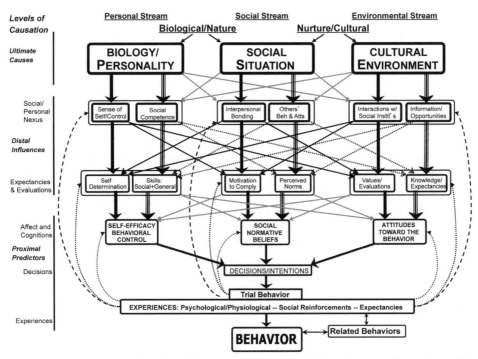

Figure 13.1.   The theory of triadic influence. Source: Adapted from Flay, Snyder, and Petraitis (2009).

peers, after-school program participation) that persons are likely to have some control over. Another step closer to behavior are evaluations and expectancies, which are general values, behavior-specific evaluations, general knowledge, and specific expectations and beliefs that result from bidirectional individual–contextual influences. Proximal-level predictors are more specific to and more immediate precursors of behavior. Youth wield control over these variables, such as their will and skill (i.e., self-efficacy) to do well in school, although proximal predictors are clearly influenced by the distal and ultimate factors described above. Decisions, intentions, and experiences are thought to directly affect a particular behavior.

Three streams of influence flow through these levels of causation as they affect PYD and influence behavior (see figure 13.1). The *intrapersonal stream* begins at the ultimate level with relatively stable biological/personality characteristics that in turn influence sense of self and competence (both general and social). These affect self-determination and general skills and converge on self-efficacy regarding a particular behavior, such as completing homework. The *interpersonal stream* follows a similar flow and begins with ultimate-level variables of the immediate social situation that in turn influence interpersonal bonding and the behaviors of role models such as parents, teachers, neighbors, and peers. The flow then continues through variables that include motivation to comply with or please various role models and perceptions of what behaviors those role models are encouraging. These influences then converge on social normative beliefs, or the perceptions of social pressures to engage in a particular behavior. Lastly, the third stream, the *cultural-environmental stream*, begins with characteristics of one's broader culture and environment and flows into variables including the nature of relationships with societal institutions (e.g., governmental, religious), along with the information extracted from the culture, such as knowledge gained from mass media (e.g., that adolescents are typically "troubled," as they are portrayed in movies). Next, the stream affects variables related to the expected consequences (expectancies) of a behavior (e.g., whether attending class is useful) and values and evaluations of those consequences. Finally, these influences converge on attitudes toward a specific behavior, such as caring for and helping an older neighbor.

In addition to the three main streams, each stream contains two substreams. One substream is more *cognitive and rational* in nature, and the other is more *affective* or *emotional, controlling* in nature and less rational. Therefore, decisions may encompass an affective or emotional component (i.e., hot cognition) as well as a cognitive or rational component (Ariely, 2009). Within the TTI, every stream ends in affective or cognitive factors (self-efficacy, social normative beliefs, and attitudes) that influence the most proximal affective or cognitive predictor of behavior, intentions. The theory recognizes that variables in one path are often mediated by or interact with variables in another path, and engaging in a behavior may have influences that feed back and alter the original causes of the behavior.

Figure 13.2 illustrates that the TTI includes ecological rings and levels of causation. The three streams of influence in the TTI are similar to the rings of influence in Bronfenbrenner's ecological-systems theory (1979, 1986, 2005); however, the TTI provides explicit detail about levels/tiers of causation within its rings. Figure 13.2 shows that time and development also influence levels of causation, and lower levels of causation often include faster processes. Time and development also influence program results; for example, PYD programs that are effective but not followed up by ongoing supportive contexts will likely have less impact over time. Much like math, reading, and science, youth should not be expected to improve developmentally and permanently gain PYD assets if prosocial skills are only briefly targeted in, for example, a one-month or one-year program.

The TTI helps explain PYD because it is integrative and recognizes interactions (i.e., moderation) and intervening variables (i.e., mediation) in a developmental, ecological framework. The appropriateness of the TTI for PYD-related work becomes even clearer after reviewing PYD-related strategies, characteristics, and outcomes of effective programs, as described in the next section. The theory also helps in understanding why some programs are more effective than others. A more detailed discussion of the TTI and its various applications can be found elsewhere (Flay & Petraitis, 1994; Flay et al., 2009).

Characteristics, Strategies, and Outcomes of Effective Programs

We are beginning to amass a body of literature that demonstrates that PYD-related approaches work. Also, research explicitly describes characteristics of effective PYD-related programs and the successful strategies they employ. However, investigation is still needed to understand why some PYD-related efforts are more effective than others, and we encourage readers to examine whether programs meet criteria for effectiveness (Flay et al., 2005). We caution that *evidence-based* is not a standardized term and

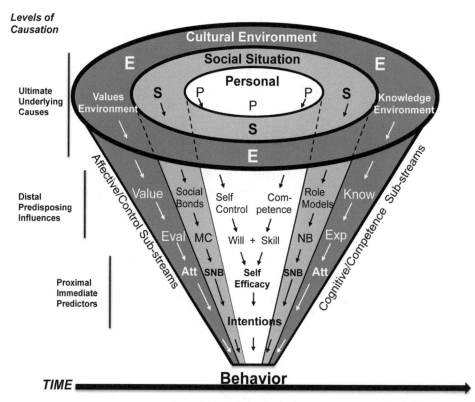

Figure 13.2. The theory of triadic influence ecological system. Source: Adapted from Flay, Snyder, and Petraitis (2009). Note: Eval = evaluation, Att = attitude toward the behavior, MC = motivation to comply, SNB = social normative beliefs, Know = knowledge, Exp = expectancies.

is often used broadly to suggest that a program has some evidence of effectiveness without regard to the quality of the research that produced the results. Further, although more work can be done to guide choices for policy and practice (Granger, 2002), we have gained a better understanding of the beneficial outcomes evinced by PYD-related programming. During the last two decades, various empirical studies and reviews have clarified effective practices and continue to advance the PYD movement (Catalano, Berglund, et al., 2004; Durlak et al., 2007; Gavin, Catalano, David-Ferdon, Gloppen, & Markham, 2010). A broad range of characteristics and strategies exist that overlap PYD and other prosocial areas of research and programming (e.g., SEL, SECD). Moreover, common themes emerge among these areas that lead to successful youth outcomes. These overlaps and common themes exemplify the usefulness of the prosocial education concept to further practice and educational theory building.

UNIQUE CHARACTERISTICS OF PYD PROGRAMMING

Some program characteristics are included in table 13.1. According to Roth and Brooks-Gunn (2003a), who surveyed U.S. youth development organizations, there are three distinguishing characteristics of youth development programs: program goals, atmosphere, and activities. Most, if not all, prosocial education interventions likely meet Roth and Brooks-Gunn's defining characteristics. While their sample is not representative of U.S. PYD organizations, and more research is needed regarding PYD organizations, the study does provide insight regarding PYD-related efforts. The researchers identified program goals that included the promotion of development (e.g., social and life skill building, academic improvement, personality development) and the prevention of unhealthy behaviors (e.g., substance abuse, violence, school dropout, gang activity). Programs offered youth-centered approaches that "create and nourish an atmosphere of hope" (Roth & Brooks-Gunn, 2003a, p. 97). Program atmospheres were supportive (e.g., relationship-focused activities); empowering (e.g., leadership training, community service); and included expectations for positive behavior (e.g., incentives or rewards). Further, program activities included opportunities for youth to pursue talents and beneficial interests, build skills, and gain a sense of achievement.

Characteristics of PYD efforts coincide with strategies of effective programs explained in recent reviews. For instance, as Catalano and colleagues noted,

> themes common to success involved methods to strengthen social, emotional, behavioral, cognitive, and moral competencies; build self-efficacy; shape messages from family and community about clear standards for youth behavior; increase healthy bonding with adults, peers, and younger children; expand opportunities and recognition for youth; provide structure and consistency in program delivery; and intervene with youth for at least nine months or longer. (Catalano, Berglund, et al., 2004, p. 114)

The authors explain further that effective programs focused on several PYD constructs, had structured curriculum and activities, and attended to fidelity of implementation. These recommendations are similar to those suggested by other scholars. For example, some have suggested four practices of effective programs (Bond & Hauf, 2004; Dusenbury & Falco, 1995; Gresham, 1995, as cited in Durlak et al. 2011). These include a sequenced step-by-step training approach, incorporating active forms of learning, a focus (and sufficient time) on social and personal skill development, and explicit learning goals, or SAFE practices (for "sequenced, active, focused, and explicit"). Effective strategies have been reiterated in the health behavior literature, and Flay (2002) has noted that programs must ideally (1) address both positive and negative behaviors; (2) be developmentally appropriate; (3) span several years, with carefully designed review, reinforcement, and extension; (4) be culturally sensitive; (5) be school- and classroom-focused, but extend beyond the school; (6) when appropriate, use peers to demonstrate skills and alter norms; (7) include proper training of personnel; (8) actively involve parents; (9) be designed with input from all stakeholders, including students; (10) include school improvement and reorganization components; and (11) incorporate ongoing evaluation at all programming stages.

Not surprisingly, these recommendations echo researchers examining other areas of prosocial education, such as character and moral education. For example, Berkowitz and Bier (2007) concluded that effective programs tend to include professional development for implementation, interactive teaching strategies, direct teaching strategies, family and community involvement, and modeling and mentoring. Many of these strategies are echoed by the Collaborative for Academic, Social, and Emotional Learning (CASEL).

These characteristics and strategies clearly relate to program expectations referenced by our integrative theory, the TTI. For example, the comprehensiveness of the TTI explains the limited impact of information-only approaches that only focus on didactic education (i.e., knowledge, in the TTI's cultural-environmental stream), value-based approaches that frequently focus only on the lower half of the cultural-environmental stream, and even more recent approaches that address the need for social skills and self-efficacy (Botvin, 1990; Botvin, Schinke, & Orlandi, 1995; Flay, 2000; Flay et al., 2009). The TTI clarifies that the most successful PYD-related programs must address all of the streams of influence. For example, programs that incorporate skill-, social-normative-, knowledge-, and value-based components are more likely to enhance social and emotional skills, attitudes, prosocial behaviors, and academic achievement (Durlak et al., 2011). Program effects can also be enhanced if programs and supports exist that address the proximal, distal, and ultimate levels of causation.

Consistent with theory, and as several key research articles have concluded, appropriately designed and implemented programs have demonstrated effects on a variety of outcomes. For instance, Catalano and colleagues (Catalano, Berglund, Ryan, Lonczak, & Hawkins 2002) found that effective PYD programs significantly enhanced multiple youth outcomes, including interpersonal skills, quality of adult and peer relationships, self-control, problem-solving abilities, cognitive competencies, self-efficacy, commitment to schooling, and academic performance. Again, not surprisingly, the results of other prosocial programs are similar, such as SEL programs, which have components overlapping with PYD. Results show that programs significantly improved social-emotional skills, attitudes, behavior, and academic achievement, with fewer conduct problems, less aggressive behavior, and less emotional distress (Durlak et al., 2011). Another recent review described beneficial effects of PYD-related programs (e.g., Aban Aya, Abecedarian, the Seattle Social Development Project, the Teen Incentives Program, the Teen Outreach Program) on adolescent sexual and reproductive health (Gavin, Catalano, & Markham, 2010; Gavin et al., 2010).

As demonstrated above and expressed elsewhere (Bernat & Resnick, 2006; Durlak et al., 2007), research as a whole has shown that PYD-related programs can promote development and prevent risk behaviors. Moreover, there is considerable conceptual overlap between youth development and prevention (Benson et al., 2006; Catalano, Hawkins, et al., 2002). As we will explain in the next section, programs can prevent health-compromising behaviors, promote development, and create contextual change by building abilities and competencies.

EXEMPLAR RESEARCH AND PROGRAMMING

Growing empirical evidence describes state-of-the-art research on PYD etiology and an array of PYD-related exemplar programs. These numerous programs are discussed in empirical reviews and meta-analyses (e.g., Catalano, Berglund, et al., 2004; Durlak et al., 2007; Gavin et al., 2010). In one PYD review, Catalano, Berglund, and colleagues (2004) described programs such as Big Brothers/Big Sisters, Life Skills Training, the PATHS Project, the Child Development Project, Fast Track, the Seattle Social Development Project, Across Ages, the Midwestern Prevention Project, and Project Northland. Other resources summarize effective PYD-related programs such as those produced by Child Trends.

As mentioned previously, PYD reviews include programs that were also included in reviews of other areas of prosocial education, such as SEL. There is sometimes no differentiation made between PYD programs and substance use prevention programs (J. V. Lerner et al., 2009). Thus, in this chapter we discuss a program that we have evaluated, Positive Action, and believe is a good example of what a PYD program encompasses and its potential impact. Positive Action serves as an example to highlight best practices and beneficial outcomes, which include an improvement in positive and prosocial behaviors, a simultaneous reduction in unhealthy behaviors, and an improvement in whole-school quality. Additionally, we discuss 4-H and an example of state-of-the-art etiology research, the 4-H Positive Youth Development Study. This etiology research supports the inclusion of both preventive and PYD approaches in programmatic efforts, such as Positive Action. The 4-H PYD study also reports evidence that suggests 4-H participants demonstrate better outcomes as compared to those participating in other out-of-school-time activities.

4-H Study of Positive Youth Development

Through land-grant university extension systems across the United States, 4-H is a PYD organization that involves nearly six million youth and adults in a variety of programs with various curricula and activities related to citizenship, science, and health. For example, 4-H citizenship programs include Citizenship Washington Focus, held in Washington, D.C., and designed to provide youth with skills to engage in civic action through field trips and leadership opportunities. 4-H science programs include curricula on renewable energy and technology; its health-related curricula include activities and training that seek to engage youth in behaviors such as preparing healthy food and participating in physical activity. Overall, 4-H offers programs and hands-on activities intended to enhance the health of youth and society.

As part of the 4-H Study on Positive Youth Development, a cross-sectional (i.e., at one point in time) analysis suggested that tenth-grade youth participating in 4-H programs demonstrated greater academic achievement and engagement in school compared to youth involved in other out-of-school-time activities (R. M. Lerner, Lerner, & colleagues, 2011). In addition, 4-H youth evinced less alcohol and cigarette use, along with lower use of other drugs. The overall goal of the 4-H PYD study and its strength, however, is to understand the processes involved in PYD (R. M. Lerner, Lerner, et al., 2005), not the effects of any one particular program.

The 4-H Study of PYD was an ambitious endeavor to gain a greater understanding of what PYD is and what fosters a healthy developmental trajectory toward an adulthood full of contributions to self, family, community, and civil society. Participant recruitment for the study began in 2002 and included 1,700 diverse adolescents and their parents located in thirteen states (R. M. Lerner, Lerner, et al., 2005; Schwartz et al., 2010). The study used a longitudinal sequential design (i.e., new groups of participants were added over time), and through wave 6 (grades 5 to 10) data were collected from 6,450 adolescents from forty-five states (R. M. Lerner et al., 2011). Adolescents in the study sample took part in numerous after-school activities, not only 4-H (R. M. Lerner, Lerner, et al., 2005). A list of publications with detailed information regarding the

4-H study is available from the Institute for Applied Research in Youth Development website (see "For More Information" section at the end of this chapter). Although the study is largely observational, its longitudinal perspective provides a good example of cutting-edge research related to PYD etiology. A brief highlight from a few of the many studies related to this project illustrates our point.

Findings from the first wave of the 4-H study demonstrated that PYD was comprised of components representing the five Cs (R. M. Lerner, Lerner, et al., 2005). The results provided support for the relationship between PYD and the five Cs as well as the sixth C, contribution. More recently, Bowers and colleagues (2010), using longitudinal data from students in grades 8 through 10, concluded that the five-C model demonstrated measurement invariance and thus suggested that PYD can be measured similarly across these age groups. In a study examining the trajectories of positive (e.g., PYD, contribution) and negative outcomes (e.g., depressive symptoms, risk behaviors), Lewin-Bizan and colleagues (2010) found that, from fifth through tenth grade, youth fit into groups that demonstrated several trajectories (i.e., patterns of intraindividual change; for example, PYD scores across grade levels) and most often followed a high trajectory of positive outcomes and a low trajectory of negative ones. Youth in the high-trajectory group were most likely to be in a decreasing risk behavior group and low depressive symptoms group. Another study (Schwartz et al., 2010) found evidence that PYD acts as a protective mechanism against alcohol, tobacco, and illicit drug use, along with unsafe sexual behavior. The researchers concluded that the results support the integration of prevention science and PYD perspectives. Overall, the 4-H Study of Positive Youth Development has provided, and continues to provide, a greater understanding of PYD etiology and how PYD relates to risk reduction.

Positive Action

The Positive Action (PA) program is a comprehensive, schoolwide PYD program designed to affect youth development in multiple affective, cognitive, and behavioral domains and create whole-school contextual change in order to reduce such problem behaviors as substance use and improve school performance. The student-focused component of the program is grounded in a broad theory of self-concept (DuBois, Flay, & Fagen, 2009; Purkey, 1970; Purkey & Novak, 1970), and the whole program is consistent with integrative, ecological theories such as the TTI (Flay & Allred, 2010).

The full PA program includes K–12 classroom curricula (consisting of almost daily fifteen- to twenty-minute lessons), a schoolwide climate development component, and family- and community-involvement components. The sequenced curricula contain teacher-friendly, scripted lessons that use a range of teaching methodologies to address different learning styles. For example, interaction between student and teacher is enhanced through structured discussions, and interaction between students is encouraged through small-group activities including games, role-plays, and practice of skills. Each grade-specific curriculum consists of 140 lessons covering six major units on topics related to self-concept (the relationship of thoughts, feelings, and actions); physical and intellectual actions (nutrition, physical activity, learning skills, decision-making skills, creative thinking); social-emotional actions for managing oneself responsibly (self-control, time management); getting along with others (empathy, altruism, respect, conflict resolution); being honest with yourself and others (self-honesty, integrity, self-appraisal); and continuous self-improvement (goal setting, problem solving, persistence). The total time students are exposed to the fully implemented program during a thirty-five-week academic year is around thirty-five hours.

The schoolwide climate development kit includes materials and activities (such as posters and school assemblies) to encourage and reinforce the six units of PA. School leaders and other personnel are involved in coordinating schoolwide implementation of the program. The family and community involvement components provide additional support and reinforcement of the PA units. For example, when the PA program is fully implemented, parents receive PA materials to guide activities in the home and a PA committee is formed to involve community stakeholders.

Both quasi-experimental and experimental trials demonstrate that PA can improve a variety of student- and school-level outcomes and that the program can prevent risk behaviors and enhance positive behaviors and development, concomitantly. Additionally, the program has been shown to create whole-school contextual change and improve school quality.

Specifically, the program has been shown to increase academic performance and decrease undesirable outcomes such as suspensions (Flay & Allred, 2003; Flay, Allred, & Ordway, 2001; Snyder et al., 2010). Snyder and colleagues (2010) utilized archival school-level data collected by the Hawai'i Department of Education to find that PA schools in a randomized trial demonstrated significantly improved standardized test scores in reading and math. At baseline, PA schools were below state averages in academic performance, and at posttest, they met or exceeded state averages. PA schools also reported lower absenteeism and fewer suspensions and retentions compared to control schools.

Other outcomes related to positive development have been examined. Washburn and colleagues (in press) examined the effects of PA on student-level positive behaviors associated with character. Utilizing data from three randomized trials (a Hawai'i trial, a Chicago trial, and a smaller trial in a southeastern state), results demonstrated that elementary-aged students in PA program and control schools showed a general decline in the number of positive behaviors associated with character across time (4 years in Hawai'i; 2.5 years in Chicago; 3 years in the southeastern state), with the PA program mitigating this decline.

The effect of the PA program on unhealthy behaviors has also been investigated. Utilizing data from the PA randomized trial in Hawai'i, Beets and colleagues (2009) found that 10 percent of fifth-grade PA students and 19 percent of control-school students had ever consumed alcohol. Less than 11 percent of fifth-grade students reported having ever engaged in behaviors related to extreme violence or voluntary sexual activity, but results showed significantly lower rates of substance use, violent behaviors, and voluntary sexual activity among students receiving the PA program compared to control school students. With data from the PA randomized trial in Chicago, Li and colleagues (2011) found that nearly one-third of fifth-grade students reported using at least one substance and engaging in at least one violent behavior, but students attending PA program schools had significantly less substance use and violent behavior compared to control school students. Overall, the studies found that the PA program reduced unhealthy behaviors even though limited or no instructional time was devoted to negative behaviors. Although substance use and violence-related behaviors (harassment, bullying, fighting, etc.) are mentioned, they are not the main focus anywhere in the curricula and are used only as example behaviors (sexual activity is never mentioned).

More recently, studies have examined mediational models whereby positive behaviors mediated the effects of the PA program on unhealthy behaviors. That is, positive development was promoted, and in the same model, risky behaviors were reduced. Snyder and colleagues (2011), using data from the Hawai'i trial, found that program effects on positive academic behavior (e.g., work hard in school, set goals, manage time wisely, try to be one's best, solve problems well) mediated the effects of PA on reducing substance use, violent behaviors, and sexual activity. In another study using longitudinal data from the Chicago study, Lewis and colleagues (2011) demonstrated that program effects on youths' general character (defined as prosocial interaction, honesty, self-development, self-control, respect for teacher, respect for parent; DuBois, Ji, Flay, Day, & Silverthorn, 2010; Ji, DuBois, & Flay, 2011) mediated the program effects on substance use. That is, students attending PA schools showed significantly better change in general character than students attending control schools, and general character, in turn, mediated the program's effects on reducing substance use. These results, in total, confirm the model underlying the PYD approach.

Regarding whole-school contextual change, a recent study (Snyder et al., in press), using school-level data collected by the Hawai'i Department of Education as part of its School Quality Survey (and independently of the evaluation of PA), showed that PA schools demonstrated improved overall school quality compared to control schools. Program schools, compared to controls, also evinced improvement on individual indicators of school quality such as school safety and well-being and student, teacher, and parent involvement. Notably, by one year posttrial, PA schools outperformed control schools and state averages on school quality. Emerging evidence continues to support the concepts that PYD-related programming can indeed improve youths' contexts and have both promotive (of positive development) and preventive (of problem behaviors) effects.

POSITIVE YOUTH DEVELOPMENT POLICY

We agree with others who have suggested that "promoting healthy youth development through programmatic means must be coupled with policy-based approaches that address the broader social determinants of health" (Bernat & Resnick, 2006, p. S14). This is evident by a quick glance at the TTI in figure 13.1. Most, if not all, policy is related to health, and policy in general is linked to PYD in some way. PYD-related policy extends beyond the educational landscape. Schools and the educational system play a role, but youth also spend time in homes and neighborhoods interacting with family, peers, and neighbors, and they are exposed to mass media. Although an in-depth discussion of many PYD-related policies is beyond the scope of this chapter, here we briefly focus on examples of U.S. federal policy and federally funded programs related to PYD and socioeconomic status. Similar to a PYD perspective, policy and program strengths and beneficial outcomes are highlighted.

Policies related to increasing the economic well-being of families play a vital role in PYD. The Earned Income Tax Credit (EITC), for instance, is one strategy responsible for lifting over four million families above the federal poverty line and increasing employment (Holtz, Mullin, & Scholz, 2001). Family-directed, in-kind support is another strategy used to increase resources for families. Strategies that are classified in this category include the Supplemental Nutrition Assistance Program (SNAP; formally known as the Food Stamp Program); the Special Supplemental Food Program for Women, Infants, and Children (WIC); the National School Lunch Program; the State Children's Health Insurance Program (SCHIP); and housing assistance programs. Many of these strategies have repeatedly been associated with improved development and health outcomes in youth. For example, WIC has been associated with a range of positive health outcomes, including improved cognitive abilities among youth (Gershoff, Aber, & Raver, 2003).

Other programs, such as Head Start and Early Head Start, include an assortment of health services for young children. In a review of Head Start research, Barnett and Hustedt (2005) reported generally positive evidence supporting the long-term benefits of Head Start. Relatedly, the Early Head Start program (Robinson & Fitzgerald, 2002) has been implemented and is designed to influence four related outcomes: child development (e.g., cognitive and social development), family development (e.g., parenting practices), staff development (e.g., training), and community development (e.g., family support services). Although there is a need for more rigorous research and evaluation of these strategies, evidence has indicated that Early Head Start has a positive influence on parents and their children, with mothers found to be more supportive and children demonstrating greater cognitive development as compared to children not enrolled (Gershoff et al., 2003).

Not only are these aforementioned policies and strategies good for the families and youth directly involved, but research demonstrates that greater equality makes societies stronger and is better for the health and well-being of *everyone* (Wilkinson & Pickett, 2010). Actualizing positive health and developmental outcomes largely depends upon policy, and although investing in youth can have a positive financial return (Newman, Smith, & Murphy, 2001), U.S. society in general has yet to make PYD a high priority. The PYD perspective and research clearly show the need to move away from an approach that attempts to fix problems (i.e., depression, substance abuse, school dropout), to one that focuses on youth development and primary prevention, a key point of the prosocial approach of this handbook. Overall, it is also important to note that programming efforts will be maximized across the life span if policy supports PYD, another point of this handbook's focus.

IMPLICATIONS FOR PROSOCIAL EDUCATION

Educators, researchers, policy makers, and the public can benefit by acknowledging the components of PYD and supporting effective PYD strategies and programs. In particular, PYD research has generated, and continues to generate, knowledge about specific youth and context strengths/assets. In this chapter we have sought to provide clarity by highlighting three key components of PYD programs: (1) a focus on youth strengths/assets and potential for positive individual development, (2) the value of supportive (asset-rich) contexts, and (3) bidirectional interactions between person and context. The implication of this is that a comprehensive PYD program by our definition includes three characteristics: (1) curricula to teach students prosocial and emotional skills and develop their intrapersonal strengths/assets; (2) activities to enrich environments (schools, families, and community) to support and reinforce the use of skills and positive behaviors by youth; and (3) activities to encourage the bidirectional influence of intrapersonal and environmental assets. Because of the relative newness of PYD, its efforts go beyond the origins of some other types of prosocial education; for example, character education, because of its far-reaching roots, was historically didactic (Berkowitz & Bier, 2004; Park & Peterson, 2009), although this is now changing. Areas of prosocial education overlap with PYD if they include a focus on youth strengths, comprehensive and integrative components, or acknowledgment of bidirectional interactions. Similar to other successful prosocial education and health promotion efforts, it is likely that the most effective approaches to PYD will include behavioral and contextual change strategies from the multiple causal levels and six substreams included in the TTI (Flay, Snyder, et al., 2009).

Although it is often difficult and frustrating to sift through the PYD-related programs without evaluation data, rigorously evaluated PYD-related programs exist and have demonstrated encouraging results on a wide array of outcomes (Catalano, Berglund, et al., 2004). Program evaluations (using randomized trials) and PYD etiology research have suggested the integration of promotive and preventive approaches. Our research with the Positive Action program suggests that focusing mainly on PYD (increasing strengths/assets/positive behaviors) can also reduce unhealthy behaviors among youth (Flay et al., 2003).

Even with the promising results of evidence-based programs, "one program, even an extraordinarily good program, cannot do it all" (Roth & Brooks-Gunn, 2003a, p. 97). Each effective programming effort plays a role, and a variety of evidence-based strategies should be implemented that meet the demands of diverse youth (Komro et al., 2011). Further, strategies need to be broader (i.e., address sociocultural influences), with sustained efforts and policy supports for long-lasting effects. Regarding sociocultural influences, more can be done by, for instance, increasing positive portrayals of youth in film media, highlighting positive youth outcomes in the news, training students to be peer advocates, creating more opportunities for community service and service abroad, offering only healthy foods at schools, changing food policy to make fresh fruits and vegetables more affordable as compared to processed and fast food, and providing youth with access to clean, safe outdoor spaces (e.g., community gardens, parks, natural areas).

Limitations

Positive youth development is comprehensive, and comprehensiveness often entails complexity. Researchers are beginning to understand the multidimensionality of PYD; however, more work is needed. Not only is PYD challenging to measure, but PYD indicators may also change across childhood, adolescence, and young adulthood. Further, although multidisciplinary work has the potential for innovation, this relatively new and multidisciplinary field is rife with overlap with other areas of prosocial education, which can make uniquely defining and understanding PYD a challenge. In many ways it appears everyone has their own unique insight regarding what PYD is and what strategies it includes. However, after a careful review of the empirical literature, several lucid themes emerge, including a focus on youth strengths/assets, the importance of supportive environments, and bidirectional youth–context interactions.

CONCLUSIONS AND FUTURE DIRECTIONS

Progress has been made in the last couple of decades toward expressing a positive view of youth development, and more research and practice will occur in the future. There will likely be growth in some PYD-related areas, such as positive psychology, while other related areas will perhaps merge together, such as SEL and SECD. Recognizing the challenges of research extending across numerous disciplines and many programs, an increased effort toward generating consistency should be made. Ideally, over time, with persistent effort, research and practice will form a more uniform terminology and approach. Consistency in theoretical understanding is one way of achieving this. Theory, when empirically tested and validated, can bring together various fields by building a common foundation on which to understand phenomena. Interconnected with a need for theory, there is a need for advancing PYD-specific measurement models to help define and delineate constructs included in PYD.

Prosocial education has much to gain by embracing a PYD perspective, which acknowledges that youth have strengths and that context matters. Indeed, public-health research shows the importance of contextual and social determinants of health (Marmot & Bell, 2009; Woolf, 2009). Overall, there is vast potential for the prosocial education focus of PYD to help answer some of the vexing questions surrounding education. For instance, PYD-related work has answered questions related to how youth are motivated and challenged to succeed and move toward a healthy adulthood: youth can be engaged in positive, meaningful activities and relationships (Larson, 2000, 2006). There is, however, more work that is needed to gain a better understanding of PYD and its influences.

To help advise and advance theory, and to understand why some PYD-related efforts are more effective than others, further research is needed related to mediation and moderation analyses (Baron & Kenny, 1986; MacKinnon & Fairchild, 2009). This will help add to the limited PYD literature consistent with theory and, further, will help in the development of PYD-specific theory (Benson et al., 2006). Methodological and statistical advances (Hayes, 2009; MacKinnon, 2008; Zhao, Lynch, & Chen, 2010) have potential to improve youth development by helping to identify how to prevent risky behaviors and promote healthy behaviors. Moreover, a better understanding of program effects can be gained. Ideally, to reduce Type I error, analysis should include comprehensive models that examine many components of a program in one theoretically justified model.

Relatedly, more research is needed to examine how positive behaviors can lead to a reduction in negative ones under differing circumstances. Evidence herein shows that a program can promote positive development and, at the same time, reduce risky behaviors; however, more work is required to better understand the complexity of this effect. For instance, does this effect occur differently for varying ages and cultures, and how can PYD be optimally integrated with risk prevention in, for example, unsafe sex prevention? Are there certain situations and contexts where increasing positive behaviors will lead to a more sustained reduction in negative behaviors? On a related note, more research is required to better understand the bidirectional nature of PYD (Benson et al., 2006; J. V. Lerner et al., 2009). For example, how do school/community efforts affect youth, and how do youth in turn affect their contexts? This calls for more longitudinal research and rigorous quasi-experimental and experimental designs.

Increased efforts could also be made examining the effect of PYD on additional behavioral outcomes, such as dietary behaviors and physical activity. Given the promising results of PYD-related programs described herein, it is likely these programs (perhaps modified) can affect behavioral outcomes that have not been examined to date. To help predict and understand the potential of a program's impact, prosocial education practitioners can refer to theory. Theory can help understand if, for example, a program will likely be behavior specific or influence multiple behaviors (Flay, Snyder, et al., 2009). Theory also helps in understanding the limits of program impacts if there are not auxiliary supports (interpersonal, environmental, or cultural, for example) in place to enhance outcomes across time.

Additionally, although some work has been done specifically with PYD among diverse youth (Lerner, Taylor, & von Eye, 2002), more cross-cultural work is needed. Further, more can be uncovered about PYD programming and etiology across ages. This includes examining the importance of PYD before a child is conceived, across gestation, through young adulthood, and into adulthood and old age.

Lastly, and perhaps most importantly, it is essential to determine which programs are effective and ready for broad dissemination (Flay et al., 2005). Many evidence-based programs exist, yet ineffective (even iatrogenic) programs continue to be implemented. Both PYD programs and other related efforts should be backed by objective data that demonstrate their positive impact; otherwise, limited resources are wasted.

To reiterate, a PYD approach seeks to instill in youth and adults the belief that humans are born with vast potential, and youth are not problems to be managed. Unhealthy development and behaviors are not inexorable, but instead, with healthy personal strengths in a supportive, asset-rich context, youth can develop positively and be more likely to have bright futures full of satisfaction, health, happiness, and contribution. This is the PYD perspective.

FOR MORE INFORMATION

Child Trends: http://www.childtrends.org

Children First: http://www.children-first.org

Collaborative for Academic, Social, and Emotional Learning (CASEL): http://casel.org

4-H: http://www.4-h.org

Institute for Applied Research in Youth Development, Tufts University: http://ase.tufts.edu/iaryd/default.htm

Positive Action (PA) program: http://www.positiveaction.net

REFERENCES

Ariely, D. (2009). *Predictably irrational: The hidden forces that shape our decisions.* New York: HarperCollins.

Baltes, P. B., Lindenberger, U., & Studinger, U. (2006). Life span theory in developmental psychology. In W. Damon & R. M. Lerner (Eds.), *Handbook of child psychology* (pp. 569–664). Hoboken, NJ: Wiley.

Barnett, W. S., & Hustedt, J. T. (2005). Head Start's lasting benefits. *Infants & Young Children, 18*(1), 16–24.

Baron, R. M., & Kenny, D. A. (1986). The moderator-mediator variable distinction in social psychological research: Conceptual, strategic, and statistical considerations. *Journal of Personality and Social Psychology, 51*(6), 1173–1182.

Battistich, V., Schaps, E., Watson, D., Solomon, D., & Lewis, C. (2000). Effects of the child development project on students' drug use and other problem behaviors. *Journal of Primary Prevention, 21*(1), 75–99.

Beets, M. W., Flay, B. R., Vuchinich, S., Snyder, F. J., Acock, A., Li, K.-K., et al. (2009). Use of a social and character development program to prevent substance use, violent behaviors, and sexual activity among elementary-school students in Hawaii. *American Journal of Public Health, 99*(8), 1438–1445.

Benson, P. L. (1990). *The troubled journey: A portrait of 6th–12th grade youth*. Minneapolis, MN: Search Institute.

Benson, P. L. (1997). *All kids are our kids*. San Francisco: Jossey-Bass.

Benson, P. L. (2003). Developmental assets and asset-building community: Conceptual and empirical foundations. In R. M. Lerner & P. L. Benson (Eds.), *Developmental assets and asset-building communities: Implications for research, policy, and practice* (pp. 19–43). Norwell, MA: Kluwer Academic Publishers.

Benson, P. L. (2007). Developmental assets: An overview of theory, research, and practice. In R. K. Silbereisen & R. M. Lerner (Eds.), *Approaches to positive youth development* (pp. 33–58). Thousand Oaks, CA: Sage.

Benson, P. L. (2008). *Sparks: How parents can help ignite the hidden strengths of teenagers*. San Fransicso: Jossey-Bass.

Benson, P. L., & Pittman, K. (2001). Moving the youth development message: Turning a vague idea into a moral imperative. In P. L. Benson & K. J. Pittman (Eds.), *Trends in youth development: Visions, realities, and challenges* (pp. vii–xii). Norwell, MA: Kluwer Academic Publishers.

Benson, P. L., Scales, P. C., Hamilton, S. F., & Sesma, A. (2006). Positive youth development: Theory, research, and applications. In W. Damon & R. M. Lerner (Eds.), *Handbook of child psychology* (pp. 894–941). Hoboken, NJ: Wiley.

Berkowitz, M. W., & Bier, M. C. (2004). Research-based character education. *Annals of the American Academy of Political and Social Science, 591*(1), 72.

Berkowitz, M. W., & Bier, M. C. (2007). What works in character education. *Journal of Research in Character Education, 5*(1), 29–48.

Bernat, D. H., & Resnick, M. D. (2006). Healthy youth development: Science and strategies. *Journal of Public Health Management and Practice, 12*(Suppl. 6), S10–S16.

Bierman, K. L., Coie, J. D., Dodge, K. A., Foster, E. M., Greenberg, M. T., Lochman, J. E., et al. (2004). The effects of the Fast Track program on serious problem outcomes at the end of elementary school. *Journal of Clinical Child and Adolescent Psychology, 33*(4), 650–661.

Biglan, A., Brennan, P. A., Foster, S. L., & Holder, H. D. (2004). *Helping adolescents at risk: Prevention of multiple problem behaviors*. New York: Guilford.

Bond, L. A., & Hauf, A. M. C. (2004). Taking stock and putting stock in primary prevention: Characteristics of effective programs. *Journal of Primary Prevention, 24*(3), 199–221.

Botvin, G. J. (1990). Substance abuse prevention: Theory, practice, and effectiveness. *Crime & Justice, 13*, 461–519.

Botvin, G. J., Schinke, S., & Orlandi, M. A. (1995). School-based health promotion: Substance abuse and sexual behavior. *Applied & Preventive Psychology, 4*(3), 167–184.

Bowers, E. P., Li, Y., Kiely, M. K., Brittian, A., Lerner, J. V., & Lerner, R. M. (2010). The five Cs model of positive youth development: A longitudinal analysis of confirmatory factor structure and measurement invariance. *Journal of Youth and Adolescence, 39*(7), 720–735.

Bronfenbrenner, U. (1979). *The ecology of human development: Experiments by nature and design.* Cambridge, MA: Harvard University Press.

Bronfenbrenner, U. (1986). Ecology of the Family as a Context for Human Development: Research Perspectives. *Developmental Psychology, 22*(6), 723–742.

Bronfenbrenner, U. (2005). *Making human beings human: Bioecological perspectives on human development.* Thousand Oaks, CA: Sage.

Bronfenbrenner, U., & Ceci, S. J. (1994). Nature-nurture reconceptualized in developmental perspective: A bioecological model. *Psychological Review, 101*(4), 568–586.

Bronfenbrenner, U., & Morris, P. A. (2006). The bioecological model of human development. In W. Damon & R. M. Lerner (Eds.), *Handbook of child psychology* (pp. 793–828). Hoboken, NJ: Wiley.

Cairns, R. B., & Cairns, B. D. (2006). The making of developmental psychology. In W. Damon & R. M. Lerner (Eds.), *Handbook of child psychology* (pp. 89–165). Hoboken, NJ: Wiley.

Catalano, R. F., Berglund, M. L., Ryan, J. A. M., Lonczak, H. S., & Hawkins, J. D. (2002). Positive youth development in the United States: Research findings on evaluations of positive youth development programs. *Prevention & Treatment, 5*(1). doi:10.1037/1522-3736.5.1.515a

Catalano, R. F., Berglund, M. L., Ryan, J. A. M., Lonczak, H. S., & Hawkins, J. D. (2004). Positive youth development in the United States: Research findings on evaluations of positive youth development programs. *Annals of the American Academy of Political and Social Science, 591*(1), 98–124.

Catalano, R. F., Gavin, L. E., & Markham, C. M. (2010). Future directions for positive youth development as a strategy to promote adolescent sexual and reproductive health. *Journal of Adolescent Health, 46*(3 Suppl.), S92–S96.

Catalano, R. F., Hawkins, J. D., Berglund, M. L., Pollard, J. A., & Arthur, M. W. (2002). Prevention science and positive youth development: Competitive or cooperative frameworks? *Journal of Adolescent Health, 31*(6 Suppl.), 230–239.

Catalano, R. F., Oesterle, S., Fleming, C. B., & Hawkins, J. D. (2004). The importance of bonding to school for healthy development: Findings from the Social Development Research Group. *Journal of School Health, 74*(7), 252–261.

Damon, W. (2004). What is positive youth development? *Annals of the American Academy of Political and Social Science, 591*(1), 13–24.

Damon, W. (2010, February). Meeting students where they are: The bridge to character. *Educational Leadership, 67*(5), 36–39.

Damon, W., & Gregory, A. (2003). Bringing in a new era in the field of youth development. In R. Lerner, F. Jacobs, & D. Wertlieb (Eds.), *Handbook of applied developmental science* (pp. 407–420). Thousand Oaks, CA: Sage.

Donovan, J. E., Jessor, R., & Costa, F. M. (1993). Structure of health-enhancing behavior in adolescence: A latent-variable approach. *Journal of Health and Social Behavior, 34*, 346–362.

DuBois, D. L., Flay, B. R., & Fagen, M. C. (2009). Self-esteem enhancement theory: An emerging framework for promoting health across the life-span. In R. J. DiClemente, M. C. Kegler, & R. A. Crosby (Eds.), *Emerging theories in health promotion practice and research* (pp. 97–130). San Francisco: Jossey-Bass.

DuBois, D. L., Ji, P., Flay, B. R., Day, J., & Silverthorn, N. (2010, June). *Further validation of the youth social and character development scale*. Poster Session presented at the fifth annual conference of the Institute of Educational Sciences Research, National Harbor, MD.

Durlak, J. A., Weissberg, R. P., Dymnicki, A. B., Taylor, R. D., & Schellinger, K. B. (2011). The impact of enhancing students' social and emotional learning: A meta-analysis of school-based universal interventions. *Child Development, 82*(1), 405–432.

Durlak, J. A., Taylor, R. D., Kawashima, K., Pachan, M. K., DuPre, E. P., Celio, C. I., et al. (2007). Effects of positive youth development programs on school, family, and community systems. *American Journal of Community Psychology, 39*(3), 269–286.

Dusenbury, L., & Falco, M. (1995). Eleven components of effective drug abuse prevention curricula. *Journal of School Health, 65*(10), 420–425.

Eccles, J., & Gootman, J. A. (2002). *Community programs to promote youth development*. Washington, DC: National Academy Press.

Elias, M. J. (2009). Social-emotional and character development and academics as a dual focus of educational policy. *Educational Policy, 23*(6), 831–846.

Flay, B. R. (2000). Approaches to substance use prevention utilizing school curriculum plus social environment change. *Addictive Behaviors,* 25(6), 861–885.

Flay, B. R. (2002). Positive youth development requires comprehensive health promotion programs. *American Journal of Health Behavior, 26*(6), 407–424.

Flay, B. R., & Allred, C. G. (2003). Long-term effects of the Positive Action program. *American Journal of Health Behavior, 27*(Suppl. 1), S6–S21.

Flay, B. R., & Allred, C. G. (2010). The Positive Action program: Improving academics, behavior and character by teaching comprehensive skills for successful learning and living. In T. Lovat, R. Toomey, & N. Clement (Eds.), *International research handbook on values education and student wellbeing* (pp. 471–501). New York: Springer.

Flay, B. R., Allred, C. G., & Ordway, N. (2001). Effects of the Positive Action program on achievement and discipline: Two matched-control comparisons. *Prevention Science, 2*(2), 71–89.

Flay, B., Berkowitz, M. W., & Bier, M. C. (2009). Elementary school-based programs theorized to support social development, prevent violence, and promote positive school climate: Description and hypothesized mechanisms of change. *Journal of Research in Character Education, 7*(2), 21–49.

Flay, B. R., Biglan, A., Boruch, R. F., Castro, F. G., Gottfredson, D., Kellam, S., et al. (2005). Standards of evidence: Criteria for efficacy, effectiveness and dissemination. *Prevention Science, 6*(3), 151–175.

Flay, B. R., Graumlich, S., Segawa, E., Burns, J. L. & Holliday, M. Y. (2004). Effects of 2 prevention programs on high-risk behaviors among African American youth: A randomized trial. *Archives of Pediatrics & Adolescent Medicine, 158*(4), 377–384.

Flay, B. R., & Petraitis, J. (1994). The theory of triadic influence: A new theory of health behavior with implications for preventive interventions. *Advances in Medical Sociology, 4,* 19–44.

Flay, B. R., Snyder, F. J., & Petraitis, J. (2009). The theory of triadic influence. In R. J. DiClemente, R. A. Crosby, & M. C. Kegler (Eds.), *Emerging theories in health promotion practice and research* (pp. 451–510). San Francisco: Jossey-Bass.

Fleming, C. B., Haggerty, K. P., Catalano, R. F., Harachi, T. W., Mazza, J. J., & Gruman, D. H. (2005). Do social and behavioral characteristics targeted by preventive interventions predict standardized test scores and grades? *Journal of School Health, 75*(9), 342–349.

Ford, D. H., & Lerner, R. M. (1992). *Developmental systems theory: An integrative approach*. Newbury Park, CA: Sage.

Gavin, L. E., Catalano, R. F., David-Ferdon, C., Gloppen, K. M., & Markham, C. M. (2010). A review of positive youth development programs that promote adolescent sexual and reproductive health. *Journal of Adolescent Health, 46*(3 Suppl.), S75–S91.

Gavin, L. E., Catalano, R. F., & Markham, C. M. (2010). Positive youth development as a strategy to promote adolescent sexual and reproductive health. *Journal of Adolescent Health, 46*(3 Suppl.), S1–S6.

Gershoff, E. T., Aber, J. L., & Raver, C. C. (2003). Child poverty in the United States: An evidence-based conceptual framework for programs and policies. In R. M. Lerner, F. Jacobs, & D. Wertlieb (Eds.), *Handbook of applied developmental science* (pp. 81–136). Thousand Oaks, CA: Sage.

Gottlieb, G. (1997). *Synthesizing nature-nurture: Prenatal roots of instinctive behavior.* Mahwah, NJ: Erlbaum.

Granger, R. C. (2002). Creating the conditions linked to positive youth development. *New Directions for Youth Development 95*, 149–164.

Haegerich, T. M., & Metz, E. (2009). The social and character development research program: Development, goals, and opportunities. *Journal of Research in Character Education, 7*(2), 1–20.

Hawkins, J. D., Catalano, R. F., Kosterman, R., Abbott, R., & Hill, K. G. (1999). Preventing adolescent health-risk behaviors by strengthening protection during childhood. *Archives of Pediatrics & Adolescent Medicine, 153*(3), 226–234.

Hayes, A. F. (2009). Beyond Baron and Kenny: Statistical mediation analysis in the new millennium. *Communication Monographs, 76*(4), 408–420.

Holtz, V. J., Mullin, C., & Scholz, J. K. (2001). *The earned income tax credit and labor market participation of families on welfare* (Joint Center for Poverty Research Working Paper). Evanston, IL: Institute for Policy Research, Northwestern University.

Ji, P., DuBois, D. L., & Flay, B. R. (2011). *Child character and social development scale: Development and initial validation with elementary school students.* Manuscript submitted for publication.

Keyes, C. L. M. (2005). Mental health and/or mental illness? Investigating axioms of the complete state model of health. *Journal of Consulting and Clinical Psychology, 73*(3), 539–548.

Komro, K. A., Flay, B. R., Biglan, A., & Promise Neighborhoods Research Consortium. (2011). Creating nurturing environments: A science-based framework for promoting child health and development within high-poverty neighborhoods. *Clinical Child and Family Psychology Review.* doi:10.1007/s10567-011-0095-2

Krieger, N. (1994). Epidemiology and the web of causation: Has anyone seen the spider? *Social Science & Medicine, 39*(7), 887–903.

Larson, R. W. (2000). Toward a psychology of positive youth development. *American Psychologist, 55*(1), 170–183.

Larson, R. W. (2006). Positive youth development, willful adolescents, and mentoring. *Journal of Community Psychology, 34*(6), 677–689.

Lerner, J. V., Phelps, E., Forman, Y., & Bowers, E. P. (2009). Positive youth development. In R. M. Lerner & L. Steinberg (Eds.), *Handbook of adolescent psychology* (pp. 524–558). Hoboken, NJ: Wiley.

Lerner, R. M. (1995). Developing individuals within changing contexts: Implications of developmental contextualism for human development research, policy, and programs. In T. A. Kinderman & J. Valsinar (Eds.), *Development of person-context relations* (pp. 227–240). Hillsdale, NJ: Erlbaum.

Lerner, R. M. (2004). Diversity in individual–context relations as the basis for positive development across the life span: A developmental systems perspective for theory, research, and application. *Research in Human Development, 1*(4), 327–346.

Lerner, R. M. (2005). *Promoting positive youth development: Theoretical and empirical bases.* White paper prepared for the Workshop on the Science of Adolescent Health and Development, National Research Council/Institute of Medicine. Washington, DC: National Academies of Science.

Lerner, R. M. (2006). Developmental science, developmental systems, and contemporary theories of human development. In R. M. Lerner & W. Damon (Eds.), *Handbook of child psychology: Vol. 1. Theoretical models of human development* (6th ed., pp. 1–17). Hoboken, NJ: Wiley.

Lerner, R. M., Abo-Zena, M. M., Bebiroglu, N., Brittian, A., Lynch, A. D., & Issac, S. S. (2009). Positive youth development: Contemporary theoretical perspectives. In R. J. DiClemente, J. S. Santelli, & R. A. Crosby (Eds.), *Adolescent health: Understanding and preventing risk behaviors* (pp. 115–128). San Francisco: Jossey-Bass.

Lerner, R. M., Almerigi, J. B., Theokas, C., & Lerner, J. V. (2005). Positive youth development: A view of the issues. *Journal of Early Adolescence, 25*(1), 10–16.

Lerner, R. M., Brentano, C., Dowling, E. M., & Anderson, P. M. (2002). Positive youth development: Thriving as the basis of personhood and civil society. In R. M. Lerner, C. S. Taylor, & A. von Eye (Eds.), *New directions for youth development: Pathways to positive development among diverse youth* (pp. 11–33). San Francisco: Jossey-Bass.

Lerner, R. M., Dowling, E. M., & Anderson, P. M. (2003). Positive youth development: Thriving as the basis of personhood and civil society. *Applied Developmental Science, 7*(3), 172–180.

Lerner, R. M., Lerner, J. V., Almerigi, J. B., Theokas, C., Phelps, E., Gestsdottir, S., et al. (2005). Positive youth development, participation in community youth development programs, and community contributions of fifth-grade adolescents: Findings from the first wave of the 4-H study of positive youth development. *Journal of Early Adolescence, 25*(1), 17–71.

Lerner, R. M., Lerner, J. V., & colleagues. (2011). *Waves of the future 2009: Report of the findings from the first six years of the 4-H study of positive youth development.* Medford, MA: Institute for Applied Research in Youth Development, Tufts University.

Lerner, R. M., Taylor, C. S., & von Eye, A. (2002). *New direction for youth development: Pathways to positive development among diverse youth* (G. G. Noam, Ed.). San Francisco: Jossey-Bass.

Lerner, R. M., von Eye, A., Lerner, J. V., & Lewin-Bizan, S. (2009). Exploring the foundations and functions of adolescent thriving within the 4-H study of positive youth development: A view of the issues. *Journal of Applied Developmental Psychology, 30*(5), 567–570.

Lewin-Bizan, S., Lynch, A. D., Fay, K., Schmid, K., McPherran, C., Lerner, J. V., et al. (2010). Trajectories of positive and negative behaviors from early- to middle-adolescence. *Journal of Youth and Adolescence, 39*(7), 751–763.

Lewis, K. M., Bavarian, B., Snyder, F. J., Acock, A., DuBois, D. L., Ji, P., et al. (2011). *Direct and mediated effects of a social-emotional and character development program on adolescent substance use.* Manuscript submitted for publication.

Li, K.-K., Washburn, I., DuBois, D. L., Vuchinich, S., Brechling, V., Day, J., et al. (2011). Effects of the Positive Action programme on problem behaviors in elementary school students: A matched-pair randomised control trial in Chicago. *Psychology & Health, 26*(2), 179–204. doi: 10.1080/08870446.2011.531574

MacKinnon, D. P. (2008). *Introduction to statistical mediation analysis.* New York: Erlbaum.

MacKinnon, D. P., & Fairchild, A. J. (2009). Current directions in mediation analysis. *Current Directions in Psychological Science, 18*(1), 16–20.

Malecki, C. K., & Elliott, S. N. (2002). Children's social behaviors as predictors of academic achievement: A longitudinal analysis. *School Psychology Quarterly, 17*(1), 1–23.

Marmot, M., & Bell, R. (2009). Action on health disparities in the United States. *Journal of the American Medical Association, 301*(11), 1169–1171.

Nelson, C. A. (1999). Neural plasticity and human development. *Current Directions in Psychological Science, 8*(2), 42–45.

Newman, R. P., Smith, S. M., & Murphy, R. (2001). A matter of money: The cost and financing of youth development. In P. L. Benson & K. J. Pittman (Eds.), *Trends in youth development: Visions, realities and challenges* (pp. 91–134). Norwell, MA: Kluwer Academic Publishers.

O'Connell, M. E., Boat, T., & Warner, K. E. (Eds.). (2009). *Preventing mental, emotional, and behavioral disorders among young people: Progress and possibilities.* Washington, DC: National Academies Press.

Park, N., & Peterson, C. (2009). Strengths of character in schools. In R. Gilman, E. S. Huebner, & M. J. Furlong (Eds.), *Handbook of positive psychology in schools* (pp. 65–76). New York: Routledge.

Payton, J. W., Wardlaw, D. M., Graczyk, P. A., Bloodworth, M. R., Tompsett, C. J., & Weissberg, R. P. (2000). Social and emotional learning: A framework for promoting mental health and reducing risk behaviors in children and youth. *Journal of School Health, 70*(5), 179–185.

Pentz, M. A., Dwyer, J. H., MacKinnon, D. P., Flay, B. R., Hansen, W. B., Wang, E. Y. I., et al. (1989). A multicommunity trial for primary prevention of adolescent drug abuse. *JAMA: Journal of the American Medical Association, 261*(22), 3259–3266.

Petraitis, J., Flay, B. R., & Miller, T. (1995). Reviewing theories of adolescent substance use: Organizing pieces in the puzzle. *Psychological Bulletin, 117*, 67–86.

Phelps, E., Zimmerman, S., Warren, A. E. A., Jeličić, H., von Eye, A., & Lerner, R. M. (2009). The structure and developmental course of positive youth development (PYD) in early adolescence: Implications for theory and practice. *Journal of Applied Developmental Psychology, 30*(5), 571–584.

Purkey, W. W. (1970). *Self-concept and school achievement.* Englewood Cliffs, NJ: Prentice-Hall.

Purkey, W. W., & Novak, J. (1970). *Inviting school success: A self-concept approach to teaching and learning.* Belmont, CA: Wadsworth.

Riggs, N. R., Greenberg, M. T., Kusché, C. A., & Pentz, M. A. (2006). The mediational role of neurocognition in the behavioral outcomes of a social-emotional prevention program in elementary school students: Effects of the PATHS curriculum. *Prevention Science, 7*(1), 91–102.

Robinson, J. L., & Fitzgerald, H. K. (2002). Early Head Start: Investigations, insights, and promise. *Infant Mental Health Journal, 23*(1–2), 250–257.

Romer, D. (2003). *Reducing adolescent risk: Toward an integrated approach.* Thousand Oaks, CA: Sage.

Roth, J. L., & Brooks-Gunn, J. (2003a). What exactly is a youth development program? Answers from research and practice. *Applied Developmental Science, 7*(2), 94–111.

Roth, J. L., & Brooks-Gunn, J. (2003b). What is a youth development program? Identificaton and defining principles. In F. Jacobs, D. Wertlieb, & R. M. Lerner (Eds.), *Handbook of applied developmental science: Promoting positive child, adolescent, and family development through research, policies, and programs* (Vol. 2, pp. 197–223). Thousand Oaks, CA: Sage.

Scales, P. C. (1999). Reducing risks and building developmental assets: Essential actions for promoting adolescent health. *Journal of School Health, 69*(3), 113–119.

Scales, P. C., Benson, P. L., Leffert, N., & Blyth, D. A. (2000). Contribution of developmental assets to the prediction of thriving among adolescents. *Applied Developmental Science, 4*(1), 27–46.

Schwartz, S. J., Phelps, E., Lerner, J. V., Huang, S., Brown, C. H., Lewin-Bizan, S., et al. (2010). Promotion as prevention: Positive youth development as protective against tobacco, alcohol, illicit drug, and sex initiation. *Applied Developmental Science, 14*(4), 197–211.

Seligman, M. E. P. (2000). Positive psychology. In J. E. Gillham (Ed.), *The science of optimism and hope: Research essays in honor of Martin E. P. Seligman* (pp. 415–429). Randor, PA: Templeton Foundation Press.

Settersten, R., & Ray, B. E. (2010). *Not quite adults: Why 20-somethings are choosing a slower path to adulthood, and why it's good for everyone.* New York: Random House.

Snyder, F. J., Acock, A. C., Vuchinich, S., Beets, M. W., Washburn, I. J., & Flay, B. R. (2011). *Preventing negative behaviors among elementary-school students through enhancing students' social-emotional and character development.* Manuscript submitted for publication.

Snyder, F., Flay, B., Vuchinich, S., Acock, A., Washburn, I., Beets, M., et al. (2010). Impact of a social-emotional and character development program on school-level indicators of academic achievement, absenteeism, and disciplinary outcomes: A matched-pair, cluster-randomized, controlled trial. *Journal of Research on Educational Effectiveness, 3*(1), 26–55.

Snyder, F. J., Vuchinich, S., Acock, A., Washburn, I. J., & Flay, B. R. (in press). Improving elementary-school quality through the use of a social-emotional and character development program: A matched-pair, cluster-randomized, controlled trial in Hawai'i. *Journal of School Health, 82*(1), 11–20.

Thelen, E., & Smith, L. B. (1998). Dynamic system theories. In W. Damon & N. Eisenberg (Eds.), *Handbook of child psycology* (pp. 563–634). Hoboken, NJ: Wiley.

Washburn, I. J., Acock, A., Vuchinich, S., Snyder, F., Li, K.-K., Ji, P., et al. (in press). Effects of a social-emotional and character development program on the trajectory of behaviors associated with social-emotional and character development: Findings from three randomized trials. *Prevention Science, 12*(3), 314–323.

Weissberg, R. P., & O'Brien, M. U. (2004). What works in school-based social and emotional learning programs for positive youth development. *Annals of the American Academy of Political and Social Science, 591*(1), 86–97.

Wentzel, K. R. (1993). Does being good make the grade? Social behavior and academic competence in middle school. *Journal of Educational Psychology, 85*(2), 357–364.

Wilkinson, R., & Pickett, K. (2010). *The spirit level: Why greater equality makes societies stronger.* New York: Bloomsbury Press.

Woolf, S. H. (2009). Social policy and health policy. *Journal of the American Medical Association, 11*, 1166–1169.

Zhao, X., Lynch, J. G., Jr., & Chen, Q. (2010). Reconsidering Baron and Kenny: Myths and truths about mediation analysis. *Journal of Consumer Research, 37*(2), 197–206.

Case Study 13A

Integrating Six Developmental Pathways in the Classroom: The Synergy between Teacher and Students

JAMES P. COMER, LARISSA GIORDANO,
AND FAY E. BROWN

Development and learning are inextricably linked. By integrating development with academics in the classroom, teachers can open up a world of opportunity for building relationships between and among students, parents, and teachers. *When these relationships thrive, so does the learning.* When in the process students are helped to better understand their own resultant development, they can also begin to understand that of their peers. With a better understanding of behavior, they can be held accountable for their actions and are more likely to take responsibility for their own learning. As this capacity grows, students tend to worry less about "why" certain things are happening or about what decisions they need to make or should have made. Greater awareness about their development and acceptance of responsibility remove a major roadblock to learning, which then allows them to focus more on what is being taught.

The integration of development and academic learning occurs best in a culture of belonging, trust, mutual respect, and collaboration, which taken together form the basis of a prosocial context for school experience. All of the stakeholders in a school, those with the greatest authority taking the lead, must intentionally create these conditions in order for the school to be a vital, dynamic place for effective teaching and learning. The Comer School Development Program (SDP) serves as a framework that, when implemented effectively in schools, helps to bring about those favorable conditions. This chapter presents a brief discussion of the model.*

THE SCHOOL DEVELOPMENT PROGRAM FRAMEWORK

The implementation of the SDP framework is guided by our theory of dynamic interaction: positive interactions between children/students and their caretakers in a supportive environment lead to powerful emotional attachments that

---

*For detailed information about the School Development Program, visit the website at schooldevelopmentprogram.org.

enable students to positively identify with, imitate, and internalize many of the attitudes, values, problem-solving behaviors, and expressive ways of their caretakers, and enable the caretakers to help make the development-driven energy of the students available for play, work, and learning.

The framework has nine elements: three mechanisms or teams (governance and management, parents, student and staff support); three operations (comprehensive school plan, assessment and modification, staff development); and three guiding principles (no-fault problem solving, consensus decision making, and collaboration).

The governance and management team is selected by, and is representative of, the stakeholder groups—educators, parents, support staff, and community partners. It establishes the school goals and creates a comprehensive school plan that addresses both academic and social issues. This team and plan provide direction and drive school activities. The parent team supports activities created in the plan. The student and staff support team provides services that promote development, desired behavior, and learning for students, staff, and parents.

The nine elements systematically pull all the many activities that must go on in a school together in a coordinated way and focus them on the critical needs of students—development and learning. Through ongoing assessment and modification of program outcomes and consistent practice of the guiding principles, representative governance helps all the stakeholders experience a sense of ownership, belonging, and responsibility for producing good outcomes. This helps to minimize relationship and behavior problems. The framework and processes encourage school community members to carry out effective problem solving and promote creative expression and growth of students, staff, and parents.

The relationship elements of the overall School Development Program framework are used to improve classroom climate, culture, and support for development—"Comer-in-the-Classroom." The following case study demonstrates how a teacher uses the Comer-in-the-Classroom elements of the School Development Program framework to improve her classroom culture and climate and effectuate significantly positive outcomes for her students.

ONE TEACHER'S EXPERIENCE

Nathan Hale is a pre-K–8 school located in New Haven, Connecticut. It serves approximately 550 students, 61 percent of whom are designated as students eligible for free or reduced-cost meals, and 9 percent of whom are designated as students with disabilities. The race/ethnic breakdown is as follows: 13 percent African American, 31 percent Hispanic, and 54 percent White. The school has made improvements in different areas within the past three years but made adequate yearly progress (AYP) for the first time last academic year, 2009–2010.

On the first day of school, I (the second author) was amazed by the twenty-seven young fourth graders in front of me. Not only did they seem self-motivated and very bright, but they were respectful and helpful and very willing to please. As the weeks passed, they were still very bright, but some were no longer willing to please, never mind be respectful. This bothered me immensely. As a teacher, I felt that it was my duty to teach and nurture these students and build relationships both with and among them so that they could better understand themselves as young people and one another as classmates. Some of my students began acting as if they were the center of the universe and no one else mattered. I could tell that something was bothering them and that they were taking it out on each other by teasing. They were probably hurting inside and wanted everyone else to feel the same way, including me. And I confess that their lack of respect toward me was making it difficult for me to want to help them—a feeling that made me both angry and guilty at the same time. I knew I needed to do something fast.

In October, the Yale School Development Program (Comer Process) started conducting a series of workshops at our school. The workshops introduced the concept of developmental pathways—physical, cognitive, language, social, ethical, psychological—which deepened my understanding of development and connected it to academic learning. The process also introduced the integration of the guiding principles of collaboration, consensus, and no-fault problem solving in the school and classroom. Not only did the Yale professionals provide workshops for the administration and faculty, but they also conducted workshops for the parents to help them understand how to support the development and learning of the children at home. With this new information and my administrator's support, I embarked on executing a plan for improving the overall climate of my classroom, with a specific goal of improved prosocial behavior.

Comer-in-the-Classroom: Getting Started

October–November

I began first by examining my own strategies of teaching and management by completing the SDP's Teacher Development and Instructional Strategies Survey (TDISS). This survey measures several variables including teachers' perceptions of their classroom practices, professional expertise, and teacher–student relationships. After reviewing the data, it became clear to me that my classroom management was too loose and inconsistent. Based on that observation, I started keeping a daily personal reflection log of the positive happenings and shortcomings of the day. I realized that although the students were learning, they were capable of so much more if I would give them more responsibility, have more confidence in them, and take more risks in challenging them to achieve. In other words, *I needed to improve my expectations for my students*. Furthermore, I noticed that I spent a great deal of time planning and mapping out objectives, big questions, and activities and too little time observing what actually unfolded in the classroom, where teachable moments were sometimes overlooked because of my rigorous adherence to my plan. I concluded that without becoming rigid I needed to be more structured and consistent with my expectations, and more observant of student needs and teaching opportunities. The structure and clarity of expectations allowed me to gradually release the responsibility for learning to the students and created a stronger, trusting relationship between us.

Given the valuable lessons I learned from completing the survey and engaging in further self-reflection, I thought the students could also benefit from doing some self-reflection. I provided an opportunity for them to complete the SDP's Student Development Survey (SDS). This survey measures students' opinions regarding various aspects of themselves as individuals, as learners, and as members of a social community. It examined not only how they felt about themselves, but how they felt others viewed them (e.g., "When I get angry, I can calm myself down," "My friends like me").

Before administering the survey, I read the questions to the students and asked them to think about what the questions were asking and to be honest with themselves. I told them that they did not have to share their answers with me if they weren't comfortable, but also that the purpose of completing the survey was not only for them to understand themselves better, but for me to better understand them in an effort to help meet their needs. Students therefore were given a choice, but they felt comfortable with me reading their answers because they wanted to reach out for help. Some of them were as unhappy with the peer relationships in the classroom as I was with my management. By completing the survey, students learned about themselves, and I learned much about them as individuals and as a class of learners. This insight led to change in how I conducted the classroom, which in turn made the management smoother because the students knew I cared, and the instruction was more closely related to them as learners. As time passed, I noticed the direct impact of my understanding and integration of the developmental pathways framework in every aspect of my teaching and overall classroom functioning. For surveys such as the SDS that do not present any psychological risks to students, we have passive parent consent; however, I also meet with parents and share with them many of the activities we do in our classroom regarding the integration of the developmental pathways, including the completion of the surveys.

Comer-in-the-Classroom: Moving Forward
After completing the survey process, which included my explaining the purpose for which they were taking the survey, I provided an overview of the three guiding principles and the six developmental pathways. Regarding collaboration, we talked about the importance of working together as members of the class to keep the room clean and tidy, restacking materials after we have used them, and being mindful of how we treat one another as a larger group and when we work in small groups. As we discussed consensus, we talked about the need for being in agreement, especially regarding how we would treat one another in the class and outside the class. We emphasized the importance of respect and integrity of self and respect for others. In terms of no-fault problem solving, we

focused on tone of voice and choice of words, discussing how they can inflame or diffuse a situation. We also discussed that as a class, when we are faced with a problem, we would do our best to not focus on blaming one another, but to try to find the best solutions to the problem.

After explaining the developmental pathways, I instituted what I called their "pathways journals." In these journals, students could record their learning about each of the pathways and also reflect on their growth along each pathway. We inserted our completed personal surveys in the opening pages and then separated the journals into chapters based on each of the pathways. I also included a section titled "Please Help Me," where students were encouraged to write about any issue of concern. They needed to identify the problem, explain it in terms of the pathway to which it was connected, and then propose a solution for solving that problem. Initially, I intended for it to be a chance for the students to write to me and I would respond in writing, but as I read a few of the journal entries and noticed some of the issues the students divulged, I knew they needed a more immediate response. I then decided that I would invite students to have lunch with me in the classroom to discuss their concerns and help them problem solve. This one-on-one lunchtime strategy proved to be very effective. Also, rather than simply reflecting in their journals once a week on Friday mornings, students often asked if they could write in their journals first thing in the morning before the teaching began, if there were issues they needed to "just get out of the way."

It is important to note that with twenty-seven students in my class, it was not possible to meet with all of them in a week or in a month. Actually, not all students indicated the need for help in any given month. Also, as the students wrote in the "Please Help Me" section of the journal, I was walking around noticing some of their entries and paying attention to body language. Some issues were taken care of at the moment of need rather than waiting until lunch. For example, one student had had an argument with her mom that morning and was allowed to call home to reconcile. Another student was writing about feeling anxious about the writing prompt that he knew he needed to take that afternoon because he "hated writing." I was able to take this child into the hallway for a pep talk. I was surprised that he hated writing because he was clearly a good writer. He thought he didn't measure up with the other students because his style was so different; so I was able to assure him that his style was different, but that's what made it so great.

Some issues that could not be addressed in the moment were discussed over lunch. Students were invited to have lunch with me either as individuals or in groups of twos or threes as the situation necessitated. If students expressed similar concerns or were involved in an issue with the student who wrote about the concern, I would meet with those students at the same time.

A More In-Depth Look at the Pathways

Over the next couple of months, in an effort to integrate the pathways in an in-depth manner in my instruction, I focused on each of them through children's books and excerpts from chapter books in which the message, theme, or characters reflected one or more of the developmental pathways. We focused on one pathway per week. Because the pathways are interconnected, in many cases all six were evident in the selected text, but we focused on one at a time until the students themselves began seeing the integration of all the pathways within the lives of the characters or message of the book. We started with a discussion about the particular pathway and connected it in terms of its relevance to our lives. Following the discussion, we read the text, stopping along points where the students noticed evidence of the pathway in a particular part of the text. After reading the text, students then shared their ideas about how a character was developing along that pathway or grappling with an issue along that pathway. The students then offered suggestions about what a character could have done to promote healthy development.

As a follow-up activity, students then had to write a reflection sheet that demonstrated their understanding of the pathway just studied and how it was relevant to their lives. They were also encouraged to include in their reflection if it was an area in which they could use more support. Throughout the week, students became increasingly verbal across the curricular areas about where they saw a pathway being developed or needing support, both within the curriculum as well as with what was happening within their own lives, in and outside of school. They were eager to share the stories with me and the class, and sometimes they added comments and suggestions in support of each other's development, such as, "I noticed that you are having difficulty with your language pathway because you don't always listen to what I am saying, and that makes me feel bad. You are a good friend, though, so I wanted to tell you and help you, because I have also done that but am trying to be a better listener." Or, "If you would only have more confidence in yourself, you would notice that you would make a great leader because you think so creatively."

January

When we returned from winter break on January 3rd, we shared some of the experiences we had during our time away. It was refreshing to see how, without prompting, we all seemed to share by focusing on our development along the six pathways. I then gave students some time to reflect in their journal—to write about any experience they chose and explain how it strengthened them as an individual or created a challenge for which they might need support in handling or resolving it. After giving the students some time to reflect, we talked about resolutions and goals. We spoke not only about how each student had grown along the pathways both socially and academically, but also about how there is always room for growth. We then discussed the importance of goals and goal setting. Given that this was January, when most of us focus on our "New Year's resolution," we talked about resolutions or promises to promote continuous self-improvement. I encouraged the students to examine themselves, focusing on their strengths and seeing if they were able to recognize personal weaknesses along the pathways that they could work on improving over the next few months, or areas in which they felt that I could provide support to help promote their development. I reminded them that I would be doing similar reflections, and that whatever they identified, it should be personal to them, with a goal that they could easily accomplish.

February

With February came Valentine's Day, or how I explained it to my students, "a day to express your feelings of friendship." I encouraged the students to not wait for this day to express their feelings, but to always use their language pathway to share feelings that boost the social, psychological, and ethical pathways, both for the person sharing and for the person receiving the compliment.

We began the day by reading the story of Amos, a mouse, and Boris, a whale, who develop a lifelong friendship. Amos, who is mesmerized by the sea, takes a boat trip on a sailing vessel which later capsizes in the rough seas. Boris comes to his rescue and brings Amos safely to land. Years later, Amos spots Boris washed up on the sand along the shore and despite his size he is able to help Boris back to his home in the sea. Despite their differences and years of separation, Amos and Boris know what it means to be a good friend. We discussed each character in terms of the developmental pathways, particularly the social, ethical, and psychological pathways. Then linking text to real life, we talked about what makes a good friend and how to be a good friend. We focused on important characteristics or qualities that ensure lasting friendships or promote healthy social relationships.

To further the conversation, each student was given a large construction paper cutout of a heart and a sheet of labels with each student's name. I then asked them to identify two specific positive qualities for each person in the class. Students then circled the room placing their label on the person's heart. The labels had items such as, "I like your sense of humor," "You have a great smile," "I like working with you in our group," and "I'm glad we're friends." This activity allowed each student to receive fifty-four positive comments that they could take home and share with their loved ones and that they could have as something tangible to revisit on days when they might feel that peer relationships were challenging.

March

The activity in February helped to decrease students' nervousness and feelings of anxiety and uncertainty that seem an inevitable part of the Connecticut Mastery Test (CMT) done in March. In preparation for these tests, I allowed students some time to talk about their test anxiety and to offer suggestions and kind words to one another. While we continued with our structured learning routine of the day, we also integrated some test-taking skills and a review of what we had been learning that year. We integrated the six developmental pathways in our discussion and reflection sheet as we shared what we were going to do to help promote a healthy mind and body to better stay focused on those tests. For example, students talked about getting more exercise and fresh air to reduce stress, drinking plenty of water, and getting the appropriate amount of rest (physical pathway). They shared that they were going to think critically when reading and problem solving or perhaps reread a text for deeper understanding (cognitive pathway). Some gave "good luck" notes to friends (social pathway), and I reminded them of the confidence I had in each of them that they would do well and had them promise that they would keep positive thoughts throughout the tests, knowing that they had the confidence to do well (psychological pathway). Students felt more prepared and confident knowing that they had the knowledge about the content and the support of their teacher and their classmates while they took the tests.

The Tests Behind Us, the Year Continues

As the CMTs came to a close and nerves began to ease, I noticed that among a few students there was somewhat of a reversal of the growth made over the previous months, particularly along the social, ethical, language, and psychological pathways. A few of them seemed to be behaving as if they were taking charge of each other and of the class community without regard for anyone's feelings. This seeming reversal was a bit surprising to me, but then I remembered a few important principles about development. For example, development is uneven and continuous; and very importantly, at this age the brain is still developing, which can account for why students from this age into their late teens seem to be inconsistent in controlling their emotions, impulses, and judgments. I also thought of the principle of no-fault problem solving.

This was early April, so we came together as a community and talked about our intolerance for teasing and for any behaviors that might feel like or sound like bullying. We talked about some of the behaviors of a bully as well as what being bullied looked like and felt like. Again, we examined ourselves along the six developmental pathways to reflect upon what happens in our language, our physical reactions, our cognitive thinking, our social behavior and interaction, our psychological mind-set, and our ability to make ethically sound decisions. I allowed students to revisit their "hearts" from February and reminded them to use their "Please Help Me" page in their journals to reach out to me so that I might know how to work with them personally to help them resolve conflicts or any other issues they were grappling with on a personal level.

May

In May, as a class we continued reflecting and, where needed, correcting past poor decisions; and although there were still two months of learning ahead, we began to focus on the positive outcomes of the year and took time to discuss how each of us had grown along all of the pathways. Each morning following math journal, a student's name was randomly chosen from my "take-a-turn" jar, and that student received the credit he or she deserved during a brief morning meeting that focused on how the selected student had demonstrated improvement along certain pathways and how that improvement was also reflected in his or her academic achievements. Many times that student would also take a minute to comment on how he or she still needed support or needed to improve along a particular pathway. The other students often commented on my comments or chose to mention specific positive details about the student of the day. This additional aspect of the student-to-student communication made it much more powerful than simply teacher-to-student feedback.

June

As the year began to come to a close, I allowed the students to again complete the survey they had completed in late October. After the self-reflection and the completion of the survey on their own, it was time for me to read the items aloud to tally the responses. In October during the first administration of the survey, I gave the students the option of putting their heads on their desk as I read the items aloud to tally their responses. They all selected to put their heads down. This time, however, the students did not feel it was necessary to put their heads down. They were proud and comfortable with how they felt about themselves, their friends, their teachers, and the school. And yes, their familiarity with having completed the questionnaire a few months earlier might also have contributed to their level of comfort sharing their responses openly. But for me as a teacher, it was enlightening to hear students stick up for one another as they raised their hands and noticed how others raised their hands to answer questions about feelings of belonging. This sharing made an enormous impact on the students and on me as their teacher to see their growth, not only in the results of the data but more importantly in the relationships that were formed and nurtured. Students were better able to understand each other because they understood themselves better. This understanding was evident in their reflection sheets about what they had learned about the pathways that year, and how this learning had helped them become better students and strengthened their confidence as individuals in and out of the classroom.

During the last week of school, I gave students the opportunity to create memory books in which they reflected on their fourth-grade school year. As I read some of their entries, I was impressed and delighted that many of them mentioned the six developmental pathways as an integral part of their learning. Following are a few examples:

My most memorable day was when my teacher gathered us on the rug to reflect on how each of us had grown and improved along our pathways. I felt so proud to be a part of such a smart class. Listening to her compliments about my specific strengths like how responsible and ethical I am in my decision making made me feel so good. The other students even chimed in and encouraged me too! I had no idea that I had such a positive effect on people around me. I realized then how important it is to always be aware of my development because it's not only about me but about my relationships with others.

My most memorable day was when the teacher was discussing feelings and how important it is to love yourself in order to love others. On my survey, I noticed I was choosing "never" a lot when it came to if I liked myself and if I found it easy to make friends. When sharing our surveys with the class, my classmates were very supportive in telling me, "That's not true, we are your friends and we love you. You should love yourself too." This made me feel very proud of myself and more confident in who I am inside. I will never forget that day when my friends really helped me to find myself, because I started the year feeling very lost.

My favorite thing about school this year was being able to express myself and learn how to not be afraid of who I am. I am able to concentrate on my work. I am learning so much more now because I am not preoccupied with how I look or whether I have designer boots on. I finally have confidence and know that others believe in me too, especially my mom. She has really noticed the difference and hugs me all the time.

Selected Examples of Student Success Stories*

Allejah

One morning, while entering the classroom, I could tell right away that something was bothering Allejah. I thought it might be a good idea to make a quick change to my lesson plan and allow for five minutes of reflection in the pathway journals. As I circled the room, I peeked at Allejah's entry in the "Please Help Me" section and noticed her eyes welling up with tears as she wrote. She was writing about needing help with her psychological pathway. I asked her to join me outside for a quick talk. She shared with me that she had an argument with her mom that morning and was feeling upset about how she left it, as she jumped out of the car for school, slamming the door behind her. Tearfully she told me she was afraid her mom didn't know that she was sorry and that she loved her. Feeling empathy for Allejah, and knowing how her state of mind might impact the rest of her day, I allowed her to use the phone to call her mom. I connected her with her mom and allowed her two minutes for her conversation. She returned to the classroom with a smile and whispered "thank you" to me as she passed. Having resolved that issue, I knew she was ready to start the day.

Jordan

It was Friday morning and Jordan was very excited, not only because it was Friday, but also because it meant that she had something positive to record in her pathways journal. Her journal was often filled with situations in which she needed support, but reflecting upon the week, this time she couldn't wait to get started. Seeing her enthusiasm, I circled to her desk to take a quick peek at what she was writing. She was writing about her development along the cognitive pathway. Specifically, she was pleased with her growth in writing. I had individually conferenced with her earlier that week and commented on how much improvement I saw in her fluency, organization, and elaboration

---

*Pseudonyms are used to protect the students.

in her writing. I told her that it was proof that if she believed in herself, took time to use the writing planner, and wrote about what she knew with feeling, her narratives would read more fluently and she would be proud of her work. Thursday she shared her story with the class about the day her baby brother was born. This was unusual for her because she often rejected any type of sharing of her work. It was the class's responsibility to note what was positive about the piece and what needed improvement. As she finished reading, the class was quiet for a second before applauding her. Although there were comments about grammar or sentence structure or using the words *I* or *said* too often, the overwhelming response was that Jordan did a terrific job in helping to create a picture in the listener's mind about what happened and what she was feeling the day her brother was born. Proudly, Jordan had noted in her journal that she was becoming a better writer—something that she had always thought was her worst subject.

Taylor

Another Friday morning I was circling the classroom as the students wrote in their journals. I saw that Taylor was trying to cover a bit of what she wrote under the "Please Help Me" section. I noticed that it involved her language pathway, but she was a bit embarrassed to let me see it at that moment. Respecting her space, I continued to circle the room, stopping by students not seeming to mind my presence. As we lined up for lunch that day, she asked if I could write back in her journal that day.

Over lunch I opened up to that page in her journal and read her entry. There, she indicated that she was having trouble with her language and psychological pathways because she gets nervous when the teacher calls on her and often doesn't want to answer in front of the class. This revelation surprised me, given her strong academic record. Although a quiet girl, it was something I should have picked up on earlier that week when I asked her to explain to the class how she solved a particular open-ended response to a math word problem. She was the only one in the class who got the correct answer. In response to my asking her to share with the class, she quietly said that she was not sure and couldn't really remember. Sadly, I had embarrassed her. She did know the answer, but now all her other classmates probably thought she was dumb, since she could barely speak. She wrote that when the teacher calls on her she gets nervous and goes blank. She mentioned that she often felt different from the other students and felt it was hard making friends because of her shyness. Rather than writing back, I asked her to bring her lunch upstairs and eat with me. First, I apologized to her for putting her on the spot in front of her classmates, and then we discussed some strategies to help her build self-confidence and maintain friendships. I reminded her that although scary, it can also be rewarding to share what you know with your peers, as long as it's in the right context and is not condescending. Within the next couple of weeks, Taylor was like a new student—actually a bit more talkative than I had hoped, but she was developing into a leader.

Malcolm

Struggling with issues along his cognitive pathway—math and reading—Malcolm tried to cover it up by acting as if he didn't care so that others wouldn't see him as not being smart. It didn't seem to require much in terms of triggers for him to act out in anger. He behaved as if he did not care about any of the other students or teachers because he was just "too cool." When I introduced the idea of writing in the pathways journal, he initially rebelled against it, but after a couple of weeks of noticing the acceptance and changes in the other students in the classroom because of their writing and sharing, he eventually began to write. It was also clear to me that his psychological pathway needed attention because it was affecting his social and cognitive pathways. I knew that the key was to work with him in a manner that would not allow him to feel like he was being targeted. So, through a variety of whole-class lessons on accepting oneself and activities aimed at building peer relationships such as the aforementioned Valentine Heart lesson, Malcolm began to settle down and open up. In one of his journal entries, he shared that he started to feel better about himself as he understood that others did not see him as he saw himself. He also came to understand that it was okay to ask for help. Because of his positive changes, his grades improved, as did his friendships.

I tutor students during part of my summer break, so after the close of the academic year, Malcolm's mom asked me to tutor him in math that summer. It was wonderful to work with him one on one and see the changes that were evident in him. I saw a boy that did care and wanted to excel and one that learned that it's not "uncool" to be smart. What touched me most was that on my first day of tutoring, as I entered his kitchen in July, I noticed the Valentine heart displayed proudly on his refrigerator.

What I Learned through This Experience

When integrated consistently throughout the curriculum, the guiding principles of collaboration, consensus, and no-fault problem solving and the six developmental pathways framework help to make significant changes in the functioning of a class and in the outcomes—for the students and the teacher. The plan I implemented in my classroom not only helped to reduce conflicts among students and helped to improve their prosocial behavior, but it also impacted their learning in ways that surprised me as I watched them take risks in their learning. Not only did their confidence increase, but so did mine as I watched my fourth-grade students develop into a community of learners.

Although this was not my first year teaching, it was my first year teaching at this school, and I felt it was my best and most productive year as a teacher. Although there is always room for growth, I felt satisfied with how I was teaching and with how the students were learning; and my "teacher passion" really came out as I reviewed my own pre- and postsurvey results and reflections and saw my growth as a teacher. I learned that trust thrives only when the students know that the teacher is on their side, and that when the students know they are cared for, they believe in themselves and want to live up to the expectations they have for themselves as well as those set by the teacher. This has been especially evident in my classroom in math, science, reading, and writing. The students tracked their growth in their data folders, which contained their assessments based on daily instruction, Developmental Reading Assessment (DRA) scores, district assessments, and Connecticut Mastery Tests (CMT). Our fourth-grade class had outstanding results on those mastery tests, especially in the area of writing.

Yearly, as August draws to a close and teachers are scurrying to get their classrooms in order, many will wonder what is going to work for the group of children that will soon be greeting them. In the past, my behavior management methods varied per different group. But, having implemented "Comer-in-the-Classroom" last year, I knew that I could think about classroom behavior and management differently. I knew that although the students change and their needs change, the developmental principles remain the same. Thus, the focus did not need to be on a particular management method, but on finding ways to support the development of each student using the Comer program guidelines.

So, I began the new school year with a newfound confidence. Welcome letters were sent out to the parents the second week in August in which I introduced myself and gave them a preview of the upcoming year. I provided an outline of the three guiding principles and the six developmental pathways as the method that would be used to foster students' development and guide the instruction. Parents were also asked to fill out a "Getting to Know Your Child" survey and to return it on the first day of school so that I would have an insight into what the parents' expectations of their children were for the upcoming year and an insight about each student who would be before me. It was a great way to get to know the students and build relationships with the parents, whose support would be needed throughout the year by both the students and me. I know that every group of students is different. I am not perfect, and I'm not looking for, nor expecting, perfect students; however, I feel more prepared than at any other point in my teaching career to handle the challenges I will face and to appreciate the surprises and the wonder of what makes every student a gift and a promise.

Lessons Learned from Larissa's Experiences

Larissa's experiences underscore the old axiom that teaching can be the most frustrating and simultaneously the most rewarding of any career. Now more than ever, our schools need great teachers, but too often many of those teachers enter the classroom without preparation that is grounded in child and adolescent development principles and practices. Without such preparation, when they are faced with the challenges that students can present, some may become overwhelmed into making decisions that are not necessarily in the best interests of their students. But all is not lost, because as explained by Larissa, her in-service professional development experiences provided her with knowledge, strategies, materials, and on-site support that helped to awaken her passion as a teacher, increase her sense of efficacy and confidence in the classroom, and, perhaps more importantly, helped her to better understand and thereby truly teach her students.

But the lesson continues because she didn't accomplish all the changes by herself in a vacuum. She had the support of her school community, especially her principal. Her principal explained to her that the school would be implementing the Comer Process, a different way of doing business. The process involved the practice of shared leadership and the empowerment of all staff; the use of the developmental pathways framework to plan and provide support for children's learning and development across the curriculum; an emphasis on relationship building in the classroom, throughout the school, and between school and home; and the collective and concerted effort of every adult connected to the school to work in support of improving the life trajectory of every child that enters through the schoolhouse door. Larissa's classroom was nested in a school in which all the stakeholders believed and practiced these aspects of the School Development Program model. As a case study, her examples provide the kind of details we hope will be beneficial to all teachers, particularly those who are just starting their journey.

Case Study 13B

Children First: It Starts with You

Karen Mariska Atkinson

Ever since I was younger, I've always felt like St. Louis Park was a place for me to flourish and grow into a great person, to get involved and make sure that other children felt the same way. I believe that the Children First initiative has everything to do with that even though as a child I wasn't aware of this community-wide asset building effort.

I became involved in Children First in seventh grade. Without this initiative, I don't think I would have found a way to get involved in my community. I have gotten to know so many new people and made so many connections. This not only made my childhood that much better, but it also has prepared me for my future.

—Leigha Sledge, Class of 2011

HISTORY OF CHILDREN FIRST

St. Louis Park is a newly urbanized community of 44,470 residents just west of the city of Minneapolis. The community has been proactive to ensure a high quality of life for all. As a first-ring suburb, St. Louis Park has instituted measures to ensure that urban blight does not impact the community. Strong housing codes and aggressive redevelopment plans have kept it a vibrant place. Likewise, the school district has continued to innovate, implementing an International Baccalaureate (IB) program in three elementary schools; the fourth is the Park Spanish Immersion School. St. Louis Park High School has Advanced Placement and IB classes along with programs to encourage academic success in low-income students and students of color. The school district's 4,300 students are 63 percent Caucasian, 22 percent African American, 8 percent Hispanic or Latino, 6 percent Asian, and 1 percent American Indian/Alaskan. Thirty-five percent of students are on free/reduced-cost lunch. St. Louis Park has 8,300 children under the age of eighteen years.

The seed for Children First was planted on March 12, 1992, when Dr. Carl Holmstrom, superintendent of St. Louis Park Schools, made a presentation about the plight of young people to the St. Louis Park Rotary Club. Carl's speech was so inspiring that two Rotarians who were entrepreneurs challenged the community to dream of a way to make life better for its young people. The question became, how does a city rally its citizens, schools, families, and neighborhoods to help all children and teenagers thrive? Armed with these questions, Dr. Holmstrom and two benefactors invited Search Institute to help St. Louis Park create a citywide effort. A yearlong process of community forums, focus groups, surveys, and interviews led to the creation of Children First, the nation's first community initiative organized to rally all its residents and institutions to nurture the healthy development of children and teenagers based on Search Institute's forty developmental assets research (Leffert et al., 1998). The developmental assets are forty commonsense positive experiences and qualities that help influence the choices young people make and help them become caring, responsible, and successful adults (Search Institute, 2011). Search Institute's research consistently shows that the developmental assets are strongly related to positive outcomes for young people across race, socioeconomic status, gender, age, family composition, and type of community.

Children First is a partnership among the business, city, health, faith, and educational communities in St. Louis Park. An eleven-member executive committee made up of top leaders representing the founding partners provides direction with the help of a staff of one. Linked by the shared vision of raising asset-rich youth, this collaborative has mobilized a significant number of citizens and organizations to promote developmental assets. Since Children First was launched in 1993, more than six hundred communities across the United States and Canada (and, increasingly, around the world) have launched similar initiatives.

Children First is not a program. St. Louis Park has plenty of good programs for young people. Instead, it is an initiative that keeps the healthy development of young people in the forefront of the community's psyche. The initiative is designed to bring both paid professionals and residents together to determine the important role that they play in young people's lives. Children First unleashes community capacity by asking its members to be intentional about their actions and to use the common language of the forty developmental assets. The Children First initiative markets, educates, trains, connects, and facilitates asset-building efforts. This is done through the Asset Champions Network—a network of individuals from all types of St. Louis Park organizations responsible for championing asset building in whatever way makes sense in their organization. Asset champions tie into systems, ignite the asset-building capacity among others in their organization, and uncover productive partnerships. The network gives asset champions ways to connect with each other, share ideas, and link to one another when appropriate.

There are 170 trained network members. They are all ages, including youth themselves, from a broad spectrum of organizations including businesses, neighborhoods, student groups, congregations, health care, law enforcement, and schools. Asset champions meet during training and later during quarterly Champion Charge gatherings where they share their accomplishments and frustrations. In March, Children First hosts an annual meeting to serve as another connecting point. In May, the Children First Ice Cream Social is a way to celebrate all that St. Louis Park offers young people during a free community celebration with entertainment, exhibits, crafts, and ice cream. Asset champions also have the opportunity to share information online through a Facebook group. All infants, children, and young people in St. Louis Park benefit from this web of asset support spanning the community.

AN INTENTIONAL FOCUS ON ASSET BUILDING

The Children First initiative serves as an instigator, encouraging community organizations and individuals to do good things for youth. Children First encourages intentional, repetitive actions that build assets in young people. The following are examples of projects that network members have developed over the past eighteen years.

Free Clinic for Youth

Park Nicollet Health System partnered with the school district to build a free clinic for infants, children, and teens. The clinic runs on a small grant offering a consistent front office and nursing staff. Medical residents work at the clinic as part of their rotation. The clinic is open two half days a week in a community center located two blocks from the high school. Once a month, dental care is offered. While a clinic is a major benefit to young people, the caring staff is what makes it an asset-rich place. An example is a doctor who while conducting a routine physical suspected that the teen was clinically depressed. After consulting with the teen's grandmother, the boy received mental health treatment. The mental health counselor explained that the young man was very depressed and the doctor likely saved his life.

Day One Celebration

Two mothers became familiar with the asset research just about the time their daughters were starting high school. After reviewing results of Search Institute's Profiles of Student Life: Attitudes and Behaviors Survey administered to St. Louis Park students in 1997, the mothers were disturbed that only 28 percent of students reported experiencing asset number 5, Caring School Climate, and 22 percent possessed asset number 7, Community Values Youth. The women sprang into action, recruiting other volunteers and raising funds for a Day One celebration to send students the message: school is important and we are happy you are here. On the first day as students travel to school, they see lawn signs dotting the landscape that say, "Kids are First in St. Louis Park, Welcome Back to School." Dozens of community volunteers greet students as they arrive. Students enjoy a free lunch from a local restaurant, and there is a lot of talk about the importance of what they will learn in the year ahead. When the Attitudes and Behaviors Survey was administered in 2003, 36 percent of students experienced the asset Caring School Climate and 28 percent felt that the Community Values Youth.

Changing Sunday School

A congregational committee viewed all of its programs with the forty developmental assets lens. As a result, the church changed how it delivers Sunday school. The curriculum remained the same, but it was reformatted so children have interaction with multiple caring adults during Sunday school, not just a single teacher.

Embedding Assets

The principles of Children First have become a part of the fabric of the St. Louis Park community. Through the local hospital foundation's grant process, community groups are required to name which assets they address. Children First is an integral part of the school district's mission statement. The city's vision statement includes a focus on young people. As the city manager explains, Children First is an economic development tool. If this is not a good community for children to live in, it's not a good community for anyone.

DOES IT WORK?

Children First has a small staff with a limited budget. Even so, a couple of tools have been used to measure its results. Search Institute's Attitudes and Behaviors Survey measures the number of assets that, on average, young people possess. A longitudinal study between 1997 and 2001 showed that for grades 6 through 12, students reported significantly higher average asset levels in 2001 compared to 1997. On the whole, youth in St. Louis Park reported having about two more assets in 2001 than in 1997 (Roehlkepartian, Benson, & Sesma, 2003).

Children First is interested in monitoring the community environment. Lots of work is focused on changing adult behavior so that they can be intentional asset builders. In the 2008 City of St. Louis Park Residential Study by Decision Resources Ltd., 56 percent of residents were aware of Children First. Among those, 46 percent were aware of the assets and 46 percent of them were actively engaged in activities to help the asset-building process, an increase of 11 percent since the 2006 survey.

Children First has conducted an online survey with asset champions to measure their commitment to community building around young people and their focus on developing and spreading the word about developmental assets. The responses of 70 asset champions in Children First's 2009 report to funders shows that through the Asset Champions Network, 78 percent have gotten to know other people in the community, 68 percent found new ideas and inspiration from others, 43 percent collaborated with others on an asset-building project, 68 percent increased their commitment to asset building, 75 percent became more familiar with the developmental assets, 70 percent talked to the group they represent about assets, 61 percent used the developmental assets in their families, 38 percent talked to youth about the assets, and 30 percent referred someone to the Asset Champions Network.

Asset champions were also asked if they "often" participate in the following behaviors. Their responses indicate that 95 percent greet young people by name, 62 percent take time to learn the strengths and talents of young people, 50 percent use the asset language when talking to others, 40 percent keep assets in mind when planning or setting policy, 30 percent recognize asset builders in their midst, and 28 percent include young people in planning and decisions.

LESSONS LEARNED
Social change efforts are often easier to start than to keep going. St. Louis Park's commitment to building assets in its young people has spanned nearly two decades. Those involved share lessons that have been learned along the way.

Partnership Is Key
Researchers and reporters that have studied Children First find this out quickly. As they talk to representatives from the partners involved, with each visit they come away with the feeling that the partner they've just spoken to owns Children First. And in fact they do; they *all* do. The leadership of the initiative rotates among founding partners, who cochair the initiative with a young person. Cochairs have included the police chief, a bank CEO, and a hospital foundation president. The relationships are authentic, and partners are just as willing to come together in tough times as they are to celebrate successes.

We're a Philosophy
Children First has stayed true to its philosophy of building assets in all people by garnering community action and support. While it can be tempting to move on to the latest grant-funding craze, Children First has not done that. It is steadfast in its commitment to be an initiative, not a program.

Give It Away
Power in a community initiative comes from giving power away, sharing information, and encouraging everyone to be involved. Everyone in the community has the power to build assets in young people. No one, or no one organization, is more important than another. That's the strength of a community initiative.

Ask, Don't Tell
When people ask what they can do, the question gets turned back to them. A frequent response is, "I don't know; what can you do?" It's not just a rhetorical question. Those in the community know best what should be done. They know what they can do, what they have the passion to do. The positive focus of the assets is perhaps one of the most important engagement tools. Many don't feel equipped to address a wide range of risk behaviors. Almost everyone can think of a positive way to build assets in kids. Usually what community members decide to do far exceeds what they would have been told to do.

Authentic Youth Leadership

Who knows better than young people what life is like at ten or thirteen or eighteen? Young people play a critical role in expanding the initiative. As our current cochairs—the school superintendent and a seventeen-year-old high school senior—the superintendent looks to her cochair for input, creativity, and leadership. At public meetings, they stand side by side as champions for young people. Young people share the message with fresh eyes, creating skits, Facebook groups, coloring books, parades, flash mobs, and even dressing the mayor as a red-caped superhero. Their mission is to inform, engage, celebrate, and have fun. The work is serious, but it can be fun, and everyone appreciates a little fun.

Even after eighteen years, the people involved in Children First would say they're still on the journey. Those involved continue to ask the question about how to rally the community to help all of our young people thrive. Many steps have been taken, but things change. There are new residents and community leaders, changing demographics, and a whole new generation of youth that weren't born when Children First was launched. The initiative is fluid, and those involved constantly pursue ways to include new routes to reach all young people. Children First may be a mature initiative, but community members are still on the path to making this the best community in America for every child.

FOR MORE INFORMATION

Children First: www.children-first.org
Search Institute: www.search-institute.org

REFERENCES

Leffert, N., Benson, P. L., Scales, P. C., Sharma, A. R., Drake, D. R., & Blyth, D. A. (1998). Developmental assets: Measurement and prediction of risk behaviors among adolescents. *Applied Developmental Science, 2*(4), 209–230.

Roehlkepartian, E. C., Benson, P. L., & Sesma, A. (2003). *Signs of progress in putting children first: Developmental assets among youth in St. Louis Park, 1997–2001*. Minneapolis, MN: Search Institute.

Search Institute. (2011). *40 developmental assets lists*. Minneapolis, MN: Author. Retrieved December 1, 2011, from http://www.search-institute.org/developmental -assets/lists

Case Study 13C

Positive Youth Development: Positive Action at Farmdale Elementary School

TERESITA SARACHO DE PALMA, MAYA FALCON AVILES,
RICARDO LOPEZ, J. CARMELO ZAMORA,
AND MONIQUE OHASHI

"You are special because you are you," said third grader Alejandra during a discussion following a Positive Action lesson, surprising the facilitator, Ms. Garcia. Alejandra came to Farmdale Elementary School at the start of the third grade. It was a new school and with it came a new family. Alejandra's whole life had been spent moving from relative to relative. Her mother's substance abuse problems had required others to step in. Her grandmother and uncles and aunts did their best to care for her by moving her to whoever was able to take her. The moves had left their mark on her. She was very guarded and quiet. She only wore dark clothes. In a simple project with modeling clay at the start of the year, she chose only the black clay. Classified as a high-risk student, Alejandra was not technically eligible for the school's Amigos program for low- to moderate-risk students, but the administration decided to let her try the program. The Amigos program uses the Positive Action curriculum to accomplish positive youth development.

As the months passed, Alejandra began to discover her own strengths. She was in a supportive environment where prosocial skills were taught not just in the Amigos group, but in the classroom and reinforced throughout the school. Every step forward Alejandra made was acknowledged so that her experience in the school was fully immersive and interactive. Alejandra began to wear brighter colors. She began to speak in class. She began to have friends at recess. By the end of the year, Alejandra had blossomed.

To the teachers and staff at Farmdale, Alejandra stands out as a student clearly reached by their conscious, structured approach to positive youth development using the Positive Action program.

POSITIVE YOUTH DEVELOPMENT AT FARMDALE ELEMENTARY SCHOOL

Farmdale Elementary School is a single-track school serving students in grades K to 5. The school is located in Local District 5 of the Los Angeles Unified School District, and it serves the Northeast Los Angeles community of El Sereno. There are 587 students enrolled: 95 percent Hispanic and 4 percent Asian, with a small

465

number of African American, Filipino, Caucasian, and Pacific Islander children. While the student attendance rate is 95 percent, there is a transiency rate of 23 percent, which indicates that about one in five students will enroll in school and leave within the year. Almost 46 percent of the students (284) are English learners (Spanish-speaking students). Eighty-five percent of the students are socioeconomically disadvantaged and receive free and reduced-cost lunch.

Since 2004, Farmdale Elementary has been a Program Improvement (PI)/ Title I school under the No Child Left Behind Act because it has not reached adequate yearly progress (AYP). The research shows that many PI/Title I schools exist in communities where children's academic performance is negatively affected by poverty and community stressors. Farmdale students are faced with daily environmental and familial stressors, thereby exposing them to additional risks of developing adjustment problems, especially at school (Los Angeles County Children's Planning Council, 2004). The El Sereno community is impacted by serious gang activity. Felonies, shootings, graffiti, vandalism, and arrests occur regularly around the schools and community. Unfortunately, many children witness violence acts, shootings, arrests, drug sales, and substance abuse on a regular and ongoing basis.

Students, teachers, parents, and school staff at Farmdale Elementary School look forward to the Positive Action Assembly Days held at the end of every month. Teachers at Farmdale Elementary select two students per classroom for recognition during the assembly. Parents are invited to be part of this celebration. A lot of work goes into making this assembly special.

Students clap as the school principal, Mrs. Saracho de Palma, announces their friends' names on the microphone. One by one, students selected begin to walk to the front to receive their Positive Action certificates and pose for pictures. Proud parents begin to quickly gather to the front to take pictures of their children being recognized by the entire school. This is a great way to acknowledge and recognize students schoolwide for their positive actions at Farmdale Elementary School.

Assembly Day is just one piece of the school's effort to implement Positive Action as part of Los Angeles Unified School District's Discipline Foundation Policy and School Wide Positive Behavior Support Programs. The policy calls for every student to be educated in a safe, respectful, and welcoming environment. In addition, every educator has the right to teach in an atmosphere free from disruption and obstacles that impede learning. Positive Action was funded in September 2009 by a School Community Violence Prevention Grant from the California Department of Education. Implementation began in the middle of the school year of 2009/10, and full program implementation started with the 2010/11 school year. The selection of Positive Action was the culmination of a process that began when the school's existing collaborative (composed of school and community stakeholders) identified behaviors such as bullying, fights, and vandalism as key school problems. The behaviors were also identified by students and parents via self-report surveys and focus groups. The school administration charged the collaborative and a local consultant, Ricardo Lopez, with the task of identifying and selecting a comprehensive, evidence-based program to address these problematic behaviors. After an exhaustive review of programs, Positive Action was selected because it addressed the problem behaviors not only with students but also with school staff, administration, parents, and other community members. The group felt it was important to target multiple systems for success. (For a further description of Positive Action, see the information provided in chapter 13 of this volume.)

For Farmdale Elementary, this multiple-systems strategy is achieved through the adoption and implementation of Positive Action to develop a consistent approach to positive youth development with schoolwide positive behavior support and a discipline plan. Farmdale Elementary School's plan consists of teaching school rules and social-emotional skills, reinforcing appropriate student behavior, using effective classroom management and positive behavior support, and providing early prevention and intervention strategies. Farmdale's plan encompasses the three key components of positive youth development—a focus on youth strengths/assets, a positive and supportive environment, and acknowledgment of bidirectional person–context interactions. Students must first be supported in learning the skills necessary to enhance a positive school climate and avoid negative behavior. Positive Action is critical in helping us reach our goals.

POSITIVE ACTION IMPLEMENTATION PROCESS

Embedded in the Los Angeles Unified School District's Discipline Foundation Policy and School Wide Positive Behavior Support Program is Response to Instruction and Intervention (RTI²). RTI² is a student-centered, multitiered approach to the early identification and support of students with learning and behavior needs. All students receive high-quality, scientifically based instruction provided by qualified personnel to ensure that their difficulties are not due to inadequate instruction. Teachers from all grade levels use the Positive Action curriculum in their classroom. All students are screened on a periodic basis to establish an academic and behavioral baseline and to identify struggling learners who need additional support. Students identified as being "at risk" through universal screenings or results on state- or districtwide tests receive supplemental instruction during the school day in the regular classroom.

Classroom Example: First Grade

"I hit her because I like her," said Joseph, a first-grade student at Farmdale Elementary. After he made that statement, the whole class looked baffled, especially Christina, the girl he "hit." It happened right after lunch recess, so Ms. Ohashi decided to reteach the concepts from the Positive Action lesson titled "My Code of Conduct" to address this particular incident.

This lesson reinforces the idea that students should treat their peers the way they want to be treated. They began the lesson by sitting in a circle in order to lower their affective filters and create an atmosphere that is conducive to open discussions. The students were then asked to discuss what they think "respect" means to them by sharing their insight with a partner. This think-pair-share activity was the introduction to their open discussion.

Since this was not the first time the students were exposed to this lesson, Ms. Ohashi did not want to teach the lesson in the same manner as she had earlier. Instead, she used various examples from the students' experiences and had them engage in role-play to help her students better understand the concept that we should treat others the way we want to be treated. By doing so, the students were able to make connections to their own personal lives and were motivated to begin to engage in positive actions.

The most challenging part about teaching these important concepts to young students is that it is not something that can easily be learned and applied after just one lesson. And even if it seems that they understand the lesson, sometimes unique situations may arise that require additional improvisation in order to better meet the needs of the students, as in the case with Joseph and Christina. Hence, taking advantage of teachable moments, along with continuous reinforcement of the concepts presented in Positive Action, is necessary in order to help students become positive, productive members of this society. One of the characteristics of positive youth development is that it takes time. A single lesson is never enough for sustainable change.

Classroom Example: Fifth Grade

Positive Action works because the school community engages in developing positive habits in and out of class. This was the consensus of Mr. Zamora's fifth-grade class, who realized that Positive Action only worked if they practiced positive behaviors outside as well as inside the school. One student said, "We all have to follow it [in order to] make it work." In Mr. Zamora's dual-language class, everyone has agreed that behavior is not a finished product—it's a work in progress.

Mr. Zamora got on board with the philosophy of Positive Action after a professional development where the school's Healthy Start coordinator, Mr. Lopez, reminded him that people come first and his relationships with his students had the power to change lives. Positive Action ensures that students are treated as people; they have both social and academic needs that need to be addressed on a daily basis. Concepts in Positive Action assist students in thinking about their actions, thoughts, and feelings and how they are really one major concept.

At Farmdale, everyone is trying to create authentic learning opportunities in a positive, supportive context for students. That has been our mission, and now with Positive Action, the mission of Healthy Start and the Farmdale community of learners initiative as well. As part of the community of learners, Farmdale has embraced the idea of working collectively to engage all students in Positive Youth Development using Positive Action.

The Amigos

To create a positive environment with effective bidirectional communication between students and the school, students' progress across a range of academic and behavioral metrics is monitored. Students not making adequate progress in the regular classroom are provided with increasingly intensive instruction matched to their needs on the basis of levels of performance and rates of progress. Intensity varies across group size, frequency and duration of intervention, and the level of training of the professionals providing instruction or intervention. These services and interventions are provided in small-group settings in addition to instruction in the general curriculum.

One of the most effective interventions is called the Amigos ("Friends") program. In Amigos, small groups are formed for those students who need extra help with social skills. The Positive Action curriculum is taught in this program using the Positive Action Counselor's Kit. Some of the students selected to be part of the schoolwide assembly are also current and former participants of the Amigos program. The group facilitator, Ms. Garcia, works with children exhibiting low to moderate school adjustment problems. A psychiatric social worker, Mrs. Aviles, and the Boys Group facilitator, Mr. Cruz, also use the Positive Action Counselor's Kit when working with their students who are exhibiting high-risk behaviors or other needs.

Alejandra was a participant in the Amigos program. Ms. Garcia noticed an increase in self-esteem and confidence in her group of students. Mrs. Aviles collected the pre- and posttests from the program using the Walker-McConnell Scale (WMS) of Social Competence and School Adjustment (Walker & McConnell, 1995), and they noticed that 83 percent of students responded well to the services using Positive Action, while others needed more individualized interventions rather than groups. The WMS is used as a tool to evaluate the effects of the Amigos program intervention on social competence and school adjustment factors as reported by teachers. Ms. Garcia also noticed that students in her groups understood the material taught and stories read. After doing a lesson on respect with her kindergarten students from unit 4 in the Positive Action Kindergarten Instructor's Kit, a child said, "I always do positive actions at home because I respect my mom." Another student in the group shared, "Positive is love, friends, and respect."

Mr. Cruz facilitated the Boys Group for fifth-grade boys displaying behavior and emotional issues. At first, group implementation was difficult because of the behavior of the boys. However, within the fourth week, the boys started understanding the Positive Action core philosophy. In one instance, after a behavioral incident during group time, without prompting, the boys used the Positive Action thoughts-actions-feelings circle to assist the boy who acted out in correcting his own behavior. "We realized that the curriculum is working!" said Mr. Cruz. Even better, the boys started referring and recruiting others boys to the group. One boy in the group said, "We do not want this group to end." Another boy said, "I changed so much."

The El Sereno Community

Farmdale Elementary School plays an important role in the mostly Hispanic and Latino community of El Sereno in East Lost Angeles. Mr. Lopez, the Healthy

Start coordinator, organized a community learning fair to help educate families on the importance of making good choices in taking care of their bodies. There were booths for the dental clinic, medical clinic, farmer's market, and local mental health agencies. Mr. Lopez integrated Positive Action with the community learning fair because the Positive Action curriculum incorporates three basic human needs—taking care of the body (physical needs), the mind (intellectual needs), and feelings (social and emotional needs).

The community learning fair team decided to recognize teachers for their strong support with the implementation of Positive Action as well as by recognizing some of the outstanding students who helped during the fair. This was an excellent way to involve the El Sereno community and educate them on how our school is using the Positive Action program.

PROGRAM EVALUATION

Positive Action lessons are monitored in the classroom by the use of an independent evaluator. The evaluator uses a fidelity checklist and monthly teacher implementation worksheets as tools. In addition, there are various evaluation tools used to measure process and outcome objectives. The findings are used to monitor Positive Action at an entire school.

Every semester, twelve to fourteen students are admitted to the Amigos program to participate in small-group lessons using the counselor's kit from the Positive Action program. Each group consists of about three to four students. Positive Action lessons run for about twenty-five minutes. Students are selected based on how they scored on the Walker Scale Instrument, which is completed by all teachers in the targeted grade level for all their students. Those students whose scores fall within the 10th to 25th percentile (low-moderate school adjustment functioning) qualify for Amigos. The program admits few high-risk students, which is agreed upon by program staff and administration. Parents are invited to an orientation to learn more about Positive Action in the Amigos program. Once the parents provide parental consent, those students are registered Amigos. The first semester targeted students in grades 1 and 3, while the second semester targeted students in kindergarten and grade 2.

In the Amigos program, data are collected by program staff prior to children beginning the program and after completing the program using the Walker-McConnell Scale. Teachers complete the scale, which measures children's school adjustment behaviors, such as social skills in and out of the classroom. Figure 13C.1 compares pre- and posttest results for a group of twelve children in grades 1 and 3 admitted to the program for the first semester (October 2010–January 2011), and figure 13C.2 shows the results for fourteen students in kindergarten and grade 2 who participated in the second semester (February 2011–June 2011). The same teacher who completed the pretest also completed the posttest for the students. Most children who participated in small-group intervention improved in their social skills.

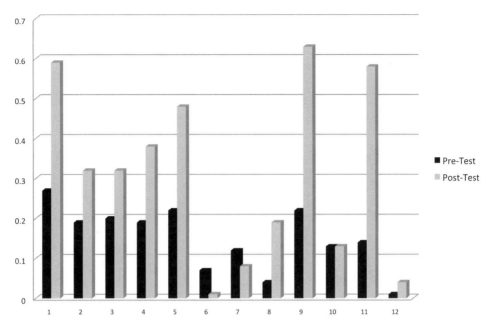

Figure 13C.1. Positive action groups 2010–2011, semester 1.

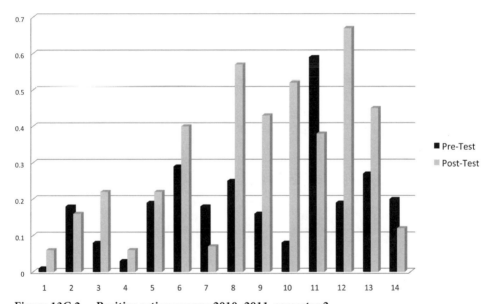

Figure 13C.2. Positive action groups 2010–2011, semester 2.

Figure 13C.1 shows results from the first semester. Eighty-three percent of students (*N* = 12) who participated in the Amigos program during the first semester did well, while 71 percent of students (*N* = 14) in the second semester (figure 13C.2) also did well using Positive Action in small-group interventions. In the second semester, four out of fourteen students were high-risk students. All four students moved up in points!

CONCLUSION

We made a substantial commitment to positive youth development when we brought in the Positive Action program. In addition to facing all the challenges of any school in a major urban school district, we took on the challenge of making Farmdale Elementary School an International Baccalaureate (IB) school. We aligned Positive Action and the IB program using components like the Positive Action words of the week.

Positive Action helped Farmdale Elementary School create a structure to enable students to recognize their own strengths; to provide a positive, supportive environment reaching into the students' homes and into the broader community; and to establish a responsive, bidirectional context-aware system of interaction. The heart of Positive Youth Development is beating at Farmdale Elementary School.

Having Positive Action at Farmdale Elementary School has given us the opportunity to train and educate everyone, including teachers, teacher assistants, and after-school program staff, on an evidence-based program that is helping us improve our school's academics, behavior, and character. In implementing this program at Farmdale, we were able to continuously monitor its application in classrooms, specialized programs, and the entire school while measuring improvement in students' academics and behaviors. Positive Action is practiced from morning before school begins and all throughout the day, including in the afternoon during the after-school program.

REFERENCES

Los Angeles County Children's Planning Council. (2004). *Los Angeles County 2004 children's score card*. Retrieved from http://www.childpc.org

Walker, H. M., & McConnell, S. R. (1995). *Walker-McConnell Scale of Social Competence and School Adjustment*. Belmont, CA: Thomson Publishing.

CHAPTER 14

Prevention of Harassment, Intimidation, and Bullying

Jan Urbanski

I have been bullied all through school. People make fun of me or just mess with me. They pull my hair, push me, and say things like I get my clothes in a thrift store. My best friend even told me once she didn't need me anymore and I make everyone's life miserable. I told a teacher once but nothing ever changed. It seems like everyone is on their side so it is really hard.

—Eighth-grade girl

I am not all that popular, but I hang out with kids who are popular. We do pick on other kids, but we are just playing. I never say anything about it or they might not like me. I don't want them to start messing with me.

—Seventh-grade boy

I am doing this because I am tired of being picked on.

—High school student expelled for making threats

I have witnessed bullying . . . he is always being picked on and called names. . . . They don't care about the cameras. They know where they are and when they are videotaping.

—Middle school boy

u r a back-stabbing jerk of a x best friend . . . I dont care about u anymore.

—Text message from a fourth-grade girl

Bullying is a reality in schools, one that has gained a good deal of recent attention. Why now? An increased awareness of liability issues, data showing a poor prognosis for children involved in bully/victim problems, emerging knowledge of the impact on academics, new state laws, and an explosion of research on bullying have contributed to this increased interest.

Students learn better when they feel safe and do not fear being ridiculed or humiliated. Bullying can create a climate of fear, and some even consider bullying prevention a human rights issue. It not only affects the student who is bullied or the student doing the bullying. A school is filled with bystanders who see the bullying or know it is happening. These youth are also impacted and may experience guilty feelings or weakened inhibition toward aggression. In comparison, when a school launches a conscious bullying prevention effort, bullying behavior decreases, and there is potential for other antisocial behaviors to decrease while prosocial behaviors increase (Pearl & Dulaney, 2006).

Promoting prosocial behavior in an environment infused with bullying is not possible. Schools must send a clear, consistent message that bullying behavior is not acceptable and work to create an environment that lets students know they are valuable, responsible individuals. This combination of a caring environment and implementation of bullying prevention strategies *can create a positive climate that discourages bullying, encourages prosocial behaviors, and provides* the foundation to support academic achievement and social-emotional growth.

Bullying in schools is not a new phenomenon. In fact, many reading this can look back on their own schooling and remember seeing or being involved in incidents of bullying. Research in this area also started with Dan Olweus studying bullying in Norwegian schools as early as the 1970s (Olweus, 1993). The problem has really come to the forefront in the United States over the last decade. In the early 1990s, a search of the PsycINFO APA database using the term *bully* would have identified few publications. The same search today will yield hundreds of articles.

Bullying is a complex behavior that we now know can ultimately cause academic and social problems for students and contribute to a negative school climate. It is also associated with poorer psychosocial adjustment, with consequences that may last into adulthood. It is a low-level, underlying kind of violence that might not be as overtly threatening as weapons but does occur more frequently in schools (Dupper & Meyer-Adams, 2002).

What used to be thought of as kids being kids can be an antecedent to more serious violence and criminal behavior in schools. Bullying threatens the development of prosocial behaviors because it allows students to achieve immediate goals without learning socially acceptable ways to interact with others (Haynie et al., 2001). The fear of physical harm or embarrassment that can occur because of bullying also creates a threat that shuts down the learning process (Mendler, 2001). Therefore, educational discourse can no longer separate academic success from a physically and emotionally safe learning environment.

This chapter will examine the issue of bullying in school. The discussion will start with an overview of what bullying is and what it is not. The various types of bullying and the characteristics of those involved will be identified. Research on prevalence and consequences as well as legal issues surrounding bullying will be presented. Once the basic understanding of bullying in school is established, the chapter will conclude with best practices to address bullying from an environmental, prevention, and intervention perspective. Incorporating these strategies into social-emotional learning programs ensures the physical, emotional, and academic growth of all students.

WHAT IS BULLYING?

To understand how to best address bullying in schools, it is important to first understand what bullying is and what it is not. Bullying is a form of peer abuse that can be defined as unprovoked aggression characterized by an imbalance of power where a more powerful person physically or emotionally attacks a less powerful one (Urbanski & Permuth, 2009). There are three characteristics that are common in most if not all bullying situations.

1. There is always a power differential between the person who is bullying and the victim. It can be something easily seen such as size, age, or number of students involved but can also be a status difference that is more difficult to discern. It might be the new kid in school or someone with more money, higher grades, or something as simple as better shoes. Whether a physical difference or a higher social status, the person who is bullying has real or perceived power over the person who is being bullied.
2. Bullying is a repeated behavior that may be the same action being done over and over again or a pattern of different types of bullying behaviors directed toward another person.
3. Although not always recognizable, bullying is a behavior that is intentional and targets a specific person. It is not a case of someone being in the wrong place at the wrong time. Rather it is someone seeking out a victim that will allow the bullying to occur either by his or her reaction pattern or inclination not to seek adult help.

Bullying is an intentional act that is repeatedly directed at a person of less strength or status. In comparison, conflict is a disagreement between two or more people or thoughts. Conflict is generally not a repeated behavior and usually occurs between people who have relatively equal status. Another common behavior seen in schools is lighthearted teasing. This type of playfully annoying or roughhousing is a normal part of growing up. However, it easily crosses the line to bullying if one person is no longer having fun.

The spectrum of bullying behavior ranges from direct, overt acts of physical violence to more indirect, subtle patterns of verbal or relational cruelty (Feinberg, 2003). These generally fall into four categories: physical, verbal, relational, and cyberbullying. It is important to note that students may engage in or be victims of just one or all types of bullying behavior.

Physical bullying involves causing harm to a person's body or to a person's belongings. It goes beyond the typical image of a big kid shoving a little kid to include behaviors such as hitting, pinching, kicking, blocking access, book checking, shanking, breaking things, stealing, and any other action that damages someone's physical property or causes bodily harm.

Verbal bullying is actually the most common type of bullying on school campuses. It involves using words to attack or threaten another person. Verbal bullying includes taunting, teasing, name-calling, extortion, or threats and can have as much negative impact as physical bullying (Windemeyer Communications, 2003).

Relational bullying is an indirect form of bullying that harms or threatens to harm a person's self-esteem or group acceptance. This type of bullying includes social isolation, exclusion, social manipulation, gossiping, spreading rumors, exclusion, alliance building, and ignoring.

Cyberbullying is a newer yet increasing manner of bullying. It is a type of indirect bullying that involves use of the Internet or other digital communication technologies to harass, intimidate, or threaten another person (Urbanski & Permuth, 2009). It can be done through personal websites, e-mail, blogs, chat rooms, social networking sites, instant messaging, text messaging, online or interactive gaming, and any other electronic form of communication. It may involve a straightforward attack in which messages are sent directly from the perpetrator to the victim, or it may be cyberbullying by proxy, which involves engaging others in the bullying, often without their knowledge.

In addition to these forms of bullying, there are several other behaviors that should be discussed to get a full understanding of what bullying entails. Contagion bullying, commonly known as group bullying, occurs when emotions and/or behaviors are spread from one person to others in the group. Due to the pressure to conform, someone who would not normally bully on his or her own is influenced by peers to take part in the bullying behavior. There is a diffusion of responsibility and guilt resulting in less personal ownership of the behavior.

Hazing involves initiation into a club or activity and is often erroneously considered tradition. Another mistaken belief is that hazing only occurs on college campuses, when in reality 48 percent of high school students who belong to groups reported being subjected to hazing activities (N. C. Hoover & Pollard, 2000). Hazing is a humiliating or dangerous process that someone participates in to join a group or to maintain status within a group. The behaviors range from minor hazing such as deception, social isolation, or disrespect to more serious actions such as verbal abuse and sleep deprivation all the way to binge drinking or expectation of illegal activity. Although bullying usually involves exclusion from a group, and hazing is part of a process to join a group, they are similar in that both behaviors are about power and control and can result in physical or emotional harm (Urbanski & Permuth, 2009).

Harassment is physical or verbal abuse directed toward someone with a legally protected status such as race, religion, age, gender, or disability. These protected classes are defined by both federal and state laws, including Section 504 of the Rehabilitation Act, Title II of the Americans with Disabilities Act, and the Individuals with Disabilities Education Act (IDEA) that deal with disability harassment; Title VI of the Civil Rights Act of 1964 prohibiting discrimination on the basis of race, color, or national origin; and Title IX of the Education Amendments of 1972 prohibiting sexual discrimination. Harassment causes significant distress for the recipient and creates a hostile environment that ultimately interferes with work or learning. It places a person in reasonable fear of harm to his or her person or damage to his or her property and has the potential to substantially disrupt the orderly operation of a school.

First Amendment rights protect a person's freedom of speech. However, if that speech is of a derogatory nature and occurs repeatedly, it can constitute harassment by federal law. Verbal harassment includes remarks that refer to someone's race, religion, sex, disability, age, or other characteristic protected by law, in negative, vulgar, or derogatory terms. Statements about inappropriate stereotypical ideas, attributes, or characteristics can also be harassment.

Not all harassment is verbal. Written or pictorial representations of graphically derogatory material about protected characteristics may be considered nonverbal harassment. This can include sending inappropriate texts or e-mails as well as unwelcome, offensive, or hostile facial expressions or body gestures. Although harassment meets the definition of bullying and the two are often grouped together, harassment carries its own legal status and ramifications.

CHARACTERISTICS AND WARNING SIGNS

Since all students are ultimately impacted by school bullying, an understanding of the problem would be incomplete without considering the different roles involved in bullying episodes. In addition to the student who bullies and the student who is being bullied, there are also bystanders who see or know what is happening.

Students Who Bully

Although the smallest percentage of students in the school, we begin with the student who bullies others. This student can be described as someone who repeatedly hurts another person on purpose. Students who do not initiate the bullying but encourage or join in also fall into this category. Students who bully seek power and control and may behave in a nonemotional, controlled, and deliberate manner. These students are generally outgoing, rebellious, and often appear angry. They attempt to get power and control by harassing or using force.

Others are more emotional and impulsive in how they bully. Those who bully in this more introverted way tend to conform to societal rules, are not rebellious, and work to stay unnoticed. They seek power and control through manipulation, smooth talking, misleading, lying, and deceiving. Regardless of the type, common behaviors that can indicate a child may be bullying others include a negative attitude toward school, difficulty conforming to rules, a need to dominate others, lack of empathy, blaming others rather than taking responsibility for one's own actions, being easily angered, defiant or hostile behavior, and an attitude of superiority. When a child exhibits any of these warning signs, it does not mean the child is definitely bullying others. Instead these indicators should be considered red flags, and an adult should investigate.

A common misconception is that students who bully have a low self-esteem. In actuality, they have equal or higher self-esteem compared to their classmates. Their grades are generally average or above average, especially in elementary school, but may begin to drop in higher grades. They are generally assertive and also good at talking themselves out of difficult situations (Nansel et al., 2001; Olweus, 1993; Slee & Rigby, 1993).

Student Who Is Bullied

The student who is a victim of bullying can be described as the student who is repeatedly targeted for aggression and other negative actions of peers. This can occur as physical attacks, verbal assaults, or psychological abuse. Although never an indication that the victim is at fault, students who are bullied may fall into one of two categories: passive or provocative.

Characteristics of the passive victim may be viewed as both the cause and the effect of being subjected to bullying behavior. These students do not assert themselves, are generally cautious and shy, and respond to bullying with avoidance and withdrawal. This type of victim is often preoccupied with personal safety, thus impairing academic learning.

Students who bully and those who are bullied are not always mutually exclusive, with nearly half of bullies reporting being victims as well (Veenstra et al., 2005). These students are known as provocative victims or bully-victims. This type of student has difficulty reading social signals, can be argumentative or disruptive, and may attempt to fight back when bullied, but usually in an ineffective manner. They may try to bully weaker students, resulting in being punished for their bullying behavior while their experience as a victim goes unnoticed. They face unique challenges since they are at risk of both the consequences related to bullying behavior as well as those of the victim.

People believe that often children are victimized because of outward appearance. In reality, accumulated research indicates that personality characteristics and reaction patterns are more significant contributors to bullying issues (Olweus, 2003). Longitudinal studies also show that students who bully gravitate toward children who are physically weak, exhibit internalizing behaviors, lack prosocial skills, and have low self-worth and perceptions of social competence (Rodkins & Hodges, 2003).

Many victims of bullying do not report it to an adult, but there are warning signs to look for. Once again, these are red flags that indicate a student may be experiencing bullying and an adult should investigate. Indicators include changes in attendance or participation in activities; leaving late, arriving early, or changing route to school; lack of interest in school; decline in grades; difficulty concentrating or being easily distracted; being withdrawn or isolated; poor social skills; being unpopular or having few friends; difficulty standing up for him- or herself; preference for being with adults; bullying others; frequent illness; being overly concerned with personal safety; and unexplained scratches, bruises, or damage to belongings.

Victims of bullying often have difficulty with social skills. Research has identified six social behaviors that were effective predictors of victimization: looks scared, gives in easily, cries when picked on, stands in a way that appears weak, talks very quietly, and looks unhappy (Fox & Boulton, 2005). A similar study investigating characteristics that predict bullying behavior reached a comparable conclusion with aggressiveness, isolation, dislikability, and gender identified as strong predictors, while socioeconomic status, parenting, and academic performance were weak predictors (Veenstra et al., 2005).

Bystanders

An often overlooked role in bullying is that of the bystander. These students are affected by the chronic presence of bullying in schools but also have a powerful role in changing the culture of the school. Bystanders are students and adults who witness or are aware of a bullying situation but do not take an active part. Instead they respond to the situation by reinforcing, observing, opposing, or defending.

Reinforcement involves offering indirect support verbally or through body language. Those who observe do not want to get involved and so ignore the bullying. Some bystanders oppose the bullying but do not know how to respond or do not feel they have the support needed, so they choose to do nothing. Defenders stand up to the student who is bullying and try to stop the behavior by intervening or reporting to an adult.

Adults can unintentionally contribute to the power differential between the student who is bullying and the one being bullied by ignoring the bullying, sending the message that it is okay. Whether ignoring by choice or due to a lack of knowledge of what bullying is, this can be detrimental to the climate of a school, creating a sense that the adults have turned over the reins of the school to the students who are bullying others.

A common fear among bystanders is that there will be retaliation if they get involved (U.S. Department of Education, 1998) or that adults will not do anything if the bullying is reported. This may account for the fact that even though the bystanders make up the largest percentage of students in a school, they seldom intervene on behalf of the victim. Playground studies have shown that peers are present in most bullying situations but intervene less than 20 percent of the time (Hawkins, Pepler, & Craig, 2001). In fact, they participate in the bullying nearly 50 percent of the time and tend to have more reverence for the person engaged in the bullying behavior. This type of behavior very well may perpetuate bullying in school.

PREVALENCE AND CONSEQUENCES OF BULLYING

As mentioned previously, research in the area of bullying prevention has recently expanded. What began as defining the characteristics of the student who bullies and the one who is bullied has grown to include the prevalence of the behaviors, the consequences for those involved, and the impact bullying has on schooling.

Although most students in a school are not bullying others or being bullied, there are a significant number who are dealing with this aggression on a regular basis. A 2010 analysis of results from the Olweus Bullying Questionnaire done with over five hundred thousand students from six thousand schools nationwide showed that 17 percent of students indicated that they had been bullied two to three times per month or more within the school semester, and 10 percent of students indicated they had bullied others two to three times per month or more within the semester (Olweus & Limber, 2010).

Comparatively, in a 2010 Josephson's Institute biennial study of more than forty-three thousand high school students throughout the United States, 56 percent of boys and 43 percent of girls reported bullying, teasing, or taunting someone at least once in the previous twelve months. Additionally, 45 percent of boys and 50 percent of girls reported that they had been bullied, teased, or taunted in a way that seriously upset them (Josephson Institute Center for Youth Ethics, 2010).

Rates of cyberbullying have also been studied. The University of New Hampshire Crimes against Children's Research Center found that one in seventeen children aged ten to seventeen had been threatened or harassed online (Florida Office of Safe and Healthy Schools, 2005). Similarly, a Canadian study of middle school students showed that 23 percent of responding students were bullied by e-mail, 35 percent in chat rooms, and 41 percent by text messaging (Li, 2005).

Has bullying in schools increased? Previous research varies. A 2003 Gallup youth survey indicated that 37 percent of teens reported being teased or picked on at school (Kiefer, 2003), while a 2001 Kaiser Family Foundation survey indicated that 74 percent of eight- to eleven-year-olds and 86 percent of twelve- to fifteen-year-olds get teased or bullied at their school (Kaiser Family Foundation, 2001). A 2001 survey conducted with eleven thousand students showed a 50 percent increase in bullying victimization when compared to earlier results from the same survey (Olweus, 2003).

Considering the dramatic increase in awareness over the last decade, it is difficult to discern if there has been an increase in the actual behavior or just an increase in recognition and reporting.

Knowing the prevalence rates of bullying in schools leads to the question, what does this mean for the students involved? Bullying prevention research shows both short-term and long-term consequences for these students (Olweus, 1993; Indiana Department of Education, 2003). The negative outcomes of bullying and victimization include an increased risk of mental health disorders, antisocial behavior, and poor academic achievement. School safety research is consistent in showing that a lack of physical and emotional safety in school also results in negative educational outcomes including violence, truancy, and poor academic performance (Kent, 2003; McEvoy & Welker, 2001; Zins, Bloodworth, Weissberg, & Walberg, 2004).

Bullying can lead to more serious violent behaviors. Without intervention, children who bully are at a higher risk for engaging in other antisocial behaviors and are more likely to have a criminal record (Olweus, 1993). They also have more cases of alcoholism and substance abuse, more antisocial personality disorders, and are more likely to drop out of school. Studies have also shown a consistent relationship between bullying and interpersonal violence. For example, results from a 2003 study indicated a greater chance of carrying a weapon, increased incidents of fighting, and a higher likelihood to sustain an injury from fighting (Nansel, Overpeck, Haynie, Ruan, & Scheidt, 2003).

There are unique consequences for students who engage in cyberbullying, since without face-to-face interaction the student who is bullying is removed from the immediate reaction of the victim. This lack of feedback indicating emotional harm to another allows for disassociation between the student who is bullying and the victim of the behavior. This can make it easier for a student to ignore the expectations, values, and norms of the family, school, and community, resulting in an increase in antisocial behaviors.

Research on cyberbullying is relatively new, but there are data that indicate it is related to involvement in school problems and delinquent behavior offline (Hinduja & Patchin, 2007) as well as risky online behaviors such as disclosure of personal information, suicide encouragement communities, risky sexual behavior, hate group recruitment, and violent gaming (Willard, 2005). Youth who are subjected to cyberbullying are also more likely to cyberbully others and experience difficulties at school, including low marks, poor concentration, and absenteeism (Beran & Li, 2007).

Being the victim of bullying can have a similar negative impact on a student's social-emotional and educational success. Experiencing bullying is associated with poor psychosocial adjustment that can last into adulthood. Students who are bullied tend to have lower self-esteem and higher levels of stress, anxiety, depression, illness, and suicidal ideation (Olweus, 1993). Victimization also correlates positively with loneliness (Telljohann, 2003). Lower grades and increased absenteeism are also higher for students who are cyberbullied (Kowalski, Limber, & Agaston, 2008).

The effects of bullying victimization carry over to school success as well. Students who are bullied have higher levels of absenteeism and drop out at higher rates. The National School Safety Center reports that an estimated 160,000 children miss school every day due to fear of attack or intimidation by other students and that as many as

10 percent of students who drop out of school do so because of bullying (Weinhold, 1999). Bullied students who do attend school are likely to spend more time thinking about ways to avoid teasing and taunting than learning.

Another concern is that students who are bullied may become detached and begin to reject social norms. They can begin a downward spiral of withdrawal, rejection, and helplessness that in the worst case can lead to violence against themselves or others. Although the student who bullies may be thought of as the aggressor in school, it is the victim who ultimately may resort to violent behavior. To underscore the importance of this, consider that the Secret Service found that two-thirds of all school shooters since 1974 had been victims of bullying prior to the shootings (Brady, 2001).

Although not directly involved, bullying also has consequences for the bystanders. They may experience a range of emotions including anger, helplessness, and even guilt for not intervening. They may also begin to believe that the school is not a safe place and begin avoiding certain areas where bullying occurs. Research has also shown that bystanders feel powerless and have difficulty with coping and problem-solving skills (Windemeyer Communications, 2003).

There can also be a negative impact on the bystanders' self-esteem if they do not respond or actually enjoy the bullying that is occurring. They can become desensitized to bullying situations and begin to have reduced empathy for the victim of bullying. Just as with contagion bullying, bystanders may develop a decreased sense of individual responsibility (Olweus, 1993), putting them at risk for joining in the bullying behavior and contributing to a culture of bullying at school. In contrast, empowering bystanders can have a positive effect on the school climate and may even decrease bullying behavior.

Research showing a direct link between bullying behaviors and academic achievement is minimal, but there is evidence that they are at least connected. Advances in brain research and learning show that there can be academic consequences for those involved in bullying. The human brain cannot engage the amygdala, the fight-or-flight area of the brain, and the frontal lobe area associated with thinking at the same time. Since the region of the brain activated during a bullying episode is the amygdala, a student who is bullied is less likely to be focused on academics and learning because the frontal lobe of the brain is not activated.

Additionally, educational literature indicates that school violence influences academic success, leading to a conclusion that physical and emotional safety is integral to the learning environment. A student's desire to be in school is linked with level of achievement (Bosworth, 1994), and students who experience bullying are more likely to be absent from school. In addition to this decreased connection to school, academic achievement is lower for students engaged in bullying behaviors (Dake, Price, Telljohann, & Funk, 2004).

LEGAL ISSUES

In addition to the psychosocial and academic consequences of bullying, there can also be legal implications when bullying in schools is not addressed. Educators are generally required to provide policy and actions to provide a safe environment for the students under their supervision. The failure to do so can open a school to litigation. There are several federal statutes and legal concepts that relate to bullying. Additionally, as of January 2011, forty-five states have enacted bullying prevention legislation. These clearly indicate that there are legal expectations that schools will address bullying issues.

The Doctrine of In Loco Parentis

The doctrine of in loco parentis provides a legal context to act "in place of the parents." From the school's perspective, it implies a sense of responsibility to maintain appropriate discipline and control to assure the safety and security of students while under the supervision of school officials. Considering this legal responsibility of parental rights, duties, and obligations, the doctrine calls for faculty, staff, and administration to provide a safe environment for schools. If school personnel fail to act when a student is bullied, they may be in violation of this "duty of care," resulting in legal action.

Negligence

A basic definition of *negligence* is a lack of supervision that results in an injury to a child. Negligence can occur in the form of a commission, doing something you should not have done, or an omission, not doing what you should have done. In relation to bullying, acts of omission are a more common complaint and can include failure to have or enforce a bullying prevention policy or rules against bullying, failure to supervise, and failure to follow designated procedures for reporting or responding to incidents of bullying.

Negligence resulting from commission might involve creating an environment that encourages bullying or willfully responding to a bullying incident in a way that is not appropriate. This legal concept implies a duty to anticipate actions that might be harmful to students and develop policies to prevent such acts, as well as an obligation to respond if the problematic action still arises. The legal responsibility of educators to address bullying prevention and respond to the actions of bullies is evident in the increasing number of lawsuits claiming negligence. Following are highlights of recent litigation.

2011—Connecticut parents filed suit on behalf of their son claiming that school officials had actual knowledge of the bullying he was experiencing yet failed to prevent or intervene. Claiming a blatant and utter disregard for their son's safety, the suit names the Berlin Board of Education, its former and current superintendents, the principal, the athletic director, and the coach of the Berlin High School football team.

2010—The family of a nine-year-old North Georgia student filed suit alleging that the staff at his school knew about the bullying he was experiencing and appropriate action was not taken. The suit names Murray County School System and two teachers.

2010—Parents of a student in the Baltimore area filed suit alleging a middle school's staff's willful neglect to address the bullying problem at the school. They claim school personnel failed to protect the student's rights to due process and equal protection by not intervening in bullying incidents. The suit names all members of the Howard County Board of Education, the principal, the assistant principal, and a substitute teacher.

2009—Parents in Chicago sued the private school their son attended, alleging that he was attacked and injured by another student known for bullying and that the school failed to act even after both the student and his parents notified school staff. The suit names the school and the Catholic Bishop of Chicago.

Disability Harassment

Since special needs students have additional protections provided by federal law, bullying of these students can easily cross the line and become an illegal act. Bullying of a special needs student might reach a level considered to be disability harassment, a form of bullying specifically based on or because of a disability. Verbal, physical, or emotional intimidation or abusive behavior that denies a student with a disability access to, participation in, or receipt of the benefits, services, or opportunities at school, thus creating a hostile environment, is disability harassment.

Federal regulations require school districts to provide a free appropriate public education (FAPE) to students with a disability. Unfortunately, equal access to educational benefits for special needs students can be eroded through bullying. When harassment or bullying is so severe, persistent, or pervasive that it creates a hostile environment, it can violate the student's rights that are protected by law. It can be argued that districts have a legal responsibility under Section 504, Title II, and IDEA to prevent bullying that could lead to disability harassment and to respond appropriately if it does occur.

Discriminatory Harassment

Discriminatory harassment is verbal or physical intimidation directed toward an individual based on race, color, religion, gender, national origin, age, or disability. In addition to the protections afforded by the laws safeguarding students with disabilities, Title VI of the Civil Rights Act of 1964, which prohibits discrimination on the basis of race, color, or national origin, and Title IX of the Education Amendments of 1972, which prohibits discrimination on the basis of sex, need to be considered when issues of bullying arise in schools. Failure to recognize and respond to discriminatory harassment may result in a violation of students' federal civil rights.

This is highlighted in the October 2010 "Dear Colleague Letter" sent to all superintendents from the Department of Education and the Office for Civil Rights. The letter reminds schools that student misconduct that falls under an antibullying policy may also trigger responsibilities under other antidiscrimination statutes. In addition to enforcing antibullying and other disciplinary policies, school personnel should take into account whether the bullying behavior also resulted in discrimination in violation of a student's federal civil rights.

First Amendment Rights

First Amendment rights protect free speech and do apply in a school setting, so they must be considered when dealing with issues of face-to-face and cyberbullying. Schools have to find a balance between free speech and the school's interest in guaranteeing student safety. Fortunately, Supreme Court rulings have resulted in standards that can help schools delineate between free speech and verbal bullying: (1) the Tinker Standard—denial of freedom of speech must be justified by a reasonable forecast of substantial disruption or material interference with school activities, (2) the Fraser Standard—a student's vulgar and offensive speech is not protected by the first amendment, and (3) the

Hazelwood Standard—educators can regulate the style and content of student speech in school-sponsored activities.

These legal standards allow schools to impose educationally based restrictions on student speech when the speech causes, or threatens to cause, substantial and material disruption at school or interferes with students' right to be secure.

There are unique First Amendment considerations when dealing with cyberbullying. When an incident of cyberbullying is brought to the attention of school personnel, the first step is to determine the school's responsibility in dealing with the problem by asking three questions: (1) Was school equipment involved? (2) Did it occur or originate at school? (3) Did it create a substantial disruption on the school campus?

If the answer to any of the questions is yes, the school may move forward with investigation and possible disciplinary action. If the answers to all of these questions is no, it is not within the nexus of the school, and disciplinary action may violate a student's First Amendment rights. Referral to law enforcement or provision of educational materials may be warranted, but disciplinary action would not be appropriate.

State Laws

The number of state legislatures addressing bullying prevention has grown dramatically over the last decade. In 1999, there were no state laws addressing bullying. In 2011 there are forty-five. Many of these statutes were enacted or strengthened following a youth suicide connected to bullying, as evidenced in these five examples.

> Florida: The Jeffrey Johnston Stand Up for All Students Act named after a young man who committed suicide after years of face-to-face and online bullying.
> Idaho: Jared's Law, named in honor of a thirteen-year-old who shot himself after experiencing multiple forms of bullying; amends the existing bullying law.
> Massachusetts: Antibullying bill passed unanimously two months after Phoebe Prince committed suicide.
> New Jersey: Antibullying bill of rights introduced and passed following the suicide of a Rutgers University student who was a victim of cyberbullying.
> Vermont: Bullying Prevention Policy Law enacted after the suicide of Ryan Patrick Halligan, a thirteen-year-old who had experienced face-to-face and online bullying.

Laws vary from state to state, but none make bullying an illegal act. Instead, most require school districts to develop a policy to prohibit bullying. Some statutes require states to provide a model policy and technical assistance. Others encourage action such as implementation of a bullying prevention program rather than requiring direct reform. Some statutes also require training for faculty and staff, education for students regarding bullying, and mandatory reporting mechanisms if bullying incidents occur.

In addition to the increased attention at the state level, there has been a heightened federal interest in bullying prevention that goes beyond the legal statutes already discussed. In 2001, the U.S. Department of Education and the U.S. Department of Health and Human Services collaborated to create the Stop Bullying Now campaign and website. Building on this interagency endeavor, the U.S. Departments of Education, Health and Human Services, Agriculture, the Interior, and Justice formed the Federal Partners in Bullying Prevention Steering Committee to coordinate the federal government's bullying prevention efforts.

In August of 2010, this committee hosted the first National Bullying Summit in Washington, D.C. Over one hundred professionals representing federal, state, and local agencies; researchers; nongovernmental organizations; corporate leaders; and youth participated in the summit working to develop a national strategy to end bullying in schools. The committee also hosted a webcast as a follow-up to the summit. Another federal effort led by this task force is the new website www.stopbullying.gov, designed to disseminate information about federal bullying prevention activities and evidence-based resources.

The federal interest in bullying problems even extends to the president himself. Following a series of suicides of youth who were being bullied for being gay, President Obama recorded an antibullying video message as part of the "It Gets Better" initiative. The First Lady, Michelle Obama, also spoke out about bullying in a television interview stating that adults can address the problem of bullying if they lead by example. In March 2011, the White House hosted a conference on bullying prevention to discuss the effects and solutions to bullying in schools. The nation was invited to join via live chats on Facebook and iVillage. MTV was also involved by announcing an upcoming original TV movie based on the true story of a bully-victim; MTV also mentioned some new safety features and presented a series of cyberbullying prevention PSAs.

Bullying is a safe school issue, and there are legal expectations as well as support for educators to become involved in the prevention process (J. Hoover & Oliver, 1996). Whether you agree with having federal oversight of the bullying problem or believe it is a local issue, the legal, social-emotional, and academic consequences are a concern for students and schools. It is time to move beyond the political arena, and past the focus on high stakes testing, and take action to address the very real bullying problem many students face every day in our schools.

BEST PRACTICES FOR BULLYING PREVENTION AND INTERVENTION

The emotional well-being and physical safety of students are an integral part of a successful learning environment. In light of the negative consequences surrounding bullying and the potential it has to influence a student's social-emotional and academic success, schools can no longer afford to ignore the problem. Fortunately, there are effective strategies to address bullying in schools. In fact, research shows that implementing a comprehensive bullying prevention program can reduce incidents of bullying as well as other antisocial behaviors (Cleary, 2000). One public official expressed it poignantly:

> We need to communicate from the first moment students come to school on the first day of the school year that bullying and harassment will not be tolerated. We don't tell kids to do a math problem once. We repeat the message. We have to do that around this.

> —Kevin Jennings, former assistant deputy secretary,
> Office of Safe and Drug-Free Schools, U.S. Department of Education

Successful antibullying programs use a multicomponent approach, are based on research, and include evidence-based strategies to reduce and prevent incidents of bullying. They increase awareness and knowledge about bullying behavior, provide strategies for confronting bullying actions, and teach skills that promote positive interactions between students and adults in school (Urbanski & Permuth, 2009). This goal can be accomplished by targeting the entire school population, not just focusing on the student who is bullying and the victim of the bullying behavior.

Substantial agreement exists among researchers on what schools can and should do to address bullying. An overview of these strategies is presented here. Keep in mind that any one strategy used alone will not adequately address the problem and can actually make it worse. For best success, the strategies should be interwoven into a comprehensive school safety plan. In order to successfully implement this type of program, a school's plan needs to include a blend of environmental, prevention, and intervention strategies.

A comprehensive program does more than interrupt negative behavior patterns. It also teaches appropriate social skills and promotes social, emotional, ethical, and cognitive learning. A systemic program that reduces bullying problems can also decrease the levels of other antisocial behaviors, improving the learning environment for all students. This can be accomplished when the program specifies clear standards about bullying and provides students with resources, knowledge, and skills to help them cope with bullying situations. Schools must go beyond the idea of solely implementing an antibullying curriculum and move to a big picture that incorporates a safe environment as the foundation for a successful prevention program (Urbanski & Permuth, 2009).

Environmental Strategies

Environmental strategies are focused on changing the aspects of the school environment that may be contributing to the bullying problem. This approach takes into consideration that bullying does not happen in a vacuum; like all behavior, it is shaped by the environment. Therefore, a systemic change may be in order to create and sustain conditions that will not support bullying.

The success of any schoolwide program begins with support from the top. However, to change the structure and management of the educational environment as well as school norms requires a shared focus with the involvement of administration, faculty, staff, students, parents, and the community. Each has a role in shaping the environment and needs to be considered in all aspects of a comprehensive bullying prevention program.

Although schools often put a high concentration of energy into dealing with the student who is bullying and the student who is being bullied, prevention methods aimed at the shared environment often produce results faster than those aimed solely at individuals. They also have the potential for permanent changes because of the broader reach, with the desired behavior becoming the norm and the prevention efforts becoming self-sustaining (Fisher, n.d.). Effective prevention plans incorporate both environmental and individual approaches. Specific strategies for developing attitudes and creating conditions that will contribute to a decrease in bullying problems in schools are indicated and presented here.

Develop a policy. The first step in implementing an effective bullying prevention and intervention program is to develop a bullying prevention policy that is in alignment with the Student Code of Conduct and other school policies. A sound policy sets the foundation by providing a framework for the school to follow and establishing clear expectations, rules, and consequences regarding bullying behavior. A review of research and policy requirements in state laws (Urbanski & Permuth, 2009) indicates that a credible policy includes the following:

1. A clear statement that bullying is prohibited.
2. A definition of bullying that includes three key elements: imbalance of power, intent to harm, and repeated behavior.
3. A noninclusive list of bullying behaviors, including cyberbullying.
4. An outline of acceptable and unacceptable behaviors.
5. An explanation of consequences.
6. Details for enforcement of the policy.
7. Procedures for reporting acts of bullying.
8. A statement regarding retaliation for reporting.
9. A statement regarding immunity for reporting in good faith.
10. Steps for investigating reports of bullying.
11. Procedures for data collection.
12. A plan for publicizing policy and providing instruction on best practices in prevention and intervention.

Bear in mind that once developed, the policy is only as good as the paper it is written on until it is disseminated and enforced. Information outlined in the policy should be posted and widely publicized so all staff, students, and families are aware of the standards and expectations. Ideally the policy should also be reviewed periodically and updated as needed.

Conduct a survey. Although rates may vary from school to school, no school is untouched by bullying. In order to obtain reliable information and to determine the extent of the bullying problem at a school, an annual survey should be given. Minimally, students should complete the survey, but triangulation of data from students, staff, and parents will provide a more rigorous evaluation of the issue. Information about where bullying happens, how often bullying occurs, and what type of bullying is most prevalent can assist with planning and identifying hot spots that may need additional supervision. It will also provide data to measure the success of the prevention efforts.

Whether a formal or informal survey is done, it should include the definition of bullying as written in the policy and should include questions such as the following:

1. Have you been bullied at school in the last two months? If so, how?
2. Where did it happen?
3. Who did you tell?
4. Have you ever bullied another student at school?
5. How did you bully?
6. How do you respond when you witness bullying?
7. How well do adults at school respond to bullying?

Sharing survey results with stakeholders is imperative to build a sense of ownership of the problem as well as the solution. It is also imperative to act on findings.

Increase supervision. Students typically engage in bullying when adults are not watching. Therefore, an effective way to reduce and even prevent bullying is to increase supervision. Using survey results to identify locations where bullying is occurring, educators can work together to monitor these hot spots. An increase in adult visibility is helpful, but all must also be prepared to intervene if bullying occurs.

Review the physical environment. A review of the physical design of the school campus can supplement the data and help create a school environment that is not conducive to bullying behavior. There should not be any physical barriers that block an adult's view of students. Stairwells, hallways, and other areas where there is only a partial view can be problematic. Keep in mind that cameras are not always a deterrent since students know where they are. Additionally, acts caught on camera are usually seen after something has happened rather than stopping it from happening in the first place.

Promote positive interactions. A safe, respectful environment is the foundation for a successful prevention program. This begins by teaching students appropriate social skills and conflict-resolution strategies as well as helping students develop strong problem-solving skills. Activities that promote positive peer and adult relationships should follow to provide practice for what students have learned. Activities that encourage shared responsibility such as class meetings, democratic rule making, class action research projects, and peer mentoring programs can help build these relationships. Most importantly, consistently modeling the expected behaviors will define clear expectations.

Supportive relationships are a key part of a respectful school environment and contribute to the social, emotional, and academic adjustment of students. Educators can build these relationships by getting to know their students and providing opportunities for students to get to know each other. Interaction and communication builds trust, which is critical in dealing with bullying. Without this, it is unlikely that students will come forward to report when something is happening or going to happen.

Relationships help develop a student's sense of school connectedness, one component of school climate. It refers to a student's relationship to school that creates a feeling of belonging to the school and being accepted by others (Blum, 2005). Research shows that students are at less risk for engaging in delinquent behaviors and are more likely to follow the norms and rules of the school community if they have a sense of attachment to the school. However, research also shows that this same connectedness does not serve as a protective factor for bullying victimization (Spriggs, Iannotti, Nansel, & Haynie, 2007).

Along with school connectedness, the interaction of human relationships, physical setting, and psychological atmosphere creates the school climate (Perkins, 2006). This climate is the shared perceptions of a school and consists of the attitudes, beliefs, values, and norms that underlie the instructional practices and operations of a school (McEvoy & Welker, 2000). The importance of a respectful school climate cannot be questioned, but is it enough to address bullying? A Johns Hopkins University survey of eleven thousand middle school students showed that although school climate improved, the self-reported rate of being bullied did not change (Bradshaw, Debnam, Martin, & Gill, 2006). So, the answer is likely no. Improving the school climate alone may not be enough to prevent bullying. A conscious effort to prevent and intervene in bullying is indicated to successfully address bullying in schools.

Consider classroom management. Classroom management can serve as either an enhancement or a deterrent to the learning environment. Although disciplinary factors are usually not considered as contributors to bullying problems, an educator's disciplinary style and strength can impact whether bullying occurs in the classroom. The frequency with which students are distracted by the misbehavior of other students and how often teachers punish students in class can have an effect on the underlying structure of the classroom and ultimately on whether bullying occurs. Elements of classroom management that may contribute to a reduction in bullying include (1) establishment of fair rules, (2) consistency in punishment for breaking those rules, (3) clear behavioral and academic expectations, (4) mutual respect between educators and students, (5) continuous monitoring of behaviors, and (6) organization and preparation for all components of the day, including transitions, in order to maintain classroom order.

Whether in the classroom, hallway, or community areas, it is imperative to provide adequate supervision to ensure students' safety. This is more than just being there and observing. Adults must respond promptly, consistently, and appropriately to stop any behavior that may be bullying.

Empower bystanders. Most students in a school are not bullying others or the victims of bullying. Most are bystanders, those who see or know that bullying is happening. Since bystanders outnumber children who bully, developing this positive peer pressure can help stop bullying at school. Empowering this group to confront bullying behaviors is critical to creating an environment that does not tolerate bullying behaviors.

Keep in mind that standing up to someone who is bullying is difficult for a student to do. However, when adults help students develop the courage to stand up for a victim and promulgate the message that bullying is not tolerated at their school, bullying behavior will decrease. Knowledge is empowering. Incorporating a teaching component as part of a comprehensive prevention program reduces bullying behavior (Olweus, 1993). Teaching students what bullying is and how to respond if they see it is a critical step for bystanders that will be discussed further in the "Intervention" section below.

Have reporting procedures in place. Ensuring that there are procedures to report bullying will help empower bystanders to act in bullying situations. Knowing what to do and how to do it will increase a student's comfort level with reporting, especially if other students have the same knowledge.

The first step is to determine a method for reporting bullying. Options include talking directly to an adult at the school, completing a reporting form, filing an online report, and calling or texting a hotline. It can be beneficial to include an anonymous reporting option for those who fear retaliation. Regardless of the method used, students should be taught to report who was involved, what happened, where it happened, when it occurred, and how often it took place. Procedures for making a report as well as the actions that will occur when a report is received should be outlined and shared with all students, staff, and parents. Once the method is chosen, staff with the capacity to act on reports of bullying should be designated to receive the reports.

When beginning a prevention program, students may believe that reporting to an adult is tattling, ratting, or snitching. Providing students with guidelines on when to report will clarify reporting procedures and ease this concern. It is important to help students understand that reporting is done when someone is in trouble and the student is telling an adult about a potentially dangerous situation to protect someone from getting hurt physically or emotionally. In contrast, tattling, ratting, or snitching is done with the intent of getting someone in trouble. It is also important to facilitate student dialogue about the benefits of reporting as well as the challenges it may pose.

Whether witnessing or experiencing bullying, an important consideration is that students will only report bullying behaviors if they believe the adult will do something about it. So, when bullying is reported, take action consistently and in a timely manner.

Extend efforts to families and communities. A school's prevention and intervention efforts can be strengthened when there is a consistency of message that can be gained by extending environmental efforts to families and the surrounding community. Parents can reinforce the environmental strategies at school by incorporating similar ones at home.

Schools should encourage parents to talk with their child about bullying, including the importance of upholding the message that it is not acceptable behavior. Parents can also make a difference by helping their child to think critically about messages in media and music. They can monitor their child's involvement and should know who his or her friends are. Most importantly, parents can discuss and model their family values as they relate to bullying behaviors.

Bullying is not just confined to the schoolhouse. It carries over and can even begin in the community. Therefore, partnering with community members in bullying prevention efforts can serve to strengthen the message that bullying is not tolerated. Community members can help on campus by volunteering or providing resources. They can also assist off campus by reinforcing the school program through posters, brochures, or using the language of the program in their place of business. Rather than simply asking for money, it is important to be creative and open to ideas when enlisting the help of the community. In fact, from the author's experience in a school district, creating a reciprocal relationship may be the most beneficial since students are also community members and may eventually be employees.

Beginning with these environmental strategies establishes the foundation for a successful bullying prevention program and sets the tone for the prevention and intervention strategies that follow. Clearly defining bullying as unacceptable and having everyone working together toward a solution to the problem creates camaraderie and ultimately a respectful learning environment.

Prevention

A bullying prevention program should help structure the school environment in a way that reduces or eliminates bullying problems to improve the learning environment for all students. A comprehensive bullying prevention program addresses the entire school population, not just the students identified as victims or students who bully. Evidence suggests that successful bullying prevention programs use a combination of school-level prevention, classroom activities, and individual interventions reinforced by administrative support, high-quality training, and integration of activities into existing school operations.

Professional development. Best practice dictates that bullying prevention initiatives begin with staff development to raise educators' awareness and increase their knowledge of bullying prevention and intervention. In order to avoid inappropriate responses to reporting, staff training should occur prior to teaching students how to intervene in and report bullying situations.

A general consensus supports fundamental components that should be included in bullying prevention training for staff. Professional development should be more than a single event but rather an ongoing process with formal workshops and informal opportunities that include staff discussions and reflection on challenges and successes.

The initial stages of professional development begin with awareness and include information about the definition and types of bullying, the difference between bullying and teasing or conflict, and the causes and effects of bullying. Formal training needs to include prevention measures and procedures to be followed when bullying is witnessed or reported so that all staff can provide an immediate and consistent response. Finally, details about the school's bullying prevention policy and program should be presented.

Additional professional development can include a review of survey data, development of a common language, reinforcement of program strategies, discussion of the social and academic problems related to bullying, and other issues identified by the staff.

Challenge myths. Education is essential in prevention and intervention. There are a number of common misconceptions regarding bullying that can interfere in the successful implementation of a bullying prevention program. It is important to dispel these myths and replace them with facts.

One common myth is that students who bully have low self-esteem. The fact is research indicates that children who bully have equal or higher self-esteem than their peers, while the victim of bullying behavior suffers from lower self-esteem. Another common myth is that most victims of bullying are targeted because of outward or physical appearance. In reality, victims are singled out because of their reaction patterns rather than their appearance. Bullying can certainly result in violence, but it is a myth that students who are bullying others are the perpetrators of mass incidents of violence. It is more common that the victim of bullying is the architect of this type of school violence. In fact, the Secret Service found that two-thirds of school shooters since 1974 had been victims of bullying prior to the shootings (Brady, 2001).

Classroom activities. Adults cannot be the only ones to work on the school's bullying prevention program. It is important to give students a voice in prevention efforts by providing them with the opportunity to talk about bullying and enlisting their support in defining bullying as unacceptable. This begins by working with students to establish classroom rules against bullying and then teaching the expected prosocial behaviors.

Topics of regularly scheduled class lessons should include a definition and description of bullying behaviors along with information about the school policy and reporting procedures. Class discussion should also include information to help students respond to bullying. Learning to safely and assertively stand up to inappropriate behavior and having a plan for intervening and reporting are key areas for dialogue. Understanding and accepting different perspectives, managing emotions, and problem solving are subjects that can be included in class discussions. Students can also have rich discussions of ethical issues surrounding bullying, such as the act of doing harm to another, being an active bystander by helping or reporting, and working to build a positive community.

Students who engage in behaviors that can be considered bullying often explain their actions as just playing around. Including strategies to help students assess their own behaviors is another topic of conversation that can be included in classroom activities. Students can learn to use three identifying questions to self-assess their behavior to determine if their actions are simply teasing or have crossed the line into bullying: (1) Is the situation fair or is it one sided? (difference in power); (2) Is the situation uncomfortable for anyone? (intentional aggression); and (3) Have similar situations happened before? (repeated behavior). If there is a difference in power and is a repeated intentional act, the behavior is likely bullying. Helping students recognize this can prevent future problems.

Depending on the climate of the classroom, assessment of victim behavior may also be a valid topic of discussion. It is imperative that this does not become a blame game, with a clear message that blaming the victim is never acceptable. Keeping the focus on behavior by avoiding use of the words *bully* and *victim*, stressing that everyone deserves respect, and engaging in developmentally appropriate discussions of civil and human rights can go a long way to prepare youth for this type of dialogue. With this in mind, a discussion of behavior can identify areas for future lessons or individual prevention efforts, possibly including strengthening assertiveness and social skills.

If choosing to purchase a curriculum for classroom activities, it should be evidence based and aligned with the goals and objectives of the school's bullying prevention initiative. It should also provide students with the skills and knowledge needed to identify bullying and teach the steps for safely intervening and reporting.

Curriculum integration. Just as with professional development for educators, sharing information with students should be more than a one-time classroom presentation. It should be discussed continuously throughout the school year in different contexts to reinforce the message that bullying is not acceptable. An effective way to ensure ongoing dialogue about bullying is to integrate prevention into the existing curriculum.

Many books can be used to discuss bullying and respectful behavior through character analysis or plot discussions. Mapping locations where bullying happens, graphing survey results, or comparing and contrasting bullying to historical events can provide additional learning opportunities. Prevention-themed art contests, development of a logo or theme song for the school's bullying prevention program, and creation of a prevention newsletter or webpage are additional ways to integrate student involvement, curriculum, and bullying prevention.

Individual prevention. Some students will need an extension of the prevention efforts presented in the classroom. The next level is individual prevention strategies that focus on improving the skills of individual students to help them avoid or deal with bullying situations. This may include individual conferences, teaching friendship skills, practicing assertiveness, developing a plan, choosing specific language to use in a potential bullying situation, or helping a student find a replacement source of power and control.

Misdirected efforts. Knowing what works in bullying prevention is foremost in creating a successful program. Just as important is knowing and avoiding what does not work. Three common approaches to avoid are zero-tolerance policies, using conflict-resolution strategies to handle bullying reports, and group treatment for students who bully others. Although these strategies can be very successful for certain types of behaviors, research does not support using them in bullying prevention efforts. Unfortunately, some can even cause more harm.

A clear message that bullying is not tolerated is not the same thing as a zero-tolerance policy. A zero-tolerance policy punishes all incidents severely and in the same manner, usually with suspension or expulsion from school. This does not necessarily encourage reporting or change the behavior. Additionally, bullying is not always clear cut and there are often differing perceptions, so consistent enforcement is nearly impossible. Instead of a zero-tolerance policy focused on punishment, bullying prevention programs should focus on creating a respectful climate and educating the school community about bullying.

Conflict is a normal part of life and happens daily at any school. Conflict resolution and peer mediation are well established ways to help students work together to resolve disputes based on those involved being of equal status and in a situation where both are partly to blame for the problem. Now consider that bullying is an intentional act of aggression. Using conflict-resolution strategies in a bullying situation can send the message that the victim was partly at fault for what happened, further victimizing the student. It can also perpetuate the imbalance of power by forcing the victim to confront the aggressor.

Although they can be helpful to create a foundation for a successful program, conflict resolution and peer mediation should never be used to resolve bullying issues. Best practice is to have adult intervention and to address the victim and the person who is bullying separately.

While group treatment can be helpful for victims of bullying, the same strategy can be counterproductive for students who bully. Anger management, empathy building, self-esteem, or other group treatment settings can provide a venue for increasing power and control, ultimately making bullying problems worse. Group members may become competitive role models for each other, thus reinforcing bullying rather than stopping the inappropriate behavior. Best practice is to work individually with students who are bullying others.

Intervention

Despite a conscientious effort to address the school environment and develop strong prevention strategies, incidents of bullying may still occur. For this reason, intervention strategies are a necessary component of a comprehensive program. The goals of the intervention program are to stop current bullying behavior and avert future bullying by providing support and protection for victims, empowering bystanders to safely and respectfully intervene in bullying situations, and redirecting students who are bullying by finding replacement behaviors.

Stop bullying behavior. The most important intervention is to address bullying behavior each and every time it is witnessed or suspected. At a minimum this means an adult intervenes by naming the behavior as bullying and stating that it is not allowed. If possible, the individuals involved should be separated and spoken to individually.

Depending on the situation, further investigation may be needed to make sure the bullying does not continue.

Investigate bullying reports. All reports of bullying must be investigated in a timely and consistent manner. The procedures for investigating incidents of bullying are similar to the procedures used for investigating other types of misconduct. The first consideration is whether the reported incident is within the scope of the school. Did it occur on school grounds, at a school-sponsored event, or while using school transportation or equipment? Did it cause or threaten to cause substantial and material disruption at the school?

If the answers are no, it may be appropriate to make a referral or provide information to assist the individuals involved, but a school-based investigation would not be indicated. If the answers are yes, an investigation should begin with separate interviews of those involved. Information to be gathered includes a description of the incident, the location of the alleged bullying, the identities of all involved, the relationship between those involved to determine a difference in power or status, the circumstances surrounding the incident, the frequency and severity of the behavior, the pattern of the behavior, and the impact of the incident on the learning environment.

Parents of involved students should be notified whenever an investigation takes place.

Protect the victim. For a variety of reasons, victims of bullying often do not tell anyone what is happening. They may be ashamed, embarrassed, afraid, or think that no one can or will help them. Therefore, when a victim does come forward and report, it is essential to send the message that it is not his or her fault and to take action.

The first step should always be to assess the student's safety and respond appropriately. Once a student's immediate well-being has been addressed, the next step is to develop a plan of action to secure the student's physical and emotional safety while the bullying problem is being dealt with. This safety plan outlines the specific steps that the student and educators will take. Each situation and resulting plan will be different, but there are several common components: areas of increased supervision, what to do if confronted by the student who is bullying, procedures for reporting any future problems, name(s) of trusted adults who will act on reports of bullying, and a communication plan to evaluate the success of the plan.

The safety plan should be developed with input from the student and parent and then be shared with other adults in the school who interact with the student and can be watchful of the situation. Exploring professional assistance or services that might benefit the student should also be part of the overall plan to help the victim of bullying. This may include counseling, role-playing assertiveness, strengthening friendship skills, helping the victim identify allies, or any other relevant service the school can provide.

Redirect behavior. An intervention program must avoid placing too much focus on punishment with too little attention paid to the underlying causes of the inappropriate behavior. Identify the reason for the action, which in cases of bullying is often about gaining power and control. Consequently, redirecting behaviors to find a positive way to meet the need for power and control is just as important as imposing consequences.

Key points to remember are to label the behavior, not the child; focus on consequences in order to teach alternatives rather than punishment as a short-term solution;

and increase observation and supervision to monitor the success of the replacement behavior in eliminating the bullying behavior.

Empower the bystanders. Bystanders are often present when bullying happens and have a choice to take part in the bullying, ignore it, or stop it. Rather than being a silent majority, this group of students can be a valuable asset to an intervention program. Encourage bystanders to be courageous and stand up against bullying at school. Set clear expectations that bystanders should not watch, encourage, laugh at, or ignore bullying situations.

Recognize that bystanders may not want to intervene because they are afraid of becoming the next target of the bullying behavior or think that intervening will make the situation worse. They may also be unsure of what to do. These concerns must be addressed so that students can take a stand. Remind students that they can be a part of the solution or a part of the problem, and then provide the knowledge and skills they need to support the school's bullying prevention program.

Help students change their perception about becoming the next target by explaining that a person who bullies looks for victims who will not stand up for themselves, so assertively intervening is actually a preventive measure. Provide a common language for students to use: "That is bullying, and it is not okay." If it is not safe to assertively address the student who is bullying, at a minimum bystanders should refuse to join in the bullying. Bystanders should also know procedures and be prepared to report bullying behavior to an adult.

Involve parents. As with all components of the bullying prevention program, parents should get involved when issues of bullying arise. Cooperation between the school and home is particularly important when an investigation is happening or when interventions are put in place. Parents may be the first ones to become aware of bullying behavior and should be educated in appropriate ways to help their child. A parent workshop can provide parents with the information and strategies they need to intervene appropriately. Workshop information includes (1) awareness of behaviors that could indicate there is a problem with bullying, (2) empathy rather than rescuing, (3) avoiding blame, (4) that fighting back or ignoring the behavior will not stop bullying, and (5) sibling bullying.

Whether notified by the school or learning about the bullying from their child, parents should communicate about the current situation and work with the school to prevent future bullying incidents. This may involve working with school personnel to create a safety plan, monitoring behavior, and suggesting replacement behaviors.

CONCLUSION

The environment in a school impacts how students learn and teachers teach. Thus, creating physically and emotionally safe schools cannot be separated from creating academically strong schools. Schools that practice prosocial education recognize that both are integral components of school and student success that are needed to address the needs of all students in a school.

Bullying is a phenomenon that negatively impacts the school environment. It has the potential to interfere with the healthy social-emotional development of students as well as their academic success. A comprehensive approach with specific strategies to increase awareness of bullying, teach students how to respond to bullying, and address individuals involved in bullying behaviors are needed to effectively address bullying in school.

The environmental, prevention, and intervention strategies presented are the foundation for a successful bullying prevention program. This comprehensive approach structures the school environment in a way that eliminates opportunities and rewards for bullying. In turn, schools will improve the learning environment for all students, which is a fundamental and minimal definition of prosocial education—that is, prosocial education creates a very good learning environment and then goes on to create the conditions for individual cognitive, moral, social, and emotional development, both short-term skills and understandings that build on each other, and long-term understanding.

The fact is that no school can be a great school until it is a safe school first.

—Arne Duncan, education secretary

REFERENCES

Atlas, R. S., & Pepler, D. J. (1998). Observations of bullying in the classroom. *Journal of Educational Research, 92*(2), 86–99.

Beran, T., & Li, Q. (2007). The relationship between cyberbullying and school bullying. *Journal of Student Wellbeing, 1*(2), 15–33.

Blum, R. W. (2005). A case for school connectedness. *Educational Leadership, 62*(7), 16–20.

Bosworth, D. (1994). Truancy and pupil performance. *Education Economics, 2*(3), 243–264.

Bradshaw, C. P., Debnam, K. J., Martin, L., & Gill, R. (2006, September). *Assessing rates and characteristics of bullying through an Internet-based survey system.* Paper presented at the Persistently Safe Schools Conference, Washington, DC.

Brady, J. (2001). *An interview with Dr. Russell Skiba of the Safe and Responsive School Project.* Retrieved June 21, 2003, from www.guidancechannel.com

Cleary, M. (2000). *Bullying information for schools.* New Zealand: Telecom.

Dake, J. A., Price, J. H., Telljohann, S. K., & Funk, J. B. (2004). Principals' perceptions and practices of school bullying prevention activities. *Health Education and Behavior, 31*(3), 372–387.

Dupper, D. R., & Meyer-Adams, N. (2002). Low-level violence: A neglected aspect of school culture. *Urban Education, 37*(3), 350–364.

Feinberg, T. (2003). Bullying prevention and intervention. *Principal Leadership Magazine, 4*(1). Retrieved June 14, 2007, from http://www.nasponline.org/resources/principals/nassp_bullying.aspx

Fisher, D. (n.d.). *Environmental prevention strategies: An introduction and overview.* Retrieved March 12, 2011, from http://wch.uhs.wisc.edu/docs/SIG/fisher-EnvironmentalPrevention Strategies.pdf

Florida Office of Safe and Healthy Schools, Department of Education. (2005, April). *SDDFS notes.* Tallahassee, FL: Author.

Fox, C. L., & Boulton, M. J. (2005). The social skills problems of victims of bullying: Self, peer and teacher perceptions. *British Journal of Educational Psychology, 75*(2), 313–328.

Hawkins, D. L., Pepler, D. J., & Craig, W. M. (2001). Naturalistic observations of peer interventions in bullying. *Social Development, 10*(4), 512–527.

Haynie, D. L., Nansel, T., Eitel, P., Crump, A. D., Saylor, K., Yu, K., et al. (2001). Bullies, victims, and bully/victims: Distinct groups of at-risk youth. *Journal of Early Adolescence, 21*(1), 29–49.

Hinduja, S., & Patchin, J. W. (2007). Offline consequences of online victimization. *Journal of School Violence, 6*(3), 89–112.

Hoover, J., & Oliver, R. (1996). *The bullying prevention handbook: A guide for principals, teachers and counselor.* Bloomington, IN: National Education Service.

Hoover, N. C., & Pollard, N. J. (2000). *Initiation rites in American high schools: A national survey. Final report.* Alfred, NY: Alfred University. Retrieved from http://eric.ed.gov/PDFS/ED445809.pdf

Indiana Department of Education. (2003). *White paper on bullying prevention and education.* Retrieved June 30, 2006, from http://www.doe.state.in.us/legwatch/docs/Bullyingpaper2004session.doc

Josephson Institute Center for Youth Ethics. (2010). *The Ethics of American Youth 2010 report: Bullying, violence, high risk behavior.* Los Angeles: Author. Retrieved February 26, 2011, from http://charactercounts.org/programs/reportcard/2010/installment01_report-card_bullying-youth-violence.html

Kaiser Family Foundation. (2001). *Talking with kids about tough issues: A national survey of parents and kids.* Menlo Park, CA: Author. Retrieved August 11, 2004, from http://www.kff.org

Kent, B. A. (2003). Identity issues for hard-of-hearing adolescents aged 11, 13, and 15, in mainstream settings. *Journal of Deaf Studies and Deaf Education, 8*(3), 315–324.

Kiefer, H. M. (2003). *Teens and bullying: Who's taking abuse?* Washington, DC: Gallup Organization. Retrieved November 17, 2011, from http://www.gallup.com/poll/10228/Teens-Bullying-Whos-Taking-Abuse.aspx

Kowalski, R. M., Limber, S., & Agaston, P. W. (2008, March). *Cyberbullying: Bullying in the digital age.* Paper presented at the annual meeting of the Southeastern Psychological Association, Charlotte, NC.

Li, Q. (2005, April). *Cyber-bullying in schools: The nature and extent of adolescents' experience.* Paper presented at the American Education Research Association (AERA) Conference, Montreal, Quebec, Canada.

McEvoy, A., & Welker, R. (2000). Antisocial behavior, academic failure, and school climate: A critical review. *Journal of Emotional and Behavioral Disorders, 8*(3), 130–140.

McEvoy, A., & Welker, R. (2001). Antisocial behavior, academic failure and school climate. In H. M. Walker & M. H. Epstein (Eds.), *Making schools safer and violence free: Critical issues, solutions and recommended practices* (pp. 28–38). Austin, TX: PRO-ED.

Mendler, A. N. (2001). *Connecting with students.* Alexandria, VA: Association for Supervision and Curriculum Development.

Nansel, T. R., Overpeck, M., Haynie, D. L., Ruan, W. J., & Scheidt, P. C. (2003). Relationships between bullying and violence among U.S. youth. *Archives of Pediatrics and Adolescent Medicine, 157*, 348–353.

Nansel, T. R., Overpeck, M., Pilla, R. S., Ruan, W. J., Simons-Morton, B., & Scheidt, P. (2001). Bullying behavior among US youth. *JAMA: Journal of the American Medical Association, 285*(16), 2094–2100.

Olweus, D. (1993). *Bullying at school.* Cambridge, MA: Blackwell Publishers.

Olweus, D. (2003). A profile of bullying in schools. *Educational Leadership, 60*(6), 12–17.

Olweus, D., & Limber, S. (2010). *Olweus answers questions, discusses data on bullying.* Retrieved from www.olweus.org

Pearl, E. S., & Dulaney, C. L. (2006). Depressive symptoms and prosocial behavior after participation in a bullying prevention program. *Journal of School Violence, 5*(4), 3–20.

Perkins, B. K. (2006). *Where we learn: The CUBE survey of urban school climate.* Alexandria, VA: National School Board Association.

Rodkins, P. C., & Hodges, E. V. E. (2003). Bullies and victims in the peer ecology: Four questions for psychologists and school professionals. *School Psychology Review, 32*(3), 384–400.

Slee, P. T., & Rigby, K. (1993). The relationship of Eysenck's personality factors and self-esteem to bully-victim behaviour in Australian schoolboys. *Personality and Individual Differences, 14*(2), 371–373.

Spriggs, A. L., Iannotti, R. J., Nansel, T. R., & Haynie, D. L. (2007). Adolescent bullying involvement and perceived family, peer and school relations: Commonalities and differences across race/ethnicity. *Journal of Adolescent Health, 41*(3), 283–293.

Telljohann, S. K. (2003). The nature and extent of bullying at school. *Journal of School Health, 73*(5), 173–180.

Urbanski, J., & Permuth, S. (2009). *The truth about bullying: What educators and parents must know and do.* Lanham, MD: Rowman & Littlefield.

U.S. Department of Education. (1998). *Preventing bullying: A manual for schools and communities.* Washington, DC: Author.

Veenstra, R., Lindenberg, S., Oldehinkel, A. J., DeWinter, A. F., Verhulst, F. C., & Ormel, J. (2005). Bullying and victimization in elementary schools: A comparison of bullies, victims, bully/victims, and uninvolved preadolescents. *Developmental Psychology, 41*(4), 672–682.

Weinhold, B. K. (1999, September). Bullying and school violence: The tip of the iceberg. *Counseling Today.* Alexandria, VA: American Counseling Association.

Weinhold, B. K. (2000). Bullying and school violence: The tip of the iceberg. *Teacher Educator, 35*(3), 28–33.

Willard, N. (2005, August). *Cyberbullying and cyberthreats.* Paper presented at national conference of the Office of Safe and Drug-Free Schools, Washington, DC.

Windemeyer Communications. (2003). *National Bullying Prevention Campaign formative research report.* Washington, DC: U.S. Department of Health and Human Services.

Zins, J. E., Bloodworth, M. R., Weissberg, R. P., & Walberg, H. J. (2004). The scientific base linking social and emotional learning to school success. In J. E. Zins, R. P. Weissberg, M. C. Wang, & H. J. Walberg (Eds.), *Building academic success on social and emotional learning: What does the research say?* (pp. 3–22). New York: Teachers College Press.

Case Study 14A

Lynch Elementary School Bullying Prevention Program

JOAN ELIZABETH REUBENS

As the staff came together for yet another monthly meeting in the 2009/10 school year at Lynch Elementary School in Pinellas County, Florida, a teacher was overheard saying, "This is about adding a bullying prevention program. Can you believe it, another program and another thing to do?" Unfortunately, this is common thinking among educational communities across the United States, and Lynch was no different. However, in this urban school of approximately 642 students, a staff that had this *one more thing* attitude gradually began to see that bullying prevention could fit seamlessly into their existing schoolwide initiatives. As a coordinator of bullying prevention for the district, I was stunned as I entered the large room that held approximately 105 staff members where the meeting was being led by the principal, Lorraine Bigelow; the behavior specialist, Mary Hickerson; and other individual staff. I had been invited to and participated in many meetings, but this one was different. Although there was some skepticism, it was obvious that everyone in that room had a stake in what was being presented and were encouraged to share their views. What was obvious and effective was the teamwork approach. Everyone's contribution counted, as was evidenced by the principal's leadership.

Lynch Elementary is one of seventy-four elementary schools in Pinellas County, Florida. With over 102,000 students, the district is the twenty-third largest in the United States. Lynch is a Title I school with 71 percent of students receiving free/reduced-price lunch. The student body is 65 percent white, 9.3 percent black, 8.1 percent Hispanic, 9 percent Asian, 0.6 percent American Indian, and 7.5 percent multiracial. The school serves 12.3 percent exceptional education students and 17.8 percent English language learning students. The mission of Lynch Elementary School staff and community is to provide quality educational experiences as a foundation for the lifelong learning of every student. The Lynch community strives to ensure that these learning experiences happen within an environment that promotes safety and respects diversity.

Looking back to the 2006/7 school year, CHAMPS, Foundations, and Commitment to Character are programs that were already being implemented to help promote a positive school climate and to instill strong character in the students. The CHAMPS and Foundations programs are both part of the Safe and Civil Schools* series and go hand in hand to promote a proactive and positive approach to classroom/campus behavior management. The Foundations program guides a school through the process of designing a proactive, positive schoolwide discipline plan. It provides a framework to help the school's staff develop and implement effective behavior management and motivational practices, including behavior support for all students. The Foundations process includes a set of specific applications to produce ongoing improvement for student behaviors. CHAMPS (Conversation, Help, Activity, Movement, Participation, and Success) is an approach to classroom management that aligns with the Foundations' schoolwide discipline component. Staff members are provided with the tools for behavior management and discipline practices. CHAMPS expectations are clarified for students using the CHAMPS tool: Conversation—can students talk during the activity? (example: inside voice); Help—how will students have their questions answered during the activity? (example: raise hand); Activity— what is the activity/lesson? (example: partner math); Movement—what kind of movement is allowed during the activity? (example: sharpen pencil); Participation—how do students demonstrate their full participation? (example: written assignment); and Success for everyone! Commitment to Character is the district award-winning model for character education.† The goal of the program is to create a school culture that is saturated with such character qualities as respect, responsibility, honesty, and self-motivation so as to promote the highest student achievement in a safe learning environment. Combined, these three programs produce ongoing improvement for student behaviors.

Each program has a core committee of faculty, staff, and leadership that guides implementation. All committees attend regularly scheduled meetings together to align and improve processes and procedures to ensure they are working at the school. The Foundations/CHAMPS team meets monthly to review data trends and issues at the school. Based on these findings, the team brainstorms new ideas for the classroom and school campus, or revisions of existing programs to meet current needs are discussed. The team is also responsible for prioritizing issues and bringing them to the staff for discussion. Issues identified by the team are discussed at monthly professional learning communities (PLC)/team leaders meetings with the ultimate goal of creating safe and civil behaviors campuswide.

The Principal's 200 Club is one outcome of this process. This incentive program focuses on positive behavioral change and increases positive interactions between students and staff across the entire school environment. It includes a dynamic feedback system, continually informing students and staff about who is following the school rules. The purpose of the program is to *catch* students following All-School Rules and behaving appropriately. Tickets are distributed to the teachers to use to recognize a student for following the rules. Students

---

*CHAMPS and Foundations, retrieved May 17, 2011, from www.safeandcivilschools.com
†Pinellas County Schools Commitment to Character brochure.

who earn these tickets make a positive trip to the office and receive kudos from the office staff, sign the 200 Club Celebrity Book and have their name mentioned in the morning announcements. Going one step further, the principal makes a personal phone call to the student's parents to congratulate them for their child's outstanding behavior. The ticket is then added to a chart in the office for a chance to be selected for a Mystery Motivator. Teachers, parents, and students would agree that this program has been quite successful at Lynch, and the students are thrilled to receive recognition for their outstanding behavior in following All-School Rules.

Despite the many positive things in place to address school climate and student behavior, through data collected during the implementation of these programs, bullying was identified as a recurring problem that needed to be addressed. Following the success of the other programs, the school recognized the need for a specific schoolwide approach. The Foundations/CHAMPS team determined that a research-based proven program needed to be put in place in conjunction with the existing programs. The idea was to integrate the programs in a seamless way that provided a one-program approach rather than having four separate programs working independently of each other. Following the process, the team researched and identified the Olweus Bullying Prevention Schoolwide Program to be implemented at Lynch Elementary School during the 2009/10 school year. The goal of the research-based Olweus program is to reduce, if not eliminate, existing bully/victim problems among students, prevent the development of new bully/victim problems, achieve better peer relations in the school, and create conditions that encourage students to respect each other. This was a natural fit with the existing programs at the school.

The Olweus program is a comprehensive process that begins with staff training for an identified core committee. Nationally certified trainers from the district's Safe and Drug-Free Schools Office led the intensive two-day training and continue with consultative services for the duration of the program. The core team, which attended the initial training to become the school experts in the area of bullying prevention, consisted of the principal, the behavior specialist, the guidance counselor, teachers from each grade level, a physical education (PE) teacher, an exceptional student education (ESE) teacher, and a support staff personnel. Since the program is a systemic approach and the implementation needed to fit with what was already in place, the team helped create PAWS for Success (PAWS is the school's mascot and refers to the school's guidelines for success) posters for all classrooms, PE locations, cafeteria, and areas for arrival/dismissal. These PAWS behaviors include self-responsibility, following the rules, being respectful, using safety and civility, honesty and trustworthiness, and the school's antibullying rules, which state, "We will not bully others, we will help students who are bullied, we will include students who are left out, and we will tell an adult at school and an adult at home if we know that somebody is being bullied."

Once the staff was trained, the program was introduced to students. Through the *We Love Your News* (WLYN) daily live student-produced news show, information about the program was introduced by reviewing the school's antibullying rules, role-plays, student-created posters, and the introduction of class meetings. This format is used for some of the ongoing teaching components of the program. DVD clips from the Olweus program help generate student discussion during classroom meetings to address various bullying prevention needs and issues on campus. Teachers have also successfully incorporated bullying issues for discussion during class meetings through classroom suggestion boxes to support class meetings. The core team also compiled a list of books from the media center that focused on bullying prevention for teachers to incorporate in their classroom read-aloud.

The Olweus program has been well received by staff and parents alike, as bullying behaviors had been an increasing issue with many students. To get everyone involved, families were notified through letters and phone calls about the school adopting the Olweus program, and families were invited to attend a schoolwide kickoff campaign designed to foster student involvement. A presentation was made to the School Advisory Council (SAC) and Lynch Boosters as well. Recognizing the need for consistency, the core team created a specific process that orients new staff as to what they need to know about the school's programs. At the PLC monthly meetings, identified staff meet with new school personnel in the media center and go through the manual step by step and provide a folder of all necessary information. This approach has lent itself as a structure for success.

Many innovative ideas have been developed and shared with teachers and staff alike to promote the Lynch antibullying campaign. This includes a variety of reporting procedures that align with the program, district policy, and state law. Many classroom teachers have used a suggestion box in their rooms for students to anonymously report bullying. Also, a campus mailbox is centrally located for all students who need to report bullying concerns. These anonymous reports are collected on a daily basis by the behavior specialist who then investigates the situations.

In December 2009, the data collected from the anonymous Olweus Bullying Questionnaire indicated the prevalence of bullying problems as well as the forms of bullying, the location and duration, and the number of incidents. An overall 22.3 percent of third-, fourth-, and fifth-grade students reported being bullied *two to three times a month*. Combined with staff input, it was noted that the cafeteria, PE area, and areas of arrival and dismissal were hot spots of concern.

In May 2011, the anonymous Olweus Bullying Questionnaire was taken again by third-, fourth-, and fifth-grade students and showed that an overall 20 percent of these students were being bullied. The hot spots that were previously noted in 2009 showed a decrease in being problematic but continue to remain as areas of concern for bullying, so supervision in these areas continues to be heightened. The results showed that there was a 2.3 percent overall decrease in the reports of bullying. Tables 14A.1 and 14A.2 show data from

Table 14A.1. Percent of Students
Experiencing Bullying at Lynch
Elementary School by Grade and Year

Grade	2009	2011
Third	24	17
Fourth	19	36
Fifth	17	14

both the 2009 and 2011 questionnaires broken down by gender, grade level, and type of bullying.

Since the core team meets regularly to discuss serious concerns from teachers and support staff, it was important for the staff to know what bullying behaviors were being most exhibited and by whom, thus generating specific strategies that would target the areas of concern. The Olweus survey results combined with a review of bullying report forms and analysis of discipline referrals provided the information about bullying behaviors. The data were used to create topics for classroom meetings so that specific behavioral areas could be addressed and additional teaching could take place. Some of the concerns include the campus hot spots for bullying and the severity of bullying behaviors on campus. These concerns were then addressed and discussed at staff meetings. The hot spots of concern have and continue to be covered with additional supervision by staff in a cooperative effort to curtail bullying behaviors.

The core team observed an increase in student buy-in for the 2010/11 school year. Students are using the language stated in the school's antibullying rules if they see bullying happen. Students are reporting more incidents of bullying, and each is handled following the district's policy against bullying and harassment guidelines. Through yearly bullying prevention training, staff know that when bullying awareness is being taught, reports of bullying may increase as well. The process has been very proactive and consistent. Now when meetings occur, comments have changed from "Can you believe it, another program and another thing to do?" to "This is just what we do and what is best for our students!"

Table 14A.2. Percent of Students Experiencing Bullying
at Lynch Elementary School by Type, Gender, and Year

Type	Girls		Boys	
	2009	2011	2009	2011
Verbal	24	24	16	21
Rumors	18	19	14	14
Exclusion	14	19	14	14
Racial	14	9	9	6
Bullied another way	13	10	14	13
Threats	9	7	12	6
Physical	6	6	9	12
Sexual	8	9	9	5
Cyber	8	6	5	2
Damage to property	5	4	8	4

Case Study 14B

Team LEAD—Leadership, Empathy, Accountability, and Discussion: Addressing Social Aggression through Bystander Leadership Groups

DENISE KOEBCKE

"Please, Mrs. K., there must be something you can do about this!" Thus began my journey into the realm of relational aggression nearly ten years ago, though at the time I didn't yet know or understand the terminology. It was a journey that began with throwing my lesson plans out the window for a day and focusing instead on simply listening to my seventh graders and letting them take the lead in solving their social issues.

My middle school in Valparaiso, a socioeconomically stable town in Northwest Indiana, just an hour outside Chicago, Illinois, houses approximately seven hundred sixth, seventh, and eighth graders. After teaching sixth-grade language arts there for approximately twelve years, I decided to move to seventh grade. My first year teaching seventh-grade language arts became a turning point for my students and me, perhaps because of the personal relationships I had already formed with so many of the kids who had been in my sixth-grade class the year before. The level of trust they had already established with me, I believe, prompted the stream of weeping girls and sullen boys who, by mid-October, seemed to continually traipse down to my new seventh-grade classroom to seek advice.

On the day in question, a student came up to my desk toward the end of homeroom and asked if I had a moment. As my homeroom kids worked on homework from other classes, she sat on the floor behind my desk and started to cry. Amid the tears tumbled out a story of hurt feelings, exclusion, poor self-esteem, and loneliness from a girl who seemingly had everything under control and everything going for her. I listened much more than I spoke, and when the bell rang for my honors language arts block to begin, she quietly rose to return to her seat, still in tears and completely miserable. I sat at the front of the room, looking out at a group of kids I knew quite well and cared about a great deal, and knew that whether I taught English that period or not, they weren't going to learn a thing until we dealt with the social issues that had apparently gotten way out of hand. I threw aside my lesson plans and simply said, "Over the past couple of months, so many of you have come to me unhappy or angry over issues with your friends this year. So today I'm not teaching English. I want to talk about what's going on that is making you all so miserable."

In that moment, my first bystander leadership team was born. Hands lifted immediately, if somewhat tentatively. Both girls and boys shared their frustrations and concerns, and it became abundantly clear to me that they had all hurt each other and been hurt in return. Most importantly, it was obvious that none of us, myself included, had all the answers. The more they spoke, though, the lighter the air in the room became, the taller they sat, and the closer they grew. As they left the room a full ninety minutes later, I recognized we had just had the most productive and enlightening lesson of the year, not in language arts, but in humanity, and it wasn't I who had done the teaching. They had also left me with a challenge I knew I had to accept: "Please, Mrs. K., there must be something you can do about this!"

Though I had always been quite confident in my ability to work with kids and understand them, our discussion that day had opened my eyes to the fact that most of the assumptions I had made about kids and a good portion of the advice I had given them concerning peer issues were not helpful and were perhaps even harmful. They left my room that day much kinder and more considerate of each other, but I knew the change would be short-lived unless I found a way to continue their growth and found it quickly. As I researched peer aggression online, I made several important decisions. First, I believed strongly that this wasn't just a girl or boy issue, but one that involved all kids equally. I needed to share the information I had gathered with the kids and give them the knowledge base from which to discuss their own experiences. Most importantly, I had to find a way to continue meeting during the school day, and it couldn't be during my language arts classes.

As the student council sponsor, I decided we would continue our discussions for the rest of the year under the student council heading, and I would allow more kids to join student council as "members at large." We met during the school day during study halls and raised money to bring in speakers on the topic of "bullying." By the end of the year, we had created enough interest in the issue to secure an Indiana safe schools grant; we used the grant to contract with the Ophelia Project out of Erie, Pennsylvania, for staff training and a high school mentor training workshop on bullying. The Ophelia Project used their Creating a Safe School (CASS) curriculum to train teachers and high school mentors in the language of peer aggression. We gained approval from both the high school and middle school administrators to institute the CASS Mentor Program, in which the high school mentors would visit the middle schools once a month, working with sixth and seventh graders on peer aggression issues.

Prompted by that one discussion with a group of seventh graders, our school district had set in motion a fledgling antibullying campaign. While bringing in professionals in this new field was exciting, I was eager to continue exploring the student energy that had created the entire movement. Therefore, as the new school year began, I moved my eighth-grade student group out of Student

Council and named it Team LEAD in order to focus specifically on bystander leadership and promoting prosocial behaviors among kids. Core values of the group were teaching Leadership, Empathy, Accountability, and Discussion in order to help kids manage their own social interactions more positively, resiliently, and productively. One goal for the group was to harness student energy and discussion as a key component in establishing a prosocial climate in our school; in addition, we wished to create a more natural progression for a broader peer mentoring and role-modeling program. How could we move our kids forward in a way that was less contrived and less dictated by adults? How could we take their concerns and give them more ownership so that they could move forward in a way that made sense to them, allowing them to initiate peer mentoring ideas and timelines? The Team LEAD concept grew from a desire to empower kids and create a more authentic leadership experience.

Based on my experience having sponsored many different leadership groups over the years, from student government to honor societies to drug-free clubs to journalism groups, Team LEAD was designed to be unique in several important ways:

1. *Members were self-selected rather than teacher selected or peer nominated to avoid creating another exclusive clique.* Students interested in becoming Team LEADers filled out extensive applications that included essay questions and self-reflective rating scales. The goal was to accept as many kids as possible; only those who were failing classes and therefore could not afford to miss study hall or those who had recent behavior referrals to the office were put on a "wait list." Teachers and sponsors would then mentor any "wait-listed" students in order to get them into the program as quickly as possible.

2. *Members attended a full-day training workshop to kick off the year with a specific emphasis on education in peer relationships and altruism and how those issues related to the Team LEAD philosophy and goals.* In speaking with kids who regularly attended other "leadership" workshops, the chief complaint seemed to be that the activities were "fun," but they didn't really "get" what they had to do with leadership or anything meaningful. In Team LEAD trainings, all activities were purposeful and processed clearly so that kids understood exactly what they had to do with our goals and the Team LEAD core values.

3. *Membership remained open throughout the year in order to encourage and support student growth.* Midway through the year or at other times if needed, Team LEAD members would run additional membership drives, inviting more students to join. By the end of the year, Team LEAD would typically have anywhere from fifty to one hundred members. Any students who had applied but had not met grade or behavior requirements met with me or another Team LEAD sponsor to discuss why we were unable to accept their applications and to help them set up a plan for resolving the issues that were blocking their membership. If and when the students achieved the improvement goals, they would become full-fledged members. This open-door policy was a win-win situation: kids in Team LEAD signed a behavior contract, and if they did not make sincere efforts to live up to that contract, they were put on a conduct sheet and removed from active membership until they resolved those conduct issues. With this safety net, we really had nothing to lose by giving every

child who was interested a chance to LEAD. The behavior contract upheld the school handbook's behavior requirements with an added emphasis on leading positively and making noticeable efforts to be kind and helpful to others.

4. *Team LEAD met every week during the school day, either for thirty minutes during lunch meetings or for forty minutes during study hall.* This point was important for two reasons. First, meeting during the school day avoided eliminating students involved in other after-school clubs or sports, so all potential leaders and members of all different social cliques had access. Allowing the group to meet weekly during the school day also sends a clear message from the staff that the group is valued and supported in their attempts to create a prosocial climate. Changing social climate takes time; thus the weekly schedule is ideal.

5. *Each Team LEAD meeting was led by the adult sponsor and followed a formula developed to both educate and bond students while promoting positive action: teambuilder, lesson, discussion, action/challenge.* This process focused on breaking down barriers among cliques and providing opportunities to practice and process prosocial behaviors in a safe environment. Lessons and discussions focused on communication skills, confidence, resilience, respect for differences, empathy, positive action in real social situations, altruism, different perspectives, individual strengths, and so on. Individualized discussions (both small group and large group) are important; each school and each group of kids will have different concerns or issues. Listening to the kids and individualizing lessons and discussions to suit their needs is the key. The goal is not to tell the kids what to do, but to help them share and process what positive actions work best for them.

6. *Opportunities to share and model new skills were provided as a natural progression and were student initiated.* As Team LEAD members were educated in leadership skills and prosocial behaviors, they naturally progressed to brainstorming how they could make a positive difference for others. At that point it was vital to offer peer mentoring opportunities with younger students and schoolwide leadership opportunities such as No Name Calling Week or Mix it Up at Lunch events for them to host. Students also came up with their own great ideas such as Free Compliment Days and Peace Patrols at lunch. Each Team LEAD group will be different, depending on the school and the group of kids. It's not a packaged curriculum; it's a system of working with and empowering kids. This format helps them own their leadership activities and gain confidence.

LESSONS LEARNED FROM MY OWN GROUP AND THOSE IN OTHER COMMUNITIES

Given a window of opportunity, student teams will readily form themselves, just as my first student team did. The question for educators becomes, what next? Student-initiated spirit weeks, dances, fund-raisers, and other concrete, finite activities or projects are things teachers understand and feel comfortable facilitating. Peer aggression and prosocial climate development, however, are not short-term, finite issues; the task is never accomplished but continually evolving. Through our continuous efforts to promote positive climate change in our schools, the kids, teachers, and I have discovered the following truths:

"Bullying" is not the problem; it is just one symptom of a much larger societal problem. American children are at risk in our society today, not just some of them, but all of them. Society has changed drastically in a comparatively short amount of time; when the "baby boomers" were born, most would agree that parents were the number-one influence on kids, and church and school were high on the list; peers were the major variable in the list. "Boomers," however, have created a new world for today's kids, one in which the media and the cyberworld have a larger impact than we ever imagined; in fact, some would argue that the number-one influence on our kids today is the media, followed by their peers. Not surprisingly, *bullying* has become this decade's buzzword in education. Why then, with such a public push toward creating safer climates, haven't we yet found a way to "end" bullying, a curriculum or a program that "works"?

The answer is twofold. Implying that we can "end" bullying or find what "works" sets up a dangerous mind-set for all involved. As adults, we know better than anyone that there is no perfect world in which everyone is kind and loving 100 percent of the time. In addition, there is rarely one right answer or solution in dealing with human relationships; so much depends on individual perspective and context. Implying to our kids that we can put an end to conflicts, misunderstandings, hurt feelings, and all forms of aggression does them a disservice because, in doing so, we set them and ourselves up for failure right from the start. If that's the standard, we will see proof of our failure every time something unpleasant happens, and the truth is, wherever human beings interact, there will be conflict. This is the very reason kids and adults throw up their hands and believe that efforts to change the social climate will never work.

In working with our Team LEAD kids, we have discovered that to effectively empower students to create positive change in this area, it helps a great deal to shift the terminology we use from "what works," a very finite, succeed-or-fail mind-set, to "what helps," the more growth-oriented mind-set. This small shift may seem insignificant, yet it empowers kids to recognize small successes and how each individual improvement can have a ripple effect, making a much larger difference down the line. In addition, we have discovered that perhaps it is time to shift the emphasis away from labels such as "bully," "target," and so on, especially in working with teenagers, who cringe at that terminology. Creating a prosocial climate for kids is not about labels such as "bully" or "target." Instead, a more real-world focus on helping kids find their strengths, explore altruism, and grow as human beings will create opportunities to practice prosocial behaviors in a more palatable, less threatening way.

Character is not developed in a vacuum; it is natural and right for kids to face challenges and conflicts and learn how to deal with them positively. If we ask a group of parents today what they most want for their child, a large percentage will say they just want their child to be "happy." Too often, however, the pursuit of happiness translates into self-gratification and self-centeredness, the child's desire to always get his own way. Does making sure our children are happy mean that we must protect them from all unpleasantness? If that kind of happiness is the goal, it is no wonder we are dealing with an alarming lack of empathy and compassion for others. How do children develop empathy, character, strength, and integrity if we shelter them from experiences in which they must meet a difficult challenge and overcome obstacles?

My eighth-grade students drove this point home for me my first year of Team LEAD. Toward the end of the school year, two of my girls came to me in tears one morning before school. They told me they had only come to school that day because they knew we would be able to deal with their problem in Team LEAD; otherwise they would have stayed home from school, unable to face their peers. It was a Monday, and over the weekend, they had gone to a party. The gist of the drama was that both of the girls had kissed one of the guys, also a Team LEAD member, and other kids were now spreading a rumor that they'd had sex. Indignantly they reported that some of the kids spreading the rumor were in Team LEAD as well. They were angry. I was angry. How could these kids be spreading rumors when we had discussed this very thing so many times? The girls asked if I could call "an emergency Team LEAD meeting" so that we could get to the bottom of this nastiness. I agreed but asked if they minded if I first spoke to the young man involved. I wanted to make sure he hadn't somehow started the rumor himself. When I spoke to him privately, though, he was just as furious as the girls. He supported holding the emergency meeting and offered to stand up with the girls. This was my first surprise; this young man was one who seemed to always be looking for approval from the other guys, and I feared he would be unable to stand up to them. I was wrong.

With the permission of the eighth-grade teachers, I called the emergency Team LEAD meeting during advisory. As all eighty of our members crammed into the Team LEAD room, I asked the injured parties if they wanted me to handle this. They looked me dead in the eye, all three of them, and said no; they wanted to do it themselves. In amazement, I watched as they took the floor, stared down their dead-silent peers, and took them to task for spreading a rumor, one that was, by all accounts, untrue. As the girls spoke, with the boy standing solidly beside them, their voices became stronger and their stature taller. The other members listened quietly, some appalled on their behalf, some tearful, some sheepish. When the young man involved stepped forward and shared his feelings of hurt and anger and then challenged anyone who was spreading the rumor to get up and leave the room because they did not deserve to be in Team LEAD, the other guys stared at him with a brand new respect. One of his friends stood up, took responsibility, and begged forgiveness. Several others also admitted to playing a part, and en masse, they stood, went to each of the three injured parties, and apologized and hugged them. All eighty students in the room vowed to shut down the rumor immediately and apologized to me for letting it happen in the first place.

After the group left, I asked my courageous three how they were doing. They said they felt great that they had been able to address the problem themselves through Team LEAD and thanked me for making it possible. They left the room with heads held high, and when I touched base with various kids later in the day and in the days following, the group had been true to its word. The rumor was stopped dead in its tracks that very day, an amazing feat in a middle school setting. Most importantly, I saw a major change in the confidence and leadership skills of the three kids who had started out as victims. Following this traumatic experience, they were much more confident leaders among their peers. They all commented to me later that while it had been awful to have a rumor spread about them, it had ended up a positive turning point for them and for the group as a whole. It was also a turning point for me and the Team LEAD philosophy. An event that I had initially considered a dismal failure had actually been one of Team LEAD's finest moments. The kids themselves had modeled exactly what Team LEAD was all about—leadership, empathy, accountability, and discussion—in that single emergency meeting. Had I stepped in and dealt with the issue as an adult, all of that growth would have been lost.

Through this experience and many others with Team LEAD kids over the years, I have come to believe we do our children a grave disservice by not allowing them the opportunities to face obstacles and challenges and overcome them, to fail until they learn how to succeed on their own, to face disappointments before they find real happiness. It is through being allowed the opportunity to overcome problems and face their fears, as we did in that emergency meeting and many other regular meetings throughout the years, that kids develop self-respect and, ultimately, empathy for others. All kids, even student leaders, will make mistakes. If we allow them to be accountable and to learn and grow from those mistakes, we empower them to become stronger, more compassionate human beings.

Children enjoy and respect being given a higher purpose; we can and must teach altruism and service. Experts in the fields of school safety and mental health encourage schools to focus on protective factors like school connectedness, empathy, and resilience. Some recent studies add a surprising new component to the list of recognized protective factors, however, one that hinges on altruism. *Hardwired to Connect: The New Scientific Case for Authoritative Communities* is a recent report by the Commission on Children at Risk (a panel of thirty-three leading professionals) and sponsored by Dartmouth Medical School, the YMCA, and the Institute for American Values. The commission set out to examine why American teenagers are suffering in epidemic proportions from drug addiction, alcoholism, depression, violence, suicide, promiscuity, emotional problems, and so on (Commission on Children at Risk, 2003). Their findings point to three protective factors that could lessen the risk for our kids: authoritative schools and families, a feeling of belonging, and a higher purpose. While the first two factors are commonly addressed in climate programs in our schools, the third factor, higher purpose, oftentimes is not. How do public schools help kids develop a sense of a higher purpose? Through Team LEAD, we were able to naturally promote a higher purpose for our kids through weekly discussion of relevant issues and by creating regular opportunities for them to address those issues using prosocial behaviors and positive actions such as mentoring and hosting pertinent schoolwide events. As one of our eighth graders so eloquently stated, "I want others to know that you can find security and comfort from being a positive difference for others in a group like Team LEAD. It changes lives."

Teaching prosocial behaviors within a character/leadership backdrop instead of an "anti-bullying" backdrop is more effective, especially for teenagers. Shifting our focus from "bullying"—a schoolyard-focused term that prompts most teens to disengage immediately—to a larger real-world perspective of character, altruism, and leadership has created a more positive and productive environment for Team LEAD kids. Inherently, a focus on "bullying" invites the labeling and judging of "bullies" and "victims" or "targets" and can therefore alienate students. What's the value of explicitly or implicitly offering them even more labels with negative connotations? We have found that if we wish to move our kids toward a climate in which they live and let live and avoid making harsh social judgments, we can model that mind-set from the start by focusing more on leadership skills and prosocial behaviors than the labels. Through Team LEAD, we helped the students themselves examine negative social behaviors and issues from their own perspectives and empowered them to support each other in creating positive change. When students have ownership of the program and issues, it means more to them; they take it more seriously, and it empowers them to be more positive leaders.

With this focus on making a difference one person at a time, we've seen some interesting progress, not just in the founding school, but throughout the five school districts, who have thus far fully implemented this system of working with kids. Given that normative beliefs determine behavior, Team LEAD focuses heavily on helping kids understand the impact they can have on others. It is important to us that kids believe they can make a difference. In data collected from 2008 in Valparaiso, we noted a 17.4 percent increase in the number of sixth and seventh graders (sample of 345) who responded "Yes" to the statement "I believe I can make a difference at school" after just five and a half months of Team LEAD programming and mentoring. From three years (2008–2010) of data on the same group of middle school kids (sample of 187), in response to the statement "I stand up more for myself and others now than I did before the program," we saw an increase in "Yes" answers each year, from 58 percent as they entered sixth grade, to 66 percent as beginning seventh graders, to 74 percent at the end of seventh grade. The School City of Hobart, Indiana, instituted Team LEAD in their schools K–12 four years ago. Superintendent Dr. Peggy Buffington writes,

Team LEAD empowers students to become leaders in their school and community. Sometimes the evidence is so obvious as in the service they provide, for example, nursing home visits, Christmas caroling, food pantry assistance, and program support in the schools and community. Then there are those profound moments when a parent tells you that if it were not for a Team LEAD member helping her child cope with the loss of a loved one, she/he would have never made it. These same Team LEAD students tackle peer aggression by identifying where it is occurring (actual maps of building) and offering solutions to stop it. There is also the taking on of social issues in the school community, including drugs and teenage pregnancy in their I RED campaign where they marketed to students to Re-evaluate Every Decision. The students in Team LEAD are leaders in every aspect because they are making a difference in young people's lives.

Team LEAD, I soon realized, was much more than an antibullying program; it was really a system of working with kids, one that empowers them to grow and become leaders. My favorite example of the power of the student leadership team philosophy involves a young girl who was one of the most disconnected middle school students I had ever seen and a middle school boy who was at the opposite end of the social spectrum.

Maria had a severe speech impediment, so severe that she rarely spoke at all because when she did, few could understand her. She didn't participate in class. She didn't speak to teachers or peers if she could help it. In fact, in the lunchroom, if other students tried to sit near her, she'd yell at them to "Go away!" If they didn't leave, she would get up and move herself. If you touched her—a pat on the back, a friendly hand on the shoulder—she would pull away and scowl. She had built a fortress of isolation around herself as a protective shield. John, on the other hand, had what some would call a privileged life, with a large support system of friends and family. He was friendly and outgoing, someone all the kids liked. In eighth grade, John had decided to join Team LEAD in order to learn how to be a more positive, active leader.

At the initial full-day Team LEAD training at the beginning of the school year, one of the discussions revolved around a U.S. Secret Service study (Vossekuil, Fein, Reddy, Borum, & Modzeleski, 2002) that involved teachers "silently mentoring" those students who seemed disconnected. After hearing of the major impact the teachers had on those students, the eighth graders discussed the potential power of peers silently mentoring each other, simply noticing each other and caring enough to say hello. John decided, unbeknownst to anyone else, that he would reach out to Maria, someone he perceived as having little support in the school. Two months after he initially began his plan, he stopped to see me after school. He explained, "You know, Mrs. K., when you told us about that Secret Service study back in August? Well, I decided to try to silently mentor Maria. Don't worry, I didn't tell anyone, but I just have to tell you what happened today!"

John went on to describe how he had started saying hello to Maria in the hallway, and how, on his first attempt, she looked at him and yelled, "Shut up, Stupid!" When I asked how he'd felt when that happened, he said, "Well, you know, it kind of hurt, but I figured that if no one had ever been nice to her, why would she trust me? So I decided to keep trying." That day, after two months of "hellos" with no response, Maria had finally looked at him and said, "Hi, John." Those two simple words were the reason John was flying high and eager to share his story with me.

Later in the week, John walked into our weekly Team LEAD meeting with Maria following silently behind. To their credit, the other kids acted like she had been there all year, and we just added her to our roster. John clearly had elicited their respect and inspired them to increase their own efforts to make a difference for others as well. Within a week or two, Maria was volunteering to make Team LEAD announcements over the intercom for the entire school in the mornings; a young lady who rarely spoke had gained the strength and courage to not only speak, but speak publicly for all the school to hear. The girl who had refused to sit with anyone at lunch now signed up to be on "Peace Patrol," the kids' name for their plan to have Team LEAD members go to lunch in pairs at least one day a week and mix it up, sitting by kids who seemed like they needed a friend. Maria signed up to do this not just one day a week, but two.

In the space of just a couple of months, one of the most disconnected kids I had ever seen had jumped right in and started connecting, all thanks to the actions of one middle school boy. As the year ended and Maria left us to go to the high school, I frankly feared that she would be eaten alive. I need not have worried. Maria joined multiple extracurricular activities and even ran for a student council office; she continues to lead and serve at the high school level.

Empowering kids to lead schools' efforts to create healthy social relationships and positive school climate is not only logical and effective but *necessary* in today's new world. Only the students themselves have direct access to and a true understanding of the constantly changing new cyberenvironment in which they live and socialize. The frightening reality is that we adults cannot control or monitor all of their social interactions today, and that will no doubt become even more difficult with each new technological advance. How do we best help them become civilized, productive adults in this new society? The answer may lie, surprisingly, in encouraging our kids to *give*, not get—to notice what they can do for others rather than what others are doing for or to them. Helping kids develop more realistic expectations for their relationships—expectations that take into account human nature and normal human conflict—can help us develop stronger leaders who will persevere rather than throw up their hands in frustration when faced with a social challenge or setback. Perhaps this is the most direct route to creating safer climates and nurturing not only good citizenship and social conscience, but individual social-emotional health and happiness as well.

REFERENCES

Commission on Children at Risk. (2003). *Hardwired to connect: The new scientific case for authoritative communities*. Poulsbo, WA: Broadway Publications.

Vossekuil, B., Fein, R. A., Reddy, M., Borum, R., & Modzeleski, W. (2002). *The final report and findings of the Safe School Initiative: Implications for the prevention of school attacks in the United States*. Washington, DC: U.S. Secret Service and U.S. Department of Education.

Case Study 14C

Building a Bullying Prevention Program from the Ground Up: Students as the Key

Michelle McPherson

HISTORY OF BULLYING PREVENTION

School District 2 is located in Moncton, New Brunswick, Canada. It is the largest school district in the province, providing services to over sixteen thousand students in thirty-eight schools. I began working as a school social worker in 1996 and transferred to School District 2 in 2004. The purpose of this case study is to provide an overview of how this district has been able to address bullying through the development of a prevention program beginning in 2009, which is not only schoolwide but districtwide. A key to what we have achieved is how we have been able to use our most valuable resources within the schools, our students. Research continues to tell us that the answer to *bullying* is the bystanders (Pepler & Craig, 2000), and our experience has underscored that by changing their own attitudes and behaviors, students are the ones who have the power to change the lives of their fellow classmates. Much of the work referred to has been done in collaboration with an Anti-Bullying District Committee that has been established in School District 2.

When I first started working with students, teachers, administrators, and senior district personnel in 1996 as a social worker, I was responsible for serving fifty-six schools. I soon realized that I needed to focus my attention on what issues were of most concern to schools rather than working with a fixed agenda. When I surveyed the schools, almost all schools reported bullying as a significant issue. In an attempt to meet the demands of the schools in regard to bullying, I began offering classroom-based presentations. I was under the assumption that if I just told the students how horrible it was to bully and how much the victims suffered, then they would simply stop. To my surprise, my entreaties did not lead to the desired outcome. I was discouraged but quickly realized I needed to change my strategy to a more effective approach. First and foremost, I came to the conclusion that support from the administration was mandatory. Without this support, a program cannot be viable within a school. I then offered staff directed workshops, with the expectation that they would be given the necessary tools to educate their own students and would be able to implement a schoolwide bullying prevention program. In addition to this, by presenting to all the staff in the school, it ensured the consistency among the staff, which was also a vital component to the program's success. Although a much better approach than classroom presentations, there were still many obstacles. The main one was that I could not possibly train all of the schools in one school year and keep ahead of the changes in administration and staff that took place on a yearly basis.

In 2009, through careful consideration, thought, and experience, I concluded that in order for a program to be successful within the school system, it required the following: the ability to reach all staff with limited resources, consistency among schools with regard to policies and interventions, a district supervisor who was well versed in the program, the ability to share updated resources among the various schools, and the ability to provide ongoing training to all of the schools. In order to meet these expectations, I met with the director of education, Gregg Ingersoll, and proposed a model of intervention. I received his full support in the development of a District-Wide Anti-Bullying Prevention Program. At the core of this program was the establishment of a District Committee, an Adult Committee, and a Student Committee. This program would not have been possible if it had not been for the leaders in School District 2, who were very knowledgeable regarding the issue of bullying. They understood the need for students to feel safe in their schools in order to reach their maximum academic potential.

STRUCTURE AND ORGANIZATION OF BULLYING PREVENTION SERVICES

The District Committee was made up of a district supervisor (Anne Bernard-Bourgeois), two administrators (Heather Welling and Christoph Becker), one guidance counsellor (Julie Campbell), two computer technicians (Mario Chiasson and Richard Daley), and myself. Most of these committee members were chosen because I had partnered with them in the past and had assisted them in implementing successful pilot antibullying programs within each of their schools. The first step of this committee was to develop a common knowledge base so that we shared a common understanding. Two books by Stan Davis were of particular value: *Schools Where Everyone Belongs: Practical Solutions for Dealing with Bullying* (2005) and *Empowering Bystanders in Bullying Prevention* (2007). Having worked at that time for thirteen years in the area of bullying in schools and having run pilot programs for a number of years, I also had a great deal of practical experience for making recommendations regarding program interventions. Although I felt confident in what I wanted to do, I felt it necessary to have the support of the District Committee. They were able to provide me with a more diverse knowledge base; they were able to turn some of my ideal approaches into more manageable, realistic school-based interventions; they were able to provide the long- and short-term goals of the anti-bullying program; and I in turn provided most of the research and practical-based tools and interventions. The committee prepared a training workbook for each school containing policy, interventions, and resources that they were expected to endorse. The District Committee had many roles and objectives, which continued to evolve and expand each school year. Their main role however was to provide ongoing training for district staff and to continually update resources, which were disseminated to each of the schools in the district.

Each school was required to set up an Adult Committee. A lead teacher was chosen from each Adult Committee and was expected to attend the ongoing training sessions conducted by the District Committee, with the expectation that they would in turn train their Adult Committee and the remaining school staff. The main objective of this committee was to assist the school in implementing the districtwide antibullying program as laid out in the training workbook.

Each school was also required to set up a Student Committee. The members of the committee were chosen for their reputation as very responsible, trustworthy, and mature citizens of the school community. It was paramount that the students selected would have the skills and respect necessary to be able to address the student body with confidence. The main objective of the Student Committee was to provide bullying prevention programs to the younger grades. They were also responsible for helping to increase bullying awareness within their schools.

Once the schools had established their Adult and Student Committees, the priority was to look at how the schools were going to implement the district program and respond to incidents of harassment, intimidation, and bullying behaviors. We anticipated that as our education efforts ramped up and awareness of the problem grew, we would see an increased number of referrals for bullying incidents. This was not because the incidents of bullying would have increased but because students would now feel that it was safe to report, as they would be encouraged by the experience that the school would do something about it when they did. This is the most important part of the program. The school must respond appropriately and consistently when a bullying incident is reported. If not, then not only will the students stop reporting, but so will the teachers.

HOW THE BULLYING PREVENTION PROGRAM WORKS

Our District Committee noted over the past few years that some staff members were getting caught up with trying to differentiate whether the behavior in question was an act of bullying or not. Consequently, this often led to adults not responding as they should have. As a result of this, the District Committee decided to call our program "If It Hurts, It's Wrong: Preventing and Addressing Hurtful Behaviours in Our Schools" (Becker et al., 2009). We emphasized that it did not matter whether the behavior could be described as bullying or not; if what the student did hurt someone else, then we responded. Many kids get away with minor forms of inappropriate behaviors in our schools. As a teacher in the classroom, if a student rolls her eyes at another student or makes a negative comment, then the teacher is left with a dilemma. Was the incident severe enough that the teacher should stop the class and deal with her, or does the teacher simply ignore it or tell the student to stop? Now, in isolation, this may not be considered a serious incident, but how do we know that this is not the fifth time today that this girl said something mean? Just as damaging, what if this was the fifth time today that someone said something mean to the victim? Seemingly minor offenses could add up to very serious implications for the victim. The kids who bully know what they are doing. They are not going to bully in front of the same teacher over and over, and for that reason they often get way with their behavior. Due to this, our District Committee looked at a way that we could respond to these seemingly minor offenses (whether bullying or not) and a way to track them. Ann Bernard-Bourgeois, of the District Committee, suggested we review and modify a resource titled "On the Spot Intervention" (www.stopbullying.gov). The intervention works as follows: If a teacher sees a student roll her eyes in the classroom at another student, the teacher simply states, "At this school we do not treat people like that; you will be tracked." The teacher does not give the student who was misbehaving an opportunity to excuse or explain her behavior. The bottom line is that what the student did was not appropriate. This intervention is used in all K–12 classrooms and works quite well because it gives teachers something specific and immediate to do, it reinforces the school's ethos and behavior standards, and it puts the student on notice. Next, the teacher fills out a behavior tracking form. Behavior tracking forms can be completed by both staff and students. The forms are not called "bullying forms," as it does not matter whether or not the behavior fits the definition of bullying. If someone engages in hurtful behaviors, then they are tracked. The purpose of the tracking forms is to identify patterns of behavior. Once a child is tracked, then a range of consequences are available based on the district's policy and depending on whether the behavior continues. I recommended to the District Committee that we categorize the interventions and consequences as either direct or indirect. It is my experience that the most effective intervention is dependent on certain particulars of the bullying incident.

Direct Interventions/Consequences

The direct interventions are primarily used and most effective when the behavior was witnessed (tracked) by a staff member or student, there is little doubt that a bullying incident has transpired, there is little worry of retaliation, and a more indirect intervention was not successful.

These interventions would entail what many schools already have in place with their code of student conduct or pyramid of interventions. This would also be part of a more rubric-based discipline system as best described by Stan Davis (2007). This is a system of consequences organized by level of severity of the infraction. Consequences might include the following (not necessarily in this order):

1. Discussion with an administrator.
2. Reflection hall: a designated place and time within the school where a student is expected to fill out a reflection form if he or she has been tracked

for a hurtful behavior. This form requires the student to provide an account of the behavior in question, why this behavior was not acceptable, what the student will do in the future to prevent this behavior, and how the student is going to repair the situation.

3. Parental contact: Stan Davis (2007) recommends that the perpetrating student call his or her parent in the presence of the administrator. The caution here is that you need to be relatively certain that the parent will respond appropriately and that there are unlikely to be negative repercussions due to poor parenting.

4. Intervention with the Adult Committee: when a student is tracked for more minor hurtful behaviors, he or she meets with members of the Adult Committee rather than having to meet with the administrator. This committee is responsible for determining the appropriate consequences. If the behavior continues, the student would then meet with the administrator. For chronic or more difficult cases, it is recommended that the administrator consult with the members of the Adult Committee.

5. Separating the child who bullied from the other students (e.g., loss of recess/lunch, detention).

6. Formative consequences (Pepler & Craig, 2000): through formative consequences, students who bully can learn to turn their negative power and dominance into positive leadership skills and acquire the insights and empathy that they are lacking. Some examples we have used successfully include the following:
   a. If this student has a particular talent (e.g., artistic, soccer), have the student deliver lessons to younger grades, with teacher supervision, during the student's unstructured time. It is very powerful when staff see the student in a more positive light, just as it is important that the student receive positive attention from others at school. To some students, negative attention is better than no attention. This is a particularly useful strategy for those students who come from homes where they receive very little attention and for those who do not have a sense of belonging to their school.
   b. The student accompanies a teacher during unstructured time with younger children and assists in resolving peer-to-peer conflicts, focusing more on the needs of the victim.
   c. Have the student do community service at a local charity or a senior citizen's home.

7. Referral to guidance: the child who engages in chronic bullying behavior may require individual counseling. There may be underlying issues that need to be addressed in order to assist the student in changing his behavior. Once a trusting relationship is formed, the student may disclose that he has been a victim of bullying in the past and is reacting as a result of this, or that he is experiencing difficulties within his own home.

8. Parental meeting: it is vital when the parents are called in that there be sufficient documentation regarding the bullying incidents, as some parents can be quite defensive. It is also important not to use the word *bullying*; this often incites further hostility, as the word has such a negative connotation. Instead, it is much more beneficial simply to describe the behaviors in question. When meeting with the parents, it is necessary that the administrator and any other

staff member that is privy to the situation in question be in attendance, keeping in mind that only necessary staff members need to attend so as not to intimidate or overwhelm the parents. It is important that the parents see this as a whole-school initiative and not just the administrator's.

9. Individual behavioral plan: this is a plan that is typically developed by the Adult Committee in consultation with the administrator. This would be used in cases of chronic bullying in which the traditional school consequences have not been successful. Some examples would be that the student receives constant supervision during unstructured time or that the student's dismissal and arrival times are altered, thus ensuring that the victim feels safe walking to and from school.

10. Suspension: the particulars of the suspension (length, in school or out of school) would be dependent on the severity of the incident.

The severity of the consequences would depend on how severe, frequent, and chronic the behavior in question is. Tracking helps to determine this.

Indirect Interventions/Consequences

Indirect interventions are primarily used and most effective when the victim fears retaliation, there were no witnesses to the bullying incident, there has been more than one student engaging in the bullying behavior and there is an obvious leader, the bullying has been relational in nature, the students engaged in the bullying had been friends or continue to be friends, and the children engaged in the bullying behavior are very young in age.

Indirect interventions are most often the first mode of intervention used when I am asked to assist in a bullying situation. In the vast majority of cases, the following kinds of interventions have proven to be most effective. When they have not been, then more direct interventions are warranted. In indirect interventions, school staff do not necessarily work directly with the perpetrator, nor do they necessarily work directly with the particulars of the bullying incident. Instead of focusing simply on the child who acted like a bully and the victim, you look beyond this, and you instill a sense of empowerment and responsibility in the bystanders. These are the students who actually have the power not only to alter the behavior of the child who has acted like a bully, but also to assist the victim in feeling a sense of belonging within the school at a time when he or she needs it most. My philosophy has always been that we have great kids in our schools, and my experience is that when students are asked to help their fellow students and are given a structured way to do it, they are more than willing. The more we create opportunities for students to participate in these support groups (led by trained Student Committee members), the more they inadvertently learn how they can intervene and help their fellow students.

Historically, however, we have not provided clear, meaningful advice about how students can and should intervene. For years we have been telling students, "Don't stand by; stand up when you see someone being bullied." However, to my dismay, students did not take the appropriate action, even though they knew and could verbally describe the expected behavior when they saw someone being bullied. The main reasons students have given for their inaction are that they do not want to be the next victim, they do not want to go against their friends, they do not know what to do in specific circumstances, and they do not want to be a tattletale. As a result, victims are left feeling that nobody cares for them, and the students who bully are left believing that everyone supports them. As I continued to hear this same story over and over, I began to realize that I needed to find a new approach to working with victims and empowering bystanders. The work of Stan Davis (2007) on social norms helped me to formalize my ideas and develop a peer support group intervention model. In essence, Davis found in talking to many young people that "they often have misperceptions about normative values and behavior. Both the youth who bully and those who are bullied commonly misperceive their school environment and see the majority of peers in support of the bully" (Davis, 2007, p. 102). He added that "social norms interventions are common and successful tools to change undesired behaviors" (Davis, 2007, p. 101).

The main objective of the bullying prevention peer support group is to make certain that the victim is left with an actual account of what the bystanders are thinking rather than their own misperceptions of the incident, as their misperceptions often leave them believing that no one cares about them, when in reality this is not the case. They need to have a clear understanding as to why the bystanders were unable to stand up for them. The victims do not want to hear from the adults that their friends are still supporting them; they need to hear it directly from their peers.

This peer support group is an indirect intervention for the victim and can be used in conjunction with the direct interventions for the student perpetrators. The District Committee recommended a developmentally tiered approach for indirect interventions with the students who have bullied others. For kindergarten to grade 3, we recommend the no blame approach by George Robinson and Barbara Maines (1997), authors of the book *Crying for Help: The No Blame Approach*. Several years ago when I first started to implement the no blame approach in schools, I added an additional last but important step, which serves as a positive incentive to be a bystander. The administrator thanks the peer group support members individually for helping the victimized student. This is an especially important intervention for the child who acted like a bully. We do not endorse this program for older children, as we feel that the child who bullied has far too much power to be included in a group as recommended by this approach.

For grades 4 to 12, in cases where the bullying incident is relational in nature, where there is more than one student who is acting like a bully, and where there is an obvious leader, such as a "Queen Bee," the District Committee recommends the method of shared concern by Ken Rigby (2005). His article, "The Method of Shared Concern as an Intervention Technique to Address Bullying in Schools: An Overview and Appraisal," is particularly useful, but with one significant modification. We do not include the leader of the students acting like bullies in the last step of the intervention, where it is recommended that the whole group be brought together with the victim. It has been our experience that the leader has far too much power and influence over the group. If the leader is included in the group discussion, then the rest of the group will not feel that they can openly express how they feel.

These indirect interventions often rely on building positive relationships and providing positive messages to all of the students, including the bystanders, the victims, and the children who acted like a bully. Through the support group structure, we have been able to teach the bystanders how they can intervene effectively and support their fellow classmates. The most important interventions that we have continued to teach the bystanders are "Tell an adult" if you see someone being hurt (ensure their confidentiality) and "Take It Away"—when you see someone hurt someone else with their words or actions, when this person walks away, go to the victim and take the hurt away. Take away the negative by saying something positive so that the victim is not left assuming that you support the one being mean.

In some cases, when the student who acted like a bully realizes how much the victim was actually suffering, the student did feel some empathy and consequently altered his or her behavior. Most importantly, it is through these indirect support group interventions that we are assisting the victims. This step is often missed if the focus is solely on punitive consequences for the child who acted like a bully.

CASE EXAMPLE

Scenario: Sam was a grade 7 student in a school of about five hundred students. Sam and his parents met with me and were all visibly upset while they were recounting the story of how Sam had been treated at school. Sam had been bullied over the course of several months by two other boys in his class. Many of his friends had since stopped hanging around with him. Sam had not been in school for the past two weeks and was asking his parents if he could transfer schools. Sam felt that at this point he did not have any friends, as no one was supporting him. He stopped reporting the incidents to the school, as the bullying was continuing and he was left with the impression that the school could do nothing to stop it. (It is very unfortunate when this happens, as the school cannot help if they do not know what is going on. Oftentimes when the student stops reporting, the school is left with the wrong assumption that the bullying has stopped.)

Plan of Action: (This plan was set up in collaboration with the school team.)

1. We set up a tracking system for Sam. He was asked to keep a running log in the back of his binder where he was to document any hurtful behaviors that were directed at him. He was to check in with the administrator each day to report how things were going. This was a very important intervention. Many students report that they stop telling the school because they told in the past and the bullying continued, so they were left with the impression that no one could help them. When this happens, the students start to feel trapped, knowing that they have to attend school each day and face the bullying and that

there is nothing that anyone can do to help them. When a student has been bullied, it is important to acknowledge up front that the planned intervention may help for the first few weeks, but then the bullying may start again. If this happens, the student is encouraged not to give up on the school and to make sure to report it. Students like Sam need to know that the intervention and support from the school will continue. Sam was asked to check in with the administrator over the next two weeks. (In most cases, this role would have been given to the guidance counselor, but in this case the student was more comfortable with the administrator.) Following the first two weeks, the administrator was asked to transition this student to the guidance counselor. The guidance counselor was then expected to meet with this student on a regular basis. This relationship was paramount, as we wanted the student to build a trusting relationship with the guidance counselor. We needed to ensure that this student had an adult in the school that he could turn to in the event that the bullying continued.

2. The administrator updated all of Sam's teachers regarding the situation and asked that they be vigilant in tracking the bullying behaviors of the two mentioned students, keeping in mind that seemingly smaller incidents could add up, as was the case in this situation.

3. The administrator met with the boys individually and conducted the first step only in the method of shared concern. (This is often a very effective strategy when an administrator has a positive connection with the student who bullied, as was the case in this situation.) She felt that she could appeal to their positive attributes. Their behaviors would be monitored closely. If their behavior continued, there would be further consequences, per the direct interventions, and parents would be notified.

4. The team ensured that Sam had something positive to do during recess break. Far too often we pull the victim from recess in order to keep him or her safe; it should really be the other way around. It is not always easy to remove the privilege of recess from the child who has acted like a bully, as the parents often question and refuse to accept this consequence. The tracking forms become very useful documentation. In this case, Sam was feeling quite isolated from his peers and did not want to go out at recess. Sam enjoyed helping out with a special needs student during recess, so this was arranged. Our goal was to slowly integrate Sam with his friends, with the help of a peer support group.

5. A peer support group for Sam was set up. We were able to enlist two boys in eighth grade to assist with this group. After we met as a group, we invited Sam to join us. As soon as Sam entered the room and he noticed his friends, he became quite emotional; his lip began to quiver and his eyes welled with tears. There was a long pause and silence. It was at that moment that the students seemed to understand the seriousness of the situation. The two older boys were able to take the lead and engage the younger boys in joining the discussion. As the support group progressed, you could slowly see Sam start to relax and some of his confidence return. They explained to Sam why it was difficult for them to stand up to the boys who had bullied him. He received the message from his friends that they did care about him and that they would support him in the future.

A week later I followed up with Sam to inquire how things were going at school. Sam stated that another boy had been teasing him, but when he told me this he did not seem upset. On the contrary, he seemed quite pleased. He went on to explain that when this happened, he went to one of the older boys who had been in the support group and enlisted his help. The older boy spoke to the student who was picking on Sam (he was able to do this, as he was quite popular and had status among his peers). Shortly thereafter, the perpetrator came over to Sam and apologized for harassing him; he went on to explain that he did not know that Sam had been having a hard time at school. Sam also said that the other older boy who was in the support group went out of his way to say hi to him whenever he saw him. I was elated when I was speaking with Sam. Sam did not seem to be bothered by the fact that he had been bullied again; the positive behavior of the other peers overshadowed the one incident.

6. The victim's parents were continually updated. Sam was able to successfully return to school, and no major incidents of further bullying were reported. This can be attributed to the fact that the administrator had a very good understanding of the interventions available through the bullying program and was able to choose the most effective interventions for the particulars of this situation.

Throughout my fifteen years of working in the area of bullying in schools, my use of interventions has continued to evolve. However, my one belief that has not wavered and that has continued to direct all that I have done in the schools is that there are wonderful children in our schools, children who are willing to help; we just need to ask them to become effective upstanders. In a school where there are hundreds of students, there is no reason that a child should be left alone. Educators often complain that there are not enough resources within the school to address the issue of bullying. I feel that we have an abundance of resources, our students; we just need to learn how to tap into this resource more effectively to successfully work on reducing bullying in our schools. I believe that through the use of student committees and peer support groups, as well as the procedures outlined above, we have started to do just that.

REFERENCES

Becker, C., Bernard-Bourgeois, A., Campbell, J., Chiasson, M., Daley, R., MacPherson, M., et al. (2009). *If it hurts, it's wrong: Preventing and addressing hurtful behaviours in our schools.* Moncton, New Brunswick, Canada: School District 2.

Davis, S. (2005). *Schools where everyone belongs: Practical solutions for dealing with bullying.* Ottawa, Ontario, Canada: Research Press.

Davis, S. (2007). *Empowering bystanders in bullying prevention.* Ottawa, Ontario, Canada: Research Press.

Pepler, D. J., & Craig, W. (2000). *Making a difference in bullying* (LaMarsh Report No. 60). Toronto, Canada: LaMarsh Centre for Research on Violence and Conflict Resolution, York University.

Rigby, K. (2005). The method of shared concern as an intervention technique to address bullying in schools: An overview and appraisal. *Australian Journal of Guidance & Counselling, 15*(1), 27–34.

Robinson, G., & Maines, B. (1997). *Crying for help: The no blame approach.* Bristol, UK: Lucky Duck Publishing.

CHAPTER 15

Establishing the Foundations

Prosocial Education in Early Childhood Development

ROSS A. THOMPSON, JANET E. THOMPSON,
AND ABBY C. WINER

It has been a rich, full day at preschool, and now it is time to clean up and get ready for closing activities. The teacher, Kiyomi Nomura, began singing the cleanup song, and soon the children were engaged in stacking blocks in the shelves, returning dress-up materials to their bins, and putting away books and art projects—all the children, that is, except for five-year-old Kyle. When Ms. Nomura asked Kyle why he was not participating in cleanup, his reply was immediate: "I didn't make this mess." Which was true: Kyle had spent most of his time in the reading corner. But Ms. Nomura replied, "Kyle, this is our classroom, and we are all responsible for it." It was a theme that Kyle had heard before in circle time: we share responsibility for our space and for each other. In a moment, Kyle joined the other children to make the classroom orderly again.

Encounters like these are a familiar feature of early childhood education, and they reflect a change that has occurred in our understanding of young children. Character development and prosocial education begin in early childhood and build on young children's developing sensitivity to others' feelings and needs, their natural interest in creating cooperative relationships with children and adults, and their desire to perceive themselves in positive ways. A thoughtfully designed early education curriculum can build on these psychological resources to promote prosocial motivation in young children.

Such a view may be unfamiliar to those steeped in the thinking of Piaget (1932/1965) and Kohlberg (1969) about moral development in young children, especially the view that young children are primarily egocentric, preconventional thinkers. Indeed, the focus on older children found in most character education curricula (and efforts to promote social-emotional learning in general) derives in part from the view that preschoolers are too self-focused and psychologically immature to benefit from interventions of this kind. This belief contrasts with the conclusion of developmental science in recent years that young children develop an early and surprisingly astute awareness of others' emotional and mental states to which they can respond with understanding and cooperation. Preschoolers may be hindered by their limited social understanding, cognitive flexibility, and self-regulatory capacities, but not by egocentrism. When this knowledge is combined with the increasingly normative experience of group care and education for young children in the United States, it suggests that character education can begin at substantially earlier ages than conventionally believed. Prosocial education in middle childhood and adolescence builds on the foundations established in early childhood.

This chapter is concerned with prosocial education in early childhood. Our goal is to describe the conclusions of research that have led to a new appreciation of the social and emotional sensitivity of young children, and the implications of this research for prosocial motivation. We then profile several promising curricular approaches to prosocial education, although work in this area is still in the early stages. The chapter concludes with some reflections on the implications of this work for policy and practice in the field of prosocial education, and for the promotion of social and emotional competence in young children more generally.

EARLY DEVELOPING SOCIAL, EMOTIONAL, AND PROSOCIAL RESPONDING

Developmental scientists have long observed young children acting prosocially and helpfully toward others (for reviews, see Eisenberg, Fabes, & Spinrad, 2006; Hay, 1994; Rheingold & Hay, 1978). But in an earlier scientific era focused on the social-cognitive limitations of young children, such observations were conventionally attributed to the rewards accompanying cooperative conduct, young children's imitative behavior, or the influence of parental instruction. With more recent understanding of how early young children derive knowledge of others' emotions, goals, and thoughts, these observations of early prosocial motivation have assumed greater significance as a foundation of concern for others.

Consider recent research by Warneken and Tomasello (2006, 2007). In a series of carefully designed laboratory tasks, they showed that eighteen-month-olds would help an unfamiliar experimenter when the adult's need for assistance was clear and toddlers knew how to provide help. They opened the doors of a cabinet, for example, when the adult tried unsuccessfully to open them to put in a stack of books filling his arms. They retrieved a marker that the adult accidentally dropped on the floor. By contrast, toddlers rarely helped when the adult's need for aid was not apparent in the adult's behavior (e.g., when a marker was not accidentally dropped but intentionally tossed to the floor). These young children were discriminating in their behavior toward an unfamiliar adult based on explicit cues of need, and they provided help independently of maternal support and in the absence of formal or informal rewards for doing so. Indeed, a follow-up study showed that extrinsic rewards undermined the helping of twenty-month-olds (Warneken & Tomasello, 2008).

These findings have been replicated by others (e.g., Svetlova, Nichols, & Brownell, 2010), including our own lab group (Newton, Goodman, Rogers, Burris, & Thompson, 2010). In our research, individual differences in toddlers' helping were predicted in some conditions by children's emotion-state language, a measure of expressive language that is often used as a proxy for emotional understanding in very young children. This is consistent with the influence of emotion in prosocial motivation in older children and adults, because many prosocial acts involve responding to the feelings of others in sympathetic or compassionate ways (Eisenberg et al., 2006).

The Warneken and Tomasello findings are important because they are part of a research program that demonstrates young children's capacities for *shared intentionality* with another person (see Tomasello, 2007; Tomasello, Carpenter, Call, Behne, & Moll, 2005). Shared intentionality refers to an individual's capacity to discern, participate in, and advance another's goal-directed behavior. It is one of the earliest examples of a young child's capacity to understand another's mental states. Toddlers' discriminative helping in circumstances in which the adult needed assistance reflects, according to this research group, toddlers' awareness of the intended goals of the adult and their willingness to contribute to achieving those goals. This conclusion is consistent with other research findings with very young children. In studies of joint attention, pointing, language acquisition, collaborative problem solving, imitation, and other behaviors, young children demonstrate their sensitivity to the goals and intentions underlying others' behavior as they seek to alter those intentions on some occasions to achieve their purposes (such as reaching while drawing mother's attention to a desired treat) or, on other occasions, sharing the intentional states of others in helpful and cooperative acts (see Meltzoff, 2007; Tomasello & Herrmann, 2010; Tomasello et al., 2005).

These early capacities to discern and share another's intentional states are in marked contrast to the assumption that young children are self-focused and cognitively limited. Indeed, even when another's goals and desires are very different from the child's own, toddlers will respond appropriately to the intentions of the other person. In one study, for example, eighteen-month-olds watched as an adult experimenter showed food preferences that were very different from the child's own while sampling from bowls of broccoli (with expressions of animated pleasure) and goldfish crackers (to which the adult expressed disgust) (Repacholi & Gopnik, 1997). When the adult subsequently extended her hand and said, "I want some more. Can you give me more?" the toddlers reliably gave the adult more broccoli, even though the children themselves preferred goldfish crackers. The capacity of children of this age to associate positive and negative emotional expressions with preferences and desires is a foundation for the subsequent development of other forms of mental understanding. Their ability to respond appropriately to the adult's preferences—even when they conflict with the child's own—reflects a developing capacity for shared intentionality.

Early Sensitivity to Emotions, Intentions, and Goals

Arguments for an early capacity for shared intentionality assume that young children do, indeed, derive inferences concerning others' intentions and goals from observing their behavior. There is considerable experimental research indicating that this occurs beginning in infancy and is based, in part, on infants' considerable experience with goal-directed activity of their own (Meltzoff, 2007; Woodward, 2009). Experiencing firsthand their own intentional efforts appears to cause infants to interpret others' behavior in terms of goals and intentions as well. By the second year, toddlers will imitate an adult's intended action, even if the adult was unable to complete that action successfully in the child's presence. After watching an adult trying to use a stick to push a button that activated a buzzer but consistently failing to do so (i.e., missing the button), nearly all eighteen-month-olds subsequently used the stick to push the button (Meltzoff, 1995).

Emotional expressions are important to early inferences of another's goals and intentions because the accomplishment of goals is often accompanied by positive emotions, and emotions like sadness, anger, surprise, and confusion are associated with the frustration of intentional activity. During the first year, infants become capable of differentiating the meaning of positive and negative emotional expressions in the face and voice and responding appropriately to the emotions they perceive (for a review, see Thompson, 2006). Thus early developing understanding of emotional expressions becomes an avenue for inferring others' desires and goals because of the emotions associated with goal achievement. One-year-olds are likely to gesture to the location of an object, for example, after they have observed a perplexed experimenter looking for the misplaced object (Liszkowski, Carpenter, Striano, & Tomasello, 2006).

As observed in the eighteen-month-olds studied by Repacholi and Gopnik (1997), therefore, toddlers are well on their way to understanding the associations between observed emotions; the desires, intentions, and goals they reveal; and the actions that contribute to satisfying those desires and accomplishing those goals. With respect to prosocial behavior, they are capable of perceiving another's emotional expressions and making simple inferences concerning why the other person might be feeling that way and, when relevant, acting helpfully, even when doing so requires comprehending intentions and preferences that are different from the child's own. In this respect, therefore, many of the conceptual bases for prosocial behavior are well established in early childhood.

Varieties of Prosocial Conduct

Prosocial behavior is not one thing, of course. Instead, there are different forms of prosocial conduct, and they involve different social and emotional requirements for young children. As earlier noted, Svetlova and colleagues (2010) showed that children as young as eighteen months can instrumentally help an adult. They also showed that young children's capacities for prosocial conduct increase significantly during the next year, with greater social and emotional understanding. Empathic responding was more difficult for eighteen-month-olds in their study, for example, and required more explicit cues from the adult experimenter about her needs, whereas altruistic responding (i.e., giving up an object of the child's own to assist the adult) was challenging even for thirty-month-olds.

Instrumental helping is one of the most direct potential behavioral outcomes of shared intentionality, as reflected in the Warneken and Tomasello research (2006, 2007, 2008). Other researchers have reported findings, consistent with theirs, of the instrumental actions of toddlers in response to the needs and desires of others (Demetriou & Hay, 2004; Lamb & Zakhireh, 1997; Zahn-Waxler, Radke-Yarrow, & King, 1979; Zahn-Waxler, Radke-Yarrow, Wagner, & Chapman, 1992). Using a laboratory environment designed to look like a typical home, for example, Rheingold (1982) showed that all of the eighteen-month-olds she observed tried to help the parent complete at least some of the household tasks (such as sweeping up and setting the table), and approximately 80 percent attempted to help an unfamiliar experimenter as well.

These findings indicate that toddlers are capable of instrumental helping, but they are inconsistent in their assistance and their responding can be situation and person specific. During the preschool years, children are capable of greater sophistication in the situations to which they respond helpfully, although they remain somewhat unreliable (Côté, Tremblay, Nagin, Zoccolillo, & Vitaro, 2002; Hastings, Rubin, & DeRose, 2005; Iannotti, 1985). Iannotti (1985), for example, found that over 70 percent of the preschoolers he observed naturalistically in their preschool classrooms exhibited helping, but only 37 percent of these children provided assistance toward an adult experimenter in a more structured assessment. This kind of variability in helping, typical for young children, arises for many reasons: the identity and behavior of the recipient, competing interests and demands, knowledge of how to provide assistance, as well as the temperament and personality of the child.

Sharing is another form of prosocial behavior that can derive from shared intentionality, in which children contribute something for another's use. Like instrumental helping, sharing begins early but also varies according to the recipient and the circumstances (Hay, Caplan, Castle, & Stimson, 1991; Hay & Murray, 1982). Sharing with a parent, for example, is different from sharing with a peer who may be a competitor. Hay and colleagues (1991) found that whereas one-year-olds were equally likely to share toys with a peer in different circumstances, two-year-olds were more likely to share when there were plenty of toys and were less likely to do so when toys were scarce. With older children, Hastings, McShane, and Parker (2007) found that preschoolers were much more likely to engage in turn taking with peers than to spontaneously share toys with them, perhaps because turn taking provides the opportunity to regain access to the toy. Taken together, these findings indicate that sharing, like other prosocial behaviors, becomes more complexly and discriminatingly exhibited with increasing age (Hay & Cook, 2007).

Finally, *compassionate responding* is also evident in early childhood. Whether manifested as empathy (a response to another's emotion that is similar to what that person is feeling) or sympathy (a response that is more generally concerned or sorrowful), compassion derives from young children's sensitivity to the emotions they observe in other people (Eisenberg et al., 2006). Toddlers in the second year often show "concerned attention" to another's distress (manifested as a downturned mouth and furrowed brow), even though a much smaller proportion of children at this age will follow this compassionate response with direct assistance (Zahn-Waxler, Robinson, & Emde, 1992; Zahn-Waxler, Radke-Yarrow et al., 1992). It is not difficult to understand why. Observing another's distress is an emotionally compelling but motivationally complex experience for a young child, and it can often be difficult for the child to know what—if anything—can be done to alleviate another's distress in everyday circumstances. When helping is exhibited by children this young, it is often in the form of emotion-specific comforting (e.g., patting the shoulder of the other person) or asking "You okay?" (Zahn-Waxler, Radke-Yarrow et al., 1992). For this reason, it is important to regard concerned attention as a prosocial response in itself, even though young children may lack the social understanding or capability to intervene more constructively to alleviate distress. With increasing age, preschoolers more often accompany their compassionate responding with inquiries about the cause of another's distress and engage in more effective forms of assistance (Knafo, Zahn-Waxler, Van Hulle, Robinson, & Rhee, 2008).

Taken together, at least two conclusions are warranted from this brief review of the research. First, a capacity for prosocial responding is evident from a surprisingly early age in simple situations to which toddlers and young children can respond constructively to the needs of other people. To be sure, it is important not to exaggerate the extent of prosocial motivation during this early period. Because of immaturity in self-regulatory capacities, social awareness, and cognitive flexibility, early helping, sharing, and compassionate behavior is inconsistently manifested and situationally influenced. Young children often do not act helpfully in situations in which we might expect them to, and indeed they may laugh or provoke another in distress, especially when they are confused about why the person is feeling that way or what to do. Prosocial behavior increases in reliability, sophistication, and scope in the years that follow (Eisenberg et al., 2006). In the context of a theoretical legacy that has doubted the capacity of young children to respond helpfully at all to the needs and interests of other people, this research underscores that a capacity for prosocial conduct emerges early.

Second, young children become more selective and discriminating in their prosocial behavior with increasing age, and individual differences in prosocial dispositions also become evident (Hay & Cook, 2007). In many respects, it would be surprising if this were not so, in light of the advances in social and emotional understanding that occur in early childhood. But it is important to recognize that prosocial responding does not increase homogeneously throughout the early childhood years, but rather selectively as young children become more attuned to social norms for expected behavior; comprehend others' behavior in more complex moral, gendered, and social frameworks; calculate the costs of prosocial conduct; begin to understand themselves as moral beings; and gradually comprehend others' goals and motives in more sophisticated ways (Hay & Cook, 2007; Thompson, 2012). The simple pleasure of a toddler who picks up a marker for another who has dropped it on the floor becomes enlisted into a more complex network of socially motivated behavior as the child matures.

One implication of this conclusion is that early childhood is a significant period for the socialization of prosocial motivation and the development of moral character (Thompson, 2009; Thompson & Newton, 2010). As young children are developing a sense of themselves and others as moral actors, the contributions of parents and educators to their developing understanding can be important to the growth of enduring dispositions to act helpfully toward others.

Early Socialization of Prosocial Motivation

Developmental researchers have focused considerable attention on the parental influences that enhance prosocial motivation in young children (Hastings, Utendale, & Sullivan, 2007). Very little attention has been devoted to the influence of early educators and care providers, although some of what is known about socialization in the home offers potentially useful ideas about comparable influences in the classroom.

In general, parent–child relationships that are characterized by security, warmth, and support are associated with greater prosocial conduct in young children, especially when parents themselves model prosocial behavior, eschew punitive approaches, and have an authoritative parenting style (Hastings, Utendale, et al., 2007). These findings suggest that young children are influenced by parental conduct that is constructive and prosocial toward them, although the findings of this research literature are not entirely straightforward. Important moderating variables include the temperament and sex of the child, as well as the overall emotional quality of the parent–child relationship.

One specific feature of family interaction that received special attention has been parent–child conversations about sociomoral and emotional events. Early childhood is a period of rapidly developing understanding of others' feelings, needs, and motivations, and shared conversation with an adult can help young children comprehend others' behavior in relation to these internal processes (Thompson, Laible, & Ontai, 2003). Consistent with this view, several studies by Garner and her colleagues have shown that when mothers talk about emotions in everyday circumstances (such as when reading stories) and explicitly approve of prosocial actions with their young children, their children are more likely to act prosocially toward peers in independent observations (Garner, 2006; Garner, Dunsmore, & Southam-Gerrow, 2008). These findings are consistent with other studies of the influence of emotion-related parent–child discourse on early moral development (Thompson, Meyer, & McGinley, 2006) and suggest that when adults explicitly connect another's feelings with its causes and outcomes, young children can better comprehend their influence on others' feelings as well.

Although this research has focused almost exclusively on mother–child conversation, there is little reason to doubt that similar influences also occur in the context of young children's conversations with other adults, including early educators and child-care providers. Indeed, as we shall see, rich conversational discourse and discussions with young children about people's feelings is a consistent feature of early educational curricula that are designed to promote social-emotional learning and character education in the early years. When this quality of adult–child conversation is combined with some of the other family influences that foster early prosocial motivation—such as warm and supportive adult–child relationships, adults acting as models of the prosocial conduct they hope children will emulate, avoidance of punitive or coercive child-management techniques, and respect for the individual characteristics of children—it is possible to generalize from the family socialization literature to the classroom practices that might advance prosocial education.

PROMOTING PROSOCIAL CONDUCT THROUGH EARLY CHILDHOOD EDUCATION

In light of these considerations, how can teachers and care providers promote prosocial behavior in young children? A cardinal principle is doing so in a developmentally appropriate fashion, which means that elements of these efforts will be very familiar to those who work primarily with older children and adolescents, and other elements may be unique to interventions with young children. Didactic verbal lessons about the importance of helping others, exposure to moral exemplars, and efforts to develop prosocial reasoning capacities are, for example, likely to be less successful with preschoolers than with older children and adolescents.

Characteristics of Early Childhood Prosocial Education

A well-designed early childhood program of prosocial education is more likely to include the following elements:*

1. Opportunities to practice helping, sharing, cooperation, and other prosocial behaviors within the context of everyday activities with peers and teachers.

---

*An outstanding resource for early childhood educators who are interested in classroom practices that promote early social-emotional learning and social competence is the Center on the Social and Emotional Foundations for Early Learning at Vanderbilt University, http://csefel.vanderbilt.edu.

2. Activities that foster young children's understanding of the emotions, needs, and perspectives of other people with whom they regularly socialize.
3. Explicitly encouraging helping, sharing, turn taking, and other forms of prosocial conduct, with adults using the examples of other children as models without acting punitively or coercively when young children fail to behave helpfully.
4. Building a classroom community characterized by cooperation and inclusiveness, in which children identify themselves as contributing members of the group who are responsible for its functioning well.
5. Encouraging young children to participate in the creation of normative behavioral expectations for group behavior based on their understanding of fairness, such as taking turns when more than one child wants to play with a valued toy, and sharing blocks when another child wants to join in.
6. Enlisting young children into activities that involve listening to and respecting the perspectives of others and building consensus—such as class brainstorming and problem-solving sessions, shared decision making, and voting—and also in strategies of cooperative conflict management, such as negotiation, bargaining, compromise, turn taking, and similar approaches that reflect mutual respect.
7. Conversations between adults and children in which teachers and caregivers help young children develop a rich understanding of the psychological connections between people's behavior, their causes, and their consequences for other people.
8. Supporting the development of self-regulatory competence, especially self-control of impulses and feelings, by equipping young children with skills of behavioral self-management, encouraging their use, and providing assistance when young children lose self-control.
9. Encouraging the development of young children's self-awareness as people who are helpful, cooperative, and responsible.
10. Models of prosocial conduct in the behavior of teachers and caregivers, who explicitly explain the reasons for their helping, sharing, and assistance to young children with reference to other people's needs, the value of the modeled behavior in addressing those needs, and respect for the rights and welfare of adults and children.
11. Ensuring that expectations for young children's sharing, helping, and other forms of prosocial conduct are developmentally appropriate (that is, that they do not exceed reasonable expectations for children of this age).
12. Promoting the development of warm, cooperative relationships between adults and children that can motivate cooperative, prosocial conduct with others.
13. Consistent with this, building bridges between the classroom and the home to enable parents to contribute to the promotion of the qualities of character and behavior that are fostered in the classroom.

In this kind of classroom environment, promoting prosocial behavior involves more than a focus on helping and sharing and includes the development of attitudes toward others and the self that provide a broad foundation for constructive conduct toward others. Viewed in this light, prosocial education occurs in the context of character development, moral awareness, and social-emotional learning. Here are some examples of how this can occur:

Three five-year-old children are on the outside merry-go-round as the teacher, Scott Smith, pushes them around and around. "Faster, faster!" shout Emma and Juanita. "No, slower!" cries Alisha, "my tummy feels sick!" Scott slows down the merry-go-round and then stops it and says, "It sounds like we have a disagreement about how fast to go." The two girls say "we want it fast!" Scott says quietly, "I know that it can be fun to go fast, but how does that make Alisha feel?" Emma says quietly, "She doesn't like it." The teacher replies, "Right. So what can we do to make sure that she has a good time, too?" All three girls think for a moment. Juanita says, "She should get off." Scott then asks, "Will Alisha have a good time then?" After a moment, Emma says, "We can have a turn for kids who want to go fast, and then a turn for the kids who want to go slow." Scott asks the three girls whether that is a good solution and receives enthusiastic nods in return. He then says, "You figured out a fair way for everyone to have a ride on the merry-go-round!"

There are several elements of best practices in early prosocial education encompassed in this vignette. First, the teacher was attentive to the experience of all three children, modeling respect for the preferences of each one. He also ensured that the girls understood clearly how each one felt and what each one wanted to do. This is because preschoolers can be limited in the cognitive flexibility to recognize competing desires and needs when they are emotionally engaged in their own activity. Once they focused appropriately on Alisha's feelings in this situation, Emma was capable of devising a balanced solution that each child endorsed. Fostering prosocial motivation thus requires attention to young children's developing social-emotional understanding.

The teacher, Scott, also enlisted the three girls' problem-solving capabilities in encouraging them to devise a solution to their problem. Such a practice would be less successful with much younger children, but for five-year-olds, this promoted their active engagement with the problem and fostered thoughtful consideration of cooperative strategies. His reminder of the need to create a solution that would be satisfactory for every child was consistent with the classroom expectations for inclusiveness that had been discussed on several occasions during circle time. Finally, Scott concluded the episode by verbalizing what the three girls had accomplished together with an emphasis on the overarching value—"a fair way"—that he intended they would generalize to other social problem-solving tasks.

Here is another example:

The four-year-old group had just begun circle time with their teacher, Will Benware, when Brian blurted out, "Where's Tien?" Indeed, the group was smaller this morning, and Brian had figured out who was missing. Will had an answer: "Yesterday Tien got very sick, sicker than when you get a cold. His parents decided to take him to the hospital to help him feel better, and that is where he is. His mother told me this morning that Tien will be in the hospital a few more days to make sure that everything is all right." The children were quiet for a few moments. Then Will asked them, "What do you think it feels like to be in the hospital?" Several children needed an explanation of what a hospital is before they could respond, but within a few moments they offered words like "sad" and "scared" and "he wishes he could be in preschool instead." Then Will asked, "Do you think there is anything we can do to help Tien feel better?" The children thought a little longer, and then Maiesha said, "We could get him some medicine!" Will replied, "The doctors are doing that. Any other ideas?" Then Jamaal said, "We can make pictures that he can look at!" The children agreed that this was a good idea, and with their teacher's help, they went to drawing tables with markers, paper, and pencils, and fifteen minutes later there was a small stack of pictures to give to Tien's mother later in the day. Will said to the children, "You have made some drawings that will remind Tien of preschool and tell him that we miss him!"

In this complex experience, these four-year-olds learned about the sudden illness of one of their classmates, the reasons that people go to hospitals, and a little about the experience of being hospitalized. Their teacher wisely did not provide information that was beyond their capacities for comprehension, but Will drew their attention to the caring actions of adults in Tien's life, such as his parents and the doctors. Will also encouraged the children's emotional role-taking capacities by asking them to imagine what Tien was feeling in the hospital. This was necessary before he could ask them subsequently to ponder whether they could do anything to help him feel better. Once again, social-emotional understanding was necessary before prosocial initiatives could be fostered in these young children.

Rather than suggesting steps the children could take, Will relied on the children's own ideas. Most of the time, this requires some filtering of practical and unpractical solutions. But once an appropriate strategy was identified, the teacher facilitated enactment of the plan by the children, who wished to participate. Finally, Will summarized with words what the children had accomplished, why it would be important to Tien, and the thoughts and feelings that would result to ensure that these connections would be clear to these young children.

These vignettes, and the one that opens this chapter, illustrate that early prosocial education—like early childhood education more generally—relies on somewhat different approaches compared to the education of older children and adolescents. Education is practical as well as didactic, incorporated into everyday experiences that are exploited by a thoughtful teacher to create learning opportunities. In the education of young children, words are used not only to provoke thought and understanding but also to make explicit the psychological processes—feelings, needs, and concerns—that underlie behavior and toward which prosocial efforts can be oriented. This is because these aspects of psychological understanding are cutting-edge conceptual developments for children of this age. Effective learning by young children is also active learning, never passive, because their most engaged thinking and understanding is provoked by meaningful, personal experiences. This requires soliciting and expanding on their own ideas and strategies and provoking their thinking with new perspectives or knowledge.

Early prosocial education is also framed by the developing competencies of young children, which are different from the emergent skills of older children and adolescents. By contrast with the salient challenges of peer pressure, responsible decision making, and intergroup understanding at older ages, in early childhood the challenges of self-regulation and the emergence of a psychological self-concept are important features of the context in which prosocial motivation develops. An effective prosocial education program must thus help young children perceive themselves as helpful, responsible group citizens and assist them with the challenges of impulse control. Finally, the relational context of learning is also central to early childhood, especially within the broader interpersonal climate of the classroom. Young children's interactions with peers as well as teachers help to provoke and motivate new understanding, especially when social interaction and psychological understanding are concerned.

Promising Curricular Avenues

Although early childhood is when the foundations of moral character and prosocial motivation begin to take shape, there has been much less attention to the development of programs to promote prosocial education in the early years compared to later ages. There are several reasons why this is true. First, across the developmental spectrum, educational curricula and intervention programs tend to focus more on remedying behavioral problems than promoting prosocial conduct. This problem-focused approach is perhaps a natural response to the concerns evoked by children's behavioral problems because these problems can be daunting and sometimes frightening (especially in older children and adolescents). Indeed, even for curricular programs with a prosocial education component, outcome evaluations of these curricula rarely focus on whether children act more helpfully or constructively as a result. Instead, the focus is on whether social problems diminish and socially appropriate conduct improves. Because it is unwise to assume that antisocial and prosocial behavior are inversely associated (Hastings, Utendale, et al., 2007), outcome studies that find diminished behavioral problems in target samples provide little insight into whether children are also acting more prosocially as a consequence.

In addition, whereas the social problems of young children are conventionally attributed to self-correcting issues of adjustment or immaturity, these problems are perceived as reflecting more concerning characterological deficiencies in older children and adolescents. Consequently, there are fewer curricular programs devoted to the behavior of young children, and some of them are derivatives of successful curricula that were previously developed for older children. Attention to the prosocial education of preschoolers tends to be low in the priorities of educational planners or intervention specialists.

This situation is beginning to evolve, however, in part owing to the recognition that problems in school achievement have early origins and that, for many young children, social and emotional difficulties help to account for early achievement outcomes. Because of this, many of these programs were designed to address the needs of at-risk young children, such as those participating in Head Start or other targeted early intervention programs, or whose families are in poverty or live in marginal neighborhoods. Even so, there is relatively little that can be confidently concluded about the efficacy of these curricula for fostering more helpful, constructive social conduct in young children, which is why these programs are described in this section as "promising." None of the programs reviewed below directly assessed prosocial behavior as an outcome of the curriculum, and in all cases a relatively small component of the curriculum was explicitly focused on fostering prosocial conduct. The larger focus of all of the curricula discussed below was on managing or averting behavioral problems and promoting socially appropriate conduct. The programs discussed below have the benefit, however, of flexible incorporation into the classroom format. Most of these curricular interventions are designed to be incorporated into existing comprehensive early childhood education curricula, such as High Scope, which contributes to their ease of implementation (for reviews, see Domitrovich, Moore, Thompson, & the Collaborative for the Advancement of Social, Emotional, and Academic Learning Preschool to Elementary Assessment Workgroup, in press; Joseph & Strain, 2003).

Preschool PATHS

One of the most promising programs for young children is Preschool PATHS (Promoting Alternative THinking Strategies) (Domitrovich, Greenberg, Cortes, & Kusche, 1999), based on the PATHS curriculum for older children (Kusche & Greenberg, 1994). The primary goals of Preschool PATHS is to promote positive peer relationships, enhance problem-solving skills, improve self-control, enhance young children's capacities to label and recognize emotions, and foster a more positive classroom environment. The program consists of a thirty-three-week curriculum with lessons in four domains: (1) prosocial friendship skills, (2) emotional understanding and emotional expression skills, (3) self-control, and (4) problem-solving skills. Methods include stories and discussions, puppets, role-playing, songs, cooperative projects and games, and other activities. Teachers are encouraged to incorporate social-emotional learning into everyday experiences in the classroom throughout the day.

In an evaluation study conducted in Head Start classrooms, child measures and teacher and parent assessments were obtained both before and after nine months of the Preschool PATHS curriculum (Domitrovich, Cortes, & Greenberg, 2007). Children in the curriculum exhibited higher levels of emotional understanding and were rated as more socially competent by teachers and parents than children in the non-PATHS comparison group. Similar outcomes were obtained when the Preschool PATHS approach was integrated with a language and literacy intervention called the Head Start REDI (REsearch-based, Developmentally Informed) program. After one year, children in the intervention group were higher in emotional understanding, social problem solving, and social behavior compared to those in the comparison group, as well as showing cognitive and language gains (Bierman et al., 2008). (For more on PATHS, see case study A accompanying Chapter 11, "Implementing the PATHS Program in Birmingham, UK.")

Second Step

Another promising program, the Second Step curriculum, was designed as a violence prevention program by the Committee for Children (1991), a Seattle nonprofit agency. It was thus intended as a primary prevention program to decrease aggression and promote more positive social behavior in preschool and kindergarten children. It consists of twenty-eight sessions provided once or twice weekly throughout the course of an academic year, with themes focusing on empathy and emotional understanding, constructive social problem solving, and emotion management. Methods include stories with puppets and photographs, role-playing activities, and discussion in the classroom. Teachers are encouraged to transfer these lessons to other classroom experiences, and there are follow-up activities that parents can use.

An outcome evaluation of Second Step was conducted in preschool and kindergarten classrooms serving children in Chicago public housing projects (McMahon, Washburn, Felix, Yakin, & Childrey, 2000). Children were interviewed and observer and teacher ratings were obtained in the fall and again in the spring of the academic year after the curriculum was concluded. Preschoolers and kindergarteners both showed significant gains over time in emotional understanding and social problem-solving skills, and observations indicated significantly decreased disruptive behavior and verbal and physical aggression, although there were no changes in teacher ratings of children's social behavior. There was no comparison group in this study, however, so it is impossible to know whether these changes might have occurred without the intervention.

The Incredible Years

A third promising early childhood curriculum is called The Incredible Years (Dinosaur School) (Webster-Stratton, 1990; Webster-Stratton & Reid, 2010). The goal of this program is to promote preschool children's social competence, emotion self-regulation, and positive social behavior with special attention to children from high-risk populations and those identified with conduct disorders. The curriculum consists of biweekly lessons over several months organized according to seven units that include emotional literacy, empathy or perspective taking, prosocial skills, emotional understanding, anger management, social problem-solving skills, and communication skills. Methods include the use of videotape modeling, role-play, puppets, games, group discussion, picture cue cards, and promotion and reinforcement of specific skills in the context of circle time activities as well as small-group activities. There is a classroom curriculum with primary prevention goals as well as a small-group therapy format for children with identified social problems. There is also a significant teacher training component of the Incredible Years curriculum and a parent training curriculum that can be used independently of the teacher and child components (see Webster-Stratton & Reid, 2007).

The Incredible Years curriculum has been the focus of numerous well-designed evaluation studies focused on different components of the program and different recipient populations (for a review, see Webster-Stratton & Reid, 2010). In one of the most recent studies, Webster-Stratton, Reid, and Stoolmiller (2008) assessed the outcomes of the combined child-focused and teacher training programs in a randomized trial with 1,768 children in preschool Head Start, kindergarten, and first-grade classrooms in socioeconomically at-risk neighborhoods. Assessments were conducted in the fall and again in the spring, after the program had been in effect for the academic year. Compared to children in the control group, children in the Incredible Years program displayed greater improvement in school readiness (indexed by behaviors reflecting self-regulation and social competence) and fewer conduct problems based on classroom observations. Child measures also indicated that Incredible Years children showed greater improvement in identifying feelings and in providing positive rather than negative solutions to a social problem-solving task. Other evaluations of this program have yielded consistent results (Webster-Stratton & Reid, 2010). In these studies, however, findings are reported for the entire study sample, including kindergarteners and first graders, which makes it difficult to know how much this program benefits preschoolers specifically.

ICPS

ICPS is a social skills curriculum that stands for I Can Problem Solve or, alternatively, Interpersonal Cognitive Problem Solving (Shure, 1992, 2001; Shure & Spivack, 1982). It is designed to be used by early childhood educators in small groups to help children solve interpersonal problems, where they are taught to identify multiple response options to the social problems they are facing, recognizing relevant thoughts, feelings, and motives, and then to evaluate each of these alternatives in a systematic manner. Methods incorporated into the fifty-nine lessons include puppets, games, dialogues, and role-playing exercises, and the curriculum lasts for three months. A review of evaluation research by Denham and Almeida (1987) indicated that preschoolers who participated in this program successfully acquired many of the intended outcomes of the curriculum and exhibited positive behavior change (see also Shure, 2001).

The Emotion Course

The Emotion Course is based on developmental emotions theory and the importance of emotional understanding and self-regulation to social competence in early childhood (Izard, 2001; Izard et al., 2001). The curriculum consists of twenty-two lessons focused on discrete emotions in which preschoolers learn to recognize and label these emotions and develop skills in emotion regulation. Methods include puppet vignettes, interactive reading and games, storybooks, emotion expression posters, and skill coaching by teachers. Several randomized-trial evaluations conducted with children in Head Start classrooms each found that children in the intervention group had, at the end of the program, better emotion knowledge and were better able to regulate their emotions (with some decrease in negative emotion expressions); in one study, they also exhibited greater social competence (Izard, Trentacosta, King, & Mostow, 2004; Izard et al., 2008).

Al's Pals

Finally, Al's Pals (Wingspan LLC, 1999) is based on resiliency research; it was designed to increase social-emotional competence and reduce risk factors for antisocial behavior, and it is oriented toward at-risk children from preschool through early elementary school. The curriculum consists of forty-six lessons over the course of twenty-three weeks, with themes of fostering positive coping, social competence, effective social problem solving, positive beliefs about the self, understanding and expressing emotions, and self-regulation, along with lessons about substance abuse and violence prevention. Curricular methods include puppet-led discussions, role-playing, reading and music, guided creative play, and brainstorming, and teachers are encouraged to incorporate curricular concepts into daily practices. There is some outcome evidence that participation in Al's Pals is associated with improved teacher ratings of child behavior problems, social competence, and coping, although the findings do not permit an assessment of whether preschoolers in particular benefit from this curriculum (see Lynch, Geller, & Schmidt, 2004).

The six early childhood curricula discussed here are the strongest of those that foster prosocial conduct and constructive social behavior in young children based on their design and on relevant evaluation research. They are also representative of other programs in the field. They reflect many of the characteristics of best practices in early childhood education identified earlier, as well as the lessons of research on early prosocial development in young children. They share an emphasis on promoting social and emotional understanding as part of a broader curriculum in character education, a focus on activities that promote young children's active learning, the use of adult–child conversations to enhance psychological understanding and social problem solving, experiences to strengthen children's self-regulatory capacities (especially skills at emotion management), enlisting children's ideas into social problem-solving exercises, and encouragement of the generalization of lessons to everyday experience in the classroom. Although the development, evaluation, and scaling up of curricular models is still in the relatively early stages—especially compared with programs for older children and adolescents—these "promising" strategies provide a good basis for future work.

There are other early childhood education curricula that are not directly focused on improving social-emotional functioning but which may have positive indirect benefits for young children. These curricular models merit attention because of additional ideas they can provide early educators about practices that may support early character education. An example is Tools of the Mind, a curriculum based on the ideas of Vygotskian theory and designed to strengthen preschoolers' self-regulatory skills (Bodrova & Leong, 2007). The core curriculum includes forty activities that focus on the development of skills of inhibitory control, working memory, and cognitive flexibility, which are key aspects of young children's self-regulatory competence (see the accompanying case study B, "Implementing an Evidence-Based Preschool Program: A Superintendent's Perspective on Tools of the Mind"). These activities often involve children working together and include pretend play, structured games involving self-regulation (e.g., the "Freeze" game), and activities that can incorporate other curricular goals (such as creating stories from picture books in pairs). Evaluation studies of this curriculum indicate that it improves preschoolers' self-regulatory skills and social conduct, although its impact on cognitive functioning remains uncertain (Barnett et al., 2008; Diamond, Barnett, Thomas, & Munro, 2007). Although it would be unwise to use Tools of the Mind as a curriculum to promote young children's prosocial conduct, it offers ideas for how early childhood educators can foster competency in self-regulation in light of how often impulsivity is an impediment to prosocial behavior.

Besides these child-focused curricula, it is important to note that there are also a handful of teacher-focused curricula that are designed to alter the quality of classroom instructional practices and teacher–child relationships. Some of these curricula are linked to the child-focused programs reviewed earlier, but their outcome evaluations typically focus on changes in teacher behavior and only secondarily on improved social and emotional behavior of children in the classroom. These curricula have not been the focus of this review, but they are discussed elsewhere (see Domitrovich et al., in press). As earlier noted, there are also a small number of parent-focused programs that are linked to the child-focused curricula described above. Taken together, some program planners have wisely understood that improving child outcomes requires multifaceted strategies that should enlist the integrated efforts of multiple adults in the child's world.

The good news, then, is that there are some outstanding program models to use and adapt for purposes of the prosocial education of young children. The bad news, however, is that despite these advances, relatively little is known about the curricular practices that specifically advance prosocial conduct in young children. Although the developmental research literature draws our attention to key ingredients—warm, supportive adult–child relationships; rich conversations that illuminate the psychological needs of other people; adults who model prosocial conduct in their behavior toward children; and avoidance of punitive or coercive child-management practices—and these ingredients have been implemented into thoughtfully designed early childhood curricula, the relevant evaluation research tells us little about the consequences of these curricula for early prosocial conduct per se. We can conclude that these program models appear to do a fine job of promoting positive social behavior and social competence in young children and of reducing the incidence of negative behavior. We must await further research to understand whether they have comparable consequences for the development of prosocial motivation.

CONCLUSION

In recent decades, administrators in departments of education throughout the country have developed statewide learning guidelines in preschool education to parallel and complement long-standing learning standards for K–12 education (Scott-Little, Kagan, & Frelow, 2003, 2006). The initial focus of these learning guidelines was on language and literacy, mathematics, and other conventional academic areas. Increasingly, however, preschool educators pushed to include social-emotional learning in these guidelines, even though they are often absent from K–12 standards, recognizing the importance of young children's emotional understanding and social functioning to their success in classroom learning. They also recognized that the difficulties of some at-risk children in early learning derive primarily not from their cognitive limitations but from problems in self-regulation, social competence, self-confidence, and other socioemotional capacities.

In a much smaller number of states, preschool learning guidelines in areas related to citizenship, responsible conduct, and even social studies have begun to appear.* Although these learning guidelines sometimes appear to have the naive intention of furthering the parallel between preschool and K–12 learning standards, in other states they seem to reflect a more thoughtful appraisal of the developmental opportunities of the early childhood years. Young children are citizens of their early education classrooms or care centers, where they learn how to get along responsibly with adults and other children. In group education and care, they develop skills in social interaction and emotional understanding in the context of daily experience with other children and adults. They learn about distributive justice (or "fairness") in the context of sharing resources during play or classroom projects. In many of their educational settings, they become acquainted with human diversity in the languages, clothing, foods, and behaviors they observe around them. And in the midst of this learning, they also have frequent opportunities to act helpfully, generously, and compassionately toward others.

Because developmental research shows that young children have an early sensitivity to the feelings, goals, and desires of other people and can share those intentional goals in helpful acts, the opportunities to foster an orientation toward prosocial conduct in the early years are profound. The field of prosocial education has much to gain from a new attention to early childhood.

---

*See, for example, California Department of Education (in press). *California preschool curriculum framework: Vol. 3. History/social science.* Sacramento, CA: Author. Accessed at http://www.cde.ca.gov/sp/cd/re.

REFERENCES

Barnett, W. S., Jung, K., Yarosz, D. J., Thomas, J., Hornbeck, A., Stechuk, R., et al. (2008). Educational effects of the Tools of the Mind curriculum: A randomized trial. *Early Childhood Research Quarterly, 23*(3), 299–313.

Bierman, K. L., Domitrovich, C. E., Nix, R. L., Gest, S. D., Welsh, J. A., Greenberg, M. T., et al. (2008). Promoting academic and social-emotional school readiness: The Head Start REDI program. *Child Development, 79*(6), 1802–1817.

Bodrova, E., & Leong, D. J. (2007). *Tools of the Mind: The Vygotskian approach to early childhood education* (2nd ed.). Upper Saddle River, NJ: Prentice Hall.

Committee for Children. (1991). *Second Step: A violence prevention curriculum.* Seattle, WA: Author.

Côté, S., Tremblay, R. E., Nagin, D., Zoccolillo, M., & Vitaro, F. (2002). The development of impulsivity, fearfulness, and helpfulness during childhood: Patterns of consistency and change in the trajectories of boys and girls. *Journal of Child Psychology and Psychiatry, 43*(5), 609–618.

Demetriou, H., & Hay, D. F. (2004). Toddlers' reactions to the distress of familiar peers: The importance of context. *Infancy, 6*(2), 299–318.

Denham, S. A., & Almeida, M. C. (1987). Children's social problem-solving skills, behavioral adjustment, and interventions: A meta-analysis evaluating theory and practice. *Journal of Applied Developmental Psychology, 8*(4), 391–409.

Diamond, A., Barnett, W. S., Thomas, J., & Munro, S. (2007). Preschool program improves cognitive control. *Science, 318*(5855), 1387–1388.

Domitrovich, C. E., Cortes, R. C., & Greenberg, M. T. (2007). Improving young children's social and emotional competence: A randomized trial of the Preschool "PATHS" curriculum. *Journal of Primary Prevention, 28*(2), 67–91.

Domitrovich, C. E., Greenberg, M. T., Cortes, R., & Kusche, C. (1999). *Manual for the preschool PATHS curriculum.* University Park: Pennsylvania State University.

Domitrovich, C. E., Moore, J. E., Thompson, R. A., & the Collaborative for the Advancement of Social, Emotional, and Academic Learning Preschool to Elementary Assessment Workgroup. (in press). Interventions that promote social-emotional learning in young children. In R. Pianta, L. Justice, S. Barnett, & S. M. Sheridan (Eds.), *Handbook of early education.* New York: Guilford Press.

Eisenberg, N., Fabes, R. A., & Spinrad, T. L. (2006). Prosocial development. In W. Damon, R. M. Lerner (Series Eds.), & N. Eisenberg (Vol. Ed.), *Handbook of child psychology: Vol. 3. Social, emotional, and personality development* (6th ed., pp. 646–717). New York: Wiley.

Garner, P. W. (2006). Prediction of prosocial and emotional competence from maternal behavior in African American preschoolers. *Cultural Diversity and Ethnic Minority Psychology, 12*(2), 179–198.

Garner, P. W., Dunsmore, J. C., & Southam-Gerrow, M. (2008). Mother-child conversations about emotions: Linkages to child aggression and prosocial behavior. *Social Development, 17*(2), 259–277.

Hastings, P. D., McShane, K. E., & Parker, R. (2007). Ready to make nice: Parental socialization of young sons' and daughters' prosocial behaviors with peers. *Journal of Genetic Psychology, 168*(2), 177–200.

Hastings, P. D., Rubin, K. H., & DeRose, L. (2005). Links among gender, inhibition, and parental socialization in the development of prosocial behavior. *Merrill-Palmer Quarterly, 51*(4), 467–493.

Hastings, P. D., Utendale, W. T., & Sullivan, C. (2007). The socialization of prosocial development. In J. E. Grusec & P. D. Hastings (Eds.), *Handbook of socialization* (pp. 638–664). New York: Guilford Press.

Hay, D. F. (1994). Prosocial development. *Journal of Child Psychology and Psychiatry, 33*(1), 29–71.

Hay, D. F., Caplan, M. Z., Castle, J., & Stimson, C. A. (1991). Does sharing become increasingly "rational" in the second year of life? *Developmental Psychology, 27*(6), 987–993.

Hay, D. F., & Cook, K. V. (2007). The transformation of prosocial behavior from infancy to childhood. In C. A. Brownell & C. B. Kopp (Eds.), *Socioemotional development in the toddler years* (pp. 100–131). New York: Guilford Press.

Hay, D. F., & Murray, P. (1982). Giving and requesting: Social facilitation of infants' offers to adults. *Infant Behavior and Development, 5*(2–4), 301–310.

Iannotti, R. J. (1985). Naturalistic and structured assessments of prosocial behavior in preschool children: The influence of empathy and perspective taking. *Developmental Psychology, 21*(1), 46–55.

Izard, C. E. (2001). *The emotions course: Helping children understand and manage their feelings.* Newark: University of Delaware.

Izard, C. E., Fine, S. E., Schultz, D., Mostow, A. J., Ackerman, B. P., & Youngstrom, E. (2001). Emotion knowledge as a predictor of social behavior and academic competence in children at risk. *Psychological Science, 12*(1), 18–23.

Izard, C. E., King, K. A., Trentacosta, C. J., Morgan, J. K., Laurenceau, J., Krauthamer-Ewing, E. S., et al. (2008). Accelerating the development of emotion competence in Head Start children: Effects on adaptive and maladaptive behavior. *Development and Psychopathology, 20,* 369–397.

Izard, C. E., Trentacosta, C. J., King, K. A., & Mostow, A. J. (2004). An emotion-based prevention program for Head Start children. *Early Education and Development, 15*(4), 407–422.

Joseph, G. E., & Strain, P. S. (2003). Comprehensive evidence-based social-emotional curricula for young children: An analysis of efficacious adoption potential. *Topics in Early Childhood Special Education, 23,* 65–76.

Knafo, A., Zahn-Waxler, C., Van Hulle, C., Robinson, J. L., & Rhee, S. H. (2008). The developmental origins of a disposition toward empathy: Genetic and environmental contributions. *Emotion, 8*(6), 737–752.

Kohlberg, L. (1969). Stage and sequence: The cognitive-developmental approach to socialization. In D. A. Goslin (Ed.), *Handbook of Socialization: Theory in Research.* Boston: Houghton Mifflin.

Kusche, C. A., & Greenberg, M. T. (1994). *The PATHS curriculum.* South Deerfield, MA: Channing-Bete.

Lamb, S., & Zakhireh, B. (1997). Toddlers' attention to the distress of peers in a day care setting. *Early Education and Development, 8*(2), 105–118.

Liszkowski, U., Carpenter, M., Striano, T., & Tomasello, M. (2006). Twelve- and 18-month-olds point to provide information for others. *Journal of Cognition and Development, 7*(2), 173–187.

Lynch, K. B., Geller, S. R., & Schmidt, M. G. (2004). Multi-year evaluation of the effectiveness of a resilience-based prevention program for young children. *Journal of Primary Prevention, 24*(3), 335–353.

McMahon, S. D., Washburn, J., Felix, E. D., Yakin, J., & Childrey, G. (2000). Violence prevention: Program effects on urban preschool and kindergarten children. *Applied & Preventive Psychology, 9*(4), 271–281.

Meltzoff, A. N. (1995). Understanding the intentions of others: Re-enactment of intended acts by 18-month-old children. *Developmental Psychology, 31*(5), 838–850.

Meltzoff, A. N. (2007). The "like me" framework for recognizing and becoming an intentional agent. *Acta Psychologica, 124*(1), 26–43.

Newton, E. K., Goodman, M., Rogers, C. R., Burris, J., & Thompson, R. A. (2010, April). *Individual differences in toddler' prosocial behavior*. Paper presented at the Conference on Human Development, New York, NY.

Piaget, J. (1932/1965). *The moral judgment of the child*. London: Free Press.

Repacholi, B., & Gopnik, A. (1997). Early reasoning about desires: Evidence from 14- and 18-month-olds. *Developmental Psychology, 33*(1), 12–21.

Rheingold, H. L. (1982). Little children's participation in the work of adults, a nascent prosocial behavior. *Child Development, 53*(1), 114–125.

Rheingold, H. L., & Hay, D. F. (1978). Prosocial behavior of the very young. In G. S. Stent (Ed.), *Morality as a biological phenomenon* (pp. 93–108). Berkeley, CA: University of California Press.

Scott-Little, C., Kagan, S. L., & Frelow, V. S. (2003). Creating the conditions for success with early learning standards: Results from a national study of state-level standards for children's learning prior to kindergarten. *Early Childhood Research and Practice, 5*(2). Retrieved November 21, 2011, from http://ecrp.uiuc.edu/v5n2/little.html

Scott-Little, C., Kagan, S. L., & Frelow, V. S. (2006). Conceptualization of readiness and the content of early learning standards: The intersection of policy and research? *Early Childhood Research Quarterly, 21*(2), 153–173.

Shure, M. B. (1992). *I can problem solve: An interpersonal cognitive problem-solving program: Preschool*. Champaign, IL: Research Press.

Shure, M. B. (2001). I can problem solve (ICPS): An interpersonal cognitive problem solving program for children. *Residential Treatment for Children & Youth, 18*(1), 3–14.

Shure, M. B., & Spivack, G. (1982). Interpersonal problem-solving in young children: A cognitive approach to prevention. *American Journal of Community Psychology, 10*(3), 341–356.

Svetlova, M., Nichols, S. R., & Brownell, C. A. (2010). Toddlers' prosocial behavior: From instrumental to empathic to altruistic helping. *Child Development, 81*(6), 1814–1827.

Thompson, R. A. (2006). The development of the person: Social understanding, relationships, self, conscience. In W. Damon, R. M. Lerner (Series Eds.), & N. Eisenberg (Vol. Ed.), *Handbook of child psychology: Vol. 3. Social, emotional, and personality development* (6th ed., pp. 24–98). New York: Wiley.

Thompson, R. A. (2009). Early foundations: Conscience and the development of moral character. In D. Narvaez & D. Lapsley (Eds.), *Personality, identity, and character: Explorations in moral psychology* (pp. 159–184). New York: Cambridge University Press.

Thompson, R. A. (2012). *Whither the preconventional child?* Unpublished manuscript, University of California, Davis.

Thompson, R. A., Laible, D. J., & Ontai, L. L. (2003). Early understanding of emotion, morality, and the self: Developing a working model. In R. V. Kail (Ed.), *Advances in child development and behavior, Vol. 31* (pp. 137–171). San Diego, CA: Academic.

Thompson, R. A., Meyer, S., & McGinley, M. (2006). Understanding values in relationship: The development of conscience. In M. Killen & J. Smetana (Eds.), *Handbook of moral development* (pp. 267–297). Mahwah, NJ: Erlbaum.

Thompson, R. A., & Newton, E. K. (2010). Emotion in early conscience. In W. Arsenio & E. Lemerise (Eds.), *Emotions, aggression, and morality: Bridging development and psychopathology* (pp. 6–32). Washington, DC: American Psychological Association.

Tomasello, M. (2007). Cooperation and communication in the 2nd year of life. *Child Development Perspectives, 1*(1), 8–12.

Tomasello, M., Carpenter, M., Call, J., Behne, T., & Moll, H. (2005). Understanding and sharing intentions: The origins of cultural cognition. *Behavioral and Brain Sciences, 28*(5), 675–735.

Tomasello, M., & Herrmann, E. (2010). Ape and human cognition: What's the difference? *Current Directions in Psychological Science, 19*(1), 3–8.

Warneken, F., & Tomasello, M. (2006). Altruistic helping in human infants and young chimpanzees. *Science, 311*(5765), 1301–1303.

Warneken, F., & Tomasello, M. (2007). Helping and cooperation at 14 months of age. *Infancy, 11*(3), 271–294.

Warneken, F., & Tomasello, M. (2008). Extrinsic rewards undermine altruistic tendencies in 20-month-olds. *Developmental Psychology, 44*(6), 1785–1788.

Webster-Stratton, C. (1990). *Dina Dinosaur's social skills and problem-solving curriculum.* Seattle, WA: Incredible Years.

Webster-Stratton, C., & Reid, M. J. (2007). Incredible Years and Teachers Training Series: A Head Start partnership to promote social competence and prevent conduct problems. In P. Tolin, J. Szapocznick, & S. Sambrano (Eds.), *Preventing youth substance abuse* (pp. 67–88). Washington, DC: American Psychological Association.

Webster-Stratton, C., & Reid, M. J. (2010). A school–family partnership: Addressing multiple risk factors to improve school readiness and prevent conduct problems in young children. In S. L. Christenson & A. L. Reschly (Eds.), *Handbook of school-family partnerships* (pp. 204–227). New York: Routledge.

Webster-Stratton, C., Reid, M. J., & Stoolmiller, M. (2008). Preventing conduct problems and improving school readiness: Evaluation of the Incredible Years teacher and child training programs in high-risk schools. *Journal of Child Psychology and Psychiatry, 49*(5), 471–488.

Wingspan LLC. (1999). *Al's pals: Kids making healthy choices.* Richmond, VA: Author.

Woodward, A. L. (2009). Infants' grasp of others' intentions. *Current Directions in Psychological Science, 18*(1), 53–57.

Zahn-Waxler, C., Radke-Yarrow, M., & King, R. (1979). Child rearing and children's prosocial initiations toward victims of distress. *Child Development, 50*(2), 319–330.

Zahn-Waxler, C., Radke-Yarrow, M., Wagner, E., & Chapman, M. (1992). Development of concern for others. *Developmental Psychology, 28*(1), 126–136.

Zahn-Waxler, C., Robinson, J. L., & Emde, R. N. (1992). The development of empathy in twins. *Developmental Psychology, 28*(6), 1038–1047.

Case Study 15A

The Early Learning Campus

JILL JACOBI-VESSELS, CHRISTINE SHERRETZ,
DOROTHY J. VEITH, AND ANN E. LARSON

I'm a single parent and work full time as a secretary at U of L. I am also a grad student. I needed a place for my daughter that was close to work and school and also affordable on a tight budget. The Early Learning Campus has been those things, but so much more—the level of quality care provided here is amazing. The staff is wonderful. The building is beautiful and well designed. There is thoughtful planning going on. It is a place I have complete confidence in for my daughter. That frees up a lot of my energy so that I can focus on my work and studies.

—Karen Habeeb, graduate program
assistant senior, University of Louisville

The Early Learning Campus has provided social interaction and learning opportunities for my son that we could not provide as working parents. The quality of staff and variety in activities is far better than what we have witnessed at other traditional "day care" facilities. We are absolutely thrilled to have been an ELC family from day one.

—Nick, Alice, and Indiana Dawson

THE EARLY LEARNING CAMPUS

The University of Louisville's Early Learning Campus (ELC) is an exemplary preschool learning community consisting of a rich collaboration of students, faculty members, and professionals committed to the development of nearly 140 young children. The campus fully embraces many of the elements found in prosocial education's philosophy, focusing on meeting children's and family's needs that could otherwise be barriers to learning. ELC is located adjacent to the Family Scholar House apartments and academic services center, a unique arrangement that primarily serves single parents seeking a college degree (see later section).

Lack of child care and stable housing are major hurdles to educational attainment. The university campus leaders identified the child-care issues of our constituents as a major factor in the amount of time it takes for students to graduate, potentially causing students to leave the university prior to completing their degrees. Child care also was identified as an obstacle to students, staff, and faculty who seek to balance professional and family responsibilities. ELC and the Louisville Scholar House (LSH) operations represent the development of a national model that enables single parents of economically at-risk families, headed primarily by women, to obtain an education and hopefully gain economic success.

ELC ensures that children in these families have the necessary developmental supports and educational experiences for infants through preschool to be fully prepared for and highly successful in school. This intrinsic link to the community is the foundation that makes the partnership between the U of L and LSH (formerly called Project Women) truly exceptional. This joint effort addresses a mutual community need for quality child care, resulting in the university opening a long-needed child-care center and the LSH expanding their housing opportunities for single parents. The partnership is aimed at eliminating disparities in education, health, economic development, and human and social services.

ELC is operated and managed by the university's College of Education and Human Development (CEHD). This facility has over twenty-five thousand square feet of space and serves children ages six weeks to four years old; during summer months and after school, children up to twelve years old participate. The building has a unique design intended to encourage the creativity of the children, resembling a child's shape sorter, with a variety of geometric shapes used for the windows. A large skylight is featured over a transparent second floor, which allows natural light to brighten the interior of the building. Classrooms with observation windows surround a piazza area on each floor, providing space for community gatherings and family conversations, a reflection of the ELC's emphasis on the Reggio Emilia approach, very much a prosocial education strategy. Reggio Emilia, named for a town in Italy that originally developed this format, emphasizes supportive relationships from parents and community in meeting young children's comprehensive needs (Lewin-Benham, 2005).* The third floor is a combination of open indoor space for gross motor activities during inclement weather, a greenhouse, and a rooftop garden.

We believe that one reason our young students succeed results from the great attention given to the look and feel of the classroom. Environment is considered the "third teacher" at ELC. Teachers carefully organize space for small and large group projects and small intimate spaces for one, two, or three children. Documentation of children's work, plants, and collections that children have made from former outings are displayed both at the child and adult eye level. The learning philosophy of the ELC embraces the knowledge that a child is first an individual with unique talents, strengths, and needs. The child

---

*For more about the Reggio Emilia curriculum approach, see pages 4 and 5 of the ELC handbook, online at http://louisville.edu/education/elc/ELC-handbook-6-11.pdf.

seeks to make meaning of the world by exploring, discovering, and mastering skills, information, and concepts. Their journeys are to be respected as much as supported by family and community. Each step of the child's journey requires the elements promoted by prosocial education, including dependable and lasting connections to the adults in their young lives.

A distinctive characteristic of the ELC is the diversity of families' educational attainment, socioeconomic levels, and ethnicities. Many learning centers, particularly those on university campuses, are "homogenous in their diversity" due to enrollment costs. Having a cohesive, diverse group at the ELC learning community provides an intrinsically rich environment that is rare and much needed in the child-care community.

ELC provides teacher candidates from CEHD with supervised fieldwork in preschool classrooms. Faculty members across campus have developed ELC opportunities for undergraduate and graduate students and medical residents for *observation* (in which there is no direct child contact, but the observation rooms are used) and *field placements* (in which there is direct contact in classrooms with children). These experiences help to achieve education goals in teacher preparation, pediatric medical residency, social work, art, music, occupational therapy, speech and language, and audiology. Faculty and staff contributions include music sessions with the School of Music, H1N1 vaccinations from the Medical School, and dental hygiene services from the Dental School.

PARTNERSHIP AND COMMUNITY ENGAGEMENT MEET COMMUNITY NEEDS

ELC is a unique project that has involved a diverse partnership since its inception in June 2007. The Kentucky governor, Family Scholar House (FSH), University of Louisville administration, and state and local officials developed ELC to support university students who are parents and to educate young children in a state-of-the-art early childhood learning center. The university made available to the FSH organization a one-half-block tract west of the Belknap Campus on a dollar-per-year lease for the housing project. Physically, the Gladys and Lewis "Sonny" Bass Louisville Scholar House Campus consists of the LSH facility and ELC, which is administered by the U of L College of Education and Human Development. Other key community partners that support the project include the Louisville metro government, the Transportation Authority of River City (TARC), Housing and Urban Development (HUD), nonprofit foundations, other educational institutions, and local businesses.

The management teams of ELC and LSH maintain a close working relationship strengthened by the shared location of offices for both organizations and the enrollment of some LSH staff members' children in ELC. The management of ELC works with LSH staff members to ensure that the needs of each family are understood and supported. The well-qualified staff have credentials directly related to early childhood development: master's degrees (four); bachelor's degrees (ten); associate's degrees (seven); Child Development Accreditation (CDA), a nationally recognized certificate in early childhood (five); entry-level staff working on degrees in the field or

CDAs (twelve); and student workers in education. The first director, recently promoted to assistant professor in early childhood education, has a PhD in teaching and learning and a master's in interdisciplinary early childhood. The current director is Dianna Zink, MEd.

LOUISVILLE SCHOLAR HOUSE AND FAMILY SCHOLAR HOUSE

Louisville Scholar House is the nonprofit organization that administers the Family Scholar House operation. FSH is the region's only nonprofit organization with a mission dedicated to assisting homeless, single parents while they obtain a college degree. The FSH theme is "Changing lives, families, and communities through education." The nonprofit organization started in 1995 as Project Women. Its mission is to end the cycle of poverty by giving single-parent university students the support they need to achieve a four-year degree. FSH recognizes the challenges that single parents face in trying to provide housing, child care, and basic necessities for their children. In the past decade, the number of homeless parents and children in Louisville has continued to increase. Over nine thousand children in the Jefferson County School system (nearly 10 percent) and their parents are homeless (according to the local Coalition for the Homeless), requiring FSH to expand its housing and program capacity. This unique combination of housing, on-site child care, and support programs successfully serves fifty-six families and also provides nonresidential programming for over five hundred families on the preresidential waiting list for housing. FSH has forty two-bed and sixteen three-bed units. All are disability compliant, and four are handicap-designated units. The Louisville site is currently the only residential housing site, but the LSH organization provides services in nineteen counties in Kentucky and seven counties in Indiana.

The university–community collaboration has resulted in a business model that is being reviewed by several cities across the country (e.g., Dallas, Cleveland, Pittsburgh). Locally, this model is being replicated at the Downtown Scholar House, a partnership between FSH and Spalding University, which opened in January 2011 and provides supportive housing and educational programs for an additional fifty-four families in the Louisville community.

The university also assists LSH residents through the Cardinal Covenant financial aid program, the first program of its kind in the state of Kentucky. Cardinal Covenant helps to make college attainable for the 22 percent of Kentucky families living at or below 15 percent of the federal poverty level, determined by the U.S. Census Bureau. Through this program, students are able to graduate debt free as long as they finish within five years and remain Pell Grant eligible each year. In addition to financial support, the university's Information Technology unit provides computers for each apartment unit and access to the main computing system, which links each LSH resident to the Internet.

The university's Department of Public Safety provides round-the-clock security for the LSH and responds to 911 calls. This important component ensures residents' safety, because 90 percent of the residents come from backgrounds involving domestic violence. In addition, LSH residents enrolled in the U of L or another local educational institution are provided other student benefits such as free bus transportation on the TARC system, university identification cards, and access to the university's libraries. Residents and their children can also utilize U of L Hospital and health services.

GROWING IMPACT IN THE COMMUNITY

The compounded impact of this exceptional program and the commitment of university and community support has created enthusiasm and excitement among the residents and university faculty. Many discussions about service provisions for individuals facing multiple challenges normally stop at identification of the problem issues and do not proceed to collaborative approaches that can be used to construct holistic solutions. The Louisville Scholar House and Early Learning Campus have created an immersion effect that truly empowers the residents of the program to succeed.

A similar community-supported model was successfully implemented and detailed in Dr. James Comer's book *Leave No Child Behind: Preparing Today's Youth for Tomorrow's World* (2005). The 2007 winner of U of L's Grawemeyer Award in Education, Dr. Comer's program involves teachers, parents, administrators, and others at more than six hundred low-performing schools in making decisions by consensus to improve the educational experience for children. LSH and ELC were created with the same goals in mind and see their fruition: *Community involvement can make a difference in the educational outcomes of children and their parents*. The ELC is experiencing the same kind of comprehensive involvement from the Louisville community. Because the ELC is only two years old, outcome data are not yet available, but stay tuned. Results are coming.

REFERENCES

Comer, J. (2005). *Leave no child behind: Preparing today's youth for tomorrow's world.* New Haven, CT: Yale University Press.

Lewin-Benham, A. (2005). *Possible schools: The Reggio approach to urban education.* New York: Teachers College Press.

Case Study 15B

Implementing an Evidence-Based Preschool Program: A Superintendent's Perspective on Tools of the Mind

LAURA MORANA, DEBORAH LEONG, AND ELENA BODROVA

Imagine a preschool classroom that has been turned into an airport. There are child-made passports, tickets, and a ticket counter. There is an X-ray frame made from cardboard boxes, complete with a smaller box that functions as the screening device for carry-on luggage. There is an airplane cockpit made out of a big piece of cardboard with child-drawn instruments, an upside-down egg carton for a keyboard, and a paper plate that functions as the "steering wheel." Nina tells her friend Joshua that she is going on a trip and that she is going to forget to take out her water bottle and then she won't get through security. Joshua says he is going to go to Puerto Rico where his grandmother lives. Nina then puts on her backpack and stands in line behind Joshua. Then, finally, it's her turn. "Where are you going?" the child behind the counter asks. "I'm going to Puerto Rico, too." "Okay," says Ava at the ticket counter. "Here's your passport and your ticket to Puerto Rico. Your flight leaves at five o'clock," she says as she hands two pieces of torn construction paper to Nina. Nina goes to another center and takes off her shoes. She puts them in a basket with her backpack. She gives it to Asam who is the security guard. He puts it on a table that has a big box on it that is open on one end and pushes it through the box. He points to a big box that has been cut open. Nina walks through the box. "Hey, you're supposed to check me," she says to Asam as she taps him on the shoulder. Asam picks up a paper towel roll, and like a TSA security guard, he waves it over her head. "Okay," he says. Miriam is standing with Nina's backpack. She is holding a bottle of water that Nina forgot to take out of her backpack. "This is more than three ounces!" "Oh, I forgot. I'll put it in my cubby," says Nina as she takes the bottle and runs to her cubby. Her next stop is the waiting room.

To the naked eye, these children are engaging in prosocial interactions; they are playing with each other in a positive, social way. They show that they engage in empathy, they share toys and work together, delaying gratification of their own desired goals until these goals are more acceptable to the group. However, these children are learning more than how to act in a prosocial way;

according to Lev Vygotsky (1967), they are also learning self-regulation, the underlying mental process that makes prosocial interactions as well as the acquisition of higher mental functions possible. There is growing evidence that self-regulation affects not only social-emotional skills, but also a child's readiness for school. Not all make-believe play promotes self-regulation. For self-regulation to develop, play must be intentional, involve symbolic props, and have roles and an evolving scenario.

CHOOSING AN EVIDENCE-BASED EARLY CHILDHOOD PROGRAM

This is the basis for the program Tools of the Mind, which is a comprehensive early childhood curriculum for children in preschool and kindergarten that has been implemented in the Red Bank School District since 2004 in prekindergarten and since 2007 in kindergarten classes. Red Bank is a small suburban community with urbanlike characteristics. Our prekindergarten through grade 8 student population of 1,100 is rich in ethnic, socioeconomic, and linguistic diversity, where 74 percent of students are eligible for free/reduced-price lunch and approximately 50 percent of our students in prekindergarten and kindergarten classes are eligible for bilingual/ESL services. Red Bank has been identified as a high-poverty and high-needs district. Despite the multiple linguistic, ethnic, and socioeconomic needs of our students, the past five years have been marked by a transformation of the school system to provide children with optimal learning opportunities that support a foundation for a successful experience at the regional high school, college, and/or career of choice. What follows is a description of why we chose this particular early childhood program, a summary of the program and how it is implemented, and how it has been effectively used in our district as a cornerstone of our pre-K to grade 3 educational program.

We chose Tools of the Mind as the basis for an expansion of the Red Bank preschool program for a number of reasons. It explicitly focuses on the role of self-regulation in learning and academic ability by using specific activities that promote self-regulation, such as make-believe play, and by embedding self-regulation promoting activities in instruction designed to build foundational skills in literacy, mathematics, and social-emotional competence.

We also felt confident about the history of the program. To date, Tools of the Mind has been implemented in seven hundred early childhood classrooms including public and private preschools, Head Start, and Even Start, as well as half-day and full-day kindergarten, and it has been aligned with early learning standards and kindergarten academic standards in nine states and forty-five districts, serving over thirty thousand children. Tools of the Mind training staff have delivered professional development and technical assistance to two thousand teachers, teacher assistants, administrators, and support staff, their educational levels varying from high school to advanced degrees (Bodrova & Leong, 2007).

Tools of the Mind curricula designed for preschool and kindergarten have the same philosophical orientation and overlap in instructional practices, but the content taught differs, matching the developmental trajectories of self-regulation and children's intellectual capacities. Information about kindergarten and the differences between the kindergarten and preschool programs are available on the Web: www.toolsofthemind.org.

MATURE MAKE-BELIEVE PLAY

To develop self-regulation, preschool- and kindergarten-aged children have to engage in mature make-believe play, which is the leading activity for that age—the activity in which there are the most gains in underlying cognitive skills like self-regulation. Although young children engage in many different kinds of play, Vygotsky (1967) argued that only a specific kind of play has the characteristics that promote the development of these underlying skills. Mature make-believe play has roles where children play specific people, and these roles have a set of rules. The passenger on an airplane does not do her own security check, for example. It has a pretend scenario where social problems emerge and are solved by the participants, like bringing more than three ounces of liquid through security. The scenario is planned in advance and evolves as the children play. There are symbolic props, like tickets made of torn construction paper. The play lasts for an extended time frame, which means it can go for hours, and continues from day to day, starting each day where the children left off the previous day.

This rich make-believe play provides a context where children practice the components of self-regulation: being regulated by others, regulating others, and voluntarily self-regulating. Being regulated by others means doing what other children want to do. The ticket taker at the airport wants Nina to take the ticket to Puerto Rico that she gives her. Maybe Nina likes a different color, but she accepts what the other child wants to do. Regulating others means that children apply the rules of interaction in the role to other children when they violate the rules. Nina does this when Asam forgets to check her the right way at security.

Most importantly, make-believe play is one of the few contexts where children actually voluntarily self-regulate. Most of the activities in a classroom are either directly or subtly teacher directed. You play a game or listen to a story because the teacher asks you to do it. It really isn't voluntary participation. Play is voluntary. You can "stay in the play" by inhibiting doing something you may want to do because you want to be the passenger. Nina had actually wanted to be the pilot of the airplane, but she decided to be the passenger so she could have a turn as pilot. She and Maddy already agreed to change roles after she flew to Puerto Rico. Because play is a child-directed activity, children voluntarily self-regulate in a way they cannot do in teacher-directed activities.

Tools of the Mind training involves helping teachers know how to set up and scaffold mature make-believe play as well as how to do activities in which self-regulation is embedded in academic activities.

WHY A PROSOCIAL CURRICULUM?

One of the goals of the instructional program is to address prosocial development in a proactive manner. Children in pre-K and kindergarten experience a curricular approach that promotes and maintains a harmonious and collaborative interaction between classmates and staff. When skills such as sharing, taking turns, demonstrating empathy, and being considerate of others' feelings and emotions have been integrated into the curriculum, students are developing the capacity for participating in large groups, small groups, working independently for extended periods of time, supporting each other, and applying creative problem solving on a daily basis.

In the absence of a developmentally appropriate curriculum with the intentional goal of promoting prosocial behavior development, the behavior of inquisitive children is often regarded as inappropriate behavior that calls for a consequence imposed by the adults, therefore never addressing the underlying root cause for the identified behavior that deviated from what was considered normal for the child's age. Prior to the implementation of our prosocial curriculum, it was not uncommon to encounter children being referred to the principal for perceived inappropriate behavior displayed in both structured and unstructured settings. For example, while in the cafeteria, two students were talking about the new skills they were learning in a wrestling class they both took privately; however, the kinesthetic approach they used to enhance the discussion led a cafeteria worker to send the two boys out to the office because their behavior was perceived as a physical altercation. A conversation with the students on this matter was most revealing, as the administrator became extremely interested in the students' account of the incident and subsequently learned how focused their conversation was on their extracurricular activities and their passion for wrestling. In a prosocial approach to managing such instances in which a student's individual learning style manifests itself through a need to actively contribute to the class discussion without regard for the interests of other students, the classroom teacher may implement a system that supports self-regulation. Using a strategy such as think-pair-share, all students can be afforded an opportunity to actively participate, therefore maximizing students' prosocial behaviors and reducing teacher and administrator reactions that impede rather than facilitate social and cognitive development.

The shift in prosocial behavior development has become focused to the extent that students feel they are truly learning strategies for responding to conflict situations in a proactive and collaborative manner with child-generated solutions. The focus at the school level has been to work toward the establishment of a common language that reflects students' understanding of teachers as caring and supportive role models who engage students in shaping the learning environment in a positive manner.

IMPLEMENTING THE TOOLS OF THE MIND PROGRAM

Tools of the Mind training involves a set of workshops, the training of teachers, in-district coaches who support implementation, and participation by other staff, such as the special education staff. The workshops roll out based on a developmental trajectory of skills that match both the self-regulation capacities of children and their growing cognitive and language skills. Tools of the Mind aims at transforming classroom practices as well as teacher under-standing of the roots of social behavior and the reasons that children might have difficulty interacting with each other. Instead of seeing aggression as a personality trait or the outcome of poor parenting, in Tools of the Mind, aggression is seen as reactive behavior by children lacking self-regulation. As children gain self-regulation through participation in all of the Tools of the Mind activities, the rate of aggression diminishes significantly. For example, classrooms that reported twenty to thirty disciplinary incidents a month prior to implementing the program lowered the rate substantially so that there were fewer than ten a year.

Expansion of this high-quality early childhood program that services all families in the Red Bank School District has been made possible by funds the district began receiving through the New Jersey State Department of Educa-tion Pre-School Expansion Initiative in September 2009.

Acknowledging the difficulty that school districts have in the design, imple-mentation, and evaluation of a standards-based and developmentally ap-propriate curriculum, our district initiated a process for creating a community of learners that will become better prepared to respond to the challenge of systemic reform and will become directly involved at all levels of the improve-ment process. This way, the vision becomes institutionalized, and the momen-tum for change and improvement is sustained regardless of any changes in the leadership at the district or school level.

The district's commitment to supporting the successful implementation and evaluation of a developmentally appropriate curriculum (pre-K–3) is char-acterized by a focused approach that includes the appropriate allocation of time and resources to support teachers and administrators in implementing, monitoring, and evaluating fidelity to the curriculum. To this end, the district emphasizes the development of classroom teachers as leaders through the identification of exemplary teachers to serve as master teachers/coaches and as grade-level team leaders. Administrators serve as true instructional lead-ers. The district's professional development reflects a data-driven approach designed to address the diverse needs of staff. Of course, a great deal of emphasis is placed on informal and formal observations and evaluations, the alignment of instruction with the curriculum, and diversified assessment prac-tices as sources of data.

The job-embedded approach to supporting staff includes superintendent/principal mentoring, master teacher/teacher mentoring, modeling, coteach-ing, leading action-research projects, and developing staff and administrators as reflective practitioners. Both formal and informal observations of instruc-tion are effective strategies for monitoring curriculum implementation that is supported by a partnership between Charlotte Danielson and Teachscape, which makes the Framework for Teaching (FTT) more practical and easier to access for ongoing professional learning. The observation and evalua-tion of teacher performance includes informal walk-throughs with feedback conducted a minimum of five times per year by multiple administrators and instructional coaches, and formal observations and an evaluation that includes a pre- and postconference with feedback (Danielson, 2007).

Staff perceptions of the overall learning environment as a catalyst for nurturing prosocial student behavior has evolved over time, further indicating that current efforts to improve the learning environment are a critical component within the teaching and learning framework. The implementation of the Tools of the Mind curriculum facilitated the establishment of classroom routines that promoted and celebrated students' ability to sustain their efforts to learn and use learning strategies in a purposeful way, engage in respectful interactions with peers and adults, and participate as productive members of a collaborative learning community. Learning through play is at the core of the Tools of the Mind curriculum, thus contributing directly to students' engagement in meaningful and creative play and prosocial behavior development and sustainability through the primary school years.

LESSONS LEARNED FROM IMPLEMENTING TOOLS OF THE MIND

We found that consistency was necessary between general education and special education. Consistency will contribute to the intentional and successful implementation of Tools of the Mind, particularly via the collection, use, and analysis of informal and formal data. A commitment to the implementation of a viable curriculum that is responsive to the multiple and diverse needs of students must be at the core of the work at the district, school, and classroom levels. A modified approach to the implementation of the Tools of the Mind curriculum in a special education setting has been found to be extremely effective in addressing varied and complex developmental delays often experienced by young children. We found that prosocial intervention might work best when children practice prosocial behaviors throughout the day in a variety of activities, rather than having the intervention as an add-on delegated to a specific activity. In addition, there must be a total commitment to the implementation, supervision, and evaluation of Tools of the Mind demonstrated via the technical support provided to staff and administrators, the development of teachers as leaders, and the strategic collection, use, and analysis of data to drive the decision-making process. The implementation of the Tools of the Mind curriculum has been reinforced via an ongoing and comprehensive professional development system that takes into account the varied readiness of teachers and administrators. District policies must reflect the commitment to offering *all* students optimal learning opportunities.

EVIDENCE OF SUCCESS

Our program also reflects best practices and is well aligned with the goals established by the New Jersey State Department of Education. The success of the program can be seen in the district's assessment data, which reveal steady growth over a three-year period. Spring 2011 student assessment results on the Primary Test for Standards, designed to assess students' progress toward achieving the knowledge and skills identified in the New Jersey Core Curriculum Content

Standards (CCCS), revealed that 98.5 percent of general education first graders and 92 percent of general education second graders scored at the advanced proficient or proficient level in language arts literacy. Comparable results were seen in mathematics, with 99 percent of general education first graders and 85 percent of general education second graders scoring at the advanced proficient or proficient level. On the other hand, the district has experienced a significant reduction in the number of referrals for special education eligibility, particularly in the social-emotional domain. Referrals at the pre-K and kindergarten levels are limited to one to two referrals per year. Subsequently, this has had a direct impact on special education programming and the cost of special education. Four percent of kindergarten special needs students in 2010/11 received in-class support through a classroom assistant. This support enables the students to meet academic expectations within a least restrictive environment (LRE).

Furthermore, our students' success has been validated by researchers and educators from prestigious universities and institutions who visited our program throughout the 2008/9 and 2009/10 school years. These included researchers from Harvard University (Rosenbaum, 2011), Georgetown University, New York University, Johns Hopkins University, the University of Pennsylvania, and Columbia University, among others. Finally, the Foundation for Child Development (Mead, 2009) and the New America Foundation have cited our Pre-K–3 program as an exemplary model that has at its core challenging, developmentally appropriate, and innovative practices to promote and sustain student learning through third grade (Takanishi, 2010). The Red Bank Borough School System is an active participant in the Preschool Research Network sponsored by the New Jersey Department of Education, which is intended to support the district's efforts via research on the most effective instructional approach to meeting the needs of English language learners while in the preschool program, with the goal of promoting sustainability in student learning through the primary school grades.

REFERENCES

Bodrova, E., & Leong, D. J. (2007). *Tools of the Mind: The Vygotskian approach to early childhood education* (2nd ed.). Columbus, OH: Merrill/Prentice Hall.

Danielson, C. (2007). *Enhancing professional practice: A framework for teaching* (2nd ed.). Alexandria, VA: Association for the Supervision of Curriculum Development.

Leong, D. J., & Bodrova, E. (2009). Tools of the Mind: A Vygotskian based early childhood curriculum. *Early Childhood Services: An Interdisciplinary Journal of Effectiveness, 3*(3), 245–262.

Mead, S. (2009). *Education reform starts early: Lessons from New Jersey's PreK–3rd reform efforts*. Washington, DC: New America Foundation.

Rosenbaum, E. (2011). *Rethinking the structures that serve children, their families, and their teachers*. New York: Columbia University Press.

Takanishi, R. (2010). *Transforming America's primary education system*. New York: Foundation for Child Development.

Vygotsky, L. S. (1967). Play and its role in the mental development of the child. *Journal of Russian and Eastern European Psychology, 5*(3), 6–18.

CHAPTER 16

After School as a Context for Prosocial Development

LISA M. DEBELLIS, CHRISTOPHER E. SMITH, AND ANNE-MARIE E. HOXIE

> Our after-school program has not only had a positive impact on the kids. It's had an impact on the staff members, the families, and the community. During the school day, the kids don't get the chance to get involved in activities that help their community. Here, they do. Our program's trademark is that we believe we can make a difference.
>
> —Helena Yordan, Program Coordinator of the Committee for Hispanic Children & Families After-School Program at PS/MS 279 in the Bronx, New York

Numerous studies have shown the positive impacts that after-school programs have on children and youth. Oftentimes, they expose children and youth to a range of new and different activities in which they can excel (Durlak & Weissberg, 2007). For many children who would otherwise be left unsupervised after the school day ends, after-school programs provide a vital service in keeping kids safe and happy. In fact, researchers have shown that children and youth who are left unsupervised after school are at risk for engaging in drug use and exhibiting both externalizing and internalizing behaviors, such as aggression and depressive symptoms (Durlak & Weissberg, 2007; Durlak, Weissberg, & Pachan, 2010; Mahoney & Stattin, 2000; Pettit, Bates, Dodge, & Meece, 1999; Vandell, Reisner, & Pierce, 2007). Participation in structured activities outside of school has also been associated with decreased likelihood of high school dropout and criminal activity and arrest in young adulthood, even for youth who displayed behaviors or characteristics that categorized them as at-risk for such negative and developmentally harmful outcomes (Mahoney, 2000). In addition, many studies have shown that participation in after-school programs helps support participants' academic performance (e.g., Durlak & Weissberg, 2007; Durlak et al., 2010; Lauer et al., 2006; Miller, 2005; Reisner, White, Russell, & Birmingham, 2004; Russell, Mielke, Miller, & Johnson, 2007).

Many research studies have also shown that after-school programs provide a place for children and youth to develop positive relationships with peers and adults, serve their communities, and improve their attitudes about themselves and others, thereby supporting their prosocial development (Arbreton, Bradshaw, Sheldon, & Pepper,

2009; Arbreton, Sheldon, & Herrera, 2005; Lerner, Lerner, & colleagues, 2009; Reisner et al., 2004). In particular, a recent meta-analysis showed that participation in after-school programs helped children and youth build self-confidence and self-esteem, promoted engagement in positive social behaviors, and reduced the occurrence of negative behaviors (Durlak & Weissberg, 2007; Durlak et al., 2010). In this chapter of the handbook, the authors will present research to support the many benefits that participation in after-school programs has on children and youth, with a particular emphasis on the research supporting how after-school programs serve as ideal contexts for the prosocial development of children and youth. Specifically, we will review the design of and research on three successful and well-established after-school initiatives, namely The After-School Corporation's (TASC's) model of after-school programming, Boys and Girls Clubs of America, and 4-H Clubs.

After-school programs provide an ideal context for children and youth's prosocial development. In response to the No Child Left Behind Act of 2001, many school leaders and educators have drastically reduced the amount of time children and youth spend in important activities, such as recess or play, the arts, music, and physical education (Grey, 2009; Pederson, 2007). They have done this in order to increase the amount of instructional time spent on the core subject areas, specifically mathematics and English language arts, in efforts for children and youth to perform well on high-stakes standardized assessments, the results of which are often tied to school funding (Grey, 2009; Pederson, 2007). Oftentimes, the types of activities that are getting cut from school schedules are the same activities that not only help children to grow intellectually but also allow them to develop positive relationships with peers and adults and practice positive social behaviors (see examples in Carlson et al., 2008; Deasy, 2002; Ginsburg, 2007). In fact, studies have shown that prosocial behaviors are not abundantly observed in traditional classroom settings (Hertz-Lazarowitz, 1983), suggesting that the classroom may not be the best place to promote children and youth's prosocial development (Eisenberg, Fabes, & Spinrad, 2006). Oftentimes, after-school programs serve as settings where children and youth get the opportunities to participate in important activities and lessons that their schools are cutting out of their schedules. In fact, throughout their history, after-school programs have often focused on educating the "whole child" (Halpern, 2002).

HISTORY OF AFTER-SCHOOL PROGRAMMING

The after-school hours have often been considered a time of "risk or opportunity" for children and youth (Hofferth, 1995, p. 1); for those children and youth who have somewhere to go and something productive to do, the after-school hours present them with opportunities for positive development. For those children and youth who are left unsupervised without a place to go or something productive to do, the after-school hours present them with an opportunity to engage in risky or undesirable behaviors. The underpinnings of after-school programs actually emerged in the late 1800s with the creation of boys clubs, which were usually housed in churches or other community buildings (Halpern, 2002). In large part, these clubs gave youth a place to go after education laws went into effect in the early 1900s, which led to an increase in school participation rates and a decrease in child labor rates (Halpern, 2002). The first actual after-school programs to emerge were founded by people who wanted to keep kids safe from the potential dangers of hanging around on the streets of big cities (Halpern, 2002). Although much has changed since those early days, after-school programs often still provide children and youth with a safe place to go after they are dismissed from school; however, many of them today have more ambitious and diverse goals, including increasing participants' academic achievement, building their social competencies, providing them with career and job training, and improving their attitudes about themselves, school, and others, to name a few.

In 1994, the federal government created 21st Century Community Learning Centers (21st CCLC) to allow for more community use of schools (James-Burdumy et al., 2005). In 1998, the focus of the funding stream specifically became dedicated to school-based after-school programs around the nation. Today, the 21st CCLC is the only federal funding stream dedicated to after-school programming in the United States, and it serves just under two million children and youth nationwide (Afterschool Alliance, 2010a). The 21st CCLC programs offer academic, artistic, and cultural enrichment opportunities and activities to children and youth in grades K–12 and their families when school is not in session. These programs currently operate in over nine thousand public schools or community centers across the nation (Afterschool Alliance, 2010a). Although this may seem like a large number of children and youth being served, many children and youth are still left without a place to go after school. Estimates are that approximately fourteen million children and youth in the United States do not have adult supervision after they are dismissed from school (Blank, 2005). The Afterschool Alliance recently conducted a national household survey of 29,754 families across the country. The results of the survey revealed that there are not nearly enough programs to support the children, youth, and families who need them. In particular, parents of the 18.5 million children and youth who were not currently participating in an after-school program (or 38 percent) said they would enroll their child in an after-school program if it were available to them (Afterschool Alliance, 2010b).

After-school programs vary widely in their range of programming and activities offered (Halpern, 2002). The 21st CCLC after-school programs are not exceptions to this. Overall, the 21st CCLC after-school programs in New York State alone focus on a variety of different activities and services. For example, according to a report from Learning Point Associates (Naftzger et al., 2007), 85 percent of the 21st CCLC after-school program coordinators from New York State reported that they spent time on recreation at their program, while 81 percent reported time spent on academic enrichment; 38 percent reported time spent on drug awareness, violence prevention, and/or character education; 34 percent reported time spent on youth leadership activities; 30 percent reported time spent on community service and service learning projects; and 21 percent reported time spent on mentoring. Nationwide, tutoring and homework help, academic enrichment, and recreation are the most common services currently offered to children and youth in the 21st CCLC–funded after-school programs (Afterschool Alliance, 2010a).

BENEFITS OF AFTER-SCHOOL PARTICIPATION

Since the 1990s, great interest has been placed on learning if after-school programs help students to improve academically (Halpern, 2002). During that time, many began to wonder particularly if after-school programs could help to lessen the achievement gap between high and low socioeconomic status children (Halpern, 2002). Although there has been variability in the findings across different studies regarding the potential academic benefits of after-school participation, many studies have shown that high-quality programs (with specific features, which will be discussed) do in fact help children and youth to improve in their academic performance. Specifically, research has consistently shown that when participants attended programs that offered academic *and* social activities, participants made the biggest improvements in achievement, providing evidence that both academic and social activities are important for after-school programs that look to help students improve academically (Durlak & Weissberg, 2007; Lauer et al., 2006; Redd, Brooks, & McGarvey, 2002).

A recent meta-analysis (Durlak & Weissberg, 2007; Durlak et al., 2010) investigated the impacts of after-school programs that promoted personal and social skills such as self-awareness, social relationships, and responsible decision making on social and academic outcomes. There were over seventy after-school programs and forty-nine prior reports represented in this study (Durlak & Weissberg, 2007; Durlak et al., 2010). The researchers chose to include only prior studies of after-school programs for children and youth between the ages of five and eighteen whose missions included promoting personal and social development. The specific impacts that were investigated included impacts on feelings and attitudes about themselves and toward their schools, school performance, and indicators of behavioral adjustment. Behavioral adjustment indicators included both the presence of positive behaviors and the avoidance of negative behaviors, including the following: presence of effective expressions of feelings, positive interactions with others, cooperation, leadership, and assertiveness in social contexts, and reduction or avoidance of noncompliance, aggression, delinquent acts, rebelliousness, and conduct problems (Durlak & Weissberg, 2007; Durlak et al., 2010).

The researchers also investigated whether or not evidence-based approaches to the promotion of social-emotional development were employed by programs and how this affected outcomes (Durlak & Weissberg, 2007; Durlak et al., 2010). In particular, the researchers coded the programs according to the presence or absence of the following four evidence-based approaches: (1) sequence (whether programs used a sequenced set of activities to teach skills); (2) active (whether the program used active learning to teach skills); (3) focus (whether the program had a specific component dedicated to personal or social skills); and (4) explicitness (whether the program targeted the development of specific personal or social skills) (Durlak & Weissberg, 2007; Durlak et al., 2010). The results showed that after-school programs positively affected students' feelings and attitudes toward themselves and their schools, promoted positive social behavior and reduced problem behavior, and boosted their school performance. These results held true only for participants who attended programs that used the four evidence-based approaches discussed previously. This research suggests that programs with distinct features that target the social-emotional development of participants are able to help students gain important benefits from after-school activities, including both social and academic benefits (Durlak & Weissberg, 2007; Durlak et al., 2010).

As previously discussed, after-school programs vary in their goals, missions, and activities. Although many programs (and the evaluations of those programs) focus on participants' academic performance, others also aim to contribute to participants' prosocial development. Three such after-school initiatives that have proven to be particularly effective in contributing to participants' prosocial development include TASC-model after-school programs, Boys and Girls Clubs of America, and 4-H Clubs. The remainder of this chapter will focus on describing how each of these initiatives works to impact participants' prosocial development and will synthesize the research illustrating their successes in this important endeavor.

THE AFTER-SCHOOL CORPORATION (TASC)

The After-School Corporation was founded in 1998 to make after-school programs accessible to all children, especially for disadvantaged youth who often do not have the same opportunities available to them after school, such as dance classes, music lessons, and private tutoring. Thus TASC sought to form partnerships between community-based organizations and public schools to offer after-school programs that give disadvantaged youth access to these types of opportunities. TASC-model after-school programs are more than drop-in clubs or child-care centers. TASC ensures that the programs provide youth with consistent, high-quality activities to promote their social and academic growth. Building on the positive impacts that are evident in their after-school programs, TASC is now seeking to reform education by insisting that the school day include these types of high-quality activities and learning experiences. Politicians and educational reform leaders are all speaking of extending our students' school days and years. TASC is currently working to ensure that the best after-school practices are infused in these efforts and has built their Expanded Learning Time initiative upon this premise. Rather than allowing school days to be extended by providing more of the same types of classroom activities during the extended hours, TASC advocates for schools to join with community partners to provide more enriching activities that have been shown to foster positive social and academic development in youth (The After-School Corporation, 2011).

Beginning in 1998, TASC built a network of after-school programs that all share common features. Program activities are provided in partnership between a school and a community-based organization, such as the YMCA or local settlement houses. Activities are available to all children in the school free of charge, and children who enroll are expected to attend from 3 p.m. to 6 p.m. each day that school is in session. Programs offer a range of activities, from academic enrichment activities such as literacy-based projects to homework help. Programs also provide opportunities for youth to participate in various art-based activities, such as theater, dance, visual arts, and music, as well as recreational activities. Most programs make social development and community engagement a key focus in all of these activities. For example, some programs have offered activities meant to encourage positive nutritional choices among youth while incorporating an element of community activism. In one program specifically, children learned about the importance of healthy eating habits and worked with their community to encourage local bodegas to offer more nutritional choices such as fruit and skim milk.

TASC-model after-school programs are meant to enhance students' social and academic learning experiences. By offering the enriching types of activities that are often the first to be eliminated by school budget cuts, such as arts and music activities, TASC-model after-school programs reinforce youths' academic development by connecting their activities to what students are learning about during the school day. Students in TASC-model after-school programs are often not exposed to these activities outside of their program. These novel activities create opportunities for youth to develop new interests while engaging in positive interactions with peers and adult staff members, which may benefit youth while in school.

TASC-model after-school programs are staffed by a blend of school day administrators, teachers, youth workers, activity specialists, and sometimes social work professionals. Programs often employ staff members from the students' communities, giving them an advantage in understanding issues that students may face day to day outside of the school building. Typically, after-school staff members, referred to as youth workers, are younger than the teachers that students work with during the school day. By encouraging interactions between youth workers and students, programs can foster close, trusting, and mentoring relationships. This staffing structure also makes the program more approachable for parents, who sometimes feel intimidated by their students' school due to their own negative educational experiences, undocumented immigrant status, or other barriers.

Since their inception, TASC-model after-school programs have been studied extensively by Policy Studies Associates (PSA; e.g., Reisner et al., 2004; Russell et al., 2007). The firm provided evaluation services to TASC to help the organization make informed decisions on program services, as well as to document how TASC has impacted schools and youth. In both studies of TASC (Reisner et al., 2004; Russell et al., 2007), PSA examined the academic and prosocial outcomes of youth. Regarding academic outcomes, the evaluations demonstrated that students in TASC-model after-school programs improved in student achievement as evidenced by standardized test score gains and improved school attendance rates (Reisner et al., 2004; Russell et al., 2007). The results of the evaluation by Reisner and colleagues (2004) showed that third- through eighth-grade participants in TASC-model programs ($N = 5,543$) had greater gains in their math standardized scores than matched nonparticipants, specifically with an effect size of .13 for one year of program participation and .79 for two years of program participation. In addition, there is evidence that participation in TASC-model after-school programs has long-lasting positive benefits for participants. Russell and colleagues (2007) conducted a follow-up study with former participants to examine whether youth experiences in TASC-model after-school programs during the middle school grades were associated with positive educational outcomes in high school. The results of the study showed that former TASC participants ($N = 2,390$) had significantly higher school attendance rates in the ninth grade than nonparticipants, with a demonstrated effect size of .26 (Russell et al., 2007). The results of this study showed that the academic benefits of attending TASC-model after-school programs in middle school can last well into students' high school years (Russell et al., 2007).

PSA's evaluation of TASC-model after-school programs also examined the implementation of activities that foster prosocial development and how participation in these activities impacted participants' social outcomes. In the first few years of the initiative, TASC-model after-school programs increased the amount of activities that centered on youth working together as a group, such as peer discussion, conflict resolution, and life skills instruction (Reisner et al., 2004). As previously discussed, schools are often limited in providing opportunities for student learning outside of the core subject areas, such as opportunities to have peer discussion and teach students about life skills. Programs fill this gap by providing youth opportunities to positively engage with their peers and encouraging positive social interactions between youth and staff members. In fact, Kahne and colleagues (2001) reported that adolescents report having more positive interactions with after-school staff members than they do with their classroom teachers. Specifically, inner-city African-American boys described their schools as notably less supportive than their after-school programs (Kahne et al., 2001). Furthermore, supportive relationships with after-school staff members are particularly important for youth who have detached relationships with their parents (Mahoney, Schweder, & Stattin, 2002). Youth who participate in after-school activities are less likely to have symptoms of depression, especially when youth deem a group leader at their after-school program particularly supportive (Mahoney et al., 2002).

In PSA's evaluation of TASC-model after-school programs, students reported that their after-school programs provided them with a positive climate in which they could develop positive relationships with their peers and adult staff members (Reisner et al., 2004). Deeper examination of TASC-model after-school programs showed that many middle school programs made explicit efforts to promote positive relationships between the staff members and the youth (Russell et al., 2007). In middle school programs that offered team-oriented activities, where staff established clear expectations for their interactions, youth were most likely to show positive peer interactions (Russell et al., 2007). Students also reported that they held a high level of trust for the staff members at their programs, and this was evident in the evaluators' observations of after-school program activities, in which staff modeled active listening skills and promoted positive behaviors while encouraging students' skill development (Russell et al., 2007). The opportunities that TASC-model after-school programs provide for positive interactions with peers and adults are very important because it is during these types of interactions that children and youth are able to practice and experience cooperation, mutuality, and reciprocity, which contribute to their prosocial development (Eisenberg et al., 2006).

BOYS AND GIRLS CLUBS OF AMERICA

Like TASC-model after-school programs, Boys and Girls Clubs of America have also provided children and youth with a safe place to learn and grow outside of school in the company of supportive adults. The first club opened over 150 years ago. Today, clubs serve approximately 4.2 million children and youth between the ages of six and eighteen in four thousand clubs around the country (Boys and Girls Clubs of America, n.d., *Facts and Figures*). The mission of the initiative is to enable young people, especially those who are disadvantaged, to reach their full potential as productive, caring, responsible citizens (Arbreton et al., 2009). Typically, clubs serve ethnically and racially diverse children and youth from mostly low-income backgrounds (Arbreton et al., 2009). To achieve their mission, Boys and Girls Clubs offer a variety of programs to children and youth that aim to do the following: (1) build their character and leadership skills; (2) help them to succeed in their academics and explore different career fields; (3) develop healthy habits and life skills; (4) foster interest, engagement, and appreciation for the arts; and (5) provide them with the opportunity to play sports, stay fit, and socialize in positive ways with their peers (Boys and Girls Clubs of America, n.d., *What We Do*).

Many studies have shown the positive effects that participation in Boys and Girls Clubs has on children and youth, including improved academic performance and attitudes towards school, reduction of risky or delinquent behaviors, giving children and youth increased access to technology, and helping them to develop and reach career goals (for a synthesis of this research, see Arbreton et al., 2005). In 2005, researchers from Public/Private Ventures began a longitudinal study examining the effects of participation in Boys and Girls Clubs on several aspects of youth development (Arbreton et al., 2009). Unlike studies that came before, the goal of this study was to understand the effects of the "whole club experience" on children and youth as opposed to focusing on specific outcomes separately (Arbreton et al., 2009, p. ii).

Over four hundred seventh- and eighth-grade participants from ten clubs across the country took part in the study. Most participants were black or Hispanic, and over 70 percent received free or reduced-price lunch at school (Arbreton et al., 2009). The researchers followed participants over a two-and-a-half-year period, through their transition into high school. The transition into high school is commonly considered a tumultuous time for adolescents, and so effects of participation during this period were of particular interest to the researchers. For this age group specifically, Boys and Girls Clubs typically emphasize the importance of offering a breadth of activities, opportunities for youth leadership, a focus on positive relationships between youth and staff members, and a space and time for teens to socialize and relax informally (Arbreton et al., 2009).

The researchers surveyed participants twice over the course of the study. The researchers also reviewed participants' club attendance records, and they interviewed several participants and their club staff members (Arbreton et al., 2009). Specifically, the researchers looked to answer how club participation may have affected youth in the following three outcome categories: good character and citizenship, academic success, and healthy lifestyles (Arbreton et al., 2009). Regarding academic outcomes, the researchers found that participation in clubs was associated with significantly fewer unexcused absences and a greater sense of effort and confidence toward schoolwork. Furthermore, the researchers found significant participant effects for reduced risk of drug use, alcohol, cigarettes, and engaging in sexual intercourse (Arbreton et al., 2009). For the remainder of this discussion, we will focus on the good character and citizenship outcomes, as these outcomes most readily relate to participants' prosocial development.

The researchers included several questions on surveys and interview protocols pertaining to good character and citizenship outcomes, which are correlates of prosocial behaviors, including questions about participants' display of fairness, integrity, open-mindedness, social competence, negative problem solving and positive conflict resolution, aggression, and shyness (Arbreton et al., 2009). Over the two-and-a-half-year period, Boys and Girls Club participants showed improvements in a number of these outcomes, including significant decreases in their levels of both shyness and aggression (Arbreton et al., 2009). They also showed significant improvements in integrity (defined as knowing right from wrong), engagement in community service projects, and leadership. Furthermore, 91 percent of participants who were surveyed in the study reported that they had opportunities to cooperate with peers at their clubs, and 91 percent reported feeling like they belonged at their club (Arbreton et al., 2009).

In interviews with staff members, the researchers asked how the clubs specifically contributed to these positive results regarding character and citizenship (Arbreton et al., 2009). Most staff members reported that they contributed to youth's positive development by giving them attention and providing them with opportunities to learn in both formal and informal ways (Arbreton et al., 2009). Similarly, participants believed that adult staff members were very supportive of them and found the staff members to contribute significantly to their development of good character and citizenship. During interviews by the researchers, staff members and participants reported that youth learned about a variety of important things at their clubs, including respecting others, collaboration and sportsmanship, listening to others, and being open-minded. Another recurring theme that emerged from the interviews included how staff members taught participants how to take responsibility for themselves and their actions and how to have self-confidence. The participants discussed how they learned about these things in a variety of ways, including specific activities offered at the clubs, informal conversations with staff members, and watching staff members themselves model positive behaviors (Arbreton et al., 2009). As shown in this study, after-school staff members play a vital role in the benefits participants receive. In supportive and structured after-school programs, mentoring in particular has been shown to be an important aspect of the program design in supporting positive social and academic outcomes (DuBois, Holloway, Valentine, & Cooper, 2002).

4-H CLUBS

Another out-of-school initiative that has been shown to influence the prosocial development of children and youth is 4-H Clubs. 4-H is the nation's largest youth development organization, with more than six million youth participating across the country (4-H, n.d., *Get Involved*). The first program was established in 1902, and their mission has evolved over time to help youth learn leadership skills and become more proactive in their communities. Youth from all parts of the country and across the world are served, and they rely on adult volunteers and mentors to implement their programming (4-H, n.d., *History*).

The national 4-H curriculum has three different concentrations: science, healthy living, and citizenship. Programs that implement the citizenship curriculum aim to engage youth in their communities and help them build decision-making skills and civic knowledge. Members participate in citizenship projects to help them accomplish these goals, and this programming is delivered through clubs, camps, and in-school and after-school services (4-H, n.d., *Curriculum*). One way that 4-H has tried to increase citizenship is through community service learning projects. Through these projects, which range from 4-H youth reading to younger children in their neighborhoods, to planting flowers near their schools, to maintaining their local parks and recreational centers, youth actively participate in service experiences that provide a direct benefit for the needs of their community. They are also given time to reflect upon their experiences and talk with their peers, which serves as a great way to connect academics and character education (Phelps & Kotrlik, 2007).

The Institute for Applied Research in Youth Development started the 4-H study of positive youth development in the 2002/3 school year (Lerner et al., 2009). This study employed a longitudinal sequential design starting with fifth-grade students, and their most recent report includes findings from the sixth wave of data collection, when the original sample had reached the tenth grade. In this report, both cross-sectional (N = 2,371) and longitudinal (N = 797) findings were presented, and 4-H participants were compared to peers in a matched comparison group who chose their levels of participation in other out-of-school programs. The cross-sectional sample of tenth graders had significantly higher scores than their peers on measures of positive youth development and contributions to others and their community. The longitudinal 4-H group also reported significantly higher levels of contribution to others and their community than their peers. In addition, the longitudinal 4-H sample scored significantly higher than their peers on a measure of civic identity and engagement, which includes items that assess participants' civic duty, civic helping (time spent helping others in informal settings), and civic activities (time spent in formal activities giving back to others). The evaluators attributed these differences, in large part, to the developmental asset building that goes on in these programs. Prior research has shown that effective youth development organizations foster positive relationships between youth and adults, and, on average, 4-H participants reported having a significantly higher number of mentors than their counterparts (Lerner et al., 2009).

Research derived from this study was used to learn more about the positive youth development and prosocial behavior that results from participation in these programs. Lerner and colleagues (2005) used data from the first wave of data collection to provide empirical evidence for the 5-C model of positive youth development. Based on literature reviews and the experiences of practitioners, researchers have long used this model to conceptualize positive youth development, consisting namely of (1) competence, defined as having a positive view of one's actions in specific areas; (2) confidence, defined as having an internal sense of positive self-worth and self-efficacy; (3) connection, defined as having positive bonds with people and institutions; (4) character, defined as having respect for societal and cultural norms; and (5) caring (Jelicic, Bobek, Phelps, Lerner, & Lerner, 2007; Lerner et al., 2009). Researchers have theorized that the presence of the five Cs in an adolescent leads to the emergence of a sixth C, contribution, which involves youth contributing positively to themselves, their families, and their communities (Lerner et al., 2005). This theory has been tested with data from the 4-H study. Using the first two waves of data, Jelicic and colleagues (2007) assessed whether fifth-grade scores on positive youth development covaried across time with measures of community contribution. Community contribution was measured as a composite of twelve items divided into the following four subsets: leadership, service, helping, and ideology. The authors found that positive youth development scores in grade 5 predicted contribution in grade 6 (Jelicic et al., 2007). Thus, participation in programs such as 4-H, which promote positive youth development, has been empirically tested and correlated with youth making more community contributions. Researchers have therefore hypothesized that the availability of activities that support the five Cs help to guide youth toward making meaningful and positive contributions to society (Lerner et al., 2009). Youth development programs like 4-H often provide the best opportunity for younger youth to connect to and contribute to their communities, thus contributing to their prosocial development.

Researchers have also examined the developmental trajectories of 4-H participants. Lewin-Bizan and colleagues (2010) sought to identify trajectories in positive youth development and contribution across six waves of data collected for the 4-H study. Overall, the authors found four trajectories for positive youth development, and the majority of 4-H participants (67.3 percent) clustered into the two highest-trajectory groups. For contribution, four trajectories were also found, and the majority of participants (79.5 percent) clustered in the two moderately high trajectory groups. Lerner and colleagues (2009) compared the trajectories for positive youth development and contribution of 4-H participants to those of youth in other out-of-school-time programs. Overall, youth who had participated in 4-H at one point throughout the fifth- to ninth-grade period were significantly more likely to have high trajectories for positive youth development and contribution. Youth who participated in 4-H for at least one year were over two times more likely than their peers to be in the highest contribution trajectory (Lerner et al., 2009). While youth who participated in 4-H during middle and/or high school appear to be on a healthy developmental trajectory, there are multiple contextual influences that can affect these pathways. Using the first and third wave of 4-H data, Urban, Lewin-Bizan, and Lerner (2009) examined whether neighborhood assets moderated the relationship between extracurricular activity involvement and positive and negative developmental outcomes. Overall, researchers found that for girls living in low-asset neighborhoods and for boys living in high-asset neighborhoods, low to moderate levels of activity involvement predicted increases in the five Cs (Urban, Lewin-Bizan, & Lerner, 2009). While more research needs to be conducted on the relationships between activity involvement, gender, and neighborhood quality, these studies provide evidence that positive prosocial outcomes emerge from 4-H participation.

Because of the expansiveness of 4-H programs, which operate in many different youth development settings, much of the data used in the 4-H study of positive youth development was not collected in after-school settings; however, 4-H after-school programs are prominent throughout the country, and many of the positive findings referenced above are relevant to out-of-school-time settings. It is clear that 4-H provides opportunities for participants to help their communities and develop relationships with adult mentors. While the discussion of the studies cited above centered on prosocial outcomes that result from participation, it should be noted that other benefits, such as decreases in the emergence of depressive symptoms and risk behaviors, were also found for 4-H participants (Urban et al., 2009).

CONCLUSION

As illustrated through a review of the research in this chapter, after-school programs not only provide a safe place for children and youth to learn and grow, but they also serve as ideal contexts for their prosocial development in several different ways. First, they provide children and youth with a safe place to relax and socialize, where they have the time and opportunity to build strong, reciprocal relationships with friends and positive adult role models. These relationships then serve as a foundation for them to explore and develop new interests and talents and to build confidence and self-esteem. After-school programs, such as the ones described in this chapter, also look to engage children and youth more fully in their communities through special programming and projects that aim to improve the neighborhoods where they and their families live. Through these programs and projects, children and youth learn how to contribute to others and their community, thereby learning how to become responsible and proactive citizens. Especially at a time when schools are held accountable mostly by their students' standardized test scores in mathematics and English language arts, and most of students' time in school is spent focusing on test preparation as a result, after-school programs may provide some children and youth with their only opportunity to learn, practice, and appreciate what it means to be prosocial.

REFERENCES

Afterschool Alliance. (2010a). *21st Community Learning Centers: Providing after-school supports to communities nationwide* (Fact sheet). Retrieved June 1, 2011, from http://www.afterschoolalliance.org/documents/factsResearch/21stCCLC_Factsheet.pdf

Afterschool Alliance. (2010b). *America after 3PM: From big cities to small towns.* Retrieved June 1, 2011, from http://www.afterschoolalliance.org/documents/AA3PM_Cities_Towns_10122010.pdf

The After-School Corporation. (2011). *ExpandED schools: A new way to increase kids' learning time & opportunity.* Retrieved from: http://www.tascorp.org/section/aboutus.

Arbreton, A., Bradshaw, M., Sheldon, J., & Pepper, S. (2009). *Making every day count: Boys and Girls Clubs' role in promoting positive outcomes for teens.* Philadelphia: Public/Private Ventures.

Arbreton, A. J. A., Sheldon, J., & Herrera, C. (2005). *Beyond safe havens: A synthesis of 20 years of research on the Boys & Girls Club.* Philadelphia: Public/Private Ventures.

Blank, S. (2005). *Hours that count: Using after-school programs to help prevent risky behaviors and keep kids safe.* New York: The After-School Corporation.

Boys and Girls Clubs of America. (n.d.). *Facts and figures.* Retrieved from http://bgca.org/whoweare/Pages/FactsFigures.aspx

Boys and Girls Clubs of America. (n.d.). *What we do.* Retrieved from http://www.bgca.org/whatwedo/Pages/WhatWeDo.aspx

Carlson, S. A., Fulton, J. E., Lee, S. M., Maynard, L. M., Brown, D. R., Kohl, H. W., III, et al. (2008). Physical education and academic achievement in elementary school: Data from the early childhood longitudinal study. *American Journal of Public Health, 98*(4), 721–727.

Deasy, R. J. (Ed.). (2002). *Critical links: Learning in the arts and student academic and social development.* Washington, DC: Arts Education Partnership.

DuBois, D. L., Holloway, B. E., Valentine, J. C., & Cooper, H. (2002). Effectiveness of mentoring programs for youth: A meta-analytic review. *American Journal of Community Psychology, 30,* 157–197.

Durlak, J. A., & Weissberg, R. P. (2007). *The impact of after-school programs that promote personal and social skills.* Chicago: Collaborative for Academic, Social, and Emotional Learning. Retrieved June 1, 2011, from http://casel.org/publications/the-impact-of-after-school-programs-that-promote-personal-and-social-skills

Durlak, J. A., Weissberg, R. P., & Pachan, M. (2010). A meta-analysis of after-school programs that seek to promote personal and social skills in children and adolescents. *American Journal of Community Psychology, 45*(3–4), 294–309.

Eisenberg, N., Fabes, R. A., & Spinrad, T. L. (2006). Prosocial development. In W. Damon & R. M. Lerner (Eds.), *Handbook of child psychology: Social, emotional, and personality development* (pp. 646–718). Hoboken, NJ: Wiley.

4-H. (n.d.). *Curriculum*. Retrieved from http://www.4-h.org/resource-library/curriculum

4-H. (n.d.). *Get involved*. Retrieved from http://www.4-h.org/get-involved

4-H. (n.d.). *History*. Retrieved from http://www.4-h.org/about/4-h-history

Ginsburg, K. R. (2007). The importance of play in promoting healthy child development and maintaining strong parent–child bonds. *Pediatrics, 119*(1), 182–191.

Grey, A. C. (2009). No Child Left Behind in art education policy: A review of key recommendations for arts language revisions. *Arts Education Policy Review, 111*(1), 8–15.

Halpern, R. (2002). A different kind of child development institution: The history of after-school programs for low-income children. *Teachers College Record, 104*(2), 178–211.

Hertz-Lazarowitz, R. (1983). Prosocial behavior in the classroom. *Academic Psychology Bulletin, 5*(2), 319–338.

Hofferth, S. (1995). Out-of-school time: Risk and opportunity. In T. Swartz & K. Wright (Eds.), *America's working poor* (pp. 123–153). South Bend, IN: Notre Dame University Press.

James-Burdumy, S., Dynarski, M., Moore, M., Deke, J., Mansfield, W., & Pistorino, C. (2005). *When schools stay open late: The national evaluation of the 21st Century Community Learning Centers program: Final report*. Washington, DC: U.S. Department of Education, Institute of Education Sciences, National Center for Education Evaluation and Regional Assistance. Retrieved from http://www.mathematica-mpr.com/publications/pdfs/21stfinal.pdf

Jelicic, H., Bobek, D. L., Phelps, E., Lerner, R. M., & Lerner, J. V. (2007). Using positive youth development to predict contribution and risk behaviors in early adolescence: Findings from the first two waves of the 4-H study of positive youth development. *International Journal of Behavioral Development, 31*(3), 263–273.

Kahne, J., Nagaoka, J., Brown, A., O'Brien, J., Quinn, T., & Thiede, K. (2001). Assessing after-school programs as contexts for youth development. *Youth & Society, 32*(4), 421–446.

Lauer, P. A., Akiba, M., Wilkerson, S. B., Apthorp, H. S., Snow, D., & Martin-Glenn, M. L. (2006). Out-of-school-time programs: A meta-analysis of effects for at-risk students. *Review of Educational Research, 76*(2), 275–313.

Lerner, R. M., Lerner, J. V., Almerigi, J., Theokas, C., Phelps, E., Gestsdottir, S., et al. (2005). Positive youth development, participation in community youth development programs, and community contributions of fifth-grade adolescents: Findings from the first wave of the 4-H study of positive youth development. *Journal of Early Adolescence, 25*(1), 17–71.

Lerner, R. M., Lerner, J. V., & Colleagues. (2009). *Waves of the future: Report of the findings from the first six years of the 4-H study of positive youth development*. Medford, MA: Tufts University. Retrieved June 9, 2011, from www.4-h.org/uploadedFiles/About_Folder/Research/Tufts_Data/4-H-Positive-Youth-Development-Study-Wave-6.pdf

Lewin-Bizan, S., Lynch, A. D., Fay, K., Schmid, K., McPherran, C., Lerner, J. V., et al. (2010). Trajectories of positive and negative behaviors from early- to middle-adolescence. *Journal of Youth and Adolescence, 39*(7), 751–763.

Mahoney, J. L. (2000). School extracurricular activity participation as a moderator in the development of antisocial patterns. *Child Development, 71*(2), 502–516.

Mahoney, J. L., Schweder, A. E., & Stattin, H. (2002). Structured after-school activities as a moderator of depressed mood for adolescents with detached relations to their parents. *Journal of Community Psychology, 30*(1), 69–86.

Mahoney, J. L., & Stattin, H. (2000). Leisure activities and adolescent anti-social behavior: The role of structure and social context. *Journal of Adolescence, 23*(2), 113–127.

Miller, B. M. (2005). *Pathways to success for youth: What counts in after-school* (Massachusetts After-School Research Study [MARS] Report). Retrieved June 1, 2011, from http://support unitedway.org/files/MARS-Report.pdf

Naftzger, N., Bonney, C., Donahue, T., Hutchinson, C., Margolin, J., & Vinson, M. (2007). *21st century community learning centers (21st CCLC) analytic support for evaluation and program monitoring: An overview of the 21st CCLC performance data: 2005–06.* Naperville, IL: Learning Point Associates.

Pederson, P. V. (2007). What is measured is treasured: The impact of the No Child Left Behind Act on non-assessed subjects. *The Clearing House: A Journal of Educational Strategies, Issues, and Ideas, 80*(6), 287–291.

Pettit, G. S., Bates, J. E., Dodge, K. A., & Meece, D. W. (1999). The impact of after-school peer contact on early adolescent externalizing problems is moderated by parental monitoring, perceived neighborhood safety, and prior adjustment. *Child Development, 70*(3), 768–778.

Phelps, C. S., & Kotrlik, J. W. (2007). The relationship between participation in community service-learning projects and personal and leadership life skills development in 4-H leadership activities. *Journal of Agricultural Education, 48*(4), 67–81.

Redd, Z., Brooks, J., & McGarvey, A. (2002, August). *Educating America's youth: What makes a difference* (Research Brief). Washington, DC: Child Trends.

Reisner, E. R., White, R. N., Russell, C. A., & Birmingham, J. (2004). *Building quality, scale, and effectiveness in after-school programs: Summary report of the TASC evaluation.* Washington, DC: Policy Studies Associates.

Russell, C. A., Mielke, M. B., Miller, T. D., & Johnson, J. C. (2007). *After-school programs and high school success: Analysis of post-program educational patterns of former middle-grades TASC participants* (Report to the Charles Stewart Mott Foundation). Washington, DC: Policy Studies Associates.

Urban, J. B., Lewin-Bizan, S., & Lerner, R. M. (2009). The role of neighborhood ecological assets and activity involvement in youth developmental outcomes: Differential impacts of asset poor and asset rich neighborhoods. *Journal of Applied Developmental Psychology, 30*(5), 601–614.

Vandell, D. L., Reisner, E. R., & Pierce, K. M. (2007). *Outcomes linked to high-quality afterschool programs: Longitudinal findings from the Study of Promising Afterschool Programs* (Report to the Charles Stewart Mott Foundation). Washington, DC: Policy Studies Associates.

Case Study 16A

The Core Five Essentials: A Prosocial Application in After-School Settings

MICHAEL W. CORRIGAN, PHILIP F. VINCENT,
AND SCOTT HALL

Each day, after the traditional school day ends and the last bell rings, millions of students attend after-school programs. For many, the after-school program is housed in their school. Others are picked up by various buses from day cares or youth groups (e.g., Boy's Club, YMCA) and then taken to a central location to wait for a parent to pick them up after work. Although many of these programs offer valuable services essential to working families, from our experience as education researchers, teachers, and parents, we know that a significant percentage of programs could do much more to complement the physical, academic, and social development of our youth. This concern for the level of quality in after-school care and the support students receive became even more relevant after consulting for a state education agency on a project that asked us to focus on researching their statewide after-school programs. As a result, we decided to develop resources to help the directors of after-school programs experience greater success. This case study provides an introduction to the five core essential components that our research and field experiences led us to include in our new program called the *Core5 After-School Program*.

When assessing if an after-school program is doing well or not, or reaching its full potential, there are a number of questions that should be asked. For example, is the program well organized? Is it based on what research tells us is working or beneficial to child or adolescent development? Is it designed to maximize the time spent with students, or is it more reflective of a haphazard "let us manage the chaos" design? Is the child receiving an opportunity for exercise, enrichment, nutrition, academics, and social support? Or is the after-school program more of a holding center to await parental pickup, or as some after-school directors have described it, "a glorified babysitting service"? Perhaps it is something in between. Unfortunately, with limited staff either available or affordable to design and manage a higher-quality program, from what we have witnessed all too often, many programs merely encourage students to complete homework on their own before socializing, playing, or consuming media. All too often, after-school programs do not capitalize on

Figure 16.A1.   Photograph by Peter C. McIntosh, Columbus, OH, pcmcreations.com.

this wonderful opportunity to provide the extra support a student needs to develop physically, academically, and socially. All too often schools overlook how this time, if approached more proactively and strategically, can provide great benefits to what we are trying to accomplish during the school day.

The question we asked when designing the Core5 After-School Program was what could or should educators attempt to ultimately accomplish in the ideal after-school program? As a result of our research and exploration into what exists and is missing in after-school programs, we concluded that there are five core components that could be fit into a normal after-school day. Those five core components are: fitness, nutrition, character, enrichment, and increasing parent involvement. Although Core5 is a new program that is still evolving, we want to share how after-school programs can improve by adopting or more thoroughly infusing all or some of these five core components. First, let us address some research-based considerations that guided our thought process to develop an after-school effort focused on supporting the development of the complete child.

RESEARCH ON ISSUES RELATED TO AFTER-SCHOOL AND CHILD DEVELOPMENT
According to the Center on Education Policy (2007), in an effort to focus more on curricula, given that school success is tied to achievement tests as dictated by No Child Left Behind, many schools have reduced the amount of physical education and recess time, which used to provide children with a chance to have a break, get a little exercise, and expend that restless energy built up from countless minutes of instruction. Although we understand the urge to try and find more time to teach the core content areas one is held accountable for, it troubles us to see such valuable time for allowing children to be creative, use their imagination, and exercise being allotted to what in most cases appears to be more direct instruction of standards-based curricula. We are also concerned about the rising tide of childhood obesity in the United States, which not only impacts the physical fitness and health of our children but has implications for their academic and social development. According to the Centers for Disease Control and Prevention (CDC), childhood obesity has more than tripled in the past thirty years, and the percentage of children aged six to eleven years in the United States who were obese increased from 7 percent in 1980 to nearly 20 percent in 2008 (Centers for Disease Control and Prevention, 2011). Similarly, the percentage of adolescents aged twelve to nineteen years who were obese increased from 5 percent to 18 percent over the same period. Besides the obvious benefits of physical fitness to the health of the body, we also recognize the neurological benefits that come from the exercise-induced endorphins that produce happiness and more efficient brain functions. Therefore, research supports the need for more exercise in our students' lives, and if physical education and recess are being reduced during the school day to make room for more instruction, then after school offers a great opportunity to address such issues of concern related to lack of student exercise.

The other component that complements exercise is nutrition. We know that many after-school programs offer nutritional snacks to kids, but in our travels we have also seen many schools and programs offer not so nutritional snacks. For those that haven't fully considered the impact of nutrition, what might happen if "snack time" actually provided a nutritional snack as well as quality nutritional information to complement the exercise? While we are developing physically fit students, which research also connects to better sense of self and a whole host of variables beneficial to education and development (Ormrod, 2011), and feeding the bodies after such exercise, we can do even more and teach them why nutrition is important. As some after-school programs have realized, taking this nutritional lesson a step further and sharing it with parents can be even more beneficial. As Epstein (1995) suggests, we should try to connect with parents. After school is a perfect time for making such connections and offering support programs that assist families with health and nutrition planning. Perhaps if we worked with the students and the parents (or guardians) on choosing and planning for positive nutritional choices within a conservative budget, families (especially lower-income parents) might make more positive nutritional choices that lead to better body and brain development. Such efforts clearly hold a strong connection to students performing better during the school day.

A comprehensive after-school program could also include lessons and opportunities to help a child develop positive social skills and better character. If the exercise and nutrition comprise about forty-five minutes of the after-school program, we still have time to utilize productively. Approximately twenty to thirty minutes could be used for structured activities that focus on addressing prosocial education issues such as bullying, social-emotional learning, and character development beneficial to better behavior and effort. As this handbook has illustrated, there is a great amount of research that illuminates the benefits of focusing on prosocial behavior.

One could also provide structured opportunities for children to receive and possibly give tutorial support to improve academic outcomes. There are a number of tutoring designs that could be used within after-school settings with a limited staff. Peer tutoring and collaborative learning are just two of the ways a limited staff could get kids focused on completing their homework assignments or working on content areas in which they need assistance or extra support.

Last, and surely not least, we decided that information could be provided to parents on how they can better support their child's social, emotional, nutritional, physical, and academic development, because, as research has shown (Corrigan, Grove, & Vincent, 2011), parental involvement is paramount to academic and prosocial developmental success. This was our line of thought for creating an ideal after-school program. And as it turns out, there is more research to support such efforts.

A 2008 study from the Harvard Family Research Project titled "After-School Programs in the 21st Century: Their Potential and What It Takes to Achieve It" validates what is needed to develop quality after-school programs to enhance the educational and developmental outcomes of students. Their analysis of multiple studies indicated that academic achievement can be enhanced through after-school programs that involve such activities as quality support, enrichment activities, hands-on activities, apprenticeships, exposure to arts, recreational opportunities, and skill building. Their analysis of multiple studies also noted that "after-school programs can contribute to better food choice, increased physical activity, increased knowledge of nutrition and health practices, reduction in BMI, improved blood pressure, and improved body image" (Little, Wimer, & Weiss, 2008, p. 8). Furthermore, a large study of after-school programs (Durlak & Weissberg, 2007) addressing social-emotional development noted that

> students involved in quality after-school programming designed to facilitate their social/emotional development experienced decreased behavioral problems; improved social and communication skills and/or relationships with others (peer, parents, teachers); increased self-confidence, self-esteem, and self-efficacy; lower levels of depression and anxiety; development of initiative; and improved feelings and attitudes toward self and school. (p. 6)

These attributes and similar others have been shown to positively impact the achievement of students (Barton & Coley, 2007; Henderson & Mapp, 2002; Sheldon & Epstein, 2005).

CORE5 IN PRACTICE

So how might the more comprehensive infusion of these five core components play out in after-school programs? We understand that not every component will be utilized every day. Some days there are various enrichment programs or activities (art, music, etc.) that are planned that might take up most of the after-school day time. On some days it just might be sunny outside, and in our opinion kids should be allowed to just go out and play. This theoretical model is designed to be the foundation for an after-school program or a resource for after-school programs wanting to complement their existing efforts. What we set out to do is design the ideal program to help others create a solid after-school program that connects to the efforts and expectations we face during the school day. What we did was combine all of the good aspects of successful after-school programs and complement them with what we know from educational psychology, academic support research, prosocial education, and health and wellness. We wanted to develop a program that can be delivered over a two-hour after-school time period with maximum benefits. Being successful in after-school programming is quite dependent upon the quality of the staff as well as the staff-student ratio. Given these and other challenges, after-school directors need support to accomplish the design proposed within the Core5 After-School Program. Therefore, to actually accomplish such goals, a program must be provided the tools needed to be successful. Thus, our goal in developing Core5 was to make it easy for a director to infuse the five components.

Figure 16.A2.　Photograph by Peter C. McIntosh, Columbus, OH, pcmcreations.com.

To illustrate how this might play out in a model Core5 after-school day (contained within the building of a traditional day school), we will consider the following example. This is how a day in a school using Core5 would ideally operate when a school infuses all five components.

The third end-of-school bell has just rung. The first bell was for the car riders and walkers, and the second bell was for the bus riders. The third bell was for students participating in the after-school enrichment program. The after-school program has a director, two full-time staff, and a network of community volunteers. The average daily attendance is seventy students. The after-school program makes use of the school cafeteria for multiple activities, but on this day, and indeed during many days, the gym is where the students start with the after-school exercise program. The students are greeted by the staff as they enter the gym. The majority of the students are in grades K–4, although there are around fifteen fifth and sixth graders. Book bags are placed around the edge of the gym, and the students move into their places to begin their after-school exercise program. The older students assist the younger students as they get in line, space themselves between other students, and prepare themselves for the video-based twenty-five-minute exercise program that is projected on a large screen via the computer so that all participants can see the video. Two of the teachers and two volunteers are also "participating" in the exercise to help the students maintain program integrity and also to get a little aerobic exercise for themselves! Both the staff and students are participating in the fitness program designed to exercise the heart, burn fat, and also develop strength, flexibility, and mobility for all participants.

The Core5 video's fitness instructor and the Core5 students in the video are very engaging. If a fitness program is to be successful with kids, it must be fun and engaging. Each week the Core5 videos focus on a different theme, and this week the students and some of the staff and volunteers are taking part in the "martial arts" theme. The focus is on keeping the moves simple and having the participants moving and engaged throughout the exercise period. Students are practicing their "kicks" as well as working to develop their arm strength and balance during this segment. The teachers are standing near the primary students to ensure they are giving it their best and are respectful of the space needed for all participants. The thirty-minute fitness program time passes quickly, as most things that are fun to students do! At the end of the fitness program, students are encouraged to practice their habits of respect toward all and to keep their caring actions focused toward each other. The students then move to the cafeteria to get a snack.

The snacks are wholesome and nutritional. There are fruits and vegetables available, as well as some more traditional snack foods that have reduced fat, sugar, and salt. The drink of choice is water, although some low-fat milk is also available. Today the students are watching a Core5 nutrition video that highlights an expert in nutrition sharing helpful hints and lessons. They are also given a flyer that the teachers downloaded off the Core5 website that helps them and their parents chart the foods they are eating. The students have around fifteen minutes to enjoy their snacks before moving into the character focus part of today's program.

Today there is a follow-up discussion planned concerning a Trevor Romain video on bullying that the group watched the day before. From opinions and insights expressed by the kids during the discussion and the looks on some of their faces, you can tell the video and discussion had an impact on their thoughts today. So, with some exercise out of the way to get the heart pumping and the endorphins flowing, a little nutrition to feed the mind and body, and a short activity to help all feel more welcome and wanted in the school, it is now time to get a little work done on academics.

Each student brings work that needs to be completed to the cafeteria. This is the tutorial and enrichment part of the program. Hopefully the students have written their homework assignments in their agendas. These are then checked as needed by the after-school staff and volunteers. The K–2 students have access to various materials including reading books, some appropriate worksheets, and some skill-building games. The third- through sixth-grade students take advantage of this time to work on their homework or receive additional tutoring from the teachers, volunteers, and other students. This school has established additional support from older students within the program who choose to tutor the younger students, as well as some students from the high school and a local college who are volunteering their time in a prescheduled time slot to assist the younger students. Student tutors may not tutor every day. Sometimes they have a fairly large amount of homework to do and choose to work on it. Other times, the tutor may choose to play games with his or her peers. This works out fine since there are staff and community volunteers who show up on a regular schedule and are available to assist the students.

From watching videos and receiving training on how to design after-school tutoring that works, the staff has developed a new system that is showing signs of success. The staff designated an area of the cafeteria for students needing assistance in mathematics and an area for those seeking assistance in reading. Those who are comfortable with the assignments and who do not need any tutoring can work independently around the tables focusing on their homework. These students are allowed to have quiet conversations as long as the staff and volunteers feel that work is being completed. Although some might think students would struggle to master this technique, these students have become comfortable, through practice tied to expectations, focusing on their homework and having quiet conversations. It is the social aspect of having a shared goal for all students to complete their homework that makes such an academic focus more attractive to students. This is a chance for older students to model for the younger students what good students do. Students who have excellent grades and have completed or gotten a good start on their homework (and feel they can complete their assignments at home) can then move back to the gym for some supervised play. On a nice day, they may go outside and play on the playground or just hang out and talk. On one recent day, a staff member was working with some students on "competitive jump-roping" while several other students were walking together around an established area marked off for mile laps. As the research shared earlier highlights, the strength of this after-school program's efforts lies in its ability to provide physical exercise, good nutrition, character building, tutoring, and homework time for the students. In addition, the after-school staff seeks out additional enrichment activities that might be intertwined within the program. This balance is essential to ensure that the students and parents value and support the after-school time.

It is now nearly 4:45 in the afternoon. Some parents are beginning to trickle into the building to collect their children. Each parent is greeted by a staff member and in many cases by a volunteer. There is a great sense of warmth on the part of all adults toward each other. If a child is struggling with the routines, a time to talk with the child and the parents is established. At the school used in this example, it seems that parents and volunteers always have something good to say to each other. Many of the parents have had some recent economic difficulties. The after-school staff provides some material concerning "Quick Training for Jobs Now!" programs at the local community college. Several of the parents took advantage of a training program in welding that was held during the day, evenings, and on the weekends. Within twelve weeks, two of the parents had their basic welding certifications and were hired by two local firms with a decent salary and benefits. Several other parents received information and training on becoming certified nursing assistants (CNA). The staff and volunteers continually receive acknowledgment of their efforts to support the families. One parent remarked yesterday that the previous week's handout under the College Club letterhead, "Talking with Your Child's Teacher," really helped in having a positive teacher–parent conference. The director responded by explaining how College Club will be meeting formally in the next week to begin a series of workshops on how to think about education after the high school years. On this day there is a handout that is given to each parent, in Spanish and English, which provides some helpful suggestions on planning nutritionally economical meals and also on how to judge television programs that are appropriate and inappropriate for young viewers. With a hug and handshakes, the parents take their children home. The last student leaves at 5:50. The volunteers and staff quickly process the day and talk about what is to be done tomorrow. By 6:00, everyone is heading home to their families.

Notice that all five elements of our Core5 after-school program were featured in this example. This does not have to be the case every day. Each program has different needs on different days. Many states or local education agencies have existing high-quality after-school programs in place that have other activities and efforts to accomplish policy-based expectations. Yet considering and planning to develop the five practices previously discussed would help any after-school program in becoming more comprehensive and educational for all stakeholders.

CONTINUOUS IMPROVEMENT

Our motivation to create Core5 followed our assignment from a state department of education to provide research on their after-school programs in order to help them distinguish which programs in their state were effective or ineffective. What we found was that many of the programs were barely meeting the grade. Most were, as their after-school leaders told us, glorified babysitting services. We also found that many of the organizations paid to provide such services in off-campus settings offered little more than disorganized social gatherings, with little attention being given to how one might maximize the time spent after school. What they were not doing was tying the after-school activities into a focused effort that could complement the school day challenges. We realized that here was a perfect opportunity for this state's schools to work more closely with many of the lower socioeconomic status (SES) kids by providing such services in a strategic manner and for such services to increase the expectations and engagement of low-SES parents. We realized during this time that if a school truly wants to increase academic achievement and bolster better behavior (reduce academic challenges), then it would make complete sense to focus on an after-school effort that addressed the five core components we have discussed.

There are millions of students under the age of fifteen who will not have a parent pick them up on the completion of the school day or greet them in the home upon their arrival by school bus or walk home. Many of the students (an estimated fifteen million) who come home after school are considered latchkey children. Millions of others participate in after-school programs until a parent can come and pick them up. It is addressing the needs of all students that is the primary focus of our theoretical model. It is our dream that after school can become such a positive developmental part of students' educational experience that all stakeholders will want to attend and support it every day.

REFERENCES

Barton, P. E., & Coley, R. J. (2007). *The family: America's smallest school.* Princeton, NJ: Educational Testing Service.

Center on Education Policy. (2007). *Choices, changes, and challenges: Curriculum and instruction in the NCLB era.* Washington, DC: Author.

Centers for Disease Control and Prevention. (2011). *Childhood obesity facts.* Retrieved September 29, 2011, from http://www.cdc.gov/healthyyouth/obesity/facts.htm

Corrigan, M., Grove, D., & Vincent, P. (2011). *Multi-dimensional education: A common sense approach to data-driven thinking.* Thousand Oaks, CA: Corwin Press.

Durlak, J. A., & Weissberg, R. P. (2007). *The impact of after-school programs that promote personal and social skills.* Chicago, IL: Collaborative for Academic, Social, and Emotional Learning. Retrieved September 15, 2011, from www.pasesetter.com/reframe/documents/ASP-Full.pdf and www.casel.org

Epstein, J. L. (1995). School/family/community partnerships: Caring for the children we share. *Phi Delta Kappan, 76,* 701–712.

Henderson, A. T., & Mapp, K. L. (2002). *A new wave of evidence: The impact of school, family, and community connections on student achievement.* Austin, TX: Southwest Educational Development Laboratory.

Little, P. M. D., Wimer, C., & Weiss, H. B. (2008, February). After-school programs in the 21st century: Their potential and what it takes to achieve it. *Issues and Opportunities in Out-of-School Time Evaluation Research, Harvard Family Research Project, 10.* Retrieved September 15, 2011, from www.hfrp.org/content/download/2916/84011/file/OSTissuebrief10.pdf

Ormrod, J. E. (2011). *Essentials of educational psychology: Big ideas to guide effective teaching* (3rd ed.). Boston: Pearson.

Sheldon, S. B., & Epstein, J. L. (2005). Involvement counts: Family and community partnerships and mathematics achievement. *Journal of Educational Research, 98*(4), 196–206.

Case Study 16B

The Committee for Hispanic Children and Families After-School Program at PS/MS 279

CHRISTOPHER E. SMITH AND LISA M. DEBELLIS

The Committee for Hispanic Children and Families (CHCF), a community-based organization operating in New York City, was founded in 1982 to be a voice for the Latino community at the local, state, and national levels, and to develop programs that address the needs of Latino children and their families. The organization provides many services, including programs focusing on early care and youth development, after school, dropout prevention, healthy living, responsible fatherhood, family literacy, and adolescent pregnancy prevention. CHCF's after-school program at PS/MS 279 Captain Manuel Rivera Jr. School is a TASC-model program that offers academic support, sports and arts enrichment, and community service opportunities to elementary and middle school students. The program is open every weekday from 3 to 6 p.m. during the school year. This program serves as an excellent model for promoting students' prosocial development in the after-school context, and in this profile, we will describe several student-run community service activities and events that they have convened.

PS/MS 279 is located in the Morris Heights section of the Bronx. The majority of enrolled students are of Hispanic descent (78 percent), and 91 percent are eligible for free or reduced-price lunch (Center for New York City Affairs at the New School, 2011). CHCF's after-school program at PS/MS 279 draws approximately three hundred students from the day school. The program offers activities and special events that address the needs of the school's students and neighboring community. Helena Yordan has served as the program coordinator since 1999, and one of her main objectives in this time has been motivating students to take responsibility for their community. She believes that a trademark of the program is the students' belief in their ability to make a difference, and they receive plenty of support from their program leaders to do so. One way staff members provide this support is through a community development activity that is offered to first- through eighth-grade attendees. In this activity, staff members teach students about the importance of community and character building.

Staff members use the curriculum materials from the generationOn youth service organization with fifth- through eighth-grade participants to promote this positive behavior (GenerationOn, n.d.). This curriculum teaches students to identify the needs and issues of their community, think about reasons why these issues are occurring, and come up with solutions that can help address these issues. For the past several years, the fifth- through eighth-grade students have created and developed several projects that have made a lasting impact, as described below. These students come up with the projects as a group and then get the younger (first through fourth grade) participants to help organize them. Older students enjoy having the responsibility of developing the projects, and younger students look up to them and eagerly anticipate the moment when they will have this opportunity. Thus, all students in this program view these community-building activities as a privilege, not an obligation.

The longest-running community project created by students in this program is an annual Breast Cancer Awareness walk. Six years ago, one student's mother was diagnosed with cancer, and he wanted to call more attention to the issue. He and his classmates developed the idea for an awareness walk, and then, with Helena's help, they started gathering information from hospitals and libraries. After learning more about the topic, students made packets with information to distribute to community members and encouraged family members and neighbors to get mammograms as part of their preparation for the event. The walk was a great success, and family and community members quickly took notice. Each year, the event has grown in stature, and this year, over 350 people in the school and community participated.

CHCF students have created several other annual charitable events at PS/MS 279. For the past five years, this program has held a coat drive for homeless citizens in November to help the less fortunate survive the winter months. Students begin to collect the coats by the beginning of October from friends, family, and community members and then accompany a staff member on Saturdays to wash them at a local Laundromat. Over two hundred coats were collected this past year, and a community church helped to distribute them. Also, each December, students collect toys to distribute to hospitalized children. Toys are collected from a variety of sources, including school and after-school staff members, family, and community members, to ensure that all children at Montefiore Hospital can receive a gift during the holidays. This past year, students made cards and wrote letters to the recipients, and staff distributed the toys at the hospital.

Their final annual event is a soup kitchen, which takes place in PS/MS 279's cafeteria. For this event, students and their family members come together to cook and serve meals to the needy. Students are involved in all aspects of this initiative. To advertise for the event, students make flyers that are sent to the local senior center, HIV center, and other targeted locations. They also draft a letter that is distributed to every participant's family, urging them to donate an item, and the response has been overwhelming. This past year, 400 to 450 people were served, and students and parents played a role in serving the food, cleaning up, and even participating in a show to entertain the audience. Incredibly, students have worked on other projects in addition to these annual events. In 2010, when an earthquake devastated Haiti, students collected medical supplies to send to the country. In addition, students started a fund-raiser for St. Jude's Children's Hospital and collected over eight hundred dollars.

How is it possible for one program to work on all of these initiatives? When presented with this question, Helena acknowledged that she has a great group of staff members and students. She also believes that day school staff members do not get an opportunity to work on these types of events in the regular school day, which is why they are eager to contribute. However, it took time for these events to garner the enthusiasm and commitment that they receive today. Program leaders needed time to learn how to organize and promote events of this magnitude. While experience helped them overcome these obstacles, funding remains a challenge. Helena admits that oftentimes her staff members must work on the weekends or stay late to finish up projects or prepare materials for an upcoming event. With a very small budget, the program often relies on extremely dedicated staff members to work extra hours to ensure that the events and activities are successful. The program has also hosted several fund-raisers to help them obtain funding for these initiatives. For example, the program hosts an annual talent show featuring students from the program. Students sell tickets to their families, friends, and community members for three dollars each. All of the money raised through ticket sales helps to pay for things like supplies and materials needed for their food and toy drives.

When asked what advice she would give to other after-school program coordinators looking to offer these types of prosocial community-building opportunities, Helena stressed the importance of teamwork. In order for the events and activities discussed above to have meaning and be successful, buy-in and cooperation are necessary from all stakeholders, including the students themselves, their families, program staff members, schoolteachers and administration, and community members. She also stressed the importance of being flexible and open to the ideas of others, especially those of the students. According to Helena, the success of the program is dependent on bringing everyone's ideas together and implementing them seamlessly. In the future, Helena would love to see her program team up with other after-school programs across the city (and maybe even across the state and country) to coordinate and participate in events that will truly make a difference in students' lives and communities.

FOR MORE INFORMATION
The Committee for Hispanic Children and Families: http://www.chcfinc.org

REFERENCES

Center for New York City Affairs at the New School. (2011). P.S. 279 Captain Manuel Rivera Jr. School. Retrieved September 1, 2011, from http://insideschools.org/browse/school/445

GenerationOn. (n.d.). *Lessons and guides*. Retrieved from http://www.generationon.org/teachers/lessons-and-guides

CHAPTER 17

Building a Prosocial Mind-Set in Teacher and Administrator Preparation Programs

Jacqueline Norris and Colette Gosselin

On the way home from teaching class one night, the following story recounted by a young middle school boy was broadcast on a radio program. I would like to share the story and the seemingly unintentional lesson learned by others because of this young student, whom we will call Jason. Jason's middle school class was on a field trip to visit the New Orleans Museum of Art. He and his peers were very excited about visiting the museum and viewing all the wonderful art that would be on exhibit inside. There had been much class preparation about the artists and the kinds of artwork that would be on exhibit. There had been lessons about art of every imaginable kind to prepare the students so that they would truly benefit from this experience and from all the effort their teacher had invested in their study about art and artists.

As Jason, his classmates, and the teacher were about to enter the museum, the class passed a homeless man on the street holding a sign that said, "Do you have food to spare?" He and his classmates walked by the homeless man, entered the museum, and set out to enjoy the experience they had been anticipating. After the museum tour, the children exited the building to enjoy an outside picnic. Remembering the homeless man, Jason looked around to see if he was still there. And indeed he was. Upon seeing him, Jason asked his teacher if he could share part of his lunch with the man. The teacher said yes and accompanied him over to the man. Seeing what Jason had done, his classmates collected enough food from their lunches to feed four other men who were nearby.

As I drove home, I could not get that story out of my head. I kept thinking, what beliefs must Jason have had to want to help as he did? What beliefs motivated the teacher to say yes, and the other students to join in? Were their beliefs nurtured in the family? Did the school support and strengthen them? These were surely prosocial behaviors—that is, the desire to help and care for others without the expectation of a reward. The behaviors were seen, but what motivating beliefs led to the acts? I thought, these are the kinds of behaviors that make a difference in our world. As a school leader educator, these are the kinds of beliefs and behaviors I intend to foster in my students and for them to use to develop schools as places where everyone in the community feels safe, affirmed, and valued.

Sharing this story and my thoughts with my colleague and coauthor, she too had the same intention for her preservice teachers. We both expect our students to be educators of the heart as well as the mind and to realize that schools are social settings that reflect and shape our society at the same time. We talked about the challenges we place before our students to examine their belief and value structures and how these structures shape the behaviors we want them to demonstrate. As they move into their future roles as school leaders and teachers, we want them to act purposefully and intentionally as agents of change and advocates for others. This chapter is a discussion of the prosocial approach and theoretical framework we use in two of our respective classes to help our students examine and strengthen the beliefs and competencies which lead to the kinds of behaviors demonstrated by the young student, his classmates, and the teacher in the story above.

OUR APPROACH TO DEVELOPING PROSOCIAL BEHAVIOR

Prosocial behavior is "other oriented." Eisenberg and Mussen define prosocial behavior as "voluntary actions that are intended to help or benefit another individual or group of individuals" (1989, p. 3). Furthermore, they explain that these acts are intrinsically motivated; that is, they are "acts motivated by internal motives such as concern and sympathy for others or by values and self rewards [such as feelings of self-esteem, pride, or self-satisfaction] rather than personal gain" (Eisenberg & Mussen, 1989, p. 3). The term *prosocial* is an umbrella term that incorporates such fields as character education, moral education, social and emotional learning, civic education, and school culture/climate. Though these approaches vary in their perspective, they all address human beliefs, attitudes, and behaviors that lead to a more caring, respectful, and responsible individual.

Our approach to developing prosocial behaviors in our students is grounded in the theories of social and emotional intelligence. In his seminal work on emotional intelligence, Daniel Goleman (1995) identified what he terms the hallmarks of character and self-discipline, of altruism and compassion—the basic capacities needed if our society is to thrive (Goleman, 1995). Goleman further describes four areas that comprise social and emotional intelligence: self-awareness, self-management, social awareness, and relationship management. Each is briefly described below.

> *Self-awareness* is the ability to recognize one's feelings while they are being felt.
> *Self-management* is the ability to act constructively on those feelings in appropriate ways.
> *Social awareness* is the ability to recognize the feelings of others without judgment and interact in ways that demonstrate caring and concern for others.
> *Relationship management* is the ability to interact effectively with others by building trust, honesty, and caring. In fact, the ability to manage one's relationships well requires all three areas listed above.

By definition, both social awareness and relationship management specifically target one's interactions with others; the connection between these two categories and prosocial behavior is relatively clear. But at first glance the connection between self-awareness and self-management and prosocial behavior may be less obvious. As we understand it, in order for a person to even possess the capacity to respond to others, that person must first be aware of feelings that are stirred *in the actual moment* of the interaction, be able to manage those feelings as they are stirred, and, finally, be able to evaluate those feelings to determine their appropriateness to the situation at hand. This process must occur quickly in order for the appropriate response to occur. In addition, we want to point out that while self-awareness and self-management may not be observable qualities, we contend that it is *in* the result that these capacities become evident and make responsiveness possible. For these reasons, we include both self-awareness and self-management as not only essential qualities but also foundational competencies for future educators.

Let's return for a moment to Jason's story. On that day outside the museum, many individuals must have passed by the homeless man. Some may have had an initial stirring of some feeling, and certainly Jason was one of those individuals. But unlike others, Jason's stirring caused him not only to feel "something" but also to know what this "something" was—*empathy*. Awareness of his feelings over time (recall that considerable time passed between Jason initially setting eyes on the homeless man and exiting the museum with his classmates) led Jason to action. In addition, Jason must also have felt a deep sense of trust in his teacher that enabled him to approach the teacher with a request to share his lunch. In turn, the teacher, in a show of caring and support for Jason, accompanied him as he walked over to the homeless man. To protect the student, a different teacher might have discouraged Jason. Instead, this teacher not only demonstrated compassion for the homeless man but also showed caring, respect, and concern for the relationship he had built with Jason. As a result, he actively encouraged Jason's prosocial actions and subsequently might have taught the most significant yet unplanned lesson of that museum field trip! As educators of future leaders and teachers, it is this type of learning rooted in care, respect, and concern for others that we intend to instill in our own students. Our hope is that by fostering this mind-set in our own classrooms, our students will in turn build schools and classroom communities that continue the cycle of prosocial behavior.

Table 17.1 provides questions drawn from *Smart School Leaders: Leading with Emotional Intelligence* (Patti & Tobin, 2006). These questions can help frame our thinking as we, teachers and leaders, self-assess and make decisions about ways we can improve in each of Goleman's four areas. Later in this chapter, we will show which of and how these questions are embedded in our course content, activities, assignments, and assessments.

OUR ORGANIZING FRAMEWORK

In higher education, we are perpetually searching for the best means to prepare future teachers and leaders. In a seminal essay that suggests a holistic approach for teacher preparation, Fred Korthagen (2004) raises two central questions for teacher educators: "What are the essential qualities of a good teacher?" And, should we be able to identify those qualities, "How can we help people to become good teachers?" As educators in two different programs, one in educational leadership and the other in teacher preparation, we have found that Korthagen's two questions sit at the core of our programmatic goals. Further, we have also extended these two questions to more deeply examine a companion set of questions in the two courses we will describe in this chapter: "What

Table 17.1. Questions Drawn from *Smart School Leaders: Leading with Emotional Intelligence* **(Patti & Tobin 2006)**

Self-awareness	**Social awareness**
How well am I aware of my own feelings?	Can I see, hear, and observe the perspectives of others?
Do I recognize my own body cues and emotional triggers?	Am I sensitive to the differences in others?
Do I see how my emotions affect my performance?	Can I listen without judgment?
Can I laugh at my mistakes and learn from them?	How well do I know the political current of my classroom/school?
Do I have presence?	Can I see and understand power relationships and utilize them positively?
Do I believe that I am good at what I do?	Do I really understand and influence the culture in which I work?
Can I hear you when you give me positive and negative feedback?	Do I know what people need to thrive? Am I available to them when needed?
Self-management	**Relationship management**
Can I remain calm under stress?	Do I mentor and coach others effectively?
Can I control my impulses?	Do I give constructive feedback to others?
Do my actions reflect my beliefs?	Do I see the strengths of others?
Am I an ethical person?	Do others view my vision as valuable?
Do I follow through on commitments?	Can I motivate others?
Can I smoothly handle all demands on me?	Do I engage others verbally and nonverbally?
Can I change my plan midstream even if I believe I am right?	Can I energize and guide others to make a needed change?
Can I make a difficult situation positive?	Do I really know how to manage conflict positively?
Do I take calculated risks?	Am I gifted at nurturing relationships and building community?
Do I set measurable goals for others and myself?	Can I work well in a team and help others to do the same?
Can I get out of the box and embrace new challenges regularly?	

essential qualities do school leaders and teachers need to promote a prosocial environment in classrooms and schools?" and "How do we help them develop those qualities in the settings in which they will work?" Before beginning to describe the courses we teach and how we set out to build a prosocial mind-set in preservice educators, we wish to first describe Korthagen's "onion model," which aptly describes the dynamic process of identity development that educators undergo and then connect Korthagen's model of change to our prosocial goals.

KORTHAGEN'S ONION MODEL

As Korthagen (2004) explains, much of the literature over the past decades in teacher preparation has focused on describing a good teacher based on two prominent themes: (1) competencies teachers should develop and (2) personal attributes that a teacher needs to develop to be effective. Much of the competency literature approach in teacher preparation stems from the middle of the twentieth century, when "performance-based" or "competency-based" models for teacher preparation gained ground. The beliefs of this approach are rooted in the idea that *if* we successfully generate a concrete list of the competencies a teacher needs to have, *then* we could use this list to train teachers. Korthagen correctly points out that one consequence of this belief has been efforts to correlate teacher competencies with student achievement. In fact, current reform efforts such as No Child Left Behind (NCLB) stem from this approach to teacher preparation. Less significant criticisms of this approach cite the unwieldy nature of the list this approach would generate and the problems it would pose should we act on competencies that are decontextualized from the settings in which they were identified. The second prominent approach that Korthagen identifies concerns beliefs about teacher personality traits, a trend rooted in the humanistic-based teacher education model, which focuses mainly on teachers' personal characteristics such as enthusiasm, nurturing ability, and love of children.

Korthagen (2004) critiques these two approaches to teacher preparation and in their place offers a holistic, dynamic model that takes both competencies and educator beliefs, not personality, into account. Briefly, his model consists of a nested set of five layers that act in concert and therefore influence each other (see figure 17.1). We find that this model provides an excellent framework to explain the goals of our two courses and our intentions of preparing educators with a mind-set that fosters the development of the requisite awareness and perspectivity needed to be prosocial, empathic actors.

External to the five concentric layers of the onion is the environment or the context in which an individual is an actor. Since the environment is where our social

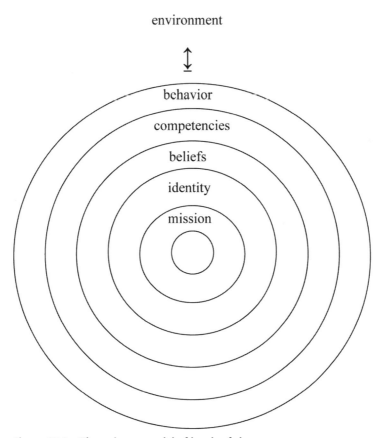

Figure 17.1. The onion: a model of levels of change.

interactions occur, it also serves as the place that affords us continuous experiences from which we learn to think, respond, and act. If we imagine the environment as an infinite number of onion bubbles, then we can begin to visualize ourselves and our own "onions" bumping into and bouncing off of an endless stream of other onions. This bumping into and bouncing off of constitutes our social life. As Korthagen (2004) explains, this bumping and bouncing is bidirectional and has a ripple effect on both the inner layers and the environment in which the onions interact. In fact, in the process of change, a bidirectional relationship or interplay exists between all concentric layers. Too, the environment can change as a result of its interaction with the outer layer of the onion bubbles.

As we review the model, we will begin by discussing the outermost layer, our behaviors. This part of our onion is the only observable layer and represents that part of ourselves that we share in our encounters within the social world as we interact with others. The significance of this layer lies in the fact that we are only privy to what we observe in other people's behaviors, and we are inclined to make decisions based on those observations. Yet these observations may not be factual and in fact tend to be laden with assumptions and misconceptions generated by previous encounters from which we have constructed meanings and labels. As Korthagen (2004) explains, we neglect the inner layers as they are simply not observable to us. If we return to the story about Jason, all that we can truly know about this story are the facts—a young boy shared his lunch with a homeless man, and his classmates followed his example. So, how then does Korthagen's model help us understand more about prosocial behavior? His model clarifies the unseen.

Below the layer of behaviors is the layer of competencies. Korthagen (2004) defines competencies as an integrated body of knowledge, skills, and attitudes that represent the *potential* for behavior. This list is almost inexhaustible, so perhaps more important than the list itself is the fact that conditions in the environment will largely determine whether or not a competency is put into practice should it already exist. Also important is that a new condition may stir the desire to learn a new competency if it does not already exist. Let's look at two different examples of how this might work. The first example involves a principal who implements a disciplinary policy with the intention of lessening disruptive behavior because he or she believes that the students require a strong external control system. This system may work well for some students but not for others who the principal notes seem to be repeatedly assigned detentions and suspensions. At this point, an effective principal will reflect on his or her decision-making process. We encourage our students to consider the possibility that the repeat offenders may require something more than those for whom the policy seems to be most effective; we suggest that they may need to rethink their beliefs about what is motivating the repeat offenders. In fact, this rethinking may lead an effective principal to not only consider new methods for disciplinary actions, but to also recognize the need for new instructional approaches and curricula that target the interests of that student population. Next, an effective principal might evaluate his or her teachers' competencies and what professional support and resources the teachers might need to positively influence the behaviors and performance of this target population. Here we see a positive interplay between the environment, the behaviors of the principal and the students, and the administrator's competencies to act by developing a policy, reflecting on the effectiveness of that policy on all students, reconsidering his or her knowledge and beliefs, and finally taking new action again.

A second example concerns a new teacher who may have learned a variety of reading strategies that students can use to effectively unpack challenging texts. However, in the teachers' workroom, the novice teacher may repeatedly hear disparaging remarks about the low performers and their inability to grapple with challenging texts. The novice teacher may challenge her peers' belief system either inwardly or outwardly. However, she might begin to rethink her own perception of her students and resort to less challenging texts. In this situation, we can recognize the interplay between the conditions of the workroom and the young teacher and how two different results can surface. Unfortunately, we also see how a negative environment can cause new teachers to abandon prior beliefs in favor of more widely held perceptions by more experienced others.

Last, as we reconsider the story about Jason, Korthagen's model helps us understand the interplay once again. It is evident from Jason's behavior that he already has the capacity to be compassionate as well as the ability to act on that compassion. Even further, his teacher's acknowledgment and support led to the reinforcement of his actions. Questions to consider in this scenario raise other possible outcomes. For instance, how might Jason's competencies to act have been impacted had his teacher responded differently? How might this affect the kind of person Jason was becoming and the beliefs he possessed about homeless people and about social responsibility?

These questions of becoming bring us to the next inner layer—beliefs. Beliefs and values stem from ideas that we construct in our social interactions; consequently they are necessarily skewed or biased. Ideas are formed by our intellect as we interpret our experiences within our own mind-set. Our mind-set, in turn, is shaped by the experiences we've had and by ideas presented to us by others. In the above illustrations, both the teacher and the principal reconsidered their beliefs about students. This reconsideration led, in both cases, to the development of new competencies. In each case, the principal and the teacher used what they now believe about challenging students to make new decisions about policies, instruction, and curriculum. However, this is easier said than done, as our beliefs are difficult to uncover, and we tend to be steadfast once we've formulated our beliefs. Typically, we need to encounter a new experience that challenges us to question ourselves, and this requires both self-awareness and a willingness to consider that our beliefs are grounded in faulty thinking. Once again, our story about Jason serves to illustrate how beliefs and competencies are linked and impacted by behaviors. Jason seems to possess certain values and beliefs about homelessness. First, he doesn't seem afraid, nor does he seem to be judgmental of the homeless man's appearance. In addition, Jason seems to also believe that he has some social obligation toward the homeless. He is compassionate and considers what it must mean to be hungry. The teacher meanwhile shares these ideas and values; he too is compassionate toward the man and in his actions reveals to us his beliefs that govern his role as teacher. In this story, the teacher perceives himself as needing to care about Jason, both for his safety and his compassion for the homeless man. That's why the teacher accompanies Jason as they walk toward the homeless man. He is affirming Jason's beliefs and conveying his agreement with social responsibility, kindness, and caring, but he also maintains his role as the protector of Jason's safety, as despite all good intentions the homeless man is unknown. A new question must now be considered: Had the teacher not shared Jason's belief about homelessness, he might have discouraged Jason from sharing his lunch. How might this have impacted Jason's beliefs regarding all aspects of this situation?

The two innermost layers of the onion model are identity and mission. For educators, both layers are represented by such questions as "What kind of leader or teacher do I want to become?" and "What is my central mission as a leader or teacher?" Both layers will be shaped by beliefs and values that the educator develops in his or her life experiences and in his or her professional programs. As both sit at an individual's core and are built on a foundation of lifelong experiences, they are the most resistant to change. Consequently, it becomes even more imperative that educational preparation programs provide numerous opportunities for preservice leaders and teachers to examine and question the basis for their beliefs, how they see themselves in future roles, and why they were drawn to the field of education initially. This kind of reflective process can assist preservice leaders and teachers to develop new competencies as they learn and grow as professionals.

Finally, we see our framework drawn from Korthagen's onion model as congruent with the questions posed by prosocial education. Though the behaviors that we desire to see in our society are ones that cause one to care for and about others, what we have come to recognize is that these desirable behaviors spring from the underlying levels of the individual's onion. By providing an ongoing challenge to our students to reach deeper into their cognitive, social, and emotional levels, it is our goal that our students will see the competencies we facilitate and expect of them and that the competencies will become a default response to the environment in which they live and work. We hope that they see the interplay of how they view themselves, what they believe and value, and the behaviors they demonstrate within the environment, and that this interplay comes from multiple perspectives, as this interplay accounts for their ability to empathize with and advocate for the members of their school or classroom communities.

Research shows that when individuals work and learn in environments that are safe, supportive, and affirming, the end result in schools is better teaching and deeper learning. This is especially important in the diverse society in which we live, given the nature of the current social ills that manifest in our schools. Students arrive at the schoolhouse door often influenced by such factors as bullying, media glorification of stereotypes, poverty, and violence. Each of these has a negative relationship to one's ability to learn and grow. In addition, the growing impact of technology in the twenty-first century allows for the potential to depersonalize and dehumanize social interactions. For these reasons, it is incumbent upon us as professors of education to prepare future leaders and teachers who have the knowledge, skills, and abilities to bring about ethical change. What follows is a discussion of two courses in our respective programs that we believe accomplish these goals.

EDUCATIONAL LEADERSHIP PROGRAM: GROUP DYNAMICS FOR SCHOOL LEADERS

There are three strands within the Educational Leadership Program in which I teach: the master's degree in education; the post-master's, which leads to principal certification; and supervision, which leads to supervisor certification. Group Dynamics for School Leaders is a course in the master's degree strand; its purpose is to provide students with a theoretical understanding of group and individual interactions, with practical applications to school situations. The emphasis is on development of the knowledge and skills, including the communication capabilities, that are essential to effective leadership. Social and emotional competencies are the foundation of my approach to meeting course goals.

The first activity presented on the first night of class is one I call "Qualities." Before we begin our discussion of what social and emotional intelligence are or why these are important competencies to possess and strengthen, I divide the class into four groups, each having a different-color marker. Each group is then given these directions: "You will discuss and generate a list of qualities or traits you believe are in the ideal person in the category you will be given." Each group knows that they must generate a list, but only they know the category of person they are given. They are not to identify that category on their list in any way. The categories are parent, principal, student, and teacher. After fifteen minutes, the lists are posted in the front of the room, and each student is given a slip of paper with the four categories of person and the four marker colors. They are given a few minutes to match which person goes with which color. Our debriefing is a very valuable tool to bring out what we truly value in people. Most of the lists include qualities such as trustworthy, good listener, honest, impartial, supportive, respectful, takes responsibilities, and open to other points of view. There is usually only one reference to cognitive intelligence. With this as a starting point, it is a natural transition to understanding that what we really want to see in the people with whom we interact are the skills of social and emotional intelligence, and it does not matter what the category of person is; what we want in the ideal parent is very much the same as in the ideal principal, student, and teacher. The ability to be open, honest, and caring are the qualities we believe should be universal.

Following the "Qualities" activity, students complete an anticipatory guide that enables them to self-assess their proficiency in each area of social and emotional intelligence identified in table 17.1. The questions are rephrased as statements, with a Likert scale from 1 to 4 for the guide. The result of this assessment becomes the first step in a self-directed learning study that continues throughout the semester. Self-directed learning is an approach to personal improvement and change developed by Richard Boyatzis at Case Western Reserve University (as cited in Patti & Tobin, 2006, pp. 39–40). This model takes the individual through five questions which Boyatzis refers to as "discoveries." I have modified his questions for the course to the following:

1. Who do I want to be?
2. Who am I?
3. What is my learning agenda?
4. What behaviors, thoughts, and feelings will I practice to the point of mastery?
5. Who will be my support system as I develop the change I seek?

Reflecting on the areas of social and emotional intelligence, students select a competency they will work to improve over the semester. They review literature on the area; they create a behavior modification plan and keep a journal of their progress. Finally, they write a paper documenting their progress toward their goal. Obviously a fifteen-week semester is not a long time to see permanent change in human behavior; however, over the seven years of teaching this course, I have seen moderate to great change in the thinking and behavior of the overwhelming majority of my students.

In Group Dynamics I also focus on creating the kind of open, honest communication skills and relationship building that would lead to successful first- and second-order change in schools. First-order change occurs when the change builds on the past structures; it is incremental and requires little deep thinking to understand it as the next obvious step. Actions such as adding a new class to a grade level or changing the textbook for a course because it is out of date are examples of first-order change. Second-order change, however, requires a new way of looking at the present and things that are familiar. It requires flexibility, organizational trust, and time (Marzano, Waters, & McNulty, 2005).

One might well think of the difference between school reform and school transformation that some educators and politicians have called for in education today as good examples of first- and second-order change. The difference may also shed some light on why the change we needed may not come by 2014 as NCLB states, or even 2020 as the proposed reauthorization of the Elementary and Secondary Education Act (ESEA) suggests.

In Group Dynamics, leadership students learn that change begins on the inside and that they must begin to see themselves as the agents of that change. They are asked to look at their espoused and core beliefs and to recognize the difference between the two—that is, the difference between those beliefs and values they profess versus those which guide their lives. Students develop greater proficiency in active listening, verbal and nonverbal communication skills, perspective taking, and empathy. Administrative in-basket activities and educational scenarios are used to provide them with multiple opportunities to practice these skills and receive constructive feedback on their performance.

Creating effective work groups or restructuring existing groups to be more effective is a major goal of the course. I use the work of David and Frank Johnson (Johnson & Johnson, 2009) to achieve this goal. We discuss the nature of groups, how to move groups from *pseudogroups* who don't commit to working together to solve a problem to *effective* and even *high-performance groups*, where the product is more than the sum of the individuals who have come together committed to work.

School leaders must rely on the knowledge, talent, skills, and abilities of their faculty to move the school closer to its vision or mission. To be successful, they must learn to work effectively and diplomatically with unique constituent groups such as parents, students, central administration, board of education members, and members of the larger school community. Decision-making strategies, conflict management, and problem solving are also part of the course content.

Interestingly, even though all of my students are presently or at some time in the recent past have been engaged in some educational experience (e.g., teaching, counseling, child study team members), they find it hard to move from their present roles to developing identities as leaders. Addressing colleagues in faculty meetings or leading professional development events may be uncomfortable, and thus they must learn to overcome former self-images and connect to new ones by adopting new behaviors.

We look at levels of knowledge: *declarative*, which is knowing that something is; *procedural*, which is knowing how to do something; and *conditional*, which is not only knowing that it is or how to do it, but also when, where, and why it should be done. These levels are very different and critically important to a school leader. People may know that change is needed; they may know what changes should be made and who should be involved; but do they know why and when is the best time to bring the changes about? Having this level of understanding can make all the difference between the success and failure of an initiative.

My culminating activity is for the students, working in groups of three or four, to devise a role-play based on an actual situation that has occurred in one of their schools. The role-play has parts that are common knowledge to the group and parts that are totally spontaneous so that it mirrors as closely as possible a real-life situation. The students have no idea how their group members plan to act and react in the scenario, though they share with me their personal intentions. It is always informative and enjoyable to see the students act and react as their peers display prosocial and antisocial behaviors during the role-plays. The debriefings, which follow the role-plays, serve to reinforce the skills presented and goals intended in the course.

LINKING ISLLC STANDARDS TO PROSOCIAL BEHAVIORS

Though I am fortunate enough to have a course specifically dedicated to these types of prosocial skills, the Interstate School Leaders Licensure Consortium (ISLLC) standards with which all educational leadership programs must align, provides a compelling rationale for these types of skills to be embedded into most leadership courses (Council of Chief State School Officers, 1996). Below we explain how other courses in the Educational Leadership Program address prosocial education through meeting ISLLC standards.

Standard 1: An education leader promotes the success of every student by facilitating the development, articulation, implementation, and stewardship of a vision of learning that is shared and supported by all stakeholders.

Standard 4: An education leader promotes the success of every student by collaborating with faculty and community members, responding to diverse community interests and needs, and mobilizing community resources.

The first course in our program, Introduction to Educational Administration, requires students to develop an educational platform—a vision of schooling—which they will continually refine as they progress through each course in the program. In Group Dynamics, they create an "elevator speech" where they must be able to articulate their vision accurately and succinctly.

Standard 2: An education leader promotes the success of every student by advocating, nurturing, and sustaining a school culture and instructional program conducive to student learning and staff professional growth.

In Curriculum Theory and Practice, the students develop an action plan to address the use of best practices and research-validated approaches to improve the academic achievement of K–12 students at a specific grade level and content area in a school setting. Here, the focus is improvement across the continuum, which is bringing the partially proficient to proficient and the proficient to advanced proficiency, as well as continuing to challenge the advanced proficient students.

Standard 3: An education leader promotes the success of every student by ensuring management of the organization, operation, and resources for a safe, efficient, and effective learning environment.

Standard 6: An education leader promotes the success of every student by understanding, responding to, and influencing the political, social, economic, legal, and cultural context.

Modules in both School Finance and School Law address issues of equality and equity, how they are different, and what consequences there might be to schools that don't understand these differences.

Standard 5: An education leader promotes the success of every student by acting with integrity, fairness, and in an ethical manner.

All courses within the program address the responsibility of school leaders to always act with the best interests of their students, faculty, staff, and community in mind. Students examine and reexamine their values, beliefs, and thoughts for inner integrity and for fairness and ethical behaviors toward others. Each and every one of the ISLLC standards calls for the school leader to advocate for and be supportive of others, thus making the leader prosocial at least in spirit. School leaders should be models for the faculty and staff, students, parents, and the larger school community. If we are not doing this in our educational leadership programs, we are not preparing school leaders who can be successful in our twenty-first-century schools. And anyone who knows anything about U.S. history knows that schools have been and will more than likely continue to be the place our society turns to address and correct the problems we face as a nation. Therefore, school leaders will continually face an environment steeped in change, both first and second order. It is imperative that they be able to adjust and respond to that change from a foundation of a deep understanding of who they are and what they believe and value, that they have a range of competencies at their disposal, and that they have the awareness to behave in appropriate and effective ways.

SECONDARY EDUCATION, UNDERGRADUATE TEACHER PREPARATION: SCHOOLS AND COMMUNITIES

At our liberal arts college in New Jersey, I teach three different courses in our undergraduate teacher preparation program, which has been intentionally designed to consider one primary foundational question: *What does it mean to teach in different contexts?* This question is central to our program for various reasons. First, our college undergraduate population is over 75 percent white, and our secondary education program serves 85 percent white students. This population is largely drawn from New Jersey suburbs, and while our students tend to be open-minded, most of them have had little experience working with diverse groups. Many of our students report living in primarily white communities, or if they do live in a diverse community, they report completing high school in an educational track that was largely populated by white

Table 17.2. "Reflecting on My EQ" (Patti & Tobin, 2006, p. 210)

Self-awareness	Social awareness
How well am I aware of my own feelings, beliefs, and values?	Can I see, hear, and observe the perspectives of others?
Do I recognize how my feelings, beliefs, and values shape my mind-set?	Am I sensitive to the differences in others?
	Can I listen without judgment?
Do I see how my emotions affect my interpretation of other's behavior?	Am I aware of the political current of classrooms/schools?
Can I hear you when I am given positive and negative feedback?	Can I see and understand power relationships?
	Do I understand how culture influences classrooms?
Self-management	Do I know what people need to thrive?
Am I aware of how my mind-set influences how I respond to others?	**Relationship management**
Do I set high expectations for myself and others?	Do I see the strengths of others?
	Can I motivate others?
Can I get out of the box and embrace new challenges?	Can I build nurturing relationships and a safe learning community?
	Can I work well in a team and help others to do the same?

students. Consequently, neither group has attended classes with students of color, nor were they friends with people of color. Many of my students express an interest in teaching in urban schools, but few have encountered what difference truly means in terms of social interaction patterns, communication styles, and the cultural needs of urban students. In addition, they do not have any experience with the demands made on students who live in urban neighborhoods.

Therefore, Schools and Communities was designed to raise my students' self-awareness of their own biases and privileges and instill social awareness of the needs of their future students who may have an entirely different cultural knapsack. Course readings provoke students to learn self-management as they are drawn into lively and sometimes heated debates over authors and situations that challenge their mind-set. Toward the end of the course, the students begin to consider how their new awareness has caused them to rethink their moral obligations to manage relationships in entirely different ways than they had expected.

Of Goleman's (1995) four areas of emotional intelligence identified previously, this course intends to specifically target the questions identified in table 17.2. Second, this course is also designed to meet the New Jersey Professional Teaching Standards (NJPTS; New Jersey Department of Education, 2004) required of all teachers who are to be certified in our state. The four standards this course meets are as follows:

Learning theory. Teachers understand how children and adolescents develop and learn in a variety of school, family, and community contexts and provide opportunities that support their intellectual, social, emotional, and physical development (NJPTS No. 2).

Collaboration and partnerships. Teachers build relationships with school colleagues, families, and agencies in the larger community to support students' learning and well-being (NJPTS No. 9).

Diverse learners. Teachers understand the practice of culturally responsive teaching (NJPTS No. 3).

Reflective practice. Teachers participate as active, responsible members of the professional community, engaging in a wide range of reflective practices, pursuing opportunities to grow professionally, and establishing collegial relationships to enhance the teaching and learning process (NJPTS No. 10).

Third, these professional standards are congruent with our own professional goals as teacher educators. As our nation becomes increasingly diverse, the cadre of new teachers entering our public schools is disproportionately white. Therefore, we see it as our professional obligation not only to develop my white students' self- and social awareness in order for them to engage in prosocial behavior, but also to provide them with the requisite knowledge and skills needed to enable them to engender prosocial behavior in their future students. While these goals inform our entire secondary education program, this chapter does not provide sufficient space for me to articulate how we enact these goals programmatically at all three levels of our students' educational experience. Therefore, we will be focusing on Schools and Communities, a course taken at the sophomore level.

Purpose of Schools and Communities

The purpose of Schools and Communities is to study the complex sociocultural context of classrooms by examining the intricate relationships between teachers and students. The course goals are to examine how classrooms, as dynamic, social environments, are co-constructed by teachers and students and for my students to learn how this dynamic impacts student learning. At the heart of this understanding is the examination of values and beliefs. I begin the first day with an activity that involves my students writing about their educational experiences, those that have been memorable and those that have been regretful. From this activity, students recognize that their memories of teachers have little to do with content but rather resonate with the classroom climate the teacher constructed and the instructional strategies the teacher implemented.

As future middle and high school teachers who hope to inspire passion for their subjects, my students are surprised that "content" is not among the list of elements drawn on the blackboard. Instead, their list is peppered with phrases inherent to prosocial behavior: caring, listening, supportive, aware of student needs, and responsive. Also among this list are other phrases that we typically associate with instruction but which in actuality are undergirded by a teacher's capacity to manage classroom relationships; students identify instructional strategies and assessments that target their intellectual and social needs as students. Phrases include *cooperative learning, creative projects*, and *real-world application*. As we discuss in class the interplay between emotional and intellectual needs, the students begin to expand their understanding of what constitutes the work of teachers.

During this first session, students also read "Looking at Classroom Management through a Social and Emotional Learning Lens" (Norris, 2003). This important essay situates prosocial behavior within the greater body of competencies teachers must develop in order to be effective managers of twenty-first century classrooms. Last, we explore their present thinking about what knowledge, skills, and attitudes might change as a result of the content in this course. In the second session, the students learn about Korthagen's

(2004) model of change, and on that day we continue the conversation about how the remainder of the course rests on the continuous reexamination of their beliefs and values, how their beliefs and values are shaped, and, as they encounter course readings that challenge their mind-sets, how their beliefs are changing. The second year this course was taught, I conducted formal interviews with students. In those interviews, the students spoke of the success of these course goals; significant numbers of students reported growing self- and social awareness and a new moral imperative that obligates them to act on this newfound awareness as future teachers (Gosselin & Meixner, 2007).

Schools and Communities Instruction

So how is this newfound awareness and moral imperative aroused and shaped? We know from Korthagen's (2004) model that for awareness or beliefs to change, individuals must encounter experiences and develop competencies to reshape their belief system. This is a tenuous process that if done poorly can backfire and in fact requires the professor to behave prosocially herself by recognizing that she needs to be self- and socially aware, be prepared to act on that awareness, and manage classroom relationships so that students feel safe to express and grapple with their intellectual conflicts. This involves tolerance of comments that are sometimes infuriating, a willingness to "put on hold" frustrations that surface when students utter naive social explanations, and patience to introduce concepts only when students reveal a readiness to *listen* to authors who anger them. One of my own learnings involved waiting to assign Peggy McIntosh's (1990) "White Privilege: Unpacking the Invisible Knapsack" until one or two students raise the specter of privilege within their own lives. It always happens; the course readings and assignments set this up.

In addition to the goal of instilling a prosocial mind-set, the preservice teachers are expected to develop interpretive and critical reflective skills for understanding how teachers' and students' lives, beliefs, and values are shaped by community and school experiences. The intent of this approach is to shift the students' interpretation of classroom dynamics and student achievement from explanations that stem from psychological models such as student motivation to sociologic models that identify competing value systems as a root cause of poor student performance. These intellectual skills are achieved through the analysis of case studies and ethnographies with a heuristic device, close readings of theoretical texts, and the completion of a fieldwork experience in a public school setting where they conduct an analysis of classroom culture.

Questions that guide the choices for course readings and classroom discussions include the following:

1. What does it mean to be an educator in a diverse society? How does this definition affect the lived experiences of teachers and students and drive the organization and culture of classrooms and schools?
2. How do family and community culture shape the values, beliefs, and mores that we use to define our role as educators? In light of that knowledge, how is our identity and mission as teachers redefined?
3. How do different cultural beliefs and values possess more or less power in shaping school practices? How does power influence the classroom practices, pedagogical choices, and curriculum designs we choose?

4. What is the relationship between white privilege, school design, and power? How does the hidden curriculum influence achievement and define our lives in schools? How do we unmask classroom and school practices that encourage the isms in social structures such as race, class, gender, and sexual orientation?

Case studies and ethnographies are carefully selected to generate opportunities that will challenge my students' social imagination to create new narratives that explain others' points of view. There is an intentional scaffolding of a complex nature of classroom and social dynamics that they encounter in these course readings. First, the students read case studies (Rand & Shelton-Colangelo, 2002) that amplify problems that a student teacher may encounter in a classroom that pertain to racism, sexism, heterosexism, or stereotyping. These case studies are very short and showcase the kinds of classroom problems the students may actually encounter when they step into the role of student teacher. For example, one case study illustrates a curriculum choice that stirs parental objections over the viewing of *Beloved* in a junior year social studies classroom. In another case study, the student teacher unintentionally sets different expectations for a Christian Fundamentalist student who is disrespectful of her more liberal peers. These case studies call upon my students' ability "to put their emotions on hold" while we interpret the social nature of the situation found in the case study as a prerequisite to considering the next step the student teacher may need to consider in order to resolve the dilemma. This interpretative process begins by examining assumptions on which the student teacher in the case study acted; we unpack our own emotional reactions aroused by the case study, and then we analyze the case study using the heuristic device (see next section).

The second type of case study we interpret and analyze is drawn from Sonia Nieto's (2004) *Affirming Diversity*. These case studies provide the preservice teachers the chance to encounter beliefs and values very different from their own. Adolescents in these case studies grapple with conflicting home and school values that impact their identity development and their school achievement. Conflicts stem from differences deeply rooted in competing social norms such as biracial, gay/lesbian, or immigration status. Frequently my students recall peers who were seemingly at the margins, who were labeled and rendered invisible in their own high schools. However, one case study involves a teenager who reflects the students in this course: a middle-class white female who espouses color blindness as a mind-set. This case study best reflects my own students' initial and well-intended understanding of social dynamics and also stands in stark contrast to the other case studies. Therefore, we read it last; this positioning of the reading requires my students to juxtapose their beliefs squarely with newly encountered differences. Many recognize themselves immediately and begin to question the moral import of color blindness as well as how this mind-set renders the experience of others invisible. They begin to recognize the harm that color blindness may cause and subsequently begin to query about "what more they now need to know."

Third, the students read and analyze one ethnographic study using the heuristic device. These ethnographies are read independently, and students work in small groups to prepare a class presentation that draws on their new interpretative skills as they analyze how social norms have defined the lived experiences of the adolescents in the ethnographies and how school and community tensions have impacted their achievement as students. A brief list of ethnographies I have drawn on include *Bad Boys*

(Ferguson, 2001); *Con Respeto* (Valdes, 1996); *Hopeful Girls, Troubled Boys* (Lopez, 2002); *Schoolgirls* (Orenstein, 1995); *Asian Americans in Class* (Lew, 2006); and *Color of Success* (Conches, 2006).

In addition to the case studies and ethnographies, the preservice teachers read a range of theoretical texts that provide them with an educational language to analyze classroom dynamics on an intellectual and practical level.

Last, the students apply their knowledge and analytic frames to an actual classroom setting. The students observe a secondary classroom in a local public school once a week for a period of five weeks. While on the surface this appears to be a very short period to draw any conclusions, the students' reports indicate that they have internalized the knowledge and skills they encounter in this course. During their classroom visits, the students take copious notes that replicate teacher and student actions over the instructional period. Elements they focus on include the manner in which the teacher welcomes and begins class, the activities the teacher has designed, how well the teacher communicates directions and lesson concepts, the quality of questioning, student engagement, the emotional climate of the classroom, and the teacher's classroom management style. The students are provided with a "handbook" that defines each of the elements that comprise their observations, and they are instructed on the sequencing and focus of each observation they conduct.

The Heuristic Device

The heuristic device (see table 17.3) used to analyze the case studies and the field-work observation assignment were course tools created by Terry O'Connor, who was among the original designers of this course. Terry, now deceased, devoted his professional career to teaching and learning especially in the domain of social interaction patterns; one of his seminal works is among the course readings. The heuristic device consists of two analytic frames that are conjoined to identify the hidden problem in the case study. The two frames, educational structures and educational themes, are used to shape the analysis or thesis of the problem the case study presents. Why use this device? My findings are that without a tool to force the students to think socially and politically, they default to explanations that result in student motivation or student behavior as the root problem. In essence, they tend to respond stereotypically and urge others to pull themselves up by their bootstraps. These analytic frames demand that they think otherwise. Students compose three different graded essays of three different case studies using this heuristic device. The use of this device is practiced regularly in class.

When reading case studies and ethnographies, students are asked to identify the central issues presented in the study by selecting what they believe is the most important educational structure and educational theme impacting the interactions. They are informed that no correct choice exists but that the facts support some structures and themes better than others. Once they've chosen their structure and theme, they compose a thesis statement and then defend their choice *based on the facts only*. They also draw on the theoretical literature we have discussed in class to additionally support and deepen their analyses. Finally, they identify the next step needed to resolve the problem and then explain how this case study has influenced or clarified their values and mission as future teachers.

Table 17.3. Heuristic Device

Education Structures	Education Themes
Classroom management: Organization of space and materials	Personal development of students: Are students' psychological, intellectual, and social development actively supported?
Student management: How are students treated?	Social development: Are students learning how to work effectively with others?
Curriculum: How is subject matter organized?	Actualization and agency: Are students learning they can positively influence their social worlds?
Learning patterns: What are the methods of instruction?	
Assessment patterns: What are the formal and informal assessment tools?	Bureaucracy: Is the school actively creating an environment conducive to all learners?
Social patterns: How do the students interact throughout the lesson?	Effectiveness: Is the school or teacher demonstrating the ability to teach all learners?
Adaptation patterns: How is instruction differentiated? How are emotions responded to? How are social structures addressed?	Fairness: Are there concerted efforts made by the school and teacher to provide everyone with a fair chance to succeed?
Counseling relationships: How does the teacher respond to individual needs?	School community: What are the characteristics of the school or classroom culture?
Peer friendships: How are student groups organized to facilitate a range of peer interactions?	Family relations: Is the school or teacher working to close the communication gap with families and the surrounding community?
	Equity: Are all students afforded the resources needed to be successful?
	Pluralism: How does the school or teacher capitalize on the assets the diverse community offers?
	Change: Are the school and teacher adapting to new technology and the new social landscapes of the community it serves?

As we work through these case studies, the students lament about not having sufficient information. We discuss this real-world problem and the role self-awareness and self-management play in examining assumptions and actions we are inclined to jump to when our emotions alone guide our decision making. The assignment demands that they suspend these hasty judgments as they consider all the facts, the details that are absent, and puzzle over the root cause of the problem. This puzzling is what I believe supports their growth most, as it asks them to reflect deeply on their ideas, the conclusions they draw from those ideas, and the hidden assumptions embedded in that thinking. Since this work is largely done privately or in small groups, students are afforded the emotional safety to engage in exposing and interrogating their personal values and beliefs as they reconsider them.

The intended end result of my course is for my students to grow in their understanding of classrooms as constructed political spaces that involve a great deal of negotiation between teachers and students, to realize that their future students will not enter their classrooms as blank slates ready to be filled with neutral knowledge and truths but rather as whole individuals with cultural assets; that it is their moral obligation as teachers to construct a well-functioning and supportive classroom that includes their own students' cultural knowledge, beliefs, and values; and that they generate opportunities, include resources, and draw upon instructional approaches that are flexible and address the intellectual and sociocultural needs of the students they will be teaching. Conversations, both formal and informal, reveal this growing mind-set among the sophomores as they exit my classroom at the end of the semester. In subsequent courses and finally in student teaching, I find that this mind-set has been internalized and serves to inform their classroom practice as student teachers. For others, this process needs continuous reinforcement and reminders for the lightbulb to remain lit. My hope and mission as a professor of education is that this mind-set will continue and follow them into their own classrooms upon graduating from our college.

SUMMARY

Our chapter began with the story of Jason, a young man whose sense of concern, perspective taking, and ethical actions motivated him to share his lunch with a homeless man he passed on the street. From this story, we drew out the qualities that characterize the kind of educator we work to shape for twenty-first-century schools. These qualities include caring, empathy, and self-awareness—values that are inherent to prosocial behavior.

We then discussed the connection between prosocial behavior and Korthagen's (2004) model of change as the framework we have drawn upon to design experiences in our respective programs to develop those qualities in our students. Using Korthagen's model, we explain the bidirectional nature of the self, the self's inner layers, and the environment. It is important to understand that while it is the outermost layer of the self (i.e., behaviors) that is observable, it is the inner layers that engender the behaviors that one demonstrates. At the same time, factors within the environment may stir up the inner layers of the self, causing different behaviors to be observed. Had the homeless man not been in the environment, Jason would not have shared his lunch. So what we really want our students to understand is that while what they bring to their schools and classrooms is important, the environment is also having an impact on them. Therefore, it is very important that they understand who they are, what they believe and value, and what their mission is in order to determine the course of action that will generate a positive end result.

The descriptions of the two courses in our programs illustrate approaches that we have found to be successful in promoting prosocial behaviors in our students. It is our hope that in reading these descriptions, others will be stimulated to first examine their own practices for what they are already doing effectively and then consider other methods that they can use to promote prosocial education in their students.

REFERENCES

Conches, G. Q. (2006). *Color of success: Race and high-achieving urban youth.* New York: Teachers College Press.

Council of Chief State School Officers. (1996). *Interstate school leaders licensure consortium: Standards for school leaders.* Washington, DC: Author.

Eisenberg, N., & Mussen, P. H. (1989). *The roots of prosocial behavior in children.* New York: Cambridge University Press.

Ferguson, A. A. (2001). *Bad boys: Public schools in the making of black masculinity.* Ann Arbor, MI: University of Michigan Press.

Goleman, D. (1995). *Emotional intelligence.* New York: Bantam.

Gosselin, C., & Meixner, E. (2007, November). *Facing developmental roadblocks in multicultural preparation in a secondary education program.* Paper presented at the conference of the National Association of Multicultural Education, Baltimore, MD.

Johnson, D. W., & Johnson, F. P. (2009). *Joining together: Group theory and group skills* (10th ed.). Upper Saddle River, NJ: Pearson.

Korthagen, F. A. J. (2004). In search for the essence of a good teacher: Towards a more holistic approach in teacher education. *Teaching and Teacher Education, 20*(1), 77–97.

Lew, J. (2006). *Asian Americans in class: Charting the achievement gap among Korean American youth.* New York: Teachers College Press.

Lopez, N. (2002). *Hopeful girls, troubled boys: Race and gender disparity in urban education.* New York: Routledge.

Marzano, R. J., Waters, T., & McNulty, B. A. (2005). *School leadership that works: From research to results.* Alexandria, VA: Association for Supervision and Curriculum Development.

McIntosh, P. (1990, Winter). White privilege: Unpacking the invisible knapsack. *Independent School Magazine, 49*(2).

New Jersey Department of Education. (2004). *New Jersey professional standards for teachers and school leaders.* Trenton, NJ: Author. Retrieved November 28, 2011, from http://www.state .nj.us/education/profdev/profstand/standards.pdf

Nieto, S. (2004). *Affirming diversity: The sociopolitical context of multicultural education* (4th ed.). Upper Saddle River, NJ: Allyn & Bacon.

Norris, J. A. (2003). Looking at classroom management through a social and emotional learning lens. *Theory into Practice, 42*(4), 313–318.

Orenstein, P. (1995). *Schoolgirls: Young women, self-esteem, and the confidence gap.* New York: Anchor Books.

Patti, J., & Tobin, J. (2006). *Smart school leaders: Leading with emotional intelligence* (2nd ed.). Dubuque, IA: Kendall/Hunt Publishing.

Rand, M., & Shelton-Colangelo, S. (2002). *Voices of student teachers: Cases from the field* (2nd ed.). Upper Saddle River, NJ: Allyn & Bacon.

Valdes, G. (1996). *Con respeto: Bridging the distances between culturally diverse families and schools.* New York: Teachers College Press.

Case Study 17A

Developing Emotionally Intelligent School Counselors for the Prosocial Classroom

SUSAN B. STILLMAN AND JOYCE A. DEVOSS

> The EQ competencies really helped me to look deeper not only at myself but it helped me to look deeper into all aspects of my life and work.
>
> —Graduate student intern

Emotional intelligence (EQ) is the capacity to integrate thinking and feeling to make optimal decisions, ensure healthy relationships, and reach one's goals. In its earliest conception in the 1990s, emotional intelligence was defined as

> the capacity to reason about emotions, and of emotions to enhance thinking. It includes the abilities to accurately perceive emotions, to access and generate emotions so as to assist thought, to understand emotions and emotional knowledge, and to reflectively regulate emotions so as to promote emotional and intellectual growth. (Mayer, Salovey, & Caruso, 1994, p. 197)

Emotional intelligence has grown tremendously in popularity through social-emotional learning (SEL), the overarching umbrella for the knowledge, attitudes, and strategies required to "develop the fundamental skills for life effectiveness" (Collaborative for Academic, Social, and Emotional Learning, 2011, bullet 1). These prosocial skills include increasing emotional literacy, recognizing patterns, applying consequential thinking, navigating emotions, engaging intrinsic motivation, exercising optimism, increasing empathy, and pursuing a noble goal (Freedman, 2007, p. 92). As the field has grown, researchers engaged in meta-analyses of school-based interventions have revealed the significant impact and power that evidence-based SEL programs have on student achievement and behavior (Durlak, Weissberg, Dymnicki, Taylor, & Schellinger, 2011). They have demonstrated that SEL is linked to decreases in antisocial behavior and aggression, school suspensions, and discipline problems while increasing personal and social competency, school attendance, satisfaction, and academic achievement (Cherniss, Extein, Goleman, & Weissberg, 2006; Durlak et al., 2011). In addition, as evidence has grown about the effectiveness of SEL and EQ on student outcomes and school climate, increasing attention is being focused on the EQ skills that adults need in order to work effectively with students, to create prosocial classrooms and schools, and to lead educational institutions in school reform, advocacy, and change efforts.

As counselor educators, we are cognizant of the fact that school counselors are expected to engage in activities that improve student social and emotional development outcomes (American School Counselor Association [ASCA], 2005). School counselors engage in activities that include teaching guidance lessons and providing small-group and individual counseling. They collect relevant data that demonstrate the effectiveness of those interventions with students. They are instrumental as school leaders and collaborators with other professionals to advocate for equity, social justice, and success for all students (DeVoss & Andrews, 2006). While school counselors are trained in counseling theory, interventions, and best practices according to the American School Counselor Association National Model (ASCA, 2005), in our experience as counselor educators, EQ and SEL training in prosocial skills such as recognizing and managing emotions, developing caring and concern for others, establishing positive relationships, making responsible decisions, and handling challenging situations constructively and ethically has been conspicuously absent from school counseling training programs.

As we thought about the needs of school counselors to be prosocial educational leaders, we realized that school counselor trainees could benefit professionally and personally from learning, practicing, and teaching EQ skills. We theorized that school counselor trainees' own development of EQ competencies would enable them to better "work the system" (Stillman, 2007), lead, and advocate (DeVoss & Andrews, 2006) for their constituencies in ethical and beneficial school reform. We theorized that developing their own EQ competencies would also enable the school counseling trainees to appropriately use selected concepts with their students and in their leadership efforts at their internship sites. We decided to introduce and teach EQ competencies in our existing school counseling training program at the point of the internship semester. We chose to use the Six Seconds model (Freedman, 2007) because it has been systematically developed and well researched. We also chose to use the associated research-validated self-report, the Six Seconds Emotional Intelligence Assessment (SEI) (Six Seconds, 2011), to measure student growth in EQ competencies over the course of the sixteen-week semester.

The learning and teaching philosophy that was used to deliver the EQ lessons derives from the constructivist belief that all learning occurs as a result of individual meaning making, as learners integrate content with their own self-knowledge and reflections. A constructivist teaching philosophy embodies the belief that learners need to be actively involved in their learning, that lessons needs to be interactive, and that the instructor needs to model, coach, and facilitate self-discovery through experimentation and discussion.

In the Six Seconds' Learning Philosophy, the authors maintain that "wisdom lives within . . . no way is *the* way . . . [and] the process *is* the content" (Freedman, 2011, para. 10; italics added). The EQ lessons we designed for our school counseling graduate students included a focus on sharing feelings, group experiences, active learning, and students being able to "engage, activate, and reflect" (McCown, Jensen, Freedman, & Rideout, 2010, p. 10). Videos, pictures, music, interactive experiential exercises, reflection, and dialogue are essential components of the teaching and learning philosophy.

INTERNSHIP CONTEXT
The graduate student interns involved in this pilot program were from one specific cohort of the MEd school counseling program attending a university in the southwestern United States in a face-to-face classroom at a distance learning site. As a key component of the MEd school counseling training program, the internship met the Council for Accreditation of Counseling and Related Educational Programs' (CACREP's) requirements, which included six hundred hours of supervised practice in K–12 settings. As faculty supervisors, we each were responsible for providing regularly scheduled group supervision over the course of the sixteen-week semester during which the internship took place. In addition, we each met with students and their field supervisors at their school sites a minimum of three times during the semester. The professional school counseling field supervisor for each student provided ongoing, one-on-one, on-site supervision. The graduate interns were placed in a variety of K–12 schools that were diverse in socioeconomic status and ethnicity. The faculty for one internship section facilitated the existing group supervision format, which included a check-in, discussion of internship accomplishments and challenges, as well as the development of skills and opportunities for leadership, collaboration, and advocacy. The faculty for the other internship section infused the traditional format with emotional intelligence competencies, including the Six Seconds' Model conceptual framework.

RATIONALE
We believe that emotional intelligence competencies are critical components of the prosocial classroom for students and adults and a prerequisite for effective school counseling leadership, collaboration, and advocacy for all K–12 students. A prosocial classroom comprises many factors, from a constructivist curriculum to proactive classroom management to democratic classroom climate and enhanced multicultural awareness. Our premise was that before the interns could work with K–12 students on their EQ competencies, it was crucial for them to understand their own EQ competencies, strengths, and areas of needed growth. It was important for the interns to develop *themselves* as emotionally intelligent leaders, role models, coaches, and change agents. Therefore, we, as faculty supervising the graduate interns as they became advocates for prosocial classrooms, believed that they

would benefit in terms of their effectiveness from training in EQ competencies, both for themselves and to use in their work in schools.

PLANNING

Over the course of the semester prior to the internship, both of us completed training on the Six Seconds model and received the Six Seconds Certification in using the Six Seconds Emotional Intelligence Assessments for use with adults and youth, called the SEI and the SEI-YV (Six Seconds, 2011). Near the start of the internship semester, one of us participated in an intensive five-day training in presentation and delivery of the Six Seconds model and received EQ certification, permitting her use of the Six Seconds model in teaching and supervision. The teaching approach in the Six Seconds model is experiential, interactive, engaging, and reflective.

We worked with one cohort of school counseling students comprising twelve females and one male of diverse age and ethnic backgrounds. With two sections of nearly equal size, determined by student self-selection and without prior knowledge of the research project, we determined that one section would receive the EQ training while the other would follow the typical curriculum focused on internship experiences and needed leadership and advocacy skills. While students in the two groups knew each other, the control group was not exposed to the intensive personal EQ training, nor did they apply it in their internship sites. It was first necessary to obtain student buy-in to participate in the program. We used the SEI assessment instrument for EQ competencies as a pre- and posttest for all students. Students in one group were requested to simply complete the pre and post assessments as part of a series of leadership assessments typically included in the syllabus. In the EQ group, students were required to reflect on their individual results and were told that group results would be discussed in class as part of the training module on emotional competency. The students and faculty member in the internship section that worked with the Six Seconds' competencies reviewed and discussed their own individual and group pretest results and used these to inform the teaching and learning for the subsequent weeks.

IMPLEMENTATION

At the first semester meeting, the faculty introduced the students in the EQ section to the overall planned program and engaged the students in the initial lesson. As part of the internship requirements, both sections of students identified advocacy projects at their internship sites and, with their supervisors and collaborators, planned interventions to address a targeted school concern. Both sections of students were required to collect data to show impact and results. The students in the EQ section were encouraged to use the competencies they were learning in their internship work. In the EQ section, the faculty member helped the interns and their school supervisors to consider the use of the SEI-YV for a school-based measure of EQ competencies for selected students who would be part of the interns' advocacy project and as one measure of guidance lesson effectiveness.

The main part of the project, the teaching of EQ skills to one section of interns during their internship group supervision seminar, was planned for the duration of the semester, or sixteen weeks. We met eight times for three and a half hours to meet the requirements of the sixteen-week semester. Since eight lessons were required to teach the eight competencies in the Six Seconds model, the time frame allowed each session to focus on one competency.

The objective of the internship seminar lessons, therefore, was to involve the student interns in an interactive, constructivist learning model, where they themselves would be engaged with the EQ activities. They would be actively learning the skills and reflecting on their own competencies and those of their classmates. Each week, the faculty instructor of the EQ group based her lesson on one EQ competency using the structure of the Six Seconds model (Freedman, 2007). The eight competencies introduced are found within the three domains of the Six Seconds model: know yourself (enhance emotional literacy and recognize patterns); choose yourself (apply consequential thinking, navigate emotions, engage optimism, and enhance intrinsic motivation); and give yourself (increase empathy and pursue a noble goal).

SAMPLE LESSON PLAN

A portion of the lesson plan, on the competency of increased empathy, is provided here. Empathy is a critical component, obviously, of all counselor education and all human interaction. It is being open to others' feelings and experiences and genuinely caring about them. Actions taken with empathy include listening, sharing, and formulating a response. Empathy is crucial for decision making, for forming trusting and long-lasting friendships, and for making connections with one's world.

The faculty instructor (Susan) began the empathy lesson with a four-minute YouTube video from an organization that she was following on Facebook, the Japan Earthquake Animal Rescue Society, in which team members rescued a disoriented dog hiding in tall grass. A dialogue followed.

> Susan. How did this video make you feel? When I first viewed this, I felt overwhelmed with emotion and couldn't stop crying. Even though this was the third time I've seen it, I guess I'm still crying! I also feel so grateful for the work of this rescue group.
>
> Martina. (Wiping her own tears.) I was so caught up with the helplessness of the poor dog and the empathy of the rescuers. . . . I'm juggling lots of different feelings, from sadness to happiness and relief.
>
> Susan. How did the rest of you respond to this video?
>
> Elise. It really helped me see a whole new complexity to empathy—how it's more than just listening to others; it involves doing something active to help and to actively express our caring.

CARLA. And it also made me realize that empathy is not just for people; your showing this to us expands for us the definition of empathy to include all living things and the natural world.

MARTINA. And, Dr. Stillman, thank you so much for sharing your feelings so openly with us.

ELISE. Right, your modeling of this gives us permission to cry or show our feelings to our own students at the right moment.

Additional parts of the lesson plan included the following:

1. Sharing perceptions about people in photos cut from magazines and discussing why certain pictures resonated with them. This exercise elicited profound discussion, sharing experiences, and challenging assumptions.
2. Reflecting about times that empathy was important in their own lives.
3. Reviewing a compendium of EQ competency exercises from *Feeling Smart* (Jensen, 2010), class members explored their own experiences of hopelessness and, reflecting on the challenges of homelessness, the need to understand others' complex experiences. One student stated, "This lesson taught me the importance of needing to get as much information as possible before forming assumptions about others."
4. Engaging in an experiential exercise. In this activity students were divided into small groups; read a scenario from *Choose to Change* (Franklin, 2009); and discussed how the protagonist and others in their scenario might think, feel, and act. One student stated she thought this exercise was a great tool for teaching empathy with her students.
5. Focusing on empathy for self, sharing things each intern did when sad, lonely, stressed, or anxious. In the ensuing dialogue, Martina said, "The EQ competency of empathy has helped me to realize that I am only human and that I need to be kinder to myself. I have started to also realize that it is okay if things are not perfect. I will admit that this is a lesson that has taken me longer to be able to grasp, but I am working on it."
6. Acting on empathy. Students made a commitment to do something in the coming week for someone they knew who needed empathy. Students were asked to consider how empathy was connected to their "noble goal" (Freedman, 2007, p. 194), the final competency in the Six Seconds model, which connects one's actions to one's values and overarching life purpose.

After learning about the EQ competencies and using them in their internship sites, the students remarked on the value of these competencies for individual, small-group, and classroom lessons and on how they informed their understanding of their own, their students', and their colleagues' needs.

KEY LEARNING

The data from the SEI self-report allowed the students to assess their competencies prior to beginning the course work; to strengthen these competencies during the semester; and then, following engagement in a complete set of eight lessons, to compare the posttest results to their pretest scores. We found that the integration of the SEI self-report pre–post assessment added to the interns' interest in and motivation for the program. In addition, we asked that the interns in the EQ group integrate the EQ lessons in their own internship sites as they learned them. The graduate students discovered and shared with us that they could regularly employ these competencies in typical school counseling settings such as individual, small-group, and classroom lessons and in their work as change agents. They learned that their own experience of the model helped them to be better counselors to their students, using the competencies for their own growth first and then for their students. The eight EQ competencies all lend themselves to counselor development as well as to counseling and consulting in the prosocial classroom.

One student, Janine, said,

> During my internship, I implemented the Six Seconds emotional intelligence model. The competencies of the model provided a framework to meet the individual needs of students and to develop an evidence-based school counseling program. Specifically, I used the Six Seconds model and the eight corresponding competencies to build the curriculum for a social skills group. The Six Seconds framework has been crucial in developing the focus of the group through the model's curriculum and assessment.

Another intern wrote about her experience with her high school students: "I really enjoyed showing my students the EQ competencies. I feel that they all got something out of it like a new perspective on how to handle difficult situations."

We learned that it was important to supplement the current leadership and advocacy focus of the internship curriculum with the addition of EQ competencies. Feedback from all students in the EQ group was that the opportunity to develop these competencies for themselves, as well as to learn about how to use them with their K–12 students, parents, and colleagues, was transformative and life changing. One intern wrote in her reflection paper, "The EQ competencies have helped me to keep a better balance in my life. Many times it is easy for people to get overwhelmed with work and their personal lives."

We also learned that, as educational leaders, it was beneficial to use our own EQ competencies to make the pilot study happen and accomplish our shared mission. We found that each competency enhanced our work and allowed us to collaborate successfully to see the project come to fruition.

Emotional literacy gives people insight into their feelings and those of others and into how these emotions drive behavior and motivation. Both faculty members engaged emotional literacy to become aware of and share their feelings with each other, including anticipation, excitement, and doubt.

Recognizing patterns requires acknowledging frequently recurring reactions in self and others, resulting in insight and masterful behavior. We knew we could trust each other to remain committed and carry out our respective roles in a timely and dedicated manner. We also recognized our respective areas of greatest strength and were able to bring these to the project to facilitate implementation.

Applying consequential thinking is an essential skill for any leader, and in the case of the prosocial educator, it is necessary for implementation of a transformational systemic change. It allows the leader to evaluate his or her decisions and potential effects. We applied consequential thinking to weigh our decisions, taking into consideration our own, our students', and others' feelings; potential obstacles; and available energy and time.

Engaging intrinsic motivation is an important competency for gaining energy from personal values. Both of us shared a commitment to emotional intelligence as a component of effective educational leadership, prosocial education, counseling, supervision, and coaching. Therefore, we wished to integrate it into our work with school counseling interns about to embark on their professional careers as school counselors. We used intrinsic motivation when the "going got tough."

Feelings provide insight and energy. The skill of navigating emotions allows people to transform the variety of emotions that occur during any project for continued effective leadership. We were able to discuss our feelings regarding ongoing accomplishments and obstacles during the process and use these feelings for furthering effective decision making.

According to Six Seconds, an optimistic perspective "allows us to see beyond the present and take ownership of the future. This skill blends thinking and feeling to shift our beliefs and attitudes to a more proactive stance" (Freedman, 2007, p. 168). Optimism allows one to see success as "permanent, pervasive, and personal" (Seligman, 2006, p. 282) and failure as temporary, isolated, and requiring personal effort to remedy. During the course of the EQ project, many options had to be considered, obstacles overcome, and accomplishments celebrated. Some problems occurred with school districts' willingness to participate. For example, at one internship site, the intern and supervisor were enthusiastic; however, the administrator vetoed the plan with no room for discussion or revision. Optimism helped us to use a solution-focused approach to implement program goals.

Empathy, as discussed earlier, is a key element of effective and resonant leadership. We used empathy in consulting with each other and making program decisions that reflected concern and caring for all involved. It is obvious to us that, in prosocial education, empathy is a key component for curriculum designers, instructors, and program leaders. The instructor for the EQ group encouraged the students to use the empathy lesson that they themselves experienced to inspire their own lesson preparation and development.

The Six Seconds model is unique in its addition of the competency of pursuing a noble goal (Freedman, 2007, p. 194). Pursuing noble goals means using one's personal vision, mission, and convictions to transform ideals into specific and concrete daily choices. Goals are accomplished with integrity and ethical behavior. We continually kept our noble goals in focus and used our collaborative vision to work toward the realization of these goals. Data are still being analyzed at this writing. Preliminary results showed a substantial gain in EQ competence in all subscale scores from pre- to posttest for the EQ group. The SEL group indicated the transformative power of the lessons and their ability to use newly strengthened competencies in their personal and professional development. The two interns who employed the comparable EQ assessment tool for youth (SEI-YV) with their K–12 counseling group students also reported substantial growth in pre- to posttest group scores.

COUNSELOR EDUCATORS PROMOTING PROSOCIAL CLASSROOMS IN COMPLEX SYSTEMS

Counselor educators working to integrate the teaching of EQ competencies into an internship seminar require a clear, intense vision and a personal alignment with the values and goals of the program. They utilize interpersonal alignment, support, and collaboration with close allies in order to convince others of the project's worth. They create many structural alignments involving required tools, models, paperwork, resources, and time to implement the program (Stillman, 2007). It is essential for prosocial educators engaged in systemic change to continually be cognizant of and build on their own emotional intelligence competencies. It is important, as well, to be aware that developing EQ is an incremental process. Prosocial classroom leaders strengthen, reflect on, and share their competencies with others as part of the work of creating and transforming systems for the greater good.

ACKNOWLEDGMENTS

We would like to express our appreciation to Six Seconds; Northern Arizona University; Amy Franklin, Ph.D.; and the Arizona School Counselors Association for resources and grants for our project. A special thanks to our Six Seconds Consultant, Deborah Havert.

REFERENCES

American School Counselor Association. (2005). *The ASCA National Model*. Alexandria, VA: Author.

Cherniss, C., Extein, M., Goleman, D., & Weissberg, R. P. (2006). Emotional intelligence: What does the research really indicate? *Educational Psychologist, 41*(4), 239–245.

Collaborative for Academic, Social, and Emotional Learning. (2011). *What Is SEL?* Retrieved from http://casel.org/why-it-matters/what-is-sel

DeVoss, J. A., & Andrews, M. F. (2006). *School counselors as educational leaders*. Boston: Houghton Mifflin.

Durlak, J. A., Weissberg, R. P., Dymnicki, A. B., Taylor, R. D., & Schellinger, K. B. (2011). The impact of enhancing students' social and emotional learning: A meta-analysis of school-based universal interventions. *Child Development, 82*(1), 405–432. doi:10.1111/j.1467-8624.2010.01564.x. Retrieved from http://onlinelibrary.wiley.com/doi/10.1111/j.1467-8624.2010.01564.x/abstract

Franklin, A. M. (2009). *Choose to change: A step by step teaching guide for fostering EQ in the classroom*. El Prado, NM: Missing Peace Press.

Freedman, J. (2007). *At the heart of leadership: How to get results with emotional intelligence*. San Mateo, CA: Six Seconds.

Freedman, J. M. (2011, January 12). What makes EQ learning work? [Web log post]. Retrieved from http://www.6seconds.org/2011/01/12/what-makes-eq-learning-work

Goleman, D. (1998). *Working with emotional intelligence*. New York: Bantam.

Jensen, A. (2010). *Feeling smart: Emotional intelligence competencies, recommendations, and exercises*. San Francisco: Six Seconds.

Mayer, J. D., Salovey, P., & Caruso, D. R. (1994). Emotional intelligence: Theory, findings, and implications. *Psychological Inquiry, 15*(3), 197–215.

McCown, K., Jensen, A. L., Freedman, J. M., & Rideout, M. C. (2010). *Self-Science: Getting started with social emotional learning* (3rd. ed.). San Francisco: Six Seconds.

Seligman, M. E. P. (2006). *Learned optimism: How to change your mind and your life*. New York: Vintage.

Six Seconds. (2011). *Six Seconds Emotional Intelligence Assessment (SEI)*. Retrieved from http://www.6seconds.org/tools/sei

Stillman, S. B. (2007). Working the system: Aligning to advantage: A grounded theory (Doctoral dissertation, Fielding Graduate University, 2007). *Dissertation Abstracts International, 68*(10), 4499.

Case Study 17B

Leading in the Middle: A Tale of Prosocial Education Reform in Two Principals and Two Middle Schools

MARVIN W. BERKOWITZ,
KRISTEN PELSTER, AND AMY JOHNSTON

There are no leader-proof schools. Great leaders will improve schools, and lousy leaders will kill them. That is why we have offered the Sanford N. Mc-Donnell Leadership Academy in Character Education (LACE) for the past thirteen years. LACE evolved from the work of CHARACTER*plus* as an advocacy and professional development resource in the St. Louis region. After about a decade of such work, its founder, Sandy McDonnell, and its executive director, Linda McKay, realized that their efforts would benefit from two additions: (1) a resident scholar with expertise in character development and education and (2) a more direct and impactful focus on principals. So the Sanford N. McDonnell Professorship in Character Education was created at the University of Missouri–St. Louis, and Marvin W. Berkowitz was hired to fill that slot. In parallel, LACE was created and was established as a core responsibility of the McDonnell Professor.

From its origins, LACE was designed as a yearlong cohort experience for principals in a geographic region (in this case, St. Louis) to help them both understand and lead the implementation of quality, effective character education. Funding came from a variety of sources, including the McDonnell endowment and various corporate and foundation gifts. Each year one or two cohorts of approximately thirty school leaders come together in January for a full year of learning and planning around character education in general and as applied specifically to their schools or districts. Throughout its history, LACE has used a once-a-month full-day workshop format for the core of this endeavor. However, there has always been a written assignment component as well, although it has evolved markedly over time and now constitutes a critical component as it has morphed into a collaborative leadership tool and vehicle for mentoring the participants in their professional growth.

The educational philosophy of LACE comprises the following ideas:

1. The most powerful way to promote prosocial development in students is through whole-school reform.

2. This depends highly, but not exclusively, on the transformation of school culture (including mission, norms, practices, policies, governance structures, etc.).
3. The leader of a school has the greatest leverage on school culture as a lead role model, social engineer, administrator, and so forth.
4. Effective comprehensive character or prosocial education ultimately requires a particular kind of leader—a servant leader, a character education expert and advocate, an empowerer, and a moral role model.

The pedagogy of LACE relies on a few key strategies:

1. *Quality professional development.* The program features a series of full-day workshops by leading experts in character education (some of the more frequent workshop leaders are Marvin W. Berkowitz, Hal Urban, Phil Vincent, Avis Glaze, Tom Lickona, Clifton Taulbert, Ron Berger, Charles Elbot, and Maurice Elias).
2. *Reflective curriculum.* We implement a monthly curriculum of collaboratively written responses to structured reflection tasks.
3. *Nurtured collaborative leadership.* We require each participant to form a stakeholder–representative leadership team for character education and to craft the monthly written reflections with that team.
4. *Expert critical feedback.* The directors of LACE read each participant's monthly reflection and provide detailed customized written feedback. This feedback is intended to be (a) shared with the leadership team and (b) then collaboratively applied to revising the originally submitted assignment.
5. *Site planning.* The curriculum of monthly assignments is designed to build the foundation for the final LACE requirement, a site-specific implementation plan which is submitted as a final report at graduation.
6. *Peer modeling.* We have learned that educators want to hear from their peers who have been there and done what they are doing. We do this in two ways. First, we take the cohort to a full day of site visits to National Schools of Character (NSOC). Second, we partner with CHARACTER*plus* to bring principals from other NSOCs around the country to St. Louis to present to LACE (and other educators).

Over the past thirteen years, nearly five hundred educators have gone through the LACE year. It is not easy, and we routinely lose 20 to 25 percent of the participants during the LACE year, generally because they were unable to fulfill the LACE obligations for a wide variety of reasons. When school leaders successfully complete LACE, there is no guarantee either that they "got it" or that they will successfully implement "it." Leading comprehensive school reform is not easy, and even if one does it well, it takes more time than most would want. Enthused LACE graduates frequently move too fast and need to be encouraged to slow down before they burn out their staffs. Nevertheless, when they do it and do it right, and do it long enough, the results can be transformative. In fact, if we start counting after LACE had been in existence for seven years and look at the following time span (i.e., 2005–2011), there have been twenty-three schools and three districts in the St. Louis region that have been named NSOC and are led by LACE graduates. That is approximately one-quarter of all NSOC schools and districts in the entire country during this time span. Let's take a quick look at just two examples. First we will look in depth at Ridgewood Middle School and then more briefly at Francis Howell Middle School (FHMS), because FHMS is featured in a separate case study in this volume (see case study 6A, "Francis Howell Middle School, Missouri" in this volume).

RIDGEWOOD MIDDLE SCHOOL (ARNOLD, MO)

While sharing some key characteristics with Francis Howell Middle School (they both are middle schools, have approximately the same number of students per grade, are National Schools of Character, overlap in key implementation strategies, and have dynamic enlightened leadership), the Ridgewood Middle School (RMS) story is quite different. Whereas FHMS went from good to great, RMS had to go from horrible to great. And FHMS has 850 students from grades six to eight, while RMS has five hundred students in grades seven to eight. FHMS serves a mostly suburban middle- to upper-middle-class population, and RMS serves a mostly rural low-SES population (43 percent eligible for free or reduced-price lunch and the remainder close to eligibility).

The beginning seems to be a good place to start the RMS story (cf., Haynes & Berkowitz, 2007). RMS began its character-education-informed school transformation journey a few years before FHMS. When then superintendent, Diana Bourisaw, came to the district, she discovered a serious mess at RMS. Over the years, her predecessors had allowed it to serve as the repository of bad teachers for the district. When a principal discovered a teacher, often tenured, who was a rotten apple, rather than fighting the system, the principal requested a reassignment to RMS. So a majority of the teachers (but certainly not all of them) did not like children and should not have been teaching. This led to a climate in which the students knew that the staff and school did not care about them and that no one cared about the school. In the words of current principal Kristen Pelster, "The appearance of the school [in 2000] was deplorable; unkempt with every inch of the bathrooms, locker rooms, and bleachers covered with graffiti, profanity, and racial slurs. A police officer had to be stationed at the school because of the daily violence and drug use. No other school in the district, not even the high schools, had a police officer. Attendance was low and standardized test scores were even lower. Only 30% of the students met the NCLB standards in communication arts and only 7% did so in mathematics" (Pelster, 2011). In the first quarter of 2001, a school of five hundred students saw six hundred failing grades posted. Bourisaw promptly brought in a new leadership team to "clean up Dodge City": Principal Tim Crutchley and Assistant Principal Kristen Pelster. Crutchley had been a middle school assistant principal in another district and Pelster an elementary school assistant principal within the RMS district (Fox School District), and they did not know each other. (As a wonderful coda to this story, they eventually fell in love and later married when Crutchley was promoted to assistant superintendent and Pelster became the RMS principal.)

First they diagnosed the problem: RMS and its staff did not care about the students, and the students knew that. Despite the abysmal academic record, they decided not to focus on the curriculum, pedagogical methods, or other areas of academics. Both of them were graduates of LACE, and so they knew that the key was to improve the school climate. They (often personally) cleaned up the physical plant, which was in utter disrepair due to neglect and abuse. They articulated a vision of a staff that served student social and emotional needs and invested in professional development to support that. They administered a needs assessment and tried to design initiatives tied to the results. However, given the nature of the staff, they experienced significant resistance. Loosely playing good cop (Pelster) and bad cop (Crutchley), they modeled good practice, implored staff to join the journey, and pressured them to change. However, many of the teachers were unable or unwilling to do so. In a critical staff meeting in the second semester of their administration, Crutchley frankly told the staff to get on board or get off the ship. He expected to be fired; but instead he discovered that about one-third of the staff were waiting for such strong leadership and vision and joined him enthusiastically. At the end of the year, about a third of the staff left, and over the next two years, another third left. This was not serendipitous but rather the result of a strategic effort by Crutchley and Pelster to either win staff over or drive them out. The departers were similarly strategically replaced with teachers who shared the vision.

Both Crutchley and Pelster also poured their lives into RMS, engaging in what can only be called supererogatory leadership. They began to call every absent student and routinely went to their homes to get them out of bed and to school. They did laundry for families at school. When they realized that teachers routinely failed students for unsubmitted assignments, they created a ZAP (Zeros Aren't Permitted) program during lunch—and they personally staffed it themselves for ninety minutes every day. (The original six hundred F grades in their first quarter are currently down to six.) They put in seventy or more hours a week, sometimes sleeping at the school. This was clearly above and beyond the call of duty, but it created near miraculous results.

Other key initiatives included an advisory program led by a leadership team of students (two per advisory). This program has been manualized (Owens & Asher, 2008). They also created a yearlong orientation program for sixth graders who were to become RMS students, largely run by the current students. The school counselor created a truancy program in partnership with the county juvenile judge. Teen Leadership is a program designed by the Flippen Group that teaches basic social and leadership skills to a diverse group of students. When a relatively new language arts teacher (Kacie Heiken-Ploen) proposed a rather daring new course for at-risk girls, Pelster (then the principal) did not balk and instead said, "At RMS it is okay to fail. Let's try it, and if it doesn't work we won't do it again." Out of Pelster's enlightened leadership and Heiken-Ploen's creativity and genuine heart for struggling girls was born Aftershock. A language arts course, its curriculum is focused on the real problems of these girls: eating disorders, suicide, abuse, cutting, and the like. Each month a topic is studied through reading and discussion, and then the students write extensively (journaling, producing a newsletter that goes out to the community to teach them about the problem, and so forth). They bring in guest speakers and engage in service learning. This course has literally saved girls' lives and clearly given them a new positive sense of self, which has led to reengagement and success in school and life. There is now a boys' version of the course, entitled ImpACT, led by a male teacher as well. As Pelster explains it, "We routinely take the kids in danger of dropping out, or much worse, and turn them into caring, prosocial leaders who succeed academically" (Pelster, 2011, p. 2).

A former music teacher and an eternally impassioned optimist, Pelster starts each school year with a theme for the year (this year it is "Stars of Character") and aligns the first day of school with it as a near carnival (e.g., one year, with a western theme, students were greeted by Pelster on horseback dressed in cowboy attire whooping it up). The philosophy is that students should go home the first day of school thinking, "Wow, this is a great place. I can't wait to come back."

Once again, the proof is in the data. From 2000 to 2010, yearly discipline referrals steadily dropped from three thousand to approximately three hundred, and the school police officer is gone. Attendance increased from 89 percent to over 95 percent. The percentage of students meeting state standards on the Missouri state student achievement test (MAP) has risen from 30 percent to 68 percent in communication arts and from under 7 percent to 71 percent in mathematics. In a nutshell, Pelster concludes,

> the clientele of Ridgewood has not changed these past 10 years. Our families still struggle with extreme poverty and a section of our attendance area is still one of the highest crime areas in our county. . . . The difference is these kids, that 10 years ago were destroying the building and each other, now know they are valued and cared about, and now take on the leadership responsibility to create a culture and climate where they value each other, their school, their character, and their academic success. Most importantly, all this was done without ever changing our academic curriculum or our textbooks. . . . What we changed was how we met the social, emotional, and character development needs of our students. (Pelster, 2011, p. 4)

FRANCIS HOWELL MIDDLE SCHOOL (ST. CHARLES, MO)

Francis Howell Middle School is different from Ridgewood. It is larger (850 students), and it has three grades (grades 6 through 8). Furthermore, whereas Ridgewood started its journey from the bottom, FHMS has a history of success. Ridgewood began with a new administrative team, and FHMS had a long-standing principal ready to try something different. Lastly, whereas Ridgewood had a low-SES population, FHMS draws from a largely suburban, privileged community. Amy Johnston, who had been an administrator at FHMS for ten years (as principal and assistant principal), recognized that she needed to counteract the sense of complacency and stagnation at the school. Something had to change, but she was not sure what. At this point it was suggested she apply for LACE, something with which she was unfamiliar. Curiosity and a sense of inertia led her to LACE, and inspiration took over her pedagogical and administrative soul (to hear it from her and her staff, see their video at http://fhm.fhsd.k12.mo.us—"Video about Us").

It is not uncommon that a principal (or other educator) discovers a new vision and becomes so enthused that she shifts into high gear without realizing that those around her do not share that fervor and will not simply start sprinting toward that vision alongside the new "prophet." Amy was a case in point—she started off like a rocket. Amy is a high-energy person and started following this dead-end path. One afternoon in June about a decade ago, Amy called Marvin Berkowitz, all excited because a district administrator had just offered her twenty thousand dollars of government funding that was about to expire. She wanted to apply this to her nascent character education initiative and had to spend the money in short order, so she made a budget and faxed it for feedback. Berkowitz read it, called her back, and told her to tear it up. It was all about buying "things." Instead, he told her to spend every dime on her staff; invest in the staff. She did, and it was a turning point for the school. She brought seventeen staff to the five-day Summer Institute in Character Education at the University of Missouri–St. Louis (it remains the largest group from one school to ever attend the institute). They spent five days immersing in character education, becoming a team, and planning for the upcoming school year.

Amy astutely and quickly realized that she needed to slow down, listen to her staff, and slowly build their interest and commitment. For example, she started by proposing to follow the experts. The Character Education Partnership suggests starting by identifying a set of core ethical values around which to build the initiative. When Amy suggested that they adopt ethical values, the staff became very uncomfortable. She suggested they adopt the virtues that Tom Lickona (1991) had identified, but they remained skeptical. So she wisely dropped that and spent more than a year building staff relations, exploring their values, and only then slowly building a school community consensus around values. In her words,

> Before we could ask our students to respect one another, we had some work to
> do as a staff. We had to discuss things like gossip, cliques, and disrespect among
> the adults in the building before we could lead those conversations with our stu-
> dents; and this is tough stuff! Instead of admitting personal flaws and working to
> change them, it is much easier to say the plate is too full. All character education
> begins in the mirror, which is why so many people reject it. (Johnston, case study
> 6A, this volume, "Francis Howell Middle School, Missouri")

As she describes it, she and they were daunted by the proposition of "teaching character" because that meant looking in the mirror at their own character. They painstakingly, as a staff and as individuals, grappled with this challenge.

She reworked the normal staff meetings to allow smaller-group time with her. She initiated a once-per-week twenty-minute advisory-like class called "Character Connection," designed after the innovative work at Halifax Middle School in Pennsylvania. Teachers were nervous about how to sit with a mixed age (sixth through eighth graders) and simply have a conversation, so she brought me in to train teachers and her Character Council (approximately sixty students who would co-lead the advisories). Amy also prioritized professional development and parent involvement. She continually supported staff going to workshops, classes, lectures, conferences, and the like. She has sent more staff to both the Berkowitz Summer Institute and to LACE than any other school leader. And she began book studies with both staff and parents. She leads a parent book study group in the evenings in which they read books about teenagers.

Finally, Amy understands that school and classroom climate are the context in which character and learning can flourish or perish. She instituted a procedure whereby the first two days of school were to be curriculum free. When she first proposed this to the staff, they were highly resistant, but she understood how important the initial experience of a school was. Staff essentially argued that they could not cover the entire curriculum as it was and could not give up two instructional days. Amy insisted. When asked what they should do instead, she said "unity builders." When they asked what that was, she handed them a sheet with suggestions (different ones for each period of the day so that students would not repeat the same activities). The staff respect and love Amy, so they begrudgingly went along with what they felt was an ill-advised policy. Partway through that year, they began to request that they begin every year with two days of unity-building activities. What they were witnessing were classrooms where students were better behaved and harder working, simply because they had invested in relationships and norms during those first two days of school.

Like Ridgewood, FHMS has the data to back up their success, and these are detailed in the FHMS case study in this volume. FHMS is doing something right. According to Amy Johnston, it is character education. In her own words, "If students graduate from here with good character, then we are doing our job."

CONCLUSION

Schools and their leaders constantly struggle with how to engage in effective school improvement while both trying to serve the dual masters of academic achievement and prosocial student development and simultaneously being pulled in different directions by the demands and constraints of educational policy; unenlightened leadership (at the federal, state, and local levels); the monomaniacal focus of many teachers' unions; dwindling material resources; and panicked and demanding parents. All of this occurs in a context of ignorance about effective practice. Therefore, it is refreshing to mentor and witness the genius of leaders like Amy Johnston, Tim Crutchley, and Kristen Pelster. The stories of Francis Howell Middle School, Ridgewood Middle School, and the Leadership Academy in Character Education bear witness to two key lessons. First, it can be done. Schools can be transformed to better serve both academic achievement and prosocial development. Second, good prosocial education is good education. Teaching harder to the test is not a path to robust sustained success (see Corrigan, chapter 23 in this volume). Creating a caring school climate that nurtures social, emotional, and moral competencies and supports the motives and skills necessary for productive work (during and after schooling) instead is the true path to success in school and life.

REFERENCES

Berkowitz, M. W. (2011). Leading schools of character. In A. M. Blankstein & P. D. Houston (Eds.), *Leadership for social justice and democracy in our schools* (The Soul of Educational Leadership Series, pp. 93–121). Thousand Oaks, CA: Corwin Press.

Haynes, C., & Berkowitz, M. W. (2007, February 20). What can schools do? *USA Today*, p. 13a.

Lickona, T. (1991). *Educating for Character*. New York: Bantam.

Owens, B., & Asher, A. (2008). *R Character Council: Empower students through character education and service learning*. St. Louis, MO: Owens/Asher Publishing.

Pelster, K. (2011). *United States Senate briefing on SEL: School climate and character education*. Arnold, MO: Ridgewood Middle School, Fox School District. Retrieved December 2, 2011, from http://www.nasponline.org/advocacy/news/2011/may/Kristin _Peltzer_statement.pdf

Case Study 17C

Prospective Teachers' Work with Homeless Youth: Articulating the Value of Service Learning in Teacher Education

Heidi L. Hallman

This case study conceptualizes service learning as having the potential to disrupt deficit theorizing on the part of teachers (Sleeter, 2008), thus encouraging teacher candidates to critically question schooling and patterns of inequity. Deficit theorizing, or blaming school failure on students' individual characteristics and backgrounds, is antithetical to prosocial education, as prosocial education encourages educators to develop strategies for positive response and empathy toward students. Because we know that many pre-service teachers learn to teach by teaching their university peers in mock teaching environments (Shrofel, 1991), many beginning teachers have little direct, field-based experiences working with youth in schools before student teaching. Therefore, the attitudes that beginning teachers express early in their careers may influence how they will develop as teachers. Service learning offers a way to reenvision the relationship between teacher and students, countering a teacher-centered model of instruction (Cuban, 1993), comprised, in part, of "a conception in which a teacher stands before students who face forward in seats and who are supposedly poised to listen and learn" (Portes & Smagorinsky, 2010, p. 236). Service learning works against this model, becoming both a counternarrative and conduit for preservice teachers to reconsider the relationship between teacher and students.

Service learning in teacher education in this case study is also framed as an early field experience for prospective teachers, and early and diverse field experiences in teacher education programs have been touted as one of the keys to successful teacher preparation (Darling-Hammond, 2006; Feiman-Nemser & Buchman, 1987; Hallman & Burdick, 2011; Sleeter, 2008; Zeichner, 2010). Holistically, such field experiences exist to promote preservice teachers' understanding and practice of culturally responsive pedagogy (Ladson-Billings, 2001), as well as to bridge beginning teachers' reflection on the constructs of theory and practice present in the teaching act (Shulman, 2004). Though field experiences have been acknowledged as an important component of teacher education programs, little work has explored the unique qualities of community-based settings as potential sites for teachers' learning (see Coffey, 2010). Coffey suggests that community-based settings have the power to transform the ways that beginning teachers think about the effects of schooling in their students' lives, as well as the extent to which social factors influence students' success in school.

Throughout the course of one academic year, I investigated how four preservice English teachers conceptualized service learning in a community-based field site. The following questions framed my inquiry:

1. What do preservice teachers reveal about the significance of service learning in a community-based setting?
2. How do they conceptualize service learning in such a space as relevant to their future work as classroom teachers?

The four beginning teachers featured in this case study completed at least forty hours of service learning as tutors/mentors of adolescents involved in an after-school initiative for homeless youth. Framed as an exploratory qualitative case study (Merriam, 1998; Stake, 1995, 2000), the study* took place in the context of Family Partnership's (all names of people and places are pseudonyms) day center for homeless families, as well as in the teacher education program at the University of Kansas. The youth at Family Partnership with whom the preservice teachers worked over the course of the year were homeless during the time of the study, and all were officially part of Family Partnership's program for homeless families. During the entire course of the study, the preservice teachers were enrolled in the Secondary English/Language Arts Education Program at the University of Kansas and were also enrolled in an English education methods course as well as other education courses that comprised their teacher education program. Consistent with the description of instrumental case studies provided by Stake (2000), the study followed this small group of preservice teachers' work in a community-based field site in a detailed manner, aligned with the commitment of preparing beginning teachers to teach in diverse educational contexts.

CONTEXT OF THE CASE STUDY
Family Promise is a national organization framed by a model with a successful history (Family Promise, 2011a). The program has been implemented nationwide in multiple communities and was adopted in Lawrence, Kansas, the community in which this study was situated, in November of 2008. Family Promise, a nonprofit organization committed to helping low-income families achieve lasting independence, is oftentimes contrasted with a "shelter model" of assisting homeless individuals and families, as the program was founded on the premise of assisting homeless families by providing "an integrated approach that begins with meeting immediate needs but reaches

*This study was funded by grants from the Conference on English Education (a constituent group of the National Council of Teachers of English) and the University of Kansas School of Education Research Support Program.

much further to help people achieve independence and to alleviate the root causes of poverty" (Family Promise, 2011b, para. 2). My purposeful selection of a community-based field site focused on serving homeless families and youth in part acknowledged that the education of homeless youth has been continually represented in scant ways in the research literature. It is now estimated that approximately fifty thousand youth in the United States are homeless for six months or longer (National Alliance to End Homelessness, 2011). Most typically, the homeless youth population has been represented as residing in the inner city with single-parent, female-headed families. Yet the "face" of homelessness has changed considerably in the past few years and continues to change. It is now estimated that fourteen out of every ten thousand people are "rural" or "suburban" homeless (as compared to twenty-nine out of every ten thousand people who are "urban" homeless) (National Alliance to End Homelessness, 2011).

The community-based field experience depicted in this case study was initially conceived as part of a course I taught entitled "Teaching English in Middle/Secondary Schools." In years prior to the fall implementation, I had included only "traditional" service learning field sites as options for preservice teachers' completion of the field experience component of the course. However, I desired to broaden the field experience to purposely include a community-based site. I initially conceptualized the community-based field site as an "option" for interested students; however, over the course of the pilot year, I came to conceptualize community-based field experiences as part of the service learning framework for the course. During the first semester of the initiative, four preservice teachers (out of nineteen total preservice teachers enrolled in the course) volunteered to work with Family Partnership's day center for homeless families throughout the fall and spring semesters of one academic year. At the time of the study, all four preservice teachers were in the process of becoming licensed teachers in the area of secondary English/language arts education at the University of Kansas.

METHOD

Ming Nguyen, Sarah Emerson, Tara Stance, and Rebecca Avery (pseudonyms) are the preservice teachers featured in the remainder of this case study. As these four prospective teachers embarked on their service learning experience, I sought to capture their perceptions concerning what the experience meant to the ways in which they conceptualized their future role as "teacher."

As a method of data collection and organization, I viewed preservice teachers' stories of "self" as opportunities to understand their service learning work at Family Partnership. On several occasions, in focus group interviews and seminar meetings, these four beginning teachers were purposefully prompted to focus on the "self" as a way to situate teacher identity as a gradual formation of "becoming" (Gomez, Black, & Allen, 2007). Throughout the remainder of this case study, preservice teachers' stories of their work with homeless youth at Family Partnership are depicted as ways to understand the "becoming" of participants' teacher identities, as well as possibilities for beginning teachers to articulate the value of service learning within the context of a community-based field site.

Preservice teachers' stories of self were captured in multiple formats: in focus group interviews with the preservice teachers in both the fall and spring semesters and in monthly seminar meetings that were held throughout the study. Stories of self were also articulated in preservice teachers' reflective journals (kept throughout the course of the year).

THEMES ILLUMINATED

Understanding the In-School/Out-of-School Connection

The beginning months of participation at Family Partnership prompted preservice teachers to focus on their perceptions of homelessness in the local community. In a seminar meeting held during the first month of the study, after preservice teachers had attended the two-hour volunteer training required by the Family Partnership program, beginning teachers were asked about their familiarity with the issue of homelessness in the local community.

I shared with the four preservice teachers that Barton (1998) writes that the issue of homelessness is often one that is "hidden" in schools and an issue that remains represented in scant ways in the research literature. Sarah, one of the prospective teachers, had been working during her first few weeks at Family Partnership with a middle-school-aged student named Cassie until Cassie and her family transitioned out of the Family Partnership program. Sarah reflected on her role with Cassie and also on what her knowledge of Cassie's life meant for her future work as a classroom teacher. In a seminar meeting in October during the fall semester, Sarah said,

> At first, I felt disappointed that I would no longer be working with Cassie in the Family Partnership program. However, I then reflected on the fact that this is the goal of the program: to transition families to permanent housing. I began to think about how my goal in teaching is not just to think of teaching as relevant to myself as "teacher" but also to what teaching means through the eyes of my students. This experience at Family Partnership really made me consider that.

Later in the fall, Sarah talked about service learning in community-based spaces as prompting her shift to focusing on both herself and her students rather than only herself as "teacher." In her journal at the end of the fall semester, she wrote,

> This experience has showed me in very real ways that students' lives outside of school really do matter to what happens in school. So many times I found myself thinking about this connection. We read about this in our [teacher education] classes, but I don't think I've ever considered it fully. Having an experience outside of a classroom allowed me to see this connection.

Resonating with Coffey's (2010) view that community-based service learning experiences have the power to transform the ways that educators see the effects of schooling in their students' lives, Sarah articulates how a service learning experience outside the more "traditional" classroom field site is beneficial for her as a future teacher. Similarly, Ming saw how situating students' reading interests and abilities was not a simple split between in-school and out-of-school arenas. Ming worked extensively with Penny, a thirteen-year-old middle school student, over the course of the fall semester. Penny was adamant about reading "vampire" books, and Ming at first viewed such books as purely pleasure reading for Penny. Yet, over time, Ming reflected on how her view of Penny's reading habits changed as she spent more time reading with Penny. Below is an excerpt from Ming's journal:

> Penny loves reading vampire books and I thought this was fine but saw it as outside of school reading. I thought that reading aloud a book like this was really only good for her fluency in reading. As we got more into the book, though, I could see how she was really imagining things about the story-world presented in the book. The book was a creative place for her mind, not just a fun book. This is what English teachers want books to do for kids and I am not so judgmental of these types of books anymore.

Ming was able to move from a conception of knowledge that is exclusively school based to one that inhabits both in-school and out-of-school spaces. Instead of dichotomizing reading choices into out-of-school and in-school books, Ming saw the value of Penny's reading choices beyond these defined dichotomies.

Embracing Multiple Visions of the Role of "Teacher"

Preservice teachers sought experiences that would lead them to inhabit a "teacher" role, and the role that they assumed at Family Partnership, in their minds, first resembled a "tutoring" role. Challenging the ways in which service learning within the context of a community-based field site was situated as "other than traditional" field experience in teacher education sought to break the binary of teacher/tutor. The teacher/tutor dichotomy stood strong in the preservice teachers' minds at the beginning of their work in Family Partnership. Challenging this dichotomy was one step in legitimizing the work that the four prospective teachers undertook at Family Partnership. To illustrate the significance of this theme, excerpts from Rebecca's and Tara's journals written early in the fall semester showed that, although they viewed their work at Family Partnership as meaningful, they continued to question the "direct relevance" their work in community-based sites had to their work as future classroom teachers. Rebecca wrote,

> When working with Jason [an adolescent at Family Partnership], I've been able to ask him about what he is good at and how this matches up with what he studies

at school. There seems to be a space for me to interact with him and a way to use his strengths to help him with school knowledge. I don't know if I could do this in the classroom.

Similarly, Tara expressed concerns that her work was more "mentoring" than "teaching." She wrote, "I think all kids need mentors just as they need teachers. I feel like I am contributing to this mentorship of adolescents when I'm at Family Partnership."

During a seminar meeting in the spring semester, Tara and Rebecca both stated that observing manifestations of teaching English in "unofficial" school spaces, such as Family Partnership, had indeed assisted them in viewing the teaching of English as a complex negotiation of multiple systems at play (Lave & Wegner, 1991). This was a shift from prior articulations in the fall semester. Tara said,

> When I started at Family Partnership in the fall, I didn't see the work we did as teaching. I saw it more as mentoring. I've been a Big Sister through the Big Brothers, Big Sisters program, so I wasn't really sure I needed to get better at mentoring. I thought that I was already good at it. I see now that the more experience you have building relationships with students, the better you get at teaching. Teaching English is not just teaching about literature or poetry or something, but about interacting with students about something.

Interacting with students, and practicing empathy and development of positive relationships between teacher and students, is at the heart of prosocial education. Through this service learning experience, teachers like Tara were able to legitimize interpersonal work between teacher and students as "teaching."

Rebecca also followed this thought in one of the focus group interviews, stating,

> Honestly, I was skeptical that my actual skills as a teacher would be built in a place like Family Partnership, but I think it helped me actually expand what I thought about teaching. I think it was good for me to do service learning outside of the formal classroom.

Over time, both Rebecca and Tara saw how service learning in a "nonschool" space helped them better understand the connection between "in-school" and "out-of-school," as well as how they connected to their future role as "teacher."

IMPLICATIONS AND CONCLUSIONS

Ming, Sarah, Tara, and Rebecca used the stories they told about their work at Family Partnership to process how they viewed both who they were as future teachers and what the work of teaching would entail. They also reflected on what they believed about the students with whom they worked, about homeless youth, and about who these youth were and what possibilities existed for them. Over the course of one academic year, they used their stories from their work at a community-based field site to imagine their future work as teachers and to deconstruct binary notions of school/community and teacher/student. Through their service learning work, preservice teachers were able to understand how limited these binaries were, in that they restricted teachers' and students' roles in and out of the classroom. The experience at Family Partnership allowed for an expanded view of what constitutes teaching; teaching in these preservice teachers' minds now included the possibility of fostering relationships between teachers and students.

Preservice teachers' service learning work in community-based field sites has tremendous potential to encourage teacher candidates to learn about their students' capabilities, strengths, and interests (Sleeter, 2008) early in teacher education programs. Most convincingly, work in community-based field sites encourages prospective teachers to deconstruct the assumed binaries of school/community, self/other, and teacher/student that so frequently limit beginning teachers' conceptualizations of teaching and learning. As a feature of teacher education programs, service learning in community-based field sites has the potential to work toward prompting preservice teachers to question and reenvision their future work as classroom teachers.

REFERENCES

Barton, A. C. (1998). Teaching science with homeless children: Pedagogy, representation, and identity. *Journal of Research in Science Teaching, 35*(4), 379–394.

Coffey, H. (2010). "They taught me": The benefits of early community-based field experiences in teacher education. *Teaching and Teacher Education, 26*(2), 335–342.

Cuban, L. (1993). *How teachers taught: Constancy and change in American classrooms, 1890–1990.* New York: Teachers College.

Darling-Hammond, L. (2006). *Powerful teacher education: Lessons from exemplary programs.* San Francisco: Jossey-Bass.

Family Promise. (2011a). *Home page.* Retrieved September 5, 2011, from http://www.familypromise.org

Family Promise. (2011b). *Our work.* Retrieved September 5, 2011, from http://www.familypromise.org/our-work

Feiman-Nemser, S., & Buchman, M. (1987). When is student teaching teacher education? *Teaching and Teacher Education, 3*(4), 255–273.

Gomez, M. L., Black, R. W., & Allen, A.-R. (2007). "Becoming" a teacher. *Teachers College Record, 109*(9), 2107–2135.

Hallman, H. L., & Burdick, M. N. (2011). Service-learning and the preparation of English teachers. *English Education, 43*(4), 341–368.

Ladson-Billings, G. (2001). *Crossing over to Canaan: The journey of new teachers in diverse classrooms.* San Francisco: Jossey-Bass.

Lave, J., & Wegner, E. (1991). *Situated learning: Legitimate peripheral participation.* New York: Cambridge University Press.

Merriam, S. B. (1998). *Qualitative research and case study applications in education.* San Francisco: Jossey-Bass.

National Alliance to End Homelessness. (2011). *Annual report 2010.* Retrieved September 5, 2011, from http://www.endhomelessness.org

Portes, P., & Smagorinsky, P. (2010). Static structures, changing demographics: Educating teachers for shifting populations in stable schools. *English Education, 42*(3), 236–247.

Shrofel, S. (1991). Developing writing teachers. *English Education, 23*(3), 160–177.

Shulman, L. (2004). Pedagogies. *Liberal Education, 91*(2), 18–25.

Sleeter, C. (2008). Equity, democracy, and neoliberal assaults on teacher education. *Teaching and Teacher Education, 24*(8), 1947–1957.

Stake, R. E. (1995). *The art of case study research.* Thousand Oaks, CA: Sage.

Stake, R. E. (2000). Case studies. In N. K. Denzin & Y. S. Lincoln (Eds.), *Handbook of qualitative research* (2nd ed., pp. 435–454). Thousand Oaks, CA: Sage.

Zeichner, K. M. (2010). Rethinking the connections between campus courses and field experiences in college- and university-based teacher education. *Journal of Teacher Education, 61*(1–2), 89–99.

CHAPTER 18

Multicultural Education Is/as/in Prosocial Education

TINIA R. MERRIWEATHER

> Education either functions as an instrument which is used to facilitate integration of the younger generation into the logic of the present system and bring about conformity or it becomes the practice of freedom, the means by which men and women deal critically and creatively with reality and discover how to participate in the transformation of their world.
>
> —Richard Shaull, Foreword to *Pedagogy of the Oppressed* (Freire, 1970/2000)

This chapter aims to connect the principles of multicultural education with the goals of prosocial education. It asserts that multicultural education *is* prosocial education. All of the key tenets of multicultural education are also prosocial in nature. The chapter also considers multicultural education *as* prosocial education. It argues that many of the aspirations of prosocial education are met by multicultural education. Finally, it explores multicultural education *in* prosocial education, connecting the ideas of this chapter to the rest of this volume. The chapter is divided into three sections. It begins with an introduction to multicultural education and the assumptions undergirding the chapter. The first section also identifies and defines key terminology commonly used in multicultural education. Specific connections to prosocial education are considered in the second section. The third section presents a theoretical framework for multicultural education, which serves as the organizing feature for the programs that are reviewed within the chapter. It also contains questions to ponder and concludes with recommendations for future inquiry.

SECTION ONE: FOUNDATIONAL UNDERSTANDINGS OF MULTICULTURAL EDUCATION

Multicultural education has emerged as a vehicle for including diverse groups and transforming the nation's educational institutions (Banks 1994a, Banks & Banks 1992). Multicultural education tries to create equal educational opportunities for all students by ensuring that the total school environment reflects the diversity of groups in classrooms, schools, and the society as a whole. (Banks, 1994, p. 4)

Multicultural Education Is Prosocial Education

Multicultural education is inherently prosocial education. Multicultural education was birthed out of a framework that involves relating to one another. It is a response to a blatantly or implicitly Eurocentric worldview offering the central idea of valuing others not as "others," but as part of a multifaceted, complex world. As we progress further into the twenty-first century, *we* undeniably means being able to interact effectively with those who are both similar to and different from us. Prosocial education involves the social, emotional, and ethical competencies that students need to develop healthy relationships with others. It also involves the transformation of schools and schooling to create the conditions for optimal development and learning. Given the demographics in the United States and the increased global interconnectedness afforded by social networking and other technology, multicultural education is a necessity. As referenced in chapter 1 of this volume, the goals of education include active learning and knowledge attainment, fostering optimal development, and socializing students into diverse communities of social and civic worlds.

Multicultural Education as Process

> What we now call multicultural education . . . is a composite. It is no longer solely race, or class, or gender. Rather it is the infinite permutations that come about as a result of the dazzling array of combinations human beings recruit to organize and fulfill themselves. Like jazz, no human being is ever the same in every context. The variety of "selves" we perform have made multicultural education a richer, more complex, and more difficult enterprise to organize and implement than previously envisioned. . . . Like jazz, multicultural education is less a thing than a process. It is organic and dynamic, and although it has a history rooted in our traditional notions of curriculum and schooling its aims and purposes transcend all conventional perceptions of education. (Ladson-Billings, 2003, pp. 51–52)

Multicultural education is education for, by, about, and inclusive of all. It also involves the process for achieving this ideal and the framework for critiquing where we fall short. It faces the fact that education has not been and is not for all with forward momentum to change. Multicultural education embraces the ultimate goals of education for learning and development in the face of the institutionalized and systemic forces that work against these goals. It actively resists being centered in whiteness, maleness, or privilege while it simultaneously examines these. It is also not centered in otherness, which is a shallow inversion of the former. Multicultural education has multiple and intersecting centers. It embraces the tensions of this intersectionality—it rests in the both/and.

Like jazz, multicultural education is a process, not a finite set of knowledge that can be memorized. It includes how teachers respond moment by moment in a classroom, frame the class, and interact with the students and their families. It also includes policy-level decisions that impact school communities. Because of its complexity, multicultural education resists a simple definition, but it is identifiable. One can know what it is—and what it is not. This process, this forward leaning into the best hopes of what education can be, is why it is prosocial.

Multicultural education is also a method for inquiry about education. Multicultural education interrogates the idea of educational or other experts, similar to the orientation of critical participatory action research (see Public Science Project program explanation in section three below), which values radical inclusion and privileges knowledge and wisdom found outside the academy (Torre, Fine, Stoudt, & Fox, 2010). Multicultural education asks critical questions: What is an expert? How did an expert get to be one? Who are the gatekeepers of expertise? Who is kept out of the expertise pipeline? Multicultural education certainly has renowned established scholars who have written extensively about the topic. Yet multicultural education does not only exist in published scholarship. Its foundation is giving a platform to voices that have gone unheard, valuing multiple perspectives, and leveraging access to opportunity. Multicultural education exists in the everyday lives of teachers and students in schools. Therefore, this chapter emerges not only out of my academic training in the field of applied developmental psychology, but it is also centered in my many years of experience as a teacher and diversity practitioner.

In diversity practitioner circles, the building blocks of multicultural competence are often described in terms of knowledge, awareness, and skills (Sue & Constantine, 2005). Much of my multicultural competence comes from engaging colleagues and students in diversity dialogues, reading books and articles, watching documentaries, taking various courses about multicultural ideas, and attending multiple multicultural professional development seminars. But some of my knowledge, awareness, and skills were formed in my everyday lived experiences of being a person of color in the United States. With the exception of my four years at Spelman College, a historically black college for women in Atlanta, Georgia, all of my experiences of school, from pre-K to graduate school—both as a student and as a teacher—have been overwhelmingly white. Several scholars have previously described this lived experience.

> It is a peculiar sensation, this double-consciousness, this sense of always looking at one's self through the eyes of others, of measuring one's soul by the tape of a world that looks on in amused contempt and pity. One ever feels his two-ness,—an American, a Negro; two souls, two thoughts, two unreconciled strivings; two warring ideals in one dark body, whose dogged strength alone keeps it from being torn asunder. (DuBois, 1903/2007, p. 5)

> The old people say being Indian today is like having your feet in two canoes. One foot in one canoe, one foot in another; one foot in one world, one foot in another. Trying to balance both canoes at the same time while the water underneath is constantly changing; trying to live in two worlds, while the rules are constantly changing. This is what it is like for my students of color, as well as for me. (Flyswithhawks, 1996, p. 35)

Author's Stance

This chapter is a negotiation of the balance of my multiple identities. As a person, I want to reflect familiar truths in an authentic way. As an educator, I want to discuss how I aim to make my pedagogy radically inclusive and progressive as I continue to challenge my students, colleagues, and myself to deeper understandings of multiculturalism. As an emerging scholar, my goal is not to fit into the academy but to transform it. I hope this chapter is useful to both scholars and educators. Because I straddle both worlds, I aim to bridge the gap between theory and practice in how multicultural education is understood. Freire (1970/2000) defines praxis as a task for radicals—as reflection and action upon the world in order to transform it. Consistent with this, my goal is to cause others to critically question, to reflect, and to enable them to act.

History of Multicultural Education

Multicultural education emerges out of several traditions. One of the earliest works cited as multicultural education is Carter G. Woodson's (1933/2006) *The Mis-Education of the Negro*. Other historical influences include African American studies, women's studies, gay/lesbian studies, Chicano studies, and other group studies. In terms of theory, multicultural education is most closely linked to the scholarship of critical pedagogy and thinkers such as Paulo Freire, but there are philosophical connections to the other critical theories, such as critical race theory, feminist theory, and queer theory. In its present form, multicultural education emerged out of the protest movements of the 1960s and 1970s in which the desire for social change included access to, equity in, and transformation of educational institutions. In the 1980s, the preeminent scholars of what we now call multicultural education began publishing. These include James Banks (1995, 2007, 2009); Geneva Gay (2010); Carl Grant (2011); Sonia Nieto (2005); and Christine Sleeter (2005). In 1990, the National Association for Multicultural Education (NAME) was formed by Rose Duhon-Sells (1991).

National Association for Multicultural Education

NAME is a nonprofit volunteer organization that works to advance equity and justice in education, with over 1,500 members in the United States. It aims to provide professional development opportunities for scholars from various disciplines and educational practitioners by maintaining an electronic repository of information related to multicultural education, holding national conferences, supporting locally organized chapters, and advocating for educational policies that support the goals of multicultural education through position papers and policy statements.

NAME emphasizes that multicultural education is a process that places students and their diverse experiences at the center. It has the goal of enabling all students and teachers to work toward structural equality in institutions by equipping them with the requisite skills for the redistribution of power equitably across diverse groups. To achieve this, schools must have a culturally competent and diverse faculty and staff, pedagogical practices that embrace multiple perspectives, and curricula that directly address all forms of injustice. Multicultural education distinguishes between equality and equity and attempts to offer all students equitable educational opportunities (NAME, 2003). The current (2011) president of NAME, Christine Sleeter, discusses how multicultural education and the current push toward standards-based education are both compatible and incompatible. The idea that every student should be presented with a rigorous curriculum is absolutely part of multicultural education, but reducing knowledge to bubbles on standardized tests is not—an idea promoted in this handbook (Corrigan, chapter 23). Fully capturing students' abilities on a standardized test is impossible; however, it is possible to integrate the skills necessary for success on these tests into a lively, engaging, culturally relevant curriculum. Nieto (2005) discusses schools for a "new majority" and challenges the idea of highly qualified teachers purported by No Child Left Behind as limited, especially given the needs of linguistically and culturally diverse students being taught primarily by what Nieto describes as a largely monolithic, monocultural, and monolingual teaching force.

Demographic Realities

In America, all education is in the process of becoming multicultural education. Demographic shifts make this an inevitable necessity. According to the 2010 census, among children seventeen and under, 46 percent are children of color and 54 percent are white. Projections indicate that by 2023, a decade from this writing, fewer than half of all children in this country will be white (Forum on Child and Family Statistics, 2011). The changing demographics of the nation are being encountered daily in the nation's schools. Many school systems, including the largest public school systems in the country, are populated primarily by students of color. In some, these statistics incite fear—fear of the unknown and of the other, fear that the browning of America also indicates its decline. Our way of dealing with this fear has a visible history in the "white flight" to the suburbs surrounding many cities that occurred in the latter half of the twentieth century. Instead of fear and flight, multicultural education presents an opportunity for encounter and embrace. In a country that is highly diverse and almost sixty years after *Brown v. Board of Education* (1954), education cannot be conceived of as for whites only. Though clearly we have moved beyond the Little Rock Nine (1957) and Ruby Bridges (New Orleans, 1960), education should not still be *The Problem We All Live With* as the aptly titled (1964) Norman Rockwell painting says. And yet it is. It cannot be "separate, but equal" over 110 years after *Plessy v. Ferguson* (1896). And yet, in many places, schools are more segregated along racial and economic lines than prior to formal integration (Orfield, Lee, & the Harvard Civil Rights Project, 2007). In a statement to the Supreme Court in 2006, 553 scholars from 201 different social science disciplines from 201 academic institutions affirmed the importance of diversity and integrated schools for both educational and community benefits (The Civil Rights Project, 2006). If prosocial education is rooted in democratic ideals for education and society, then multicultural education is a method for making this possible because such societal shifts are welcomed rather than feared. While some have systematically benefitted from the implicit power structure, all have also been damaged by it, not just those who have been oppressed (Wise, 2011). Because multicultural education sets itself against reinforcing the current inequitable system with a goal for educational excellence, equity, and justice for all, all will benefit. Diversity multiplies our strengths.

Recognizing the heavy costs already borne by those marginalized in education, multicultural education does not subscribe to the scarcity-dominated, inequality-reproducing idea that there is a limited supply of power. Rather, it rests in embracing the notion that the supply of power is endless and can be regenerated (Tuck, 2009a). Certainly multicultural education is not naive about the realities of differential access to resources and inefficient, inequitable funding streams (Rutter & Maughan, 2002). There are real implications of changing the socioeconomic power structures of the current educational system, yet philosophically reimagining education as equitable and just is the source of the idea that all will truly benefit.

The Importance of the Language of Multicultural Education

In multicultural education, how language is used is key. In the 2011 introduction to the fortieth-anniversary edition of Freire's *Pedagogy of the Oppressed*, Macedo explains that the word *oppressed* was chosen for a reason—to denote action. The oppression of people does not exist by happenstance; people and systems actively oppress other people.

> Imagine that instead of writing *Pedagogy of the Oppressed* Freire had written *Pedagogy of the Disenfranchised*. The first title utilizes a discourse that names the oppressor, whereas the second fails to do so. If you have an "oppressed," you must have an "oppressor." What would be the counterpart of disenfranchised? (Macedo, 2011, p. 2)

Because of the importance of language, I am choosing to use the actual language of various scholars to allow their ideas to speak for themselves, thus reinforcing the notion that multicultural education is about valuing multiple perspectives. Tatum (2003) explains the significance of choosing language carefully when identifying groups of people.

> I have used the term people of color to refer to those groups in America that are and have been historically targeted by racism. This includes people of African descent, people of Asian descent, people of Latin American descent, and indigenous peoples (sometimes referred to as Native Americans or American Indians). Many people refer to these groups collectively as non-Whites. This term is particularly offensive because it defines groups of people in terms of what they are not. (Do we call women "non-men?") I also avoid using the term minorities because it represents another kind of distortion of information which we need to correct. So-called minorities represent the majority of the world's population. While the term people of color is inclusive, it is not perfect. As a workshop participant once said, White people have color, too. Perhaps it would be more accurate to say "people of more color," though I am not ready to make that change. (Tatum, 2003, p. 15)

A good rule of thumb for naming groups is to be as specific as possible and to use the terms preferred by members of the group, while recognizing that groups of people are not monoliths; therefore, there will be no perfect terms, and terms change with the times (Castania, 2003). For example, when referring to people of African descent in the United States—a group of which I am a member—some prefer the term *African American*, while others prefer *black*. I will not attempt to speak for all the members of my group, but I can illuminate the language I use and why. In casual conversation, I use the terms interchangeably, but I prefer *black* in part because my parents came of age during the Black Power movement and "Black Is Beautiful" era, and *black* is the term I heard in my home. To me, being black is much deeper than color; it is my culture and my consciousness. When being formal, however, I use *black* to refer to my race and *African American* to refer to my ethnicity. My understanding is that *African American* refers to the descendents of the slave trade in the United States. Immigrants from African countries or other parts of the African diaspora, even if descendent from the slave trade in the Caribbean Islands or in South America, are not technically African Americans. Though in subsequent generations, people from these groups who grew up in the United States may embrace the term *African American*.

Similarly, multiple names abound in other groups. Some may prefer *Native American*, others may prefer *First Nations*, or *American Indian, Native, indigenous, First American*, or the specific group involved, such as *Cherokee*. Naming groups is not an exact science. Throughout this chapter, when I use the term *people of color*, in the U.S. context, I am referring to black, Latino, Asian, Pacific Islander, Native American, Middle Eastern, and multiracial peoples living in the United States. Like Shakespeare, when he asked, "What's in a name?" some may question whether finding the right name to refer to a group is worth the trouble. Castania (2003) explains—

> It is work for all of us, but with time, the process will feel as natural as driving a standard shift car: we will feel more at ease trying new terms, asking questions comfortably, and not letting mistakes interfere with our willingness to build relationships across differences. (Castania, 2003, p. 1)

Language is not only important in describing individuals and groups of people; it is important to be clear about concepts, as well. Therefore, it is critical to define how I am using some key terms of multicultural education.

Key Terminology in Multicultural Education
- Multiculturalism—of many cultures that are equally valued; a qualitative experience of this value.
- Diversity—similarities and differences in social identity categories; can be measured quantitatively. "The goal of diversity is to undo itself" (C. Robinson, personal communication, August 11, 2011).
- Social identifiers—these are relatively fixed social identity categories that exert both individual and intersectional influences on individuals and groups. While some diversity practitioners use slightly different versions, these eight are most common: (1) physical, mental, and emotional *ability*, including the ability to learn; (2) *age*; (3) social *class* and socioeconomic status (*SES*); (4) *ethnicity*, including nationality and first language; (5) *gender* and gender identity; (6) *sexual orientation*; (7) *race* (in a U.S. context); and (8) *religion*, including spirituality.
- Some multicultural educators have found the eight too exclusive given multicultural education's goal of inclusion and the multiple other facets of identity that are relevant to education (Batiste, 2010). Other important identities include (1) immigration status, including undocumented, first-generation, and so forth; (2) language fluency, including bilingualism, monolingualism, and speaking with an accent; (3) appearance and body image; (4) living in a geographic region of the United States; and (5) family structure. The importance of these multicultural social identity categories is to remind us that these and other identities (political party affiliation, first-year teacher, new student, smoker, etc.) are both important but also exist at the surfaces of our lives. Multicultural education helps us to honor each other's visible and invisible identities and those we use to describe ourselves, as well as creating supportive schooling structures in which we each can explore those identities and those that we come to believe and know are common to us all.

Intersectionality
Some have argued that even within the Big 8, there exists a hierarchy. Some have posited a Big 3 of race, class, and gender, or a Big 4 of race, class, gender, and sexual orientation. Still others have argued that at least in the U.S. context, race supersedes all other identifiers (Carter, 2000). These scholars assert that all other identities are

experienced through the lens of race. So, for example, I experience my gender as a black woman, not just as a woman, which leads to the idea of intersectionality in identity. Many research studies only examine identities in relative isolation, although in schools and in society these identities themselves do not have isolated impacts. Strolovitch (2006) adopted the term *intersectionally marginalized* to describe such overlaps, coined by a legal scholar, Kimberlé Crenshaw (1989). This term is appropriate to consider in schools that serve students of color in poor neighborhoods. While even a passing glance at census statistics would show that there are many citizens of color who are not in poverty, and there are many families in poverty who are not people of color, the prevailing image of an "inner-city student" is one who is in fact a person of color, particularly African American or Latino, and poor. Overall child poverty is estimated at one in five children in the United States. While the poverty rate is higher in some communities of color, in raw numbers, the majority of U.S. children in poverty are white. Data from 2009 report the numbers of American children in poverty by race as follows: white (507,000), black (259,000), some other race (99,000), and children of two or more races (160,000) (U.S. Census Bureau, 2010). Though poverty and people of color are often inaccurately and stereotypically conflated, there are historical underpinnings to the confound between class and race.

Class structures are connected to the history of race in the United States. Early in the nation's history, measures of wealth included land and slaves, both of which have racial implications—from the displacement of indigenous peoples and the seizure of their land to the institution of slavery in which African people were considered property. More recently, the impact of the GI Bill, which was intended as an equalizing policy but benefited whites disproportionately, and the current class struggles of undocumented workers—many of whom are people of color—as well as the persistent health disparities along both racial and socioeconomic lines are examples of a continued linked legacy. Because of these confounds and because of the reality that many students are impacted based on the intersection of race and class, scholars should begin to examine these effects with an intersectional understanding of the combined effects of multiple identities, which may be different and likely even greater than their individual impacts (Cole, 2009).

Reframing the Deficit Model

One of the ways that race and class affect how schools treat students rests in a deficit ideology. Multicultural educators reject the common tendency to problematize students, families, communities of color, and poor communities of any racial or ethnic background. This chapter posits that the myriad problems plaguing the schools that serve students of color and/or poor students are the result of systemic inequities, not deficiencies within the individuals in the school communities (see also Artiles, 2011). For instance, it is useful to reframe the "achievement gap" as an "opportunity gap" (Hill, 2010). This term suggests that the structural supports and resources necessary for students to achieve should be accessible to all and equitably distributed. Achievement can only be understood in the context of the opportunities provided for students to achieve (Ladson-Billings, 2006, 2007).

It is also critical to interrogate the metrics used in assessing achievement. White students should not be the standard against which all other students are measured

(D. Sawyer, July 6, 2011, personal communication). Using measures of white students' achievements as the target for students of color reinforces two things that are antithetical to multicultural education—the idea of white as "normal" or the standard and the negative implications of the deficit model. Instead, excellence should be the universal standard.

Another important term to examine and reframe is the term *at risk*. This term, too, is a symptom of deficit thinking—wrongly ascribing the risk to students. Marginally better is the term *placed at risk*, which at least conjures the conditions in which students find themselves. Gordon and AERA (2004) argue that the term *resilience* must also be reconceptualized, coining a new term, *defiance*.

> Our introduction of the concept of defiance into the literature on resilience involves more than a semantic shift. The difference between resilience and defiance is best understood as a difference between survival in the face of challenge, and acts of active resistance to a challenge and pushing against obstacles standing in the way of personal achievement. (Gordon & AERA, 2004, p. 124)

Similar deficit terminology, such as *underprivileged, disenfranchised, inner-city*, and *minority* all connote images of black and Latino youth in the "ghetto," with associated educational hardships and failures. Fine and Ruglis (2009, p. 20) suggest the idea of "circuits of dispossession" to describe the experiences of these youth, which places the onus on the system itself rather than on those dispossessed by it. This is an example of a key goal of this handbook—that is, to underline, emphasize, and insist that the work of prosocial education is to change and optimize schooling and schools for the development and achievement of students; thus, the various orientations of prosocial education stress universal interventions for school change, not targeted or selected programs to change only some students, such as those defined by a deficit model.

Schools Are Racialized Spaces

School experiences exist in racial contexts. For many of the issues plaguing education, such as chronic low achievement and high dropout rates, race is paramount. While an intersectional understanding of race, class, and to a lesser degree gender is crucial to understanding some of the problems of education, the reality is that too often these problems happen disproportionately in schools that serve students of color because of the circuits of dispossession and the opportunity gap. Even in schools in high-SES neighborhoods, racial experiences still manifest. From the institutional racism that is perpetuated by school systems (Taylor & Clark, 2009), to the implicit bias perpetrated unintentionally by teachers (Chugh, 2012), to the stereotype threat experienced by students on standardized tests (Steele, 2010), race matters. When using race, I will not merely be referring to black/white relations in the United States. Certainly, the historical implications of black/white relations and landmark decisions such as *Brown v. Board of Education* (1954) are still relevant today. For example, the restructuring of the Memphis school system planned for 2013 is bringing many racial and economic tensions to the surface (Dillon, 2011). However, the racial landscape in the United States has broadened since the civil rights movement, and so must the discussion. I will not use race as a euphemism for black, which is inaccurate and misleading. Nor do I assume that the effects of racial experiences are only felt in communities of color (Chugh, 2012; Wise, 2011). But I consider schools to be racialized spaces, which means that there are racial impacts on all students and adults—black, white, Asian, Latino, Native American, Middle Eastern, and multiracial.

Multicultural Education Is Not Color-Blind

Some mistakenly think that color blindness is a desired outcome of multicultural education. They have romanticized the line in Dr. King's famous "I Have a Dream" (1963) speech, about not judging his four little children by the color of their skin but by the content of their character, to mean that color should not be noticed. This is problematic on many levels. First of all, race is more than color—it includes culture and consciousness as well as other facets of the social construct noted in the definition above. Secondly, none of us is blind to race, not even babies (Katz, 2003). Thirdly, as Bond (2003) noted, to be color-blind is to be blind to the consequences faced by communities of color in the United States. Similarly, Gorski (2010) observed, "Colorblindness denies people validation of their whole person." When naive educators suggest that they don't see color, not only are they lying, but they are also committing racial microaggression (Sue, 2010).

An Equity and Justice Framework

The ultimate goal of multicultural education is equity and justice in education, from the classroom level through educational policy. While many want to see this goal come to fruition, there are some who call themselves multicultural educators who do not share this goal. Some are content with the heroes, holidays, foods, and festivals brand of multicultural education, but I most certainly am not. To have students wearing sombreros and eating tacos but to not address the historical and current implications of U.S.–Mexico relations is to do a huge disservice to educating our young people (Gorski, 2008). Beyond the fact that there are many distinct cultures found in Central and South America, there are so many issues more relevant to the education of Latino/a students than hats and food. Given current political controversy about whether or not undocumented students should have access to a quality education and higher education, there are implications for all Latino students and other immigrant groups, whether citizens or not.

Conversations about access and equity are not easy, nor are steps to making significant social change to ensure educational quality for all. Sue and Constantine (2005) have noted that some have inappropriately utilized multicultural education as a scapegoating practice to avoid difficult dialogues about race. Initiating conversations about religion and gender in the name of multicultural education, but with the aim of ignoring racial and class privilege or shifting the conversation away from the hard truth with false color blindness, is fundamentally opposed to the goals of multicultural education. There is danger in having too broad a focus in multicultural education because it could dilute its power to transform educational institutions for equity and justice, especially if it allows educators to feel that they are celebrating diversity without making substantive changes in their curriculum and pedagogy (Gorski, 2010).

Equity vs. Equality

Neither color blindness nor equality is a goal of multicultural education. Equality means giving every student the same. Equity means giving every student the opportunity to have what she or he needs to be successful. Given how inequitable education currently is, treating every student the same would perpetuate inequity. Underresourced schools that have been underserved by the educational system require more than equal resources to achieve equity. Equity and educational justice from a multicultural perspective goes beyond proposals for longer school days or cutting time from the arts and physical education for standardized test preparation. Equity means accessible opportunities fitted to the needs and strengths of all students. Every student must have highly qualified teachers, rigorous content taught in an engaging and skillful manner, academic feedback and guidance, technological resources, safe and clean school buildings, creative and critical thinking opportunities, physical and aesthetic education, and other means of developing the whole child.

Hope

Finally, multicultural education is possible and it is transformative. While many inequities in schooling exist, there are also many schools that fulfill the goals of multicultural education. And even in schools where the institution as a whole might fall short of the goals, individual educators within the school do uphold them. A belief in the ability of people and institutions to become more equitable and just is necessary. Radical transformation does not happen overnight, but it can happen. Every step in the direction of equity and justice moves us closer. For many of us, the process of getting there is multicultural education. These goals of equity, justice, and transforming schools are consistent with the goals of the prosocial interventions and perspectives discussed in this handbook.

SECTION TWO: MULTICULTURAL EDUCATION AND PROSOCIAL EDUCATION

Multicultural education can be considered prosocial education because it is the vehicle for socializing students into our diverse society. The chapters of this handbook demonstrate that prosocial education affects human development through its expression of values, ethics, and morality, and it fosters and motivates academic and life learning (chapters 1, 5, and 25). Multicultural education meets these three essential criteria.

Multicultural Education and Development

Multicultural education's effect on development is fairly straightforward. Schools are the most important extrafamilial context for development. If schools allow some young people to develop academically and socially but hinder others' ability to do so, this has an impact. We know that finishing high school is a key milestone, with those students earning a high school diploma having better outcomes on a variety of indicators and better life chances. We also know that there are contextual influences found in schools that promote or hinder students reaching this milestone. These conditions—opportunity, access, and resources, along with pedagogical and school structures—are what is examined in multicultural education. High schools that are "dropout factories," meaning that the graduating class is less than 60 percent of the ninth-grade class, are schools that disproportionately serve students of color and students in poverty. This is a multicultural issue and a developmental one as well. Too many students are dropping out of school, or rather, as some have reframed it (Brownstein, 2009), being pushed out of school. This has far-reaching developmental implications for these students—and the next generation of students. But even before the extreme of leaving school without a diploma, a school's impact on a student's self-esteem, identity development, academic knowledge, social skills, and a host of other developmental indicators is paramount. All of these indicators are of great concern to multicultural and prosocial educators.

While specialized school settings designed to meet the developmental needs of students may seem like a positive trend, when students of color, particularly black and Latino males, are routinely, disproportionately overreferred to them, both prosocial and multicultural education must shine a light on this practice. Why is this happening? On the other side, students of color are dramatically underrepresented in gifted programs given their proportion in local populations and across the nation. Research has demonstrated that teachers overlook markers of giftedness in students of color (Kern, 2009).

On the more positive side, research has shown that people who have interracial friendships as children have less prejudiced racial attitudes as adults (Aboud, Mendelson, & Purdy, 2003; Dayanim, 2006) and that vicarious experiences with diversity through curricula, videos, and simulations, even in homogenous school settings, have a positive effect. The impact of relationships is key in children's development in the school setting. The quality of teacher–student and student–peer relationships is also integral to multicultural education. Class climate and school culture have also been shown to have profound positive impacts on interracial friendships (Hallinan & Williams, 1987; Power, Higgins, & Kohlberg, 1991).

Multicultural Education and Society's Values

Society uses schools to reinforce its values and provide continuity into the future; however, society also recognizes the power of education to question the status quo and to keep alive its ideals (Higgins-D'Alessandro, chapter 1, in this volume). Multicultural education, with its roots in critical race, feminist, queer, and other status-quo challenging theories, is also a framework for examining when society is not living up to its values—or for calling society out when its values fail to live up to its ideals. Like other social movements throughout the history of this country, multicultural education can use words espoused in our country's sacred documents—for example, "liberty and justice for all"—as a litmus test for its values. In this sense, multicultural education offers a critique to prosocial education for socializing students into a value system without specifically examining the ramifications of reproducing the social inequities of the system.

Multicultural Education and the Knowledge Base

Multicultural education also raises questions about how scholars contribute to the knowledge base. In an era where "evidence-based practice" is a new buzz term, it critically questions the evidence on which we should base our practice (Torre, 2009). Because of a long historical legacy of exclusionary, multiculturally misguided, and inappropriate research that produced harmful evidence (Guthrie, 2003), this is an important concern. Is the research paradigm situated in a deficit ideology? To what end is the research being conducted? Are the measures being used culturally sensitive? How will the results be used? Is the sample culturally and economically diverse? Is there economic diversity within the racial diversity and vice versa? Even as scholars have attempted to have more diverse samples—or at least acknowledge the lack of diversity as a limitation—Tuck (2009b) warns against retelling what she refers to as damage-centered narratives, for example, negative statistics of underachievement and stories only of hardship and struggle, and suggests a desire-based framework as an alternative. Toldson (2010) also resists the idea of reinforcing negative stereotypes with statistical evidence, noting that inappropriate metrics are often used, and misleading conclusions can be drawn. Like any field, multicultural educators and scholars should and do value evidence, but it resists evidence that may not share assumptions of equity and justice.

Multicultural Education in Prosocial Education

There are many connections that can be made between multicultural education and specific assumptions or foci of prosocial education. Each prosocial education area has to deal with the multicultural contingencies placed on a society with changing demographics. Some share assumptions of equity and justice and have been "multicultural" before this term was popular. However, other areas that have not traditionally explicitly espoused a multicultural focus will need to grapple with the reality that being multiculturally competent is an integral part of what it means to be prosocially competent in the twenty-first century.

Service Learning

One potential place of conflict is in service learning. Chapter 10 and its case studies also make this point and give examples. Because service learning has a helping orientation integrated into the learning process, service learning must ask, who is the helper and who must be helped? When the helper/helpee divide cuts across diversity dimensions and multicultural lines, this must be examined in a sensitive manner. For example, when wealthier schools go to poorer areas to perform community service, care must be taken to not invoke a deficit ideology by pathologizing the communities and the people who are being served. This can be particularly problematic in magnet schools or independent schools where students come from many types of neighborhoods. School trips to do service in what may very well be a student's own community set up an interesting duality for that student. Also, students should not encounter certain communities only in the context of needing help, especially if they haven't encountered the resources and strengths of these communities in other ways. Valuing the knowledge of the community agency personnel and clients is critical in not setting up a "Great White Hope" dynamic where students are inadvertently reinforced for thinking of themselves as saviors and of others as in need of saving. While certainly there are people and communities in need, and students benefit tremendously from the act of serving others, service learning programs must be careful not to reinforce stereotypes in the process.

SECTION THREE: FIVE DIMENSIONS OF MULTICULTURAL EDUCATION

James A. Banks, past president of the American Educational Research Association (AERA), is arguably multicultural education's preeminent scholar. Banks (1995) describes multicultural education across five dimensions: content integration, knowledge construction, equity pedagogy, prejudice reduction, and creating an empowering school culture. He created these five dimensions to help educators recognize that they each can play a role in multicultural education. This section illustrates the range of multicultural education efforts by using examples to illustrate each of the five dimensions. Narrow conceptualizations of multicultural education as simply content education falsely make it the domain of English, history, and social studies (Banks, 1995). Banks points out that math and science teachers have a responsibility to include mathematicians of color and women scientists. Failing to do this, we render students vulnerable to what Adichie (2009) describes as the danger of a single story. Without being "taught," students "know," for example, that Albert Einstein was a scientist. Without meaning to, teachers who do not consciously introduce students to other scientists reinforce a single story of what it means to be a scientist in children's minds, potentially leaving them with the image of scientists as white and male. Content integration is the first dimension of multicultural education.

Content Integration

The work of multicultural educators over the last few decades has done much to include more diverse perspectives in the curriculum. Curriculum has a significant impact on students; it is intricately connected to how students see themselves and others. Emily Style (in Nelson & Wilson, 1998) described curricula as a function of both eyesight and insight, arguing that multicultural curricula should serve both as a window and a mirror. While this is a complex topic worthy of its own volume (Sleeter & Stillman, 2005), it suggests that students should have access to worlds they are not members of through curricula, and equally important, they should see themselves reflected in the materials presented in classes. A multicultural perspective on curricula includes learning about the authors of literature and textbooks, the characters in stories and historical figures, and contexts and illustrations of oppression, discrimination, injustice, justice, and peace.

While there is still much more that can be done, many schools now use curricula that include more women, more people of color, more gays and lesbians, and so forth. The idea is not to just include something as an add-on, but to fully integrate these perspectives throughout the curriculum on an ongoing basis. One should also go one step further than inclusion, but one should also examine the representation in the inclusion. For example, an English teacher should not just include the one book from a certain group each year if the characters in that book reinforce stereotypical notions, such as a black family being poor and trying to save their farm or a Latino family trying to learn to speak English, lose accents, and assimilate to the mainstream culture. Some teachers think including these stories makes their curriculum more multicultural, and on some levels this is true, but if the multicultural representation creates or reinforces more stereotypes than it dispels, then it likely does not serve the goals of equity and justice well.

Teaching Tolerance is a program that aids educators in content integration (see table 18.1).

Table 18.1.   Review of Teaching Tolerance

Program	Teaching Tolerance
First dimension: Content integration	Teaching Tolerance is best known for their curricular materials, which support teachers in exposing students to diverse content. Some Teaching Tolerance's resources, such as the Teaching Diverse Students Initiative (2009) and ongoing professional development tools, also illustrate other dimensions of Banks' framework.
Origin	Teaching Tolerance was begun in 1991 by the Southern Poverty Law Center (SPLC). SPLC was founded in 1971 as a nonprofit civil rights organization by two civil rights lawyers, Morris Dees and Joseph Levin Jr.
Mission	Teaching Tolerance is dedicated to reducing prejudice, improving intergroup relations, and supporting equitable school experiences for children in the United States.
Format	The program provides free educational materials including the free self-titled magazine *Teaching Tolerance*, which is sent to approximately four hundred thousand educators twice each year. Other resources include a website with curricular downloads, documentaries, and support materials for school activities, such as National Mix It Up Day, which is geared toward helping students eradicate social boundaries.
Connections to prosocial education	Teaching Tolerance uses the term *tolerance* to refer to the broad range of skills that people need to live together peacefully. The term *prosocial* is used in the explanation of what the organization stands for. The definition of tolerance from the UNESCO Declaration on the Principles of Tolerance (1995) is used as the philosophical underpinning of the organization. Teaching Tolerance views tolerance as a method of thinking, feeling, and acting to promote the human values of peace and respect and the courage to act on them.
Successes	Teaching Tolerance has won two Oscars, one Emmy, two Golden Lamp Awards, and twenty other awards for its work.
Challenges	• The term *tolerance* has some negative connotations associated with it, such as having to deal with something unpleasant rather than full acceptance. Though the organization is explicit about their understanding of and use of the term, Teaching Tolerance is frequently questioned about the idea of tolerance not going far enough in promoting acceptance and harmony. • The SPLC which supports Teaching Tolerance is a 501(c)(3) charitable organization that operates solely from donations and receives no government funding. The current financial status of the organization and its endowment are deemed sound according to the SPLC website.
Empirical support	There are references to scientific surveys, but no links to research studies were found on either the Teaching Tolerance or SPLC websites. After an extensive search through the ERIC and PsycINFO databases, only two articles were found, but neither were research studies on the impact of the program in schools.

Sources:
Organization websites: http://www.tolerance.org, http://www.splccenter.org.
Articles: Peebles-Wilkins (2006), Stevens and Charles (2005).

Knowledge Construction

The second dimension of Banks' (1995) theory of multicultural education is knowledge construction. This dimension challenges teachers and students to examine the assumptions about how knowledge bases are built over the years. When U.S. history textbooks (Loewen, 2007) include chapters about "Westward expansion," this dimension asks, "From whose perspective is this author writing?" As Banks points out, it wasn't west for the Lakota Sioux; it was home—the center of their universe. It wasn't west for Mexicans; it was north. It wasn't west for the Japanese; it was east. It was west for a particular group of people, the European settlers, which in too many cases is taken as the norm, and as such has gone unexamined.

Understanding processes of knowledge construction is critical to both multicultural and prosocial education. Both approaches foster students' abilities to take the perspectives of others in the classroom and through the curricula of past and future others. Some multicultural education efforts offer further development of perspective taking and critical thinking, encouraging students to explicitly examine processes of knowledge construction. As Howard (2006) pointed out in the poignant title of his book, *We Can't Teach What We Don't Know*, if we educators weren't taught to critically examine basic ideas such as the "discovery of America," which negates the presence of the indigenous peoples that first inhabited the "New World" and ignores the accomplishments of other explorers like the Afro-Phoenicians who "discovered" the area previously (Loewen, 2007), how will they help their students to build a full, rich picture of historical epochs? In 2010, an educator friend of mine was given a textbook, *Bound for America* (Meltzer, 2002), to teach sixth grade social studies. This title ignores the perspectives of those first Americans who were already here. My friend immediately noticed the unfortunate use of the term *bound*. For some, the word may invoke feelings of being excited for a new journey, but to others, it may conjure images of the millions of people who were literally bound in chains as they were stolen from their continent and brutally forced into more than four hundred years of unpaid labor in the construction of this nation. This dimension of multicultural education uncovers these hidden truths by asking the hard questions about how knowledge is constructed.

Construction of knowledge operates on many levels—in examining curricular texts, in the dynamic processes of the classroom, and in research. The Public Science Project (see table 18.2) is an organization that utilizes critical participatory action research as a method that co-constructs knowledge.

Equity Pedagogy

The third dimension of the framework is equity pedagogy. Equity pedagogy means that teachers employ teaching methods that allow for equitable achievement by students from all backgrounds. This dimension incorporates ideas for modifying and enriching the kinds of pedagogy normally used in classrooms to ensure the success of each student. Successful examples are cooperative learning groups, collaborating on problem solving, and student leadership opportunities, among many others. Natural ties to prosocial education are evident as prosocial educators also employ these and other pedagogical strategies to enhance individual learning.

Table 18.2. Review of the Public Science Project: Center for Critical Participatory Action Research (cPAR)

Program	Public Science Project
Second dimension: Knowledge construction	cPAR exemplifies knowledge construction because it is built upon the democratization of the systematic production of knowledge. It expressly values knowledges that have been traditionally undervalued in the academy and in education. cPAR is rooted in the co-construction of new knowledge by empowering those who may traditionally have been "the researched" to become "the researchers" by leveraging various capacities within research collectives, usually made up of youth, scholars, and practitioners or community members.
Origin	The Public Science Project is a center for Critical Participatory Action Research (cPAR) at the Graduate Center of the City University of New York under the direction of Maria Torre, PhD. cPAR's use of social historical context is an extension of the ideas of Wilhelm Dilthey (1883) and W. E. B. DuBois (1898, 1903), with roots in liberation scholarship (Freire, 1970) and social psychology (Lewin, 1946). cPAR research is grounded in critical theories (i.e., critical race theory, feminist theory, queer theory, disability theory, etc.), in action research, and in qualitative methods.
Mission	The goal of the Public Science Project is to conduct research honoring the following principles, among others: • To value knowledges that have been historically marginalized and delegitimized (i.e., youth, prisoner, immigrant) alongside traditionally recognized knowledges (i.e., mainstream scholarship). • To share various knowledges and resources held by individual members of a research collective, across the collective, so members can participate as equally as possible. • To collaboratively decide appropriate research questions, design, methods, and analysis as well as useful research products. • To conceive of action on multiple levels over the course of the cPAR project. • To think through consequences of research findings for actions. • To negotiate conditions of collaboration over time.
Format	cPAR is an epistemology rather than a program. It is a way of approaching research design, research methods, data analyses, and empirical results sharing through a lens of democratic participation.
Connections to prosocial education	cPAR is intricately connected to prosocial education because of its focus on democratic participation and is explicitly used by some civic education approaches. The collaboration necessary to engage in a cPAR project, on both individual and institutional levels, is inherently prosocial in theory, process, and outcome goals. Its goal of using research as a strategy for a more just world resonates with the goals of prosocial education.
Successes	The Public Science Project publishes scholarly articles, presents at conferences, and consults widely; just as important, it directly reports findings to community agencies emphasizing action steps. Its biggest successes may lie in the capacity built within youth who before may have been trapped in circuits of dispossession (Fine, 2010) and afterward see themselves as valuable contributors as researchers and change agents in their communities.
Challenges	There are many challenges at multiple levels in undertaking research projects aimed at undoing systemic injustice, from getting IRB approval and the ethical challenges in working with vulnerable populations, including negative legacies of history and unrealistic promises of change, to providing youth or others opportunities to learn and to co-construct research goals and methods.
Empirical support	cPAR is well documented empirically; theoretical articles include Torre, Fine, Stoudt, and Fox (2010); Fine and Torre (2006); and Tuck et al. (2008). Various cPAR projects have also been documented in videos, performances, websites, and other data-sharing products (Fine et al., 2004). Links to data-sharing products can be found at http://www.publicscienceproject.org: Red Flags, the Food Justice Project, Polling for Justice.

Sources:
 Websites: http://www.publicscienceproject.org, http://www.thefoodjusticeproject.org.
 Videos:
  Red Flags: http://www.viddler.com/explore/mestizoartsactivism/videos/2.
  Polling for Justice: http://www.publicscienceproject.org.
 Articles: Fine et al. (2004); Torre et al. (2010).

Equity pedagogy relates to actions teachers take to ensure that all students are successful. This can take various forms depending on the situation. In schools where many students have the means to procure outside tutoring at exorbitant rates, a teacher committed to equity pedagogy would ensure that every student had the opportunity to be successful by securing school funding for all students to have access to an outside tutor, providing extra one-on-one assistance to students unable to get a tutor, or communicating proactively with all families. In schools where parental participation is minimal, equity pedagogy might mean thinking creatively about how to involve parents and being flexible about means of communication. Because this dimension refers to process, the National SEED Project is an excellent illustration (see table 18.3).

Prejudice Reduction

Prejudice reduction is the fourth dimension and involves facilitating the development of positive multicultural attitudes. Because research indicates that students come to school with prejudices about different groups (Killen, Rutland, Ruok, & the Society for Research in Child Development, 2011; Pfeifer, Brown, Juvonen, & the Society for Research in Child Development, 2007), it is important for teachers to counteract any false and negative stereotypes with positive experiences. From this perspective all teachers are accountable, regardless of subject area expertise. Sometimes math, science, physical education, or other teachers may feel that they cannot be as involved in multicultural education as teachers of history or English, but this dimension emphasizes equal opportunity and equal responsibility for prejudice reduction. When students make prejudicial comments to one another; imitate or otherwise make fun of students with disabilities; or tell racist, sexist, or homophobic jokes, all teachers have a responsibility to intervene.

Reducing prejudice, obviously, is an important goal of prosocial education. But, as is pointed out by many authors in this volume, prosocial education involves more than diminishing antisocial behavior; it must also promote positive social interactions and ultimately productive citizenry. Similarly, Banks (2009) holds that positive multicultural attitudes can be developed and lead to positive social interactions across groups. The People's Institute for Survival and Beyond is an organization that works toward the dismantling of racism in individuals and institutions (see table 18.4).

Empowering School Culture

The fifth and last dimension moves outside of the individual classroom to the school level to focus on empowering school culture and social structure. This dimension examines an entire school's policies and programs for equity. Grouping, tracking, labeling practices, participation, and leadership within the curriculum and in extracurricular activities are reviewed. Disproportionate rates of underachievement and discipline referrals and policies that contribute to disproportionality are also explored. If, for example, physical bullying carries an automatic suspension, but relational or social bullying, the bullying in which girls are more likely to engage (Swearer, Espelage, Vaillancourt, & Hymel, 2010) does not, then this is inequitable. If students of different groups receive different punishments for the same offenses, this also should be examined and rectified. Gregory, Skiba, and Noguera (2010) reviewed several studies

Table 18.3. Review of the National SEED (Seeking Educational Equity and Diversity) Project

Program	The National SEED Project
Third dimension: Equity pedagogy	SEED is involved in ensuring that the curriculum, teaching methods, and school climate become more multicultural; thus it fits multiple levels of the framework. However, since it is process oriented and run by teachers for teachers, it is best located in the equity pedagogy dimension.
Origin	The SEED Project, founded in 1985 by Peggy McIntosh, PhD, is an outgrowth of her (1983, 1990) Interactive Phases of Personal and Curricular Re-Vision theory. SEED's philosophy is that teachers are the authorities on their own experiences and as such can seed the process of school transformation. SEED is both an acronym and a metaphor. SEED Project's website highlights its philosophy. "Though I do not believe that a plant will spring up where no seed has been, I have great faith in a seed. Convince me that you have a seed . . . and I am prepared to expect wonders."—Henry David Thoreau.
Mission	Its mission is to have faculty-driven faculty development in which teachers examine the textbooks of their lives in conversation with other faculty in order to transform themselves and their schools. A key SEED idea is that personal faculty development needs to be supported over time for real change to happen; once teachers are the center of their own growth processes, they can in turn put students' growth and development at the center of their educational goals.
Format	School-based, three-hour SEED seminars are held monthly with a SEED group leader (a teacher involved in a weeklong intensive summer institute) and faculty volunteers. SEED purposely seeks diverse and various participants to cocreate their summer institutes.
Connections to prosocial education	SEED's emphasis on interactive exercises, group dialogue, and democratic process makes it prosocial. Like prosocial education, it can be a preventive intervention. It is proactive and exemplifies the equitable distribution of respect, power, access, support, and opportunity.
Successes	SEED seminars have been led by almost two thousand SEED leaders in schools throughout the United States and across the world for more than twenty-five years. Participants report that SEED had an impact on multiple aspects of their lives, including how they teach, learn, make policy, and relate to students (Nelson, 1991).
Challenges	Because participants volunteer, SEED may not reach faculty in need of this type of reflective training in pedagogy. Each SEED seminar is a unique reflective process, so by design, standardization across SEED groups is difficult.
Empirical support	SEED is housed in the Wellesley Centers for Women. Articles by the founder, Peggy McIntosh, PhD, and current directors, Emily Style, MA; Brenda Flyswithhawks, PhD; and Emmy Howe were found. No empirical articles by other scholars were found.

Source:
  SEED project website: http://www.wcwonline.org/Active-Projects/seed-project-on-inclusive-curriculum.

Table 18.4. Review of the People's Institute for Survival and Beyond (PISAB): Undoing Racism

Program	The People's Institute for Survival and Beyond: Undoing Racism
Fourth dimension: Prejudice reduction	The PISAB Undoing Racism workshop is an example of prejudice reduction. Banks argues that all educators should be involved on an ongoing basis in prejudice reduction. This workshop helps participants understand more about how the system of racism works so that they can be empowered to work toward dismantling it. Although the Undoing Racism workshop is focused at the structural level and Banks frames this dimension in terms of individual responsibility, the Undoing Racism workshop provides systemic analysis with the aim of increasing individual agency in deconstructing racism.
Origin	The People's Institute for Survival and Beyond (PISAB) was founded in 1980 by Ron Chisom, a community activist in New Orleans, Louisiana, and Jim Dunn, PhD, a professor at Antioch College in Yellow Springs, Ohio. PISAB is a national and international collective of antiracist, multicultural activists and educators committed to social transformation through helping individuals, communities, organizations, and institutions move beyond addressing symptoms of racism to undoing its causes with the goal of creating a more just and equitable society. Undoing Racism is PISAB's signature program.
Mission	Its mission is to build a multicultural and antiracist movement for social change. The organization believes that if racism was constructed, it can be undone. The Undoing Racism workshop focuses on understanding what racism is, where it comes from, how it functions, why it persists, and how it can be undone. The workshop is founded on several antiracist principles including undoing racism, learning from history, sharing culture, developing leadership, maintaining accountability, networking, analyzing power, gatekeeping, undoing internalized racial oppression, and identifying and analyzing manifestations of racism.
Format	Undoing Racism is a two-day intensive workshop led by a multicultural team of facilitators. The training is intentionally grounded in communities of color, which, while inclusive of all, purposely resists the dominant culture. It utilizes large-group presentations and dialogue. It also incorporates participant reflection, role-playing, and strategic planning. The goal of the workshop is to create effective organizers for justice.
Connections to prosocial education	Similar to prosocial education efforts (e.g., Character Education Partnership, Association for Moral Education), one of its goals is to build coalitions. Moreover, working together toward the common goal of social transformation is prosocial. The use of multiracial teams of trainer/facilitators models collegial working relationships across dimensions of difference for participants.
Successes	The program has trained almost five hundred thousand individuals in its thirty years. It has a wide variety of participants including youth groups, parent groups, educators, social service agencies, community activists, civic organizations, and schools. It was recognized by the Aspen Institute as a leading racial justice organization in 2002.
Challenges	Its theory of change rests on antiracism and multiculturalism, which remains in need of greater theoretical research and support according to Paluck and Green's (2009) review of what works in prejudice reduction.
Empirical support	The Aspen Institute's review of several racial justice training programs is the only scholarly reference outside PISAB's own materials that was found. As a practitioner, I have encountered several references to Undoing Racism, including in multiple trainings at the Ethical Culture Fieldston School, Fordham University's Office of Multicultural Affairs, and the Dorothy Day Center for Social Justice, and recommendations from other diversity practitioners at schools in the New York City area.

Sources:
  Website: http://www.pisab.org.
  Training for Racial Equity and Inclusion: A Guide to Selected Programs by the Aspen Institute (Shapiro, 2002).
  Personal interaction with some of the PISAB trainers, several personal recommendations about the program by recent participants.

and found race as a significant predictor of school discipline reports when controlling for SES. They found disproportionality in disciplining black students, especially black male students, at much higher rates than any other group. Discipline patterns should be examined alongside patterns of academic achievement for different groups. Gregory et al. (2010) interpreted findings of interactions between the discipline gap and the "achievement gap" as grounded in societal stereotypes, implicit bias, and cultural mismatch between teachers and students. Further research is needed in this area.

The demographic composition of the school faculty and staff as compared to the student body is key information from a multicultural education standpoint, as it sends implicit messages about who has authority and who can become teachers and other professionals, which influences students' sense of autonomy and possibility. For example, if the kitchen and maintenance staffs are entirely Latino, but only a small percentage of the faculty are Latino and they only teach Spanish language classes, the message to Latino students can be that they should limit their aspirations. In the case of an almost entirely white student body, this would mean that most of the students' interactions with Latinos exist in a service capacity. In the case of a largely Latino student body, this would mean that the students would not see themselves represented broadly in various facets of the school in the adult population. The Equity Collaborative exists to help educators collaborate with colleagues at other schools to transform their school cultures (see table 18.5).

The five dimensions put forth by Banks (1995) support the goals of prosocial education as well as illuminate the goals and strategies of multicultural education. Schools that are successful in fully implementing multicultural education demonstrate evidence of all five dimensions on an ongoing basis; they also would likely be exemplary prosocial education schools as well. Multicultural education is an ever-evolving process in which educators continually strive to enhance their knowledge, awareness, and skills toward the full development and learning of all students and the creation of equitable schools whose existence and graduates will help move our society toward greater justice.

The preceding section explained the prevailing theoretical framework for multicultural education, illustrated by existing programs that connect theory to practice. The first sections of this chapter elaborated the assumptions and principles of multicultural education and explicated parallels with prosocial education. I will conclude with further thoughts about bridging theory and practice in schools.

CONCLUSION: POINTS TO PONDER

Given the richness of Banks' (1995) theoretical framework and the context provided by this chapter on the history and practice of multicultural education, I think it is most fruitful to consider each dimension's implications for school policies and practices.

Content integration. Multicultural curricula should be infused throughout. Regular audits of curricular content should be examined both horizontally (across grade level in every discipline) and vertically (across each discipline at every grade level Pre-K–12) for inclusion of multicultural educational principles and ideas. They should be transformative of curricula rather than additive (Gorski, 2008). Style's windows and mirrors theory (in Nelson & Wilson, 1998) can be a useful framework. Given that

Table 18.5. Review of the Equity Collaborative

Program	The Equity Collaborative
Fifth dimension: Empowering school culture	The Equity Collaborative fits the fifth dimension because it focuses on organizational development and building school teams working in various roles to support multicultural education antibias programming for students. Teachers, school leaders, student support people, and parents all attend the Equity Collaborative to work together to create an empowering school culture.
Origin	The Georgetown Day School Equity Collaborative was founded in 2007 by the Equity and Social Justice Program under the leadership of Elizabeth Denevi and Mariama Richards at the Georgetown Day School (GDS) in Washington, D.C. GDS opened in 1945 as an integrated school in a segregated city, and it continues to be a model multicultural education school. It is the 2004 recipient of the National Association of Independent Schools Leading Edge Award for Equity and Justice.
Mission	Its goal is to help educators develop institutional road maps for creating and supporting multicultural education and antibias curricula in both public and independent schools. A focus on organizational development and strategic planning for equity and diversity initiatives in essential school teams is a unique feature. The GDS Equity Collaborative defines an essential school team as two school leaders (such as heads of school or principals), two student support people (such as deans or directors of diversity and multicultural affairs), and one classroom teacher.
Format	The Equity Collaborative is a leadership program held in June when schools dismiss for the summer. This weeklong intensive session for educators consists of workshops, speakers, field trips, and sustained dialogue in small and large groups. Groupings include school planning groups; school role affinity groups (i.e., teachers, principals, directors of diversity, etc.); participant choice workshops; and so forth. It emphasizes participants and facilitators learning from one another and provides an online forum for continued dialogue throughout the next school year.
Connections to prosocial education	The Equity Collaborative is prosocial in its name and processes. Prosocial education approaches all emphasize the Equity Collaborative's prevailing idea that educators should be enabled to support one another in creating just and equitable schools. Like prosocial education, it focuses on students' lives, inclusive of but also beyond academic learning; thus both approaches recognize the importance of including student support staff in their training. Finally, the process of the leadership program employs many prosocial ideas, specifically with the explicit focus on the establishment of positive community norms.
Successes	The Equity Collaborative has been held for the past five years, with many alumni returning. Not only have participants spoken highly of their experiences, but they have shared testimonials about leveraging knowledge gained at the collaborative toward institutional transformation during the following school year. The essential school team model of organizational development used during the summer workshop is rare in diversity trainings that focus primarily on individual awareness. The Equity Collaborative also attempts to forge partnerships between public and independent schools, another feature that sets this program apart.
Challenges	The intensive, intimate nature of the Equity Collaborative, which seems to be key to its success, may make this program difficult to scale up; therefore the program has intentionally remained confined to a relatively small community. The regular fees of approximately $1,500 per person may be out of reach for some schools.
Empirical support	Because the program is new, small, and grassroots based, it has not been empirically validated; however, various features of the program are built on empirical support. Guest speakers are often scholars from major research universities who connect contemporary, relevant research findings to program features.

Sources:
Website: http://www.equitycollaborative.org.
Personal experience as a collaborative participant in 2008 and 2009.

students have multiple, intersecting identities, the way that they see themselves and others throughout curricula should address these intersections. Even curricula that attempt to be multicultural can fall into the trap of being one dimensional. For example, if a unit on protest movements in the United States highlights only black men in the civil rights movement and white women in the women's suffrage or women's liberation movements, where will black young women see themselves mirrored? This too frequent failure to represent intersectional identities resulted in the aptly titled black women's studies book, *All the Women Are White, All the Blacks Are Men: But Some of Us Are Brave* (Hull, Scott, & Smith, 1993).

Every student in the classroom should have windows and mirrors. If the classroom is not demographically diverse, this does not let teachers off the multicultural education hook. *What If All the Kids Are White?* (Derman-Sparks, Patricia, & Edwards, 2011) gives suggestions for incorporating multicultural education in every classroom.

Knowledge construction. Students must be taught the skills of critically analyzing sources of knowledge. Rather than being empty receptacles for deposits of information, students are active, engaged learners who ask critical questions. Students must also be encouraged to recognize the validity of multiple narratives as well as the idea that conflicting narratives can occupy the same space at the same time and both be right and true.

Equity pedagogy. When educators, school systems, and scholars reject deficit ideologies and recognize that every student has a right to high-quality educational opportunities, equity pedagogy helps to ensure equity and justice. Equity pedagogy can be measured. If certain groups are being "left behind," the answer is not more testing but changing school structures. Equity pedagogy is the commitment to ensuring that all students get what they need to be successful and recognizes strengths in diversity of curricula, classrooms, and educational opportunities. Diversity equals academic excellence (Denevi & Richards, 2009). Gurin and colleagues (2003) found that students who learn in diverse environments demonstrate both academic and social growth, in fact with differential effects for white students and students of color. White students tended to benefit more than students of color from diversity efforts. Gurin discusses the idea that interaction with white students is less novel to students of color given the prevalence of their access to white students in this culture. Keeping this in mind, many schools have created affinity groups for students of color to allow them to have a safe space to discuss racial experiences in their school. Some schools have also instituted clustering policies, so that no student of color is an "only" in a class when there are options to do otherwise.

Because family involvement is important for ensuring student success, equity pedagogy is also involved in collaborating with families. Schools need to think carefully about how communication with families is handled. Some schools have new, green, sustainable initiatives that require all communication to be sent electronically—from notices about PTA meetings to student report cards. If not all families have easy, regular access to the Internet, this is inequitable. Sending all communication in English to families with limited English proficiency is also inequitable. Equity pedagogy means thinking through scenarios proactively and in the moment. For example, in a school that is accessible to people with disabilities with an elevator, what is the contingency plan for when the elevator is not working? Can a student's classes all be temporarily moved to the first floor? Will a parent be able to reach the conference room for a meeting? These everyday multicultural contingencies make up equity pedagogy. The key question to ask in these situations is how do we ensure that every student and family has the opportunity to get what they need to be successful?

Prejudice reduction. Educators have the responsibility to become involved in reducing prejudice in their school communities. While many educators would likely interrupt the use of derogatory racial slurs, some choose not to intervene when other types of prejudice occur in schools, for example, using the phrase "That's so gay." This is heard countless times per day at schools all over the country, but not every educator recognizes the saying as one that is rooted in a stereotype, nor do all educators feel empowered to stop it. Other expressions, such as "Don't throw like a girl," can also be heard regularly. Educators need to step up and stop even these little, insidious acts of prejudice whenever they are found. Students also need to be empowered in this regard to no longer be bystanders but to become upstanders for equity and justice in schools.

Empowering school culture. This dimension incorporates all of the above dimensions into a cohesive school culture that is supportive of multicultural education. There are real implications for school policies and programs in whether or not a school culture is empowering. Tatum (2003) distinguishes between active racism and passive racism with a metaphor that explains the need for an empowering school culture.

> Because racism is so ingrained in the fabric of American institutions, it is easily self-perpetuating. All that is required to maintain it is business as usual.
>
> I sometimes visualize the ongoing cycle of racism as a moving walkway at the airport. Active racist behavior is equivalent to walking fast on the conveyor belt. . . . Passive racist behavior is equivalent to standing still on the walkway. No overt effort is being made, but the conveyor belt moves the bystanders along to the same destination as those who are actively walking. Some of the bystanders may feel the motion of the conveyor belt, see the active racists ahead of them, and choose to turn around, unwilling to go to the same destination as the White supremacists. But, unless they are walking actively in the opposite direction at a speed faster than the conveyor belt—unless they are actively antiracist—they will find themselves carried along with the others. (Tatum, 2003, p. 11)

Tatum's airport people-mover analogy provides an excellent rationale for the comprehensive model of creating an empowering school culture. Though her work talks specifically about race, it can be applied to other dimensions of diversity and the totality of multicultural education. If the media inundate students with stereotypes, schools must present even more contrary, positive examples. If adult society models relatively segregated social behavior, schools must provide explicit, active opportunities for interracial friendship formation. If part of our culture dictates that discussions involving diversity and multiculturalism are taboo, or at least politically incorrect, schools must open the dialogue in a meaningful way, including constructive methods for dealing with conflict, which in turn can be used as catalysts for learning. Schools must be proactively involved in creating an empowering school culture that supports both multicultural and excellent education. Faculty and staff hiring and retention play a key role in this effort. As Irvine (2003) put it, "They Bring More Than Their Race:

Why Teachers of Color are Essential in Today's Schools." Given the proliferation of stereotypes that abound in the media, society and mainstream culture may be moving schools along in a racist, sexist, and homophobic direction. This is likely unintentional, but it is the result of an unexamined status quo. The media, along with the cultural norms, expectations, and socialization practices of our society, bombard young people with detrimental stereotypical information regularly. The only way to offset this is for schools to move in the opposite direction—toward multicultural education, equity, and justice—and move toward this goal faster.

This chapter connects the principles of multicultural education with the goals of prosocial education. Multicultural education is prosocial education. All key tenets of multicultural education, such as inclusion, equity, and justice are prosocial in nature. The chapter also considered multicultural education as prosocial education. The ideals of prosocial education are met by multicultural education in its optimization of the developmental context of school; its emphasis on understanding, accepting some, and critiquing other societal values—so that society itself becomes more multicultural; and its interrogation of and contribution to the existing knowledge base. Multicultural education is also found throughout prosocial education, such as in service learning; civic, moral, and character education; after-school programming; and other areas. The programs explored as illustrations of the five dimensions of Banks' (1995) theoretical framework represent different models of multicultural education. Finally, because multicultural education is an ever-evolving process, the work is never finished; however, through focusing on multicultural education, practitioners and researchers grow closer to the ideal of equitable and just schooling for all.

REFERENCES

Aboud, F. E., Mendelson, M. J., & Purdy, K. T. (2003). Cross-race peer relations and friendship quality. *International Journal of Behavioral Development, 27*(2), 165–173. doi:10.1080/01650250244000164

Adichie, C. (July, 2009). Chimamanda Adichie: The danger of a single story [Video file]. Retrieved from http://www.ted.com/talks/chimamanda_adichie_the_danger_of_a_single_story.html

Artiles, A. J. (2011). Toward an interdisciplinary understanding of educational equity and difference: The case of the racialization of ability. *Educational Researcher, 40*(9), 431–445.

Banks, J. A. (1994). Transforming the mainstream curriculum. *Educating for Diversity, 51*(8), 4–8.

Banks, J. A. (1995). Multicultural education: Historical development, dimensions, and practice. In J. A. Banks & C. A. M. Banks (Eds.), *Handbook of research on multicultural education* (pp. 3–24). New York: Macmillan.

Banks, J. A. (2007). *Educating citizens in a multicultural society* (2nd ed.). New York: Teachers College Press.

Banks, J. A. (2009). Human rights, diversity, and citizenship education. *Educational Forum, 73*(2), 100–110.

Banks, J. A., & Banks, C. A. M. (2006). *Multicultural education: Issues and perspectives* (6th ed.). Hoboken, NJ: Jossey-Bass, an imprint of Wiley.

Banks, J. A., Cookson, P., Gay, G., Hawley, W. D., Irvine, J. J., Nieto, S., et al. (2007). Essential principles for teaching and learning for a multicultural society. In W. D. Hawley & D. L. Rollie (Eds.), *The keys to effective schools: Education reform as continuous improvement* (2nd ed., pp. 173–188). Thousand Oaks, CA: Corwin Press; Washington, DC: National Education Association.

Batiste, G. (2010, May 25). Sample cultural identifiers (Online resource page). Retrieved from http://nais.org/equity/article.cfm?ItemNumber=153165&sn.ItemNumber=142552

Bond, J. (2003, June). *Ware lecture*. General assembly of the annual meeting of the Unitarian Universalist Association of Congregations, Boston, MA.

Brownstein, R. (2009). Pushed out. *Teaching Tolerance, 36,* 58–61.

Carter, R. T. (2000). Reimagining race in education: A new paradigm from psychology. *Teachers College Record, 102*(5), 864–897. doi:10.1111/0161-4681.00082

Castania, K. (2003). *The evolving language of diversity*. New York: Cornell Cooperative Extension.

Chugh, D. (2012, January). Implicit bias in institutions. *What's on Your Mind? A Talk on Unconscious Bias.* Lecture given at the Ethical Culture Fieldston School, Bronx, New York.

Chugh, D., & Brief, A. P. (2008). 1964 was not that long ago: A story of gateways and pathways. In A. P. Brief (Ed.), *Diversity at work* (Cambridge Companions to Management; pp. 318–340). New York: Cambridge University Press.

The Civil Rights Project. (2006). PICS: Statement of American social scientists of research on school desegregation submitted to the U.S. Supreme Court.

Cole, E. (2009). Intersectionality and research in psychology. *American Psychologist, 64*(3), 170–180.

Crenshaw, K. (1989). Demarginalizing the intersection of race and sex: A black feminist critique of antidiscrimination doctrine, feminist theory and antiracist politics. *University of Chicago Legal Forum,* 139–167.

Dayanim, S. (2006). *Ethnic stereotyping and attitudes toward America and her policies among preadolescents in relation with television viewing behavior.* ProQuest Information & Learning, U.S.

Denevi, E., & Carter, R. (2006). Multicultural seminar: A new model for professional development. *Multicultural Perspectives, 8*(2), 18–24.

Denevi, E., & Richards, M. (2009). Diversity directors as leaders: Making the case for excellence. *Independent School, 68*(3). Retrieved from http://www.nais.org/publications/ismagazinearticle.cfm?ItemNumber=151664

Derman-Sparks, L., Patricia, G. R., & Edwards, O. (2011). *What if all the kids are white? Antibias multicultural education with young children and families.* New York: Teachers College Press.

Dillon, S. (2011, November 5). Merger of Memphis and county school districts revives challenges. *New York Times.* Retrieved from http://www.nytimes.com/2011/11/06/education/merger-of-memphis-and-county-school-districts-revives-challenges.html

Dilthey, W. (1883/1989). *Introduction to the human sciences* (R. A. Makkreel & F. Rodi, Eds., pp. 185–219, 431–440). Princeton, NJ: Princeton University Press.

DuBois, W. E. B. (2007). *The souls of black folk.* New York: Oxford University Press. (Original work published in 1903)

Duhon-Sells, R. (1991). *Multicultural education is essential for the academic success of schools in the 21st century.* Retrieved from the ERIC database (ED347126).

Fine, M. (2004). The power of the Brown v. Board of Education decision: Theorizing threats to sustainability. *American Psychologist, 59*(6), 502–510.

Fine, M., & Ruglis, J. (2009). Circuits and consequences of dispossession: The racialized realignment of the public sphere for U.S. youth. *Transforming Anthropology, 17*(1), 20–33.

Fine, M., Torre, M. E., Boudin, K., Bowen, I., Clark, J., Hylton, D., et al. (2004). Participatory action research: From within and beyond prison bars. In L. Weis & M. Fine, *Working method: Research and social justice.* New York: Routledge.

Flyswithhawks, B. (1996). The process of knowing and learning: An academic and cultural awakening. *Holistic Education Review, 9*(4), 35–39.

Forum on Child and Family Statistics. (2011). *America's children: Key national indicators of well-being, 2011. Demographic background*. Retrieved from http://www.childstats.gov/americaschildren/demo.asp

Freire, P. (2000). *Pedagogy of the oppressed, 30th anniversary edition* (M. B. Ramos, Trans., 30th ed.). New York: Continuum. (Original work published 1970)

Gay, G. (1997). Connections between character education and multicultural education. In A. Molnar (Ed.), *The construction of children's character, 96th yearbook of the National Society for the Study of Education, Part 2* (0077-5762; pp. 97–109). Chicago: National Society for the Study of Education.

Gay, G. (2010). *Culturally responsive teaching* (2nd ed., Multicultural Education Series). New York: Teachers College Press.

Gordon, E. W., & American Educational Research Association. (2004). Closing the gap: High achievement for students of color. *AERA Research Points, 2*(3).

Gorski, P. C. (2008). Good intentions are not enough: A decolonizing intercultural education. *Intercultural Education, 19*(6), 515–525.

Gorski, P. C. (2010). *Beyond celebrating diversity: 20 things I can do to become a better multicultural educator* (EdChange). Retrieved from http://www.edchange.org

Gorski, P., Shin, G.-T., Green, M., & National Education Association. (2000). *Professional development guide for educators* (Multicultural Resource Series, Vol. 1). Washington, DC: National Education Association.

Grant, C. A., & Sleeter, C. E. (2011). *Doing multicultural education for achievement and equity* (2nd ed.). New York: Routledge/Taylor & Francis Group.

Grant, C. A., & Zwier, E. (2011). Intersectionality and student outcomes: Sharpening the struggle against racism, sexism, classism, ableism, heterosexism, nationalism, and linguistic, religious, and geographical discrimination in teaching and learning. *Multicultural Perspectives, 13*(4), 181–188.

Gregory, A., Skiba, R. J., & Noguera, P. A. (2010). The achievement gap and the discipline gap: Two sides of the same coin? *Educational Researcher, 39*(1), 59–68. doi:10.3102/0013189X09357621

Gurin, P. Y., Dey, E. L., Gurin, G., & Hurtado, S. (2003). How does racial/ethnic diversity promote education? *Western Journal of Black Studies, 27*(1), 20–29.

Gurin, P., Nagda, B. (Ratnesh) A., & Lopez, G. E. (2004). The benefits of diversity in education for democratic citizenship. *Journal of Social Issues, 60*(1), 17–34. doi:10.1111/j.0022-4537.2004.00097.x

Guthrie, R. V. (2003). *Even the rat was white: A historical view of psychology* (2nd ed.). Boston: Allyn & Bacon.

Hallinan, M. T., & Williams, R. A. (1987). The stability of students' interracial friendships. *American Sociological Review, 52*(5), 653–664. doi:10.2307/2095601

Hill, M. L. (2010, March). *Men of color and education: A discussion on the pursuit of excellence.* Panel discussion at Avery Fisher Hall, hosted by Teach for America, New York, New York.

Howard, G. R. (2006). *We can't teach what we don't know: White teachers, multiracial schools* (J. A. Banks, Ed., 2nd ed.). New York: Teachers College Press.

Hull, G. T., Scott, P. B., & Smith, B. (Eds.). (1993). *All the women are white, all the blacks are men, but some of us are brave: Black women's studies.* Old Westbury, NY: Feminist Press at CUNY.

Irvine, J. J. (2003). *Educating teachers for diversity: Seeing with a cultural eye.* New York: Teachers College Press.

Katz, P. (2003). Racists or tolerant multiculturalists? How do they begin? *American Psychologist, 58*(11), 897–909.

Kern, A. H. (2009, January 1). *Ashe City Schools' journey to recognize, nurture, and respond to the potential in all children via U-STARS-PLUS*. ProQuest LLC.

Killen, M., Rutland, A., Ruok, M., & the Society for Research in Child Development. (2011). Promoting equity, tolerance, and justice in childhood. *Social Policy Report, 25*(4).

Ladson-Billings, G. (1995a). But that's just good teaching! The case for culturally relevant pedagogy. *Theory into Practice, 34*(3), 159–165.

Ladson-Billings, G. (1995b). Toward a theory of culturally relevant pedagogy. *American Educational Research Journal, 32*(3), 465–491.

Ladson-Billings, G. (2003). New directions in multicultural education: Complexities, boundaries, and critical race theory. In J. A. Banks & C. M. Banks (Eds.), *Handbook of research in multicultural education* (2nd ed., pp. 50–65). San Francisco: Jossey-Bass.

Ladson-Billings, G. (2004). Landing on the wrong note: The price we paid for "Brown" (DeWitt Wallace–"Reader's Digest" Distinguished Lecture). *Educational Researcher, 33*(7), 3–13.

Ladson-Billings, G. (2006). From the achievement gap to the education debt: Understanding achievement in U.S. schools. *Educational Researcher, 35*(7), 3–12.

Ladson-Billings, G. (2007). Pushing past the achievement gap: An essay on the language of deficit. *Journal of Negro Education, 76*(3), 316–323.

Ladson-Billings, G., & Donnor, J. (2008). The moral activist role of critical race theory scholarship. In N. K. Denzin & Y. S. Lincoln (Eds.), *The landscape of qualitative research* (3rd ed., pp. 371–401). Thousand Oaks, CA: Sage.

Lewin, K. (1997). Action research and minority problems (1946). *Resolving social conflicts and field theory in social science* (pp. 143–152). Washington, DC: American Psychological Association.

Loewen, J. W. (2007). *Lies my teacher told me: Everything your American history textbook got wrong*. New York: Touchstone.

Macedo, D. (2011). Introduction. In P. Freire, *Pedagogy of the oppressed* (40th ed., M. B. Ramos, Trans., pp. 1–9). New York: Continuum.

Mayo, P. (2004). *Liberating praxis: Paulo Freire's legacy for radical education and politics*. Westport, CT: Praeger.

McIntosh, P. (1983). *Interactive phases of curricular re-vision: A feminist perspective* (Working Paper No. 124). Wellesley, MA: Wellesley College Center for Research on Women.

McIntosh, P. (1990). *Interactive phases of curricular and personal re-vision with regard to race* (Working Paper No. 219). Wellesley, MA: Wellesley College Center for Research on Women.

Meltzer, M. (2002). *Bound for America*. Tarrytown, NY: Benchmark Books.

National Association of Multicultural Education. (2003). *Definitions of multicultural education*. Retrieved from http://www.nameorg.org

National Association of Multicultural Education. (2012). *About NAME*. Retrieved from http://www.nameorg.org

Nelson, C. L. (1991). The national SEED project. *Educational Leadership, 49*(4), 66–67.

Nelson, C. L., & Wilson, K. A. (Eds.). (1998). *Seeding the process of multicultural education: An anthology*. St. Paul: Minnesota Inclusiveness Program.

Nieto, S. (2005). Public education in the twentieth century and beyond: High hopes, broken promises, and an uncertain future. *Harvard Educational Review, 75*(1), 43–64.

Nieto, S., & Jenlink, P. M. (2005). Affirming diversity: A conversation with Sonia Nieto, professor of language, literacy, and culture, University of Massachusetts, Amherst. *Teacher Education and Practice, 18*(2), 175–184.

Orfield, G., Lee, C., & Harvard Civil Rights Project. (2007). *Historic reversals, accelerating resegregation, and the need for new integration strategies*. Civil Rights Project/Proyecto Derechos Civiles.

Paluck, E. L., & Green, D. P. (2009). Prejudice reduction: What works? A review and assessment of research and practice. *Annual Review of Psychology, 60*, 339–367. doi:10.1146/annurev.psych.60.110707.163607

Parks, G., & Hughey, M. W. (2011). *The Obamas and a (post) racial America?* New York: Oxford University Press.

Peebles-Wilkins, W. (2006). Affirm diversity: "Mix it up." *Children & Schools, 28*(1).

Pfeifer, J. H., Brown, C. S., Juvonen, J., & the Society for Research in Child Development. (2007). Prejudice reduction in schools: Teaching tolerance in schools—lessons learned since Brown v. Board of Education about the development and reduction of children's prejudice. *Social Policy Report, 21*(2).

Power, F. C., Higgins, A., & Kohlberg, L. (1991). *Lawrence Kohlberg's approach to moral education.* New York: Columbia University Press.

Rutter, M., & Maughan, B. (2002). School effectiveness findings 1979–2002. *Journal of School Psychology, 40*(6), 451–475. doi:10.1016/S0022-4405(02)00124-3

Shapiro, I. (2002). *Training for racial equity and inclusion: A guide to selected programs by the Aspen Institute.* Queenstown, MD: Aspen Institute.

Shaull, R. (1970) Foreword. In P. Freire, *Pedagogy of the oppressed* (M. B. Ramos, Trans., pp. 9–15). New York: Continuum.

Sleeter, C. E. (2000). Strengthening multicultural education with community-based service learning. In C. R. O'Grady (Ed.), *Integrating service learning and multicultural education in colleges and universities* (pp. 263–276). Mahwah, NJ: Erlbaum.

Sleeter, C., & Stillman, J. (2005). Standardizing knowledge in a multicultural society. *Curriculum Inquiry, 35*(1), 27–46.

Steele, C. M. (2010). *Whistling Vivaldi: How stereotypes affect us and what we can do.* New York: Norton.

Stevens, R., & Charles, J. (2005). Preparing teachers to teach tolerance. *Multicultural Perspectives, 7*(1), 17–25.

Strolovitch, D. Z. (2006). Do interest groups represent the disadvantaged? Advocacy at the intersections of race, class, and gender. *Journal of Politics, 68*(4), 894–910. doi:10.1111/j.1468-2508.2006.00478.x

Sue, D. W. (2010). *Microaggressions in everyday life: Race, gender, and sexual orientation.* Hoboken, NJ: Wiley.

Sue, D. W., & Constantine, M. G. (2005). Effective multicultural consultation and organizational development. In M. G. Constantine & D. W. Sue (Eds.), *Strategies for building multicultural competence in mental health and educational settings* (pp. 212–226). Hoboken, NJ: Wiley.

Swearer, S. M., Espelage, D. L., Vaillancourt, T., & Hymel, S. (2010). What can be done about school bullying? Linking research to educational practice. *Educational Researcher, 39*(1), 38–47. doi:10.3102/0013189X09357622

Tatum, B. D. (2003). *"Why are all the black kids sitting together in the cafeteria?": A psychologist explains the development of racial identity* (5th ed.). New York: Basic Books.

Taylor, D. L., & Clark, M. P. (2009). "Set up to fail": Institutional racism and the sabotage of school improvement. *Equity & Excellence in Education, 42*(2), 114–129.

Toldson, I. A. (Ed.). (2010). The happy bell curve: How misguided research on race and achievement is duping black progressives and liberal Americans into accepting black inferiority. *Journal of Negro Education, 79*(4), 443–445.

Torre, M. E. (2009). Participatory action research and critical race theory: Fueling spaces for nos-otras to research. *Urban Review, 41*(1), 106–120. doi:10.1007/s11256-008-0097-7

Torre, M. E., & Fine, M. (2011). A wrinkle in time: Tracing a legacy of public science through community self-surveys and participatory action research. *Journal of Social Issues, 67*(1), 106–121. doi:10.1111/j.1540-4560.2010.01686.x

Torre, M., Fine, M., Stoudt, B., & Fox, M. (2010). Critical participatory action research as public science. In P. Camic & H. Cooper (Eds.), *Handbook of research methods in psychology.* Washington, DC: American Psychological Association.

Tuck, E. (2009a). Re-visioning action: Participatory action research and indigenous theories of change. *Urban Review, 41*(1), 47–65. doi:10.1007/s11256-008-0094-x

Tuck, E. (2009b). Suspending damage: A letter to communities. *Harvard Educational Review, 79*(3), 409–427.

Tuck, E., & Fine, M. (2007). Inner angles: A range of ethical responses to/with indigenous/decolonizing theories. In N. K. Denzin & M. D. Giardina (Eds.), *Ethical futures in qualitative research: Decolonizing the politics of knowledge* (pp. 145–168). Walnut Creek, CA: Left Coast Press.

U.S. Census Bureau. (2010). *Child poverty brief 2009 and 2010: Rates by race and Hispanic origin by state.* Retrieved from http://www.census.gov/hhes/www/poverty

Wise, T. (2011). *White like me: Reflections on race from a privileged son* (Rev. Ed.). Brooklyn, NY: Soft Skull Press.

Woodson, C. G. (2006). *The mis-education of the Negro.* San Diego, CA: The Book Tree. (Original work published 1933)

Case Study 18A
Facing History and Ourselves*

DENNIS J. BARR AND BETTY BARDIGE

Facing History and Ourselves calls for you to expand your obligations and to care for the many hurting people in the world. . . . It calls for you to take action when you see something wrong with the environment we live in. . . . I faced history one day and found myself.

—Facing History and Ourselves student

Facing History dares to pose the question, how do I affect the moral and intellectual development of my students? We must ask this question about all of the students with whom we work, students from all walks of life, whether their paths have been windy or straight, paved or dirty, and even though we do not know where they will lead. If the answers come too quickly, they are probably false. If they don't come at all, then we are all in trouble—teachers, students, and ultimately the society of which we are a part.

—Facing History and Ourselves teacher

Facing History and Ourselves is an international educational and professional development organization whose mission is to engage students of diverse backgrounds in an examination of racism, prejudice, and anti-Semitism in order to promote the development of a more humane and informed citizenry. Facing History and Ourselves believes that by studying the historical development of the Holocaust and other examples of dehumanization, collective violence, and genocide, students can make essential connections between history and the moral and civic choices they confront in their own lives.

Facing History and Ourselves has nine offices in North America, an international hub in London, and a network of twenty-nine thousand educators who reach nearly 1.9 million students each year. For this purpose, the Facing

*The authors acknowledge, with gratitude, Marty Sleeper, Margot Strom, Doc Miller, the members of the Facing History Core Knowledge working group, Jocelyn Stanton, and Karen Murphy for their contributions to this chapter.

History and Ourselves "program" refers to the application of Facing History principles, content, and methodology to teacher professional development and classroom implementation. Facing History's work encompasses a broader range of activities, however, including a model for systemic reform in schools, districts, and school systems internationally. In addition, since neither schools nor school systems exist in isolation from the communities of which they are a part, Facing History reaches audiences beyond the classroom through major public events such as a traveling multimedia exhibition, speaker series, and academic conferences in partnership with major universities. Facing History's website (www.facinghistory.org) and online resources attract more than seven hundred thousand visits from 215 countries and territories annually.

CORE TENETS OF FACING HISTORY AND OURSELVES

Facing History and Ourselves assumes that democracies are human enterprises that can only remain vital through the active, thoughtful, and socially responsible participation of their citizens. Education can be used as a critical tool for building and preserving democratic civil society. At the same time, history has shown how education can also be used to dehumanize and marginalize some groups and as a tool to subvert the values that are essential to preserving human rights and democracy. Facing History highlights the importance of creating learning environments that encourage reflection, deliberation, debate, and questioning processes that allow teachers and students to develop well-informed perspectives and judgments about complex social, moral, civic, and political issues.

Moral development is a lifelong process, beginning in early childhood and extending through adulthood. It takes on special urgency in adolescence, however, when children need to be seen as moral philosophers (Kohlberg & Gilligan, 1971) as they develop a sense of moral agency, principled self-worth, and voice. Similarly, adolescence is a critical period for the development of civic knowledge, skills, and dispositions. Adolescence is, by definition, a time of transition, when young people begin to take their places as responsible and participating members of their communities. As young people weigh their future choices, they wrestle with issues of loyalty and belief. The adolescent's central developmental questions are "Who am I?" "Do I matter?" and "How can I make a difference?" They seek people and paths that are worthy of their loyalty and commitment, challenge hypocrisy, and bring passion and new perspectives to enterprises that capture their imaginations and engage their involvement (Bardige, 2011).

Facing History brings historical and moral dimensions to civic education. To become informed and thoughtful citizens of their communities and of the increasingly interconnected and interdependent world, adolescents need civic education that goes beyond the traditional civics class. They must develop sufficient background in history and world affairs—as well as in science and the humanities—to know what to make of new information, or at least how to find it. Students need to understand the major controversies and conflicts of today's world; the national and international institutions and processes that protect or imperil human rights, freedoms, and well-being; and the pivotal events and processes that have shaped our world and continue to influence our common destiny.

In addition to knowledge of history and other social sciences, and moral and civic competencies and dispositions, tomorrow's world citizens will need literacy and media skills that enable them to find, interpret, and evaluate information and to communicate their views with integrity and persuasiveness. They will need to develop "habits of mind" that encompass multiple-perspective taking, admit divergent views and discrepant information, tolerate uncertainty and ambiguity, and ultimately form integrated understandings and judgments on which they can base individual and collective action.

If as adults we want the next generation to join us in building more compassionate and inclusive communities, in standing up to injustice and preventing cruelty and violence, we will need to stretch their imaginations—and our own—as together we attempt to walk in unfamiliar shoes and communicate across cultural and ideological divides. At the same time, young people will need worthy models to emulate and challenge their thinking. We will need to engage them in discussions and take their questions and positions seriously. And we will need to give them many opportunities to develop their own opinions and voices and to practice empathy, ethical decision making, and civic participation in caring communities as well as in circumstances that call forth their moral outrage and challenge them to put their beliefs into action.

THE FACING HISTORY AND OURSELVES PROGRAM

The Facing History and Ourselves program integrates compelling content and rigorous inquiry, not a specific lesson sequence. As a model of professional development, studying, and teaching, Facing History encompasses the teacher's intellectual and emotional engagement, which along with the particulars of her classroom situation guides mindful selection of resources, activities, guiding or "essential" questions, and assignments. The journey that each class takes is shaped by the insights and questions these experiences spark for that particular group of teacher(s) and students. At the same time, each journey is built around a core of common elements—regardless of whether the "course" being taught is seen as primarily history, literature, art, humanities, civics, or ethics; whether it is taught to adolescent or adult learners; whether it is a unit within a longer sequence, a core or elective course, or a yearlong or multiyear program; and regardless of the particular time and place in which it is offered.

The common core elements of a Facing History course are designed in a "scope and sequence" framework that organizes the inquiry and shapes the journey that students and teachers will take together. The scope and sequence begins with what students know and care most about—themselves and the social/moral worlds they inhabit. Through evocative literature, art, and individual and group activities, students probe themes of identity, individuality, conformity, stereotyping, group loyalty, and responsibilities to those beyond one's immediate circle. They explore how society influences individuals and how individuals can influence their society. They examine how, for individuals, communities, and nations, in-group identity and cohesion can come at the expense of exclusion, stereotyping, marginalization, and dehumanization of those in "out-groups." They see people who fell down in terms of their moral actions, but they also see people who stood up. As they will again and again when they look at distressing history, they face their own propensities to participate in or overlook cruelty and to ignore opportunities to help (Bardige, 2011).

In the early part of their journey, students and teachers begin to build a common language, a "vocabulary of ethical decision making." It includes words like *victim*, *victimizer*, *bystander* and *upstander*, *democracy*, *citizen*, *civic participation* and *patriotism*, *stereotype*, *propaganda*, *ostracism*, *racism*, and *anti-Semitism*. This core vocabulary will serve students well as they study the past and make connections to the present. It will also expand and deepen as historical examples and students' judgments of their protagonists' actions and/or inaction give new meanings and resonance to the words.

After an exploration of questions about identity and membership, courses examine a historical case study in depth. The foundational resource book, *Facing History and Ourselves: Holocaust and Human Behavior* (Strom, 1994), focuses on the failure of democracy in Germany and the events leading to the Holocaust. It provides a rich set of materials to support student and teacher inquiry. The history is examined as something that did not have to happen, the result of choices made and neglected by individuals and groups at all levels of society. Finally, it provides multiple entry points into explorations of related historical content and present-day issues, enabling individual classes and students to "go deeper" into content that holds particular interest or relevance for them. Examining the collapse of democracy in Weimar Germany, the rise of the Nazis, and the role of propaganda, conformity, and obedience in turning neighbor against neighbor provides students with new perspective on the present as well as the past.

In all Facing History and Ourselves materials, history is looked at through multiple lenses, incorporating eyewitness accounts and other primary sources along with interpretative material and reflections on root causes. Why, a course may ask, do some people willingly conform to the norms of a group even when those norms encourage wrongdoing, while others speak out and resist? Students' answers will be stretched by their study of history; by the findings and reflections of psychologists and social scientists; by the reflections of artists, writers, scholars, and eyewitnesses; and by their own intellectual, moral, and emotional reasoning and that of their teachers and classmates. Studying resources such as an interview with a concentration camp commander, a story of a German university professor whose colleagues were expelled and whose activities became increasingly constrained, and a video about a village in France where Jews were hidden may offer students entry points for a rich discussion of issues of compassion, courage, and resistance in their own worlds. At the same time, such readings can provide needed distance and perspective on issues and events that may yet be too raw, painful, or controversial to discuss directly.

Having delved into a historical period, students who had been initially asked to suspend their prejudgments and prejudices are asked to reflect on and form judgments about the actions and inactions of the people whose lives they have studied. How has the world judged these historical actors? Do students feel that justice has been served? In addition, students consider what needs to be remembered and memorialized and the ongoing consequences or legacies of the history they studied. What paths to restitution or reconciliation have been, or might be, taken?

The final section of the scope and sequence involves connecting what students have been studying to questions about prevention, civic engagement, and their own participation in society. It usually begins with study and reflection—delving into the choices of those who have "made a difference" in large and small ways. For many individual students and sometimes for a whole class, it leads to a student-initiated action or project—as simple as writing a letter to a politician, helping with a community fund-raiser, or not laughing at an ethnic joke, or as complicated as staging a protest march or exhibition, orchestrating a discussion of class or school norms that changes policy and behavior, or starting a blog or a service club. And often, of course, the important choices are made long after the course has ended.

There is an ongoing interplay between "facing history" and "facing ourselves" throughout this scope and sequence. The meaning students make of core themes of the course, such as issues of inclusion and exclusion, are informed both by personal experience and their study of history. Students' perspectives on in-groups and out-groups in their school or community, for example, can provide the teacher with critical information about what is relevant to them and how their moral imaginations might be stretched through the Facing History journey.

One eighth grader, Patty, wrote in her Facing History journal about the teasing of immigrant students in her school, "I know how I feel, which is that it's wrong. But I'm not planning on standing up for those people even though I know it's wrong, 'cause I mean, it's not that big of a deal. Even though if it happened to me it would be."

Though she judges the way the immigrant students are being treated as "wrong," she also sees it as "not that big of a deal." The vocabulary, content, and pedagogy of Facing History may provide the opportunity for Patty and her classmates to think more deeply about their involvement in relation to such issues. Patty might come to see, for example, that she does not include "those people" in her universe of responsibility (a concept Facing History courses address), and to consider how her decisions are both shaped by and influence the culture in the school.

In this particular school, a culture of fear influenced students' responses to everyday ethical issues. Another girl, Jenny, put it this way, "Like if you see someone else getting picked on, in your mind, like a part of you thinks it's wrong but another part is like, yes I am glad they're being picked on so then I won't be picked on, so then you join in so then they won't look at you, you know?"

Jenny and Patty, like many students in similar school cultures, grapple with conflicting motivations, such as the wish to act according to their values but also to stay psychologically and physically safe. Facing History helps students to gain new perspective on these kinds of dilemmas and the consequences of their daily choices.

Pedagogical Emphases

As we have seen, the content of a Facing History and Ourselves course can be laid out on a scope and sequence map, but its power to build the knowledge, skills, and dispositions of civic learning grounded in historical and moral considerations comes from the fusion of content and pedagogy. To Facing History, pedagogy is an active, always challenging process of engaging young people in an intellectual, emotional, and ethical enterprise worthy of their commitment. This enterprise requires personal reflection and active interaction with others.

The first pedagogical emphasis is intellectual rigor. Adolescents, by and large, are keenly interested in questions of historical veracity and moral integrity, but a lack of historical knowledge and memory can skew their perspectives. At the same time, most are just developing the cognitive capacity to grasp the ways in which an outcome can be influenced by multiple interacting factors. They may believe that there are "two sides to the story" and seek out alternative views, yet they may have difficulty holding in mind more than one explanation or recognizing that the "two sides" they see do not carry equal moral or explanatory weight (Bardige, 1983). Intellectual honesty in teaching adolescents, therefore, requires that historical narratives not only be factually accurate but also authentic in their use and portrayal of eyewitness accounts and other primary sources; unbiased in their inclusion of multiple relevant perspectives; and truthful in their representations of scope and scale, competing causal explanations, the weight of evidence favoring one explanation, conclusion, perspective, or judgment over another, and the limitations of current knowledge.

Historical content must also be explored in sufficient depth to allow students to follow the historical narrative and reflect upon its implications. Teachers help students to resist the urge to frame a neat story of the triumph of good or evil so that students can engage with the complexities of what actually happened and understand the relationships among historical events. When history is read as a human story—full of complexity and challenge, propelled by the decisions of individuals who could not always anticipate their consequences—it comes alive. History becomes a body of knowledge that adolescents can think and debate about and can mine for lessons with present-day relevance.

The second pedagogical emphasis involves allowing for and attending to students' emotional engagement with the historical content and with the views and feelings shared in class discussions. When the arc of a historical narrative resonates with adolescents' own emerging stories, they can "take in" the emotions of others, grapple with the complexities of their life situations, empathize with them, and learn from their experiences.

The active and ongoing participation of the teacher is critical in assessing what her students know and can do, what they feel strongly about, what they want to know more about, and what will engage and stretch their hearts, minds, and values. Curricular materials and approaches must be integrated with tools that provide teachers with insight into students' thoughts and feelings, including thought-provoking assignments, curriculum-embedded assessments, and engaging group discussion activities. And any program of study must be backed up by a set of well-chosen, well-organized resources that enable teachers and students to extend their investigations and enlarge their understanding. When history is taught and learned in this way, intellectual rigor is not opposed to emotional engagement, but rather stimulates it. Stories chosen for their emotional resonance are especially compelling when they are both true and authentically told.

The third component at the heart of Facing History's pedagogy is ethical reflection. The complexities of history and life can stimulate ethical reflection that, in turn, promotes more sophisticated moral reasoning (Lieberman, 1981). Complicating one's thinking is especially critical in the realms of social perspective taking (Selman, 2003) and moral reasoning (Power, Higgins, & Kohlberg, 1989). When teachers seek to highlight the ethical dimensions of history, they ask different kinds of questions than when they only seek to promote dispassionate understanding (Reimer, Paolitto, & Hersh, 1979).* They focus on moments of choice and call students' attention to the moral dilemmas they pose. They help students articulate their own perspectives as to the right or best choice, explain their reasoning, and then step into others' shoes and take their perspectives into account. Such discussions help students to learn from the failures of history and steer a path between the dangers of dogma and the "anything goes" abyss of moral relativism. Both extremes have often proved dangerously seductive to adolescents and young adults, who are looking for something to believe in and at the same time testing their ability to choose their own paths. Nowhere is this clearer than in the history of the Holocaust and the events that led up to it.

Facing History teachers deepen students' historical understanding by sparking rigorous analysis, emotional engagement, and ethical reflection that feed and are fed by each other. Students actively engage with what they are reading, hearing, and seeing. They respond with empathy, concern, or outrage;

---

*In a discussion of a videotape of her teaching, Margot Strom explained how focusing on the ethical questions raised by a hypothetical dilemma influenced the questions she asked her students, how their thinking was stretched through the discussion, and how she adapted the technique to deal with the greater complexities of real events in history.

they examine their initial reactions in light of new or discrepant information or a teacher or classmate's question; they rethink their beliefs and commitments and deepen their understanding in light of what they have learned. In sum, within the context of an emotionally supportive, intellectually stimulating, and ethically focused classroom, students are challenged to face history, face themselves, and practice the skills and habits of informed, reflective, and ethically grounded democratic citizenship.

The fourth pedagogical emphasis makes historical analysis, emotional engagement, and ethical reflection possible and fruitful: creating a safe, reflective, and engaging classroom. Reflection, conversation, and debate are known to be essential to fostering social and moral growth. The distinctive teaching philosophy of Facing History and Ourselves relies on the moral discourse of history to deepen adolescents' understanding of humanity. It takes a special kind of learning environment, what Facing History calls a "reflective classroom community," to achieve such a goal (Miller, 2009).

To create the reflective classroom that is essential to teaching Facing History and Ourselves, teachers must (1) promote a climate of respect, (2) model a culture of questioning, (3) nurture student voice, (4) create space for diverse viewpoints, (5) deepen reflection through thoughtful silence, and (6) honor different learning styles.

In reflective classrooms, students' knowledge is constructed rather than passively absorbed. Students are prompted to join with teachers in posing problems to foster "critical consciousness" (Freire, 1994). In reflective classrooms, teaching and learning are conceived as *social* endeavors in which a healthy exchange of ideas is welcome. Students are encouraged to engage in dialogue within a community of learners, to look deeply, to question underlying assumptions, and to discern underlying values being presented. Students are encouraged to voice their own opinions and to actively listen to others, to treat different students and different perspectives with patience and respect, and to recognize that there are always more perspectives and more to learn. Learning in these contexts nurtures students' humility as well as confidence— humility because they come to see that they have no "corner" on the truth, and confidence because they know their opinion will still be taken seriously. Perhaps this is why the educator Diane Moore has argued that "encouraging students to take themselves seriously and inspiring in them the confidence to do so are two of the most important roles of an educator in a multicultural democracy" (Moore, 2006, p. 11). As John Dewey has argued, classrooms like these are not training grounds for *future* democratic action but rather places where democracy is already enacted (Dewey, 1916).

The following example illustrates what can happen when a teacher skillfully fosters a reflective classroom that is intellectually rigorous, emotionally engaging, and ethically rich. The context is a yearlong humanities course in a public high school in an urban community. The class, composed of sixteen students, all of whom are recent immigrants to the United States, had been using Facing History resources to study the Rwandan genocide. The teacher describes the background for a lively class discussion that incorporates key themes and resources of the course and engages diverse perspectives:

My students have been working on their digital stories, which are stories of moral dilemmas and universes of obligation. The students had a choice: they could write a story pertaining to their community project or they could write a story about Rwanda. We have been working on community projects for the last two months, and students have been observing, researching, and questioning their communities around a key issue. We also just finished a unit on the Rwandan genocide, where students wrote and debated issues of obligation and accountability. Together, we decided to create a collection of community dilemmas of people trying to understand their moral obligations during complex times. Each student wrote a script for their story. They recorded someone reading it, and then they found or created images to illustrate it. The final step is combining both the audio and visual into a three minute movie called a "digital story." After a class period of editing and searching for images, a student asked me if we could have a "sophisticated conversation" about the story-making process. The rest of the class agreed that a discussion would be helpful to their projects.

We began. The students admitted that they were struggling with finding images to best represent their stories. One student, Elizabeth, said to the group, "You know, many of our stories are about violence, and I don't know how to represent violence. I don't know what would be an appropriate image. I don't want to do something inappropriate."

Immediately, Omar answered her, "Who says what is appropriate? Who says what is inappropriate? If it's truth, if you think it represents your story, it's appropriate. It has to be your story, not someone else's story."

From there, with no help from me, students starting drawing connections to *Fahrenheit 451*, which we read together in September. One student said, "I connect this to *Fahrenheit 451*, and how the people burned books. They said that some ideas shouldn't be in society, and so they burned them. It's like saying what images are appropriate or not. Who says what should be in society? It's like limiting our freedom of speech."

From there, Abdoul chimed in. "I see your point, but I think there are some books that should be burned. Hitler's book is one of those books."

The students all jumped in. "But if Hitler's book is burned, how will we learn about him? How will we learn about history? What examples will we have of how genocide happens? If we burn his book, aren't we being just like him? If we start burning books we disagree with, then someone might burn our books one day."

Abdoul argued, "We can learn about the Holocaust in other ways. I take Elie Wiesel as an example. His book is a better book to use to learn about the Holocaust."

"But how can you decide what books people should learn from?" another began. "We need different ideas to understand different societies. Different people have different ideas. We have to accept that."

A student named Fatoumata interjected, "I am from Africa. You are from Africa. Where is our history? Do you carry it with you? How would you feel if they burned our history? Don't you want people to know our history?"

The conversation continued. From there, the class connected the discussion to the essential question I used to frame the first unit in September: "What is the nature of humans? Are humans born good or evil?"

"I think humans are neutral!" Ankita firmly said. "It's not like you're evil and you're good and I'm this and you're that. It's that you do evil things or good things sometimes. You make choices."

"Right," one said, "but can humans be trusted to live with all the different ideas in society? Can we trust humanity enough to not burn books?"

"It's all about trust," another agreed. "You have to trust humanity with all types of speech."

"But how do you know you can trust someone?" Sunny asked the group.

The answers varied:

"You can see it in their face."

"You can't."

"I don't trust people until they really know me."

"You can trust someone by being trustworthy yourself."

"You can trust someone by being the change."

"You have to be the person you hope others will be to you."

"However, maybe we trust people who look like us and sound like us," Ankita admitted. "Maybe we need to start trusting people who don't look like us."

"I think it depends on your experience with trust and your experiences with different people," Abdoul suggested.

"I think it's all about fear, and fear of people who aren't like you. We have to trust people when they say they are trustworthy." Omar offered.

"We keep saying that if we trust people, the world will be better. But look at our community projects. All of us are now talking about violence. How can we trust in a world where all we see is violence?"

At the end of the conversation, our class only had more questions. But for me, as their teacher, I was left with something more. These conversations showed me that my students were engaged; engaged with the curriculum, with choice-making, and with creating a society where all can participate. I often ask how educators can help create a more informed and active citizenry. After a discussion like this, I felt one step closer to the answer. (Stanton & Sleeper, 2009)

The students are talking about many different things—their histories; book burning in Nazi Germany; the Holocaust; violence in their worlds; and trust in the people they see, read about, and interact with. They have explored all of these topics in more focused discussions during their course, and now they are doing the hard work of thinking about what such issues mean in their own lives. But most of all they are talking about humanity. The essential lesson with which they are grappling is how to cope with and understand differences in the world in which they live. In doing so, they are coming to grips with the question, how do I make a difference?—a question constantly on the minds of young people and one fundamental to any construction of civic education.

Preparing and Supporting Teachers and Schools

Since its founding in 1976, Facing History and Ourselves has recognized that teacher effectiveness is at the heart of educational success for students. Facing History provides professional development seminars, workshops, coaching, and print and online resources for teachers, helping them to create reflective classrooms and to use the content and pedagogy to promote their students' growth as thoughtful participants in society, as well as their academic achievement.

Teachers come to Facing History and Ourselves by many paths. Some are sent or mandated by administrators; others come at their own initiative, either alone or with like-minded colleagues. Some come having already made a commitment; others are merely curious. Most find that what the program has to offer is meaningful to them as adults as well as teachers, and the task of sharing it with students is one that requires not only their own courage, thoughtfulness, and willingness to be a student again, but also the support of mentors and colleagues.

To become effective Facing History and Ourselves educators, teachers first need time to step back and reflect together with colleagues. During professional development seminars and workshops, they get time as learners to explore the concepts at the core of the scope and sequence and to deepen their understanding of the history they intend to teach. They look at and experience a variety of ways they can constructively engage their students in the study of this history and its implications for how we live today. All of this is done in community with the support of Facing History staff, colleagues, scholars, and ideally also school administrators and parents. At the same time, teachers build relationships with colleagues who will share their challenges and with a staff member who will provide ongoing support.

In its teacher preparation efforts, Facing History and Ourselves is explicit both about the need for support and effective methods of obtaining it. Administrators and supervisors need to understand the program and value its aims and content so that they can adjust schedules and respond to parent and community concerns when needed and can foster a schoolwide culture that builds upon the lessons of Facing History and supports civic learning beyond the classroom. Facing History urges teachers to make their efforts visible to parents, other teachers, administrators, and community members, inviting them to sit in on classes and professional discussions, offering curriculum night presentations or extended study group opportunities, or linking them with adult education offerings in the community. Facing History staff continually follow up with teachers who have attended their seminars, listening to teachers' observations and concerns, suggesting additional resources, arranging for speakers, and sharing the joys of uncovering students' moral insights and growing sense of the importance of their education and their "choices to participate."

APPLYING FACING HISTORY AND OURSELVES IN NEW CONTEXTS

From its beginnings, Facing History and Ourselves has been international, with outreach to educators and scholars from around the world. Facing History has staff in Toronto and London supporting extensive work in Canada and the UK, and it provides professional development and follow-up coaching to educators in dozens of other countries. Partnerships with educational organizations in South Africa, Northern Ireland, Rwanda, and Israel have allowed the work to expand broadly in those locations.

Since 2003, the global work of Facing History and Ourselves has included the facilitation of teacher professional development seminars in South Africa, Rwanda, and Northern Ireland and the development of appropriate follow-up strategies tailored to each country's needs and educational context. Importantly, each of these countries is emerging from a history of violence, division, and trauma, and each is at a significant point in the process of transition. These countries are places where the legacies of recent conflict remain painfully present and where teachers, charged with the responsibility of teaching historical narratives that themselves remain the subject of intense controversy, are struggling with the burden of their own memories. Facing History's experience in each of these countries demonstrates the enormous challenges that confront educators who too often are left to address conflicts and promote reconciliation without the necessary tools and support (Murphy, Sleeper, & Strom, 2011).

In these postviolence societies where the program has been introduced, Facing History, working as an outsider, has acted as a medium for bringing together individuals and groups who have been on opposite sides of the conflict. Its approach to history education meets the need to look at history from multiple perspectives, to explore issues of ethics and decision making, to not treat historical events as inevitable, to locate individual moral agency, and to understand the process of history making itself. By introducing a discussion of historiography, teachers are brought into the process of transition within the context of history education, providing them with tools to understand and deconstruct the official narrative as well as to better understand the basis and background for the curriculum they have been given to teach. The Facing History model of continual interchange between facing the present and confronting history has allowed participants in professional development seminars to reflect upon their own identities, to think about the impact of identity on behavior, to contemplate how such thinking and actions can produce a sense of "we and they," and to use those reflections as entry points to their own history. Further, using a case study of another time and place in which universal themes of human behavior, choice, and decision making are embedded has been critical to eliciting significant discussion and reflection upon the particulars of that history and its legacy for the present and future.

The salient challenge for teachers in these countries is for them to confront their own past and then help their students find meaning and connection to the present. In order to do so and to help students develop the skills necessary for democratic participation, teachers need to practice these things themselves. In the three postconflict societies where Facing History has been introduced, traditional pedagogies, with an emphasis on lecturing and exams, have been the dominant mode of instruction. Increasingly, education departments are recognizing that the interactive strategies and participatory methods that characterize Facing History represent a needed opportunity for modeling and practicing democracy. Facing History professional development seminars have allowed teachers to develop new skills that can then be integrated and modeled for their students. Evaluations of Facing History's efforts in South Africa and in other countries in transition have demonstrated positive effects on teachers and students and have been used to adapt the approach for each country (Tibbetts, 2006).

HOW DO WE KNOW FACING HISTORY AND OURSELVES WORKS?

Throughout the organization's history, Facing History and Ourselves' evaluation staff and independent researchers have carried out more than one hundred studies that have yielded a large body of knowledge about the model's effectiveness, as well as knowledge about teacher and adolescent development more generally (Barr, 2010; Brabeck, Kenny, Stryker, Tollefson, & Strom, 1994; Schultz, Barr, & Selman, 2001; Tibbetts, 2006). Independent experts and review panels have repeatedly validated the program's effectiveness based on the findings of evaluation studies. Facing History was selected for membership in the U.S. Department of Education's National Diffusion Network (NDN) from 1980 to 1996 as an exemplary program (Lieberman, 1993). Since that time, research on Facing History's model has been reviewed and provided the basis for external validation as a promising approach under the U.S. Department of Education's Safe, Disciplined, and Drug-Free Schools initiative (U.S. Department of Education, 2001) and as a best practice in the fields of civic education (Fine, 2004); character education (Berkowitz & Bier, 2005); and Holocaust education (Isaacs et al., 2006).

Evaluation and basic research studies have examined different aspects of the following proposition: when teachers develop the knowledge, skills, confidence, and commitment needed to create safe and reflective learning environments and to use Facing History content and pedagogy to engage students' hearts and minds, treating them as moral philosophers, capable of deeply examining the moral dimensions of history, students develop greater social, moral, intellectual, and civic maturity.

In 2009, independent researchers completed an ambitious randomized experiment studying the impact of Facing History and Ourselves on teachers and students (the National Professional Development and Evaluation Project: Barr, 2010; Boulay et al., 2011).* The study investigated the causal impacts of a Facing History professional development on high school teachers' sense of professional efficacy and satisfaction, and on their students' historical understanding and social and civic growth. Schools and teachers near Facing History's U.S. offices that had not been exposed to Facing History were eligible to participate in the study. The study involved 134 teachers and 1,371 of their students in seventy-six schools in eight regions of the United States. Half were randomly assigned to receive Facing History training and implement the program in the first year, and half served as a control group and received these services a year later.

---

*The study was funded by the Richard and Susan Smith Family Foundation. Data collection and analysis were carried out by Abt Associates Inc. Dennis J. Barr, Melinda Fine, Ethan Lowenstein, and Robert L. Selman served as coinvestigators.

The results demonstrate that Facing History's educational model is scalable beyond those teachers and schools who actively seek to use Facing History. The professional development provided by Facing History had a statistically significant and educationally meaningful impact on all aspects of teacher self-efficacy that were measured, as well as on teacher satisfaction and professional growth* (Boulay et al., 2011). Specifically, Facing History teachers felt more capable than the control group teachers, on average, of creating community and learner-centered classroom environments and implementing teaching practices to promote students' historical understanding, civic learning, ethical awareness, and character development.

In addition, Facing History teachers were more energized and motivated by their professional development experiences than were teachers in the control group and felt a greater sense of accomplishment, engagement, and growth as teachers. No differences were found between Facing History and control teachers in the degree of their emotional exhaustion or depersonalization (disengagement from their work). These findings were sustained longitudinally over two years and were replicated with a second cohort of teachers.

Facing History students outperformed control students, on average, in their historical understanding and in certain civic learning outcomes. Historical understanding involves skills for interpreting evidence, for analyzing what leads people to make ethical choices, and for thinking critically about cause and effect. In the area of civic learning, Facing History had a statistically significant impact on five civic learning outcomes: civic efficacy; valuing the protection of the civil liberties of people with different views on social and political issues; awareness of the dangers of prejudice and discrimination; students' perceptions of their class climate as safe, inclusive, and respectful of differences; and students' perceptions of their class as offering them the opportunity to learn about meaningful civic matters. These academic and civic findings were replicated with a new group of students in an exploratory study that did not use an experimental design, suggesting that program effects are sustained in schools over time if the program is implemented fully.

Taken together, the teacher and student findings suggest that Facing History teachers not only felt a greater sense of efficacy in promoting student academic and civic learning than control teachers, but they were also, in fact, *effective in practice* because student outcomes were found in the same areas. Although the relationship between specific teacher and student changes was not the focus of this study, the alignment of these outcomes suggests that Facing History prepares teachers to address the following critical needs in education:

1. Creating safer and more engaging learning environments.
2. Promoting respect for the rights of others whose views differ from one's own.

---

*P values for group differences on all efficacy outcomes range from .0004 to .0047. The effect sizes range from .49 to .85. The *p* value for the satisfaction with professional development, expertise, and engagement variable is .0001, and the effect size is 1.00. The *p* value for the personal accomplishment variable (one aspect of teacher satisfaction) is .0011, and the effect size is .49.

3. Fostering awareness of the power and danger of prejudice and discrimination.
4. Promoting critical thinking about history and contemporary events.
5. Increasing students' belief that they can make a difference in society.

In sum, this rigorous study and the many other studies carried out over nearly four decades provide a robust picture of Facing History's effectiveness in enhancing teachers' sense of efficacy for promoting students' abilities to participate in society as thoughtful, informed, caring, and active citizens.

CONCLUSION

Martin Niemoeller, a leader of the Confessing Church in Germany, voted for the Nazi party in 1933. By 1938, he was in a concentration camp. He survived the war, later reflecting,

> In Germany, the Nazis came for the Communists and I didn't speak up because I wasn't a Communist. Then they came for the Jews and I didn't speak up because I wasn't a Jew. Then they came for the trade unionists, and I didn't speak up because I wasn't a trade unionist. Then they came for the Catholics, and I didn't speak up because I was a Protestant. Then they came for me, and by that time there was no one left to speak for me. (Strom, 1994, p. 206)

Niemoeller considers the tragic consequences of indifference for those he did not see as belonging within his universe of responsibility. If we study history in depth and with rigor, using narratives such as this, we complicate and deepen our understanding of who we are as individuals. Looking at ourselves through lenses of group and national membership, we see how our identities and actions have been shaped by larger historical events and the actions and perceptions of those within and outside our groups. At the same time, of course, our growing self-understanding deepens our understanding of history—and may cause us to question interpretations or constructions of historical narratives. This is the interplay at the heart of the Facing History approach.

REFERENCES

Bardige, B. (1983). *Reflective thinking and prosocial awareness: Adolescents face the holocaust and themselves*. Doctoral dissertation, Harvard Graduate School of Education, Cambridge, MA.

Bardige, B. (2011). *Introductory essay in "Facing History and Ourselves": Core ideas in brief: A series of conversations among theory, research and practice*. Unpublished manuscript. Brookline, MA: Facing History and Ourselves National Foundation.

Barr, D. J. (2010). *Continuing a tradition of research on the foundations of democratic education: The National Professional Development and Evaluation Project*. Brookline, MA: Facing History and Ourselves National Foundation.

Berkowitz, M. W., & Bier, M. C. (2005). *What works in character education: A research-driven guide for educators*. Washington, DC: Character Education Partnership.

Boulay, B., McCormick, R., Gamse, B., Barr, D. J., Selman, R. L., Lowenstein, E., et al. (2011). *Effects of Facing History and Ourselves on teachers and students: Findings from the National Professional Development and Evaluation Project*. Manuscript in preparation.

Brabeck, M., Kenny, M., Stryker, S., Tollefson, T., & Strom, M. S. (1994). Human rights education through the "Facing History and Ourselves" program. *Journal of Moral Education, 23*(3), 333–347.

Dewey, J. (1916). *Democracy and education*. New York: Free Press.

Fine, M. (2004). *Making our children more humane: Facing History and Ourselves as civic education*. Report prepared for Facing History and Ourselves.

Freire, P. (1994). *Pedagogy of the oppressed*. New York: Continuum Press.

Isaacs, L. W., Rosov, W. J., Raff, L., Rosenblatt, S., Hecht, S., Rozenek, M, et al. (2006). *Best practices in holocaust education: Report to the San Francisco Jewish Community Endowment Fund*. New York: The Berman Center for Research and Evaluation in Jewish Education, Jewish Education Service of North America. Retrieved December 5, 2011, from http://www.sfjcf.org/endowment/grants/programs/SFJCEF-JESNA%20Holocaust%20Education%20Full%20Report.pdf

Kohlberg, L., & Gilligan, C. (1971). The adolescent as a philosopher: The discovery of the self in a post-conventional world. *Daedalus, 100*, 1051–1086.

Lieberman, M. (1981). Facing History and Ourselves: A project evaluation. *Moral Education Forum, 36*–41.

Lieberman, M. (1993). *Project submissions to U.S. Department of Education Joint Dissemination Review Panel in 1980 (285:80-33), 1985 (451:80-33R), and submission to U.S. Department of Education Program Effectiveness Panel*. Unpublished report.

Miller, W. (2009). *Creating a reflective learning community: A foundation for teaching Facing History and Ourselves*. Unpublished paper. Brookline, MA: Facing History and Ourselves National Foundation.

Moore, D. (2006). *Overcoming religious illiteracy: A multicultural approach to the study of religion in secondary education*. New York: Palgrave.

Murphy, K., Sleeper, M., & Strom, M. S. (2011). Facing History and Ourselves in post-conflict societies. *International Schools Journal, 30*(2), 65–72.

Power, F. C., Higgins, A., & Kohlberg, L. (1989). *Lawrence Kohlberg's approach to moral education*. New York: Columbia University Press.

Reimer, J., Paolitto, D. P., & Hersh, R. H. (1979). *Promoting moral growth: From Piaget to Kohlberg*. New York: Longman.

Schultz, L., Barr, D. J., & Selman, R. L. (2001). The value of a developmental approach to evaluating character development programmes: An outcome study of Facing History and Ourselves. *Journal of Moral Education, 30*(1), 3–27.

Selman, R. L. (2003). *The promotion of social awareness: Powerful lessons from the partnership of developmental theory and classroom practice*. New York: Sage.

Stanton, J., & Sleeper, M. (2009). Learning democracy: Facing History and Ourselves in a high school classroom. *Newsletter of the National Social Studies Supervisors Association*.

Strom, M. (1994). *Facing History and Ourselves: Holocaust and human behavior*. Brookline, MA: Facing History and Ourselves.

Tibbetts, F. (2006). Learning from the past: Supporting teaching through the Facing the Past History Project in South Africa. *Prospects, 36*(3).

U.S. Department of Education. (2001). *Exemplary and promising school-based programs that promote safe, disciplined and drug-free schools*. Retrieved December 5, 2011, from http://www.ed.gov/admins/lead/safety/exemplary01/panel_pg3.html

Case Study 18B

Educating American Indian Students: Creating a Prosocial Context

HOLLIE MACKEY

> Culture seems to be those words, artifacts, social phenomena, and ideas that one cherishes, that one builds belief systems and values . . . that people feel they must protect. . . . Cultures are not static. They are not momentary, like the bolt of lightning across the evening sky, but last as long as the people they encompass endure.
>
> —Richard Littlebear (2009, p. 89)

The ideal of multicultural education in American schools, that is, education for, by, about, and inclusive of all, often falls short in regard to the lived experiences of American Indians. Cultural pluralism has become a norm for the American education system, which represents progress from the Anglo-conformity goals espoused by educational leaders of the early 1900s. However, American Indian groups are not fully represented or adequately included in the curriculum. This poses special problems for educators' ability to teach American Indian students and include them in school life.

There are a number of challenges that arise when it comes to meaningful inclusion of American Indians into contemporary school culture. Most notable is the fact that there are 565 federally recognized tribes listed on the Federal Register as of 2010, along with a host of tribes that have acquired individual state recognition. While similarities exist among tribes, each has its own unique set of customs and history. Public school curricula commonly group tribes into regional categories that overlook the possibility of several hundred different tribal perspectives and contributions. From a curricular standpoint, inclusion of each individual tribe would be overwhelming; however, omission of individual differences is obvious to members of the very people targeted for inclusion. Another critical challenge includes the common misunderstanding of the context of the American Indian experience throughout American history, specifically as it relates to the sovereign status of tribes and the unique relationship defined within the U.S. Constitution regarding the status of American Indians within this country. This can lead to the perpetuation of stereotypes such as the notion that all American Indian students are provided a free college education and health care or that all native people receive a check from the government each month. The reality is that college tuition waivers and scholarships are dependent upon state legislatures and each respective tribal group to determine, and in many instances, there are contingencies for qualification and maintenance of such waivers and scholarships such as course load and GPA minimum requirements. Health care is typically available to American Indians living on or near reservations; however many live outside of the home reservation boundaries and designated nonreservation boundaries, which prohibits them from receiving care at no charge. Each tribe has the autonomy to determine the allocation of funds stemming from obtained revenue, whether that be from federal use of resources on tribal lands or gaming money, and while some tribes do receive a monthly check, many do not. The sovereign status afforded to American Indians allows for tribal leaders to make such decisions through tribal legislation. Additionally, American Indians tend to be relegated to a historical context that is devoid of contemporary issues and experiences, and often there is a lack of knowledge of the resources available to classroom teachers to help them facilitate or fully explore nuanced regional and tribal differences. These challenges can have a detrimental effect on the education of American Indian students and on native communities as a whole. In this case study, I explore a few of the ways in which many American Indian communities have chosen to address these issues through their schools. Moreover, I try to look beyond the strategies that educators of American Indian students have incorporated and seek to provide meaning as to why these strategies are important for supporting and improving American Indian education in general.

WALKING IN TWO WORLDS
It is important for those who are unfamiliar with American Indian education to understand the basic notion of "walking in two worlds" as it can often be heard described in native communities. Under this premise, students must be taught to understand and negotiate the social rules, norms, and expectations of both the native and nonnative environments that they will inhabit in order to fully realize successful adulthood and become a contributing member of society. While seemingly neutral facially, the phrase has the potential to be heavily value laden and can be viewed either as an asset or from a deficit perspective. For example, political voice at the state and federal levels requires American Indian leaders to interact and communicate citizens' needs beyond the confines of the tribal boundaries while maintaining the confidence of those they represent. Tribal leaders who cannot communicate effectively between tribal and nontribal members run the risk of alienating one or both sets of people, so it is imperative that they can walk in and out of both worlds fluidly. Conversely, when cultural differences become an extraordinarily heavy burden, walking in two worlds can be perceived as an additional and unfair responsibility that American Indians should not have to bear any more than

non-Indians. In this respect, we are forced to confront an institutionalized system that requires nondominant cultural groups to conform to the dominant group while there is no requirement for reciprocity. Regardless of where an individual falls on the spectrum, the basic premise of "walking in two worlds" acknowledges existing cultural pluralism and ethnic differences.

Similarly, native communities recognize and respect that cultural pluralism exists between nondominant ethnic groups as well. Many American Indian students identify with more than one tribal or ethnic affiliation; for example a student might identify as Cheyenne-Arapaho, Afro-Seminole, or any number of tribal and ethnic combinations based upon family history. Schools serving American Indian students typically identify all ethnic affiliations represented within the school and strive to include each distinct group into conversations of multiculturalism. In this sense, students are taught respect for all racial and ethnic groups and are provided prosocial instruction that develops skills for navigating through the similarities and differences among all people. One example of this is the use of restorative justice practices for resolving disputes or repairing relationships among students. These practices include participation of all stakeholders involved in a particular dispute and promote conversation and subsequent actions that work to promote healing and harmony for both the victim *and* the offender. The use of restorative justice practices is effective because they allow students to voice thoughts and feelings while acknowledging the thoughts and feelings of others. Through mutual understanding, students learn to discern the differences between themselves and others while developing strategies for getting along with one another. This allows students to effectively walk in multiple worlds in and across a number of ethnicities.

MORE THAN ONE CULTURE OR TIMEFRAME

American Indian communities have a distinct strength when it comes to promoting multicultural ideals. That strength stems from the innate understanding that there is not *one* native culture, but rather American Indian tribes create a rich tapestry of traditions and values that may or may not overlap with other tribal groups. American schools attempt to delineate differences by categorizing Native American curricula into regional constructs such as the Plains tribes or the Southwestern tribes; however there are differences and similarities in and among these categories that, if ignored, prevent full inclusion.

To date, there are two states, Montana and New Mexico, that have passed legislation mandating that their public schools fully recognize and teach about specific tribal affiliations within the state rather than group all represented tribes into one category. Not only does this respect the full sovereign status afforded individual tribes by the U.S. Constitution, but it also allows the space for individual tribal members to be meaningfully included and feel valued. The goal is not to place stress on educators by demanding they know and teach every tribe in the nation, but to encourage them to (1) help students understand that these individual differences exist and (2) provide greater understanding of specific tribal groups within the students' home state.

Omission of unique tribal affiliation can have the opposite effect. I distinctly recall one experience that illustrates this point clearly. Upon moving to a new school in another state, I watched as an American Indian boy was introduced into his new classroom. He was excited to learn that they would be engaged in a nine-week Native American curriculum, something familiar and comfortable for him. I watched as he excitedly scanned the classroom, taking in the themed bulletin boards, artifacts, and books spread throughout the room. His eyes lit up when he noticed a big map of the United States that designated the federally recognized tribes. Wanting to share his "home" with his new teacher, the boy pulled her toward the map, and as he pointed to where his tribe should have been located, his face fell with dismay. The little boy's tribe was not included on the map. I listened as the teacher explained to the boy that his tribe was actually included because it was considered a Plains tribe (this general territory was labeled), even if the specific name was not on the map due to lack of space. The boy shook his head and said very quietly, "No, I don't belong to the 'plain' tribe; according to *your* school, I don't exist." It was a truly profound experience to hear an eight-year-old Indian boy discuss with greater understanding than a professional educator the importance of belonging and inclusion for historically marginalized ethnicities.

It is an understatement to point out that it would be impossible for the lay educator to incorporate every ethnicity and minority group into the limited amount of time provided for social studies. The critical issue for American Indians is not necessarily centered on full individualized content for instruction, but rather providing culturally appropriate curricula, instructional materials, classroom activities, and supplemental resources that recognize the broad concept of inclusion. Understanding this, a number of organizations such as the U.S. Department of Health and Human Services, the Census Bureau, and Montana's Office of Public Instruction have created resources available at no charge to educators. These resources include the K–12 Diabetes Education in Tribal Schools (DETS) curriculum, tribal land maps, statistics, demographic trends, and an extensive compilation of lesson plans created by each of the Montana tribes spanning multiple subject areas (both online as PDFs and through iTunes).

A number of steps can be taken to ensure that American Indian students are not excluded by default. First, school librarians should review all books containing content about native people. Even within schools serving American Indian students, a number of books have been discovered and removed because they contained inaccurate or stereotype-perpetuating content (i.e., Indians referred to as "savages" and described as impediments to westward expansion). Moreover, librarians should seek to locate books and other references for both students and teachers that address the inaccurate portrayal of this population. One very reputable source for locating appropriate books (and a list of books to avoid) can be found at http://www.oyate.org. Second, while teachers do not have the ability to learn about and teach all tribes, they can verify that the teaching resources they use such as maps and other bulletin board materials are current and reflective of a modern understanding of native people. Last, many state and tribal departments of education have developed fully vetted instructional materials to ease the burden many educators feel in trying to compile information on their own. These materials can be found with relative ease through an Internet search engine. I encourage those who are not familiar with local or regional tribal affiliations to contact their state departments of education since most have the ability to connect educators to personnel in regional tribal offices.

American Indian communities are also careful to discuss and reinforce both historical *and* contemporary native issues. The key difference I have observed between schools serving Indian students and those who serve predominantly non-Indian students in terms of teaching social studies is the general tone and context of the supplemental teaching materials. Images, books, and content of the curriculum in non-Indian schools often portray American Indians as a singular culture that once existed in the not-too-distant past. Omitted are references to contemporary American Indians from many tribes who continue to help shape contemporary culture in native communities. Educators in schools serving American Indian students have found ways to integrate native and nonnative elements almost seamlessly and are as proactive in teaching the historical context of American Indians as they are a more contemporary context.

One of the best examples I have observed of this seamless integration is in the sciences. Many schools will integrate multiple ethnic constructs and time frames through the use of a traditional teaching technique such as the use of the buffalo. Students are exposed to traditional ways of hunting and tribal values through an organized buffalo hunt, followed by lessons on ceremonial and modern practical uses for the different parts of the buffalo as students experience the act of skinning and preserving different parts of the animal. Spiritual and moral teachings are often infused through the hunt and dressing of the buffalo. Teachers will then move to connecting to the contemporary biology curriculum, health curriculum (safe handling and preservation of meat), and even social justice concepts. Native science classes are by no means limited to this one tradition, and these classes often use ethno-botany and the spaying/neutering of stray dogs to teach other core cultural lessons that have contemporary applications as well. Schools without American Indian students could learn from these seamless methods and use them in thematic units or apply the same methods for highlighting the cultures of ethnic minorities that are prominent in their school.

TO CHERISH AND PROTECT

Communities across America choose to address multicultural education in various ways, and understanding the many components of full cultural inclusion can be daunting. American Indian cultures recognize the enormity of the task but seem to have different reasons for making it an important priority. These cultures fully grasp the necessity of nuanced recognition for the multitude of ethnic facets for two specific reasons. First, the majority of American Indian students are of mixed tribal and ethnic backgrounds; therefore, in order to create a space where all students are valued, multiple cultural backgrounds must be incorporated. Second, tribal differences and acknowledging the existence of several hundred perspectives, customs, languages, and traditions is not something that native people have to learn; they simply know that these many differences exist. They also understand that native cultures cannot exist in a vacuum separate from the dominant cultural aspects that guide American schools. These basic understandings have created an approach to multicultural education that blends a myriad of cultures and transitions smoothly between past and present contexts.

Non-Indian educators already demonstrate this thinking through the inclusion of multicultural perspectives within the curriculum; however, these perspectives are often presented in silos or as compact units of instruction. The strength in the approach used in American Indian schools is that it reinforces the commingling of cultures rather than stressing the sense of "otherness" present in the silo approach. If multicultural education is to realize the goal of being education for, by, about, and inclusive of all, schools must step away from a categorical approach to teaching about other cultures and ethnicities and embrace a more holistic and fluid approach.

THE ROLE OF PROSOCIAL EDUCATION
American Indian communities have endured monumental forces that have tried to eradicate, assimilate, and deny their very existence. This endurance is both evidence of and ammunition for cherishing and protecting the cultural values that have provided core stability for tribes and communities. In a very real sense, multicultural inclusion between both dominant and nondominant groups as well as between equally nondominant groups provides the space to continue to define and teach traditional customs and values without denying the greater societal expectations.

Effective prosocial education in American Indian schools begins with careful identification of community values and stresses the importance of belonging. Students are often provided the opportunity to compare and contrast the characteristics of identified native values to seemingly similar values of non-native communities. American Indian value sets blend both moral and performance values that complement one another. For example, coupling the moral value of "generosity," that is, the *quality* of being kind and generous, with the performance value "perseverance," or continuing *to do* something despite difficulty, promotes both a state of being and an action attached to such a state. Similar to the delivery of multicultural education, prosocial education in American Indian schools becomes infused throughout the curriculum and culture of school rather than isolated into specific units of time on specifically assigned days. This prosocial teaching is often shared with the community at large so students see that the values being taught are not just school values but values held in the community at large.

It is through inclusion of all cultural groups that we preserve our own heritage. Multicultural and prosocial education in native communities is not about what we do; it is about who we are and about intentionally moving forward in ways that allow our children to understand how they fit within our own cultures as well as how they fit into the greater society simultaneously. Nonnative schools might find it beneficial to use a similar approach that uses prosocial education as a means of defining a way of being rather than as a means of correcting problems and issues. As the ethnic complexity of American society continues to grow, there will be an increasing need for educators to help all children learn how to develop an identity in a multicultural world; what can be learned from the way in which multicultural education is woven deeply into the education of American Indian children can serve as a very useful, even revolutionary, model. American Indian communities should not relinquish the reins of proactively addressing the importance of local culture, nor will they abdicate the responsibility of preserving the dignity and history of local communities. It is through this approach to multicultural education that we cherish and protect our heritage. It is through this approach that we believe others can cherish and protect their heritages.

REFERENCE

Littlebear, R. (2009). Understanding American Indian cultures. In L. S. Warner & G. E. Gipp (Eds.), *Traditions and culture in the millennium: Tribal colleges and university* (pp. 89–92). Charlotte, NC: Information Age Publishing.

Part III

VOICES FROM THE FIELD

Who Does Prosocial Education
and How Do They Do It?

CHAPTER 19

The District Superintendent's Role in Supporting Prosocial Education

SHELDON H. BERMAN, FLORENCE C. CHANG, AND JOYCE A. BARNES

Across the nation, superintendents feel pressure to raise students' academic performance. No superintendent can—or would want to—give short shrift to these expectations. Yet the role of the superintendent is also to see the big picture for the long term. Doing so requires thoughtful attention to the social settings in which student learning takes place. Having recently been appointed to my third superintendency, I have witnessed the difference that prosocial education can make in districts large and small. I have also learned that such a focus can succeed only if the superintendent is philosophically and operationally committed to it and provides leadership to the staff, board, and community in several key steps: framing the vision for prosocial education, policy development, understanding and applying the findings of research, selecting or modifying high-quality social education programs appropriate to each grade level, integrating the academic and social curricula (including service learning and cultural competence), and supporting and recognizing teachers and administrators through professional development, as well as the allocation of classroom time, the collection of data, and the analysis of program impact.

In the interest of promoting improved student outcomes in other districts, I am pleased to share the following discussion of my work in the area of prosocial education in two demographically disparate school systems. I appreciate the contributions made by coauthors Florence C. Chang, evaluation specialist, who collected and analyzed much of the data, and Joyce A. Barnes, specialist, who assisted in transforming this information into a comprehensive report. Both of these colleagues are with the Jefferson County Public Schools in Louisville, Kentucky.

—Sheldon Berman, EdD, superintendent, Eugene (OR) School District 4J

To perform at their highest level, students need to feel safe to take intellectual risks, they need the social skills to exchange ideas and collaborate with others, and they need to feel supported by the peers and adults who form their community of learners. Although school district leaders feel tremendous public pressure to concentrate on the academic curriculum, the social environment of the classroom and the school are equally critical to student learning. In fact, the nature of the classroom social environment can determine whether learning will thrive or flounder. The social environment creates the foundation on which productive learning can occur.

GROUNDED IN RESEARCH

Phillip Jackson and other educational theorists referred to this social curriculum as the "hidden curriculum of schooling" because it communicates to children what is valued, what behaviors are acceptable, and who has power and authority in the classroom. Since Jackson's pioneering work (1968), we have learned much about the impact of the social environment of the classroom on children. In essence, whether we are explicit about how we construct that social environment or not, it creates the conditions for both social and academic learning. Therefore, it is far better that educational leaders thoughtfully consider how best to create an environment that supports children's social, emotional, and academic growth than to leave this key factor to chance.

The research supports this concept. Durlak, Weissberg, Dymnicki, Taylor, and Schellinger (2011) examined over two hundred school-based programs, involving over 270,000 students, that aimed to improve the social and emotional climate in schools. All the studies reviewed had a control group, and about half of the studies utilized a randomized design. The meta-analysis found that, compared to the control groups, students in schools that promoted a supportive school climate demonstrated on average an eleven-percentile-point gain in academic achievement.

Not only has school climate been shown to impact student achievement, but a positive school climate has also been shown to be related to a variety of outcomes, including reduced student absenteeism, reduced suspensions and behavior problems, lower rates of alcohol use, reduced psychopathology, and increased student connectedness to school (Battistich, Solomon, Kim, Watson, & Schaps, 1995; Battistich, Solomon, & Watson, 1998; Kasen, Johnson, & Cohen, 1990; Pianta & Stuhlman, 2004; Reid, 1982; Schaps & Solomon, 1990; Solomon, Battistich, Kim, & Watson, 1997; Wu, Pink, Crain, & Moles, 1982). A study by Rimm-Kaufman, Fan, Chiu, and You (2007) found that the Responsive Classroom approach in elementary schools led to significant gains in reading and math, with the greatest impact being in those schools that had utilized the Responsive Classroom approach for at least three years. The Search Institute, a nonprofit group focused on the well-being of young people, also conducted a series of studies on the impact of a caring school climate. In these studies, a caring school climate was associated with higher grades, higher engagement, and lower grade-retention rates (Scales & Leffert, 1999).

In addition, many experts point out that it is not simply the impact on test scores that matters, but the impact on student motivation that is the ultimate outcome of forming successful lifelong learners (Cohen, 2006). A positive school climate has been shown to increase academic motivation to learn (Goodenow & Grady, 1993), whereas a less supportive school climate has been shown to decrease student motivation (Eccles et al., 1993). The degree to which students feel safe, respected, and connected to school has a profound impact on whether students are able to and desire to learn (National School Climate Council, 2007).

Therefore, district leaders have good reason not only to think through how best to support a positive and productive environment for students, but also to think carefully about the strategies and social structures that teachers and administrators use to create such an environment in the first place.

SOCIAL DEVELOPMENT IN PRACTICE

What also emerges clearly from the research on prosocial development is that it is necessary, but not sufficient, to teach children basic social skills. Children must learn these skills within the context of a caring community in which they feel connected to and cared about by others, where conflict resolution and collaboration are modeled in the daily realities of the classroom, where students have a voice in decision making, and where they have opportunities to act constructively and make a difference for others and the community at large. In essence, they need to experience a sense of community and the opportunity to put into practice—in real situations—the positive social skills they are learning in the classroom. However, creating this kind of environment is just as challenging as providing high-quality reading and math instruction. It requires the use of research-based strategies embedded within the school day, emanating from thorough professional development of faculty and administration in the use of these strategies and in understanding children's social development.

To arrive at this point in the classroom entails working at multiple levels simultaneously. At its heart, teachers need to build a sense of community in the classroom wherein both the adults and the students feel that they are known and valued as individuals. To achieve this goal, students need opportunities to learn such social skills as viewing a situation from another's perspective, solving problems collaboratively, and resolving conflicts positively. Even as adults, we sometimes struggle with these skills; therefore, teaching them to children requires self-reflection and a predisposition toward personal growth. How teachers and administrators interact with students, deal with conflict situations, and work collaboratively with students to solve problems is critical to the success of their efforts to build community and nurture social development. In fact, the way teachers and administrators communicate and work with other adults in the building, as well as with students, not only models these behaviors for students but makes an important statement about what adults value and what standards they hold for themselves.

In addition, young people need to experience the effectiveness of these skills in the world around them. While it is vital that the safety of a caring community first be evident in the classroom, in order to change and shape their own behavior, students need to see the utility of these skills on the playground, in the cafeteria, on the bus, in their neighborhoods, and with their parents, relatives, and friends. Applying these skills in multifaceted situations requires practice and dialogue. Classroom time is wisely spent enabling students to discuss their experiences and suggest strategies for how to best handle conflict or problem situations. It also helps to create situations in which students are of service to others, so that they not only demonstrate the helping behaviors they are learning but experience the affirmation of their own efficacy in assisting others. Finally, social development efforts need to engage parents through strategies that bring them into that sense of community that has been created in the classroom and school and that assist them in learning parallel strategies for addressing issues at home.

Just as there is a developmental sequence for the teaching of reading and math, there is a developmental sequence in teaching prosocial skills and social responsibility

(Berman, 1997). Consistency among teachers and administrators is important—very much like the consistency we encourage parents to have in their child rearing at home. Employing a systemic and consistent approach across classrooms and across schools enhances the individual efforts of teachers and ensures the significance of the impact it has on student learning. It also facilitates students' integration into a new setting as they change schools, either when moving up a level or as a result of family mobility, and discover that the same social norms apply. It is the role of leaders, particularly the superintendent, to set a vision that encompasses prosocial development and to set district priorities so that this vision is achieved.

A SYSTEMIC APPROACH

As a superintendent first in Hudson, Massachusetts, and later in Louisville (Jefferson County), Kentucky, I had the opportunity to put this research into practice. In both districts, we initiated comprehensive and systemic social development programs to teach students basic social skills and build a caring sense of community in the classroom and school. While these programs were in part homegrown, they were intentionally based on the rich experience and effective professional development provided by other organizations that are recognized leaders in this field. Hudson and Jefferson County also incorporated social development into their mission statements and theories of action.

Small District

In Hudson, we combined several programs to achieve our prosocial education goals, presaging a core message of this handbook (see chapter 1). The preschools adopted the Adventures in Peacemaking curriculum produced by Educators for Social Responsibility. This engaging set of activities provided a solid foundation among the early childhood population. The elementary schools chose a program from the Committee for Children—entitled Second Step—and supplemented it with conflict resolution material from Educators for Social Responsibility. Second Step focuses on teaching children to manage their anger in constructive ways and to demonstrate empathy for others. Beginning at the kindergarten level, the program offers thirty lessons per grade that involve students in role-playing and discussions. The intent of these lessons is to help children learn to identify the feelings of others and to reflect on and practice appropriate ways of responding to situations. Second Step also includes a parent component to stimulate related conversations and behaviors at home. A study of this program, funded by the Centers for Disease Control and Prevention, found that it was successful in decreasing physical and verbal aggression and in increasing prosocial behavior (Grossman et al., 1997).

Where Second Step takes a direct-instruction approach to developing students' social skills, the Responsive Classroom program—developed by the Northeast Foundation for Children—targets teachers' strategies for structuring and managing their classroom. Nearly all of the elementary and middle school teachers in Hudson were trained in this program, which provides teachers with a framework for creating a classroom environment that fosters the integration of prosocial skills. Based on a belief that the social and academic curricula are equally important and integrally connected, Responsive Classroom guides teachers to effectively use class meetings, rules and their logical consequences, classroom organization, academic choice, and family communication to create a caring classroom environment even as they foster children's academic and social success.

Service Learning

Of course, the point of prosocial education is not simply to facilitate classroom interactions and learning but to prepare students for positive social interactions in all aspects of their lives. To enable students to hone and apply their emerging skills within the community, the Hudson school district initiated a comprehensive service learning program. However, service learning was not interpreted as a single-event participation in local charitable efforts, such as collecting canned goods for the food bank or raising money for medical research. Rather, it became an ongoing activity that was woven into each year's curriculum, promoting students' mastery of core concepts while providing a means for authentic assessment. Since service learning was designed into a unit of study from the outset with clear expectations and outcomes, it not only supported the acquisition of content knowledge but enabled students to apply the social skills and prosocial behavior they were learning at school to a context in which they were actually of service to others. This service learning gave them a sense of empowerment and grounded their social skills in the real life of their community.

High-quality service learning programs can assume many forms. In Hudson, each grade level designed a project and integrated it into the districtwide curriculum, thereby giving students consistent experiences with service learning throughout their school years. For example, as kindergartners were learning essential math and reading skills, they wrote and laminated math and alphabet books to be sent to children in Uganda. Fourth graders who were studying ecosystems performed field research and environmental reclamation work in nearby woodlands and wetlands. Fifth graders served as reading buddies for first graders and for special needs students. Sixth graders studying ancient Greek and Roman cultures staged an educational culture fair for younger students. Ninth graders grappling with their civics course developed and implemented proposals that addressed a variety of community needs. What made this service learning approach particularly effective is that the students' experiences were deeply integrated into the regular curriculum and so concurrently furthered curricular, prosocial, and civic engagement goals.

Large District

To accomplish similar goals in Jefferson County (Louisville), we have blended the preschool Adventures in Peacemaking program from Educators for Social Responsibility and the Caring School Community (CSC) program of the Developmental Studies Center for grades K–5 with several other programs into a program we call "CARE for Kids." The program is aimed at providing significant and engaging learning opportunities that allow students to experience membership in a safe and caring community. In 2010/11, a total of seventy out of ninety elementary schools and twenty-one out of twenty-five middle schools were implementing the program.

CARE for Kids Principles

CARE for Kids embodies six core principles:

1. At the heart of a caring school community are *respectful, supportive relationships* among and between students, educators, support staff, and parents.
2. Learning becomes more connected and meaningful for students when social, emotional, and ethical development is an integral part of the classroom, school, and community experience.
3. Significant and engaging learning, academic and social, takes place when students are able to construct deep understandings of broad concepts and principles through an active process of exploration, discovery, and application.
4. Community is strengthened when there are frequent opportunities for students to exercise their voice, choice, and responsible independence to work together for the common good.
5. Classroom community and learning are maximized through frequent opportunities for collaboration and service to others.
6. Effective classroom communities help students develop their intrinsic motivation by meeting their basic needs (e.g., safety, autonomy, belonging, competence, usefulness, fun, pleasure) rather than seeking to control students with extrinsic motivators.

CARE for Kids Components

The primary activities and components of CARE for Kids include the following:

1. *Caring classroom community:* developing classroom community and unity building through activities such as cooperative and collaborative learning across content areas and class meetings.
2. *Morning meetings:* special type of class meeting where students greet each other, share experiences in their lives, listen carefully to others, discuss the agenda for the day, and build relationships with their classmates.
3. *End-of-day meetings:* brief closing meetings in which students reflect on their day and share something that stood out for them, something they learned, or something that someone did to help another person.
4. *Developmental discipline/logical consequences:* proactive, preventive approach to discipline that uses a teaching/learning approach with an emphasis on relationships, modeling, skill development, moving students to self-control, and responsibility.
5. *Homeside activities:* designed to stimulate conversations between students and their family members.
6. *Buddies:* matches older students with younger students for collaborative mentoring activities facilitated by the teachers.
7. *Schoolwide activities:* designed to link the students, parents, teachers, and other adults in the school with a focus on inclusion and participation, communication, cooperation, helping others, taking responsibility, appreciating differences, and reflection.

At its core, the program in Jefferson County engages children in a variety of thoughtful class meetings that provide students with a voice in their classroom community. These class meetings teach basic social skills and help students grow socially and ethically through dialogue about classroom and school issues. Morning meetings drawn from the Responsive Classroom program build community among students. End-of-day meetings ask students to not only reflect on their day academically but also to reconnect with the sense of community established in the morning. Teachers use a model of developmental discipline that provides logical consequences for behavior and gives children opportunities to reflect on and correct their behavior. In addition, the program engages older students in service opportunities through mentoring younger students. Finally, the program engages parents in this community-building and social development initiative through activities that children take home to complete with their parents or other family members, and through schoolwide activities that engage parents and caregivers in social and academic events at school. Although modified at the middle school, these same key elements provide a continuum from preschool through eighth grade. As at Hudson, the comprehensiveness and systemic nature of the program nurtures prosocial development in a consistent and developmentally appropriate way.

INTEGRATION WITH ACADEMIC CURRICULA

In addition, both districts selected academic curricula that support and further the development of social development goals. For example, the social and collaboration skills that students acquire through the prosocial programs are critical to the effective use of such inquiry-oriented and collaborative learning math and science programs as Investigations in Number, Data, and Space; the Connected Mathematics Project; and the Full Option Science System (FOSS), which are used in Jefferson County. At the same time, these inquiry-oriented academic programs facilitate students' social development by giving them practical and immediate application of their social skills. The schools in both Hudson and Jefferson County introduced a reading comprehension program entitled Making Meaning and a writing program entitled Being a Writer, developed by the Developmental Studies Center. Through these programs, students read high-quality literature with prosocial themes and then learn strategic comprehension and writing skills through activities that are structured to also teach social skills. To further enrich the reading program, we added historical fiction that depicts people facing social and ethical dilemmas and choosing to make a difference through service or social activism. Examples of these fictional texts include *Uncle Jed's Barbershop* by Margaree King Mitchell, *The Long March* by Marie-Louise Fitzpatrick, *Coolies* by Yin, and *Pink and Say* by Patricia Polacco. Any district that is weighing the idea of layering programs to create this type of comprehensive, systemic effort should remember that one of the essential rubrics that must be used in selecting curricular programs is the quality of social and collaboration skill development embedded in the program. This alignment enhances the consistency between the academic and social curricula.

CULTURAL COMPETENCE

There is yet another strategy integrated into the CARE for Kids program that is key to fostering a socially responsive classroom for educators across all grades, and that is cultural competence (see chapter 18). Most teachers and other educators are the product of middle-class homes and have little or no experience with the economic, family, and language differences that are present among so many students, particularly in urban school districts. Consequently, teachers' level of caring often far outstrips their level of understanding. Unacknowledged and unaddressed, the lack of cultural sensitivity and competence among both adults and students can undermine students' sense of worth and security, particularly for those most at risk. To address this underlying barrier to student success, Jefferson County has undertaken a systemic effort to promote cultural competence. Through intensive workshops and institutes, staff members at all levels of the organization are engaging in simulation activities and frank conversations designed to help them confront stereotypes and prejudices and understand different lifestyles and cultural norms. As teachers, in particular, are sensitized to the diversity among students' everyday lives, they are more likely to make valid observations about why some children respond as they do and to find more effective ways of reaching out and building strong relationships with these students. Cultural competence training also enables teachers to connect students' cultures to the curriculum, thereby assisting children to feel safe and respected within the classroom setting. However, the impact is clearly felt in the prosocial behavior it models and encourages in students, laying the foundation for all students to act in a socially caring and responsible way toward others.

HIGH SCHOOL IMPLEMENTATION

In Jefferson County, as in Hudson previously, the program took on a different form at the high school level, which can be a challenging level for building community because of the larger student population; nevertheless, personalization of the secondary experience remains a critical element. In both districts, the ninth grade is taught by teams of teachers in a freshman academy model that supports students' transition from middle school to high school. The teachers share a common planning time that enables them to discuss and address the needs of students, meet with parents, and plan ways to build a sense of community among students. Students are a part of a smaller and supported community of learners in which they feel known and respected.

In addition, each district formed small learning communities for students in grades 10 through 12 that extend ongoing support in an environment where each student is known by the adults in the school and feels a part of the larger student community. These clusters, as they were known in Hudson, or schools of study, as they are known in Jefferson County, do not restrict students' ability to enroll in a wide range of courses, but instead provide a community of interest among students and teachers around broad career themes. Again, the opportunity to connect with peers and adults who share similar career interests encourages students to engage in collaborative work and demonstrate respect for the contributions of others. The high school years present an apt time for students to consider the broader social and ethical implications of individual actions on their school, their community, and the larger social world. Again, in both districts, we developed a core ninth-grade social studies civics course that poses the essential question: "What is an individual's responsibility in creating a just society?" This course draws heavily from the Facing History and Ourselves curriculum (see chapter 18 case study A), which engages students studying the roots of genocide, including the Holocaust and the Armenian genocide. By asking how it is that a nation of everyday people can allow genocide to become state policy, this course confronts young people with the human potential for passivity, complicity, and destructiveness.

It poses significant ethical questions and raises awareness of the ramifications of injustice, inhumanity, and the abuse of power. On a broader level, because it helps discourage students from accepting simple answers to complex problems, the curriculum also supports inquiry-based course work in other classes. In the process of studying the individual and social forces that have spawned genocides throughout history, students come face to face with their own potential for passivity and complicity, their own prejudices and intolerances. As the classroom dialogue promotes new perspectives and social reasoning skills, students develop a deeper sense of moral responsibility and a stronger commitment to participate in making a difference. They come to view their school as a microcosm of society, and they reflect on their own responsibility for creating a more just and compassionate school community.

As a result of the comprehensive layering of each of these programs, students build positive relationships with peers and adults and develop prosocial and conflict resolution skills. However, what is actually most important is that students experience what it means to be a responsible member of a community and they come to realize that their action—or lack of action—has an impact on others around them and on the quality of life in the community.

SUSTAINABLE IMPLEMENTATION

Implementation of any new curriculum or program requires thoughtful planning and in-depth professional development. It requires staging the integration over time so that teachers and administrators can make sustained and steady progress. As with any program, that integration is best supported by high-quality curricula and professional development. Most important, the program needs to have the strong backing and encouragement of district leadership so that staff know they can take the risks and make the effort necessary to create an effective approach to reaching its stated goals.

Allocating Classroom Time

One of the immediate tensions that emerges in implementing a comprehensive social development program is that it requires teacher–student interaction time. Initially, class meetings, morning and end-of-day meetings, buddy programs, and community-building activities appear to deduct time from instruction. Over the long term, however, the impact on instruction is precisely the reverse of what initially seemed to be the case. Because students are better able to work together and resolve their interpersonal differences, there are fewer discipline issues in the classroom, fewer disruptions, and far greater efficiency and productivity in cooperative and collaborative classroom activities and projects. Teachers also become adept at interweaving academic and social reflection into the class meetings. Essentially, as teachers implement the program, they start viewing the class meeting time as critical instructional time. Not surprisingly, attendance improves and tardiness declines because students don't want to miss the important and productive social time with their classmates.

In addition, programs in social development are absolutely critical to the smooth and effective functioning of inquiry-based curriculum programs in math and science and of literacy programs such as Readers and Writers Workshops. These programs are designed to build student engagement and interest and make extensive use of group work and group problem solving. The skills students develop through a social development program enable teachers to more effectively use these programs and enable students to gain the conceptual benefit these programs were designed to offer. Although social development programs require making a commitment to regularly scheduled time during the school day and week, that time facilitates higher and deeper levels of learning in a more productive environment.

Professional Development

Building community and resolving conflicts are not simple skills for teachers to develop. The focus of most universities' preservice teacher development programs is on managing the classroom and planning lessons to effectively teach content. Few new teachers have either background or instructional experience in the area of prosocial development (see chapter 17). For veteran teachers, focusing on social development by engaging students in classroom problem solving can cause them to feel that they are relinquishing control of the classroom and the order they have so carefully established. One of the powerful lessons of teaching is that by engaging students, one gradually acquires more—but less obvious—control as students assume greater responsibility for the interaction between peers and the management of the classroom. However, this process takes time, quality professional development, and on-site coaching by those who have had success in building a sense of community in their classrooms.

Nurturing social development requires facilitating problem-solving and conflict-resolving dialogue among students. It requires being aware of one's own tendency to intervene with a solution instead of allowing the students to find their own workable solutions. It requires reflection on the way the class day is structured, the opportunities students may have to make choices, and the language and approach the teacher uses in difficult situations. Just as encouraging student thinking about an investigation in science requires attention to asking the right questions, leaving sufficient wait time to stimulate student thought, and organizing the lesson in a way that engages student discovery and reflection, facilitating social problem solving requires similar instructional thoughtfulness. In essence, teachers are supporting deeper levels of conversation about the social dynamics of the classroom and school so that children can begin to better understand and take a positive role in those dynamics. Therefore, successful, sustainable implementation necessitates that teachers acquire new proficiencies. To do so entails providing them with opportunities to participate in high-quality professional development, observe teachers proficient in these skills, be observed by and mentored by colleagues, and collaborate with other teachers on implementation.

Program Selection

Essential to high-quality implementation is the use of well-developed, research-based programs that have been shown to produce the desired results. If a program is of high quality, it can be instrumental in furthering a teacher's knowledge and skill by providing the guidance and structure to support effective implementation. Although Hudson and Jefferson County selected a particular set of programs to create the right blend of skill instruction and modeling for our circumstances, there are a number of excellent programs available to schools that are equally effective. Such programs as the Educators for Social Responsibility's Resolving Conflicts Creatively Program, the Wellesley College Stone Center's Open Circle, and others are effective avenues for teaching these skills. In each of these programs, not only are students given direct instruction in basic social and emotional skills, but the whole school becomes involved in creating a caring community that models respectful and empathetic behavior. The Collaborative for Academic, Social, and Emotional Learning (CASEL) has published valuable reviews of programs and is an important resource organization in supporting program selection and implementation.

SUPERINTENDENT'S ROLE IN LEADING THE LEADERS

In addition to allocating adequate time, using high-quality programs, and supporting teachers through in-depth professional development, sustainable implementation requires the superintendent's leadership in policy development and administrative support and recognition. The pressures of school and district accountability based on state standards and tests are ever increasing. It is easy to lose focus on anything that appears extraneous to what is being tested. Unless administrators endorse and encourage a focus on social skills comparable to that on academic skills, teachers will not feel they can take the time necessary to hold the kinds of meetings and pursue the kinds of activities that promote social skill development. District and building-level administrators have to clarify that this area is also a priority and that, without a focus on social development, students won't achieve at the levels we hope for in their academic work. District-level administrators need to allocate the resources for program materials, professional development, and coaching. In both Hudson and Jefferson County, I designated a central office director to facilitate this work, and coaching was provided either through teacher mentors or staff developers. This support made an important statement to teachers that the district was going to provide the resources necessary for them to be successful in implementing a comprehensive and high-quality social development program.

SUPERINTENDENT'S ROLE IN POLICY DEVELOPMENT AND RECOGNITION

It is also important that this emphasis be built into policy and regular forms of recognition for teachers and students. Over the course of several months and multiple conversations with staff and board, I led both districts to develop thoughtful mission statements and theories of action that addressed the concept of social development and established its role within the curriculum. There were regular school board presentations about the program and its impact on students. The districts recognized teachers and students for their success, both by honoring high-quality implementation through articles and videos and by service awards and recognitions for students. Although public recognition may seem ephemeral, it makes an important statement to those who receive it as well as to those who observe that the administration and school board members take the time to acknowledge that this is important work for the district to be doing.

DATA COLLECTION

Results matter, no less for social development than for academic development. As a small district, Hudson did not have the capacity to do in-depth program evaluations.

Although there was improvement in attendance, behavior indicators, and academic performance, the district was in the midst of numerous reform initiatives, and it was impossible to determine the degree of impact the initiatives around prosocial development had independently. However, since Jefferson County possesses an experienced and talented group in its research and evaluation department, assessment of the CARE for Kids program was tracked from its inception. As CARE for Kids was being implemented, the logic model for outcomes was that the implementation of the program would first yield positive differences in school climate. As students felt more supported and respected, the next logical outcome would be to see improvements in the areas of behavior, attendance, and achievement. The data for the program support this logic model. The implementation of the program has resulted in positive growth in school culture, improved attendance and behaviors, and, finally, improved academic achievement.

Baseline Data

Prior to the rollout of CARE for Kids, it was important to have the baseline data and program-aligned assessment tools developed so that (1) the program could be closely monitored for quality implementation and (2) school data could be examined pre- and post-implementation of the program. The year prior to the CARE for Kids implementation, the district's Comprehensive School Surveys (CSS) were redesigned so that the surveys gathered not only perceptions of academic content, but also perceptions of the social-emotional, civic, and moral connections that are vital to student learning. Each year since 2007, the district has administered the redesigned CSS to all school staffs, intermediate elementary students, and middle school students. Students answer on a 1-to-4 scale (1 = strongly disagree; 4 = strongly agree) the extent to which they agree with statements such as "I really like other students in my school" and "I enjoy going to school." The CSS surveys have consistently yielded strong reliability coefficients (Muñoz & Lewis, 2009). Because the survey is given annually, it was possible to examine the change in any school's culture pre- and post-implementation of a program.

Classroom Observations

In addition to the survey assessment of school climate, another critical aspect of successful rollout of the program was the development of an implementation rubric to identify and define observable components of the program. The district specialists for CARE for Kids worked alongside the district research department to develop a reliable walk-through tool. Subscales include routines and procedures (e.g., classroom norms displayed), relationship (e.g., respectful interactions between teachers and students), language (e.g., utilization of reflective language), and student-centered environment (e.g., students collaborating with each other). The walk-through instrument was used to randomly observe schools each year, so we had data on how to better support implementation. For example, after the first year of the program, it was observed that while relationships were strong, schools were struggling with having student-centered classrooms. Focused support was developed to address that component the following year, and as a result the largest gain seen in the walk-throughs in 2010/11 has been in the area of student-centered environment. The walk-through instrument also served as a tool to the in-house school leadership teams to provide internal support.

Survey of Implementers

Each year, the district's research department also administered an annual survey to gather perceptions and implementation levels of the CARE for Kids program. Because Jefferson County is such a large district, it was not feasible for district personnel to observe every teacher implementing the program. The annual survey allowed staff the opportunity to identify aspects of the program that were working well and areas in which they needed support. By utilizing all three pieces of data—the CSS, walk-throughs, and CARE for Kids surveys—the district was able to continuously understand how to better support implementation. For example, after the first year, one of the insights that emerged from the surveys was that teachers almost unanimously agreed that their principals were supportive of the program. However, the key to higher implementation was found among teachers reporting that their principals actually observed their classrooms and provided feedback on implementation. Based on this observation, we shared with principals that their support alone was insufficient; instead it was crucial that they visit classrooms and have a continuing dialogue with their staff on areas of improvement.

PROGRAM IMPACT: SCHOOL CULTURE

In terms of outcomes, the district is large enough to allow for matched comparison groups of schools that have implemented a program and schools that have yet to implement the program. Analyses of the data each year (including from 2010/11) reveal *statistically significant differences* in growth of school culture, with CARE for Kids schools outperforming the non–CARE for Kids schools in growth of positive school culture across the subscales. Students who attended CARE for Kids schools showed more growth in the areas of school satisfaction, school engagement, school belonging, school discussion, personal safety, political discussion, and positive character than did students at non–CARE for Kids schools (see figure 19.1). The growth represented a difference of one-half to one full standard deviation in school climate, depending on the subscale.

When examining attendance and suspensions for elementary schools, data show that there was a significant correlation between CARE for Kids implementation and attendance and suspensions. The higher the implementation of CARE for Kids (as defined by staff survey and walk-through data), the more likely the schools were to increase student attendance and decrease suspensions. At the middle school level, the findings were similar, with high implementers of CARE for Kids decreasing their number of suspensions at a significantly higher rate than did low implementers of CARE for Kids.

Correlations between implementation data and change in attendance and suspensions showed that higher implementation was significantly related to growth in attendance and a decline in suspensions, $r(54) = 0.44$, $p < .01$ and $r(54) = -.37$, $p < .05$, respectively. The average attendance rate at an elementary school in 2009/10 was 95.07

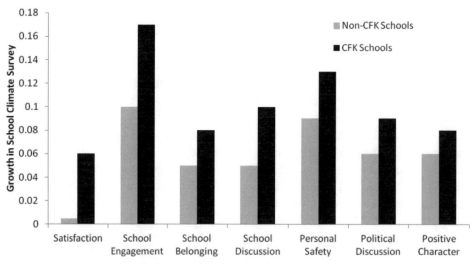

Figure 19.1. Growth in student comprehensive survey subscales.

percent. When examining high and low implementers of CARE for Kids, high implementers showed an increase of .05 percent in attendance, while low implementers showed a decline of .16 percent. High implementers of CARE for Kids also decreased their number of suspensions, while low implementers had an overall increase in the number of suspensions from pre- to post-implementation of CARE for Kids.

PROGRAM IMPACT: ACADEMIC ACHIEVEMENT

In the area of academic achievement, the Kentucky state achievement test is given each year in April and yields an academic index score (on a scale of 0 to 140) that is reflective of the percent of students who score at the novice, apprentice, proficient, and distinguished levels in reading and math. At the elementary level, schools that had implemented CARE for Kid for two years outpaced a matched comparison group, as well as the district as a whole, in their growth in reading, social studies, and writing on the 2010 Kentucky state achievement test. For elementary schools that had been implementing CARE for Kids for only one year, high implementers improved significantly more in reading and math than did low implementers. At the middle school level, high implementation of CARE for Kids was also related to higher academic achievement. Table 19.1 shows the difference in the index scores for reading and math for high and low implementers of CARE for Kids at the elementary level.

Table 19.1. Implementation of CARE for Kids and Impact on Academic Achievement

Group	Reading Index Change	Math Index Change
Low implementers	.86	−4.19
High implementers	3.09*	1.84*

*Indicates statistically significant difference between high and low implementers.

Data examining the impact of CARE for Kids on school climate and academic achievement also support the logic model. Schools that were higher implementers showed higher growth in school climate, and schools that showed the growth in school climate were schools that made academic gains. Although this evaluation is for the initial stages of implementation, it clearly indicates that the high implementation of a comprehensive prosocial development program has an impact on school culture, attendance, behavior, and academic achievement. However, the most important result of this research is that students enjoy school more and feel more comfortable in their classrooms because they have learned basic social skills that allow them to collaborate more effectively and learn from each other.

PROGRAM IMPACT: TEACHERS AND STUDENTS

Perhaps the most illuminating data from the evaluation of CARE for Kids come from the voices of the students and teachers. Focus groups and surveys were conducted with teachers and students in CARE for Kids schools. Table 19.2 shows themes and quotes that have emerged from the data.

Not only have our efforts shown positive results, but our results confirm the growing research base showing that consistent programs such as these have a strong impact on students' academic success, social-emotional skills, and sense of belonging in school.

Table 19.2. CARE for Kids Program—Impact on Teachers and Students: Voices from the Field

Theme	Quote
CARE for Kids Teachers	
Social skills	"Better behavior through community building on the kids' part has allowed for more time to have on-task activities, which is directly attributed to CARE for Kids."
	"CARE for Kids has improved the way children interact with each other and adults in the building. They just seem happier."
	"It enables the children to talk with each other, respect each other, and live among the diversity."
Ready to learn/ academic	"CARE has had the greatest impact on my teaching. I have learned to interact to a greater extent with my students and in turn they with each other."
	"Students are very happy and well adjusted, which creates an atmosphere for learning."
	"CARE for Kids is a great program—it opens up the communication in the classroom by starting and ending each day with a meeting to allow the students to reflect on their school day and what they learned."
Students in CARE for Kids Schools	
Caring community	"Teachers take time to get to know you and learn what you are interested in."
	"In morning meetings, you get noticed before the day starts."
	"We have learned how to communicate and respect each other more."
Interactions with other students	"I like working with partners because I get to know them better. I can learn from them, and they can learn from me."
	"I have changed—I never used to show respect for others."
	"My class is like a family and having brothers and sisters. Sometimes we fight, but we always work it out."

CONCLUSION

While each district is unique, the role of the superintendent is key to whether or not prosocial education becomes a pivotal component of the curriculum. The superintendent must develop a strong understanding of the vision among the leadership team; communicate commitment and support; guide curricular integration through program review and professional development; assist the board, community, and parents to understand and reinforce the effort; and promote sustainability through evaluation of impact.

Our work with children has a profound and long-lasting impact. Thoughtfully constructing the social environment so that young people grow up knowing what it means to be responsible and caring members of a community is equally important to preparing them for the contribution they will one day make to their community's economic life. In fact, educators' failure to help young people see that they, too, are responsible for building viable communities—where people can resolve differences positively, work cooperatively with others to solve significant community problems, and reach out in caring ways to support others in need—may actually compromise the essence of civic life in the United States.

If you stop people on the street and ask them to define the mission of education, they are almost certain to respond with such phrases as "teach fundamental academic skills" or "prepare students for a future career" or perhaps "motivate students to be lifelong learners." All of these responses are good ones; yet they are less than complete, because education has a broader purpose as well. To be truly educated, people need to fully comprehend their capability and responsibility in the myriad social settings in which they find themselves. Nurturing students to assume their vital role as reflective and caring citizens cannot be an afterthought of teachers, principals, or superintendents. Our work in structuring the classroom social environment should be at least as intentional as our work in formulating our math and language arts curricula. To do less is to leave the larger mission of education unfulfilled.

A critical facet of my role as superintendent, and that of all superintendents and district and school leaders, is to continue to remind our staff, our parents, and our communities that there is a larger mission to public education. That mission is to give young people the knowledge, skills, and attitudes to sustain our democracy and help create a safer, more just, and more peaceful world, the kind of world we all want for our children, the kind of world we should be shaping in our classrooms today.

REFERENCES

Battistich, V., Solomon, D., Kim, D., Watson, M., & Schaps, E. (1995). Schools as communities, poverty levels of student populations, and students' attitudes, motives, and performance: A multilevel analysis. *American Educational Research Journal, 32*(3), 627–658.

Battistich, V., Solomon, D., & Watson, M. (1998, April). *Sense of community as a mediating factor in promoting children's social and ethical development.* Paper presented at the annual meeting of the American Educational Research Association, San Diego, CA.

Berman, S. (1997). *Children's social consciousness and the development of social responsibility.* Albany, NY: SUNY Press.

Cohen, J. (2006, Summer). Social, emotional, ethical, and academic education: Creating a climate for learning, participation in democracy, and well-being. *Harvard Educational Review, 76*(2), 201–237.

Durlak, J. A., Weissberg, R. P., Dymnicki, A. B., Taylor, R. D., & Schellinger, K. B. (2011). The impact of enhancing students' social and emotional learning: A meta-analysis of school-based universal interventions. *Child Development, 82*(1), 405–432.

Eccles, J., Wigfield, A., Midgley, C., Reuman, D., MacIver, D., & Feldlaufer, H. (1993). Negative effects of traditional middle schools on students' motivation. *Elementary School Journal, 93*(5), 553–574.

Goodenow, C., & Grady, K. E. (1993). The relationship of school belonging and friends' values to academic motivation among urban adolescent students. *Journal of Experimental Education, 62*(1), 60–71.

Grossman, D. C., Neckerman, H. J., Koepsell, T. D., Liu, P., Asher, K. N., Beland, K., et al. (1997). Effectiveness of a violence prevention curriculum among children in elementary school: A randomized controlled trial. *Journal of the American Medical Association, 277*(20), 1605–1611.

Jackson, P. (1968). *Life in classrooms.* New York: Hart, Rinehart, and Winston.

Kasen, S., Johnson, P., & Cohen, P. (1990). The impact of social emotional climate on student psychopathology. *Journal of Abnormal Child Psychology, 18*(2), 165–177.

Muñoz, M., & Lewis, T. (2009). *Comprehensive School Surveys (2008–09): Strengthening organizational culture.* Retrieved on March 1, 2011, from http://www.jefferson.k12.ky.us/Departments/AcctResPlan/PDF/ReportsForCSSWebSite/CSS_Eval_REPORT2009.pdf

National School Climate Council. (2007). *The school climate challenge: Narrowing the gap between school climate research and school climate policy, practice guidelines, and teacher education policy.* Retrieved on March 1, 2011, from http://nscc.csee.net

Pianta, R. C., & Stuhlman, M. W. (2004). Teacher–child relationships and children's success in the first years of school. *School Psychology Review, 33*, 444–458.

Reid, K. (1982). Retrospection and persistent school absenteeism. *Educational Research, 25*(2), 110–115.

Rimm-Kaufman, S. E., Fan, X., Chiu, Y.-J., & You, W. (2007). The contribution of the Responsive Classroom approach on children's academic achievement: Results from a three year longitudinal study. *Journal of School Psychology, 45*(4), 401–421.

Scales, P. C., & Leffert, N. (1999). *Developmental assets.* Minneapolis, MN: Search Institute.

Schaps, E., & Solomon, D. (1990). Schools and classrooms as caring communities. *Educational Leadership, 48*, 38–42.

Solomon, D., Battistich, V., Kim, D., & Watson, M. (1997). Teacher practices associated with students' sense of the classroom as a community. *Social Psychology of Education, 1*(3), 235–267.

Wu, S., Pink, W., Crain, R., & Moles, O. (1982). Student suspensions: A critical reappraisal. *Urban Review, 14*(4), 245–303.

CHAPTER 20

The School Principal's Role in Planning and Organizing Prosocial Education

JOHNCARLOS M. MILLER

With positive character and prosocial development of students so critical to everything that we do in education, why do high-stakes testing and the demand for accountability take precedence over developing the well-balanced children we so desperately need to sustain our society? Why is there no major push at the federal and state levels to include a prosocial focus in the curriculum? I hope the rationale is *not* that high-stakes testing and accountability take precedence over children's character. My contention is that we must have a prosocial education focus in our schools. In my school, the prosocial focus is called character education.

President Theodore Roosevelt stated, "To educate a man in mind and not in morals is to educate a menace to society." Evidence of his statement unfortunately is seen too often in the lives of some our more recent societal nightmares such as Theodore Robert Cowell, also known as Ted Bundy, and Theodore Kaczynski, known as the Unabomber. These men were intelligent in their own rights. Both attended universities on either full or partial scholarships, but their intelligence would not prohibit them from using their savvy to kill other innocent human beings. As an educator, I wonder what path they walked in their developmental and grade school years. In these men's wakes, however, were left trails of heartbroken mothers, fathers, sisters, brothers, and children. It is my belief that the Reverend Dr. Martin Luther King Jr. hit the nail on the head when he said, "Intelligence plus character—that is the goal of true education." In many of our nation's schools, there are fights occurring in the office between kids sent there for fighting. Staff members are leaving the schools and even the profession because they feel unsafe in many schools. Parents are going before boards of education seeking an alternative to sending their children to certain schools because of the horror stories that are unfolding in many schools daily. As a result of the instructional time lost and disruption to the entire learning process, many schools and students are failing to meet their academic as well as social and moral goals.

OUR SCHOOL

This was the story at Northeast Middle School (NEMS) in McLeansville, North Carolina, when I arrived and became the principal during the 2007/8 school year. The school was home to 911 students of whom over 65 percent received free or reduced-price lunch. White students comprised 37 percent of the population while African American students represented 45 percent of the student body. Hispanic students made up 11 percent of the population, with the remaining 7 percent of students identified as multiracial, American Indian, or Asian. Northeast Middle was a school in crisis. The school was about to be a candidate for reconstitution, in which all staff, including the principal, must reapply for their jobs. The year I came, there was an exodus of several career, probationary, and interim status teachers because they had given up all hope. Being part of an ongoing research study funded by a U.S. Department of Education Partnerships in Character Education Program (PCEP) grant, however, we were provided the services of an external evaluator, Multi-Dimensional Education Inc. (MDed). As part of the evaluation efforts for the research grant, MDed had assessed our school using the following seven dimensions: community engagement, curriculum expectations, developmental perspectives, educational attitudes, faculty fidelity, leadership potential, and school climate (Corrigan, 2007). The multidimensional formative data helped illustrate to what extent we were engaging with our parents and community, supporting and pushing our students through the curriculum, assisting in positive youth development, improving the educational attitudes of our students, building trust as a faculty, communicating as leaders, and providing a healthy learning environment. I suspected that school climate would be assessed as the lowest dimension for our school because during informal meetings the summer before the school year began, 90 percent of the teachers stated that the "kids are running the school" (see figure 20.1). They advised that there appeared to be no respect toward any school official, principals included. MDed's assessment confirmed that school climate was, by far, the lowest dimension for NEMS. And we used the MDed data to guide our action plan.

OUR PLAN

With the input of our leadership team, our school committed to a strategic character education program that would simply teach our students the behaviors that were expected in all the school's venues such as the hallway, classroom, cafeteria, bathrooms,

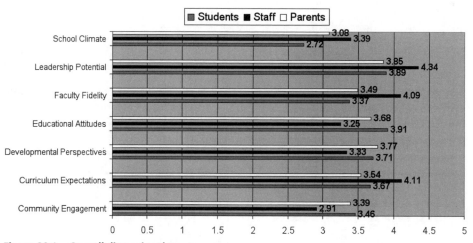

Figure 20.1. Overall dimensional mean scores.

and so forth. Our school's character development team posted behavioral expectation matrices throughout the school, but our teachers also had daily specific character education lessons to teach. These lessons were derived through our character team consisting of teachers and the administrative team in conjunction with input from our students and parents. Students were not only taught how to handle certain situations, but teachers also were expected to model consistently for students the process to follow in those situations. In other words, effective character education is not just about teaching character to students, it requires an equal focus on reminding the adults in the building what character means and to become an example of good character.

Northeast Middle experienced a record 557 out-of-school suspensions the year before I arrived as principal. Reasons for suspensions included noncompliance with school personnel directives, drug/alcohol possession and use, assault against students and staff, and fighting. Needless to say, there were incredible challenges to overcome, and our school community had to make a decision—change our school culture or succumb to the negative environment that permeated our school. Our character development initiative coupled with a strong standard mode of dress (SMOD) program and positive behavior support (PBS) system led to a significant reduction in out-of-school suspensions to 369 after the first year of implementation.

Our students were beginning to practice the behaviors that had been modeled for them by the entire staff, and it was starting to reap positive benefits for our school. Professional golfer Gary Player once suggested that the harder he practices, the luckier he gets (Brubaker & Coble, 2005). Our children were getting luckier each day practicing what was expected of them. It was as if they had been reading Wynton Marsalis' book *Moving to Higher Ground*. They began swinging with a matter of equilibrium, of balance, of knowing when, how, and how much (Marsalis, 2008). They were not the only ones. The NEMS staff took calculated swings as well, and as a result there were no further power struggles to see who was the strongest, the loudest, or got the most attention (Marsalis, 2008). We began teaching the students the pillars of character education by beginning with respect. Respect is summed up by the Golden Rule: *Do unto others as you would have them do to you*. Because our schools tend to be melting pots of various cultures and values, some may question the validity of respect. However, respect is paramount all over the world. Several religions have offered their interpretation of the Golden Rule (U.S. Department of Education, 2005):

1. *African traditional religion:* One going to take a pointed stick to pinch a baby bird should first try it on himself to see how it hurts.
2. *Buddhism:* Hurt not others with that which pains thyself.
3. *Hinduism:* Do nothing to thy neighbor which thou wouldst not have them do to thee.
4. *Islam:* No one of you is a believer until he loves for his brother what he loves for himself.
5. *Judaism:* What you hate, do not to anyone.

We showed students what respect looked like. Treating others fairly regardless of their race, age, or sex is respect. Avoiding put-downs and cruel remarks is respect. Teachers as well as students had to understand this because it is a given fact that children learn to respect others when they are treated with respect themselves. Our character education program helped our teachers understand that as the adults in the school building, our modeling played an integral part in our students' social and academic development. We communicated our beliefs through our actions. Teachers understood that not returning papers when promised sent the message that they were not responsible or trustworthy, two of the character pillars. Expecting students to perform tasks just because someone says so is no longer effective or efficient. Adults must exhibit the expectation of being good to their students in all that they do. Calling custodians Terry, Jay, Maria, or Dorothy and everyone else Mr. and Ms. sent the message that respect should only be shown to certain people within the building. There was no longer acceptance for a teacher to reprimand students for being late to class when that teacher was late to class coming from the copy room with class activities or arriving at work at 8:30 a.m. when school began at 8:35. Our goal was to model the behaviors for students that we expected from them.

Simply put, if we are to have civil schools, the adults in the building charged with educating the students should be willing to begin the character education message by first looking at themselves (Vincent, 2006). The teachers and students in NEMS were able to transform a school on the brink of utter failure to one that was recognized by Guilford County Schools as a Most Improved School out of 117 schools in the district in 2009. Achieving this honor was one of the goals we set out to achieve when we began working together during the 2007/8 school year. In addition, the state of North Carolina also recognized NEMS as a Model School for Positive Behavior Support. This recognition was achieved by providing evidence of reconstructing a school culture for better academic and social success via teaching and encouraging prosocial skills and behaviors. Evidence-based behavioral practices were also implemented with fidelity and accountability while simultaneously monitoring student progress and performance consistently.

OUR RESULTS

Within a three-year time frame, NEMS reduced its out-of-school suspensions from 557 before character education to 194. Northeast Middle School students also achieved high growth according to North Carolina accountability standards and adequate yearly progress (AYP), meeting twenty-nine of twenty-nine targets, which had not been done in the prior six years. I had promised staff and students when we began our journey together that if we made AYP and achieved growth, we would celebrate our accomplishments. The promised celebration was a necessity because "when you have a big success, don't keep the news under wraps" (Hernez-Broome, McLaughlin, & Trovas, 2009, p. 41). We had a party the likes of which no one at NEMS had ever seen. These types of celebrations are crucial to "rejuvenat[ing] our own energy," as Holcomb suggests (2004, p. 223). I believe this celebration ignited an already blazing fire of commitment in our staff, students, and school community. Our students appreciated the gesture and have continued to succeed. As mentioned before, the number of out-of-school suspensions for students fell below two hundred—a feat that had not been achieved for multiple years.

The Northeast Middle School climate became one in which the students and staff were friendly enough to greet visitors and each other, often saying "Hi!" Students and staff were working harmoniously together, whereas years before everyone had been just surviving under the negative climate due to extreme pressure. Teachers were finding it easier to get to know students and each other, which led to several impromptu staff gatherings at local restaurants and other venues.

There are those that would argue that with the curricular demands on teachers and students, prosocial education does not have a place in a school's daily routine. I submit that the prosocial aspect of education is not comprised of initiatives, programs, or here-today-gone-tomorrow gimmicks. It is a way of life for everyone who embraces it, for when it is done with fidelity and intentionality, there are multiple positive results that can transform the school culture. More importantly, when good character is modeled for students, it breeds the type of environment in which significant teaching and learning can take place. It also cultivates the type of academic success on standardized tests of which many schools dream. I strongly contend that to solve many issues within our nation's schools, we have to first recognize there is a problem and, secondly, commit to resolve it.

Lastly, everyone within the building, from administrators to certified and classified staff, must reiterate the same message—we will be a school of positive character founded on prosocial development! When this is done, the thrill of academic success is realized for all school stakeholders, as listed in table 20.1. This table illustrates how in the accountability year 2007/8 the school data improved. Please note that the state reading test was renormed, and the data could not be compared with the year prior; however, table 20.1 represents the results for math and reading in all Northeast subgroups after the character education implementation.

Often an increase of one year is hard to sustain during the second year. However, we were determined that we could do better. We reexamined our comprehensive data reports. We celebrated our strengths and developed strategies to address the concerns with greater intensity. What was interesting was that data from the research study were showing improvement within the seven dimensions. Some growth was significant, but much was pointing to a more gradual growth model. Meanwhile, as the dimensions developed, the 2008/9 school year resulted in the achievements and growth shown in table 20.2.

For anyone who disputes the necessity of solid character education in our twenty-first-century schools, I would advise that they cannot afford *not* to model positive character in schools. I am committed to modeling good character at whatever school I am found in. Our state and federal governments need to get with the business of placing prosocial education at the forefront of schools' agendas. Without it, schools

Table 20.1. Accountability, 2006–2008 (in percentages)

Subgroups	Reading, 2007–2008	Math, 2006–2007	Math, 2007–2008
All	50.1	54.5	67.6
African American	41.5	43.2	60.4
Hispanic	44.6	40.9	69.6
White	60.7	67.0	74.8
Free/reduced-price lunch	41.7	42.7	64.0
Limited English proficient	23.6	24.4	50.9
Students with disabilities	16.2	26.0	46.2

Table 20.2. Accountability, 2007–2009 (in percentages)

Subgroups	Reading, 2007–2008	Reading, 2008–2009	Math, 2007–2008	Math, 2008–2009
All	50.1	62.3	67.6	80.6
African American	41.5	54.8	60.4	74.8
Hispanic	44.6	55.6	69.6	84.0
White	60.7	75.7	74.8	88.0
Free/reduced-price lunch	41.7	55.0	64.0	74.9
Limited English proficient	23.6	35.8	50.9	79.2
Students with disabilities	16.2	32.7	46.2	53.5

are much less likely to experience the environmental and cultural shifts experienced at NEMS, which I am convinced, based on my observations and the MDed data, is the foundation for academic gains and improved learning conditions that all can agree are an important goal.

THE PRINCIPAL'S ROLE

Although for many of us prosocial education is the foundation of success, there are still many among us who might not agree with such a theory. Local boards of education and other community constituents may view prosocial education as a detractor from a school's instructional program and therefore consider any thought of pursuing it a mistake. Needless to say, the age of high-stakes accountability in which schools effectively have to raise the academic performance of all its students to a set standard or at least post a 10 percent reduction of nonproficiency in its subgroups presents a discomfort for many. It would have been easy to consider these sentiments as most do and respectfully decline the opportunity to present this prosocial change vehicle to the NEMS staff and community; however, as a principal, one must accept the reality of improving a school that has everything to lose, including its children. Once that principal accepts that truth, it's time to begin the business of getting better.

As the NEMS principal, I spoke about the prosocial approach we chose for improving our school (character education) knowing that the first question posed would be, "How is this going to impact your student's academic performance positively?" I spoke with my supervisors about my thoughts on how our school could improve our students' academic performance. Simply put, our school had nowhere to go but up. Northeast Middle School was a good school that had all the potential to become great; however, becoming great can only be realized through the concerted effort of a school community. Once I had the nod from my supervisors, we moved forward on the road to greatness.

Meeting with the staff, students, and parents of our school was the first order of business but was not the easiest of tasks. As the principal, there are so many different personalities and opinions with which to contend. Students want to blame teachers who want to blame the parents, and the ordeal continues. The role of the principal is to listen to the commonalities of the school's stakeholders' concerns and lead the discussion in developing what will work best for all involved. The principal is charged with being the most optimistic cheerleader for his or her school despite what circumstances may suggest. Our role is to become an advocate for the prosocial movement within our buildings and abroad. The real tragedy of prosocial development in a school is not that students come to school deficient in certain expected positive behaviors. What is tragic is that upon leaving our schools, the students are still deficient.

As principals, it is imperative that we report our success as we progress along the road of continuous improvement. The principal's role is to ensure that all stakeholders are aware of what Dr. Larry Coble calls "'priests and priestesses' who 'bless what goes on' and who 'take confessions' regardless of what the leaders say is important" (2007, p. 41). These people are important in the cultivation of a prosocial education environment in the school and community. We must enlist the unwavering support of these stakeholders in the movement for the benefit of the school. Countless school improvement dreams become nightmares when the principal does not communicate the intent of such initiatives and the resulting impact it should have on children. The principal should establish a system of mutual trust and respect via keeping stakeholders apprised of progress and roadblocks. Doing so assists in setting the stage for shared decision making that will propel student and school community success forward.

Within the school is where the work toward the prosocial education of our children deepens. The principal must organize a group of teachers who are well liked and respected by most students. These educators are often viewed as problem solvers for their students. They should have a warm and friendly personality, which results in consistent smiling. Most importantly, these teachers are known for the high expectations that they hold for students. This group, along with the principal, makes plans for how facets of prosocial education may be embedded in the everyday operations of the school. In every school, there are cynics who can potentially circumvent the intent of the prosocial movement. Their pessimism may be derived from the myriad here-today-gone-tomorrow initiatives that have riddled the school. These unbelievers should be consistently encouraged by the group in an effort to win their hearts. Positive messages left in the in-box or mailbox, praise for a prosocial lesson taught, and round-the-clock guidance in the prosocial way are simple, cost-effective means the principal or the group can employ to get these folks on the right path to embracing prosocial education and subsequent school improvement.

The principal's role is to provide an improvement framework for this group as they devise and produce the plans that will be the foundation for the school's prosocial education community. Everyone within the group should have clearly defined roles so that overlap is kept to a minimum. These roles include the following: discipline referral data entry, discipline data collector, academic data collector, behavioral matrix coordinator, and public relations liaison, to name a few. The group, comprised of no more than seven staff members, should meet regularly to determine the prosocial rollout plan for staff. The plan should be ingrained in each professional development day a school is afforded, particularly on any days in which students are released from school early. This group also works with the staff through weekly grade-level, content area, or departmental meetings to ascertain the level of implementation and corresponding positives and areas for improvement within the prosocial plan. Ultimately, the group should ensure that all staff understand their role in educating the students in accordance with the plan. In the event that there is a misunderstanding or questions, the group is charged with identifying key staff members who can serve as the prosocial champions at the school. I would suggest that the champions reflect a member of each grade level and/or content area within the school such that correlations may be made between education and delivered instruction. As the principal, I am charged with communicating the school data to parents, staff, students, and supervisors. Bright spots in the data should be accentuated to reflect the work of the staff and students in realizing the growth and success of the school; however, the needs for improvement should also be discussed with school stakeholders to modify the plan in suggested areas. When done with fidelity, the prosocial development of students can produce success the likes of which may have never been experienced in a school.

REFERENCES

Brubaker, D., & Coble, L. (2005). *The hidden leader*. Thousand Oaks, CA: Corwin Press.

Coble, L. (2007). *Lessons learned from experience: A practical developmental source book for educational leaders*. Greensboro, NC: On Track Press.

Corrigan, M. W. (2007). *Meaningful dimensions of education*. Costa Mesa, CA: MDed Inc.

Hernez-Broome, G., McLaughlin, C., & Trovas, S. (2009). *The truth about sucking up*. Greensboro, NC: Center for Creative Leadership Press.

Holcomb, E. (2004). *Getting excited about data: Combining people, passion, and proof to maximize student achievement*. Thousand Oaks, CA: Corwin Press.

Marsalis, W. (2008). *Moving to higher ground*. New York: Random House.

U.S. Department of Education, Office of Safe and Drug-Free Schools. (2005). *Helping your child become a responsible citizen*. Washington, DC: Author.

Vincent, P. (2006). *Restoring school civility*. Thousand Oaks, CA: Corwin Press.

CHAPTER 21

The School Specialist's Role as a Champion of Prosocial Education

BECKY WILSON, VONDA MARTIN, AND BETTY STRAUB

"Getting everybody to do a little bit—everyone in the community—that's how we meet students' needs." This theme for the Spencer County (Kentucky) Family Resource and Youth Service Centers has served to create a system for an unbelievable level of cooperation to help our kids. We focus on our goal: *Reducing barriers to learning.* Our centers, therefore, embrace the whole philosophy undergirding prosocial education, with our goal inspiring us to serve as a critical support mechanism that investigates and attends to the comprehensive needs of the whole child and families. Our processes focus on ways to operate outside the school building and to bring needed services into the schools.

Since 1991, our rural community has relied on the Centers' mission to provide a process much like case management for our school district's children and families. Collectively called the FRYSC (pronounced "Friskee"), the Family Resource Center serves the two elementary schools, and the Youth Service Center assists the middle and high schools. We are the two FRYSC coordinators, employed as school staff with education and social work degrees; we are not school counselors. Expertise in community collaboration is a nonnegotiable requirement for our positions. For the most part, we do not offer direct services ourselves but act as referral agents for a wide variety of concerns that affect families (e.g., mental and physical health, basic needs, day care, financial assistance, housing, after-school programs, jobs, and job training).

We are a very close, tight community that has little industry and no large businesses, leaving us with a small tax base available to help families in need. FRYSC was the catalyst for getting the community to communicate and collaborate to identify the kind of outside-the-classroom assistance that would ensure students could focus on learning. Our structure connects people who are willing to help gather and distribute very limited resources, and we continue to find more people almost on a daily basis. Our story that follows illustrates how we reduce learning barriers.

The Advisory Council is the heart and soul of the FRYSC, a remarkable testament to our continuing success. Required by the state, this group has at least forty members that have continued to meet bimonthly since 1991 to catalog activities and needs, provide updates, and celebrate the successes we build upon. The council's members

717

represent the diversity of the county: parents; school staff; community organizations (health, multipurpose, mental health and substance abuse prevention agencies, the Ministerial Association and individual churches, community businesses); and other volunteers. Even with the recent state budget being cut for FRYSC staff hours, our council continues to find resources for our ongoing programs, which include many unique opportunities to get parents involved in our schools. To get a sense of services and programs that make up the FRYSC efforts, let's follow a typical client.

FINDING FRYSC

Margie at First Baptist Church meets with Bess, who just discovered that her husband has lost his job. Referred by a neighbor who has volunteered multiple times with the Advisory Council, Bess didn't know where to begin to find help. Margie calls us at FRYSC, since Bess has one child at each school level (elementary, middle, and high), and we contact the Multipurpose Community Action Agency to connect the many dots necessary to respond to Bess's needs. We first find transportation to Mary's Closet, run by the Methodist Church, where Bess finds clothing for one of her children. Vonda at the Youth Service Center conveys to the students that it's nobody's fault that Dad lost his job and can't afford to buy school clothes. She emphasizes that decisions they make about taking care of their needs will ensure they perform well in school.

Bess's husband is invited to Donuts with Dads and finds several leads for job interviews in Louisville, the largest nearby city, where many county residents work. Bess attends Muffins with Moms, hears a skills presentation on parenting teenagers, and finds two babysitting jobs for her sophomore daughter. Bess's children are worried about school supplies until they attend the Health Fair/Readifest with sixty booths, one loaded with backpacks full of school supplies.

There's an interesting story about these backpacks. When FRYSC state funding for materials was exhausted, our churches stepped up, each one selecting an item needed for school, including the backpack itself. The churches purchase five hundred to one thousand of each item and then send volunteers to fill the backpacks. We have many children that wouldn't have school supplies each year without this kind of generosity from our churches.

Back to Bess. She and her family attend our annual festival that starts the school year off on the right foot. The Health Fair/Readifest has gotten bigger every year, held the first Saturday before school begins. Booth sponsors turn away no one, regardless of income level and need, so Bess is thrilled to find so much help in one place. She and her family enjoy activities that include health screenings from volunteers outside the county (Jewish Hospital from Shelby County) and helpful school and community-related publications (Publishers Printing from Bullitt County provides printing for ten thousand materials). North Central Health Department is one of our big contributors, with T-shirts for volunteers and a major item each year, so Bess's three children each get a bike helmet this year.

Because all school agencies take part in Readifest, Bess's family sees presentations on martial arts, cheerleaders performing, and school clubs sponsoring information booths. She is so delighted at this chance to meet over one thousand people who attend, many who urge her to sign up for a variety of school activities. Our Health Fair/Readifest really works to get whole families involved early in the year.

Now that the school year is under way, Bess's elementary-age son Bart participates in Backpack Buddy. At Taylorsville Elementary, Kaye is the home/school/community liaison who coordinates donations from churches, school staff (who sign up for monthly payroll deductions to help with funding), and private citizens. On Friday for under three dollars, Bart picks up a backpack filled with food that will last over the weekend. Bess had to give parental permission that identifies any food allergies. Last year, 184 students enrolled in the program, serving kids who didn't have to do without food, literally, on the weekend. This program doesn't happen during summer, so Bess will continue to struggle. To meet that need, Dare to Care programs (one supplies fresh produce for backpacks) are available at four sites in the county on the second week each month; food stamps are distributed during the first week of the month. Bess experiences for herself that the community sees need and meets it.

THE KIDS NEED COUNSELING: CAN FRYSC HELP?

Bess realizes she has to figure out how to get individual counseling for her children to help them cope with pressures of a father out of work and its impact on the family. She's in luck. We FRYSC coordinators are connected to multiple mental health services, including school counselors, to which we refer students and their family members. Counseling needs are critical for some students, and we are diligent in protecting confidentiality when they express that need to us. That's a primary reason that our offices are located in the schools at a considerable distance from the schools' administrative offices. Parents especially appreciate our protective stance regarding confidentiality.

Mentoring, a robust FRYSC component, provides additional help for Bess's kids. The program began when a new principal came to Spencer County. He immediately started working hand in hand with our staff to create an effective mentoring project that continues to this day. He placed the home/school/community liaison, who is also the school's parent involvement coordinator, in the office next to the FRYSC. When our current superintendent came, he had the school board agree to require all staff members to mentor a student—on school time. That act alone has really contributed to mentoring being one of our biggest successes. The role model that mentors provide has led to improved attendance and academic performance and has increased participants' self-confidence. Administration support is the absolute key. Mentors meet with students at lunchtime and during recess. Several of our male mentors are retired workers from General Electric who share mechanical expertise and teach bicycle repair. Other mentors are ministers, retired school teachers, and insurance salesmen. Speaking of lunchtime, Spencer Elementary has a lunch backpack program where students go to their pods to eat privately with their mentors. If a student is having a bad day, the mentor stays longer to provide extra needed time to help. The program is referral based; we always have a waiting list.

In addition to mentoring, Bess has discovered a world of volunteer projects through one of FRYSC's basic elements, a broadly disseminated monthly newsletter that goes to local legislators, parents, students, principals, and teachers. We want everyone to know about our work, and yet we believe we only reach a small proportion of the county's need. We work closely with community members primarily to reduce duplication. Bess is just one of so many examples of the great good hearts we touch. She gave back from the day she began receiving assistance. For example, she helped a great-grandmother who provides care for three of her great-grandchildren (ages two, four, and eight years old) and needed clothing, bedding, diapers, and furniture. Bess took her to places like Mary's Closet, operated by the Methodist Church for children (infant to size 8), and filled every need. Lots of families help with the Father-Daughter Dance for the elementary schools, which promotes the Fatherhood Initiative originally funded by a state grant from Community Collaboration for Children; moms help with food for the event. This event has been sustained by our many local partners—our heroes.

Bess is finding that nearly all activities in Spencer County somehow involve FRYSC. We have sites set up all around the county due to transportation problems that many families have in this hilly, rural area. At Vacation Bible School at many churches, our summer feeding program provides breakfast or lunch for children. We deliver flyers during the community library's summer Story Hour to inform parents that breakfast or lunch is available at Taylorsville Elementary. A local resident works in Louisville for a large management company that removes stoves and refrigerators during renovations. She stored the discarded appliances in her garage and gave them to families as FRYSC told her about families in need. This is so typical. People hear about furniture needs; someone calls up and donates to fill the need.

One bit of anxiety for Bess is the coming holidays. She begins seeking FRYSC sources. A grandmother, working at CVS, arranges for seasonable merchandise to be given to FRYSC. A one-thousand-dollar value, we distribute donations like this through the Christmas Assistance program to families who otherwise wouldn't have a holiday for their children. One church always asks for fifty angels each year, followed by smaller requests from our other churches, Girl Scouts, Boy Scouts, various student clubs, and private citizens. Similar to the Salvation Army's Angel Tree, we provide lists to these special helpers who anonymously buy and wrap gifts for hundreds of families in Spencer County.

We used Christmas Assistance as a way to increase parent involvement. To participate, we make it a different requirement each year to keep participants interested and to prevent families just coming every year for a handout. We believe that you need to help yourself. One year, parents had to volunteer twelve hours, of which four hours could be for community events or spending time in the library reading to their children. Eight hours must be devoted to such school-related activities as PTA meetings and events, open houses at the start of the school year, or attending board of education meetings. The next year, we added a parent–teacher conference per child. It has worked beautifully. Parents are proud to carry the sheets of paper that verify hundreds of volunteer hours they've donated so that their families can have a Christmas. Students also are involved in community volunteer projects as their way of giving back for the assistance.

INVOLVEMENT OF OTHER AGENCIES

Not all FRYSCs across Kentucky are like ours. Others depend more on social service agencies to refer for needs, or they have big corporations that provide help. We accomplish so much of what we do by word of mouth. Two of our staff—Kaye (the liaison) and Vonda's assistant—go to meetings with the Chamber of Commerce and Ministerial Association to inform them and stay informed about county needs and news. As you can likely tell, the churches are great partners; some churches directly buy the food for the Backpack Buddy program. Without our churches, we wouldn't exist. Regular funding donations come from other organizations and multiple private citizens. When there are special events, various groups take the lead. The PTA comes up with volunteers whenever we need them and develops project ideas for which we reciprocate their incredible support. The local University of Kentucky Extension Office agricultural center might provide information to homes about good nutrition. The 4-H agency recently distributed hygiene items around the time flu shots were being given. Vonda coordinates events around prom and graduation, involving numerous organizations and volunteers in helping to keep our seniors safe and alive on these important nights in their lives.

The Area Health Education Center is another powerful, multi-serving partner. At the high school, its members discuss health careers; for elementary and middle schools, its Scrubby Bear teaches good hand-washing technique. The University of Louisville Dental School sends great role models for our kids on October 31—dental students in lab attire, the tooth fairy, or Mr. Decay to talk to every classroom about eating candy, providing free toothbrushes and toothpaste. Later, in mid-November, the Smile Kentucky Dental Program helps FRYSC reach students. The largest dental event in the United States, Smile Kentucky is led by the Louisville Water Company's collaboration with the U of L Dental School to provide free dental screenings for third through sixth graders and dental educational programs for grades K–6. The Colgate corporate van is on-site, outfitted like a dental office with free brushes and toothpaste for participants. Volunteer dentists, hygienists, and other providers analyze the results of our students' screenings and arrange for needed treatments at no cost that occurs in February each year. This project addresses our students' serious lack of dental insurance.

WITHOUT FRYSC, WHO'S GOING TO DO IT?

We often ask ourselves this very question. Other school staff members do not have the time to attend meetings, make contacts, and coordinate the resources. To illustrate, one of the important tasks we perform to sustain FRYSC and its ongoing resources is our work with legislators. We keep them informed about learning barriers and challenges families face in our rural setting. When Spencer County hosted one of our Region Six Coordinators quarterly meetings, several local legislators attended at our invitation. They regularly express interest in our FRYSC focus and outcomes, and they provide resources. One state senator recently hosted a booth at Readifest to meet residents and answer their questions. Legislators annually attend a FRYSC reception at the capital in Frankfort in February to hear updates about our work and pressing needs. We also coordinated the legislative page program selection process this year, and two of our middle school students participated in the daylong program.

Getting everyone to do a little, FRYSC will continue. We can't depend on one person to do it all, or it will simply end. One church volunteer takes vacation time to work an entire week at Christmas to distribute the gifts gathered by the church for families. A single mother, referred to Mary's Closet, has become a church member and now helps gather and distribute clothing. She is an example of learning that time given is more important than nice clothes or money, a philosophy that we share with many of our county's residents.

We believe that we only reach a small portion of the needs in our county. Summer stops the external funding, but the need never ends, so the staff continues to meet and collaborate throughout the summer to help families. Our basic philosophy hinges on meeting needs so children can learn. Why not? Without clothes, children can't attend school. We can't change the circumstances that parents and children are experiencing. It's a hard reality, but *with resources* the students can make conscious decisions about succeeding at school. Vonda actually tells students, "You don't have to give up; you have choices."

Editor's note: New Jersey is one state that replicates Kentucky's FRYSC model. With its School-Based Youth Services Centers (SBYSC) in all twenty-one counties for all youth ages ten to nineteen, New Jersey is serving students in sixty-seven high schools, eighteen middle schools, and five elementary schools through the one-stop-shopping format. A three-year evaluation of the SBYSC program indicated that SBYSCs are effective in providing services useful for adolescents to address problems and meet their needs. Funded by the Annie E. Casey Foundation and conducted by the Academy for Educational Development (AED), the evaluation concluded that SBYSC made important differences in the lives of vulnerable students. Specifically, involved youth showed (1) increased educational aspirations and higher accumulation of credits toward graduation; (2) diminished feelings of unhappiness, sadness, depression, and suicidal thoughts; (3) improved sleep habits and less worrying; (4) less destructive behavior and feelings of anger; (5) decreased use of tobacco and alcohol; (6) more and improved interaction with families and friends; and (7) better use of contraceptives to prevent pregnancy and sexually transmitted diseases (State of New Jersey, 2011).

REFERENCE
State of New Jersey. (2011). *About school-linked services: School-based youth services program.* Retrieved on November 28, 2011, from http://www.nj.gov/dcf/prevention/school

CHAPTER 22

The Teacher's Role in Implementing Prosocial Education

JUDY ROSEN

INTEGRATING THE PROSOCIAL AND ACADEMIC CURRICULA: TWO SIDES OF THE SAME COIN

It's not easy to be a young and developing high school teacher. A complex and confusing array of challenges—academic curricula, individual personalities, group dynamics, the developmental needs and interests of adolescents, and our societal need for an engaged and thoughtful citizenry—all hover in every classroom. I spent thirty-three years in those classrooms, trying to juggle and balance those challenges as I taught history and some of the other social sciences to teenagers in blue-collar Pittsburgh, rural Upstate New York, and suburban Westchester County. The deepest truth that pervaded my professional life in the beginning and intermittently throughout was that I had no idea what I was doing; I knew nothing. It was only my classrooms full of expectant and hopeful faces, and even the less hopeful ones with their downcast eyes, who challenged me to find an even deeper truth: that teachers and students create knowledge together by jointly finding questions worth answering and pursuing the answers collaboratively.

Questions of right and wrong, and the decision-making process for answering those questions, are inherently interesting to teenagers, especially when the questions come from real-life experience. What we label "moral education" was the most effective tool I slowly and painstakingly discovered for imparting the analytic skills and unwieldy information in the academic curriculum. Employing this approach works most efficiently in a school whose structures and culture value moral education, but framing curricular material around compelling questions of right and wrong can, in any school, open the minds of those students who believe that education holds no hope for improving their lives, as much as it opens doors for the most achievement oriented. The "right" questions are the key, and finding the right questions involves really knowing one's students and supporting them to create a classroom climate that promotes curiosity, risk taking, and exposure, no easy task in any classroom in any school, but one that is infinitely worth pursuing.

When I started teaching at the Scarsdale Alternative School in 1985 (see Rodstein, case study 8C for more detail about the school), it was already affiliated with Lawrence Kohlberg and the Harvard Graduate School of Education (Kohlberg & Wasserman,

1980). Each school year began with a six-day orientation in which students were introduced to the ideas of moral development and spent long days getting to know each other and the faculty. Making the rules by which our school would be governed and voting on those rules became the source of our community building. We discussed and argued about everything from whether we should have a community service requirement to what obligations each of us had to ensure that classes went well, obligations like getting there on time, coming to class prepared, not coming "high." This experience taught me that classroom and school climate could be explicitly created rather than being the default setting that teachers and students were compelled to live within.

When I went back to teaching in a traditional school, I took that lesson with me and spent the beginning of each year creating class expectations with each of my classes. Instead of handing out a list of rules on the first day of school as I had previously done and as teachers traditionally do, I asked students to make a list of the conditions necessary for them to enjoy and be engaged in learning. Before I did this, I asked them to describe an enjoyable and satisfying situation in which they learned something that they valued. It could be anything from how to bait a hook or change a diaper, to how to solve a quadratic equation or write an argumentative essay. Having a concrete example in mind made it easier for many of them to think about what kind of environment would most promote their learning. They shared their answers with the class, getting to know each other a little as they did so, and we discussed and voted on which of the items on the list we wanted to live by in our classroom. I typed those lists up, hung them prominently, and when things got out of hand throughout the course of the year—as they inevitably did—we'd go back and reevaluate the list and our behavior. In my experience, hypocrisy is one of the greatest sins to teenagers, so their pledge to abide by rules to which they agree can go far toward creating a climate in which moral questions can be taken seriously. It was important for the students that I was required to meet their expectations as much as any other member of the class. I hoped that my willingness to try to do this would signal my respect for them and might convey the necessity of our working together.

In my first twelve years of teaching, before I got to the Scarsdale Alternative School, I had no idea how to create a climate of respectful, enthusiastic engagement in learning or, as I think it's labeled today, how to "manage" a classroom, a euphemism for rewarding good and punishing bad behavior. In reflecting on that period, I believe that most of my classes worked because I genuinely respected my students; called them on their disrespectful or disruptive behavior; tried to think about the roots of that behavior, both with them and on my own; and reached for the good student inside every troublemaker.

An example of the struggle to do this took place during one of my first years of teaching in a rural Upstate New York school. The halls of the school smelled of the manure on the students' boots because they had been up milking cows at five in the morning before they got to school. I was teaching world history to a tenth-grade "non-regents" (not college bound) group. The mood of the class swung wildly from out-of-control boisterousness to somnambulant. They told me that the subject matter was useless to them, refused to do any reading outside of class, and got restless whenever I asked them to do any work that involved reading in class. Two minor interventions turned this around. In addition to the fact that they saw no connection between what we were studying and their own lives, most of them couldn't read very well. I decided to try an experiment. I called the County Agricultural Extension Agent and asked for some pamphlets relevant and useful for the kind of dairy and cattle farming at which my students worked. The day I brought in a huge box of those pamphlets, the room was silent, and everyone was reading—or struggling to read—material they saw as useful. They begged to sign the pamphlets out so they could finish reading them at home, an indication that they were capable of doing homework when motivated to do so. In the days after that, we did have to get back to world history, but something shifted both in their willingness to work and in their relationship to me. They knew I had listened to them and heard them, and thus they were more willing to listen to me.

Perhaps this example seems far from prosocial education. While no explicit moral dilemma was raised, the building of trust between students and their teacher is essential to their willingness to think deeply when moral dilemmas are presented, as was evidenced by the second "intervention" that really turned this class around. We had read something about how many more people throughout the world could be fed daily if Americans gave up eating beef one day a week (since the grain a cow eats could feed so many more people than the cow itself). I asked the class whether it would be right, beneficial, and fair for us to give up meat one day a week for this reason. I was shocked at the firestorm of impassioned opinion on all sides of this question, though I shouldn't have been so surprised, given the fact that many of their families' farms grew cattle for slaughter. The class got so involved in this question that they each went home and asked their families what they thought and what would happen on their farms if Americans ever made such a shift. They came back and asked their math teachers to help them with some statistical questions and then decided to conduct a schoolwide poll. After that project, for the rest of the year, they joined me for the study of world history because they came to see that they had a teacher on their side and that interesting questions might come up just where they least expected them. Also after that, I was inspired, by the courage they displayed in pushing past their limitations to carry that project through, to find new ways to teach them more effectively. Even in teaching situations where the curriculum is packed and standardized testing is breathing down everyone's necks, I have found it worthwhile to take the time to do whatever is necessary to make students feel heard and to aim the course content toward their interests. Doing so saves the countless unpleasant hours it takes to "manage" disruptive behavior, and in terms of moral education, it is essential to build the kind of trust that flows from these kinds of interactions.

Another critical factor in creating the kind of classroom climate that fosters moral development, ironically, takes place outside the classroom. The kinds of relationships students observe as their teachers interact with each other and with administrators teach potent lessons about respect, concern, helpfulness, and power. In my experience, high school hallways teach as much about social organization as social studies classes do. Just as a school where every department chair and administrator is a man contradicts its paying lip service to the idea that "girls can be anything they want," teachers sharing materials or helping each other when technology has one of its inevitable breakdowns, even when they are busy with their own class, models what we want our classroom climate to be. In contrast, schools in which the teachers gather in clusters to gossip mirror the adolescent hierarchy of cliques, a hierarchy that works powerfully to silence many potential participants in class discussions. While as an individual teacher I was often frustrated when the larger school climate clashed vehemently with what I was trying to teach in my classroom, I tried to give voice to those silent lessons and let students talk about what they observed. This sometimes made me unpopular with colleagues or administrators, but it hopefully taught my students that social relationships are open to question and thus to change, laying an additional foundation for raising moral questions within the curriculum.

I was lucky to come of age in a historical period when the civil rights and student, peace, labor, and women's movements questioned and challenged every part of the political, economic, and foreign policy structures of American society. That same questioning found its way into the teaching of history in what was, at that time, called the "inquiry method" as part of the "New Social Studies" (Fenton, 1966; Fenton & Good, 1969), or using documents to help students figure out what they thought happened in various periods of American and global history. Today this method has trickled down to elementary and middle school and is included in the high school AP American history exam in the form of "document-based questions." DBQs started in the AP exam; then high schools started to use them, which meant that middle schools, preparing students for high school, started to use a modified form of DBQs, and ultimately elementary schools went the same route. While this method is nothing more than allowing students to experience and practice the process of creating and writing history, the analytic skills it involves are some of the same ones employed in the teaching of ethical decision making: making logical inferences from information, considering multiple perspectives, and finding one's way to the other side of the cognitive dissonance created by deeply considering conflicting accounts. Although I had been trained in the inquiry method, I only got to use it occasionally in the conservative schools in which I first taught, both in rural New York and working-class Pittsburgh. It is impossible to raise moral questions from a teacher-centered lecture, unless the teacher is telling the students what to think. Even at the Scarsdale Alternative School, lecture and discussion was the prevailing norm in academic classes until our affiliation in the early 1990s with the Brown Coalition of Essential Schools validated the idea of student as learner, teacher as coach (Sizer, 1984). It is ironic that it took us so long to integrate this principle in our classes since community meetings and all the other Just Community foundations of the school promoted moral development through hands-on experience, discussion, and debate, where the students were the workers, the teachers the coaches. Fortunately, as the Alternative School embraced the reforms that the Coalition of Essential Schools promoted, academic classes there started emulating the process of moral education that was happening in the other forums of the school. The coalition's impact on high schools that were much more traditional than the Scarsdale Alternative School similarly laid the groundwork for this kind of teaching.

My students and I were the lucky recipients of these reforms because they freed me from within the confines of the social studies curriculum to ask moral questions. I experimented with different kinds of questions, and my students let me know which were the most compelling to them. A question that became the backbone of the many

American history courses I taught at all levels, from classes for the least able students to AP classes, was the question of whether and in which situations the use of violence is justified. I first saw this question in a social studies series (the name of which I can't remember, and it has been out of print for years) where a short piece recounted the history of events during the 1760s and 1770s leading up to the American Revolution, from the Stamp Act riots to the arming of the colonists at Lexington. A question at the end of the reading listed the various forms of protest the colonists used from boycotting to tarring and feathering Loyalists and asked students which form or forms were justified and why. The passionate student reactions on every side of each form of protest were fascinating to witness and easy to duplicate in the sadly recurrent theme of the use of violence in American history. I stumbled upon the usefulness of this question and looked for ways to expand upon it every year after the first one when I saw how much it captured the interest of teenagers who, age appropriately, are protesting and considering social mores in their search for identity. Because the question of how and when to rebel is central to their stage of development, the historical consideration of the question is organically interesting. There were years when my classes hosted "peace conferences" to prevent the War of 1812, considering the conflicting views of expansionist western settlers and northeastern merchants. Other years we tried Abraham Lincoln for provoking the Civil War and suspending civil liberties, or compared the Declaration of Independence, the Declaration of Sentiments that launched the feminist movement, and the Black Panther Party's platform "to determine the destiny of [the] Black Community." In all of these cases, students had to gather information from conflicting viewpoints, argue from an assigned perspective, weigh the merits of the varied positions against what could and could not be established as facts, and synthesize an array of material into their own personal positions. Besides the intellectual challenges of each of these tasks, activities that are organized this way have the additional benefit of seamlessly "differentiating instruction" because students' roles can be assigned based on their level of difficulty, giving each of them a greater chance at success and each of them the necessity of listening to all of the others.

The same kinds of moral questions can easily find their way into other aspects of the social studies curriculum as well. In a senior elective I often taught on gender roles, one question that deeply captured student engagement was whether parents should raise their children without regard to gender roles. To answer this question, they had to consider why gender roles are useful and beneficial, the extent to which these roles limit opportunities for both men and women, and what the consequences of eliminating them would be for individual children and for society as a whole. In American government courses, simulations of Congress can raise infinite moral questions with regard to whether given legislation should be passed: from social questions regarding abortion or the right to die, to political/economic questions of whether society has an obligation to provide health care to all. In my experience, moral questions like these introduce and build the research and analytical skills that schools are designed to impart in a way that draws students in. At the same time and in its own right, teaching students to consider moral questions is, in my opinion, our best shot at making our society and our world more humane.

Teaching can be a torturous experience. The sheer number of interpersonal interactions taking place within any one forty-nine-minute class is exhausting to take in, let alone try to manage, to say nothing of the curricular content one is trying to guide her students to master. In discussing ways to integrate moral education into the academic curriculum, I have tried to emphasize that it is not only fine, but necessary, to stumble and to get lucky. Even the most experienced teachers are constantly creating their courses anew because each classroom of students is different from every other, and for new teachers, the many-layered demands and challenges can be truly overwhelming. The process of learning to teach students to think about right and wrong was, for me, an exciting way out of being overwhelmed. It helped me make sense of an always too-packed curriculum, and it brought me closer to the teenagers with whom I spent my days. I have been surprised that, in trying to write about the academic curriculum, I ended up devoting so much of this chapter to classroom climate and student–teacher relationships. Doing so has made me realize how essential those elements are to the process of moral education and how rich the experience of teaching can be on those days when the students, the curriculum, and the teacher create in their classroom a glimpse of a more moral social order, one where passionate disagreement is valued and where conflict and cognitive dissonance lead to progress and growth.

REFERENCES

Fenton, E. (1966). *Teaching the New Social Studies in secondary schools.* New York: Holt, Rinehart, & Winston.

Fenton, E., & Good, J. M. (Eds.). (1969). Report on Project Social Studies. *Social Education, 29.*

Kohlberg, L., & Wasserman, E. R. (1980). The cognitive-developmental approach and the practicing counselor: An opportunity for counselors to rethink their roles. *Personnel & Guidance Journal, 58*(9), 559–568.

Sizer, T. R. (1984). *Horace's compromise: The dilemma of the American high school.* Boston: Houghton Mifflin.

Part IV

SUMMARY AND RECOMMENDATIONS

CHAPTER 23

The Body of Evidence Supporting the Call for Prosocial Education

Michael W. Corrigan

For more than a century now in the United States and abroad, educators, psychologists, philosophers, and researchers from many other disciplines have produced a body of evidence that quantitatively and qualitatively informs us as to what has worked and not worked in education. As this handbook has shared, a respectable portion of this body of evidence on what works in education is supportive of the present-day benefits of practicing prosocial education and its historical roots in the American education system. As the chapters and case studies in this handbook have documented, since our education system began, prosocial educators and education researchers have admirably been exploring the best ways to help our youth learn better while simultaneously developing into not only good students but good people—productive citizens. This is the dualistic goal of prosocial education. As the research shows, prosocial education has served as a critically important complement supporting the academic side of the educational coin. During the past few decades, however, the United States has been moving away from using prosocial education research and practice to inform and guide the totality of educational improvement efforts and turning progressively toward standards and accountability systems to determine how to best measure the effectiveness of our curricula.

In other words, within a few decades, we have moved our main research and practice focus away from informing what we do as educators and how best to help our students learn content material and develop into model citizens, to a focus or policy centered more specifically on how well our students score on standardized tests. As a result, many educators have been forced to change from a data-driven focus of applicability (how to use rubrics, test scores, and other data to improve our practice) to accountability (how to use rubrics, test scores, and other data to document the effectiveness of our practice). This would be fine if our existing practice was actually producing effective results, but as the body of evidence to be shared here documents, this is not the case.

It would appear our policy makers continue to ignore a large body of evidence highlighting the prosocial-based approaches or practices most beneficial to academic success. They continue to ignore a large body of evidence showing how social-based variables (e.g., socioeconomic status [SES], parent involvement, motivation to learn) can account for a large part of the discrepancies or variances in student tests scores. And at the same time they continue to ignore the fact that the accountability high-stakes testing approach we are taking is not producing higher test scores but in the process is dismantling what was once the model of education that many countries have strived to become. As this chapter will explain, the testing obsession in itself is one of the biggest threats to improving what we do in education and serves as an indicator that our nation's current approach to improving education is shortsighted to say the least.

Ask any honest educator behind closed doors, and they will tell you that we now focus almost entirely on the input of standards-based curriculum and the output of test scores. Such a focus is so time consuming that many are now ignoring a large majority of the variables conducive to the learning process as well as the input, process, and formative data we could realistically be using to truly educate ourselves on what needs to be done to actually help test scores rise. Instead of focusing on how best to improve our schools, we now focus on how best to improve our scores. If the last few decades of minimal gains in proficiency have taught us anything, these two foci of improvement cannot be approached separately. As the chapters and case studies in this handbook have illustrated, your challenges will be far greater if you only focus on improving test scores and ignore efforts to help students improve developmentally, socially, behaviorally, ethically, and emotionally. Instead of using higher standards of evaluation and a system of accountability to fix what aspects of our education need more support and provide change we can believe in, we have developed a case of tunnel vision that has blurred the insight of far too many policy makers and lawmakers, and tied the hands of an even larger number of educators.

Unfortunately, what started out as a promising way to assess our progress or status has now turned into a mandate-driven system that has far too many educators scared to take time away from standards-based curricula and focus on what prosocial education practice, research, and common sense tells us works. If we know how to help students develop socially, behaviorally, ethically, and emotionally and we know that such prosocial development complements a student's academic development, then why are we still so heavily focused on only academics, standards-based curricula, pacing guides, and test scores after a decade of failure? If we also know (as documented in numerous chapters throughout this handbook) that focusing on improving school climate and increasing the civic and community engagement of our schools promotes both academic achievement and prosocial development while also helping students to develop stronger attachments to school, higher motivation to learn, and greater affect for learning, then why do we continue to test our students (and subsequently teachers) into submission? Given the overwhelming amount of evidence and research available suggesting that greater success and satisfaction exists when a symbiotic relationship between prosocial education and academic achievement is embraced, it is truly a conundrum to me that the powers that be have not solved this simple riddle. Apparently for some this conundrum still needs to be unraveled a bit more. This is why we enlisted experts across a range of fields to write this handbook.

We asked our friends and colleagues, respected leaders in the field of education with a focus in prosocial development, to help us compile a body of evidence to support you the reader in helping others better understand why we need more prosocial education to make real change, real academic reform and improvement. This chapter is mainly written to summarize the body of evidence we have provided in this handbook. But if you will indulge me, I would like to first address in a bit more depth the academic outcomes we have experienced during the past decade of the high-stakes testing movement that has in many aspects separated itself from prosocial education. My goal is to provide a rationale that clearly shows that if we continue to do what we have been doing, then we will continue to get the same results: no significant increase in proficiency, no significant decrease in dropouts, and no significant increase in retention of highly qualified educators. My goal in critiquing the high-stakes testing movement is to show that what could truly make our test scores rise is a stronger focus on prosocial education. After more than ten years of failure under No Child Left Behind (NCLB), and the introduction of the Common Core State Standards Initiative (CCSSI) promising to not be much different, it is time to have an honest discussion of the policies at hand. It is time to reconnect prosocial education to our academic achievement efforts and solve this conundrum so that we can once again get back to being the education system other countries seek to emulate.

I see this conundrum having two sides that need to be systematically explored. First I want to document what is not working (our current policy) and then discuss what holds great potential for improving our education efforts. What I hope to show by using this step-by-step approach is that the two sides of the conundrum are interconnected and to some degree reliant upon each other. My goal is to connect the dots so to speak so that it becomes crystal clear as to how, if we truly want to increase achievement, we must expand our conceptualization of academic achievement to reach far beyond test scores, and we must stop ignoring the prosocial education side of the coin.

In the first part of this discussion of the body of evidence, I will examine our existing approach to standardized testing. I will share how the standardized tests we use annually at so many grade levels came about and have evolved. I will then address how these tests were intended to improve where we rank in the world in education today but have not produced such success. To me, this is where an abundance of evidence exists supportive of prosocial education, because as we unravel how our existing approach has not worked to increase tests scores (and certainly not to support the development of the full potential of students), it becomes evident how prosocial education might be the missing piece of the puzzle. In unraveling this first part of the conundrum, I will discuss briefly how this testing fixation began as well as the Programme for International Student Assessment (PISA) scores that are used presently to rank education systems internationally. If our goal is to use our standards-based focus to improve our standards-based standardized test scores in hopes of improving our international ranking (that evidence also suggests we have not accomplished what we wanted), then all education stakeholders should understand how our standardized test scores are used and what they actually are and are not capable of measuring in the current design. Furthermore, in this first part of the body of evidence, I will also examine what variables are accounting for better international tests scores. In the last year, some very interesting analysis of the PISA scores has uncovered once again how socioeconomic status and parent involvement are two variables related to prosocial education that are having a great impact on how students score no matter what country they live in.

Next, I will explore how others that are scoring better than us internationally are actually approaching assessment, and more importantly how their education system is designed to do so well. For example, in the latest set of PISA scores released, Finland once again is among the top-scoring countries. Therefore I would like to briefly share with you how Finland approaches standardized testing and what they do within their education system to produce superior scores. Not to ruin the ending, but what you will find is that Finland is focused heavily on prosocial education efforts, and the annual testing of students (beyond PISA) typically only takes place when they turn sixteen years of age. You will also find that they do not hold teachers accountable or school systems hostage for such test scores. In the discussion of the other side of this body of evidence, and assuredly not least, I will review what we have shared in this handbook—the evidence and promise of prosocial education. After dissecting these two sides of the body of evidence, in the final part of this chapter I will discuss how these two sides could be and should be joined together to reap greater benefits for all educational stakeholders, and just maybe increase those coveted test scores significantly. Let's begin by addressing when this movement toward a higher-stakes test-centered approach began and the rationale behind such an approach.

THE PARALYSIS OF ANALYSIS

As hundreds of the educators I work with have told me, they feel paralyzed by the high-stakes testing movement. What started out as a *calling* to inspire youth has turned for many into a *career* that has taken the wind out from under their sails. So when did this paralysis of analysis begin? Well, depending on which educational historian or policy expert you ask, and as the next chapter on policy shares, you will probably find a few different answers or starting points as to when this movement actually began. Yet according to Wynne (1972), early output accountability measures began in 1895 with the introduction of spelling tests and written exams as a means to measure the quality of education in schools. The Elementary and Secondary Education Act (ESEA) of 1965, however, required funded programs to conduct evaluations that used basic skills tests as the measurement of student and program success (Popham, 2001). This brought about the idea that programs and school performance could be measured or evaluated by the performance of students on standardized testing measures, and by the 1980s, many states had developed statewide testing programs, which for all intents and purposes were utilized as an early accountability system in the United States.

On April 26, 1983, the concern for low-performing schools and their connection to test scores was escalated when the Reagan administration released a report on the status of America's schools, *A Nation at Risk*. This criticism of the public education system that basically blamed teachers and schools for the decline in student performance was prepared by a prestigious committee, given the endorsement of the secretary of education (William Bennett), and warned that this decline would be the demise of America's industrial clout (Berliner & Biddle, 1995). Through the power of the media (with a great amount of help from the agenda-setting gurus working in our nation's capital under the Reagan administration), the idea was branded and to some degree accepted that America's future business prominence would only be as strong as the student test scores being produced in America's public schools. To many, this was the tipping point when the movement toward a competitive testing environment and mandates for evaluation gained great momentum (Corrigan, Grove, & Vincent, 2011).

As the next chapter on policy highlights, however, the arguments put forth in the mid-1980s (or even during the Cold War for that matter) are not that different from the claims made prior to putting No Child Left Behind in place or the rhetoric associated with today's Common Core State Standards Initiative and the call for a new common core standards-based national test. This reoccurring belief or claim is that our tests scores and greater need to improve our focus on STEM subjects is the fulcrum on which our ability to continue to compete globally in science, technology, and industry rests. Such claims are scary. That's probably why they have had so much success in re-directing our education's focus. I would agree that the quality of our education system will be one of the deciding factors as to whether our country will remain a world leader. But I am not so sure that the test scores we are putting so much value on will necessarily be the most reliable or valid indicator of the extent of our success or failure. Let's hope not, because as the research to follow suggests, our standardized test scores do not look too promising. So in an effort to expedite this historical synopsis and fast-forward to the *lessons learned* part of this brief chronological overview, let's move forward from the 1980s and parachute pants to the year 2011 and skinny jeans, where we find standardized tests to be the latest fashion.

IT'S ALL THE RAGE

We all know that No Child Left Behind commendably set out to shrink the achievement gap between blacks and whites, mandated that schools demonstrate adequate yearly progress (AYP), put state standards in place, and assessed such efforts through testing. But has a focus on achievement tests helped to increase achievement scores or our international standing? To answer this question, given that PISA didn't begin until 2000, let us take a moment to consider the National Assessment of Educational Progress (NAEP).

The National Assessment of Educational Progress is the largest nationally representative and continuing assessment of what America's students know and can do in various subject areas. The NAEP is often referred to as our nation's report card. If it is our report card, the next question to ask is, how are we doing according to the NAEP? Based on a five-hundred-point scale, the scores for the 2011 administration of the National Assessment of Educational Progress (National Center for Education Statistics, 2011) show the following for fourth and eighth graders in reading and math:

1. In math, fourth and eighth graders scored on average one percentage point higher in 2011 than 2009. Both grades scored more than twenty points (four percentage points) higher in 2011 than in 1990 (when the test was first given). But please note that most of these gains were experienced in the 1990s, prior to NCLB.
2. In reading, fourth-grade scores did not change from 2009 but were four points higher than in 1992, when the reading test was first given. Eighth-graders scored on average one point higher in 2011 than 2009 and five points higher than in 1992.
3. The overall achievement gap between white and black students showed no real change between 2009 and 2011, and it remains wide. There persists, according to the NAEP scores, a twenty-five-point gap in reading in both tested grades and in math among fourth graders.

4. The gap between Hispanic eighth graders and non-Hispanic white students in reading and math closed slightly. It went from twenty-four points in 2009 to twenty-two points in 2011; in 1992, it was twenty-six points.

So if we are to use the NAEP scores as our indicator of success, it would appear that our focus on testing has not produced any significant gains in test scores. As Valerie Strauss (2011) of the *Washington Post* wrote, "Someone should be printing up a T-shirt about now that says: 'My nation spent billions on testing and all I got was a 1-point gain'" (para. 1). Strauss also points out that "it is important to remember that even NAEP has its critics, some of whom point out that the test cannot measure many of the qualities students must develop to be successful, and others who say that the NAEP definition of 'proficiency' is unnaturally high" (para. 17). I would agree that rarely can a test assessing content and subject knowledge, with a splash of critical thinking, assess all that teachers teach students and all that students learn. This is where the many measures utilized in prosocial development could help. The NAEP, however, is the one consistent test we currently have that has sampled students from states across the United States (at different grade levels) for more than two decades. And since we are currently unable to compare scores from all of the states that basically use a different standardized test to assess student achievement based upon the different standards and levels of proficiency adopted by each state under NCLB, regardless of the shortcomings associated with the NAEP, it is still the best longitudinal assessment of educational progress we have. Yet I would agree that the NAEP might be setting their standards for proficiency a bit too high.

As Peterson and Hess (2008), state,

According to NAEP standards, only 31 percent of 8th graders in the United States are proficient in mathematics. Using that same standard, just 73 percent of 8th graders are proficient in math in the highest-achieving country, Singapore, according to the AIR [American Institute of Research] study. In other words, bringing virtually all 8th graders in the United States up to a NAEP-like level of proficiency in mathematics constitutes a challenge no country has ever mastered. (p. 70)

In fact, a study conducted by a former acting director of the National Center for Education Statistics, Gary Phillips, showed that most of the countries that participate in the international tests called the Third International Mathematics and Science Study (TIMSS) would not do well under NAEP's definition of proficiency (National Center for Fair and Open Testing, 2011). Phillips' study found that of forty-five countries who took part in the TIMSS, only six have a majority of students who would score proficient on NAEP's eighth-grade math test.

If the NAEP's definition of proficiency is too high, demanding, or stringent, then should we assume that the standardized tests used in each state are a better or fairer measure of proficiency? The answer to this question rests upon how you define better or fairer. When we compare our state-based tests (that currently rest upon assessing students' subject content knowledge aligned with state content standards) to national assessments such as the NAEP (which focuses more on critical thinking skills than most states' tests), however, we find that the two different measures rarely paint the same picture. Take for example in West Virginia where 81 percent of students were proficient in reading according to the state's standardized achievement test, while only 22 percent were proficient in reading on the NAEP, and while 73 percent were proficient in math according to the state's test, only 18 percent were proficient in math according to the NAEP (Rosenberger, 2008). This type of discrepancy when comparing state achievement tests to NAEP scores is not uncommon or exclusive to Appalachia. Discrepancies between NAEP and state tests are even larger in Georgia, Tennessee, and Oklahoma. If you take the time to explore such discrepancies on the NAEP website, as did Peterson and Hess (2008), you will find that all but three states' tests (Massachusetts, Missouri, and South Carolina) fall short or far short of the NAEP proficiency expectations. It would appear that while the NAEP expectation for proficiency is too stringent, for the majority of the states the level expected for proficiency is not stringent enough. Yet despite the fact that a large portion of the body of evidence related to testing suggests that most states are giving a test that is far too lenient in assessing proficiency, some *still* believe that our differing states' standardized tests provide a more feasible alternative to assessing academic success. If this is the case, how does our adequate yearly progress look when we consider our states' tests?

Before I answer this question, for those not familiar with our high-stakes testing system (or for those who are just trying to make sense of it—and I sincerely wish you luck), I suspect I should first address briefly in a bit more detail what AYP is, how AYP is calculated, and more specifically how a level of proficiency achieved on the states' standardized achievement tests is determined by each state for assessing AYP. Sounds kind of convoluted, doesn't it? Well, to be honest, it is. In theory, the idea of requiring schools to make adequate yearly progress seemed like a good idea; as did leaving no child behind. But when you begin to dig into what this acronym (*AYP*) actually represents, you can see it has many flaws as well. For brevity's sake, please allow me to give you the CliffsNotes on this little caveat of our testing system. Basically, under NCLB, the federal government wanted to make sure that schools were making progress each year. The goal was to get states to set achievable annual goals that helped them to gradually stair step to 100 percent proficiency by 2014; this part sort of makes sense if you believe 100 percent proficiency to be achievable. But to determine a way to actually gauge AYP, states first had to determine (in the early years of NCLB) what score would constitute a proficiency level on the standardized achievement tests adopted or created by the states at the beginning of NCLB. For example, some states created quartiles to categorize their scores and then designated a certain quartile (i.e., cut scores) to be reflective of proficiency.

Unfortunately, as you might surmise, each state has a different level of proficiency that was calculated in different ways based upon the variation of scores collected on their tests at the beginning of NCLB. Therefore, the discrepancies between NAEP scores and state test scores are not necessarily due to the standards set forth or the test that is being given but are also heavily reliant upon what proficiency level the state determined for such standards-based tests. Therefore, it would require far too much explanation to detail how each state has designated what test scores represent a proficient score. Regardless, the goal of AYP was to use this proficiency level to show that more students were becoming proficient in the tested content areas as NCLB matured.

So, in order to show how the states would reach or accomplish 100 percent proficiency by 2014, and to keep funding coming in, they developed different plans to meet AYP. For example, if a state was at 64 percent proficiency at the beginning, they might have said they would increase proficiency by 3 percent every year for twelve years (3% × 12 = 36%; and 36% + 64% = 100%). Other states knew how hard it would be to increase proficiency every year, so they took a different approach (i.e., an ARM loan approach, if you will) and said they would increase 1 percent every year and then in the last few years they would make huge gains. These states most likely were hoping that NCLB would go away before they were required to meet their end goal. So how did the efforts to meet AYP (show gains in proficiency) based upon state tests work out?

Unfortunately, even when we set the NAEP scores aside, we are still not seeing progress in proficiency or AYP. According to the Center on Education Policy (Usher, 2011), and based upon using the states' standardized test scores, "An estimated 38% of the nation's public schools did not make AYP in 2011. This marks an increase from 33% in 2010 and is the highest percentage since NCLB took effect" (p. 2). In other words, even using each state's standardized achievement tests (that they were allowed to create and set the level of proficiency for) did not yield adequate yearly progress. Even after allowing states to "renorm" or "improve" their tests (i.e., create new tests), the bottom line here is that we are not seeing the improvements that the billion-dollar testing policy set out to achieve. So the question that still lingers for many (who have not yet unraveled the conundrum and moved on to the question of how we actually improve our scores) is how do we create a fair and accurate measure of proficiency for what some like to call or think represents academic achievement? Personally, I believe the question should be whether it is even possible to create a fair measure of proficiency at national or international levels. Regardless, this is the challenge that our next line of policy, the Common Core State Standards Initiative, could and should address as well as fix. Unfortunately, as I will share with you next, I am not sure that what has been proposed will provide us with any major progress.

COMMON SENSE VERSUS COMMON CORE

Next, I would like to address the role of common sense in testing. And to do this, before I go any further and address how the system will be "improved" under the Common Core State Standards Initiative, please allow me to clarify where I stand on testing. I am not suggesting we need a world free of testing. I think testing and holding *students* accountable on what they should be trying to learn is an essential component to providing a rigorous learning environment. Using tests, or even better, in some instances, using projects (or writing assignments) to test understanding and knowledge, is essential to helping a student get better. Such forms of testing are some of the best ways to help teachers better understand how to help and guide students. And only with the rigor that comes from testing, and providing the academic and social support needed to succeed in testing, can we help a student rise to the challenge and actually hit that zone of proximal development (ZPD) that Vygotsky (Ormrod, 2006) set for our ideal target. I am not saying to throw the baby out with the bathwater when it comes to testing, but it has been more than ten years that we have labored under this testing policy, and we might at least consider changing the stagnant, stinky bathwater before it becomes toxic.

I do believe test scores are important. I am a parent, a former teacher who taught in a juvenile detention center, and currently a professor, and I want my children and students to score well on tests. I also have researched more than a half dozen federally funded grants that required longitudinal and experimental designs to document success based upon test scores. I want my children and students to be challenged by tests. In many instances, I want my children and students to reach mastery on tests. But a well-designed test in a world cursed with the reality of the normal distribution of intelligence, should rarely ever produce all passing grades or for that matter 100 percent proficiency. If it is truly testing the knowledge or ability levels of all our students, it should mirror a spectrum of scores reflective of our students' differing intelligence, knowledge, ability, motivation to learn, work ethic, and prosocial support levels.

If you ask any of my students, they will tell you that I am a believer in (yet not necessarily a practitioner of) normal distribution. I tell my undergraduates the first day of class that to me an A is for excellence, a B is for good, a C is for average, a D is for diploma, and an F means you *forgot* to drop my class. I explain to them on the first day that I am a fair grader, and the grades I assign will reflect how well they performed based upon the grading scale. But I also explain that from my experience, the performance of my students normally reflects a normal distribution, and I doubt that all in the class (for many reasons beyond intelligence) will reach excellence. Not a semester goes by that I do not give a wide spectrum or distribution of grades ranging from A to F. Is it possible that one semester I might have a group of driven, motivated, and intelligent students who receive all high grades? Sure it is, and that is what keeps me motivated to help all in my classes do their best work. But I do believe that if used wisely and created to assess critical thinking skills and content knowledge accurately, tests can be beneficial to educators and students. But the tests are only beneficial when we use them to guide our efforts with individual students and use them as an assessment to help each student improve in his or her weaker areas.

To make standardized tests useful instructional tools rather than mainly instruments of accountability, we need to start using the tests to diagnose student needs and progress, not as indicators of whether the class (i.e., teacher) or school has made adequate yearly progress (AYP). If we are going to spend billions of dollars more on testing annually, with only 2.6 percent of our federal budget going to education and states experiencing some of the largest deficits in educational funding to date (i.e., an underfunded education system), we need to invest more wisely and start developing tests that actually allow us to track an individual student's growth and ability level. We need to create tests that inform what we are doing rather than just serving as an indicator of our being.

Furthermore, we need to stop using a cross-sectional comparison of last year's student test scores to this year's student test scores to hold teachers and schools accountable, as our current all-knowing analysis relies upon. If you are unaware of this analysis, you might be surprised to learn that we don't actually use the tests to longitudinally track if individual students are increasing their test scores. Instead, we use the tests to compare Mrs. Jackson's class test scores from last year to Mrs. Jackson's class test scores this year. At best this cross-sectional approach only provides us with an assessment of how smart this year's kids are compared to last year's kids. And if the

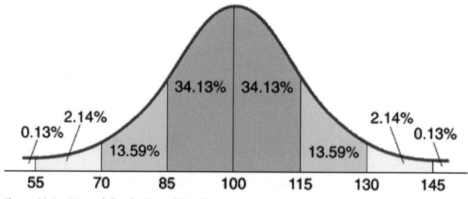

Figure 23.1. Normal distribution of intelligence.

normal distribution of intelligence research (see figure 23.1) provides us with a bell curve, historically showing that when assessed by an IQ test (heavily reliant upon reading and math skills) a great majority of individuals (68 percent) fall within one standard deviation of the norm (100-point IQ), shouldn't we assume that each year will provide a normal distribution of intelligence in our classes? And if our standardized tests are also heavily reliant upon reading and math skills (just like the IQ tests), shouldn't we also expect a normal distribution of standardized achievement scores each year?

Basically, what our tests are showing us is that we have little change taking place when we only compare last year's class to this year's class. In my opinion, beyond showing a normal distribution of intelligence (not to mention a normal distribution of motivation or effort put forth due to a test that does not hold students accountable), what the scores show us is that we have hit a ceiling, and if we continue this strict focus on testing void of common sense and an equal focus on prosocial education, we probably cannot increase our scores to the subjective level set to somehow miraculously take us to 100 percent proficiency by 2014. We have not made the gains expected even after allowing the states to change their tests annually if for some reason after they have not met their goals they feel it might be due to the tests they are using. We have not made the gains even after some states give a "practice" test that coincidentally is very similar to the real test. We have not made adequate yearly progress even after we have basically dismantled all other activities not related to the tested subject matter. Even after some have gotten rid of physical education, art, music, recess, and a great number of prosocial education efforts such as character education, we still cannot find enough instructional time to reach such unrealistic heights. And instead of realizing that such unreachable goals will lead to desperate people doing desperate things (e.g., the cheating scandal in Atlanta Schools), we continue to "stay the course." Instead of being honest and forthright, our leaders at the highest levels and their federally funded research wings continue to shake the shiny keys and say "look over here—we have a new test and new standards." Instead of discussing the fact that we have not made any adequate progress over several decades, all we seem to hear about is that NAEP is not fair, the state tests need to focus on a common core of standards and use a common test, and we need to continue our pursuit of the mirage known as 100 percent proficiency.

This is basically what the Common Core State Standards Initiative (CCSSI) is trying to accomplish. Through political strong-arming (e.g., if states do not agree to adopt the common core state standards, they will not be allowed to apply for certain federal monies), the decision makers at the federal government level have been able to push this new policy through. But when we look at who funded this program, we find that it is funded through the organizations and corporations that provide the testing services and subsequent texts developed to teach the new standards (Corrigan et al., 2011). Now that is truly scary. Even a student at only 27 percent reading proficiency could read the writing on the wall that there might be a problem (conflict of interest) when a large publishing company (such as Pearson) is funding (i.e., committing resources to) a federal movement to rewrite standards so that they conveniently *might* have a role in writing the new test, printing the new test, and/or publishing the new books to teach to the test. But welcome to Washington, D.C., where common sense is not that common anymore.

Furthermore, though some of the new CCSSI standards have been provided for educators to begin teaching, the curricula and different content subject knowledge tests are not quite ready. As a result, for the first few years of the CCSSI, many will be teaching new standards with inadequate resources and using old tests that measure different standards while the powers that be create, pilot, and set new proficiency levels for the new test. I am very curious, however, how the news of the first CCSSI test scores will be handled. I am also very curious as to what method they will use to determine the proficiency level for the tests and how such proficiency levels will compare to NAEP scores. I should mention that in some states such as California and Massachusetts, there is debate over whether the common core state standards are actually lower standards than the current California and Massachusetts standards used for NCLB (Stotsky & Wurman, 2010). Regardless, we know what is needed to move from a cross-sectional comparison of test scores to a more meaningful assessment that allows us to track whether educators are actually helping individual students get better academically. But with the rumors leaking out from behind the closed doors where these tests are being created suggesting they are developing another battery of content subject–based knowledge tests with a pinch of critical thinking that cannot be compared between grade levels (i.e., tracked longitudinally), it would appear that the new tests will not be used to track individual student progress. To steal President Obama's words from the 2008 presidential election that caused so much debate, "You can put lipstick on a pig, but it's still a pig."

And despite the uproar in response to using such assessments of academic success as a means to hold teachers and administrators accountable, we will probably see these new CCSSI tests being used as some sort of "value-added" indicator of teacher effectiveness. This seems strange given that the test typically only starts in fourth grade and then often skips grades up to the junior or senior year. How can such an approach be fair to the teachers who teach the grade levels tested compared to those who do not? How can such a test be used fairly to assess teachers who teach pre-K through third grade or the primary or secondary grades not tested? And given that the tests typically only assess math, reading, history, and science, how will the tests be used to assess teachers who teach the few existing nontested subjects? And not to avoid the eight-hundred-pound gorilla in the classroom, why aren't we taking this opportunity to incorporate age-appropriate developmental measures into the new tests to assess the developmental level of our students and possibly the impact of all the other prosocial education efforts put forth by a teacher or principal to help students develop? Because what I tell many of my students is that what some might call a learning disability is actually just developmental delay that can be remedied with a prosocial focus. Furthermore, even though policy does not mandate and in some instances does not even encourage prosocial education, many educators still focus on prosocial education and should be commended and rewarded for such efforts. To many, in addition to me, this standardized testing path we continue to stumble down as some states use their monies to theoretically Race to the Top makes absolutely no sense at all.

Why do we continue to think we can move so many test scores from the left of the normal distribution curve (and the middle) to the far right, turning a bell curve of scores into a graph resembling a tsunami? Why do we think a system so focused on academics can change historical research which finds that intelligence is somewhat innate (inherited from nature and for the most part not nurture dependent or changeable) (Simonton, 2001) or that we can rarely increase our intelligence more than one standard deviation (fifteen points) (Flynn, 1999)? Some might think my analogy comparing IQ tests to standardized tests is problematic. I find this resistance strange and ironic because it is as if some believe you don't have to be intelligent to do well on a standardized test that is heavily reliant upon reading and math skills. Some think teaching to the test can actually help students memorize hundreds of answers regardless of their intelligence level. Such a perspective might explain why there are an endless number of students in classrooms across the United States who are being *drilled and killed* (not *drilled and thrilled*) with a plethora of test-based worksheets daily. I guess their educational psychology professors didn't teach them the limitations of rote memory–based instruction. It is as if some want to state that intelligence has nothing to do with our ability to think critically when it comes to scientific inquiry, how well we can read and comprehend, how well we can do mathematical analysis, or how well we can recall history correctly and comprehend how historical events play a role in shaping our society. If standardized tests don't measure intelligence, then what else are they measuring?

To play devil's advocate against myself, it is quite possible the test scores are not reflecting intelligence in some instances. I am sure there are a great number of students who are highly intelligent that do poorly on the standardized tests. I know this for a fact because I was one of those students who, when told my IOWA test did not matter to my grades or moving on to become a sophomore, proceeded to fill in the letter *C* (for *Corrigan*) in order to complete the test more efficiently. I would say the standardized tests (in addition to reflecting one's intelligence and subject matter knowledge, or lack thereof) are also measuring motivation to learn, intrinsic motivation, and work ethic (or lack thereof). I think the standardized test scores also reflect whether a student is actually interested in taking the test or even cares about his or her test score. An experiment led by Duckworth (University of Pennsylvania, 2011) was conducted in which researchers observed video footage of adolescent boys taking a standard IQ test to rate their motivation and then measured how well they fared in terms of criminal record, job status, and educational attainment more than a decade later. According to Duckworth, one's motivation to take a test and IQ scores were nearly equally predictive of the adult outcomes of years of education, employment status, and criminal record. "What we were really interested in finding out was when you statically control for motivation, what happens to the predictive power of the IQ tests? What we found is that the predictive power goes down significantly," Duckworth said (University of Pennsylvania, 2011, para. 6). From my experiences and from reviewing research similar to Duckworth's, I believe that our low test scores are not necessarily a reflection of lack of intelligence (or lower reading and math ability) but quite possibly a reflection of lack of motivation.

I have spoken to a great number of students (from elementary to high school) who tell me that they know their scores will not influence whether they move on to the next grade. They have told me that they know it won't affect their grade point average (GPA). And a few have even told me that they know the only person these test scores will impact is the teacher. From the devilish smile on a few of the faces that shared such news, I could only predict that they did not try that hard because it appeared they did not like their teacher. That is why I tell my students (i.e., preservice teachers and teachers getting a graduate degree) that if you want your test scores to rise, you must first focus on building relationships with your students and their parents. I share the old saying with them often, "They don't care how much you know until they know how much you care." And to do this, a teacher must use prosocial education to be successful.

But if you take the time to research how tests for IQ originated, you will find that Alfred Binet (of the Stanford-Binet test) created the IQ test in France in 1905 to determine which kids were not smart enough to be in public schools (Ormrod, 2006); therefore, both IQ and standardized tests were developed for similar uses to assess students' cognitive abilities as they relate to public schooling. Furthermore, as mentioned earlier, the standardized tests and IQ tests are both heavily reliant upon reading and math abilities. In fact, if you take the time to analyze standardized test scores as I have on quite a few grants, you will often find collinear relationships between reading, math, science, and history scores. In other words, students' reading abilities account for the lion's share of the variance in their other subject area test scores and vice versa. This makes good common sense. Because how can one do well on one of those tricky algebraic math problems that require you to read and comprehend how long it takes a train to get from point x to point y at z speed if one does not have good reading comprehension skills? Furthermore, according to a study by Lynn, Meisenberg, Mikk, and Williams (2007) titled "National IQs Predict Differences in Scholastic Achievement in 67 Countries," in an analysis of TIMSS assessments and IQ, the average correlation between IQ and mathematics scores was .89, and the average correlation between IQ and science scores was .86. In laymen's terms, this means that IQ scores accounted for (predicted, if you will) 79 percent of the student math scores and 74 percent of science scores.

One might argue that the criterion-reference test requirement of No Child Left Behind is a fairer approach, as it is less dependent on a forced normal distribution and more dependent on a reflection of student content mastery. The hope of 100 percent proficiency even on a test that theoretically everyone could pass remains an unobtainable goal for many, and studies show that distributions of student proficiency on criterion-reference tests can have a normal distribution or be negatively skewed due to the test being a minimum proficiency test (Fusarelli, 2004). Therefore, because intelligence is one of the strongest predictors of high achievement, even for criterion-reference tests, IQ and mastery remain difficult to separate (Corrigan et al., 2011). The bottom line is that regardless of IQ, motivation, test anxiety, and the many other variables that possibly lead to testing fatigue or whatever it is one chooses to place blame on for the lack of stellar proficiency scores, there are many who still debate whether a challenging curriculum and intensive instruction within a public setting can actually improve intelligence significantly, which ultimately leads theoretically to increased test scores reaching 100 percent proficiency. One might debate whether we can do anything to raise our level of proficiency to 100 percent. But while we debate this construct of 100 percent proficiency, and even possibly my theory of how the normal distribution of intelligence relates to proficiency, let's set aside the NAEP scores and the state standardized test scores and for a few moments more see if our efforts to increase achievement while separating it from a prosocial education focus have helped to increase our scores internationally.

IT DEPENDS ON HOW YOU SLICE THE PISA

If this whole accountability movement, however, is based to some extent upon the belief that the fate of our nation's industrial or economic clout (our ability to compete globally) is dependent upon how well our students score on tests, let us continue by looking at how our international test scores compare to other countries. As the research shared so far suggests, our efforts to increase proficiency by using the standardized tests we have created at home have not garnered the success we had hoped for with NCLB. But just maybe our problems lie within the testing challenges that we have with the NAEP and states' tests (the ability to accurately and fairly assess proficiency), and just maybe by some strange serendipitous occurrence this focus has helped us to test better at the international level. If you have not read this research before and you are hoping for good news, I suggest that you not hold your breath.

The Organisation for Economic Co-operation and Development's (OECD's) Programme for International Student Assessment, is an international comparison of fifteen-year-olds' scholastic performance in more than sixty-five countries. According to the OECD's website, "the Programme for International Student Assessment is an international study which began in the year 2000. It aims to evaluate education systems worldwide by testing the skills and knowledge of 15-year-old students in participating countries/economies. Since the year 2000 over 70 countries and economies have participated in PISA" (OECD, 2011b, para. 1). The PISA is administered every three years. The PISA assesses reading, mathematical, and scientific literacy as well as problem solving. Please note, however, that the content areas are not designed to assess "merely in terms of mastery of the school curriculum, but in terms of important knowledge and skills needed in adult life" (OECD, 2012, para. 1). In fact, if you take some time to explore some of the questions they ask (which I strongly encourage), you will find that they truly do require a fifteen-year-old to think, not just recall a fact or circle a multiple-choice answer.

To some it seems that the United States has been in a free-fall on the international education rankings for several decades now. As President Obama stated in his January 2011 State of the Union address, "America has fallen to *ninth* in the proportion of young people with a college degree" (Obama, 2011, para. 34); we were once number one. In the 1970s, we were number one in high school graduation and now we have fallen to thirteenth, and the United States now has the highest college dropout rate in the industrialized world (Symonds, Schwartz, & Ferguson, 2011). And when it comes to how well we have performed on the PISA, which started around the same time as NCLB, "unfortunately, the USA's performance on the four rounds of PISA over the past decade has been uniformly mediocre" (Symonds et al., p. 18). The 2009 PISA scores, the most recent scores analyzed, did not help to improve the picture.

The 2009 PISA scores ranked the U.S. average at fourteenth out of thirty-four OECD countries for reading skills, seventeenth for science, and a below-average twenty-fifth for mathematics. There is some news that a few desperate individuals might call good. In mathematics, no countries moved ahead of the United States since 2006, and the United States caught up with nine countries that previously had higher average scores. The best news rested in the science scores, where the United States went from 489 in 2006 to 502 in 2009—on par with the average OECD score. Additionally, the United States caught up with six countries in science and moved ahead of six other countries, though it still scored below twelve of them. In reading, despite the states' efforts to increase their Sustained Silent Reading blocks to longer time allotments than what research shows kids are capable of paying attention (this is why I call it Sustained Silent Daydreaming), the United States had no change in reading from previous years. So once again, on a whole other level of testing, we are seeing no progress with our existing efforts to increase achievement and proficiency. But as the subheading suggests, how well we performed on the PISA administered in 2009 depends on how you look at the data; it depends on which slice of data you choose to digest.

While some reading this chapter might think I am being harsh when it comes to criticizing standardized tests and this proficiency movement, when you read the plethora of criticism of the PISA coming from the United States, you will think I have been nice. As a methodologist who spends a great amount of his time designing, reviewing, and critiquing research studies, I know all too well the increased challenges that arise as you add in an exponential number of covariates (variables that one can typically only statistically control for) and when you increase the diversity and size of the sample you are studying. For the individuals running the PISA, it has to be a nightmare at times. All of the tests are translated into the language of each participating country and then tested for reliability and validity. Some countries have a true sample of their students take part, while other countries, such as China, handpick which cities and schools take the test (while avoiding the rural poorer and less-educated areas). Some countries are quite diverse and have a large number of nonnative language speakers, while others are quite homogeneous. And some countries have a large number of what we might title low-socioeconomic-status students, while other countries (typically more socialist-based countries) do not have such a disparity of income and social support.

After the most recent PISA scores were released, there were a great number of naysayers who came out in the media to point out the shortcomings of the PISA. They brought up many of the methodological challenges I have just listed; "We have more diverse schools," "We have the most kids in poverty of any other industrialized nation" (note to self: be careful what you use as an excuse, because it might make things worse), "We have 20 percent that do not speak English at home," and "We test all of our kids" and "do a true random selection of schools across the states." And from a psychometric standpoint, I would have to agree with them. It seems like a heroic effort that would have to be completed to validate the assessment tools as being equally reliable and accurate after they have been translated into so many languages. Also, the sampling procedures are equally challenging. How could it be fair to have one nation (such as the United States) have a truly random sample of a diverse group of individuals of different races and income levels take the test while another nation does not even have to worry (like the United States does) that 20 percent of the participants don't even speak the native language fluently that they are being asked to read on the test? But the United States is not the only country that has its challenges with PISA. For example, in Germany, fifteen-year-olds are enrolled in five different grade levels, leaving them with 34 percent of fifteen-year-olds being in lower grades than expected (as compared to other countries) (Stanat et al., 2002). But what I found truly interesting is the research on socioeconomic status and parent engagement as it relates to the international PISA test scores.

SENDING OUT AN SES

For quite some time now, research has established that there is a strong relationship between socioeconomic status (SES) and academic achievement (Henry, Cavanagh, & Oetting, 2010; Kruse, 1996; Lee, Daniels, Puig, Newgent, & Nam, 2008). It makes sense that a child who grows up in a home where the parent or parents have lower education levels, possess fewer resources and skills to provide for good nutrition and academic support, and spend much less time on average helping their children with schoolwork or emphasizing schoolwork as an important part of life would by these circumstances be delayed (or at least challenged) developmentally, and as a result challenged when it comes to tests that rely heavily on reading comprehension. For example, Hart and Risley (1995) found that vocabulary growth differed sharply by SES class and that the gap between the classes opened early. By age three, children from professional parents had vocabularies of about 1,100 words, while children of parents on welfare had vocabularies of about 525 words. The children's IQs correlated closely with their vocabularies. The average IQ among the professional children was 117, while the welfare children had an average IQ of 79. To throw insult after injury, by age three, the average child of a professional heard about 500,000 encouragements and 80,000 discouragements. For the welfare children, the situation was reversed: they heard, on average, about 75,000 encouragements and 200,000 discouragements. You do not have to be a developmental psychologist to understand how such early developmental challenges translate into academic challenges that persist into adolescence. As early as 2002, Germany had connected the lower PISA test scores with their low-SES students (Stanat et al., 2002).

Most recently Gerald Tirozzi, executive director of the National Association of Secondary School Principals, brought the SES debate to the forefront again in relation to how U.S. reading scores on PISA compare with the rest of the world's by stating, "Once again, we're reminded that students in poverty require intensive supports to break past a condition that formal schooling alone cannot overcome" (as cited in McCabe,

2010, para. 6). The head of the National Association of Secondary School Principals took a closer look at how U.S. reading scores compared with the rest of the world's by overlaying the statistics on the tested students receiving the government's free and reduced-price lunch program (provided to all students below the poverty line) to the PISA scores. Here's what he found:

- In schools where less than 10 percent of students get free or reduced-price lunch, the reading score is 551. That would place those U.S. students at number two on the international ranking for reading, just behind Shanghai, China, which topped the ranking with a score of 556.
- In schools where 75 percent or more of the students get free or reduced-price lunch, the reading score was 446. That's off the bottom of the charts, below last-place Greece's 483. (as cited in McCabe, 2010, paras. 3–4)

Basically what Tirozzi is showing is that if PISA scores used SES as a covariate and controlled for this variable statistically, our scores and rankings would quite possibly be much higher in international rankings. Tirozzi also points out that other nations sort students into professional and labor tracks in the early teen years. In other words, many of the countries that take part in the PISA do not expect all students to be viable candidates for higher education and use their governmental powers to dictate that some are better suited for vocational careers or a trade. As a result, in some of the participating PISA countries, they only have the students heading to higher education actually taking the test. Not so in the United States, where educators must commit to educating all students and encouraging all in the belief that they too can go to college. Tirozzi goes on to say, "The release of the (Programme for International Student Assessment) data gives school leaders occasion to recommit to that goal [of helping low-SES students break past a condition that formal schooling alone cannot overcome]." Tirozzi added, "And we hope policymakers and all with a stake in the success of U.S. schools will take this occasion as well not merely to consider the problem, but to recommit with us to solving it" (as cited in McCabe, 2010, para. 8). What Tirozzi is asking policy makers to do is to focus on what we call prosocial education.

So how do we solve the problem? Do we adopt a policy where we allow one's SES to dictate one's achievement and thus dictate one's education? "I'm sorry, Mike, but your IOWA test was horrible and your reading scores are too low due to your cultural upbringing, and there is nothing we can do to help you. . . . You will be a great janitor someday," states my imaginary counselor. At what age would we "tell" a student he or she will not be pursuing the college prep track and instead will go to vocational school? Is it at fourteen so we can strategically increase our PISA test scores? I hope not. As a child of a single mom who survived on food stamps, I am very hesitant to say or suggest that students of poverty due to their academic performance should be destined for blue-collar work. This is the United States (not communist China and not fairly socialist Germany for that matter) and this is not part of the American dream. We believe that all deserve equal opportunity, and if our education system is not equipped to help students overcome the social challenges children of poverty face, then we need to revamp our education system. At the same time, it sure would be nice if we did revamp our education system to actually allow students of whatever SES the option to pursue a vocation or trade. Given that most students drop out of school due to not seeing how the material taught relates to what they want to do in life, a stronger commitment to vocational schooling offers true hope of not only reducing our dropout rate but engaging students in understanding how different careers, vocations, and trades are reliant upon the content knowledge and skills they learn in high school. Schools and teachers should have the support to be able to develop these connections in classes, in service learning, and in other out-of-school opportunities.

As this handbook has suggested, another possible way to solve (or at least address) the poverty issue (which may or may not be highly correlated with the vocational school movement when all is said and done) is to put more time toward helping low-SES students get the social support they need to compete with the other children who have many of the resources that low-SES students do not. And as this handbook suggests, this will require the powers that be to actually widen their educational lens to focus on the prosocial side of education. This will require our policy makers and others who play a role in the educational lobbying arena to read the research so they actually understand what is happening. One such area that prosocial education holds great potential for improving is parent involvement. As I will address next, parent involvement also is a variable that has been found to greatly impact PISA scores. The point is that those with lower-SES backgrounds may lack the developmental support needed to help them reach higher levels of proficiency (or possibly excellence) by the age of fifteen. More instruction and more testing have not produced these results. Yet as the prosocial education research this handbook has shared shows, we do know how to help them. We just need to make time for it.

HOME SWEET HOME

Parent involvement probably holds the greatest potential for helping us solve the effects of poverty on education—the differing scores between the "haves" and the "have nots." Epstein (1995) argues that school, family, and community are important *spheres of influence* on children's development and that a child's educational development is enhanced when these three environments work collaboratively toward the same goals. Many of the foundational learning and developmental theories and philosophies taught to preservice teachers (and shared in chapter 5 and many case studies as well as other chapters) focus on these same spheres of influence. Vygotsky, Piaget, Erikson, Kohlberg, Dewey, and many others stressed the importance of the larger community's and parent's impact on developing the whole child and helping them accomplish higher levels of learning. Numerous literature reviews (e.g., Mitchell, 2008) and meta-analyses (e.g., Fan & Chen, 2001) clearly demonstrate the relationship between parent involvement and a student's success in the test of life as well as the life of tests. We know that no matter what one's economic status, having an involved parent can be the difference between academic success and failure.

Most of the individuals at the top of the food chain in education know this to be a fact. This is why increasing parent involvement, communication with parents, and surveying of parents were actually requirements under NCLB Title I efforts. Unfortunately, most educators did not have time to focus on all that NCLB set out to fix and instead decided to focus on increasing test scores in order to keep or get more funding.

Some at the federal level continue to ignore research that highlights how poverty and parent involvement in education are tied together. Some even choose to live in a state of denial. One such person in a position of power with the ability to make a positive impact on education is Bob Wise, president of the Alliance for Excellent Education and the former governor of West Virginia. "The good news is that the free-fall seems to have stopped—and it was a free-fall for a while," says Wise. He adds that he's encouraged by the fact that 30 percent of the United States' students who are low-income performed in the top quartile. "That says to me . . . that the child's income level is not determinative of how well they can do" (as cited in Paulson, 2010, para. 8).

Really, the fact that 30 percent of low-income students performed in the top quartile shows that poverty does not determine academic success? Maybe he is confused and actually thinks it is the child's income and not their family's income. Maybe he meant to say that "it is encouraging that a child's SES is not the sole determinant of how well they can do." But if not, it makes me wonder how Governor Wise got elected to run a state that suffers from mass poverty. I guess during his one term of office, which included constant clog dancing with his constituents, he did not find the time to see first-hand how poverty impacts education. But as a professor who has taught for more than nine years in West Virginia and evaluated several federally funded longitudinal studies in the state, I can tell you with 100 percent confidence that it does. I guess he never met any of the kids I met who lived in homes without electricity or running water and whose role models consisted of a drug-addicted relative or a parasocial relationship with someone such as Dr. Phil. Maybe he didn't meet any of the poverty-ridden parents who relied upon their children to read the mail because they did not finish ninth grade and thus could not help their children with schoolwork as other more affluent and educated parents could. There is ample evidence, however, that might explain to individuals such as Governor Wise why 30 percent of low-SES students do better than the others on the PISA. It just makes me wonder if they know and don't care (or care to tell the truth), or if they just don't understand the research.

To better understand why some students do well on the PISA tests, and others not as well, Andreas Schleicher of OECD was encouraged by the countries participating in the PISA to look beyond the classrooms. So, starting with four countries in 2006, and then fourteen more in 2009, her PISA team went to the parents of five thousand students and interviewed them about how the children were raised and then compared that with the test results. The OECD study found the following:

- Fifteen-year-old students whose parents often read books with them during their first year of primary school show markedly higher scores on PISA 2009 than students whose parents read with them infrequently or not at all.
- The performance advantage among students whose parents read to them in their early school years is evident *regardless of the family's socioeconomic background*.
- Parents' engagement with their fifteen-year-olds is strongly associated with better performance on PISA. (OECD, 2011a, p. 1)

According to the OECD, differences in performance that are associated with parental involvement partially mirrored the differences in the socioeconomic backgrounds of households. The study states that typically students in socioeconomically advantaged households experience an environment that is more advantageous to learning in many ways, including having more involved parents. However, even when comparing students of similar socioeconomic backgrounds, those students whose parents regularly read books to them when they were in the first year of primary school scored fourteen points higher, on average, than students whose parents did not. What they found was that when parents read with students at an early age, or discussed with their children what they had done that week in school, or even cared enough to ask how their day was, students did better in school. Furthermore, when parents were willing to discuss political or social issues, books, movies, or television programs, the kids did better on the tests. And the more involved the parents were, the smaller the test score gap was between those of lower socioeconomic status and others.

Who were the 30 percent of the lower-SES students that Governor Wise says are proof SES doesn't matter? I would be willing to bet that 95 percent of the time they have some very caring parents (or grandparents) at home who want to help them break the cycle of learned helplessness that haunts his native state of West Virginia. I would also be willing to bet they have some great teachers and principals who welcome them every day at school and make them feel like someone actually cares about them and wants them to succeed. Finding out what truly is helping our low-SES students excel academically should be pushed to the forefront of our national research efforts. But there is plenty of research beyond this study that should lead us to be more prosocially focused on getting parents more involved.

Darling-Hammond (2011), in her latest book, *The Flat World and Education*, says the school reform challenge is all about equity. Darling-Hammond uses the example of Singapore, where "80% of families live in public housing, yet its 4th and 8th-grade students scored first in the world in both mathematics and science on the TIMSS assessment in 2003" (p. 5). Darling-Hammond's statement highlights the investment in the schools themselves and in teacher training and support the country has initiated. As a side note, it's not coincidental that we often see representatives from the Singapore ministry of education at prosocial education conferences in the United States. They attend to learn more about character education and social-emotional learning every year and are focused on building social skills into the national curriculum.

According to researchers Karen Smith Conway and Andrew Houtenville (University of New Hampshire, 2008), in order to experience the same achievement results gained by parent involvement, schools would have to increase per-student spending by more than one thousand dollars. Research suggests that there is a significant, positive relationship between parent involvement and student educational experiences, including improved academic outcomes (Barton & Coley, 2007; Henderson & Mapp, 2002). The literature explains that parent and community involvement activities associated with student learning have a greater effect on academic achievement than general forms of involvement (e.g., volunteering in schools, event attendance) (Henderson & Mapp, 2002). More specifically, parental involvement has an even greater impact when the involvement revolves more around specific academic needs such as mathematics (Sheldon & Epstein, 2005). Such increased parental involvement has an impact on secondary students (Tonn, 2005) and an even greater impact in some circumstances on elementary students (Horvat, Weininger, & Lareau, 2003; McNeal, 1999).

Research also shows us that greater parental involvement and helping parents (or guardians) better understand the social-emotional learning and socialization challenges their children encounter, can greatly complement teachers' efforts to get students more engaged, and can reduce behaviors that create barriers to effective instruction and learning (Spoth, Randall, & Shin, 2008). As Boethel (2003) explains, "Relationships are the foundation of parent involvement in schools" (p. 71). And at the end of the day, this is what prosocial education aims to bring to the table—a way to bring the social side of education back to the forefront of our education efforts. Nearly every chapter in part 2 of this handbook links prosocial efforts to working more closely with parents. Nearly every chapter in this book holds some tie to communicating to parents that we (educators) care about their children and not just test scores. As an old saying in education reminds us, they don't care how much we know until they know how much we care.

LET ME FINNISH

Research shows that during the past ten years of NCLB and the PISA, we have made no significant gains in improving our NAEP or state standards–based test scores, nor our international ranking; and sadly, according the PISA we are scoring at average to below-average levels. There are very few teachers or principals I have worked with who would disagree that as we have moved deeper into testing as our focus, we have moved further away from allowing our teachers the time and resources to focus on developing the whole child and promoting prosocial education. Though some might say that our early childhood development efforts requiring pre-K in many states' schools and the fact that some states now require all-day kindergarten equates to a focus on prosocial education or prosocial development, in reality this effort is not enough, and to many it is obvious that these efforts are just an attempt in many instances to get our kids up to speed academically and theoretically prepared to be ready to better excel on the more demanding standards set for elementary school. Finland, however, doesn't have children start formal schooling until seven years of age (Sahlberg, 2011). As I will explain next, Finland basically does education nearly completely differently than the United States. Finland focuses on prosocial education, and Finland is doing great in the PISA rankings. Furthermore, Finland was not performing well educationally in the 1970s, when the United States was the unquestioned education leader in the world. As the United States has fallen in the ranks, Finland has soared to the top. The process of change is basically the reverse of policies in the United States. "Over the past 40 years, Finland has shifted from a highly centralized system emphasizing external testing to a more localized system in which highly trained teachers design curriculum around the very lean national standards" (Darling-Hammond, 2010, para. 12). Therefore, I would like to take a moment to explore what Finland has done to help them improve so much and score as well as they do.

First, however, I didn't pick Finland because of all the press they have received for being one of the top dogs in the PISA race. I picked it because a colleague and I were having a discussion about the Finnish approach to education and how they are very prosocially focused. My nine-year-old daughter overheard the discussion and said, "I wish I went to school there!" Reflecting back to when she was younger and we spent part of a summer in Ireland and Great Britain while I did several lectures, she enthusiastically suggested, "You could get a professor's job there!" Why did she suggest such a career move for me? Is it because she heard us say they don't start school until they are seven? Is it because she heard us say they don't bring homework home during the elementary grades? Is it because she heard us say they don't do widespread standardized testing until they are sixteen? Knowing full well that my daughter, being the youngest in her class and being as gifted as she is, loves school and is an amazing student who sees grades as a competition to be the best in her class, she still is a kid at heart who would much rather come home and be able to find time to just be a kid. Therefore, the answer to all of these questions of why my daughter would suggest such a move is probably yes. All of what Finland does sounded great to my daughter, and her enthusiasm made me realize even more so how Finland's approach holds great promise for the United States. Why? Because Finland understands that in order for students to be excellent they must first have a chance to grow up, and we must help them to actually like going to school. They understand that children first need to actually experience childhood. They don't expect children to take more courses than a college student while they are in fourth grade. Finland focuses on helping each child develop individually. This is why I feel that Finland is a perfect example to use to show how the United States could once again get back to prosocial education, and that, among other things, could be the conduit to higher test scores.

Finlandophilia is a term that has been used to define the world's infatuation with the Finnish education system. While some might think we cannot learn from other countries that are not like us (i.e., Finland is a socialist country that many believe to be a very homogeneous population that speaks a common language), others disagree and strongly suggest that if we are to improve, the answer rests in adopting or, more importantly, adapting what other more successful PISA-scoring countries do so well to our education system (Symonds et al., 2011). Some believe that the U.S. student population is too diverse ethnically and economically to adopt a Finland-like approach. Although the United States does have some very diverse and multicultural schools (mainly located in urban areas), given that the majority of our schools rest in rural and suburban areas typically populated by a majority of English language speaking Caucasian students, to me this is not the case. But the facts are that Finland has a fairly diverse population. According to Darling-Hammond (2010), "One recent analysis notes that in some urban schools the number of immigrant children or those whose mother tongue is not Finnish approaches 50 percent" (para. 7). Although most immigrants come from places such as Sweden, the most rapidly growing sectors since 1990 have been from Afghanistan, Bosnia, India, Iran, Iraq, Serbia, Somalia, Turkey, Thailand, and Vietnam. These recent immigrants speak more than sixty languages. Yet achievement has been climbing in Finland and produces a highly equitable distribution of achievement for its growing share of immigrant students. Sure we are a more diverse country than Finland, but if their system is working in their homogeneous and also in their rather diverse urban schools, I think it would be wise to at least consider for a moment what they have learned and accomplished during the forty years we have digressed.

To me there are many aspects we can learn and adopt/adapt from Finland in regard to how prosocial education is the foundation for a better education system. In fact, much of what they do is diametrically different from our current approach. Dr. Pasi Sahlberg (2009, 2011), a Finnish educator, author, and director general at the Finnish Centre for International Mobility and Cooperation, states,

1. The first six years of education are not about academic success or measuring academic success. It's about being ready to learn and finding a student's passion.
2. Finland does not have high-stakes testing.
3. Finnish students do little homework.
4. Finland does not have a thick tome of national standards. Instead they are designed more at the local level.
5. The notion of caring for students educationally and personally is a central principle in the Finnish schools.
6. There is meaningful technical and vocational education in Finnish schools.
7. More than 99 percent of students now successfully complete compulsory basic education.
8. About 90 percent complete upper secondary school (i.e., 10 percent dropout rate).
9. Two-thirds of the graduates enroll in universities or professionally oriented polytechnic schools.
10. And most interesting of all to me is that he says it is harder to get into teacher education than law or medicine.

According to Sahlberg, at the University of Helsinki where he teaches, 2,400 people competed last year for 120 slots in the (fully subsidized) master's program for school teachers. "The Finns have worked systematically over 35 years to make sure that competent professionals who can craft the best learning conditions for all students are in all schools, rather than thinking that standardized instruction and related testing can be brought in at the last minute to improve student learning and turn around failing schools" (Sahlberg, 2009, p. 22). Finland has a productive teaching and learning system that was created by investing purposefully in ambitious educational goals using strategic approaches to build teaching capacity (Darling-Hammond, 2010). Finnish schools are generally small (fewer than three hundred students) with relatively small class sizes (in the twenties) and are uniformly well equipped. Students receive a free meal daily, as well as free health care, transportation, learning materials, and counseling in their schools so that the foundations for learning are in place. "Most visitors to Finland discover elegant school buildings filled with calm children and highly educated teachers. They also recognize the large autonomy that schools enjoy, little interference by the central education administration in schools' everyday lives, systematic methods to address problems in the lives of students, and targeted professional help for those in need" (Sahlberg, 2009, p. 7).

There are many things we can learn from Finland. Can we actually just fully transplant what they do to our education system? I would think that such an effort would fail. As Sahlberg said quoting an old Finnish saying once in an interview, "Only dead fish follow the stream." The reason they succeeded was because they went completely against the stream and developed something unique to their schooling and then allowed each school to personalize it even more. And as if that were not enough, they allow each teacher to do what he or she needs to do to help each student succeed in school and life. In reality what they are doing is a better job of creating citizens capable of running a democracy than we are doing.

DIVIDED WE FALL

I do believe the great divide that exists between policy makers, educators, and not to forget parents and students is that we disagree on what the most important outcome (or possibly outcomes) should be for our education system. Showing realistic improvement in proficiency on the basic content knowledge currently tested is a worthy endeavor. We can and should try to increase the number of academically proficient students in our schools. But as the critics of the NAEP suggest, a test cannot measure all that we do or accomplish in a classroom. Furthermore, scores that do not reach our goals of proficiency should not be our only concern or sole focus. As this handbook has shared, there are so many other prosocial education related variables that should be of major concern to educators, parents, and lawmakers. If our education system is the fulcrum our nation's clout rests upon, this means we are hoping our education system produces not only the knowledgeable workers we need to be astute in subjects such as math, science, and reading, but also the ethical workers we need who will have the social skills and perseverance to truly put such knowledge to work. As this handbook has put forth, our education system was created to develop the citizens we need to make our democracy (or republic) work and thrive.

We must stop limiting our focus to testing and curricula. We must stop treating the symptoms of our education system's ailments with first-order changes (surface-level changes such as a new test with common core state standards or the latest curriculum) and begin addressing the causes of the illness (Corrigan et al., 2011). For example, we can often revive a person who is having a heart attack, but if we do not help that person understand the life changes they need to make in diet and exercise, the probability is great he will find himself again under emergency medical care. We need to be more proactive and preventive in our approaches so that we do not find ourselves in ten years creating another bastardized version of NCLB because we have once again failed under CCSSI to increase proficiency. We must focus on the vital signs (e.g., our students' prosocial needs) to take a more comprehensive approach. This is crucial. To provide long-term health for the patient (the students our education system produces) demands a more prosocial education systemic focus capable of making second-order or more meaningful change. We must get back to assessing and focusing on what we do that helps students do better and develop into the citizens we need to compete globally and flourish locally, as well as help teachers experience greater success and satisfaction. And we must move away from overtesting our students and inducing the boredom that results.

As my colleagues and I wrote in our recent book focused on data-driven education reform,

> GPA and standardized testing supposedly offer insight into one's academic achievement. Yet most of us know a smart child who is not motivated to learn or take a test. Motivation is a key factor to learning (Skinner, 1969) that typically accounts for a significant percentage of achievement (10+%) (Uguroglu & Walberh, 1979). Also one's feelings (affect) for the subject matter or schoolwork play a key role and account for an equally significant

percentage of academic achievement. As a result, improving educational attitudes is often the answer to improving learning and increasing test scores. In reality, if a student is not held accountable for his or her test scores and the scores do not have any impact on their GPA, moving to the next grade, or graduating, why would they try hard on the tests? One answer is that they actually feel intrinsically motivated, empowered to do well, and want to show how smart they have become. Another possibility for trying harder is that students know it is the teacher and school that are held accountable for their test scores, and they like you the educator (and the school) and want to do well to help you. How about considering the students' feelings toward school or testing? How about seeking more information as to how one might build an intrinsic drive to learn or achieve? (Corrigan et al., 2011, pp. 34–35)

I do believe that if we continue to overfocus on standards-based testing we will continue to see more students grow bored and disillusioned with school and learning. And given that we still have approximately one-third of our students dropping out of school (as discussed and cited in chapter 5), ignoring efforts to focus on prosocial education, increase motivation to learn, and make the material we teach more meaningful to students is something we cannot do. Furthermore, if we are losing a high percentage of our new teachers within three to five years of starting their careers and seeing some of our best teachers taking early retirement or leaving for jobs in other sectors (which as chapter 5 explained is related to the testing focus), we must focus equally on what we can do to help teachers overcome the side effects that result from the overfocus on testing. If we are to escape this paralysis of analysis, we must move to a broader conceptualization of what measures, or more importantly helps us to achieve, a broader definition of academic success.

THE BODY OF PROSOCIAL EDUCATION EVIDENCE
In this handbook we have shared with you different levels and kinds of evidence for prosocial education. The persuasive stories in the case studies and the thematic analyses addressed in the chapters provide an abundance of anecdotal and qualitative evidence. The well-designed randomized controlled trial (RCT), quasi-experimental, and experimental studies cited within the chapters have added to the body of prosocial education evidence sound quantitative research to further support the efficacy of prosocial education. From small-sample qualitative studies to large longitudinal quantitative studies, a great number of hypotheses have been answered with data supporting the impact that prosocial education can have on a range of developmental and academic outcomes and suggesting that prosocial education holds great potential for turning around the not-so-successful results we have experienced with our efforts to increase proficiency and our international standing.

The body of evidence that relates to prosocial education shows that educators and education researchers are using their heads, hearts, and hands to actually improve education. The body of prosocial education research is focused on (1) the developmental needs of students and (2) the needs of educators and school systems to make the climate and culture conducive to student learning and growth (i.e., fixing an archaic, broken system overly focused on standards and testing). The body of prosocial education evidence provides a logical response (or alternative) to the challenges of today that show that much of the current programmatic, political, and reform agendas guiding our education efforts are bankrupt or corrupt, misdirected, or simply ineffective or inadequate. We need standards and good reading programs, but if the school culture is dehumanizing, it becomes an unproductive hidden curriculum that dominates daily life and overpowers the academic goals for many or most kids.

One such chapter that provides strong evidence supportive of prosocial education is Kidron and Osher's chapter, "The History and Direction of Research on Prosocial Education." This chapter shows how the debate over the role of education in improving prosocial behavior and prosocial development (i.e., prosocial education) has been on-going for quite some time. But this chapter also provides you with results from a great number of federally funded studies that have produced evidence suggesting not only that such efforts can be accomplished by schools to try to make a difference, but also that such efforts can make a statistically significant difference. In its practice guide from the What Works Clearinghouse (Epstein, Atkins, Cullinan, Kutash, & Weaver, 2008), the Institute of Education Sciences identified five research-based, prosocial education practices for reducing problem behavior in elementary school classrooms. Character education, civic engagement, and life skills training are just a few of the programmatic foci that have produced quantitative evidence showing that such efforts work toward improving education and instruction while reducing the risky and problem behaviors that hold so many classrooms back from increasing academic achievement.

Sheldon Berman's chapter, "The District Superintendent's Role in Supporting Pro-social Education," is a wonderful combination of evidence and narrative that shows how the social environment creates the foundation on which productive learning can occur. Cohen's chapter, "School Climate and Culture Improvement," shares an abundance of prosocial education research showing indirect and direct relationships between school climate and academic success. The Snyder and Flay chapter, "Positive Youth Development" (PYD), shows how PYD-related approaches are beginning to amass a body of literature that demonstrates how PYD programs work to augment youth development that can contribute greatly to improving the positive effects of instructional efforts. As we contemplate solutions for problems such as declining academic motivation and achievement; escalating school dropout rates (Battin-Pearson et al., 2000); and increasing school bullying and aggression (Swearer, Espelage, Vail-lancourt, & Hymel, 2010) that our current policy is not helping to improve, Schonert-Reichl's chapter, "Social and Emotional Learning and Prosocial Education," as well as Durlak and colleagues' meta-analysis on social-emotional learning (Durlak, Weiss-berg, Dymnicki, Taylor, & Schellinger, 2011), supports the assertion that a focus on our youth's mental well-being is greatly needed. All of these slightly different areas of prosocial education research point to the systemic nature of human development and the relational systems, including children, parents, and teachers, that are needed for education to be effective. When you begin to connect these slightly different areas of prosocial education research, you can begin to see the systemic nature demanded for education to truly work. In order for true academic or educational success to occur, we must begin connecting how the environment (climate, culture) provides a place for youth to develop physically, ethically, mentally, socially, and emotionally before we can hope to see the academic developmental gains our current federal policy focuses upon.

The chapters on character education, civic engagement, service learning, prevention of bullying and harassment, and after-school efforts provide even more evidence showing how educators, who have developed a mind-set (philosophy) to help students develop prosocially, have made incredible and commendable gains to broadening the focus and success of their education efforts when they developed a process to approach education reform systematically. And even though we set out to develop a handbook that stresses process over programs, we still shared within this handbook a great number of examples of successful programs supported by research. Too Good for Violence, Positive Behavior Supports, Facing History and Ourselves, and the Olweus approach to preventing bullying and harassment are just a few of the programs cited within the chapters and case studies that have strong quantitative and qualitative evidence. Please note, however, that these are programs that all stress process and are adaptable to different classes and schools.

Furthermore, the chapter on the emerging field of contemplative education, "Supporting Educational Goals through Cultivating Mindfulness," demonstrates how to build a research program based on evidence from different sources. They cite Benson's work on the relaxation response (thirty years old); Kabot-Zinn's work showing an impact on the chronically ill, which is translated to prevention with more diverse groups; and neuropsychology research, which is now directing hypothesis testing and program design in schools. The moral-reading intervention case study is a good example of how to build in evaluation from the beginning of a new program. Though moral education (e.g., Kohlberg) has a very strong quantitative and qualitative evidence base built off of the research performed several decades ago on moral dilemma exercises integrated into social studies classes and curricula (which both the Cohen and Powers chapters refer to), today the research is resurfacing again stronger than ever under the efforts of *Just Communities* and *democratic classrooms* as described by the Powers chapter on moral education. Therefore, the evidence provided in this handbook offers insight as to how numerous prosocial education fields are continuing to evaluate and replicate interventions and programs in different contexts, classrooms, and countries and to document the evolution of school policy changes over the decades since they started. To me this is a very important point.

Though there is a great amount of excellent longitudinal research taking place, in my opinion, too often in academia we perform what some might refer to as one-shot studies. A professor, graduate student, or group of researchers sets out (with possibly some grant monies) to study how one variable (e.g., an intervention) impacts other variables or practices. They spend anywhere from a day to years performing the study. Some collect data on the sample as the study is taking place, while others might perform what they want to believe is a causal analysis on an archived (secondary) data set. These studies produce results that are either found to be statistically significant or not significant. Unfortunately, all too often, once the study is completed and the conference papers and manuscripts are presented and published, they move on to another focus of study, which is typically not related to the variables they first investigated. Instead of replicating studies (which is truly needed to establish anything close to claiming causation), in educational research we seem to too often be in search of the next discovery. In prosocial education, however, when you begin to read the mass of research as presented in this handbook, you can begin to see how the research has been built up for decades and generations. From decades of research on prosocial education, you can see how the qualitative research has fed and informed the quantitative research. And what I find most admirable, for which we editors are truly grateful to the authors of the chapters and case studies in this handbook (as well as the hundreds of others who research prosocial education), is that despite a tenure of policy that has taken us away from a focus on prosocial education, they have not given up. They continue to replicate studies to produce evidence for the day when the powers that be come to the realization that what we are doing is not working and come back to a state of common sense. They continue a research focus with an emphasis on building school processes that acknowledge the two sides of education—prosocial and academic—are sealed together.

Between this chapter, the following chapter on education policy, and chapter 1, we editors have given you a rich array of arguments, theories, examples, and stories that should have persuaded you about the importance of starting with prosocial education as the necessary basis of educational and school reform and the promotion of student learning, excellence, and preparation for life. This brings us to summarize the major points that we introduced in chapter 1 of this handbook.

1. All educational policies should foster schools that are safe, humane, respectful, and caring because all human beings (in this case the children and adolescents and their teachers and school personnel) have intrinsic worth and should not be abused or neglected or overcontrolled. The editors of this handbook believe that bad schools are guilty of neglect in the same way that parents can be guilty of neglect. The problem is that when schools neglect children, we accept it because we think there is not enough money to tackle the problem, teachers are too overburdened, neighborhoods are poor or communities are uncommitted to education so there is no tax base, and so forth. Yet none of these excuses hold water. This handbook and the abundance of research cited within it demonstrate that many schools are caring and intellectually stimulating places in which students and adults thrive. The authors herein offer many variants on the fundamental recipe that integrates prosocial education with academic learning.

2. All educational policies should permit, that is, not hinder, the fullest development of each child's social, emotional, self-regulatory, and cognitive skills. The basis for this is the same as above, the intrinsic worth of each human. To acknowledge the intrinsic worth of someone means that she should be treated as you yourself would want to be treated, as you seek to be treated, and as you try to get others to treat you—that is with deep respect.

3. Educational policies must also be based on science, on evidence. This book compiles evidence of all kinds about specific programs that *all* focus on prosocial development—so there is a good and growing evidence base that shows we have the practical knowledge and skills to create the positive conditions demanded by points 1 and 2.

4. Specifically, moral education promotes perspective taking, empathy, and social reasoning; SEL programs promote self-regulation and emotional growth skills; character programs promote positive attitudes and prosocial behaviors; better school climate promotes safety; and so on. The theoretical point to be made is that there are strategies and programs that effectively target and promote child development and conditions in which children can thrive (points 1 and 2).

5. Most importantly, there is evidence from many of the authors cited in our handbook that shows that prosocial processes enhance motivation to learn and academic achievement. This is a key point for policy, as we all know.

SOMETIMES NOTHING IS SOMETHING

This chapter has focused mainly on research and data supportive of the need to focus on prosocial education and also on data supportive of changing the dysfunctional strictly focused, standards-based testing approach. But I would like to end this chapter by posing a question that I am sure many individuals in education have wrestled with at some point in the past: If something cannot be accurately measured or tested, if we are unable to place a numerical value on a specific effort's worth or contribution, does that mean it has no value? I pose this question because some still question the research findings of specific studies in prosocial education while neglecting to consider the totality of the body of evidence that supports it.

I wrote this question down the other day as one of my graduate students left my office. While working on a research proposal focused on the contribution that teaching the arts (more specifically, teaching art instruction in schools) provides to academic achievement, she had discovered that research supportive of the arts' ability to *directly* influence positive improvements in academic achievement was not that easy to find. She was disappointed to discover that the few studies completed which suggested that such a direct relationship existed held many limitations such as small sample sizes (studies performed on a few art students taught by one art teacher in one school), bias in research design (e.g., nonexperimental studies on the arts funded by large arts organizations), and questionable psychometrics (lack of reliable and valid assessment tools used to measure the outcomes). After nearly a semester of researching the topic she wanted to study as an aspiring art teacher, and a lifetime of striving to become a great artist, I could see the disappointment on her face. This is when I decided to share with her the difference between the belief in additive models versus mediated models.

I shared with her Anderson's (1982) work on school climate that explains how "the simplest models are purely additive. That is, they assume that variables directly influence student outcomes in a separate but additive way" (p. 384). For example, some still seek (often to no avail) to support that a new curriculum can by itself increase achievement. While from a simplistic research design additive models appear easy to use (i.e., you only have to theoretically capture a variable assumed to measure whether art instruction took place and compare it to achievement scores), these models do not adequately reflect reality, where many highly related variables are constantly interacting (Burstein, 1980; Levin, 1970). For example, wouldn't variables such as the quality, frequency, duration, or types of art instruction have a role in the impact that art instruction could make? Furthermore, what other challenges exist in the schools studying whether art instruction can improve academic achievement that might also be holding back efforts to increase achievement? Is it even feasible to think that art instruction given a few hours a week could overcome the academic challenges related to socioeconomic status (SES) and lack of parent involvement? I explained how often a distal (long-term) goal such as increasing academic achievement is frequently reliant upon many mediating variables. We discussed how there are many variables that impact a school's or teacher's ability to increase achievement such as school climate, peer relationships, motivation to learn, student attitudes toward education, school leadership, and parent involvement. We talked about the many other variables that students face when trying to increase achievement, such as getting adequate sleep, nutrition, academic support, and time to study, not to mention wrestling with the intelligence they were innately granted at birth (and which quite possibly has not been nurtured to the highest extent). We talked about how many of these mediating variables can and should be addressed from a more short-term or proximal perspective, and we discussed how they impact each other in more of a systemic way. In other words, in order to accomplish your long-term goal, there are a great number of short-term variables that will impact and predict whether you are able to accomplish the long-term goal. And as a result, under a mediated model, you should be including these many variables as part of your focus.

In order to truly capture (statistically) the potential power of art instruction, many of these variables mentioned would also need to be addressed in the research design or at least statistically accounted for or controlled for in the analysis. If we only look at a few variables, the existence of art instruction and academic achievement, we probably are not going to find much evidence suggesting that art instruction helps achievement, because as numerous studies cited within this chapter suggest, the majority of the variance in test scores is typically accounted for by prosocial variables such as motivation to learn, affect toward the subject matter or school, socioeconomic status, parent involvement, and IQ. Studies that only consider a few variables are just flawed shortsighted studies in my opinion. And the truly sad part is that these types of studies are often the majority of studies that are published. Even more disappointing, typically journals will not publish studies that do not find statistical significance; therefore we truly only see the portion of these studies that actually find something. As a result, people in charge of making policy decisions in the age of data-driven education are left with little evidence to make critical decisions. Furthermore, they use this type of research to make statements that could be paraphrased as "the arts have no significant impact on achievement." But for those who understand Type I and Type II errors in statistics, we must be careful not to assume that what we find to be true is true, because it might actually be false. We must also be careful in assuming that what we find to be false is false, because it might actually be true. In other words, that which apparently has no value, worth, or power statistically might actually be very significant to our efforts.

The research my colleagues and I have produced suggests that educational success (or academic achievement, for individuals who have not yet accepted the prosocial side of the education coin) is reliant upon a multidimensional assortment of variables and efforts (Corrigan et al., 2011). And though measuring the impact of instruction in the arts (e.g., arts, music) might be hard to capture and link directly to increases in academic achievement, in reality, if the arts increase creativity, inspire critical thinking, and provide a class that students actually enjoy being part of, then logic would suggest that to some degree the instruction of arts in schools holds great value. I then shared how there are also very few studies on specific curricula showing a direct impact on achievement scores.

I share this little anecdotal story because I think it relates closely to the evidence existing in education today related to academic achievement (and curriculum) as well as the evidence supporting prosocial education. In my opinion, we are making too many education policy decisions based upon not enough research or research that needs more research (replication). I think part of this is due to the publish-or-perish mandate that many in academia are forced to work under. It is much easier and more efficient to produce and publish a great number of small studies than it is to truly adopt a research agenda and stay focused on that agenda for quite some time while still producing the publications required for tenure and promotion. I think part of this approach to research, however, is due to the fact that as a society we are often directed and dictated by headlines. We read one headline saying "Study Finds Character Education to Be Ineffective," and suddenly we believe that character education holds no value. As the evidence presented in this handbook suggests, this could not be further from the truth. Character education and the many prosocial efforts we have shared have great value. And though some of the studies might be methodologically or statistically challenged, it is the body of all of the evidence, the totality of decades of research, that must be the main point of consideration. When we consider the totality of the evidence, it becomes overwhelming and obvious that our education system must widen the focus of our efforts to move far beyond the academic tunnel vision we suffer from today.

Why did I spend the first half of this chapter focused on achievement scores? Now that is a good question. As I was writing I kept thinking about a bumper sticker my father had on one of his old dilapidated cars. The bumper sticker said, "If it works, don't fix it." I was lucky enough to be given this car when I was in college—and I say this with great sarcasm. This car was a piece of junk. Yet his idea of what constitutes "working" was much different from mine. It worked for him because it started, and though shaky and stinky of burning oil (a sign that the engine was soon to explode), it got him to work every day. But once I had the car, I soon realized that this working car could not go faster than forty-five miles per hour without nearly falling apart and jumping off the road. The inside of the car reeked of years of neglect. I actually coached football during my college years at a local middle school. At first I was glad to receive the car, but then I realized it would cost more for me to fix it on a weekly basis, and it was more of a headache and an embarrassment than it would be if I just parked the car and went back to riding my bike. Just working is not enough. This is the education system we are stating that our future rests upon. Furthermore, the U.S. government is not my dad, and I am sure they have much more money and resources than a drug/alcohol counselor at the VA would have to upgrade the vehicle that can get us someplace tomorrow.

Yet despite our great amount of wealth and assets we hold as a country, we still underfund our education. And despite an underfunded education, the fulcrum our success as a nation rests upon, we still expect excellence. How can we give so little and expect so much? With undersupported teachers responsible for too many students in too few classrooms lacking today's technology, air conditioning, and operational heating systems, we still continue to blame the teachers. With antiquated school buildings made of cinder block and surrounded by fencing resembling the architecture of the county jail, we blame school systems. Instead of fully funding our education system, we throw the cost back onto tax-paying citizens who are far too often voting down bond issues due to being strapped in a horrid economy. And still we say that our test scores are the biggest predictor of our country's future success. As a result, we spend a large portion of the little monies we have on testing. If our kids' test scores, the effectiveness of their teachers, and the climate of the school buildings are the predictor of our future success, why are we only putting 2.6 percent of our federal budget to education? The answer is politics and lobbyists. And we need you to help us help the powers that be to better understand what is needed to make real change in education. And as this handbook has shared, a stronger focus on prosocial education should be a part of this change.

Doing versus Being

For quite some time now, research has suggested that if we truly want to improve the quality and productivity of our learning environments we should focus on variables in education that measure "doing" and not focus as much on "being" (Bloom, 1976, 1980; Mood, 1970; Wolf, 1966). In other words, as Bloom and others proposed back during the decades when our education system was still actually considered to be one of the best in the world, we should focus on what our educators and students *do* and not as much on the outcome assessments telling us how well our students might *be* performing on tests. To me this makes good common sense.

When it comes to today's data-driven side of education, however, too often school-level administrators and teachers are told what scores or statistics they will be responsible for rather than being provided with the scores and statistics they need to improve what they are responsible for (Corrigan et al., 2011). If you have ever tried to lose weight, you know that getting on the scale every morning and staring at the number will not help that number significantly improve. No matter how much we wish or pray we would lose weight, it does not happen until we actually do something. Now we could just adjust the scale so that it appears we lost weight, but that would not be right. You could also change your diet. And for some this will help. But though it might help you drop your weight, it might not help improve your health, cardiovascular fitness, or muscular definition. For most of us trying to get healthy (trying to get stronger and better), we have to change our diet, and we also have to change our daily routines. We often have to add different types of exercise to the schedule. We often need to eliminate unhealthy practices. In order to change our "being," it is normally reliant upon changing what we are "doing" (Corrigan et al., 2011). If we want to figure out why our students are doing well or not so well on tests, it will require that we look at research on education-related variables and measures that go far beyond student test scores. This is where the body of evidence related to prosocial education can help.

For educational leaders who are growing frustrated with focusing on achievement and proficiency scores and long for the flexibility to get back to focusing on developing the whole child, this handbook is written to help them by presenting a more rational argument for how one can truly improve academic success, not to mention the satisfaction and effectiveness of teachers. This handbook holds many of the answers for educators who continue to look at their test scores and wish (and pray) they would improve. We wrote this handbook for the educational leaders who have embraced a new "diet" of curriculum that helped to improve things a little but did not get their schools to where they want them to be. We wrote this handbook to provide educators with an exercise regimen that helps them to focus on the prosocial side of education. And no matter how many times we "improve" or "renorm" the standardized tests (i.e., adjust the scale), from the static scores holding so many schools back from meeting the requirements of NCLB (100 percent proficiency), it would appear we need to widen the focus of our lens to once again encompass the prosocial side of education. If what we are doing is not changing the being of our test scores, we need to refocus on fixing what we are doing. As a friend of mine likes to quote one of those pithy Zen sayings, "Having lost sight of our goals, we must now redouble our efforts."

REFERENCES

Anderson, C. (1982). The search for school climate: A review of the research. *Review of Educational Research, 53*(3), 368–420.

Barton, P. E., & Coley, R. J. (2007).*The family: America's smallest school.* Princeton, NJ: Educational Testing Services.

Battin-Pearson, S., Newcomb, M. D., Abbott, R. D., Hill, K. G., Catalano, R. F., & Hawkins, J. D. (2000). Predictors of early high school dropout: A test of five theories. *Journal of Educational Psychology, 92*, 568–582. doi:10.1037/0022-0663.92.3.568

Berliner, D., & Biddle, B. (1995). *The manufactured crisis: Myths, fraud, and the attack on America's public schools.* Cambridge, MA: Perseus Books.

Bloom, B. S. (1976). *Human characteristics and school learning.* New York: McGraw-Hill.

Bloom, B. S. (1980).*The new direction in educational research: Alterable variables. *Phi Delta Kappan, 61*, 382–385.

Boethel, M. (2003). *Diversity: School, family, & community connections.* Austin, TX: Southwest Educational Development Laboratory.

Burstein, L. (1980). The analysis of multilevel data in educational research and evaluation. In D. C. Berliner (Ed.), *Review of research in education* (Vol. 8, pp. 158–233). Washington, DC: American Educational Research Association.

Corrigan, M. W., Grove, D., & Vincent, P. F. (2011). *Multi-dimensional education: A common sense approach to data-driven thinking.* Thousand Oaks, CA: Corwin Press.

Darling-Hammond, L. (2010). *What we can learn from Finland's successful school reform.* Washington, DC: National Education Association. Retrieved January 10, 2012, from http://www.nea.org/home/40991.htm

Darling-Hammond, L. (2011). *The flat world and education: How America's commitment to equity will determine our future.* New York: Teachers College Press.

Durlak, J. A., Weissberg, R. P., Dymnicki, A. B., Taylor, R. D., & Schellinger, K. B. (2011). The impact of enhancing students' social and emotional learning: A meta-analysis of school-based universal interventions. *Child Developments, 82*(1), 405–432.

Epstein, J. L. (1995). School/family/community partnerships: Caring for children we share. *Phi Delta Kappan, 76*, 701–712.

Epstein, M., Atkins, M., Cullinan, D., Kutash, K., & Weaver, R. (2008). *Reducing behavior problems in the elementary school classroom: A practice guide* (NCEE #2008-012). Washington, DC: National Center for Education Evaluation and Regional Assistance, Institute of Education Sciences, U.S. Department of Education. Retrieved November 25, 2011, from http://ies.ed.gov/ncee/wwc/publications/practiceguides

Fan, X., & Chen, M. (2001). Parental involvement and students' academic achievement: A meta-analysis. *Educational Psychology Review, 13*, 1–22.

Flynn, J. R. (1999). Searching for justice: The discovery of IQ gains over time. *American Psychologist, 54*, 5–20.

Fusarelli, L. (2004). The potential impact of the No Child Left Behind Act on equity and diversity in American education. *Educational Policy, 18*(1), 71–94.

Hart, B., & Risley, R. T. (1995). *Meaningful differences in the everyday experience of young American children.* Baltimore, MD: Paul H. Brookes.

Henderson, A. T., & Mapp, K. L. (2002). *A new wave of evidence: The impact of school, family, and community connections on student achievement.* Austin, TX: Southwest Educational Development Laboratory.

Henry, K. L., Cavanagh, T. M., & Oetting, E. R. (2011). Perceived parental investment in school as a mediator of the relationship between socio-economic indicators and educational outcomes in rural America. *Journal of Youth and Adolescence, 40*(9), 1164–1177.

Horvat, E. M., Weininger, E. B., & Lareau, A. (2003). From social ties to social capital: Class differences in the relations between schools and parent networks. *American Educational Research Journal, 40*(2), 319–351.

Kruse, K. (1996). *The effects of a low socioeconomic environment on a student's academic achievement* (Research study submitted for the requirements of CNE 579, Research in Education). Huntsville, TX: Sam Houston State University. (ERIC Document Reproduction Service No. ED 402380). Retrieved January 18, 2012, from http://www.eric.ed.gov/PDFS/ED402380.pdf

Lee, S., Daniels, M., Puig, A., Newgent, R. A., & Nam, S. (2008). A data-based model to predict postsecondary educational attainment of low-socioeconomic-status students. *Professional School Counseling, 11*(5), 306–316.

Levin, H. M. (1970). *A new model of school effectiveness: A report on recent research on pupil achievement.* Stanford, CA: Stanford Center for Research and Development on Teaching, Stanford University. (ERIC Document Reproduction Service No. ED 040 252)

Lynn, R., Meisenberg, G., Mikk, J., & Williams, A. (2007). National IQs predict differences in scholastic achievement in 67 countries. *Journal of Biosocial Science, 39*(6), 861–874.

McCabe, C. (2010, December 9). The economics behind international education rankings. *NEA Today.* Retrieved January 3, 2011, from http://neatoday.org/2010/12/09/a-look-at-the-economic-numbers-on-international-education-rankings

McNeal, R. B., Jr. (1999). Parental involvement as social capital: Differential effectiveness on science achievement, truancy, and dropping out. *Social Forces, 78*(1), 117–144.

Mitchell, C. (2008). *Parent involvement in public education: A literature review.* Philadelphia: Research for Action. Retrieved October 17, 2010, from http://www.maine.gov/education/speced/tools/b8pi/reports/review.pdf

Mood, A. M. (1970, February). *Do teachers make a difference?* Washington, DC: U.S. Office of Education, Bureau of Educational Professions Development. (ERIC Document Reproduction Service No. ED 040 253)

National Center for Education Statistics. (2011). *National Assessment of Educational Progress.* Washington, DC: Author. Retrieved January 24, 2012, from http://nces.ed.gov/nations reportcard

National Center for Fair and Open Testing. (2011). *Would foreign students score proficient on NAEP?* Jamaica Plain, MA: Author. Retrieved December 28, 2011, from: http://fairtest.org/would-foreign-students-score-proficient-naep

Obama, B. (2011, January 25). *State of the Union address.* Washington, DC: White House. Retrieved December 29, 2011, from http://www.whitehouse.gov/the-press-office/2011/01/25/remarks-president-state-union-address

Organisation for Economic Co-operation and Development. (2011a). *What can parents do to help their children succeed in school?* Paris: Author. Retrieved from http://www.pisa.oecd.org/dataoecd/4/1/49012097.pdf

Organisation for Economic Co-operation and Development. (2011b). *What PISA is.* Paris: Author. Retrieved December 27, 2011, from http://www.pisa.oecd.org/pages/0,3417,en_32252351_32235907_1_1_1_1_1,00.html

Organisation for Economic Co-operation and Development. (2012). *Programme for international student assessment*. Paris: Author. Retrieved January 31, 2012, from http://www.oecd.org/department/0,3355,en_2649_35845621_1_1_1_1_1,00.html

Ormrod, J. E. (2006). *Essentials for educational psychology*. Columbus, OH: Pearson.

Paulson, A. (2010, December 7). US students halt academic "free-fall," but still lag in global testing. *Christian Science Monitor*. Retrieved December 23, 2011, from http://www.csmonitor.com/USA/Education/2010/1207/US-students-halt-academic-free-fall-but-still-lag-in-global-testing/%28page%29/2

Peterson, P. E., & Hess, F. M. (2008). Few states set world class standards. *Education Next, 8*(3), 70–73.

Popham, J. (2001). *The truth about testing: An educator's call to action*. Alexandria, VA: Association for Supervision and Curriculum Development.

Rosenberger, B. (2008, March 21). Study: State must improve test scores. *Herald-Dispatch*. Retrieved January 18, 2012, from: http://www.herald-dispatch.com/news/x2087241981

Sahlberg, P. (2009). Educational change in Finland. In A. Hargreaves, M. Fullan, A. Lieberman, & D. Hopkins (Eds.), *International handbook of educational change* (pp. 1–28). New York: Springer.

Sahlberg, P. (2011). *Finnish lessons: What can the world learn from educational change in Finland?* New York: Teachers College Press.

Sheldon, S. B., & Epstein, J. L. (2005). Involvement counts: Family and community partnerships and mathematics achievement. *Journal of Educational Research, 98*(4), 196–206.

Simonton, D. K. (2001). Talent development as a multidimensional, multiplicative, and dynamic process. *Current Directions in Psychological Science, 10*, 39–42.

Skinner, B. F. (1969). *Contingencies of reinforcement*. New York: Appleton-Century-Crofts.

Spoth, R., Randall, G. K., & Shin, C. (2008). Increasing school success through partnership-based family competency training: Experimental study on long-term outcomes. *School Psychology Quarterly, 23*(1), 70–89.

Stanat, P., Artelt, C., Baumert, J., Klieme, E., Neubrand, M., Prenzel, M., et al. (2002). *PISA 2000: Overview of the study design, method and results*. Berlin, Germany: Max Planck Institute for Human Development. Retrieved January 18, 2012, from http://www.mpib-berlin.mpg.de/Pisa/PISA-2000_Overview-2.pdf

Stotsky, S., & Wurman, Z. (2010, July). *Common core standards still don't make the grade: Why Massachusetts and California must regain control over their academic destinies* (White Paper No. 65). Boston: Pioneer Institute.

Strauss, V. (2011, November). What the new NAEP test results tell us. *Washington Post*. Retrieved December 28, 2011, from http://www.washingtonpost.com/blogs/answer-sheet/post/what-the-new-naep-test-results-really-tell-us/2011/11/01/gIQADSOtcM_blog.html

Swearer, S. M., Espelage, D. L., Vaillancourt, T., & Hymel, S. (2010). What can be done about school bullying? Linking research to educational practice. *Educational Researcher, 39*, 38–47.

Symonds, W. C., Schwartz, R., & Ferguson, R. F. (2011). *Pathways to prosperity: Meeting the challenge of preparing young Americans for the 21st century*. Cambridge, MA: Pathways to Prosperity Project, Harvard University Graduate School of Education.

Tonn, J. L. (2005, June 8). Keeping in touch. *Education Week*.

Uguroglu, M. E., & Walberh, H. J. (1979). Motivation and achievement: A quantitative synthesis. *American Education Research Journal, 16*(4), 375–389.

University of New Hampshire. (2008, May 27). Parental involvement strongly impacts student achievement. *Science Daily*. Retrieved January 18, 2012, from http://www.sciencedaily.com/releases/2008/05/080527123852.htm

University of Pennsylvania. (2011, April 26). Penn research demonstrates motivation plays a critical role in determining IQ test scores. *Penn News*. Retrieved January 19, 2011, from http://www.upenn.edu/pennnews/news/penn-research-demonstrates-motivation-plays-critical-role-determining-iq-test-scores

Usher, A. (2011, April 28). *Update with 2009–10 data and five-year trends: How many schools have not made adequate yearly progress?* Washington, DC: Center on Education Policy. Retrieved January 10, 2012, from http://www.cep-dc.org/displayDocument.cfm?DocumentID=357

Wolf, R. (1966). The measurement of environments. In A. Anastasi (Ed.), *Testing problems in perspective* (pp. 491–503). Washington, DC: American Council on Education.

Wynne, E. (1972). *The politics of school accountability*. Richmond, CA: McCutchan Publishing.

CHAPTER 24

Prosocial Education

Weaving a Tapestry to Support Policy and Practice

PHILIP M. BROWN AND MAURICE J. ELIAS

SETTING THE STAGE: WHY POLICY MATTERS

Like other services that must be delivered to meet the needs of individual citizens, education in America is a joint responsibility of the federal, state, and local governments. The contemporary debate regarding control of educational policy draws its intensity from a complex mix of history, politics, and economics and is all too rarely guided by research or informed practice regarding how schools can help children grow up to be successfully functioning twenty-first-century human beings. The threads of prosocial education represented in this book weave a tapestry that when viewed as a whole speaks to the human condition in our time, to our responsibility to nurture and teach the next generation so it can thrive. It is a tapestry that can be seen in the warp and woof of well-designed, research-based practices that make it strong. The quality of the fabric can be felt through the deft and often calloused hands of the teachers, principals, and researchers who have created it. It is a tapestry that is rich in technical know-how about what it takes for educators to support the development of children and young adults so they are equipped to handle the tests of life, not just a life of tests. Our purpose is to turn the heads of policy makers from Washington, D.C., to local boards of education so that they have the opportunity to view the richness of this tapestry. The chapters in part 2 of this book enable these readers to identify the qualities that make the prosocial tapestry useful and long lasting. The case studies that accompany these chapters are designed to speak as well to practitioners, to assist them in understanding the decisions they must make in choosing a tapestry of adequate design, color, and texture that will facilitate their work to move all children forward.

This chapter argues that there is good reason to consider promoting prosocial education for policy purposes because it is based on sound principles of human development and years of convergent research. Prosocial education is an umbrella concept that is inclusive and integrative of the various strands that have been presented in this book; as we have mentioned, these strands can be woven into a variety of strong, beautiful, functional tapestries that are more durable and valuable than any one or two of the strands themselves. The aim of policy is to articulate positions that when implemented have a broad and potentially powerful impact on systems. As we have seen so clearly during the reign of the No Child Left Behind Act (NCLB), policy decisions at high levels can and do drive and constrain decisions down the line at the state and local levels. Virtually every teacher in every classroom in every public school in the country has been affected in one way or another by the implementation of NCLB in terms of curriculum taught, time spent preparing for high-stakes standardized tests, and how district and school resources are allocated. Research and practice in prosocial education create a mandate for policy makers to ensure that educators focus on important developmental outcomes that are in fact essential for academic success and closing the achievement gap (see chapters 9, 11, 13, 15, 19, and 23).

The challenge and need for new ways to explain the threads of prosocial education is illustrated in a report prepared by the RMC Research Corporation and commissioned by the Foundation for Character Development, a Colorado organization that was searching for ways to gain traction in communicating with policy makers and lawmakers as well as with prospective funders of their work. RMC interviewed eight national and twenty-two state and local experts and supporters and found no consensus about what language to use to frame their work. Their conclusion was that character development needs to be rebranded "to focus on outcomes that are important primarily to schools but also to parents, community members, and the business community" (Billig, 2009, p. i). The report notes that the respondents had multiple terms they used to describe this work. The terms "tended to either connote the need to help young people develop specific knowledge, skills, and/or dispositions (individual character) or the need for a system to play a role in supporting youth development by encouraging specific types of connections, relationships, or climate (system support)" (Billig, 2009, p. 3). The complexity of the challenge as well as a direction in which to head is signaled by one of the study respondents who said, "People want to see responsibility and ethics nurtured in children, but it has to be blended into the larger context of adolescent growth and youth development" (Billig, 2009, p. 11).

THE HISTORICAL THREAD

The research cited throughout this book, much of it conducted in the last twenty years, has greatly strengthened the case for prosocial education. Proponents of free public education from Thomas Jefferson to Horace Mann have similarly argued that it is not enough simply to be born into a democracy; individuals must learn to engage in democratic action if they are to continue to govern themselves. As Margaret Branson discusses in chapter 7, for more than 150 years public schools have been viewed by Americans as the primary state institution *to provide opportunities for young people to become civically engaged.*

Education reforms from the 1980s to the present day have focused primarily on establishing and meeting educational standards and on making sure young people are well prepared for higher education or the workplace. But comparatively little attention has been paid to what it means to prepare young people to participate fully in our democracy—especially in those dimensions of participation that go beyond mere knowledge of government to include the development of skills, attitudes, and dispositions needed to sustain and continually renew our traditions of self-governance. In creating a democratic self, young people need to learn how to bring their fellow citizens together around common concerns; how to give a loud but articulate voice to their ideas, support, and objections; how to persevere when faced with disagreement or opposition; and how to not lose heart when they have lost a battle.

Education policy in this country has gradually sidelined much of what has been learned that could be applied to enhancing student development and enabling schools to become nurturing places. Instead of fostering the full growth of human beings, contemporary schooling too often is limited to focusing on a narrow set of academic skills. How did this come to be?

Unlike the systems of most other countries, education in the United States is highly decentralized. Those who have attempted to take on the task of setting a national education policy direction in such a decentralized system have discovered that it is a messy affair. Historically, the federal government and Department of Education have not been heavily involved in determining curricula or educational standards; until the enactment of the No Child Left Behind Act of 2001, this was left almost entirely in the hands of state agencies and locally elected school boards. The structure of education finance in America reflects this predominant state and local role. Of an estimated $1.13 trillion being spent nationwide on education at all levels for school year 2010/11, a substantial majority will come from state, local, and private sources. This is especially true at the elementary and secondary level, where about 89.2 percent of the funds will come from nonfederal sources (U.S. Department of Education, 2011). The interplay between federally targeted and block-granted funding and state and local funding, with the accompanying regulatory and reporting requirements, creates a complexity that maps well onto the complexity of decision making that faces educational administrators at all levels.

Sputnik and the National Defense Education Act

A number of events took place in the last half of the twentieth century that began to shift the perception of national policy and government leaders and increased the receptivity of the public to a greater federal hand in guiding the curriculum and expectations of their schools and teachers. Sputnik 1 was launched by the Soviet Union on October 4, 1957. This small satellite, only about twenty-three inches in diameter and weighing less than two hundred pounds, was a projectile heard about around the world. Although the Eisenhower administration had announced plans to orbit an artificial satellite in the International Geophysical year, the Soviets unexpectedly beat the United States to it. In the context of the Cold War, this was understood by the United States not as an admirable accomplishment for mankind, but as a direct threat to our military and technological supremacy. With the fear still alive of how close Germany could have come to world domination if it had created better rockets or an atomic bomb, and the realization of how critical it was in this new age to have the best-prepared scientists in the world, it was easy to sell increased federal funding on education to the American public (Peoples, 2008).

Within less than a year of Sputnik, Congress passed, and President Eisenhower signed, the National Defense Education Act, which was the most far-reaching federally sponsored education initiative in the nation's history to that point. The bill authorized expenditures of more than $1 billion for a wide range of reforms including new school construction, fellowships, and loans to encourage promising students to seek higher education opportunities (*Encyclopedia Britannica*, 2011).

From ESEA to NCLB

Work on crafting the Elementary and Secondary Education Act (ESEA), which began during the Kennedy administration, already had as a backdrop the implications of the Supreme Court's 1954 *Brown v. Board of Education* decision outlawing public schools that were organized to separate the races. It was clear that national policy needed to address the politics of school funding for as yet segregated schools, particularly in the South. After Kennedy's assassination in November 1963, President Lyndon B. Johnson made education and civil rights the foundation of his War on Poverty. The Civil Rights Act was signed into law in 1964, and the ESEA followed on its heels and was signed into law in 1965, launching a comprehensive set of programs, including the Title I program of federal aid to disadvantaged children to address the problems of poor urban and rural areas, which began to tie together the issues of poverty, race, and educational opportunity (U.S. Department of Education, 2011).

Not long after ESEA was enacted, Congress commissioned James Coleman, a Johns Hopkins University professor, to conduct a study for the purpose of better understanding the extent of education inequality in the United States. This study of six hundred thousand children in four thousand schools titled "Equality of Educational Opportunity" (or often simply called the "Coleman Report") was issued in 1966 and argued that student background and socioeconomic status are much more important in determining educational outcomes than are differences in school resources (Hanushek, 1998). During the 1970s, two pieces of legislation were enacted that were consistent with the aims of the civil rights movement and reflected the ongoing influence of the Coleman Report. In 1974, the Equal Education Opportunity Act (EEO) was passed, which outlawed discrimination in public education on the basis of race, color, sex, or national origin. Among other provisions, EEO ushered in different approaches to educating English language learners. This was followed in 1975 by the Education of All Handicapped Children Act, often referred to by its legal reference, PL 94–142, which secured the entitlement of disabled children to a public education that met their individual needs in the least restrictive environment. Over time both of these laws have changed the face of American educational policy and practice at the state and local levels. They also are important anchors for the goal of prosocial education to support students in reaching their developmental potential. The principle of inclusion of all students in public school classrooms is at the heart of a prosocial vision of the civic mission of education.

Other progressive and conservative movements of the 1970s were also influential in setting the stage for twenty-first-century educational policy debates. There was the open classroom movement that called for a student-centered approach to instruction; the emergence of community and alternative schools that experimented with new democratic structures; values clarification, a relativistic version of teaching values that lacked standards; and the back-to-basics movement which became an increasingly powerful reaction against these and other progressive reforms. The final act of the 1970s was the creation of the U.S. Department of Education. There was no cabinet-level federal education agency until 1979, when it was established by Public Law 96–88 and signed into law by President Jimmy Carter. The creation of the agency was opposed by many Republican lawmakers, and its very existence has remained a bone of contention since its inception, with conservative politicians, starting with President Ronald Reagan, calling for its abolition.

The Reagan administration began looking for a way to establish its own educational policy, and in 1983, following eighteen months of study, its National Commission on Excellence in Education issued a report, *A Nation at Risk* (U.S. Department of Education, 1983), that started policy makers down a path that eventually led to the revision of the ESEA in 2001, the No Child Left Behind Act. The lofty rhetoric of the report begins with a statement that sets the tone not only of the report but of the school reform efforts that succeeded it:

> Our Nation is at risk. Our once unchallenged preeminence in commerce, industry, science, and technological innovation is being overtaken by competitors throughout the world. This report is concerned with only one of the many causes and dimensions of the problem, but it is the one that undergirds American prosperity, security, and civility. We report to the American people that while we can take justifiable pride in what our schools and colleges have historically accomplished and contributed to the United States and the well-being of its people, the educational foundations of our society are presently being eroded by a rising tide of mediocrity that threatens our very future as a Nation and a people. What was unimaginable a generation ago has begun to occur—others are matching and surpassing our educational attainments. (para. 1)

A Nation at Risk is widely credited with getting the public's attention regarding the need to make schools function better. But it also had significant critics. As John Goodlad (1997) put it in a paper on school reform, the report directed the country to narrow the original focus of ESEA,

> using military language in charging our schools with instrumentality in ensuring our nation's leadership in the global economy. Local districts and states were to carry out the crusade. Theodore Sizer wrote a little piece in reply that would have been hilarious had it not been so tragically true. There was to be no mounting of the necessary weaponry, he contended. The country folk would do battle with their customary shovels, hoes, and rakes. State-appointed commissions wrote thousands of pages of reports, selecting carefully and repeating endlessly the same data and horror stories designed to arouse the populace from its perceived over-satisfaction and lethargy regarding the schools. A self-fulfilling rhetorical prophecy of school failure was engendered and tied to a narrative of dire consequences for what Neil Postman refers to as the god of economic utility. (para. 8)

Tying the purpose of education to economic utility continued to gain momentum as the dominant theme in school reform. In both the Bush and Clinton administrations, market reforms of various kinds were advocated for public education. The idea that public school structures were remnants of the industrial age took hold, with business leaders advocating realignment with the practices of high-performance private sector organizations (Ravitch, 2010). Thus was born the search for uniform standards, the charter school movement, an emphasis on accountability, and the search for objective measures of teacher and school success through student output on standardized tests. After a politically charged reaction to the attempt to form national standards for history curricula under the first Bush administration, the Clinton administration presided over the Goals 2000: Educate America Act in 1994 and provided funding to states to develop their own standards, which was part of a reemphasis on state-led educational reform.

By the dawn of the twenty-first century, the themes that had emerged in the previous fifty years became a perfect storm, with calls for innovation, further deregulation, privatization through school choice, and attempts to require or incentivize large-scale adoption of research-based programs. At the same time came renewed calls for equitable distribution of resources and continued legal wrangling regarding the limits of desegregation. The stage was set for the No Child Left Behind legislation enacted with broad support in 2002.

As McGuinn (2006) points out, the original ESEA legislation was narrowly targeted; mainly it directed federal funds to support the needs of disadvantaged students and contained few federal mandates. In contrast, NCLB embraces a much broader scope. Its requirements apply to all public schools and students, and "it focuses on outputs (measuring academic performance), and is remarkably prescriptive" (p. 1). There is general agreement that NCLB directed our consciousness to the wide disparities in achievement between economically advantaged and disadvantaged students, majority and minority students, native speakers of English and students for whom English is a new language, and regular education students and students with exceptional needs. In this sense it attempted to tighten the federal reins on the promise of the civil rights acts of the 1970s by flagging differences in student performance based on disaggregating data by these categories, thus shining a light on long-standing inequalities. The law is also credited with having brought useful attention to the qualification of teachers, an issue of particular importance in schools serving low-income, minority children (Darling-Hammond, 2010).

However, Pedro Noguera, sociologist and urban school authority, puts it succinctly: "Drawing attention to the problem is not the same as solving it" (Noguera, 2011, para. 7). As he looks over the current status and impact of NCLB, Noguera sees inequities and gaps in resources and reform strategies that work against the stated goal of the law. He agrees with others that implementation of the law appears to have exacerbated some of the very problems it hoped to address. As Rose (2009) points out, for example, by focusing on a "no excuses" stance toward the unacceptable record we have with the targeted populations and by using a model of mind that defines development in terms of "test scores, rankings and the technology of calibration and compliance" (p. 52), NCLB has shifted attention from the larger economic and social conditions that affect academic achievement. Eugene Garcia (Rebell & Wolff, 2009) traces the history of changes in federal policies from the first passage of ESEA and argues that NCLB is out of sync with practices that could reduce the learning gaps it seeks to close. He calls for an inclusive approach to pedagogy that "argues for the respect and integration of the students' values, beliefs, histories, and experiences and recognizes the active role that students must play in the learning process" (p. 99).

The NCLB Scorecard

Linda Darling-Hammond (2010), one of our most astute observers of educational reform efforts, credits a few states, such as Connecticut, North Carolina, and New Jersey, with producing standards that have clarified and upgraded instructional goals to guide student learning, invested in high-quality learning materials and teaching, and/or constructed assessments thoughtfully. In these states, education for underserved students has improved. However, in states where low-quality tests have driven a narrow curriculum and states like California where investment has been low and policy mismanaged, "discouraged students and overwhelmed schools have produced higher dropout rates rather than higher standards, leaving the society to contend with a greater number of young people placed into the growing school-to-prison pipeline" (p. 67).

What are the results of the new federal education policy? States have made progress in setting their own standards and grading their own progress, which has led to vastly inflated claims of progress and confusion about standards, all in the hope that we will become more competitive with other nations that have been more successful in preparing students for the twenty-first-century workforce. The NCLB measure of school-level progress in meeting reading and math goals is annual yearly progress (AYP). For 2011, the most recent year for which data were available, states as diverse as Florida, New Mexico, Missouri, Vermont, and New Hampshire all reported that more that 70 percent of their schools failed to make AYP test score targets (McNeil, 2011). According to Eric Schaps, the founder and president of the highly regarded Developmental Studies Center, the problems with NCLB can be traced back to the 1980s and the *Nation at Risk* report, which began a rhetorical stance that has denigrated and disempowered American schools and educators. He believes that the current result has been a disaster for those who believe in Dewey's vision of progressive education (see more on Dewey's contribution to the tenets of prosocial education in the case study "Philosophy as Pro social Education" accompanying chapter 8).

> Even in schools [that he has worked with] where there is courageous, enlightened leadership, over the past few years there has been a gradual knuckling under to the untoward, counterproductive, short-term pressures created by cheap, test-based high-stakes accountability systems. The result is that classroom practice and the curriculum gets highly distorted as the amount of time for test-prep goes up, up, and up and the autonomy and morale of teachers goes down, down, and down. (E. Schaps, personal communication, June 13, 2011)

We agree with historian Diane Ravitch's (2010) point of view in characterizing the essential failure of NCLB as a blueprint for educational change. She calls it a technocratic approach to school reform that measures success only in relationship to standardized test scores in reading and math. By focusing on accountability measured by such a narrow definition of education, she says, "NCLB essentially ignores the importance of having a rich, well-balanced, and coherent curriculum and degrades the importance of knowledge itself" (p. 29). "There is a certain irony in the NCLB name, which was appropriated from Marian Wright Edelman of the anti-poverty advocacy group, the Children's Defense Fund, who used it to refer to children's health and welfare, not to testing and accountability" (p. 93). Prosocial education embraces the call for a comprehensive approach to development that promotes children's health and welfare, which includes intellectual, social, emotional, and moral development. Examples of schools that do all of this well are seen in many of the case studies presented in part 2 of this book. Take a look at the Ridgewood Middle School in rural Missouri (see the case study "Leading in the Middle: A Tale of Prosocial Education Reform in Two Principals and Two Middle Schools" accompanying chapter 17), where over a ten-year period disciplinary incidents declined from three thousand to three hundred and state achievement scores in mathematics rose from 7 percent to 71 percent, and all this was done without changing academic curriculum or textbooks; they changed how they met the social, emotional, and character development needs of their students. Or look at the Arts and Technology Academy charter school in a high-poverty and crime-infested area of Washington, D.C. (see the case study accompanying chapter 9, "School Climate: The Road Map to Student Achievement"), where there has been a 42 percent drop in behavior referrals and an increase in academic achievement levels each of the past four years. How did they do it? The school used a comprehensive school climate survey as the basis for making collaboratively driven decisions that focused on areas such as staff and student trust and relationship building.

What have other countries done that are frequently looked to as reform models with good results? Finland is one of the world leaders in successful educational systems transformation, accomplished during the same period the country experienced growing ethnic and linguistic diversity. Starting in the 1980s, Finland dismantled its rigid tracking system and eliminated its state-mandated testing system, replacing it with a focus on upgrading the teacher preparation system and a curriculum "focused on problem solving, creativity, independent learning, and student reflection" (Darling-Hammond, 2010, p. 5). Prosocial educators could look for guidance at the Finnish reform model. Finland has focused on the long term, creating systems that select good people, prepare them well, and support their development over time and over their careers (E. Schaps, personal communication, June 13, 2011). In a succinct statement of the drivers behind its reform efforts, Finnish policy analyst Pasi Sahlberg describes the framework his country has adopted this way: "Finnish education policies are a result of four decades of systematic, mostly intentional development that has created a culture of diversity, trust, and respect within Finnish society, in general, and within its educational system, in particular" (Sahlberg, 2009, p. 10). At or near the pinnacle of that culture of respect are teachers, who are recognized socially, professionally, and financially as crucial to the health of the entire nation.

SOCIAL REALITY IN AMERICA: WHAT PART CAN PROSOCIAL EDUCATION PLAY?

There are many ways of diagnosing social ills that can help shape our understanding of what kind of people we are and what steps we should take to reduce problems that affect our personal and collective aspirations and create the kind of society we want to live in. While it is not the intent here to describe the current state of social affairs in America, it is important to identify significant signposts and patterns that may serve to clarify our condition and help contextualize the need for prosocial education.

One such signpost is the nation's penchant for attempting to solve the problems that result from our social ills by incarceration. The high rates of school failure and dropping out that plague many American cities and rural areas have a variety of repercussions. A study of incarceration among black men born between 1965 and 1969 based on administrative, survey, and census data estimates that 60 percent of high school dropouts went to prison by the time they were thirty-five years old (Pettit & Western, 2004). As Linda Darling-Hammond (2010) points out, failure in school feeds the school-to-prison pipeline. In California, it costs forty-six thousand dollars per year to incarcerate a prisoner, but the state spends less than ten thousand dollars per year to educate a child (California Department of Education, 2011). While there is little public financial support for prosocial education, many of the protective factors that have proven effective in keeping kids in school are embedded within prosocial education (see chapter 13).

We appear to have brought our search for individual accountability into education by implementing a punitive national educational policy framework that punishes failing schools just as we punish recreational drug users, addicts, and sellers. We seek accountability measures first before we have understood or acknowledged the depth and origins of the problem; we devise a hodgepodge of standards to measure success or failure, provide some funds for failing schools without adequate guidance or support, and then we punish schools that fail to meet the standards. As Eric Schaps puts it,

> All of these reforms were launched with almost no research base. They had an ideological logic to them that was appealing, a business ideology or belief that the current systems are moribund and need to be dismantled however they can be. Research rarely drives policy; it adorns policy decisions that are made on other bases. (personal communication, June 13, 2011)

Narcissism, Violence, the Digital World, and Its Impact on Prosocial Values

In addition to our fear of being outperformed by our competitors in the global economy and our willingness to pay for better jails instead of investing in better schools, other social forces are at work that are a challenge to prosocial values. We will briefly examine two features of the current social and educational landscape that help illuminate the complexities of the dilemmas we face and the opportunities that prosocial approaches offer to understand them better. First, we look at what we know or may not know about the role of media and the digital revolution in influencing both antisocial and prosocial behavior and what has been characterized as the growing trend toward more narcissistic views and behaviors of America's youth. Then we examine the prevalence of cheating in America's schools and what it seems to imply about the impact of current educational policy on the prosocial behavior of both students and educators.

With the proliferation of access to information, entertainment, and interpersonal communications that has occurred due to the digital revolution, it is fair to ask whether schools are the main place where socializing influences take place. As we shall see, the jury is still out regarding whether the digital access to our world is having a predominantly prosocial or antisocial impact. As with all learning technologies from the pencil to the iPad, the key questions are how are they being used, by whom (think developmentally), and for what purpose? The reason for concern is obvious: children from birth to age six spend more time on entertainment media than on reading, being read to, and playing outside combined (Rideout, Vandewater, & Wartella, 2003). In a meta-analysis of seventy-two different studies of American college students conducted between 1979 and 2009, Konrath and colleagues found a decline in both empathic concern and perspective taking (Konrath, O'Brien, & Hsing, 2011). When comparing college students of the late 1970s with today's students, the study found that college students today are less likely to agree with statements such as "I sometimes try to understand my friends better by imagining how things look from their perspective" and "I often have tender, concerned feelings for people less fortunate than me." In a related but separate analysis of these data, Konrath found that nationally representative samples of Americans see changes in other people's kindness and helpfulness over a similar time period. According to Konrath (as cited in Fisher, 2010):

> The increase in exposure to media during this time period could be one factor [influencing this change]. . . . Compared to 30 years ago, the average American now is exposed to three times as much nonwork-related information. In terms of media content, this generation of college students grew up with video games, and a growing body of research, including work done by my colleagues at Michigan, is establishing that exposure to violent media numbs people to the pain of others. (para. 9)

Children spend more time consuming entertainment media than engaging in any other activity besides school and sleeping (Roberts, Foehr, Rideout, & Vrodie, 1999). And the content of media, including news, video games, and general prime-time television, contains an increasing amount of violent programming (Media Awareness Network, 2010). A national study of television violence in 1998 (Wilson et al., 1998) reported that 61 percent of programs on television contain some violence. Perhaps more disturbing was the finding that 96 percent of all violent television programs use aggression as a narrative device for entertaining the audience. In other words, violence becomes the story line. The study notes that much of the aggression on television is made more tantalizing so viewers can identify with the perpetrators: 44 percent of the violent interactions on television programs represent perpetrators who have some attractive qualities worthy of emulation. How worried should we be about the impact and effect of this level of antisocial acts of violence on our children and our behavior?

In July 2011, the U.S. Supreme Court ruled 7–2 in *Governor of California et al. v. Entertainment Merchants Association et al.* that the state's attempt to shield young people from violence in video games violates the First Amendment (Walsh, 2011). Writing for the majority, Justice Antonin Scalia described the California law that sought to regulate the sale of violent video games to minors as one more in a series of campaigns to censor violent entertainment for minors. So far in the United States, obscenity is the only grounds for restricting access to entertainment. A public television network can be liable for a musician revealing an unclad female human breast, but a video gamer can kill and mutilate the body of an opposing player in the virtual reality that so many young people inhabit for hours every week. Clearly, the psychological research community has not done enough to persuade the justices of the well-established impact of video game violence on behavior. In his opinion, Justice Scalia wrote, "Psychological studies purporting to show a connection between exposure to violent video games and harmful effects on children do not prove that such exposure causes minors to act aggressively" (*Brown et al. v. Entertainment Merchants Assn. et al.*, 2011, p. 13). What is the state of the evidence that Justice Scalia finds unconvincing? A summary of the research on violent television and films, video games, and music (Anderson et al., 2003) indicates

> unequivocal evidence that media violence increases the likelihood of aggressive and violent behavior in both immediate and long-term contexts. Short-term exposure increases the likelihood of physically and verbally aggressive behavior, aggressive thoughts, and aggressive emotions. Recent large-scale longitudinal studies provide converging evidence linking frequent exposure to violent media in childhood with aggression later in life, including physical assaults and spouse abuse. (p. 81)

What are the mechanisms that translate media violence into antisocial behavior? According to Anderson and his colleagues (2003),

> Media violence produces short-term increases by priming existing aggressive scripts and cognitions, increasing physiological arousal, and triggering an automatic tendency to imitate observed behaviors. Media violence produces long-term effects via several types of learning processes leading to the acquisition of lasting (and automatically accessible) aggressive scripts, interpretational schemas, and aggression-supporting beliefs about social behavior, and by reducing individuals' normal negative emotional responses to violence (i.e., desensitization). (p. 81)

In summarizing the impact of media violence on youth, the report notes that it has become common parlance to describe our use of entertainment media in nutritional terms, such as "media consumption" and "a steady diet of violence." Implicitly, perhaps, we

> recognize that nourishing children's minds through the media is like nourishing their bodies. In both cases, from a public-health perspective, today's consumption patterns are far from optimal. And for many youths, they are clearly harmful. The challenge is to discover how to provide more nourishing fare. (p. 106)

In their meta-analysis of changes in empathy of college students over time, Konrath and colleagues (2011) suggest that in addition to the impact of media exposure on antisocial behavior, the increased use of personal technology and social media may also play a role in a drop in empathy. They conjecture that the ease of making friends online may have the effect of making people less likely to respond to others' problems on- and offline. It is also reasonable to think that the speed and truncated nature of digital communications, such as text messaging, as well as the inability to convey subtle emotions, are not conducive to the deep listening that evokes empathic responses. The content of media to which we are exposed is also a potential factor in altering the interpersonal landscape. For example, Konrath points to the dominant popularity of reality programming on television (Murray & Ouellette, 2008, as cited in Konrath et al., 2011) and notes that these shows commonly portray narcissistic characters (Young & Pinsky, 2006, as cited in Konrath et al., 2011) who do not serve as empathic role models.

For the time being, efforts to reduce the impact of media violence on children and our social well-being is in the hands of parents, educators, and the general public. There is no sign that the government will push back against the commercial interests that dominate both digital devices and media content.

Prosocial Media and Games

If the research evidence points to the impact of media and digital game violence on aggressiveness and antisocial behavior, can prosocial entertainment media have positive behavioral outcomes? In an attempt to answer one aspect of this question, researchers in Singapore, Japan, and the United States reviewed correlational, longitudinal, and experimental studies of the effects of prosocial video games played by three different age-groups of youth on prosocial behaviors (Gentile et al., 2009). In the Singapore study of middle school students, those who played more prosocial games behaved more prosocially; in the Japanese study which followed students from childhood into adolescence, prosocial game play was predictive of later prosocial behavior; and in the experimental study, "U.S. undergraduates playing prosocial games behaved more prosocially toward another student than those who did not play the games" (p. 753). In summarizing their review of the three studies, the authors conclude that the content of digital media games matters, particularly because games are excellent teachers:

> Video games are not inherently good or bad, just as any tool is not inherently good or bad. For example, an axe can be used to split logs for a fire to keep people warm on a cold day or it can be used as a weapon. Likewise, video games can have both positive and negative effects. Violent content in video games can lead people to behave more aggressively. Prosocial content, in contrast, can lead people to behave in a more cooperative and helpful manner. (p. 762)

How will the Internet play a role in the next generation's involvement in our democracy? A panel study assessed more than 2,500 young people (ages sixteen to twenty-one), 400 of whom were followed for more than three years, regarding the kinds of online activities that were associated with civic and political activity (Kahne, Middaugh, Lee, & Feezell, 2010). A number of the findings from this study contradicted conventional wisdom. Spending time in online communities appears to promote engagement with society. The research suggests that young people who become very involved with online communities tend to increase their offline prosocial activities such as volunteering, work with charities and with neighbors, community problem solving, and protest activity. The study findings indicate that the Internet can provide a gateway to greater civic and political engagement, that young people benefit from formal assistance in learning to use the digital resources, and that media literacy education can dramatically increase students' exposure to diverse perspectives.

Another example of how the Internet offers avenues of prosocial action that would have been unheard of at the turn of the century is the ability to generate petitions that go viral. A *New York Times* article by Nicholas Kristof, "After Recess: Change the World," tells the story of a class of fourteen Massachusetts fourth graders who were upset when they discovered that the website advertising the Universal Studios film version of the Dr. Seuss story "The Lorax" ignored the environmental themes at the heart of the story. So they started a petition on Change.org. They demanded that Universal Studios "let the Lorax speak for the trees." The petition quickly gathered more than fifty-seven thousand signatures, and the studio updated its movie site with the environmental message that the students had dictated. This is no longer an isolated case, and, as Kristof says, it's a good example of how these students "have shown that the Web can turn the world upside down" (Kristof, 2012, para. 4).

Education policy makers should carefully consider the role schools can play in helping children to manage this interface between the media and digital world and their role as active participants in the social fabric. It seems fair to ask, for example, are young people turning to civic engagement via the Internet because their schools are not giving them live opportunities to have a voice and participate in making changes in their schools and communities? There are many examples of the power of these experiences on students, teachers, and school culture documented in this volume—see, for example, the chapters and accompanying case studies on service learning (chapter 10) and civic education (chapter 7).

Cheating

Prosocial education is not only important because it facilitates healthy developmental outcomes and helps create capable people. The moral and ethical acumen that is necessary for successful community building and democratic institutions that serve us all is as important as social and cognitive skills. Man-made disasters from Enron to the 2008 economic meltdown were caused by the immoral acts and antisocial behavior of smart people at the highest level of the corporate world, sometimes in tacit collusion with equally smart government officials. It is important to look at the cultural conditions we have created that have led to these costs. One view into the normative behaviors that may lead to unfettered self-aggrandizement is the acceptance of cheating to get good grades in school.

Cheating in school is hardly a recent phenomenon. Cheating in college has been well documented since 1964 when a study by William Bowers found that three-quarters of all students engaged in some kind of cheating (Bowers, 1964). McCabe and colleagues (2001) conducted surveys throughout the 1990s and found a slightly higher prevalence of cheating in higher education institutions, but their studies revealed that more serious cheating, on exams for example, increased significantly during the decade. McCabe and Treviño (1993) summarized what they learned about the primary context for this increase:

> The strong influence of peers' behavior may suggest that academic dishonesty not only is learned from observing the behavior of peers, but that peers' behavior provides a kind of normative support for cheating. The fact that others are cheating may also suggest that, in such a climate, the non-cheater feels left at a disadvantage. Thus cheating may come to be viewed as an acceptable way of getting and staying ahead. (p. 533)

Why has it become so necessary to be at the top of the pack, and what are the repercussions for later adult behavior? It is a common mantra now that in the knowledge economy, finding a good job depends on getting a good education, or more precisely, getting a college degree, and increasingly, graduate degrees. The pressure to get a degree from a high-status institution persists although there is little evidence that bright students from lesser schools are not as capable. In *The Cheating Culture*, David Callahan (2004) describes the relationship between the obsession with degrees from branded colleges and getting on the track to the "winning class." The earning gap between those with high school educations and college and professional degrees more than doubled between 1975 and 1999 according to U.S. Census Bureau data (2002). This pressure translates down into how parents understand their desires for their children's success and their responsibility for guiding them. Should we be surprised that cheating is on the rise when our children get the message that what matters is getting the grades that will get them into the schools that meet their parents' expectations? Or as McCabe and colleagues (2001) put it,

> With increasing competition for the most desired positions in the job market and for the few coveted places available at the nation's leading business, law, and medical schools, today's undergraduates experience considerable pressure to do well. Research shows that all too often these pressures lead to decisions to engage in various forms of academic dishonesty. (p. 220)

Both individual and organizational or contextual factors are sources of influence on cheating behaviors (McCabe et al., 2001). Individual differences in cheating are influenced by factors such as the pressure to get high grades, having lower grades, parental pressures, a desire to excel, pressure to get a job, laziness, a lack of responsibility, a lack of character, poor self-image, a lack of pride in a job well done, and a lack of personal integrity. Students engaged in athletics and other extracurricular activities reported more cheating, and McCabe and colleagues (1997, 2001) conjecture that this may be due to the time demands that these activities place on students, leading to their decision to take shortcuts to remain competitive in their course work. Students who cheat commonly engage in neutralization processes to explain away their dishonest behavior through rationalization, denial, deflecting blame to others, and condemning their accusers (Haines, Diekhoff, LaBeff, & Clark, 1986).

In examining organizational or contextual factors contributing to widespread academic cheating, McCabe and Treviño (1993, 1997) cite institutional factors such as the lack of clear rules regarding unacceptable behavior and the perceived likelihood of getting caught; the degree to which a school has a supportive, trusting atmosphere; competitive pressures; the severity of punishments; and peer pressure to cheat or not to cheat. Bertram-Gallant and Drinan (2006) have a more expanded view of how organizational context impacts student cheating behaviors. When getting an academic credential is viewed as more important than how you get it, the ground has been tilled for a cheating culture, in which cheating is tolerated as normative or acceptable behavior. Norms require language to support them, and for students this can begin with talking about fulfilling class requirements as playing a game to get the desired results. Situational dishonesty is considered acceptable and divorced from the essential integrity of the person. The peer culture then becomes more dominant than institutional values and expectations in governing behavior for many students. Students may ignore or condone cheating among their peers because they recognize the pressures and competition they all face and understand cheating as a necessary coping mechanism. Prosocial education works best when it is embedded in and recognized as a dominant aspect of school culture. This is supported by McCabe and colleagues (2001), who found that one of the main features identified by students in effective honor codes is the degree to which the code is deeply embedded in a culture of integrity.

And what happens when students who have learned cheating as a normative behavior in college or professional schools go on to the workplace? A 2001 study of one thousand business students on six campuses found that "students who engaged in dishonest behavior in their college classes were more likely to engage in dishonest behavior on the job" (Nonis & Swift, 2001, p. 76). Baldwin and Daugherty (1996) found that the best predictor of cheating in medical school was having cheated previously in one's academic career, either in high school or college. Fass (as cited in May, 1990) observed a correlation between cheating in school and cheating in public arenas such as income tax payment, politics, and college athletics. When students leave a cheating culture in school and enter occupations where results and the bottom line are all that matter, instrumentalism pushes other moral imperatives and ethical considerations aside. As Kaplan and Mable (1998) put it, instrumental communities create an egocentric climate in which an individual's needs take precedence over the claims of the community. It is remarkable how well this mirrors descriptions of the ethos inculcated in employees on the Enron trading floor.

This is no less true for the K–12 institutional environment. When values of trust and responsibility are authorized from the top down but are not experienced and reinforced in the daily life of students and staff and in their relationships with one another, this erosion leaves an open field for alternative, instrumental, and self-serving values derived from other sources, such as peer culture or competitive academic survival, to prevail. This corrupts the ethos of school as community and corrodes the purpose of education as the public institution responsible for providing a model for and an introduction to civic life.

What happens to school systems and educators when professional identity and economic survival are threatened by increased accountability unaccompanied by sufficient resources or assistance is vividly portrayed by the large-scale cheating that has occurred in some classrooms, schools, districts, and states under NCLB. A July 13, 2011, article in *Education Week* entitled "Report Details 'Culture of Cheating' in Atlanta Schools" (Samuels, 2011a) reveals how far some Atlanta public schools went to raise test scores in one of the nation's largest-ever cheating scandals:

> Investigators concluded that nearly half the city's schools allowed the cheating to go unchecked for as long as a decade, beginning in 2001. The report names 178 teachers and principals, and 82 of those confessed. Tens of thousands of children at the 44 schools, most in the city's poorest neighborhoods, were allowed to advance to higher grades, even though they didn't know basic concepts. Administrators—pressured to maintain high scores under the federal No Child Left Behind law—punished or fired those who reported anything amiss and created a culture of "fear, intimidation and retaliation." Schools that perform poorly and fail to meet certain benchmarks under the federal law can face sharp sanctions. They may be forced to offer extra tutoring, allow parents to transfer children to better schools, or fire teachers and administrators who don't pass muster. Teachers were either ordered to cheat or pressured by administrators until they felt they had no choice,

authorities said. Experts say the Atlanta cheating scandal has become the new rallying cry for education advocates and parents in other urban districts like Philadelphia, Los Angeles and Washington, D.C., where cheating investigations are ongoing. (para. 4)

In a follow-up article in *Education Week* entitled "Cheating Scandals Intensify Focus on Test Pressures," Christina Samuels (2011b) reminds us of a wise admonition by one of the grandfathers of statistical research in the social sciences:

> While scholars who have attempted to study how wide-spread cheating is in general have reached the conclusion that it ranges from about 5–10%, in cases where the pressure to perform is higher, those number can escalate greatly. Scholars often say such cheating incidents are examples of "Campbell's law" at work. Donald T. Campbell, a social scientist, wrote in the 1970s that "the more any quantitative social indicator is used for social decision making, the more subject it will be to corruption pressures and the more apt it will be to distort and corrupt the social processes it was intended to monitor." (para. 6)

The good news is that this needn't be so. This volume is replete with examples of educators and schools where consensually derived democratic values, the quality of relationships, and the vision of a common purpose to serve the developmental needs of students combine to provide a different model of schooling. Prosocial education lives at the heart of Shelly Berman's successful work in the urban environment of the Jefferson County schools (chapter 19), in preschool (chapter 15) and after-school (chapter 16) programs, and in the many case studies throughout part 2 that describe the way dedicated professionals using a combination of evidence-based approaches and their own ingenuity and experience can create environments that support the development of the whole child.

POSITIVE SIGNS

Now let's take a look at some positive signs that the social fabric in America is not so torn asunder that developing a prosocial education agenda is a hopeless task. We will begin with a brief look at young people's eager involvement in service activities, a sign of their desire to contribute to the welfare of others, as well as to the vitality of their own schools and communities. Next, we will review some of the governmental and private sector supports for programs and approaches that fit with the prosocial education agenda.

Participation in Youth Service

According to Peter Levine of the Center for Information and Research on Civic Learning and Engagement (cited in Fleming, 2011), the most important trend in youth service is a substantial increase over the past forty years. Three-quarters of high school seniors say they volunteer through school, religious, or community organizations, which is up from 63 percent in 1976. The rates of participation vary considerably, says Levine, based on the degree to which different states and localities have traditions of civic engagement, more welcoming civic organizations, and more policies that support service. Approximately 10.6 million young people, or 38 percent of the youth population, have engaged in community service that takes place as part of a school activity or requirement (Corporation for National and Community Service, 2006).

In her chapter on civic education (chapter 7), Margaret Branson mentions a study of eighteen- to twenty-four-year-olds' political attitudes which reveals that almost six in ten (59 percent) said that they were personally interested in engaging in some form of public service to help the country.

An analysis by Fox and colleagues (n.d.) of the motivation behind volunteering for older high-school-age students engaged in thirty-two 4-H service projects in Louisiana supports the relationship between youth service and prosocial education. The most highly rated reasons for volunteering were "I feel compassion toward people in need; I am concerned about those less fortunate than myself; Volunteering allows me to gain a new perspective on things; and I can learn more about the cause for which I am working" (pp. 8–9).

With this good news about the evidence of young people's willingness to serve if there is community support comes a caution. A study by the Search Institute found that from 2000 to 2004 the percentage of public schools participating in service learning declined at every school level (Scales & Roehlkepartain, 2004). The authors believe it is likely that these declines in participation are due to the stringent achievement levels and compliance codes that went into effect with the No Child Left Behind Act of 2001. For more information on the history of service learning and a summary of research on its effects, as well as three stories demonstrating the range and depth of prosocial learning that takes place when students participate, see chapter 10 and the related case studies.

Federal Government Programs

It is safe to say that the very size and complexity of the issues facing our society are reflected in the organizational complexity of the federal government's responses in recognizing and addressing these issues. This frequently leads to incongruous laws, regulations, and fiscal policies. While the policy framework of NCLB is not likely to advance prosocial education, there are federal programs that have the potential to do just that. The following are a few examples.

The U.S. Department of Education (USDOE)

In 2010, the USDOE awarded $38.8 million in Safe and Supportive School (SSS) grants to eleven states to measure school safety and climate at the building level and to provide federal funds for interventions in those schools with the greatest needs based on the assessment data. The ultimate goal of the grants is to create and support safe and drug-free learning environments and increase academic success for students in these high-risk schools (U.S. Department of Education, 2010b).

Funds may be used by state education agencies to develop measurement systems that will enable them to assess conditions for learning within individual schools, including school safety, school engagement (including the relationships between the members of the school community and the extent to which members participate in school activities), and students' perception of the fairness of disciplinary policies, and to make this information publicly available. Using these data, states will work in collaboration with participating local educational agencies to improve the learning environment within schools facing the biggest challenges (U. S. Department of Education, 2010a).

The Centers for Disease Control and Prevention (CDC)

In 2009, the CDC identified school connectedness—the belief held by students that adults and peers in the school care about their learning as well as about them as individuals—as an important protective factor that discourages a range of high-risk behaviors among youth, such as drug use, gang involvement, and early sexual activity (Centers for Disease Control and Prevention, 2009). The CDC school connectedness initiative identifies six prosocial strategies that parents, teachers, and school staff can use to foster social learning environments that facilitate healthy development as well as discourage high-risk behavior:

1. Create decision-making processes that facilitate student, family, and community engagement, academic achievement, and staff empowerment.
2. Provide education and opportunities to enable families to be actively involved in their children's academic and school life.
3. Provide students with the academic, emotional, and social skills necessary to be actively engaged in school.
4. Use effective classroom management and teaching methods to foster a positive learning environment.
5. Provide professional development and support for teachers and other school staff to enable them to meet the diverse cognitive, emotional, and social needs of children and adolescents.
6. Create trusting and caring relationships that promote open communication among administrators, teachers, staff, students, families, and communities. (p. 9)

The CDC initiative also notes the research indicating that students who feel connected to their school are also more likely to have better academic achievement, including higher grades and test scores; have better school attendance; and stay in school longer (CDC, 2009).

Department of Health and Human Services (DHHS)

In 1995, with support from DHHS, the University of California, Los Angeles, established the Center for Mental Health in Schools as part of the federal mental health in schools program. The codirectors of the project, Howard Adelman and Linda Taylor, have created a conceptual framework they call student learning supports as a component in school improvement efforts. Student learning supports are designed to address barriers to learning and teaching, including reengagement of disconnected students (Adelman & Taylor, 2010a). While much of the thrust of the project's work is oriented toward preventing mental health problems and connecting helping systems, the fundamental principles overlap considerably with prosocial approaches. The key learning supports concepts are described below:

1. enhancing regular classroom strategies to enable learning (e.g., improving instruction for students who have become disengaged from learning at school and for those with mild to moderate learning and behavior problems);
2. supporting transitions (i.e., assisting students and families as they negotiate school and grade changes and many other transitions);
3. increasing home and school connections;

4. responding to and where feasible preventing crises;
5. increasing community involvement and support (outreaching to develop greater community involvement and support, including enhanced use of volunteers); and
6. facilitating student and family access to effective services and special assistance as needed. (Adelman & Taylor, 2010b, p. 3)

It is significant that at least three states have adapted this model as part of their school reform efforts, and specifically as ways to reduce student disengagement, which Adelman and Taylor believe are causes of antisocial acts such as disrespecting, bullying, and the resulting overclassification of students as ADHD and learning disabled. Hawaii calls their program the Comprehensive Student Support System, Louisiana's initiative is called the Comprehensive Learning Supports System, and Iowa refers to their program as the System of Supports for Learning and Development.

Private Sector Contributions to Prosocial Education

ASCD's Whole Child Initiative

ASCD is one of the premier practitioner-oriented educational publishing and professional development organizations in the United States and internationally. Its primary members are educational supervisors, administrators and curriculum developers, and university faculty and deans, along with significant numbers of teachers and school support personnel. The five tenets of its Whole Child Initiative are consistent with a broad view of the educational purpose of prosocial education.

1. Each student enters school *healthy* and learns about and practices a healthy lifestyle.
2. Each student learns in an intellectually challenging environment that is physically and emotionally *safe* for students and adults.
3. Each student is actively *engaged* in learning and is connected to the school and broader community.
4. Each student has access to personalized learning and is *supported* by qualified, caring adults.
5. Each graduate is *challenged* academically and prepared for success in college or further study and for employment in a global environment. (The Whole Child, n.d., para. 3)

According to Molly McCloskey, managing director of Whole Child programs, the initiative was born from a combination of visionary leadership and important influences at the right time. ASCD's executive director, Gene Carter, had deepened his understanding of the importance of child health to learning through his contacts with the Centers for Disease Control and Prevention (M. McCloskey, personal communication, June 9, 2011). ASCD had also been a signatory to a 2004 document called Pathways to Civic Character, the result of a Wingspread conference that was eventually publicized by twenty national education organizations. It begins,

At the heart of our shared vision for excellence in education is an abiding commitment to high academic achievement, civic and social responsibility, healthy social and emotional development and moral character for all students. In order to sustain and expand the American experiment in liberty and justice, students must acquire civic character—

the knowledge, skills, virtues and commitment necessary for engaged and responsible citizenship. Civic character is responsible moral action that serves the common good. (Pathways, n.d., para. 1)

While ASCD had become a successful practice-oriented educational publisher and center for professional development with 160,000 members, Carter took the position that ASCD had to see its mission in the broader sense of making a difference in national educational policy. McCloskey says ASCD realized that "we as an organization need to stand up for what we know is research-based and true about learning, teaching, and leadership" (personal communication, June 9, 2011). ASCD convened a commission or luminaries, including Nel Noddings and James Comer (see their contributions to this volume in the case study accompanying chapter 13 and in the foreword), to advise them about how to proceed, and in 2005 the Whole Child initiative was born. From the beginning the vision was that the initiative would serve as both a clearinghouse and a community "designed to be supportive for teachers who may feel isolated and frustrated by the emphasis on testing mentality" (M. McCloskey, personal communication, June 9, 2011). It was intentionally designed to be kept separate from ASCD's business side, although the organization is committed to supporting the initiative by creating resources that would be available to complement the initiative. For example, the engagement tenet is one that McCloskey identified as more difficult to link to obvious practices, so ASCD's publishing wing developed resources and tools to talk about engagement strategies, such as how to do project-based learning.

McCloskey (personal communication, June 9, 2011) summarized her perspective on the status of school reform and federal government support with two comments:

Too often educational reform focuses on too narrow a variable: for example, the Gates Foundation emphasis on small schools. Small was not the critical variable as they discovered; relationships is the critical variable. Small can be a facilitator of relationships, but only if it is intentional. There is a dichotomy, a disconnect, between federal rhetoric and action (in the Obama administration). The rhetoric does talk about the importance of community schools, school climate, social-emotional learning, and civic participation, but the policy does virtually nothing to reflect that.

Once started down this road, ASCD has not shied away from making its voice heard regarding federal proposals. In early May 2011, Rep. Duncan Hunter (R-CA), the chairman of the U.S. House Committee on Education and the Workforce introduced HR 1891, the *Setting New Priorities in Education Spending Act*. The bill, which was the first Republican proposal to reauthorize and overhaul the ESEA, called for the elimination of forty-three Education Department (ED) programs such as Elementary and Secondary School Counseling; Safe and Drug-Free Schools and Communities, State Grants; and Parental Information and Resource Centers. Within days, ASCD policy director David Griffith issued a position statement in response that read, in part,

After carefully reviewing this bill, (ASCD) is concerned that the programs eliminated disproportionately affect a whole child approach to education.

Any true definition of college, career, and citizenship readiness is not confined merely to proficiency in reading and math, but must also include all core academic subjects and the comprehensive knowledge and abilities required of students after high school graduation. Eliminating programs that support physical education, arts education, school counselors, school leadership, and the Teaching American History program indicates that these important activities that promote healthy, safe, engaged, supported, and challenged students are no longer a federal priority. (ASCD, 2011a, para. 1)

ASCD's Whole Child Initiative asks the rhetorical question, what works best for children? What must we all—educators, families, policy makers, and community members—do to ensure their success? In part it answers the question by stating,

> The demands of the 21st century require a new approach to education policy and practice—a whole child approach to learning, teaching, and community engagement. Measuring academic achievement is important and necessary; no one is arguing otherwise. But if we fail to move beyond a narrow curriculum and accountability system, we will have failed to adequately prepare children for their futures. (ASCD, 2011b, p. 2)

Through its initiative, ASCD has partnered with national, state, and local leaders in attempting to move the country to action in adopting policies and practices to better educate the whole child, one of the broadest and most coherent of current efforts to promote a vision of prosocial education.

The George Lucas Educational Foundation: The Interface between Digital Technology and Prosocial Education

Earlier in the chapter we briefly examined the world of the Internet and computer gaming in terms of ethics, learning, and development. The much larger question educators and school systems are faced with is how to understand and respond to the impact and implications of the digital revolution. New terms and concepts abound in the search for language to describe the nature and scope of the digital world. It has been posited, for example, that most current K–12 students, who qualify as "digital natives" because they have grown up surrounded by the new technology, think and process information fundamentally differently from their predecessors. The rest of us, including most teachers (and all the authors of this volume), are "digital immigrants" who are faced with the task of learning and adopting the new technologies as adults (Prensky, 2001). One of the central issues to consider for educators is how the complex learning afforded by digital technologies can find recognition and authenticity in school. It has been suggested that the magnitude of this change "will require a significant shift in how we conceive of childhood, learning, and schooling" (Downes, as cited in Brown & Davis, 2004, p. 6).

Regardless of the specific digital device, platform, or network, learning is a social enterprise, transmitting varieties of information between people. Human beings have developed as social animals, and our learning capacities are exquisitely designed to enhance the survival of the individual and the species. But the skills and process of information transmission are essentially value neutral until applied to specific goals with purposeful content: both Adolf Hitler and Franklin Delano Roosevelt were master speakers and motivators; Facebook and Twitter can be used to start a revolution or to tell police where to go to squash a demonstration. The digital revolution can be either antisocial or prosocial.

One of the organizations that has taken on the challenge of assisting schools to use digital technology in the service of educational goals is the George Lucas Educational Foundation (GLEF) and its implementation wing, Edutopia. In discussing the genesis of Edutopia, Lucas says that he and his colleagues originally focused on three uses of information: helping students to "know how to *find* information, how to *assess* the quality of information, and how to *creatively and effectively use* information to accomplish a goal" (as cited in Chen, 2010, p. xi). Edutopia's vision of how to improve the K–12 learning environment goes beyond the idea of digitizing the classroom and has expanded upon that initial focus in a way that signals an understanding of prosocial values, content, and skills:

> Our vision is of a new world of learning, a place where students and parents, teachers and administrators, policy makers and the people they serve are all empowered to change education for the better; a place where schools provide rigorous project-based learning, social-emotional learning, and access to new technology; a place where innovation is the rule, not the exception; a place where students become lifelong learners and develop 21st-century skills, especially in information literacy so they can find, assess, and use information effectively and creatively; work cooperatively and constructively with others; use their strengths and talents to become empowered, productive citizens in our democratic society and the world at large. (George Lucas Education Foundation, n.d., para. 2)

In an interview with Phil Brown regarding how the organization had come to include a prosocial view in its work, GLEF's executive director emeritus, Milton Chen, talked about taking a whole child perspective in determining its core agenda. That agenda includes prosocial curriculum innovations such as project-based learning, social-emotional learning, and cooperative learning (personal communication, June 22, 2011). He agreed that we can't separate developmental goals form academic goals: "We can do both—we can create caring and compassionate human beings at the same time we give them the knowledge and skills to be innovators and leaders in the new kind of economy." How are these goals emphasized? Chen indicated that it has been helpful to refer to the Partnership for 21st Century Skills project, "where they emphasize that the modern work force is about teams and groups working together, collaborating, and learning to resolve conflict and to build on each other's ideas" (personal communication, June 22, 2011). It was striking how clear the implications of this approach are when Milton Chen applied them to other education issues.

On the teacher's role:

> It can be very liberating for teachers to realize that they don't need to be the most important or sole source of knowledge in the classroom. Their job should be to convey the knowledge they have, but also to understand that the knowledge that needs to be mastered is on the Internet. So the teacher can become more a coach and work with smaller groups, working more directly with students, which is why most teachers went into the profession to begin with.

On current policy issues:

The debate about charter schools, high-stakes testing, and teacher accountability is a distraction from the main issues we should be focusing on. It's very important to lead educators and particularly policy makers to take a more integrated view of what is needed to make improvements. I wish our leaders were more focused on the kind of learning day and month and year needed to create innovative school systems and the kind of support teachers need to meet these goals instead of the rhetoric about the knowledge economy.

On learning:

The real drivers behind educational policy debates should start with questions that the digital revolution has placed on our doorstep. [The questions are] what should the classroom look like, what should teachers do, what should students do, and when should they do it? In the last fifteen years we have made it possible for students to always access the information they need, to share the information they are creating 24/7/365, when you have a school system that runs on a 6/5/180 timeframe that doesn't encompass the learning opportunities [opened up by the digital revolution]. The genius of George Lucas is his understanding that documentary film could be used to show what a classroom looks like. Schools today are so tightly wrapped around policy and compliance systems that you rarely see what the best classrooms look like. (M. Chen, personal communication, June 22, 2011)

The issue of how digital technologies are transforming the time when students learn and the place where they learn is a critical issue, Chen believes, and the change has happened within the ten-year history of Edutopia. When they started, Edutopia disseminated video cassettes of best practice and books. Now almost everything they do is online; the same content is available, but at a much lower cost. But the implications for student learning are more profound. What we have learned over the past fifteen years of experimenting with digital devices in the classroom, Chen says, is that in order for it to be transformative technology, the ratio of devices to students needs to be one-to-one. This enables us to take advantage of out-of-school time; to enhance areas such as physical activity, art, and science; and to discover innovative ways to engage students in collaborative and authentic learning, all important elements of a prosocial learning climate (personal communication, June 22, 2011).

NATIONAL STANDARDS

The idea that schools should be able to define what they want students to know and be able to do so at each grade level and for all major curriculum content areas has a transparent logic to it. The intent of standards is to form clear educational goals with benchmarks that can be assessed. As noted earlier, the effort to have national standards that provide such definitions foundered on the effort to agree upon history standards in the Bush 1 era, and instead, states have been left to determine their own standards, consistent with the long-held division of educational decision-making policy. Under the conditions of NCLB, however, the requirement for high-stakes assessments aligned with state standards further increased the importance of having high-quality learning standards. The Collaborative for Academic, Social, and Emotional Learning (CASEL) had earlier taken a leadership role in promoting rigorous research on the relationship between academic and social-emotional learning (SEL) goals (see chapter 11), and so it was a natural extension for CASEL to see the connection to state standards. In 2010, CASEL began conducting a state scan of SEL learning standards, preschool through high school.

The preliminary results of the policy scan were reported in 2011 and showed that while most states have integrated SEL skills into various curricular areas or titles (e.g., interpersonal communications, problem solving, wellness), only Illinois, with which CASEL worked intensively, had distinct standards focused on a comprehensive set of SEL skills (Dusenbury, Zadrazil, Mart, & Weissberg, 2011).

There are three different concerns that prosocial educators face at this point in the evolution of the standards approach to school reform. First is the fact that without nationally accepted standards, the piecemeal approach of integrating select skills into different curriculum areas is unlikely to result in either comprehensive or evidence-based programs of professional development. Second, focusing only on skill development is an inherently inadequate approach to whole child development, which must include moral and civic education goals as well to fulfill the prosocial mission of the schools. Third, there is a danger that focusing only on curriculum and instruction ignores the need to address the organizational reforms in other areas of school life necessary for institutional and cultural change. This volume contains rich examples of what that change looks like (see, for example, the chapter and case studies for school climate [9], character education [6], service learning [10], and positive youth development [13]). Having meaningful prosocial skills standards may be a necessary condition for true reform, but it is unlikely to be a sufficient condition to engage teachers and students in the heart of teaching and learning (Palmer, 2007).

CONCLUSION

Prosocial Education: The Challenge of Studying Complex Systems

The field of prosocial education, while not named or recognized as such, has come a long way in the last twenty years in defining relevant constructs rooted in sound developmental and social change research and in developing programs grounded in theory. One of the difficulties that face policy makers and researchers alike is that schools are not static institutions where conditions of critical organizational functions and structures, such as a stable administration, faculty, and student body, hold or can be controlled over the period of time needed to do multiyear research studies. Therefore, attributing causation to either positive findings or negative results is hazardous (see chapter 23), and drawing firm conclusions about what will work and should guide broad policy actions needs to be approached cautiously. One of the lessons from NCLB is that unintended consequences may often be more powerful than well-intended interventions.

As can be seen in the diverse and compelling case studies in this volume, the on-the-ground evidence is convincing that well-implemented prosocial programs can result in significant changes in student behaviors in comportment, engagement, and academic outcomes. Firsthand accounts of the successful efforts schools have made to implement prosocial programs are an important primary source of evidence of the transformative potential of prosocial education. When administrators, teachers, and stakeholders such as parents and school board members testify to their experience of how prosocial education approaches have made an important difference in their schools and students' lives, we should treat it as more than just anecdotal evidence. Our sobering and enlightening conclusion from observing these changes at close range over the past thirty years is that no evidence-based program sufficiently accounts for these changes. Scientifically sound prosocial programs implemented with fidelity by well-prepared teachers can serve to provide needed skills for students and can sometimes ignite the conditions leading to broader change. But sustainable change requires significant alterations of policies and practices at the school level over a period of three to five years. Furthermore, research studies rarely describe the wonderfully complex conditions that result in meaningful change, precisely because the scientific methods used in quantitative research by necessity focus on what can be controlled. While newer statistical methods, such as hierarchical linear modeling, are beginning to change this picture, it is very difficult to actually measure enough to get all we need to into the data. Our research is limited by the number of variables we can handle and conceptualize at one time. In complex organizations like schools, one change, such as a new principal, can alter the entire field of play in a school, with repercussions that are not easily accounted for or adequately understood when interpreting cross-sectional or self-report survey data. The prosocial field should support longitudinal, mixed-methods, repeated-measures studies that look at organizational as well as individual issues, indicators, and variables. Researchers and policy makers need to provide educators with data that inform them about how to improve their schools and classrooms, rather than just summative outcomes that only tell them how they performed.

Prosocial Education: The Rich Tapestry of Threads Woven Together by Research and Practice

Should our mantra be "Leave no child behind" or "Move all children forward"? If the former, then we should be concerned about reducing problem behaviors to zero. This is a good thing, but it does not equip children for success in school and life. If the latter, then we want to focus on enhancing student strengths and strengthening the environments in which they learn and interact. The more caring, supportive, challenging, healthy, and engaging the environments kids are in, the more they will thrive. The more they aspire to have lives with positive purpose, the more they will want to learn and excel. Opportunity to advance leads to growth. Opportunity to not be negative, to have passing scores on state tests, leads to a kind of okayness that should not be our highest aspiration for our students or for our schools.

Schools are organized as semi-independent entities and function as interdependent ecological niches in a complex policy and practice landscape. By highlighting the formative role of emotion and supportive relationships, the integrating role of character formation, the actualizing role of skill development, and the sustaining role of social context, all within a developmentally continuous frame, prosocial education provides the glue that allows for a synergistic joining of related educational policy streams that have been flowing in our schools and communities unchanneled. The following are two principles of prosocial education that may be persuasive to even hard-core members of the American branch of the teach and test club.

First, Academic Learning and Performance Are Linked to Prosocial Education Practices

Dewey's holistic, constructivist, and action-oriented view of learning has been cited by a number of authors in this volume as an inspirational influence. The field of confluent education believes that content knowledge is the organizing factor in learning. "Confluence" involves the application of reflection, inquiry, introspection, physically active learning, and mind-body awareness to lessons in each discipline (Hackbarth, 1997). Gardner's (1993) multiple intelligences theory similarly advocates multichannel learning, speaking particularly to the importance of noncognitive modalities and both intrapersonal and interpersonal factors for many learners. Moral and character education (Noddings, 2002; Nucci & Narvaez, 2008; Power & Power, chapter 8—"Moral Education," this volume) raises awareness that educators must be concerned with the creation of a caring environment as well as with the congruence of learning and the learner's perception of him- or herself. Caring implies the competence to make a difference in someone else's life: "It is the strong, resilient backbone of human life" (Noddings, 2002, p. 101). Goleman's (2006) popularization of emotional intelligence began to put a long-overdue spotlight on the pervasive role of emotion on how and what students learn, influencing attention, focus, and retention. Recently, Davidson (2007) provided initial evidence, from imaging studies, that some prosocial education programs sustain their effects in individuals by producing changes in brain structure and functioning. Memory is impaired by high degrees of anxiety and stress, and learning is enhanced by calmness and cooperation (see chapter 12).

The very nature of school-based learning is relational, and social and emotional skills are essential for building and sustaining learning relationships of the kind needed for academic success, citizenship, a civilized and nonviolent classroom, and effective inclusive education. More than a decade ago, Sylwester (1995) pointed out that memory is event coded, linked to social and emotional situations, and that the latter are integral parts of larger units of memory that make up what we learn and retain—including and especially what takes place in the classroom. In his words, by separating emotion from logic and reason in the classroom, we've simplified school management and evaluation, but we've also then separated two sides of one coin—and lost something important in the process. While each of us needs individual emotional skills to function optimally, it's impossible to separate emotion from the social relationships that govern most of the important activities of life. Students must have an array of emotion recognition and management skills if they are to be able to focus on the increasingly sophisticated academic agenda being put before them. And they require interpersonal skills and a moral compass to successfully navigate the field of relationships that define their social world.

Second, Our System of Democracy Is Linked to the Prosocial Values and Attitudes and Emotional Intelligence of Voters

Every student must graduate with the competencies needed to be an involved citizen in our democracy. How do we prepare students to follow candidates' arguments, listen to their words, consider all of the candidates' positions as well as their own, think through the consequences of various proposals under consideration, and actively join in civic life? John Dewey (1916) recognized that education in a democracy had to provide students with the tools for exceptional capacities of discernment. Such discernment requires considerable analytic and reflective skills, self-knowledge, and cultural and contextual awareness, all elements in Dewey's constructivist pedagogy. Ultimately, education is not about producing talented students and the highest test scores; it is about producing talented *people*. It is about teaching *all* children to have the patience, interest, and skills to think about the complex issues all citizens face and to have the knowledge, inclination, and skills needed for civic participation. Although hinted at in writings about democratic schools (Apple & Beane, 1995), current thinking with regard to twenty-first-century schools and civic involvement identifies social-emotional competencies and character and ethical education (Berman & McCarthy, 2006; Truesdale, 2008; Wilczenski & Coomey, 2007) as the foundation of democratic participation and engaged citizenship. The development of these skills and values begins within schools as arenas for student participation and leadership. How are students helped to understand their role as "citizens" of their school? What allows children to see that school has relevance and importance to their everyday lives and that they are important to the school?

Paradoxically, President George W. Bush provided the reply in his remarks at the White House Conference on Character and Community on June 19, 2002: "The thing I appreciate is that you understand education should prepare children for jobs, and it should also prepare children for life. I join you in wanting our children to not only be rich in skills, but rich in ideals. Teaching character and citizenship to our children is a high calling" (cited in Spring, 2004, p. 3). As we approach the reauthorization of NCLB, we must give this high calling high priority and adequate resources. Children need the skills of discernment as well as participatory competence (Dalton, Elias, & Wandersman, 2007). These skills reflect the extraordinary amount of information children have to process on their path to adulthood and the ways in which advertisers, politicians, and other parties with interests seek to subtly (and at times, brashly and unashamedly) persuade children to believe their version of facts and truth. Cognitive and marketing research seems to make it ever easier to learn how to "package" information to enter the zone of truth, past the sensors of discernment. Prosocial skills, including emotion recognition, situation analysis, problem solving, decision making, and understanding the ethical frames and hidden moral perspectives in situations are essential for bolstering discerning judgment. These and other prosocial skills are also vital for children to have in order to grow up with the confidence and competencies needed to participate effectively in a global and highly politicized world, where being part of the mechanisms of democracy, community life, family, and workplaces is going to be challenging. Identifying "the missing piece" of prosocial education may create a challenge, but it also outlines a path. The evidence from theory, research, and practice is growing that education at all levels—preschool through college—must focus explicitly on the integration of social, emotional, moral, and academic learning as part of the process of preparing, humanizing, and educating students.

Students are not vessels to be filled with information and skills, but individuals with developing personal and social identities, in the process of cocreating meaningful lives of value. School communities form the boundaries and support for this process, and teachers create the relationships, guidance, and nurturance to foster growth. Prosocial education is and should be considered an essential cornerstone of genuine progress in the education field and essential for enduring school reform. Those concerned with educational policy may want to consider approaching the task with a mind-set consonant with a new title, ACMF (All Children Moving Forward), and then focus on providing the infrastructure and resources needed to vigorously and relentlessly accomplish this attainable goal.

Making policy in a democracy necessarily entails persuasion. Prosocial education is an idea that must be advanced through a process of exploring and advancing the research and practice terrain. As Roger Weissberg, CASEL's president, puts it,

> The field needs to do its homework, to be able to tell policy makers and educators: here is a clear agenda now, with roadmaps. . . . The burden of the work is to move from programs to schoolwide, to district, statewide, and federal policies, and to approach this holistically in terms of promoting positive development [of children] instead of categorically by talking about a problem-centered approach—a war on this issue or that issue. Now we are in a position to move from "What does the research point us to do next?" to "What's the policy environment for us to do it?" and then next to "What do we need to implement this systemwide?" (personal communication, August 24, 2011)

For the good of our civilization, the goals of prosocial education are very much worth pursuing, because if the moral and social development of our children is not as worthy of attention as our drive for academic success in the service of economic productivity, we will inadvertently foster the kind of cultural impoverishment and ethical misconduct that undermines our ability to thrive as a nation.

Each of the scholars and practitioners represented in this volume has been engaged in developing and testing formal and informal theories of action designed to bring about improvements in teacher and administrator preparation, school culture and climate, and student learning and growth. This volume is itself an attempt to draw the threads together in a way that has not happened before, a step in creating a tapestry that can serve as a rich portrait of the contribution educators can make to nourish our children's development so that they can flourish as adults. The editors invite those who support this work to form a community of prosocial educators whose combined voices can speak in harmony to those creating educational policy.

Recommendations

The following recommendations are what we believe policy makers and educators should most closely pay attention to as they consider the key ideas in this book that have the potential to change the face and heart of our efforts to develop young people as happy, caring, and productive citizens.

1. Prosocial education should be embraced as a critical and integral part of all school reform and renewal efforts. Prosocial education is a process rooted in human development theory and research. Prosocial education is not a particular program but a process of individual and institutional change that must include social-emotional skills, moral and character development, and opportunities for civic engagement.

2. Education policy and practice must acknowledge the importance of school climate in achieving both whole child growth and academic achievement. A school climate conducive to learning rests on the pillars of positive adult and student relationships, mutual respect, trust, and engagement. Shared leadership and collaborative professional development based on mutual respect are necessary conditions for sustained growth.

3. Schools should adopt a collaboratively shaped and coherent prosocial mission, with associated and well-defined norms and behavioral expectations for faculty, staff, and students; articulate it clearly; and share it widely. The core values of American life need to be continually reexamined by educators and students as we strive to understand and address the changing nature of our biological, social, and civic environment.

4. There should be an emphasis on pedagogical methods of prosocial education that are known to be effective (e.g., cooperative learning, service learning, moral dilemma discussions, teaching of social-emotional skills) and that link implementation strategies to measurable qualitative and/or quantitative outcomes. These methods can be used to promote a core set of prosocial developmental processes, among them, self-regulation, reflection, perspective taking, empathy, and personal and interpersonal problem solving. Emphasis should also be given to longitudinally coordinated instruction to foster internalization of these processes, leading to enduring intrinsic motivation and fostering meaningful prosocial activities and civic engagement with both other youth and adults.

5. Preservice preparation should be provided for both school staff and administrators based on theory, research, and evidence-based practices that are foundational for both social and academic development. Advances in child and adolescent development; the establishment of professional, ethical learning communities; and prevention science need to be taught in the context of implementation within daily school life. This should have equal footing alongside cognitive skill development, curriculum, and instructional methods. Teachers should be brought to a deep understanding of how their own character and behavior impacts the lives of students in their care, and that there is a profound relationship between how they act and respond to children and what children learn from what they teach.

The editors and authors invite readers to join with us in working to make this vision a reality in American education.

REFERENCES

Adelman, H. S., & Taylor, L. (2010a). *Mental health in schools: Engaging learners, preventing problems, and improving schools.* Thousand Oaks, CA: Corwin Press.

Adelman, H. S., & Taylor, L. (2010b). *School policy alert: Improving outcomes for students and schools requires a comprehensive system of learning supports.* Los Angeles, CA: UCLA School Mental Health Project/Center for Mental Health in Schools. Retrieved August 9, 2011, from http://smhp.psych.ucla.edu/pdfdocs/improvingoutcomes.pdf

Anderson, C. A., Berkowitz, L., Donnerstein, E., Huesmann, L. R., Johnson, J. D., Linz, D., et al. (2003). The influence of media violence on youth. *Psychological Science in the Public Interest, 4*(3), 81–110. doi:10.1111/j.1529-1006.2003

Apple, M. W., & Beane, J. A. (Eds.). (1995). *Democratic schools.* Alexandria, VA: Association for Supervision and Curriculum Development.

ASCD. (2011a, May 16). *ASCD responds to first ESEA reauthorization bill.* Retrieved August 9, 2011, from http://www.ascd.org/news-media/Press-Room/News-Releases/ASCD-Responds-to-First-ESEA-Reauthorization-Bill.aspx

ASCD. (2011b). *Making the case for educating the whole child.* Alexandria, VA: Author. Re-trieved August 9, 2011, from http://www.wholechildeducation.org/resources/WholeChild MakingTheCase.pdf

Baldwin, D. C., & Daugherty, S. R. (1996). Cheating in medical school: A survey of second-year students at 31 schools. *Academic Medicine, 71,* 267–273.

Berman, S. (1990). Educating for social responsibility. *Educational Leadership, 48*(3), 75–80.

Berman, S., & McCarthy, M. H. (2006). The connection between character, service, and social-emotional learning. In M. Elias & H. Arnold (Eds.), *The educator's guide to emotional intelligence and academic achievement* (pp. 46–57). Thousand Oaks, CA: Corwin Press.

Bertram-Gallant, T., & Drinan, P. (2006). Organizational theory and student cheating: Explanation, responses, and strategies. *Journal of Higher Education, 77*(5), 839–860.

Billig, S. H. (2009). *Promoting character development in Colorado schools: Evaluation report.* Denver, CO: RMC Research Corporation.

Bowers, W. J. (1964). *Student dishonesty and its control in college.* New York: Columbia University Bureau of Applied Social Research.

Brown et al. v. Entertainment Merchants Assn. et al., 422 U.S. 205 (LexisNexis 2011).

Brown, A., & Davis, N. (Eds.). (2004). *World yearbook of education: Digital technology, communities and education.* London: Routledge Falmer.

Brown, J., D'Emidio-Caston, M., & Benard, B. (2000). *Resilience education.* Thousand Oaks, CA: Corwin Press.

California Department of Education. (2011). *Fiscal, demographic, and performance data on California's K–12 schools.* Retrieved August 9, 2011, from http://www.cde.ca.gov/ds

Callahan, D. (2004). *The cheating culture.* Orlando, FL: Harcourt.

Centers for Disease Control and Prevention. (2009). *School connectedness: Strategies for increasing protective factors among youth.* Atlanta, GA: U.S. Department of Health and Human Services.

Chen, M. (2010). *Education nation: Six leading edges of innovation in our schools.* San Francisco: Jossey-Bass.

Cohen, J. (2006). Social, emotional, ethical, and academic education: Creating a climate for learning, participation in democracy, and well-being. *Harvard Education Review, 76*(2), 201–237.

Collaborative for Academic, Social, and Emotional Learning. (2003). *Safe and sound: An educational leader's guide to evidence-based social and emotional learning (SEL) programs.* Chicago: Author.

Comer, J. (2003). Transforming the lives of children. In M. J. Elias, H. Arnold, & C. Steiger-Hussey (Eds.), *EQ + IQ: Best practices in leadership for caring and successful schools* (pp. 11–22). Thousand Oaks, CA: Corwin Press.

Corporation for National and Community Service. (2006, December). *Volunteer growth in America: A review of trends since 1974.* Washington, DC: Author. Retrieved August 9, 2011, from http://www.cns.gov/pdf/06_1203_volunteer_growth_factsheet.pdf

Dalton, J. H., Elias, M. J., & Wandersman, A. (2007). *Community psychology: Linking individuals and communities* (2nd ed.). Belmont, CA: Wadsworth.

Darling-Hammond, L. (2010). *The flat world of education: How America's commitment to equity will determine our future.* New York: Teachers College Press.

Davidson, R. (2007, December). *The neuroscience of social, emotional, and academic learning.* Keynote address, Forum of the Collaborative for Academic, Social, and Emotional Learning, New York, NY. Retrieved January 23, 2012, from http://casel.org/wp-content/uploads/2011/04/FORUMreport8.25.08.pdf

Dewey, J. (1916). *Democracy and education: An introduction to the philosophy of education*. New York: Macmillan.

Durlak, J. A., Weissberg, R. P., Dymnicki, A. B., Taylor, R. D., & Schellinger, K. B. (2011). Enhancing students' social and emotional development promotes success in school: Results of a meta-analysis. *Child Development, 82*, 474–501.

Dusenbury, L., Zadrazil, J., Mart, A., & Weissberg, R. (2011). *State learning standards to advance social and emotional learning: The state scan of social and emotional learning standards, preschool through high school*. Retrieved August 22, 2011, from http://casel.org/wp-content/uploads/2011/04/Brief-on-the-State-Scan-4-18-2011.pdf

Elias, M. J. (2001). Prepare children for the tests of life, not a life of tests. *Education Week, 21*(4), 40.

Elias, M. J. (2009, November). Social-emotional and character development and academics as a dual focus of educational policy. *Educational Policy, 23*(6), 831–846.

Elias, M. J., & Arnold, H. A. (Eds.). (2006). *The educator's guide to emotional intelligence and academic achievement: Social-emotional learning in the classroom*. Thousand Oaks, CA: Corwin Press.

Encyclopedia Britannica. (2011). National Defense Education Act. Retrieved August 9, 2011, from http://www.britannica.com/EBchecked/topic/404717/National-Defense-Education-Act

Fisher, C. (2010, May 30). College students do not have as much empathy. *Behavioral Medicine Report*. Retrieved January 23, 2012, from http://www.bmedreport.com/archives/13176

Fleming, N. (2011, April 11). Participation in youth service. *Education Week*. Retrieved August 22, 2011, from http://blogs.edweek.org/edweek/beyond_schools/2011/04/youth_service.html

Fox, J., Machtmes, K., Tassin, M., & Hebert, L. (n.d.). *An analysis of volunteer motivations among youth participating in service-learning projects*. Retrieved from http://appl003.lsu.edu/slas/ccell/facultyinfo.nsf/$Content/Publications/$file/Analysis.pdf

Gardner, H. (1993). *Multiple intelligences: The theory in practice*. New York: Basic Books.

Gentile, D. A., Anderson, C. A., Yukawa, S., Ihori, N., Saleem, M., Ming, L. K., et al. (2009). The effects of prosocial video games on prosocial behaviors: International evidence from correlational, longitudinal, and experimental studies. *Personality and Social Psychology Bulletin, 35*(6), 752–763.

George Lucas Educational Foundation. (n.d.). Retrieved August 9, 2011, from http://www.edutopia.org/mission-vision

Goleman, D. (2006). *Social intelligence: The new science of human relationships*. New York: Bantam.

Goodlad, J. I. (1997, October). *Beyond McSchool: A challenge to educational leadership*. Paper presented at Reflecting on Sputnik: Linking the Past, Present, and Future of Educational Reform, a symposium hosted by the Center for Science, Mathematics, and Engineering Education, Washington, DC. Retrieved August 22, 2011, from http://www.nationalacademies.org/sputnik/goodlad.htm

Governor of California, et al. v. Entertainment Merchants Association, et al., 08 U.S. 1448 (2011).

Hackbarth, S. (1997, March). *Reflections on confluent education as discipline-based inquiry*. Paper presented at the annual meeting of the American Educational Research Association, Chicago, IL. (ERIC Document Reproduction Service No. ED409322)

Haines, V. J., Diekhoff, G. M., LaBeff, E. E., & Clark, R. E. (1986). College cheating: Immaturity, lack of commitment, and the neutralizing attitude. *Research in Higher Education, 25*, 342–354.

Hanushek, E. A. (1998). Conclusions and controversies about the effectiveness of school resources. *Economic Policy Review, Federal Reserve Bank of New York, 3*, 11–27.

Johnston, L. D., O'Malley, P. M., Bachman, J. G., & Schulenberg, J. E. (2011). *Monitoring the future national survey results on drug use, 1975–2010: Vol. 1. Secondary school students*. Ann Arbor, MI: Institute for Social Research, University of Michigan.

Kahne, J., Middaugh, E., Lee, N., & Feezell, J. T. (2010). *Youth online activity and exposure to diverse perspectives*. Irvine, CA: DML Central, Youth & Participatory Politics Project. Retrieved January 23, 2012, from http://dmlcentral.net/sites/dmlcentral/files/resource_files/YouthOn lineActivityDiverseExposure.WORKINGPAPERS.pdf

Kaplan, W., & Mable, P. (1998). Students' perceptions of academic integrity: Curtailing violations. In D. D. Burnett, L. Rudolph, & K. O. Clifford (Eds.), *Academic integrity matters* (pp. 22–31). Washington, DC: National Association of Student Personnel Administrators. (ERIC Document Reproduction Service No. ED452577)

Konrath, S. H., O'Brien, E. H., & Hsing, C. (2011). Change in dispositional empathy over time in American college students: A meta-analysis. *Personality and Social Psychology Review, 15*(2), 180–198. doi:10.1177/1088868310377395

Kristof, N. D. (2012, February 5). After recess: Change the world. *New York Times*, p. SR11.

Lickona, T., & Davidson, M. (2005). *Smart & good high schools: Integrating excellence and ethics for success in school, work, and beyond*. Cortland, NY: Center for the 4th and 5th Rs (Respect and Responsibility) and Washington, DC: Character Education Partnership.

May, W. W. (Ed.). (1990). *Ethics and higher education*. New York: Macmillan.

McCabe, D. L. (1992). The influence of situational ethics on cheating among college students. *Sociological Inquiry, 62*, 365–374.

McCabe, D. L. (1993). Faculty responses to academic dishonesty: The influence of student honor codes. *Research in Higher Education, 34*, 647–658.

McCabe, D. L., & Pavela, G. R. (1997). Ten principles of academic integrity. *Journal of College and University Law, 24*, 117–118.

McCabe, D. L., & Treviño, L. K. (1993). Academic dishonesty: Honor codes and other contextual influences. *Journal of Higher Education, 64*, 522–538.

McCabe, D. L., & Treviño, L. K. (1997). Individual and contextual influences on academic dishonesty: A multicampus investigation. *Research in Higher Education, 38*, 379–396.

McCabe, D. L., Treviño, L. K., & Butterfield, K. D. (1996). The influence of collegiate and corporate codes of conduct on ethics-related behavior in the workplace. *Business Ethics Quarterly, 6*, 461–476.

McCabe, D. L., Treviño, L. K., & Butterfield, K. D. (1999). Academic integrity in honor code and non-honor code environments: A qualitative investigation. *Journal of Higher Education, 70*, 211–234.

McCabe, D. L., Treviño, L. K., & Butterfield, K. D. (2001). Cheating in academic institutions: A decade of research. *Ethics and Behavior, 11*(3), 219–232.

McGuinn, P. J. (2006). *No child left behind and the transformation of federal education policy, 1965–2005*. Lawrence: University of Kansas Press.

McNeil, M. (2011, August 3). Are 82% of schools "failing" under NCLB, as Duncan warned? *Education Week*. Retrieved from http://blogs.edweek.org/edweek/campaign-k-12/2011/08/are_82_of_schools_failing_unde.html?qs=Are+82%+of+schools+%27failing%27

Media Awareness Network. (2010). *Violence in media entertainment*. Retrieved August 22, 2011, from http://www.media-awareness.ca/english/issues/violence/violence_entertainment.cfm

Murray, S., & Ouellette, L. (2008). *Reality TV: Remaking television culture*. New York: New York University Press.

Noddings, N. (2002). *Educating moral people*. New York: Teachers College Press.

Noguera, P. (2010, January 11). Revising NCLB. *Teachers College Record*. Retrieved from http://tcrecord.org

Nonis, S., & Swift, C. O. (2001). An examination of the relationship between academic dishonesty and workplace dishonesty: A multicampus investigation. *Journal of Education for Business, 77*(2), 69–77.

Nucci, L., & Narvaez, D. (Eds.). (2008). *Handbook of moral and character education.* New York: Taylor & Francis.

O'Neil, J. (1997). Building schools as communities: A conversation with James Comer. *Educational Leadership, 54,* 6–10.

Palmer, P. J. (2007). *The courage to teach.* San Francisco: Wiley.

Pathways to Civic Character. (n.d.). Retrieved August 22, 2011, from http://www.slcschools.org/departments/curriculum/character-education/documents/Pathways-to-Civic-Character.pdf

Peoples, C. (2008). Sputnik and "skill thinking" revisited: Technological determinism in American responses to the Soviet missile threat. *Cold War History, 8*(1), 55–75.

Pettit, B., & Western, B. (Eds.). (2004). Mass imprisonment and the life course: Race and class inequality in U.S. incarceration. *American Sociological Review, 69*(2), 151–169.

Prensky, M. (2001). Digital natives, digital immigrants, part 1. *On the Horizon, 9*(5), 1–6.

Ravitch, D. (2010). *The death and life of the great American school system: How testing and choice are undermining education.* New York: Basic Books.

Rebell, M. A., & Wolff, J. R. (2009). *NCLB at the crossroads: Reexamining the federal effort to close the achievement gap.* New York: Teachers College Press.

Rideout, V. J., Vandewater, E. A., & Wartella, E. A. (2003). *Zero to six: Electronic media in the lives of infants, toddlers and preschoolers.* Menlo Park, CA: Kaiser Family Foundation.

Roberts, D. F., Foehr, U. G., Rideout, V. J., & Vrodie, M. (1999). *Kids & media @ the new millennium.* Menlo Park, CA: Kaiser Family Foundation.

Rose, M. (2009). *Why school? Reclaiming education for all of us.* New York: New Press.

Sahlberg, P. (2009). Educational change in Finland. In A. Hargreaves, M. Fullan, A. Lieberman, & D. Hopkins (Eds.), *International handbook of educational change* (pp. 1–28). Netherlands: Kluwer Academic Publishers. As quoted in Darling-Hammond, 2010, p. 168.

Samuels, C. A. (2011a, July 13). Report details "culture of cheating" in Atlanta schools. *Education Week.* Retrieved August 22, 2011, from http://www.edweek.org/search.html?qs=Report+Details+%27Culture+of+Cheating%27+in+Atlanta+Schools

Samuels, C. A. (2011b, August 10). Cheating scandals intensify focus on test pressures. *Education Week.* Retrieved August 22, 2011, from http://www.edweek.org/search.html?qs=Cheating+Scandals+Intensify+Focus+on+Test+Pressures

Scales, P. C., & Roehlkepartain, E. C. (2004). *Community service and service learning in U.S. public schools, 2004: Findings from a national survey.* St. Paul, MN: National Youth Leadership Council. Retrieved August 9, 2011, from http://www.search-institute.org/system/files/2004G2GCompleteSurvey.pdf

Spring, J. (2004). *American education* (11th ed.). New York: McGraw-Hill.

Sylwester, R. (1995). *A celebration of neurons.* Alexandria, VA: Association for Supervision and Curriculum Development.

Truesdale, V. (2008). Partnership for 21st century success. *Education Update, 50*(7), 2.

U.S. Census Bureau. (2002, July). *The big payoff: Educational attainment and synthetic estimates of work-life earnings* (by J. C. Day and E. C. Newburger; Special Studies, P23-210). Retrieved August 22, 2011, from http://www.census.gov/prod/2002pubs/p23-210.pdf

U.S. Department of Education. (1983). *A nation at risk.* Retrieved January 12, 2012, from http://www2.ed.gov/pubs/NatAtRisk/risk.html

U.S. Department of Education. (2010a). *Safe and supportive schools: Fiscal year 2010 information and application procedures* (CFDA #84.184Y). Retrieved August 22, 2011, from http://www2.ed.gov/programs/safesupportiveschools/2010-184y.pdf

U.S. Department of Education. (2010b). *U.S. Department of Education awards $38.8 million in safe and supportive school grants* (Press release). Retrieved August 9, 2011, from http://www.ed.gov/news/press-releases/us-department-education-awards-388-million-safe-and -supportive-school-grants

U.S. Department of Education. (2011). *The Federal role in education.* Retrieved January 12, 2012, from http://www.2.ed.gov/about/overview/fed/role.html

Walsh, M. (2011). Supreme Court rejects violent video game law. *Education Week.* Retrieved August 22, 2011, from http://blogs.edweek.org/edweek/school_law/2011/06

Watson, M. (2006). Long-term effects of moral/character education in elementary school: In pursuit of mechanisms. *Journal of Research in Character Education, 4*(1–2), 1–18.

The Whole Child. (n.d.). About. Retrieved August 9, 2011, from http://www.wholechildedu cation.org/about

Wilczenski, F., & Coomey, S. (2007). *A practical guide to service learning: Strategies for positive social development in schools.* New York: Springer.

Wilson, B. J., Kunkel, D., Linz, D., Potter, J., Donnerstein, E., Smith, S. L., & Grayi, T. (1998). Violence in television programming overall: University of California, Santa Barbara Study. In M. Seawall (Ed.), *National television violence study* (Vol. 2). Thousand Oaks, CA: Sage.

Young, S. M., & Pinsky, D. (2006). Narcissism and celebrity. *Journal of Research in Personality, 40,* 463–471.

Index

ability, 641

academic education: character education and, 140–41; district-based approaches and, 697; focus on, effects of, 96, 742, 754–55, 779–80; positive youth development programs and, 431; relationship to prosocial education, 6, 93–98, 723–28, 792

accountability, school climate intervention and, 712–13, 713*t*–714*t*

achievement: after-school programs and, 561–62; character education and, 131; deficit model and, 642–43; district-based approaches and, 704–5, 704*t*; focus on, effects of, 779–80; moral education and, 217; positive youth development programs and, 431; relationship to testing, 739; school climate and, 232, 253–61, 258*f*–259*f*; service learning and, 284; social and emotional learning and, 323; socioeconomic status and, 746–48

achievement gap, 168, 562, 642, 655, 735–36

action: moral education and, 187–88; in service learning, 274, 297

Adams, John, xiii, 149

adequate yearly progress (AYP), 96, 466, 735; issues with, 737–38; school climate and, 254, 269

ADHD. *See* attention deficit hyperactivity disorder

Adler, Felix, 230

administrators: and history of prosocial education, 40–41; preparation programs

for, 589–608; and school specialists, 719. *See also* principals; superintendents

adolescence, moral development in, 666

adult culture in schools: and bullying prevention, 517; character education and, 116, 139–40; and civic education, 158–59; importance of, 117; modeling prosocial behavior in, 79; preparation programs and, 589–608; recommendations for, 75; and RULER Approach, 332; teachers and, 725–26

Adventures in Peacemaking program, 694–95

African American students: and achievement, 735; term, 640

after-school programs, 559–72; benefits of, 561–63; case studies on, 559–72; history of, 560–61

age, 641; and civic engagement, 155; and political knowledge gap, 153; and service activities, 276

aggressiveness: case studies of, 505–14; PATHS curriculum and, 328; programs on, 59–60; reduction of, factors affecting, 61–62. *See also* bullying prevention

alignment problem, 84

Al's Pals, 538–39

Althof, Wolfgang, 71–90

American Indians: and cultural preservation, 685–86; prosocial education and, 681–87; term, 640; walking in two worlds, 682–83

American Recovery and Reinvestment Act, 277

Burke, Edmund, 182
Burke, Eileen, 295
burnout, teachers and, 372, 376–77
Bush, George H. W., 157, 276
Bush, George W., 54, 56, 771, 793
bystanders, 478–79; consequences for, 481; empowerment of, 489, 495, 505–14, 520–21

California: and civic education, 163, 167–70; and positive youth development, 465–72; and standards, 741, 773
Callahan, David, 780
Camilleri, Vanessa A., 253–61
Campbell, Donald T., 782
Campbell, Julie, 516
Campus Compact, 44, 161, 276–77
Campuses of Service, 277
Campus Outreach Opportunity League, 276
Canada: and bullying prevention, 515–24; and social and emotional learning, 320, 321*t*
Captain Manuel Rivera, Jr. School, 585–88
CARE. *See* Cultivating Awareness and Resilience in Education
care, duty of, 482
CARE for Kids program, 695–97; components of, 696–97; effectiveness of, 701–5, 704*f*, 704*t*–705*t*; principles of, 696
caring practice, CARE program on, 381–82
Caring School Community (CSC), 130–31, 324–25, 694–95
CART. *See* Compendium of Assessment and Research Tools
Carter, Jimmy, 771
CASEL. *See* Collaborative for Academic, Social, and Emotional Learning
case studies: on after-school programs, 559–72; on bullying prevention, 499–524; on character education, 137–48; on civic education, 167–78; on early childhood prosocial education, 545–57; on mindfulness approaches, 399–414; on moral education, 186–87, 211–21; on multicultural education, 665–87; on positive youth development, 445–72; on school climate, 253–70; on service learning, 289–309; on social and emotional learning, 347–70; on teacher preparation programs, 609–34

CASS curriculum, 506
Castania, K., 641
Catholic schools, 52
CCSSI. *See* Common Core State Standards Initiative
CEB. *See* Cultivating Emotional Balance
CEI. *See* Character Education Inquiry
celebration: in positive youth development, 461; in school climate intervention, 712; in service learning, 275, 298
Center for Critical Participatory Action Research (cPAR), 651*t*
Center on the Social and Emotional Foundations for Early Learning, 531
Centers for Disease Control and Prevention (CDC), 47, 57, 784
CHAMPS program, 499–500
Chang, Florence C., 691–707
character: after-school programs and, 576; and bullying prevention, 509–10; types of, 183
Character Counts!, 181
character education, 115–36; case studies on, 137–48; controversies over, 72; definition of, 117–18; effects of, 62–63; history of, 43, 56, 117–27; implementation of, 64, 127–28; practices and approaches in, 127–28; principals and, 619–26, 709–16; public schools and, 53; and service learning, 301–2; terminology in, 768. *See also* moral education
Character Education Inquiry (CEI), 121–22
Character Education Partnership, 127–28, 139, 265–66, 269, 304–5; website of, 246
CHARACTER*plus*, 130–31
charity. *See* service
cheating, 225, 740, 779–82
Chen, Milton, 788–89
Chiasson, Mario, 516
Child Development Project, 130–31, 324
Children First, 436, 459–64; history of, 459–61
Children's Mental Health Act, Illinois, 320
Child Trends, 436
Chisom, Ron, 654*t*
citizenship education, 52, 149–65; case studies on, 167–78; prosocial education and, 792–94
City University of New York, 651*t*

conflict, versus bullying, 475, 493
conflict resolution education (CRE), 366–67; versus bullying prevention, 493; research on, 59
confluent education, 792
conformity, versus moral behavior, 188
connectedness: and bullying prevention, 488; CDC on, 784; effects of, 62; promotion of, 64–65; school climate and, 241–42
Connecticut: and positive youth development, 445–58; and standards, 773
Connolly, Maureen, 295–99
constructivism, 84, 93, 102, 610
contagion bullying, 476
contemplative education. See mindfulness approaches
contemplative practices, elements of, 373
contemplative science, 374–75
content integration, in multicultural education, 648, 649t, 655–57
continuous improvement: after-school programs and, 582; schools and, 238–43
controversy, dealing with, 72
Core Five After-School Program, 573–83, 574f, 578f
Corporation for National and Community Service (CNCS), 277–79
Corrigan, Michael W., xvii–xxii, 91–111, 573–83, 731–66
Coughlin, K. A., 289–91
counselors: school specialists and, 719–20; training in emotional intelligence for, 609–18
cPAR. See Center for Critical Participatory Action Research
CRE. See conflict resolution education
Creating a Safe School (CASS) curriculum, 506
Crenshaw, Kimberlé, 642
criminal justice system: versus education spending, 775; and moral education, 211–21
criterion-reference tests, 743–44
critical consciousness, 672
Crutchley, Tim, 621
CSC. See Caring School Community
CSCI. See Comprehensive School Climate Inventory

Cultivating Awareness and Resilience in Education (CARE), 379–82, 409–14; program schedule, 380t
Cultivating Emotional Balance (CEB), 378–79
cultural competence, district-based approaches and, 697–98
cultural-environmental stream, 424–25
cultural pluralism, 681–83
culture. See school climate
curriculum: for American Indian education, 684–85; balanced, 93–98; and bullying prevention, 492; CASS, 506; character education and, 140–41, 145–46; civic education and, 160; default, 181, 189–90; district-based approaches and, 697; hidden, 14, 91, 369; multicultural education and, 648; Relaxation Response, 389; service learning and, 272, 305; social and emotional learning and, 332
cyberbullying, 476; consequences of, 480; prevalence of, 479
Czarnecki, E. Janet, 301–9

Dachnowitz, Eileen, 268
Dalai Lama, 378, 411
Daley, Richard, 516
dame schools, 41
Damon, W., 106, 118, 182
Danielson, Charlotte, 555
Darling-Hammond, Linda, 750–52, 773, 775
data collection, superintendents and, 701–2
Davenport, Roberta, 366, 369
Davidson, Richard, 375–76, 401
Davis, Stan, 516, 518–19, 521
Dawson family, 545
DeBellis, Lisa M., 559–72, 585–88
decision making: prosocial education and, 20; social and emotional learning and, 316t. See also democratic decision making
declarative knowledge, 599
Dees, Morris, 649t
default curriculum, 181, 189–90
defiance, term, 643
deficit model, 627; reframing, 642–43
Delli Carpini, Michael X., 151
democratic decision making: civic education and, 175; moral education and, 223–26;

prosocial education and, 792–94; recommendations for, 78

demographics, and multicultural education, 639

demonstration, in service learning, 275, 298

Denevi, Elizabeth, 656*t*

Department of Health and Human Services, 784–85

development, 4; and civic engagement, 156; mindfulness approaches and, 390–91; multicultural education and, 645–46; relationship to learning, 13; and testing, 741–42

developmental discipline, 79–80

developmental psychology, 418

Developmental Studies Center, 336

developmental system theory, 422

DeVoss, Joyce A., 609–18

Dewey, John, 42–44, 52, 99, 123, 202, 672; and democracy, 793; and philosophy, 204–5; and service learning, 275; and social and emotional learning, 321; work of, 121, 172

Diamond, Larry, 158

digital world, 775–78; and prosocial education, 787–89; status in, 787

Dilthey, Wilhelm, 651*t*

direct instruction, in character education, 122–23

disability harassment, 483

discipline: CARE for Kids program and, 696; character education and, 131, 139–40; developmental, 79–80; moral education and, 189–90, 225–26; social and emotional learning and, 368

discrimination, 476; legal issues in, 483

discussion: and bullying prevention, 491–92, 505–14; in early childhood prosocial education, 532; and empathy development, 613–14; Facing History and Ourselves program and, 668–69, 671–74; moral, 184–86, 189; philosophical, 126, 197–209

dispositions, civic, 157–59

distal causes, 423

district-based approach to prosocial education, 691–707; for large districts, 695; for small districts, 694–95

district superintendents: and leadership, 701; and policy, 701; and prosocial education, 691–707; role of, 691

diversity: definition of, 641; Finland and, 752; and respect, 711; Teach for America and, 46

document-based questions, 726

doing, versus being, 762–63

dropping out, 15, 94; bullying and, 480–81; multicultural education and, 645–46

drug abuse prevention. *See* substance abuse prevention

Drug-Free Schools and Communities Act, 54

Du Bois, W. E. B., 637, 651*t*

DuFour, Rebecca, 146

DuFour, Richard, 146

Duncan, Arne, 57, 92, 496

Dunn, Jim, 654*t*

Durkheim, Émile, 191

dynamic systems theories, 422

early childhood prosocial education, 525–44; case studies on, 545–57; characteristics of, 531–35; programs for, 535–40

Early Head Start, 433

Early Learning Campus, 545–49

Earned Income Tax Credit (EITC), 433

ecological-systems theory, 99, 425

economic issues, and service learning, 278

Edelman, Marian Wright, 773–74

education: current status of, xiii, 7, 25–26, 94–95; funding for, 740, 761–62, 769; goal of, 159–60, 754–55; responsibility for, 43; stability and, 10; structural aspects of, 9, 13–14; value of, 12. *See also* prosocial education

Education of All Handicapped Children Act, 770

Education Sciences Reform Act, 56

Edutopia, 787–89

Edward M. Kennedy Serve America Act, 277

egocentrism, types of, 180

Eisenhower, Dwight D., 54, 769

Eisenhower, Milton S., 54

EITC. *See* Earned Income Tax Credit

Ekman, Paul, 378

Elementary and Secondary Education Act (ESEA), 734, 770–72; Amendments, 54

feedback: in LACE, 620; in mindfulness approaches, 403–4

Fenton, Ted, 185

Finland, 751–54, 774

Finlandophilia, term, 752

First Amendment: and bullying, 483–84; and violence, 776–77

First Things First, 101

Five Cs, in positive youth development, 421, 430

Flanagan, Constance, 155, 157, 162, 171–77

Flay, Brian R., 415–43

Flook, Lisa, 401

Florida, and bullying prevention, 499–503

Foulks Ranch Elementary School, 167–70

Foundation for Character Development, 768

Foundations program, 499–500

4-H Clubs, 567–69; and positive youth development, 428–29, 436

4Rs program, 325–26, 365–70

Framework for Teaching (FTT), 555

Francis Howell Middle School, 137–42, 623–25

Franklin, Benjamin, 41–42, 149

Fraser Standard, 483

free appropriate public education (FAPE), 483

Freire, Paulo, 637–38, 651t, 672

Gaiman, Neil, 213

Gallay, Erin, 171–77

Galston, William, 152

games, prosocial, 778–79

Garcia, Eugene, 772

Gardner, Howard, 792

Garrison Institute, 379, 381–82

Gay, Lesbian, and Straight Education Network (GLSEN), 235

Geller, Karen, 263–70

gender, 641; education for girls, 41, 44; justice system and, 217–18; and political knowledge gap, 153; student inquiry on, 727; women as teachers, 120

GenerationOn curriculum, 586

genocide, Facing History and Ourselves program on, 672–74

George Lucas Educational Foundation, 787–89

Georgetown Day School, 656t

Georgia, and cheating, 781–82

GI Bill, 275

gifted programs, 646

Giles, Kathy, 406

Giordano, Larissa, 445–58

GLSEN. See Gay, Lesbian, and Straight Education Network

goals: doing versus being and, 762–63; early sensitivity to, 527–28; noble, effects of, 501, 616–17; prosocial education and, 11–12; setting, shared, 79

Goals 2000: Educate America Act, 772

Golden Rule, 711

Goleman, Daniel, 315, 319, 367, 590, 792

Goodlad, John, 771

Gordon, Mary, 353

Gorski, P. C., 644

Gosselin, Colette, 589–608

Governor of California et al. v. Entertainment Merchants Association et al., 776–77

Gregory, Maughn, 197–209

Griffith, David, 786–87

Grimley, Michelle, 289–93

Grode, Deirdra, 271–88

Groundswell, 171–77

group bullying, 476

group dynamics, for school leaders, 597–99

Grove, Doug, 115–36

Growald, Eileen Rockefeller, 315

guided meditation, 371, 413–14

Guthrie, James, 97

Habeeb, Karen, 545

Habermas, Jürgen, 152

habits, character education and, 117

Hale (Nathan) School, 445–58

Hall, G. Stanley, 121

Hall, Scott, 573–83

Hallman, Heidi L., 627–34

Hallowell, J. H., 157

Hantman, Lisa, 290–91

harassment, 476–77; legal issues in, 483. See also under bullying

Harrisburg, PA, mindfulness approaches in, 409–14

Hartshorne, Hugh, 121

Hazelwood Standard, 484

hazing, 476

Head Start, 433; REDI program, 536

health-related disciplines, 47

heart, head, and hand approach, 85; in character education, 139

Hecht, Deborah, 271–88

helix metaphor, for prosocial education, 103–5

heroes. *See* upstanders

Hess, F. M., 736

heuristic device, 605–7, 606*t*

Hickerson, Mary, 499

hidden curriculum, 91, 181–82, 189–90, 369; term, 14

Higgins-D'Alessandro, Ann, xvii–xxii, 3–38, 91–111, 230–31, 238

higher education: child care and, 545–49; civic mission of, 160–62

high school: district-based approaches and, 698–99; implementation of prosocial education in, 723–28

Hine, Jennie, 347–52

HiPlaces Model, 239

Hispanic children: and achievement, 736; after-school programs and, 585–88

history: for American Indians, 681–87; Facing History and Ourselves program on, 665–80

Hoboken Charter School, 271

Holmstrom, Carl, 459–60

Holocaust, Facing History and Ourselves program on, 668–69

homelessness: empathy development and, 589; teacher preparation programs and, 627–34

home-school connections: CARE for Kids program and, 696; character education and, 131; recommendations for, 77; school climate and, 229, 267–68; school specialists and, 717–22; teacher preparation and, 630–31; and test performance, 748–51

hope, multicultural education and, 645

Hopkins, Cheryl, 347–52

Hosseini, Khalid, 214

hot spots, for bullying, 236

Howell (Francis) Middle School, 137–42, 623–25

Hoxie, Anne-Marie E., 559–72

Hoy, Wayne, 234

Hudson, MA, school district, 694–95

Hunter, Duncan, 786

ICPIC. *See* International Council for Philosophical Inquiry with Children

ICPS, 537–38

identity: civic, 177; development of, 592–96, 593*f*, 627–34

IEE. *See* Integrated Ethical Education

IES. *See* Institute of Education Sciences

Illinois: and bullying prevention, 505–14; Children's Mental Health Act, 56; and social and emotional learning, 320

immigrants/immigration: civic education and, 159; education and, 52; status, 641

Imperato, Christina, 268

implementation of prosocial education, 71–90; approach to, 91–111; of character education, 127–28; of counselor training, 612–13; of district-based approaches, 698–701; in early childhood, 554–56; gap with ideals, 81–82; grassroots, 82–83; naming problem in, 82; recommendations for, 74–80, 86; of school climate program, 257; of service learning, 278–80; teachers and, 723–28; time for, 106; variations in, 63–65. *See also* case studies

Improving America's Schools Act, 54

incarceration, 775

inclusion, moral education and, 190–91

incoherence, as problem, 84

The Incredible Years, 537

indoctrination, versus civic education, 158

Industrial Revolution, 42

infant development, lessons on, 311–12, 330, 355

Ingersoll, Gregg, 516

in loco parentis doctrine, 482

Inner Children program, 388

Inner Resilience Program (IRP), 385–86

inquiry: community of, 200; method, 185; philosophical, 197–209; teachers and, 726

Institute for Applied Research in Youth Development, 430, 436

Institute of Education Sciences (IES), 56, 58, 60

Institute of Social and Religious Research, 121

institutional environment, school climate and, 231

instrumental helping, 528–29

Integrated Ethical Education (IEE), 187

722; and service learning, 271, 276,
301–9; and standards, 773; and teacher
preparation programs, 601–2
New Mexico, and American Indian
education, 683
New York: and after-school programs, 559,
585–88; and mindfulness approaches, 381;
and multicultural education, 651*t*; and
service learning, 276, 283–84, 295–99; and
social and emotional learning, 365–70
Niemoller, Martin, 679
Nieto, S., 638
no-blame approach, and bullying prevention,
521
No Child Left Behind (NCLB) Act, 12, 54–55,
57, 560; and civic education, 149–50;
effects of, 94, 96, 773–74; goals of, 735;
and parents, 748; passage of, 772; and
school climate, 264; and testing, 743–44
Noddings, Nel, ix–xi, 189, 792
Noguera, Pedro, 772
Nomura, Kiyomi, 525
normal distribution, 739–40, 739*f*
norms, and school climate, 242
Norris, Jacqueline, 589–608
North Carolina: Northeast Middle School,
709–16; and standards, 773
Northeast Middle School, 709–16
NSBA. *See* National School Board
Association
NSLC. *See* National Service Learning
Clearinghouse
Nuss, Judith, 409–14
nutrition, after-school programs and, 576,
579–80

Obama, Barack, 57, 485, 741, 744–45
Obama, Michelle, 57, 485
obesity, childhood, 575
O'Brien, Mary Utne, 311–45
OECD. *See* Organisation for Economic
Cooperation and Development
Office of Safe and Drug-Free Schools
(OSDFS), 56
Ohashi, Monique, 465–72
Olweus program, 501–2
onion model, 592–96, 593*f*
Ophelia Project, 506

Organisation for Economic Cooperation and
Development (OECD), 744, 749–50
OSDFS. *See* Office of Safe and Drug-Free
Schools
Osher, David, 51–70
Ould Deluder Satan law, 119
outcome measures, 22; character education
and, 131; school climate and, 260, 269–70;
service learning and, 282–83, 298–99

PA. *See* Positive Action program
Pacific Institute for Research and Evaluation
(PIRE), xiii–xiv, xix
packaged programs, current status of, 83
Page, Tyler, 415
Paley, Vivian, 190
Palmer, Parker, 138
PARC model, in service learning, 273–75,
296–98
parents: and after-school programs, 576, 581;
and bullying prevention, 490, 495, 519–20,
523–24; and character development, 117,
119; and early childhood development,
530–31, 545–49; as partners, 77; and
school climate, 229, 267–68; and school
specialists, 717–22; and service learning,
298; and test performance, 748–51. *See
also* home-school connections
Partnerships in Character Education
Program (PCEP), xvii, 55, 291, 710
PATHS program, 327–28, 347–52; preschool
version, 536; website of, 336
pathways journals, 449
PBIS. *See* Positive Behavioral Interventions
and Supports
P4C. *See* Philosophy for Children
Peace Corps, 44, 275
pedagogy: in LACE, 620; in multicultural
education, 650–52, 657–58, 670–74;
in Philosophy for Children, 200;
recommendations for, 795; in service
learning, 273–75
peer interactive strategies: after-school
programs and, 576; bullying prevention
and, 521, 523–24; CARE for Kids program
and, 696; character education and, 116;
recommendations for, 77
Peirce, Charles, 121

tribal affiliation, 682–84
truancy, 15
trust: erosion of, and cheating, 781; and school climate, 76, 240; teachers and, 725; theory on, 100
Twemlow, Stuart, 242
21st Century Community Learning Centers, 561

ultimate causes, 423
United Nations Educational, Scientific and Cultural Organization (UNESCO), 649t
United States, social conditions in, xiii–xiv, 371–72, 774–82; positive signs for, 782–89
United States Department of Education, 28, 56–57, 770–71; Office of Special Education Programs, 55–56; Partnerships in Character Education Program (PCEP), xvii, 55, 291, 710; Safe and Supportive Schools program, 236, 245, 783; Strategic Plan, 56
universities, civic mission of, 160–62
University of Louisville, Early Learning Campus, 545–49
Upper Merion Area Middle School, 263–70
upstanders, 237, 241–42
Urban, Hal, 138
Urbanski, Jan, 473–98

values: American Indian, 686; and character education, 117; and civic education, 158; and democracy, 792–94; multicultural education and, 646; Philosophy for Children and, 202–3; prosocial education and, 20; and school climate, 264–65; and teacher preparation, 595–96
values clarification, 123–24
Vanderbilt University, Center on the Social and Emotional Foundations for Early Learning, 531
variables, multiplicity of, and research, 759–60
Veith, Dorothy J., 545–49
verbal bullying, 475
Vessels, Gordon, 118
victims of bullying: protection of, 494; signs of, 477–78
video games: prosocial, 778–79; and violence, 776–77
Vincent, Philip, 115–36, 146, 573–83

violence, 775–78
violence prevention, 57–58; research on, 58–61
virtue theory, 186, 211–12, 215–16
vocational education, 747–48
Volunteers in Service to America (VISTA), 44, 275, 277
Vygotsky, Lev, 99, 378, 552–53, 738

Walker-McConnell Scale (WMS), 469
walking in two worlds, 682–83
Wallace, Alan, 378
Washington, D.C., school climate in, 253–61, 258f–259f
Weissberg, Roger, 45, 794
Welling, Heather, 516
West Virginia, and poverty, 749
White House Conference on Youth, 44, 54, 276
whole child education, private sector and, 785–89
Whole Child Initiative, 3, 278–79, 785–87; website of, 246
Wilson, Becky, 717–22
Winer, Abby C., 525–44
Wisconsin: and character education, 143–48; and mindfulness approaches, 401–6
Wise, Bob, 749
witnesses. See upstanders
WMS. See Walker-McConnell Scale
Wooden, John, 301
Woodson, Carter G., 638
Worthen, Doug S., 399–408
Wynne, E., 182

yoga, for children, 386–87
Yordan, Helena, 559
youth: psychological disorders in, 313–14; risk factors for, xiii–xiv; stresses on, 371–72
Youth Engagement Zones, 277
Youth Service America, 276
Youth Service Center, 717–22
Youth Virtues Scale, 213

Zamora, J. Carmelo, 465–72
zero-tolerance policies, 493
Zink, Dianna, 548
zone of proximal development, 738
Zorbaugh, H., 52

About the Contributors

Wolfgang Althof is the Teresa M. Fischer Professor of Citizenship Education at the University of Missouri–St. Louis where he also serves as the director of the Citizenship-Education Clearing House (CECH) and as codirector (with Marvin W. Berkowitz) of the Center for Character and Citizenship. He has a PhD from the University of Fribourg, Switzerland, and a "Habilitation" (higher-level doctorate; Dr. habil.) from the University of Oldenburg, Germany.

Karen Mariska Atkinson has been director of Children First since 1994. Children First is a pioneering community initiative in St. Louis Park, Minnesota, focusing on the healthy development of young people. Karen has consulted with people interested in this community engagement model from communities across the United States and four other continents. Prior to this, she was vice president of the TwinWest Chamber of Commerce. Karen has a degree in public relations from the School of Journalism and Mass Communications at San Jose State University.

Maya Falcon Aviles is the psychiatric social worker at Farmdale Elementary School in Los Angeles. She has been working with students, families, school staff, and the El Sereno Community, where Farmdale is located, for seven years. Mrs. Aviles obtained her master's degree in social work, her bachelor's degree in psychology, and her Pupil Personnel Services credential from the University of California, Los Angeles. As a new parent, Mrs. Aviles hopes that her daughter Atziri will benefit from programs like Positive Action that promote positive behavior and character in instruction.

Nick Axford, PhD, is a senior researcher at the Social Research Unit, Dartington, UK. He has fourteen years of experience measuring child well-being and service use and of using the data to inform service design. He has also worked at several sites in the UK and Ireland to ensure the successful implementation and evaluation of evidence-based programs. He has a PhD in social work from the University of Exeter and a master's in European social policy analysis from the University of Bath.

Betty Bardige, EdD, is an educator and developmental psychologist who has worked with Facing History and Ourselves as a board member, volunteer, parent, and consultant for more than thirty years. She has written numerous books and articles for early childhood professionals and the general public, including *At a Loss for Words: How America Is Failing Our Children and What We Can Do about It*. She currently chairs the board of the Brazelton Touchpoints Foundation. She holds a doctorate in human development from the Harvard Graduate School of Education.

Joyce A. Barnes, EdS, currently a specialist in the Office of the Superintendent for Jefferson County Public Schools (Louisville, Kentucky), has served the district for forty-four years as both a teacher and administrator. Her work has encompassed elementary education, exceptional child education, resource development, and communications. She earned a BS in elementary education from Spalding University in Louisville and both an MEd in neurological impairment and an EdS in educational administration from the University of Louisville.

Dennis J. Barr, EdD, is director of evaluation for Facing History and Ourselves and an adjunct lecturer on education at the Harvard Graduate School of Education. He has conducted evaluation and other research in the context of programs designed to promote social, moral, historical, and civic learning in youth for more than twenty years. Dr. Barr earned a BA in psychology from Occidental College and an EdM and EdD from the Harvard Graduate School of Education. He is also a licensed clinical psychologist in the Commonwealth of Massachusetts.

Anna Bateman is a coach consultant project manager for the PATHS social-emotional learning curriculum in Birmingham, UK. She has eighteen years of experience working within primary schools and for Birmingham Education Authority as a teacher, advisor, and consultant, with a particular focus on children's emotional and social development. She has a degree in Early Childhood Education and a postgraduate certificate of education.

James M. Bentley is a sixth-grade teacher in Elk Grove, California; has taught sixteen years in grades 8 through 5; and served as districtwide trainer for math, reading, writing, and word study. Mr. Bentley also works as a state and national trainer with the Center for Civic Education as California's Third Congressional District coordinator for the We the People: The Citizen and the Constitution and We the People: Project Citizen curricula. In 2007, he codirected Elk Grove Unified School District's School Violence Prevention and Demonstration Program. He earned his BS in social sciences with special emphasis in cross-cultural studies.

Marvin W. Berkowitz, PhD, the McDonnell Professor of Character Education, President Thomas Jefferson Professor, and codirector of the Center for Character and Citizenship at the University of Missouri–St. Louis, is a developmental psychologist specializing in character development and education. He is author of more than one hundred book chapters and journal articles and coeditor of the *Journal for Research in Character Education*. Dr. Berkowitz earned his BA at the State University of New York at Buffalo and his master's and doctorate at Wayne State University.

Sheldon H. Berman, PhD, served as superintendent of Hudson Public Schools in Massachusetts for fourteen years and superintendent of Jefferson County Public Schools in Louisville, Kentucky, for four years. He was appointed superintendent of Eugene (Oregon) 4J School District on July 1, 2011. He was a founder and president of Educators for Social Responsibility and is the author of numerous articles, books, and chapters on civic education, character education, service learning, virtual education, and education reform. He received his master's and doctorate of education degrees from the Harvard Graduate School of Education, an MEd from the University of Maine, and his BA from the University of Wisconsin.

Melinda C. Bier, PhD, is associate director of the Center for Character and Citizenship at the University of Missouri–St. Louis. She has extensive experience in the adoption of K–12 educational innovations, in designing and managing professional development for geographically and culturally diverse teachers, and in the philanthropic sector. Her recent work spans the fields of character education, professional development, and the investigation of youth-produced media to achieve academic, character, and health outcomes for youth and communities.

Elena Bodrova, PhD, is a principal researcher at the Mid-continent Research for Education and Learning (McREL) and a research fellow at the National Institute of Early Education Research at Rutgers. Jointly with Dr. Deborah J. Leong, she has written extensively on the applications of the Vygotskian approach to early childhood education and codeveloped Tools of the Mind curriculum. She received her PhD in educational psychology and child development from the Russian Academy of Educational Sciences and her MA in educational psychology and child development from Moscow State University.

Satpal Boyes is a coach consultant in the PATHS social-emotional learning program for Birmingham Local Authority (UK). She qualified as a teacher in 1988 and has taught in primary and secondary schools across Birmingham.

Margaret Stimmann Branson, PhD, is associate director of the Center for Civic Education. Previously, she was assistant superintendent for Kern County Schools, California. Dr. Branson was associate professor of education at Holy Names University and director of secondary education at Mills College, Oakland, California. She has authored numerous textbooks and professional articles. She was one of the editorial directors and principal researchers and writers of the *National Standards for Civics and Government*. She served on the management team for the 1998 National Assessment of Educational Progress (NAEP) in Civics, on the International Education Association National Expert Panel on US Civic Education, and on the Res Publica: An International Framework for Education for Democracy development committee.

Patricia C. Broderick, PhD, is author of Learning to BREATHE, a mindfulness curriculum for adolescents. She is a research associate at the Penn State Prevention Research Center and a licensed clinical psychologist, school psychologist, and school counselor. The fourth edition of her developmental psychology textbook, *The Life Span: Human Development for Helping Professionals* (Broderick & Blewitt) will be published in 2013 by Pearson Education.

Fay E. Brown, PhD, is associate research scientist at the Yale Child Study Center. She is also the director of child and adolescent development for the Comer School Development Program. Her major focus in working with schools is to help them create and maintain developmentally appropriate conditions that will foster academic learning and ensure the holistic development of every child.

Philip M. Brown, PhD, is a fellow of the Graduate School of Applied and Professional Psychology at Rutgers University where he founded and directed the Center for Social and Character Development. He served in student services–related management positions in the New Jersey Department of Education and the Pennsylvania Department of Health for twenty-five years. He has served as principal investigator on several research grants from the US Department of Education; as a school board director; as a Global Advisory Board member of the Human Dignity and Humiliation Studies Network; as president of the New Jersey Alliance for Social, Emotional and Character Development; and as a member of the National School Climate Council. He received his doctorate in adult developmental psychology and the addictions from the Union Institute and University.

Vanessa Camilleri is director of student support services at the Arts and Technology Academy, Public Charter School, in Washington, D.C. She is currently completing her doctoral studies in education leadership and policy at the University of Maryland. She has published and presented widely and remains committed to designing schools that aim at developing academically, socially, and emotionally competent individuals.

Florence C. Chang, PhD, is evaluation specialist for Jefferson County Public Schools (JCPS) in the Department of Accountability, Research, and Planning. She has been a researcher and evaluator for nine years and has been the lead evaluator on several major evaluation studies related to the social and emotional development of students. Previous to JCPS, Dr. Chang was a researcher at the FPG Child Development Institute at the University of North Carolina–Chapel Hill. She earned her doctorate in cognitive development from the University of Louisville.

Jonathan Cohen, PhD, is president and cofounder of the National School Climate Center and adjunct professor at Teachers College, Columbia University, and at the School of Professional Studies, City University of New York. He is also the cofounder and cochair (with Terry Pickeral) of the National School Climate Council and has authored eighty-five papers and books, including *Educating Minds and Hearts: Social Emotional Learning and the Passage into Adolescence* and *Caring Classroom/Intelligent*

Schools. He earned his PhD in clinical psychology from the City University of New York and completed postdoctoral fellowships at New York Hospital–Cornell Medical Center and the Memorial Sloan Kettering Center.

James P. Comer, MD, is the Maurice Falk Professor of Child Psychiatry at the Yale University School of Medicine's Child Study Center. He is known nationally and internationally and has received numerous awards for his creation in 1968 of the Comer School Development Program (SDP), the first modern school reform program based on the centrality and application of child and adolescent development principles to school practice. He is the author of ten books, including *Maggie's American Dream* and *Leave No Child Behind*, and the recipient of many honors and awards, including forty-seven honorary degrees.

Maureen Connolly, EdD, is an English teacher at Mineola High School in Long Island, NY. She has developed many service learning projects that link community outreach, character education, and classroom content. Dr. Connolly has also coauthored a book on the Common Core State Standards for ELA entitled *Getting to the Core of English Language Arts Grades 6–12: How to Meet the Common Core State Standards with Lessons from the Field*. She earned her doctorate at St. John's University.

Michael W. Corrigan, EdD, is associate professor and director of research at Marshall University in Huntington, West Virginia. He teaches educational psychology, human development, and research methods. Dr. Corrigan's more recent large-scale research projects include five US Department of Education grants studying character development and academic achievement in Florida, Ohio, North Carolina, Tennessee, and West Virginia, as well as a National Science Foundation grant collaborating with NASA that studies the impact of science-based inquiry on academic achievement in at-risk youth. His earlier research into the deviant behavior of youth in relation to community engagement was funded through the Department of Justice. Dr. Corrigan is the founder of the nonprofit Neighbor's Day Initiative Group, which seeks to build safer communities for youth, and his community work has been featured in the *Christian Science Monitor* and other national publications.

E. Janet Czarnecki, MA, is assistant principal at Lake Riviera Middle School (eight years). She previously taught special education for sixteen years at LRMS and in the Elizabeth School District. In 2000, Mrs. Czarnecki became chair of LRMS's Character Education Initiative. During these eleven years, LRMS was named a New Jersey School of Character from 2009 to 2013, a National School of Character for 2011, and a recipient of several grants through Learn and Serve America, Rutgers University, and the New Jersey Department of Education. Mrs. Czarnecki received her MA in urban education from New Jersey City University, Jersey City.

Lisa M. De Bellis, MA, is a doctoral candidate at Fordham University in the Applied Developmental Psychology Program. She has worked on the evaluation of several after-school and out-of-school-time initiatives for over five years.

Ms. Teresita Saracho de Palma is principal at Farmdale Elementary School, an International Baccalaureate World School located in the El Sereno community in East Los Angeles. A native of El Sereno, she has worked at Farmdale Elementary School for fifteen years and for the Los Angeles Unified School District for thirty-four years. Ms. Saracho de Palma began as a teacher of autistic students. She has worked in special education programs and bilingual programs, both of which have been integrated at Farmdale Elementary. Ms. Saracho de Palma obtained her master of science degree in education from the University of Southern California and a second master of arts degree in educational administration from California State University, Los Angeles. She is dedicated to helping improve the academic, behavior, and character development at Farmdale Elementary by implementing Positive Action schoolwide.

Joyce A. DeVoss, PhD, is associate professor in the Department of Educational Psychology at Northern Arizona University. She is currently coordinator of the MEd School Counseling Program at Northern Arizona University in Tucson, cochair of the Arizona School Counseling Association (AZSCA) Research Committee, and coeditor of the journal *School Counseling Research and Practice*. Dr. DeVoss coauthored the book *School Counselors as Educational Leaders* (2006), has published articles and book chapters, and has presented at local, state, national, and international levels.

Maurice J. Elias, PhD, is professor and director of clinical PhD training for the Psychology Department at Rutgers University and serves as academic director of Rutgers' Civic Engagement and Service Education Partnerships Program. He is past president of the Society for Community Research and Action/Division 27 (Community Psychology) of the American Psychological Association, and director of the Rutgers Social-Emotional Learning Lab. He is the author of numerous books for the general public and professional articles, and he writes a blog on social-emotional and character development (SECD) for the George Lucas Educational Foundation at www.edutopia .org. He received his doctorate from the University of Connecticut.

Connie Flanagan, PhD, is professor in the School of Human Ecology at the University of Wisconsin–Madison in a program on civic action and research in civil society. Her work focuses on the development of political theories and commitments in adolescence. Her doctorate in psychology is from the University of Michigan.

Brian R. Flay, DPhil, is professor of health promotion and health behavior at Oregon State University. He has been conducting school-based randomized trials in schools (in Canada, California, Chicago, and Hawaii) for thirty years. Most of his past work has concerned the development and evaluation of programs for the prevention of substance abuse, violence, and AIDS. Recent studies focus on positive youth development, including social-emotional and character education. He is currently conducting several studies of the Positive Action program.

Erin Gallay has been a practitioner of service learning and environmental education for nearly fifteen years, focusing primarily on youth civic action projects involving environmental issues. She has worked with K–12 schools, universities, and community organizations throughout the state of Michigan. She holds degrees in environmental education and secondary science instruction from the University of Michigan and Eastern Michigan University.

Karen Geller, EdD, is associate professor at Immaculata University, teaching supervision and evaluation and the principalship. She is also principal of grades 5 and 6 at Upper Merion Area Middle School, a 2010 National School of Character and a 2011 Johns Hopkins National Network of Partnership School. Dr. Geller is a leader in the character education field and focuses on the integration of character throughout the curriculum.

Larissa Giordano, MA, is a fourth-grade teacher at Nathan Hale School in New Haven, Connecticut. She has been a teacher in that urban school system for nine years. As a teacher, her greatest passion is nurturing her students to feel confident about themselves, as individuals and as learners, as they work toward realizing their full potential. Recently, under the guidance of Dr. Fay Brown, she has been working with other teachers in the district, helping them to integrate knowledge of the six developmental pathways into all aspects of their classroom practices.

Colette Gosselin, EdD, is assistant professor and coordinator of secondary education at the College of New Jersey where she teaches undergraduate and graduate courses in educational foundations. She has over fourteen years of experience teaching in higher education and five years as a high school biology teacher. She has an EdD in the social and philosophical foundations of education from Rutgers University. Her areas of research include both the relationship between emotions and learning and preservice teacher development.

Maughn Gregory, PhD, JD, is associate professor of educational foundations at Montclair State University, where he is faculty advisor to the Institute for the Advancement of Philosophy for Children and Director of the Classroom Inquiry Project in Newark. He publishes and teaches in the areas of philosophy of education, pragmatism, philosophy for children, gender and education, and critical thinking. Dr. Gregory regularly conducts workshops on these topics throughout the United States and around the world.

Michelle Grimley, LSW, is assistant director for GEAR UP at the School District of Philadelphia. She has worked in programmatic and administrative roles in Philadelphia nonprofits, AmeriCorps, and the school district since 1998. She earned a BA in sociology, social psychology, and education from Lehigh University, and a master's in social services from Bryn Mawr.

Doug Grove, PhD, is director of the Graduate Program in Education and associate professor of education at Vanguard University in Costa Mesa, California. Dr. Grove has taught English, business, and physical education in public and private school settings. He has worked as a high school vice principal, coordinator of a county office assessment unit, and a school board member. Dr. Grove has broad experience in educational evaluation including management of numerous state and federal grants, as well as many other local education agency–based initiatives on the West Coast. Dr. Grove has been lead evaluator on five Partnerships in Character Education grants funded by the US Department of Education and its Office of Safe and Drug-Free Schools.

Scott Hall, MAT, teaches sixth grade at a middle school in Columbus, Ohio, where he coaches football and wrestling and serves on the district Wellness Committee. He is certified in Taekwondo (black belt) and personal training. In addition to eight years of middle school experience, Hall has competed successfully in power lifting for fifteen years. He has over thirty years of weight training, fitness, and nutrition experience. He is one of the founders of the Core5 After School Program, which focuses on improving academics, fitness, nutrition, social and emotional wellness, and parent/community involvement. Hall received his bachelor of science in education from Otterbein College in 1997 and his master of arts in teaching from Marygrove College in 2005.

Heidi L. Hallman, PhD, is assistant professor at the University of Kansas where she teaches graduate and undergraduate courses in English education. She earned a PhD from the University of Wisconsin–Madison, and prior to working in higher education, she taught high school English.

Deborah Hecht, PhD, is an educational psychologist and senior principal investigator at the Center for Advanced Study in Education, part of the Graduate Center for the City University of New York. Dr. Hecht is engaged in research, evaluation, and development of educational innovations and reform efforts with a focus in the areas of service learning, character education, and STEM (science, technology, engineering, and mathematics). She has worked with K–16 schools and educators to bring about systemic change and has been on numerous national committees that seek to connect research and practice in meaningful ways. She was a founding board member of the nationally recognized Hoboken Charter School.

Ann Higgins-D'Alessandro, PhD, is director of the Applied Developmental Psychology Graduate Program in the Psychology Department and faculty coordinator of the new multidisciplinary Center for Community-Engaged Research (CCER) of Fordham University. Her major research focus is on schools and workplaces as contexts for adolescent and adult social-moral and identity development, included authoring the School Culture Scale (1997) that has been used in several European and Pacific Rim countries. Her career began conducting action research on Just Community schools (*Lawrence Kohlberg's Approach to Moral Education*, 1989). She has served as principal investigator on over a dozen grants and most recently completed two US Department of Education four-year evaluation projects of the Community of Caring intervention in New York and New Jersey schools. In 2002 she coedited *Science for Society*, an SRCD New Directions volume. Consulting with the US Department of Education, she coproduced *Mobilizing for Evidence-Based Character Education* (2007) to promote effective educator/evaluator partnering. She consults widely on the development of school-specific civic, democratic, and moral education interventions and is a member of the National School Climate Council. In 2000, Dr. Higgins-D'Alessandro received the highest award of the Association for Moral Education for her research and service to the profession.

Jennie Hine is a PATHS coach consultant working in Birmingham, UK. She has eleven years of experience working within the education system, and her work has encompassed teaching in mainstream classrooms as well as within a specialist social-emotional unit, working as assistant educational psychologist and also as inclusion manager within a mainstream school. She has a degree in psychology and a postgraduate certificate of education from the University of Birmingham.

Cheryl Hopkins has worked in local government in the United Kingdom for over thirty years, commencing her career as a psychiatric social worker. She worked for the Birmingham City Council from 2004 until recently, leading an ambitious and widely endorsed early intervention, long-term strategy and transformation program called Brighter Futures, a strategic process for innovative service design that links comprehensive data, systematic reviews of evidence targeted to specific outcomes, and evaluation methods including randomized control trials. Each innovation engaged all stakeholders and resulted in a financial return on the investment. Cheryl retired from Birmingham City Council at the end of 2011 and now works as an independent consultant.

Anne-Marie Hoxie, PhD, is director of research at The After-School Corporation (TASC). She is responsible for conducting research on issues that strengthen after-school and expanded learning time fields and overseeing all of TASC's program evaluation activities. Dr. Hoxie holds a PhD in developmental psychology from Fordham University and has researched and evaluated youth health interventions, school-based initiatives, and OST (out-of-school time) programs for over ten years.

Jill Jacobi-Vessels, PhD, is assistant professor in early childhood education in the College of Education and Human Development at the University of Louisville. She earned her PhD in teaching and learning and an MEd in interdisciplinary early childhood education at the University of Louisville. Her experience includes five years at the University of Louisville Early Childhood Research Center and fifteen years directing and coordinating child development centers, children's programs, and family support programs.

Patricia Jennings, MEd, PhD, is senior director of the education initiative at the Garrison Institute and research assistant professor in human development and family studies at Pennsylvania State University. Her current research focuses on developing and testing interventions designed to reduce stress and promote social and emotional skills among teachers. Her background includes over twenty years as an educator and teacher educator.

Amy Johnston, MA, has been in the field of education for thirty-one years. She taught high school, served as a middle school counselor, and has been in administration for the past seventeen years at Francis Howell Middle School. She has spoken on her character education leadership journey to educators at conferences in five states. Her efforts have earned her the St. Louis Area Middle School Principal of the Year Award and the Dean's Award for Excellence in Character Education. In 2007, her school was named a Missouri School of Character, and in 2008 Francis Howell Middle was named a National School of Character. She has master's degrees in both education administration and counseling.

Bridget Kerrigan is program manager for the Troubled Families Programme at Birmingham City Council. The program takes a holistic approach to supporting families with complex needs, which includes a focus on evidence-based early intervention programs. She has worked in local government for over twelve years and earlier served in various policy roles within the disability sector. She is a graduate of the University of Birmingham in public and social policy management and holds a master's degree in public sector management.

Yael Kidron, PhD, is senior research analyst at the American Institutes for Research (AIR). She specializes in research reviews, translation of research into practice, and social-emotional learning. She currently serves as project director and task leader of projects that aim to inform practice of state, district, and school administrators and educators, including the U. S. Department of Education Doing What Works Initiative and the National High School Center. She received her PhD in psychology from the University of Haifa, Israel.

Denise Koebcke, MEd, has been an educator for nearly twenty years in the Valparaiso Community School System in Northwest Indiana. She founded Team LEAD LLC, a bystander leadership program for schools, community agencies, and businesses, and is currently Team LEAD consultant in multiple school systems across the Midwest. She earned her BA in education from Purdue University and her master's degree from Indiana State University.

Tony Lacey is head teacher of Arden Primary School, a large, inner-city Birmingham, UK, school serving a largely Muslim population in a deprived area of the city. This is his second headship, and he has been at the school since 2005. He has always had an interest in positive behavior management, ensuring that children develop an understanding of empathy, consequences, and an ability to articulate feelings. He is on the steering group for the Primary Behavior Strategy, which aims to ensure that children and schools with behavior issues have the best support to help them succeed. His school was one of the original schools to pilot the PATHS social-emotional learning curriculum.

Jennifer Lane, MAT, is a teacher at Lake Riviera Middle School for eighth-grade science and coadvisor of the National Junior Honor Society. She has taught for eight years at the middle school level, where she demonstrates her passion for character education, service learning, and prosocial education. She earned her master of arts in teaching in elementary education from Monmouth University, West Long Branch, New Jersey.

Linda Lantieri, MA, has been in the field of education for over forty years in a variety of capacities—classroom teacher, elementary assistant principal, and middle school director in East Harlem, New York City, as well as education faculty member in the Department of Curriculum and Teaching, Hunter College. Currently, she is director of the Inner Resilience Program and cofounder and senior program advisor for the Collaborative for Academic, Social and Emotional Learning (CASEL). Her most recent book is *Building Emotional Intelligence: Techniques to Cultivate Inner Strength in Children* (2008).

Ann E. Larson, PhD, is vice dean of the College of Education and Human Development and professor in middle and secondary education at the University of Louisville. Her scholarship currently focuses on assessment and accountability in educator preparation, teacher preparation, teacher development, and curriculum studies. Dr. Larson earned her PhD in curriculum and instruction from the University of Illinois, Urbana-Champaign.

Minna Lehtonen, BSc (Hons.), is a research assistant at the Social Research Unit Dartington. She has worked as special needs teaching assistant and on the implementation of evidence-based programs in Birmingham, UK. She earned a BSc (Hons.) in psychology from the University of Bedfordshire, UK.

Deborah Leong, PhD, is professor emerita of psychology at the Metropolitan State College of Denver. She is director and codeveloper of the Tools of the Mind curriculum project designed to promote self-regulation and executive function skills in young children. She has written with Elena Bodrova on the Vygotskian approach to early education and on intentional make-believe play. She has also written with Oralie McAfee on child assessment. She is a research fellow at the National Institute of Early Education Research at Rutgers. She has a PhD in educational psychology, a BA in psychology from Stanford University, and an MEd from Harvard University.

Donna Letchford has a wide-ranging background working as a primary school teacher, an early childhood educator, and in adult education as a parent worker. After thirteen years with the Roots of Empathy organization, she has delivered over twenty Roots of Empathy programs and worked extensively as a trainer and mentor, nationally and internationally.

Ricardo Lopez, MSW, is the Healthy Start coordinator and psychiatric social worker for Farmdale Elementary School, El Sereno Middle School, and Wilson High School in Northeast Los Angeles. Mr. Lopez has been a social worker for seventeen years and has worked for various government agencies (Los Angeles County Probation, the Department of Children and Family Services, and the Los Angeles Unified School

District) and nonprofit social service agencies. Mr. Lopez has specialized in providing therapeutic prevention and intervention services for young boys and men. Mr. Lopez obtained his master of social work degree and Pupil Personnel Services credential from California State University, Long Beach. Mr. Lopez earned his undergraduate degree from Whittier College, Whittier, California.

Vonda Martin is coordinator for the Youth Service Center in the Spencer County Public School District, Kentucky. She engages the middle and high schools in community-wide collaborative groups that focus on reducing disparities and meeting the needs of the district's children and families, especially low-income families.

Jennifer McElgunn is a primary school teacher in Toronto, Ontario, who has had the Roots of Empathy program in her grade 3 class for three years. She has over sixteen years of teaching experience in K–5 settings. She earned a BA in sociology and psychology from Trent University and a BEd from the University of Maine.

Tinia R. Merriweather is completing the PhD program in applied developmental psychology at Fordham University. Her dissertation examines equity of opportunities for students in classroom-level processes and associated teacher characteristics. With sixteen years of classroom experience, she has taught at all levels from elementary through graduate school, but her passion is middle school. She currently teaches in the Ethics Department and works on diversity initiatives at Ethical Culture Fieldstone School. Tinia holds a BA from Spelman College and two MA's from Fordham University and Teachers College, Columbia University.

Johncarlos M. Miller, currently high school principal at Weaver Academy in Guilford County Schools (Greensboro, NC), has served the district for fifteen years as teacher and administrator at the middle and high school levels. He has provided professional development on the power of character education and its impact on school culture and student achievement locally, regionally, and nationally. He earned a BS in chemistry secondary education from North Carolina A&T State University and an MS in school administration from the University of North Carolina at Greensboro, where he is currently pursuing the EdD in educational leadership and cultural foundations.

Laura Morana, EdD, began her career as a teacher, eventually serving as supervisor of special education, middle school principal, director of staff development, and assistant superintendent for curriculum and instruction, and in 2006 she assumed the role of superintendent of the Red Bank Borough School System. Her leadership has focused on pre-K through twelfth-grade curriculum improvements, fostering partnerships between school districts and local businesses and colleges, and championing the critical link between home and school. She earned a BA in education from Kean University, an MA in special education, and an EdD in educational leadership from Rowan University.

Jacqueline Norris, EdD, is professor and coordinator of educational leadership at the College of New Jersey. She has more than forty years of experience in the field of education having been a teacher at both the elementary and secondary levels and principal and assistant superintendent for curriculum and instruction in the K–12 setting. Dr. Norris is passionate about her commitment to ensuring that school leaders understand the critical role that prosocial skills and decision making play in creating effective schools for the twenty-first century. She earned her doctorate at Rutgers, the State University of New Jersey.

Judith Nuss, MA, is an independent consultant for CASEL and AIR presently working in Cleveland, Austin, and Sacramento school districts. She is former director of social and emotional learning in Harrisburg School District, PA, where she led districtwide implementation of SEL. She has over thirty years of experience in teaching and school leadership as well as research experience with Penn State University Prevention Research Center. Judy earned her BS in elementary education from Temple University and her MA in community psychology and social change from Pennsylvania State University.

Mary Utne O'Brien, PhD, (deceased) was a research professor of psychology and education at the University of Illinois at Chicago. She joined the Collaborative for Academic, Social, and Emotional Learning (CASEL) as associate director in 1999. Working closely with CASEL president Roger Weissberg, she quickly became a key leader not just for CASEL but for the entire field of social and emotional learning (SEL). In 2004 she was appointed as CASEL's executive director. When CASEL incorporated as a not-for-profit organization in 2007, she became vice president for strategic initiatives, responsible for strategic planning, development of collaborative partnerships, and exploration of new projects. She received her doctorate in social psychology from the University of Wisconsin–Madison.

Monique Ohashi, MEd, is a first-grade teacher at Farmdale Elementary School, an International Baccalaureate World School in Los Angeles, California. Her eleven years of teaching experience have enabled her to continue to promote social justice and international-mindedness at the elementary level. She obtained her teaching credentials and master of education degree from the University of California, Los Angeles (UCLA), and her undergraduate degree from the University of California, Riverside (UCR), where she graduated cum laude.

David Osher, PhD, is vice president at American Institutes for Research (AIR). He is a nationally recognized expert in prevention research; social-emotional learning; youth development; the social and emotional conditions for learning, teaching, and healthy development; and culturally competent interventions. Dr. Osher consults with federal, state, and local officials and with offices in the US Departments of Education, Health and Human Services, and Justice and has served on multiple interagency work groups with federal officials. Dr. Osher serves on numerous expert panels (e.g., Preschool and Elementary School Assessment Workgroup and research advisory boards for America's Promise and the Collaborative for Academic, Social, and Emotional Learning).

Kristen Pelster, SEd, an educator for nineteen years, is administrator at Ridgewood Middle School in the Fox School District of St. Louis Missouri. In 2000, she took over a failing middle school and used character education to achieve four "Top Ten Most Improved" awards for test scores in Missouri and an 84 percent decrease in discipline referrals. She and her school have received numerous state and national awards, including Inspire by Example (state education department) and National School of Character (Character Education Partnership). Kristen earned a BA in music education from Missouri Baptist University and a master's and specialist degree in education administration from the University of Missouri–St. Louis.

Laura J. Pinger, MS, is senior outreach specialist at the Center for Investigating Healthy Minds at the Waisman Center on the University of Wisconsin–Madison campus. With over twenty years of teaching experience in Madison public schools and twelve years of teaching affiliation with the UW Health Center for Mindfulness, Laura develops and teaches secular mindfulness-based curricula to educators and students as part of translational research investigating attention, emotion regulation, and well-being.

Ann Marie R. Power has been director of undergraduate studies in the Department of Sociology at the University of Notre Dame since 2000. She received her PhD in the sociology of education at the University of Notre Dame. Her publications focus on educational attainment, social capital in schools, social responsibility among youth, and the moral culture of schools.

F. Clark Power has been teaching at the University of Notre Dame since 1982. He is professor in the Program of Liberal Studies (PLS), concurrent professor in the Department of Psychology, a member of the graduate faculty in education, and director of the Play Like Champion Character Education through Sports Program. He received his EdD in human development from Harvard University and wrote his thesis under the direction of Lawrence Kohlberg. His publications focus on moral development and education, civic engagement, and school climate.

Joan Elizabeth Reubens works as a bullying prevention specialist for Pinellas County Schools, Florida. She works with the district's Policy against Bullying and Harassment and the Teen Dating Violence and Abuse Policy, in addition to teaching workshops on prevention and intervention strategies and being a Nationally Certified Olweus trainer. Joan coauthored *Bullying . . . Not in This School: 40 Weeks of Bullying Prevention Activities*. Joan has a bachelor's degree in behavior disorders from the University of South Florida and a master's degree in educational leadership from Nova Southeastern University.

Howard Rodstein, director of the Scarsdale Alternative School and a tenth-grade English teacher, has worked in Scarsdale, New York, public schools since 1978. His "Just

Community" school is based on an application of Lawrence Kohlberg's theory of moral development to six core structures. He is also an Annenburg Institute–trained Critical Friends Group coach, training teacher-leaders in suburban New York. He earned his bachelor's degree at Brandeis University and holds two master's degrees from Teachers College, Columbia University, and Bank Street College of Education.

Robert W. Roeser, PhD, MSW, is professor of psychology and human development in the Department of Psychology at Portland State University in Portland, Oregon. He received his BA with honors in psychology from Cornell University and his PhD from the Combined Program in Education and Psychology at the University of Michigan. In 2005, he was a US Fulbright scholar in India, and from 1999 to 2004, he was a William T. Grant Foundation faculty scholar. Dr. Roeser's research focuses on school as a primary cultural context of adolescent development and on professional development of public school teachers. His current research is focused on how mindfulness training can be used to cultivate the positive development of adolescents and teachers alike.

Judy Rosen retired as a teacher from the Scarsdale, New York, school system in 2007, where she served ten years as a Scarsdale Alternative School teacher and fifteen years in Scarsdale High School. She previously taught at three other high schools in New York State and Pittsburgh. Rosen taught social studies and team taught in several innovative interdisciplinary courses, including civic education with an English teacher and a guidance counselor, American studies with an English teacher, and a health course called "Mind-Body" with a science teacher.

Kimberly A. Schonert-Reichl, PhD, is associate professor in the Faculty of Education at the University of British Columbia. For more than twenty years, Kim's research has focused on the social and emotional learning (SEL) and development of children and adolescents. Her research has particular emphasis on identifying processes and mechanisms that foster children's positive human qualities such as empathy, altruism, and resiliency, and school-based promotion of SEL. Following her work as a middle and high school teacher, Kim received her master's degree from the University of Chicago and her PhD from the University of Iowa.

Alesha D. Seroczynski, PhD, is a research fellow in the Institute for Educational Initiatives at the University of Notre Dame and founder and director of Reading for Life, a character education diversion program for juvenile offenders. She has over twenty years of experience with delinquent and at-risk youth, including internships at the Center for the Homeless in South Bend, Indiana; Madison Center, Indiana's largest community mental health center; and the Western Psychiatric Institute and Clinic at the University of Pittsburgh. Alesha earned her MA in counseling psychology and her PhD in developmental psychology from the University of Notre Dame.

Christine Sherretz, EdD, is assistant professor at the University of Louisville, where she primarily teaches reading courses and works as university liaison at a local elementary school. She has over twenty years of teaching experience in P–5 settings and in higher education. She has an EdD in curriculum and instruction, with emphasis in instructional improvement, from Georgia Southern University.

Christopher E. Smith, MA, is program director of evaluation services at The After-School Corporation (TASC), where he is responsible for managing TASC's external evaluation of 21st Century Community Learning Centers. He is pursuing his doctorate in applied developmental psychology at Fordham University. He has researched and evaluated out-of-school time (OST) science, technology, engineering, and mathematics (STEM) programs.

Frank J. Snyder, PhD, MPH, is a postdoctoral fellow in the Division of Prevention and Community Research in the Department of Psychiatry at the Yale School of Medicine. His research focuses on the complex array of factors that influence youth development and risk behaviors. He earned a PhD in public health with emphasis in health promotion and behavior from Oregon State University, an MPH in community health from Idaho State University, and a BS in nutritional sciences from Michigan State University.

Susan B. Stillman, EdD, is a counselor educator at Northern Arizona University and is on the graduate faculties in educational leadership at Fielding Graduate University and the School of Education at Northcentral University. She also is currently chair of the Social Emotional Learning (SEL) Special Interest Group (SIG) American Educational Research Association, coeditor of *School Counseling Research and Practice*, a member of the Arizona School Counselor Association (AZSCA) Research Committee, and reviewer for the *Grounded Theory Review*.

Betty Waters Straub, EdD, is director of research for the Center for Health Promotion and Prevention Science at the University of Louisville, where she holds a faculty position in health education and has taught since 1982. She served as director for the national Character Education and Civic Engagement Technical Assistance Center (2004–2010) for the US Department of Education. She earned her doctorate in education in student development and higher education administration, her master of arts in teaching, and her bachelor's in health promotion at the University of Louisville.

Mike Swartz is currently superintendent of schools for the School District of Jefferson (Wisconsin). He has served as teacher, coach, assistant principal, principal, athletic director, assistant superintendent of schools, and superintendent of schools during his forty-three years in public education. He earned a BS in education from Western Michigan University and an MS degree in school administration and leadership from Central Michigan University.

Sandy Swartz became volunteer coordinator of the School District of Jefferson's (Wisconsin) character education initiative by agreeing to assist the district for six months to get the initiative off the ground. Nine years later, she continues to serve as coordinator of a program that reaches into the entire community, in addition to five schools. She is a graduate of the Indiana University School of Philanthropy and attended Western Michigan University and Alma College in Michigan.

Janet E. Thompson, MA, is director of the Early Childhood Laboratory at the Center for Child and Family Studies at the University of California, Davis. As an early childhood educator, her interests focus especially on the growth of social and emotional competency and its contributions to early learning. With Ross Thompson, she was primary author of Preschool Learning Foundations and Preschool Curriculum Frameworks for Social-Emotional Development recently adopted by the California Department of Education. She earned her BA from Occidental College and her MA from the University of Michigan.

Ross A. Thompson, PhD, is distinguished professor of psychology at the University of California, Davis, where he directs the Social and Emotional Development Lab. The research of the lab focuses on development of emotional understanding, conscience and prosocial behavior, empathy, and other constructive social capacities in the early years. He also works on the application of developmental science to problems in child and family policy. He earned an AB in psychology from Occidental College and AM and PhD degrees from the University of Michigan.

Jan Urbanski, EdD, is director of the Special Projects Office for Pinellas County Schools in Largo, Florida, where she has supervised the Safe and Drug-Free Schools office and held other positions since 1991. She is technical assistance consultant and national trainer for the Olweus Bullying Prevention Program for Clemson University and has cowritten two books and numerous articles on bullying prevention. Dr. Urbanski holds a doctorate in educational leadership with a focus on bullying prevention and school connectedness, a specialist degree in educational leadership, and a master's in education, all from the University of South Florida, and a bachelor's in elementary education from Eastern Connecticut State College.

Dorothy J. Veith serves as director of marketing and communications for the College of Education and Human Development at the University of Louisville in Kentucky. She has worked at the university for more than fourteen years, where she earned her bachelor's and master's degrees.

Philip Vincent, EdD, is director of the Character Development Group and a partner with Multi-Dimensional Education Inc. A former teacher and school administrator, Dr. Vincent has worked for fifteen years in numerous school districts in the United States and Canada on enhancing, evaluating, and developing comprehensive character education initiatives. He has also authored, coauthored, or edited thirty books published in the United States and Australia. He earned his doctorate in education from North Carolina State University.

Becky Wilson is director for the Family Resource Center in the Spencer County Public School District in Kentucky. She engages the two elementary schools in community-wide collaborative groups that focus on reducing disparities and meeting the needs of the district's children and families, especially low-income families.

Abby C. Winer, ABD, is a doctoral candidate at the University of California, Davis, with the Social and Emotional Development Lab. She earned her AB in psychology with distinction from Georgetown University. Her current work involves studying a variety of parent–child relational influences on individual differences in young children's prosocial behavior and motivations. Having worked as both a child-care researcher and provider, she is committed to applications of developmental science to early education programs.

J. Carmelo Zamora has been an elementary school teacher for almost eighteen years, currently at Farmdale Elementary School in Los Angeles. He has a bachelor's degree in literature from Occidental College and a master's degree in education from National University. His educational philosophy includes listening and working with school staff and the community. His educational goal is to nurture critical thinkers and life-long learners who care about real-world issues. Presently, he is in his second year working in a Spanish/English fifth-grade dual-language immersion classroom.